*Understanding*

# Foundations in Human Development

Second Edition

### JERRY J. BIGNER, Ph.D
*Department of Human Development and Family Studies*
Colorado State University

### TROIANNE GRAYSON, M.A.
*Department of Social and Behavioral Sciences*
Florida State College at Jacksonville

### AVIDAN MILEVSKY, Ph.D
*Department of Psychology*
Kutztown University of Pennsylvania

BVT
PUBLISHING
**Custom Publishing Division**

PROJECT AND DESIGN MANAGER: Brae Buhnerkemper

EDITORS: Susan Gall and Rhonda Minemma

PHOTO RESEARCHER: Della Brackett

COVER DESIGN: Brae Buhnerkemper, Jason James, and Dan Harvey

ILLUSTRATIONS: Dan Harvey

TYPESETTER: Rhonda Minemma

ISBN: 978-1-60229-721-0

Copyright © 2010 by BVT Publishing, LLC

*From J. J. Bigner:*

**For Duane—Partner, Mentor, Best Friend, my Hero,**
*The wind beneath my wings.*
**And for Todd, Shannon, and Katy—**
*Once again with feeling!*

*From T. Grayson:*

**For Glenn, Whisper, Haley, Alexa, Lance, and my Lord**
*I couldn't have written this without your support, love, patience, and strength. Thank you!*

*From A. Milevsky:*

**For Liora, Tamar, Uzi, and Mati**
*Thank you for triggering my interest in child development—and for making me laugh.*

# TABLE OF CONTENTS

# PREFACE

*Foundations in Human Development*, Second Edition is a comprehensive and engaging introduction to life span development. With a unique blend of classical studies and cutting-edge research, the reader is provided a context in which he or she is able to appreciate the historical foundations of life span development, as well as current themes and findings. The reader is consistently encouraged to apply the text material to his or her own life, in order to encourage retention and increase interest.

After the first two chapters, which focus upon introducing the field of human development and biological beginnings, each chapter is organized into three parts. The first part of each chapter emphasizes biological development. The second part emphasizes cognitive development. The third part emphasizes socioemotional development. The central task of these chapters is to help students learn basic concepts that relate to developmental changes affecting individuals throughout each stage of the life span.

There are some important pedagogical features to the text that distinguish it from others as well. First, each chapter is written using the SQR3 (S-Q-R-R-R) method. This is a method designed by Dr. Francis Robinson to facilitate effective learning of written material. The first step in learning this material is to survey (S) each chapter. The second step is observed with questions (Q) that are raised as a result of reading a section. The third step is to read (R) each chapter carefully, one section at a time. The fourth step is recitation (R) where you may make notes, underline, or use the learning objectives or pause and process questions within each section to check for comprehension of main points. The final step is review (R) where you might test your comprehension by performing the self-quiz given at the end of a chapter, rereading your notes, or rereading a chapter, for example.

Second, learning objectives are given at the beginning of each chapter. Throughout the chapter, key terms and concepts appear in **bold face** print. These terms are defined in the glossary. At the end of each section of the chapter, pause and process questions are given so that a student may gauge his or her understanding for each segment of the chapter.

Third, a summary at the end of each chapter explains important concepts for that chapter. The summary could also be read prior to reading the whole chapter, in order to gain a preview of what the chapter contains.

Fourth, each chapter contains a self-quiz that may be used in the recitation and review steps of learning. It also may be interesting to test yourself prior to reading a chapter and also upon completing the steps in learning the material to observe your progress.

Fifth, the theoretical and empirical foundation of the material will be expanded by providing qualitative accounts of the concepts using the words of those experiencing the actual process covered. Based on interviews conducted by research assistants with various individuals, the narrative of the text will be peppered with these accounts providing a personal context to the material. Each chapter will include several of these *"In Their Own Words"* qualitative accounts using various types of people at differing developmental stages.

Sixth, to expand on the practical application of the material a feature titled *"Development in the Real World"* will include interviews with various professionals who in their daily work apply the concepts discussed in the text. The feature will begin with an introduction to the individual interviewed and a description of the work they do, followed by the responses to the questions. The questions presented to these practitioners will include inquires about their work setting, type of work conducted, how they apply developmental psychology in their work and their job satisfaction. This feature will be extremely valuable for students looking for the real world way in which the material can be applied.

Finally, part of the human condition is that individuals can differ in their views on controversial issues. Because of this, a few controversial topics are discussed within the text. Research on these topics is presented and students are encouraged to think critically about these issues and form their own opinion. Some controversial topics discussed in the text include stem cell research, the cohabitation effect, whole versus partial-brain death, and euthanasia. Coverage of these societal controversies should pique the student's interest in the field of human development as a whole.

# The Field
# of Human
# Development

CMPS

# THE FIELD OF HUMAN DEVELOPMENT

*LEARNING OBJECTIVES:*

1. *Understand the reasons why it is important to learn about human development over the life span*
2. *Awareness of the historical issues that guide human development theories and research*
3. *Describe the main foundational theories and principles of development*
4. *Identify the major approaches to the scientific study of development*

# WHY DO WE STUDY DEVELOPMENT?

Humans have had a long history of being curious about their surroundings. Great scientists, explorers, artists, and architects have all been driven by the need to know and understand the world. Developmental psychology is driven by this similar quest for knowledge. However, in the study of human development the quest is amplified by the need to understand ourselves. Humans are a complex species and in our daily interactions with ourselves and others we are constantly asking why? Why did that person say that? Why did he look at me this way? Why is she acting this way? Why am I thinking that? Why did I buy that? Why am I sad? Why is my sister so different than me? The need to understand ourselves has been the focus of many disciplines for several millennia. From religion, to philosophy and psychology, the goal has been to shed some light on the mysteries of our thinking, emotions, and personality. The ancient Greek aphorism "know thyself" found on many Delphic monuments and temples and quoted by Aristotle as a well known saying, is motivated by this quest for understanding the human condition.

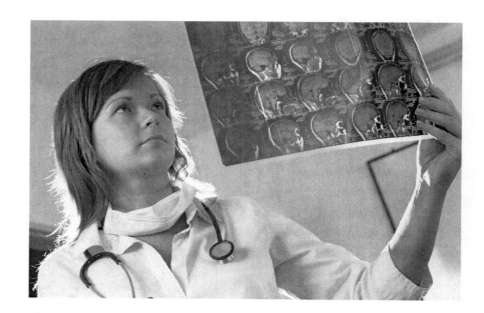

*Disciplines such as neuroscience have greatly contributed to the understanding of human development. (iStock)*

*Human development begins at the earliest stages of life. (iStock)*

However, the study of development is driven by more than this need to understand ourselves. The benefits resulting from this understanding is immense. By comprehending how we develop and why we act the way we do, we have the ability to manipulate the areas of development that are in our hands and hopefully assist in creating a more adaptive life for others. Knowing what variables play a role in positive development can shed light on what we as teachers, parents, social workers, psychologists and policy makers (Galatzer-Levy & Cohler, 1993; National Research Council & Institute of Medicine, 2000) can do to improve the human condition. The exceptional advances in many social services that we have seen over the past century have been driven by new and evolving science emanating from the study of development. Many questions that are asked in relation to enhancing the human condition can be informed with the study of development. For example: Should grandparents have visitation rights if parents divorce (or never marry)? What information should be on file from sperm donors in case their children someday have questions about their biological father? How should juvenile offenders be treated differently than adult offenders? Should taxpayers pay for parental leave, daycare, or elderly care? Should kindergarten last half a day or a full school day? Should expectant parents be required to obtain a license prior to childbirth? How old is to too old to have children? How young is too young to have children? What is the best age to get married? All of these questions are actively discussed in our society, some at official, legislative levels, and others around the office cooler. Regardless, the way we treat individuals and create social policy is largely based upon our knowledge of human development.

Our understanding of developmental delays, **psychopathology**, and therapy is also based upon our knowledge of human development (Galatzer-Levy & Cohler, 1993;

**Psychopathology**

The branch of medicine dealing with the causes and processes of mental disorders.

National Research Council & Institute of Medicine, 2000). Many preschool children have imaginary friends. Such imaginary playmates cause little concern in parents. However, parents would begin to raise their eyebrows if their nine-year-old had an imaginary friend. Professional intervention would probably be sought if a family's teenager had an imaginary friend. As you can see, the "normalness" of imaginary playmates depends upon a person's age and development. Normal and abnormal development often lie upon the same continuum, and our understanding of abnormal is dependent upon our understanding of normal development.

Intervention and therapy should also be based upon an individual's stage of development. A counselor would need to use different strategies and techniques for a five-year-old who underwent a traumatic event versus a twenty-five-year old. Along a similar line of reasoning, a bereavement counselor must consider a client's developmental understanding of death prior to ascertaining the best course of action in assisting in the grieving process.

Finally, studying human development provides a person with enormous understanding of the multiple pathways and timetables development can take (Galatzer-Levy & Cohler, 1993). Ultimately the possibility of contributing to a better world by understanding what is best for humans, from pregnancy to death, is the reason why we study development.

# THE HISTORICAL PERSPECTIVES

Although the scientific study of development is a relatively recent discipline, the attempt to understand humans has had a long history. Considering that some of you may have decided to take a psychology class to avoid taking history allow me to convince you why a brief analysis of the history of the study of development is warranted.

First, understanding what people thought about humans in the past helps us to further understand humans. Knowing what was thought in the past about humans can teach us something about those people who thought these things which in turn can help us understand humans in general better. Additionally, knowing what was thought in the past can help us critically examine what we think we know now about development. By comparing what has been thought in the past and what current advances in the sciences tell us now, we have the ability of challenging our thinking which in turn will help us clarify current approaches further.

## *What We Thought About Children*

The immaturity we often attribute to children can be seen in historical record as well. Recent archeological findings from excavations in the Middle East and northern Africa reveal distinct pottery art depicting childhood play. Apparently children were given the time and resources even back then to indulge in their need to play indicating a similarity to the current state of childhood.

However, an integrated approach to understanding childhood originates only in the Middle-Ages (500-1500 CE). The pervasive approach to children at the time was termed "original sin". This approach, based heavily on religious teachings, describes children as being born of sin and possessing an evil inclination from the first moment of life. Considering the influence of religion during the middle-ages it is no surprise that the accepted view of children would be based on religious and biblical references. The bible contains several passages depicting children as sinful "every product of the thoughts of his heart are but evil always" (Genesis 6:5) and requiring harsh discipline "He who spares the rod, hates the son" (Proverbs 13:24). Viewing children as such require harsh discipline techniques designed to subdue the evil and direct the child toward good. In relation to current theories of development, elements of the original sin view can be seen in Psychoanalytic theory which will be examined in a future section.

*Spotlight*

Which philosopher believed that humans are born basically good and that it is civilization that corrupts the human race?

By the end of the middle-ages and the dawn of the enlightenment a new approach toward children begins to surface in the writings of the English philosopher, and first of the British empiricists, John Locke (1632-1704). In his Essay Concerning Human Understanding (1689) he described children as being born with a "tabula rasa", or blank slate. Blank slates are neither evil nor good; they are blank like a white sheet of paper ready to be written on. Individuals become a function of the environment they grow up in. Children are written on by the people, places, and things they know which in turn makes them the way they are. The current approach to psychology emphasizing behaviorism, which will be discussed late in this chapter, draws from this original blank slate idea.

*Spotlight*

What are three views of human nature?

The third historical approach to children was described by Jean-Jacques Rousseau (1712-1778) in his book The Social Contract (1762) as innate goodness. The Genevian philosopher believed that children are born "innately good" and if we allow children to develop uninterrupted they will naturally mature adaptively. He further suggested that individuals seen as being bad later in life is a function of the society in which they developed which corrupted their natural good. In relation to current theories, innate goodness can be seen in many of the assertions of Humanistic theory.

## *What We Thought About Adolescents*

The focus on adolescence as being a distinct and somewhat tumultuous stage of development can be traced all the way back to the Bible. Written according to the most egalitarian views beginning at about 900 BCE (Ehrlich, 2009), the Bible in the 37th chapter of Genesis recounts the story of Joseph the second to last son of Jacob. The chapter elaborated on this 17-year-old "youth" who is extremely idealistic, is obsessed with his appearance, gets into fights with his siblings, and is having a hard time communicating with his father. It sounds like the bible is describing not a religious figure living in the wastelands of Canaan but a teenager living in suburban Chicago.

The Greek philosopher Plato (424-348 BCE) believed that adolescents had a growing capacity for reason which in turn, allowed for the beginning of the study of science and math. His disciple Aristotle (384-322 BCE) stated that adolescents were "heated by nature as drunken men by wine". By comparing adolescents to the intoxicated he was suggesting that adolescents could be as volatile as drunken men. Now we know why high schools have a zero tolerance policy for drinking, just imagine what happens when you combine both adolescence and drunkenness.

Fast forward to the Middle Ages, during the height of the crusades when a group of youths decided to organize the Children's Crusade at about 1212 CE. Many teens from various areas in modern day Europe decided to marched in their own crusade. Their goal was to reach Israel, the holy land. They marched south through Italy towards the Mediterranean Sea with a goal of crossing the sea and reaching Israel. They got to the tip of Italy and tried to march through the water. They believed that God would part the sea for them as he did in the past for the wandering Jews en-route from Egypt to Israel. As they entered the waters expecting a miracle many of the youths drown. This historical episode highlights the idealism common in adolescents which often leads to self destruction.

During the enlightenment Jean-Jacques Rousseau describes the adolescent period as the "Stormy Adolescence" believing that adolescence was a tumultuous time of life.

By the end of the nineteenth century a new focus was emerging on adolescent issues. This Age of Adolescence (1890-1920) ushered in new school and labor laws. These laws forced adolescents to attend school and limited the number of hours adolescents could work.

Soon after began the scientific age of adolescents. With the work of the first president of the American Psychological Association G. Stanley Hall (1844-1924), who coined the phrase "Storm and Stress" to describe adolescence, a new focus was emerging in the scientific study of adolescents. In his seminal two volume book Adolescence, Hall (1904) suggested three key aspects to the adolescent experience: conflict with parents, mood disruptions, and risky behavior.

The next shift in the discipline's thinking about adolescence came with the work of anthropologist Margaret Mead (1901-1978). After spending a considerable amount of time studying adolescence in the south pacific island of Samoa she concluded that adolescent storm and stress was not universal. She believed that an adolescent's experience was based on culture. While studying adolescent Samoans, she discovered that the transition into adulthood was marked by very little strife and suggested that the stress found in western cultures was based on social and cultural elements.

## *What We Thought About Adults*

Historically the study of development has focused on childhood and adolescence. It is only in more recent times that adulthood became a focus of investigation. This trend is due to the historical belief that growth and development were only possible in the early years. Furthermore, considering the minimal life expectancy throughout history the developmental stage of adulthood was short lived and hence an area of less focus.

However, due to recent advances in the study of development, highlighting the continuous growth throughout the life-span, and the increase in life expectancy during the past 100 years, from 47 years to about 78 years, current work on development is beginning to include work on the entire life-span.

# DEVELOPMENTAL THEORIES

Theories are important because they help us to understand our observations. A good theory is a testable theory that can either be supported or not supported by research. There are several guiding theories in the study of human development and A basic foundation in these theories is vital in order to have a common starting point for all future chapters. Look at these theories as the foundation on which all other topics in this book are built on.

The theories in this section are categorized into broad categories based upon if their emphasis is on intrapsychic processes, cognitive processes, environmental processes or biological processes. However, you must keep in mind that such classifications have their shortcomings. Most of these theories cover multiple aspects of development; these groupings are based upon where most of the theory grounded.

Keep in mind, as you read about these theories, that the theories differ in their approaches to the most fundamental questions asked about the human condition. The theories provide different explanation for following fundamental questions:

NATIVISM VS. EMPIRICISM: Are humans born preprogrammed for development and growth or does development only occur through learning? The classic manner that this question has been asked is the nature/nurture controversy. Are we a product of our genetic makeup or a product of the environment we grow up in?

ACTIVE VS. PASSIVE KNOWLEDGE: Is knowledge acquired through active participation in the learning process or is knowledge acquired in a more passive manner.

CONTINUOUS VS. DISCONTINUOUS: Is growth throughout life slow and steady, like a life ramp, or does development occur in distinct stages, more like life steps? If development is slow and steady that would be continuous; but if development happens in stages then we would term development as discontinuous.

UNIVERSALISM VS. RELATIVISM: Are life experiences similar in all healthy humans across the globe or is development more relativistic and based on the specific culture in which development occurs?

Thinking about the above questions as they relate to the upcoming theories can help in narrowing down the various ideas found in these theories and can help in providing points of comparison between the various theories.

# THEORIES THAT FOCUS ON INTRAPSYCHIC PROCESSES

The theories discussed in this section address important issues regarding the nature of human beings. As such, they have had a significant impact on both researchers and practitioners in the field of human development. Psychodynamic and psychosocial theories laid the foundation for many contemporary methods of psychotherapy, for example, and parents and educators have applied these theories to child rearing. The common denominator of these theories is the belief that our development in often driven by internal, often subconscious, mechanisms that operate without our awareness. The construction of these internal mechanisms occurred during early childhood experiences.

## Psychodynamic Theories

Few individuals had more influence on modern psychology than Sigmund Freud (1856-1939). To much of the public, in fact, "psychology" is synonymous with "Freudian psychoanalytic theory." Though Freud's ideas about human **personality** development are still controversial, they are widely known and drawn upon by mental health professionals.

Freud was a physician who spent most of his life in Vienna, Austria. As a young doctor working in France in the late 1800s, Freud became interested in people's emotional disorders. He began experimenting with hypnosis as a means to study emotions. He also was interested in the role and function of dreams as emotional expression. As a result of his investigations, Freud proposed a theory of personality development that he expounded on in various books and professional articles in the early 1900s (Crain, 2005).

Freud's theory centers on how the individual progresses through a series of stages during childhood and adolescence that shape adult personality (Crain, 2005). Personality in Freudian theory refers to inner behavior that represents the true inner self as well as to outward actions manifesting that inner self. Personality also refers to the collection of emotional traits that are unique to the person.

**Personality**

The inner behavior that represents the true inner self as well as to outward actions manifesting that inner self.

What is personality?

Sigmund Freud (1856–1939), an Austrian physician, proposed the progressive development of the personality in distinct but related stages of psychosexual development. (AP)

Freud used the term psychosexual in referring to the stages of personality development. He derived the characteristics and nature of these stages through a process called psychoanalysis, which involved using hypnosis and by asking people to recall their experiences when growing up. The majority of people Freud studied would today be diagnosed as emotionally ill. From his studies of these patients, Freud came to believe that events from a person's past determined that person's behavior in the present.

Another theme in Freud's writings about personality development relates to the basic nature of human beings. Freud believed strongly that children's behavior was rooted in basic animalistic instincts that came to be controlled as they matured. These instincts, which he thought were irrational in content, became channeled into appropriate, acceptable behavior patterns as the individual grew up.

**BASIC CONCEPTS:** Freud was convinced that much human behavior is influenced by the unconscious mind, especially by the conflict between instinctual drives and social constraints against their expression. Basic personality structures are involved in mediating this conflict. Because the conflict is unbearable, people block off their awareness of their basic drives by repressing them in the unconscious part of their minds. Defense mechanisms are used to ward off the anxiety generated by conflict. Some of the common defense mechanisms employed by individuals are repression, which is when an individual conceals a disturbing memory or thought deep in the subconscious, displacement, which is when an individual redirects feelings from one person to another, and denial, when an individual blocks reality from sinking in.

But the drives do not disappear; they seek expression in some manner. Freud and others proposed that repressed drives are often expressed as physical symptoms, which the person finds to be more acceptable than the direct expression of forbidden emotions. Freud believed that the role of a psychoanalytic therapist was to help patients release these repressed emotions—to bring into the conscious (aware) mind what had been delegated into the unconscious (unaware) mind.

Early experience plays a prominent role in Freudian theory. The periods of infancy and early childhood are thought to be crucial for development in the later years of life. Interactions with parents during these years are especially important, according to Freud, in determining how healthy a person's personality development is in these years.

Freud thought that an individual's personality structure included three components. The first component of the personality is the id, which contains the person's life force. The id is composed of the drives that seek gratification of elemental needs for food, water, sex, and warmth, and contains the emotions basic to all human beings, such as anger, joy, love, and fear. The id is unconscious and operates according to the pleasure principle—that is, it is attracted to those things that are enjoyable and repelled by those things that produce discomfort. The id is largely illogical and very mysterious. Dreams are the best means for learning how a person's id functions, according to this theory. The id wishes to satisfy its needs, and does not care how it

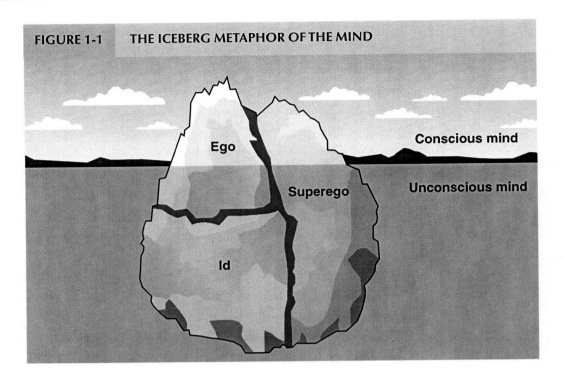

FIGURE 1-1    THE ICEBERG METAPHOR OF THE MIND

does so. If it is hungry, it doesn't care if the person buys the food or steals the food, as long as the food is obtained and eaten.

The second component of personality is the ego, which is responsible for contact with day-to-day reality. The ego emerges slowly and becomes noticeable only after a child's first birthday. This part of the personality is guided by the reality principle—that is, the ego analyzes reality in relation to past experiences, alternatives, and options for action. It also predicts probable outcomes of behavior choices. Although the ego operates fairly independently of the id, it also guides the expression of basic impulses that arise from the id.

The third part of the personality is the superego. This structure functions to control and override the id's attempts to express basic drives in ways that are socially unacceptable. It is similar to the traditional notion of conscience in that it contains information and decision-making processes that produce guilt when the person transgresses its standards. The superego is often likened to an internalized judge or parent figure guiding the person's behavior according to social and moral ideals. That is why the superego is said to operate according to the **perfection principle**.

The interaction of these three structures as they seek to express themselves in an individual constitutes personality, according to Freud.

**STAGES OF DEVELOPMENT:** Freud described the progression of personality development through stages. These are experienced in the growing years of infancy, childhood, and adolescence. The role of sexual feelings or emotions is prominent in all the stages. Freud believed that much behavior in the early years of life was dominated by the struggle to

**Perfection principle**

An internalized judge or parent figure guiding the person's behavior according to social and moral ideals.

bring the id under control of the other personality structures. Because the id operates on the pleasure principle, this means that children participate in behaviors that are sexually satisfying to them and only learn with time to control their expression.

As the person experiences each stage of development, the general sexual energy, or libido, becomes concentrated in a specific body region called an erogenous zone. Through the years of infancy and childhood, the principal erogenous zone shifts to different body locations. The sequence of the shift from one body area to another is determined by the maturation of the body as well as by experiences.

**Fixation**

Occurs when attempts to satisfy needs at a certain stage of personality development are continually frustrated.

Freud also concluded that development can be retarded by **fixation**. A fixation occurs when attempts to satisfy needs at a certain stage of personality development are continually frustrated. When tensions are experienced later in life, the person will revert to behaviors that were effective in managing frustrations at an earlier time in life.

Freud proposed five psychosexual stages based on his clinical observations and research.

## Oral Stage

The age range of this stage is birth to about 1 and a half years of age. In the oral stage, infant's pleasure centers on the mouth. Infant are constantly placing objects in their mouth to gratify this urge. Abundance or a limitation in this gratification, for example by means of over- or under-feeding, can result in an oral fixation. This fixation will reveal itself later in life in the form of an adult with an oral personality who is an overeaters, smokers, or coffee drinker.

## Anal Stage

The age range for this stage is 1 and a half to 3 years old. In the anal stage, the child's pleasure centers on the anus. The child enjoys defecation and control over anal stimulation. Overly harsh or very permissive toilet training can lead to a fixation at this stage. Harsh techniques may lead to an adult with an anal retentive personality who is obsessed with cleanliness, perfection, and control. On the other hand permissive toilet training may lead to an adult with an anal expulsive personality who is usually messy and disorganized.

## Phallic Stage

The age range for this stage is 3 to 6 years old. In the phallic stage, the child's pleasure centers on the genitals. As a result masturbation during this stage may be common. An additional dynamic operating during this stage is the Oedipal and Electra Complexes. In the Oedipal Complex boys have a sexual desire towards their mothers and hence compete with their fathers for maternal attention. Similarly, in the Electra Complex girls have a sexual desire towards their fathers and therefore become rivals with their mothers. Children overcome this stage by identifying with the same sex parent. A fixation at this stage is exhibited by the inability to identify leading to over-identification with the opposite gender. A child who over-identifies with the opposite gender parent, for example a boy over-identifying with his mother, may subconsciously want to be like the opposite gender leading to homosexuality.

## Latency Stage

The age range for this stage is 6 years old to puberty. In the latency stage, the child suppresses sexual interests and exhibits a greater interest in social and intellectual pursuits. During this time girls and boys tend to play with same sex peers. However, although not at forefront, sexuality remains in the subconscious anticipating the arrival of the next sexually explosive stage.

## Genital Stage

The age range for this stage is puberty onward. This stage is characterized as a sexual reawakening. An obsession with sexuality emerges and the source of sexual pleasure becomes someone outside of the family. Fixations that occurred during previous stages explode to the surface during adolescence. In fact, current studies indicate that often self-reports of same-sex-attraction and occurrences of obsessive-compulsive and eating disorders surface during the adolescent years, supporting Freud's fixation surfacing ideas.

It is important to remember that although controversial Freudian theory has generated much interest in the developmental processes involved in personality changes. Freud emphasized the influences of the unconscious mind and early experience on later development. These are outstanding contributions to our understanding of developmental changes across the human life span.

## Neo-Freudian Theories

Freud had many disciples that built upon his psychodynamic theory, making changes where they saw fit (Hergenhahn, 2005). Alfred Adler (1870–1937) is one such theorist. Like many neo-Freudian's, Adler thought that Freud overemphasized the biological aspects of human nature and underemphasized the psychosocial aspects. He was interested in how a person reflects upon his or her past and uses those reflections to direct development in the future and other aspects of goal-directed behavior. The ideas of inferiority and striving for superiority run throughout his work. Adler is also well-known for his theories on birth order and sibling relationships (Corey, 1991; Fadiman & Frager, 1976).

Carl Jung (1875–1961) altered Freud's theory on the personality structure to include elements such as the collective unconscious, the persona, and the shadow. Beyond that, much of popular culture's ideas about a midlife crisis come from Jung's theory, and he discussed aging and late adulthood development. Additionally, he discussed the importance of archetypes and religiosity when facing death. Besides psychodynamic theory, Eastern philosophy was highly influential to Jung's ideas (Crain, 2005; Fadiman & Frager, 1976; Jung, 1964).

## *Erikson's Psychosocial Theory*

Most modern development theories focus on the development of children. They offer extensive abstract explanations of how heredity and environment interact to influence the changes that take place during infancy, childhood, and adolescence. Our society considers the changes that occur during these periods to be the most significant life changes. Therefore, few developmental theories explain or interpret the changes that occur after adolescence. In fact, it is only within the last few decades that developmentalists have become convinced that changes do occur during adulthood.

The psychosocial theory of Erik Erikson (1950, 1964, 1982, and 1986) is a notable exception to this cultural belief. His approach is an exception also to the notion that individual development happens only under the influence of psychological and biological forces.

Erikson's theory recognizes that changes occur throughout the life span. His explanation of psychosocial development builds upon Freud's theory. Erikson expanded upon the ideas that Freud first presented, but differed from Freud in major ways about how changes are experienced, the forces that motivate changes, and the process by which changes are experienced.

Erikson's concept of development emphasizes the individual experiencing a "series of childhoods"—or changes—throughout life. Psychosocial changes occur as an evolutionary process, meaning one based on a sequence of stages involving biological, social, and psychological events that take place during life. A person enters each stage of psychosocial development with the goal of developing the specific skills and competencies considered appropriate for that time in life. Erikson sees the person as having a *dynamic* rather than a *static* personality. Thus an individual constantly experiences the reshaping and revising of personality configuration over the life span (Maier, 1965).

Each stage of psychosocial development has its own theme, which Erikson terms a **psychosocial crisis**. A psychosocial crisis is a central problem that the person is expected to master in order to make healthy progress to the next stage. Changes are enhanced or retarded by the way the person confronts and handles the central crisis of each particular stage of psychosocial development. If the person successfully deals with the crisis, she or he will experience "normal," healthy changes that lead toward happiness and personal fulfillment. If, however, the person has overwhelming difficulties in accomplishing what is expected at a particular stage, the result will be a failure to establish healthy changes not only at that particular stage but at future stages as well. As you can see, Erikson's theory incorporates epigenesis—the notion that development occurs in a stepwise manner.

**Psychosocial crisis**

A central problem that the person is expected to master in order to make healthy progress to the next stage.

**Significant others**

Those people who are singularly important at each particular stage of a person's psychosocial development.

Erikson's theory strongly refutes the idea that changes are triggered simply by some pre-set biological programming. Changes occur through interaction with social and psychological events as well as from biological programming. As the person grows older, he or she is influenced by an increasing number of people. Changes are fostered by interactions and relationships within the family context first, and then within an ever-expanding social radius (friends, the school environment, and so on). **Significant others** are those who are singularly important at each particular stage of a person's psychosocial development. These others influence the person's changes positively or negatively. Readiness to progress to a subsequent stage occurs when she or he is ready or has completed the requirements at a particular stage.

The psychosocial crisis at each stage of Erikson's theory is thought to challenge the person to acquire a corresponding psychosocial sense or attitude. Each psychosocial sense is an attitude or general feeling resulting from how adequately the person meets the crisis.

Erikson describes eight stages of psychosocial development. There are two opposing attitudes that are possible at each stage. Experiences lead the person to feel one attitude in the pair more predominantly than the other. Erikson acknowledges that it is unrealistic to expect no negative experiences at any stage. The desirable outcome is to resolve the overall developmental challenge of each stage so that more healthy than unhealthy attitudes are acquired over the life course.

| TABLE 1-1 | ERIKSON'S TIMETABLE OF DEVELOPMENTAL STAGES | | | |
|---|---|---|---|---|
| **STAGE** | **PSYCHOSOCIAL CRISIS** | **SIGNIFICANT OTHER** | **THEME** | **PERIOD OF LIFE SPAN** |
| I. | Trust vs. Mistrust | Maternal person | To get; to give in return | Birth–18 months |
| II. | Autonomy vs. Shame and Doubt | Paternal person | To hold on ; to let go | 18 months–3 years |
| III. | Initiative vs. Guilt | Family | To make; to make like | 3–6 years |
| IV. | Industry vs. Inferiority | School | To make things; to make things together | 6–12 years |
| V. | Identify vs. Role Confusion | Peers | To be oneself; to share being oneself | 13–18 years |
| VI. | Intimacy vs. Isolation | Partners | To lose and find oneself in another | 18–24 years |
| VII. | Generativity vs. Self-absorption | Life partner | To make be; to take care of | 24–54 years |
| VIII. | Integrity vs. Despair | Humankind | To be, through having been; to face not being | 54 years–death |

It is this successful resolution that enables the person to progress in psychosocial development. In the early years of childhood, for example, children are thought to experience a psychosocial stage where they have the opportunity to develop a sense of autonomy (positive) or a sense of shame and doubt (negative). Healthy development, of course, requires the child to achieve a sense of autonomy. At each of the eight stages of psychosocial development over the life span, healthy progress depends on acquiring the positive rather than the negative sense in the pair of attitudes possible for that stage.

Erikson's theory is basically optimistic in that it provides for the possibility of redemption at each stage if unhealthy attitudes were acquired at earlier stages. Someone who failed to develop a healthy psychosocial sense at one stage is not condemned to an unhealthy path of change for the rest of his or her life. But failure or difficulty in meeting the developmental challenge of one stage does slow down healthy progress in the next stages. Still, Erikson believed that a person could transform negative attitudes acquired at one stage into positive attitudes later in life.

Erikson's theory of psychosocial development is an extension of Freudian theory. Erikson's theory stresses (1) the discontinuity of psychosocial development over the life span; (2) the resolution of a central psychosocial crisis at each stage of the life span; (3) the establishment of an associated psychosocial attitude at each of his stages; and (4) the important influence "significant others" have on the individual's psychosocial development at each stage. Erikson described eight stages of psychosocial development that extend from birth until death: Trust vs. mistrust (infancy), Autonomy vs. doubt and shame (2–3 years), Initiative vs. guilt (preschool), Industry vs. inferiority (elementary school), Identity vs. role confusion (adolescence), Intimacy vs. isolation (young

| TABLE 1-2 | A COMPARISON OF CONCEPTS IN FREUDIAN AND ERIKSONIAN THEORY | |
|---|---|---|
| **CONCEPT** | **FREUD** | **ERIKSON** |
| Development | All behavior and change are determined by instinctual drives. Psychic energy propels change. | Changes occur as an evolutionary process according to a sequence of biological, social, and cultural events. |
| Dynamics of Change | Individual experiences a series of stages marked by certain characteristics. | Individual resolves psychosocial crises while progressing through a series of related stages. |
| Factors Influencing Changes | The unconscious mind; libidinal energy; the id, ego, and superego; nature of instinctual drives. | Experiencing the sequence of epigenetic stages; significant others. |
| Socialization | Maturing ego and superego gain increasing control over the id. | Establishment of identity; intrusive behavior; increasing radius of significant others. |

adulthood), Generativity vs. stagnation (middle adulthood), and Integrity vs. despair (older adulthood). We will discuss each of Erikson's stages of psychosocial development in detail when we discuss socioemotional development at each stage later in the book.

## *Humanistic Theory*

Humanistic psychology describes the human experience differently than other theories (Crain, 2005; Hergenhahn, 2005). Some people consider this approach to be diametrically opposed to behavioral theory (discussed later in this chapter). Humanistic theory views the individual as a dynamic force who seeks self-fulfillment over the course of life. Continuity of change is therefore an ever-present reality in human beings. The individual seeks her or his own destiny by setting goals, attempting to meet inner-self needs, and expressing creative energies. Humanistic theory denies the exclusive influence of either the environment or unconscious drives. Self-understanding and fulfillment—the ultimate goals of life span changes in this view—result from a conscious choice. Individuals willfully seek to maximize their experiences.

## *Maslow's Concepts*

Abraham Maslow (1970) is probably the most prominent humanistic psychologist. Maslow's approach stresses that people are motivated to make changes in order to achieve their personal full potential. He called this the drive to **self-actualization**.

**Self-actualization**

A person's drive to achieve their personal full potential.

**Needs hierarchy**

A person's need to satisfy certain basic needs before they attempt to realize self-actualization.

This state in the personal developmental path is at the pinnacle of a **needs hierarchy** common to all humans. Maslow proposed that people have to satisfy certain basic needs before they can attempt to realize self-actualization. The needs he describes are ranked in terms of priority. The most essential needs, those addressed first, relate to basic survival. These include the creature comforts of having food, warmth, shelter, safety, and so on. After these basic needs are satisfied, individuals then seek love and social contact with others. Once these needs have been satisfied, the individual turns to self-worth and self-esteem needs. These particular needs are satisfied by interactions with others that produce the conviction that the person is valued by peers, colleagues, and others. After all these needs have been fulfilled, the individual addresses the need for self-actualization. As the person experiments and learns to express his own unique nature, he may achieve self-fulfillment.

Maslow and others (Shaffer, 1978) believe that the process of achieving self-actualization is not usually begun until people reach middle or even late adulthood. Earlier in life, people tend to focus on fulfilling the lower-ranked needs. Adolescents, for example, are developmentally unready to do what is necessary to fulfill their self-actualization needs because the need for belongingness is typically addressed at this time in life. Early adulthood is the developmentally appropriate time for addressing self-esteem needs.

**FIGURE 1-2        MASLOW'S HIERARCHY OF NEEDS**

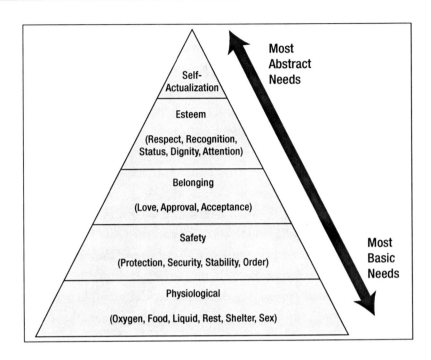

**Peak experiences**

The feeling of great joy, ecstasy, and cosmic identification with the whole universe.

Making the changes in our thoughts and behaviors that lead us to be all that we can be is what life is all about, according to Maslow. Self-actualization can be a near-mystical experience. According to Maslow, the self-actualizing person has **peak experiences**. These are feelings of great joy, ecstasy, and cosmic identification with the whole universe.

## Rogers' Concepts

**Client-centered therapy**

Also known as person-centered therapy, it is a non-directive approach to therapy based upon humanistic theory. This approach believes that the client has the necessary inner resources to cope with his or her problems.

Carl Rogers is another humanistic psychologist. In contrast to Freud, Rogers (1961) believed that human behavior is driven by impulses that are basically healthy and positive. Roger's concept of human nature is similar to Maslow's.

Unlike Maslow, though, Rogers was a practicing psychotherapist. His humanistic orientation led him to promote a style of interaction with clients termed **client-centered therapy**. Rogers' approach is less formalized than Maslow's; it has no stages. Rogers shared Maslow's conviction that reaching one's personal potential is the ultimate goal of developmental changes, but he saw the need for some people to turn to others for assistance in working through their problems. He created a style of psychotherapy that differed greatly from psychoanalysis. It stresses the attitude of the therapist. Rogers promoted a therapeutic attitude of **positive regard** toward clients. Positive regard is characterized as being warm, genuine, and giving total attention and acceptance to the client. Rogers felt that such an attitude would help the client to become more self-accepting and to achieve the greatest degree of personal growth possible (Shaffer, 1978).

**Positive regard**

Characterized as being warm, genuine, and giving total attention and acceptance to the client.

## *Implications*

Freud's psychodynamic theory of psychosexual development has generated much fruitful debate about the nature of humankind and the manner in which individual personality development occurs. However, there are difficulties with this theory that cast doubt on its validity in explaining personality development.

First, it is hard for scientists to test the concepts, principles, and propositions of Freud's theory. For instance, researchers have a hard time operationally defining some of Freud's key concepts, such as id, ego, or superego. Any good theory must be a testable theory, and so far it has been extremely difficult to test psychodynamic theory. However, new advances in neuroscience are making the testing of the unconscious mind more feasible (Galatzer-Levy & Cohler, 1993).

Second, psychodynamic theory may be biased in several ways. First of all, the theory is criticized as culture-bound and therefore limited in its application. Freud derived his concepts and principles from adults reminiscing about their past. Errors in memory are quite likely under these circumstances. It should be noted here as well that Freud drew his ideas about personality development from people who were emotionally maladjusted. His theory may better explain unhealthy personality development than normal development. Beyond being culturally biased, psychodynamic theory has been accused of being gender biased (Crain, 2005; Hergenhahn, 2005).

Third, the theory is imprecise about the nature of personality development, making it difficult to predict how people will change over time. However, it did in many ways begin the psychological study of personality and development. Additionally, psychodynamic theory has great appeal because it is such a broad-based explanation of personality development. Despite its shortcomings, Freud's psychodynamic theory has done much to increase awareness of the importance of early life experiences on later development.

Erikson's psychosocial theory attempted to extend psychodynamic concepts and stages beyond adolescence. Psychosocial theory is also significant for its emphasis on the normal rather than the abnormal aspects of developmental changes. Erikson was optimistic about human nature. His psychosocial theory allows for the possibility of later resolution of problems and tasks left unresolved at a previous stage of development. His theory also acknowledges the impact of significant others who influence the individual's psychosocial changes for better or worse throughout life. Psychosocial theory is used extensively in the fields of psychology and education as a teaching device. It helps students to understand the course of human development from a social-psychological perspective.

One of the main criticisms of Erikson's theory is its vagueness (Crain, 2005). Its explanation of the role of maturation in adulthood, for instance, is neither clear nor specific. The theory does not fully mesh with Freud's ideas and concepts on some points. Finally, this theory has generated only limited research either substantiating or refuting it.

Humanistic explanations of development offer an important alternative to learning theory and psychosocial explanations. This approach encourages an examination and appreciation of individual differences in the course of developmental changes. It stresses that certain goals cannot be accomplished until certain fundamental needs are addressed. The humanistic approach has influenced educational programs for children.

Critics judge this approach to be as imprecise as psychoanalytic theory and equally difficult to test empirically. They regard concepts such as self-actualization, peak experiences, self-fulfillment, and positive regard skeptically. They insist on the need for objective measurement of both concepts and therapeutic outcomes.

# THEORIES THAT FOCUS ON COGNITIVE PROCESSES

There are many theories that focus upon cognitive processes in development. However, one of the best-organized and most comprehensive explanations of how human beings acquire their thought processes and problem-solving abilities was proposed by Jean Piaget (1896–1980). We will discuss the foundation of Piaget's cognitive development theory in this section, laying the groundwork to discuss his stages in detail later in the book. Lev Semenovich Vygotsky (1896–1934) provided the framework for a social-historical theory of cognitive development before his life was cut short by tuberculosis at the age of thirty-eight. We will also be laying the foundation of his theory in this section. Finally, a number of theories fall under the blanket term "information-processing theory." Because the general assumptions and tenets of information-processing theory will be important when we learn about memory, problem-solving, and other cognitive processes later in the book, we will introduce some of its core concepts here.

## *Piaget's Cognitive Development Theory*

Piaget's training was in biology, although he devoted most of his life to child psychology. His intent was to learn as much as he could about how intellect developed. Ultimately, he wished to explain how human knowledge was acquired, used, and limited in scope (Crain, 2005; Dixon, 2005).

Piaget based much of his theory of cognitive development on observations of, and interviews with, children (Crain, 2005; Dixon, 2005). He also intently observed his own children to learn about the mental development of infants. Although he began publishing his findings and thoughts in 1921, his work went largely unnoticed in the United States until the 1960s (although Vygotsky knew of Piaget's work and critiqued it). His works have probably stimulated more research and educational programming for children than those of any other theorist in this area of development (Beilin, 1994).

**Cognition**

Those processes, such as perception, thinking, reasoning, and problem solving, by which one comes to know and understand the world.

**BASIC CONCEPTS**    Several concepts are central to Piaget's thoughts about the development of the intellect. **Cognition** and cognitive development are terms that refer to the way in which people come to know and understand the world. A variety of related processes—perception, problem-solving, judgment, and reasoning, for example—are involved in how people organize their mental life.

Cognitive development also refers to the changes that take place as people acquire a general understanding of the world. Piaget proposed that individuals go through a series of four stages in infancy, childhood, and adolescence (Beilin, 1994; Crain, 2005; Wadsworth, 2004). These lead to more complex and sophisticated ways of understanding the world. The ages at which people proceed through these stages are somewhat variable, though the sequence of the stages is invariable (i.e., you must go through the stages in order and not skip any stages).

A **schema** (or scheme) is a building block in cognitive development. This term refers to any consistent, reliable pattern or plan of interaction with the environment. Schemas are usually goal-oriented strategies that help the person to achieve some type of intended result from his or her behavior (Wadsworth, 2004).

**PIAGET PROPOSED TWO TYPES OF SCHEMAS: SENSORIMOTOR AND COGNITIVE**   Sensorimotor schemas are formed during the years of infancy and early childhood. These are the first rudimentary ideas about how the world functions and how the young child may operate or act to make things happen. Sensorimotor schemas have a strong base in early reflexes and motor behavior. Sucking is an early sensorimotor schema, for example. This motor act is used by babies to define and understand their world as well as to receive nourishment. It satisfies some goal and can be initiated by babies even when they are not hungry.

Cognitive schemas are derived in part from sensorimotor schemas. Cognitive schemas refer to ideas or patterns that are based largely on the individual's experiences in operating upon the environment. They differ from sensorimotor schemas in having a strong basis in mental imagery. They reflect the person's ability to use symbolism and abstract reasoning or thinking. Cognitive schemas begin to be formed in early childhood, and are continually formed throughout life. Mathematical processes, for example, are a type of cognitive schema. Once you master the mathematical operation of addition, you are then able to perform the operation using imagery rather than needing to have concrete objects before you. Visualizing objects or symbols becomes automatic through trial-and-error learning and practice.

Piaget proposed that individuals use two processes to modify schemas (Dixon, 2003; Wadsworth, 2004). **Assimilation** is the process by which people acquire new knowledge or information and match it with or incorporate it into their existing schemas. **Accommodation** refers to the process of altering existing schemas in order to bring about congruence with reality. For example, a child after repeated experiences with dogs may understand, or build a schema for dogs and from that point on will assimilate every dog they see into this existing schema. However, if this child sees a giraffe one day for the first time he will not know what it is and in an attempt to make sense out of this odd looking animal he may call it a dog, assimilating this information erroneously. Once the child spends a few more days at the zoo he will eventually understand the difference between a dog and a giraffe and will accommodate by building a new schema called giraffe. The

**Schema**

Any consistent, reliable pattern or plan of interaction with the environment.

**Assimilation**

Incorporating information from the environment into previously known ideas.

**Accommodation**

Altering existing schemas to help in understanding new information.

processes of assimilation and accommodation function throughout life to provide the means for changing and modifying schemas.

Central to Piaget's theory is the idea that mental life is devoted to active organization of one's personal understanding of the environment (Crain, 2005; Dixon, 2003; Wadsworth, 2004). Progression through the stages of cognitive development does not occur automatically, either from biological maturation or from genetic programming. Rather, people progress cognitively as they learn to organize their understanding of the world in more complex ways. Experience in interacting with the environment is the cornerstone for producing changes as people grow older. Because of this factor, each person has his or her own unique interpretation of the environment. In essence, Piaget believed that we derive our own singular understanding of the world based on our personal experiences. It is these individual meanings that we attach to what we observe that give rise to the emotional reactions we experience (Burns, 1980).

## *Vygotsky's Social-Historical Theory of Cognitive Development*

Vygotsky lived in Russia during the Communist Revolution and at a time when Marxist theory was a topic of active discussion. In fact, Vygotsky built his theory of development utilizing some of the key concepts of Marxism (Crain, 2005). This means that although Vygotsky valued both biological and environmental forces in development, he tended to spend more energy focusing on the environmental forces. Specifically, he appreciated the importance of social processes in guiding development and the value of culturally-based, psychological tools in cognitive processes (Crain, 2005; Vygotsky, 1978; Wertsch & Tulviste, 1994). Finally, Vygotsky believed that one absolutely must consider the social-historical context in which a human is developing in order to study cognitive development.

Speech, writing, our number system, and memory aids are all psychological tools which we use to mediate our behavior in the world. Vygotsky felt that although intrinsic maturational processes are enough to motivate cognitive growth the first few years of life, these cultural systems are necessary to maintain cognitive growth after that (Crain, 2005). Therefore, one of the main ideas to take away from social-historical theory is that one must understand the historical and social context of development if thinking is to be understood. We will be returning to Vygotsky's theory when we learn about language development.

**Zone of proximal development**

The range between what a child can accomplish alone and what can be accomplished with assistance.

**Scaffolding**

Provides a framework to assist a child learning a new skill initially through small steps.

As interesting as the above discussion of Vygotsky's theory is, it is not what most Americans think about when they think about Vygotsky. Instead, it is his impact on the educational system with which most Americans are familiar. Vygotsky proposed the idea of the zone of proximal development. The **zone of proximal development** is the range between what a child can accomplish alone and what they can accomplish with assistance. For example, a child may be able to "read" only a picture book on his or her own, but with some help sounding out words, he or she could read a beginning Dr. Seuss book.

Another important term to Vygotsky and modern education is **scaffolding**. Scaffolding provides a framework to assist a child learning a new skill initially through small

*Teaching a child a new skill through small steps is referred to as scaffolding. (shutterstock)*

steps. Initially, the parent or teacher provides a lot of support and assistance, then incrementally reduces the assistance as the child can complete more of the skill or task independently. For example, let's say that a child wants to learn to make a salad. Initially, the parent would probably gather and prepare all of the necessary ingredients and simply have the child toss everything into the salad bowl. Over time, maybe the child can gather the ingredients, the parent will do the necessary washing/cutting/cooking, and the child will combine the ingredients in the bowl. Ultimately, the child will take over the task in its entirety having been guided through the process time and again by the parent via a scaffolding process.

## *Information-Processing Theory*

As mentioned at the beginning of this section, information-processing theory is actually an overarching term for a group of theories. We will learn about the specifics of memory, language, and problem-solving development across the life span. All we seek to do in this section is provide you with the general framework all information-processing theories share. Below are the general assumptions in information-processing theory (Siegler, 1998):

**Information-processing**

How information is represented, processed, and applied in reference to memory constraints at any given age.

1. The term **information-processing** is synonymous with thinking. Thinking can be defined as how information is represented, processed, and applied in reference to memory constraints at any given age.

2. Information-processing researchers seek to understand the specific mechanisms that allow for cognitive development.

3. Cognitive development is guided by constant self-modification in thinking.

Future chapters will further illuminate the complexity of topics studied within information-processing theory. We will learn about types of memory, cognitive processes, and age-related changes in both of these areas.

## *Implications*

Theories that focus on cognitive processes in development share much in common yet have some marked differences. All of these theories seek to understand how thinking develops across the life span. Piaget sees cognitive development as discontinuous, or occurring in stages. Vygotsky emphasizes the importance of the social and historical context in cognitive development. Information-processing theories view cognitive development as a continuous, self-modifying process.

The most important impact all of these theories have had in the United States would be upon education. For example, the sequence of learning in a curriculum, what topics should be covered at each grade level, how children's intelligence should be measured, how children learn best and through what types of teaching methods, and what information should be taught to children, have all been developed based upon research with these theories. Beyond education, these theories have also impacted parenting advice and psychotherapy approaches.

# THEORIES THAT FOCUS ON ENVIRONMENTAL OR CONTEXTUAL PROCESSES

Reflecting back on the philosophical issues discussed in the first section, the theories discussed in this section have two main assumptions. First, humans are born as blank slates that will be shaped by their environments. Second, empiricism (or learning by experience) is far more important in shaping human development than nativism. Although the degree of rigidness on these issues varies across the theories in this section, these basic assumptions are crucial in these theories.

**Classical conditioning**

The pairing of a neutral stimulus with an unconditioned stimulus in order to achieve a desired response.

**Operant conditioning**

The use of reinforcers and punishers to control behavior.

## *Behavioral Theory*

Behavioral theory is sometimes referred to as learning theory. The two terms will be used interchangeably in this text. Behavioral theory stresses the role of an individual's interactions with the environment in shaping developmental changes. Learning is thought to take place in several ways. Behavior is modified or changed as a result of experiences and interactions with factors external to the individual.

There are two major ways learning is believed to occur in behavioral theory: **classical conditioning** and **operant conditioning**. Ivan Pavlov is the name associated with classical conditioning. He was a Russian physiologist who won the Nobel Prize in 1904 for his studies of the digestive system. Pavlov became involved in learning research

## FIGURE 1-3    PAVLOV'S CONDITIONING APPARATUS

An apparatus similar to that used by Pavlov to study classical conditioning in dogs. (From An Introduction to Psychology, by Ralph Norman Haber and Aharon H. Fried, 1975. Copyright © by Holt, Rinehart and Winston. Reproduced by permission.)

unintentionally when he was using dogs as subjects in studying the digestive process. Whenever he placed meat powder on their tongues to stimulate salivation, an unconditioned stimulus, the salivation reflex was automatically performed by the dogs, an unconditioned response. Then, Pavlov noticed that the salivation reflex was also initiated when the dogs heard their caretaker approach at mealtime, when they saw or smelled food, and when they heard noises associated with their meal preparation. All these are now termed conditioned stimuli producing salivation which is a conditioned response. The dogs had learned to respond to a new stimulus that had come to replace the original stimulus. This process of pairing a new stimulus with one that automatically produces a particular response is called classical conditioning. After this serendipitous finding with his dog subjects, Pavlov proceeded to investigate the development of classical conditioning techniques as a learning theory of behavior.

You may be thinking that although all this talk of dogs and meat and salivation is fascinating, what on earth does it have to do with human beings. Well, you have been classically conditioned and you probably don't even realize it. Put simply, classical conditioning builds new reactions built on pre-existing reflexes. Let's work through an example.

What would you feel if someone poked you with a needle? You would probably flinch or cringe and withdraw from the needle. You didn't need to learn this response; it was a reflex with which you were born. Now imagine that every time that you were poked with this needle you heard a particular sound. Eventually, just that sound alone would be enough to cause you to flinch or cringe in anticipation of the needle poke—that is, you would be classically conditioned to respond to a previously neutral stimulus in a way you responded to the original stimulus. If you don't believe this, imagine—right now—the sound of the dentist's drill (made you cringe). The first time you heard a dentist's drill, that sound meant nothing to you. However, because it has been paired with pain over and over again, just the sound of the drill is enough to cause a cringe reaction. The same can be said of food poisoning/food aversion or the smell of perfume/cologne your ex-girlfriend or ex-boyfriend wore. All of us have been classically conditioned at some point in life, and this conditioning impacted our development.

John B. Watson (1878-1958) expanded this idea into the psychological realm. Using the famous case of Little Albert, J.B. Watson created an association between a rabbit, a neutral stimulus, and a harsh noise, an unconditioned stimulus, producing within Albert a fear response to the rabbit alone. The rabbit now is termed a conditioned stimulus producing a fear conditioned response.

Let us now turn our attention to operant conditioning. Behaviorism received a great deal of attention in the 1950s and 1960s owing to the works of psychologist B. F. Skinner (1957). His contributions focus on the role and function of the consequences of behavior to learning. There are two broad categories of consequences to behavior: reinforcements and punishments. **Reinforcers** are meant to increase the behavior they follow, whereas **punishers** are meant to decrease the behaviors they follow. In general, reinforcers are more powerful in shaping behavior long-term. If you ever received praise (a reinforcer) for a good grade, or grounding (a punisher) for a bad grade, you have been operantly conditioned. A behavior can be reinforced by providing the subject a reward, a positive reinforce, or by taking away an aversive situation, a negative reinforce. When you put on your seatbelt in the car in order to stop the bothersome buzz coming out of the dashboard you are behaving as a result of a negative reinforcement. However, theoretically if a mechanical hand would come out of the car dashboard with a chocolate cake every time you put on your seatbelt your putting on the seatbelt behavior would be as a result of a positive reinforcement.

**Reinforcers**

Are meant to increase the behavior they follow.

**Punishers**

Are meant to decrease the behaviors they follow.

## Social Cognitive Theory

This theory is sometimes referred to as social learning theory. In some textbooks, it would have been discussed under behavioral theories, in other texts it would be discussed under cognitive theories. We will honor this theory with its own subsection, but please realize that not everyone will agree with our choice.

Social cognitive theory is an extension and application of behavioral theory. You see, hard core behavioral theory thought that all human behavior could be explained

*A child playing dress up to imitate a mother is an example of modeling and imitation. (iStock)*

**Observational learning**

Learning that occurs through observing others.

**Modeling**

The process by which behavior is acquired and modified through observing and replicating the behavior of others.

via external circumstances—that there was no need to consider a person's thinking. At the same time, the environment that directed a person's development had to be experienced first-hand. Social cognitive theory turned both of these assertions on their head. First, social cognitive theory recognized the importance of cognition. Second, social cognitive theory recognized that we could learn by observing the impact of the environment on others.

One of the proponents of this approach is psychologist Albert Bandura (1977). He agrees with Skinner that social learning occurs by reinforcers and punishers, but differs from Skinner in proposing that **observational learning** also shapes or changes social behavior (Bandura & Walters, 1963). **Modeling** and imitation are key ideas in social cognitive theory. Bandura believes that many kinds of behavior are acquired by watching the behavior of another person, and then coming to model one's own behavior on that of the others. This interconnection between behavior, the environment and our personal and cognitive factors is termed by Bandura as *reciprocal determinisms*.

Research into this style of learning investigates how children learn to express such social behaviors as sharing, cooperation, and aggression by imitating role models in their environment. Role models include both real people and characters on television shows or video games. Research reveals that when children see a model being rewarded for aggressive behavior, for instance, they are more likely to demonstrate that same kind of aggressive behavior in their own play.

Social cognitive theory also explains how people acquire social values and attitudes as well as occupation skills in adulthood. Social roles are learned by modeling. Children imitate behaviors they observe in adults and in other children they perceive as role models. Some aspects of human development are not so efficiently explained in social learning terms, however, as we will see throughout the book. Despite these limitations, social learning theory has significance in explaining how at least some of our different types of behavior are shaped and how learning occurs over the life span.

## *Other Contextual Theories*

There are several other theories that focus upon the environment or context of development. Bioecological theory, sociocultural theory, and family systems theory are three examples that are currently receiving a lot of attention.

**Bioecological theory** was developed by Urie Bronfenbrenner (Bronfenbrenner, 1979, 1995). This theory focuses on layers of development, much like the nested Russian dolls, that can be visualized as a series of circles. The innermost circle is the person and his or her biology (e.g., genetics, sex, age, etc.). The next circle is called the microsystem and it includes the person's immediate environment (e.g., family, friends, neighborhood, etc.). Now think briefly back to your teenage years. Did your parents and friends always get along? Interactions among the elements in your microsystem are referred to as the mesosystem, and that is the next level of context. Beyond the mesosystem is the exosystem. The exosystem involves elements that influence a person's life indirectly, such as parents' jobs or vacations. The macrosystem is the final, outside circle and includes the culture and society in which a person develops. Beyond all these circles, Bronfenbrenner includes the chronosystem, or historical time period in which an individual develops. We know this is a lot of circles and systems to wrap your brain around—the theory is dense and uses confusing terminology. Still, bioecological theory is comprehensive in tearing apart the numerous contexts in which we develop; hence, allowing researchers to zero in on the influence of specific layers of the environment on development. It may be helpful for you to sketch out your own bioecological context of development, listing influential factors to your development at each level.

**Sociocultural theory** is still evolving, largely due to the work of Barbara Rogoff. Although this theory could be viewed as neo-Vygotskian and included in the cognitive development section of this chapter, Rogoff's cross-cultural research has touched upon so many different aspects of human development (not just cognitive), that we felt it needed to be placed, on its own, in this section of the chapter. Rogoff (2003) believes that "Human development is a cultural process … people develop as participants in cultural communities. Their development can be understood only in light of the cultural practices and circumstances of their communities—which also change" (pp. 3–4). Rogoff's research not only seeks to investigate how culture creates unique patterns in human development, but also what is universal in development across cultures. She also explores the diversity of goals in human development.

**Family systems theory** describes the family as a social system. This approach theorizes that families operate as a system in the ways in which they make decisions and take actions that govern behavior, help the group meet its goals, and enable the group to maintain stability over time. Maintaining dynamic equilibrium is a challenge to a family. It must adapt as a group to the changing nature of its members as each experiences different rates of developmental change. Several concepts describe the family as a social system: wholeness, interdependence, self-regulating patterns, equifinality, adaptation, open versus closed boundaries, relationships among members, and homeostasis (Becvar & Becvar, 1982; Galvin & Brommel, 1986; Olson et al., 1983; Olson, Sprenkle & Russell, 1979; von Bertalanffy, 1974a/1974b).

---

**Bioecological theory**

A theory by Bronfenbrenner that emphasizes the nested environments that influence human development.

---

**Sociocultural theory**

A theory that cognitive development is dependent upon social interactions.

---

**Family systems theory**

The approach that theorizes that families operate as a system in the ways they make decisions and take actions that govern behavior, help the group meet its goals, and enable the group to maintain stability over time.

*Under the family systems theory families operate as a system which enables the group to maintain stability over time. (AP)*

## Implications

Theories that focus on the environment or context of development have generated a substantial amount of research into human development. Behavioral and social cognitive theories have had a broad impact on educational programs as well as on therapeutic methods for treating a variety of behavioral problems such as phobias, learning disabilities, and stress management.

Behavioral theory emphasizes the role of experience and environmental interactions that produce changes in behavior. Critics of behavioral theory have pointed out several limitations of these approaches. First, these theories emphasize the environment to the point of bias. Hereditary and biological factors also play important roles in shaping changes in behavior. Second, behavioral theory is limited to explaining specific types of behavior (neglecting cognitive processes and emotions). Third, behaviorism has been criticized for depicting the individual as rather like a machine whose performance can be controlled through conditioning. Fourth, research on behavioral theory is usually conducted in laboratory settings in which small segments of behavior are isolated, which makes the application of their findings to everyday life dubious. Critics also note that studies of behavioral theory have focused extensively on the behavior of lower animals and it is difficult to generalize these studies findings to humans. Despite all these criticisms, behavioral theory still provides some of the best approaches we know of in the treatment of autism and phobias.

The bioecological theory has led developmentalists to appreciate the nested environments that impact development, and sociocultural theory has enhanced our appreciation of the impact of culture on development. Family systems theory encourages us to see individuals as part of a system of mutual influences. All of these theories have impacted research in human development, social policy, and therapy.

# THEORIES THAT FOCUS ON BIOLOGICAL PROCESSES

Some theories emphasize the importance of biological processes on development. These theories may emphasize genetics, the process of maturation, or evolution; nevertheless, they all still understand the importance of the environment for development as well. This section will discuss some of the more commonly known theories of human development that emphasize the influence of biological processes.

## *Evolutionary Theory*

Charles Darwin (1809–1882) is largely credited as the founder of evolutionary theory. Although many contributed to and shared his thoughts, he was the most thorough in presenting and documenting his theory (Desmond & Moore, 1991; Hergenhahn, 2005). In terms of human development, key concepts in evolutionary theory would include the ideas of adaptation and fitness. **Fitness** would be seen as how well an individual is suited for his or her environment and the ability to survive and reproduce. Adaptation is traditionally posed in terms of **adaptive features**. "Adaptive features are those features that are conducive to survival in a given environment, whatever those features may be" (Hergenhahn, 2005, p. 275). In purely Darwinian terms, adaptation does not imply progress, improvement, or anything of the like. In Darwin's view, evolution lacks strategy or direction. This tends to run counter to what most of us think of when we use the terms adaptation or evolution. Evolutionary theory has been highly influential in the field of sociobiology—commonly referred to as evolutionary psychology—(Hergenhahn, 2005).

**Fitness**

How well an individual is suited for his or her environment and the ability to survive and reproduce.

**Adaptive features**

Those features that are conducive to survival in a given environment, whatever those features may be.

## *Sociobiology (or Evolutionary Psychology)*

**Sociobiology**

The study of the biological bases of social behavior.

**Sociobiology** theorists believe that genetic makeup and functioning are the prime basis of social behavior (Hergenhahn, 2005). They recognize, however, that developmental changes result from the interaction of heredity with the environment. A species tends to resist the alteration of its basic genetic pattern from one generation to another. This resistance, called phylogenetic inertia, is the nature part of the developmental

*After Charles Darwin published* On the Origin of Species *in 1857, scientists began to use animal studies to gain insight into human physiology and behavior. (Library of Congress)*

*Genes are passed down through each generation which enables the survival of genetic material. (iStock)*

change equation in the sociobiological framework. Factors from the environment, however, force a species to undergo a change in its genetic pattern over several generations. This change happens because it is beneficial to survival. Some environmental factors that force genetic change upon a species are a shortage of shelter, floods that destroy food, and disease that incapacitates or kills many individuals of the species.

Sociobiologists propose that several levels of such factors explain why individuals behave as they do. The ultimate goal of all individual behavior and developmental change, in this theory, is the survival of genetic material. All behavior relates to this basic premise: life exists in order that genes may be replicated and survive from one generation of a species to another. All living organisms adapt their behavior to ensure the survival of these basic elements of life.

Sociobiologists have studied a variety of social behaviors to test their ideas: altruism (concern for the welfare of others), competition, socialization, mating behavior, and communication, for example. Their research attempts to uncover the genetic basis underlying these behaviors—in other words, to find the biological source of developmental change.

## *Ethology*

**Ethology**

The field of inquiry that studies the biological bases of behavior patterns in animals and humans.

**Ethology** is the field of inquiry that studies the biological bases of behavior patterns in animals and humans. Several basic concepts that are used to explain behavior are briefly discussed here.

Ethology focuses on learning about the innate basis of behavior and the hereditary factors that influence developmental changes (Crain, 2005; Hergenhahn, 2005). Ethologists remind us of our animal origins. They believe that many of our behavior patterns are innate and are linked to past ancestral traits. Several researchers have stressed the role of genetic programming in the functioning of human behavior patterns. For example, Noam Chomsky (1957, 1965, 1968, and 1975) believes that the demonstrated ability of human infants to learn any particular language points to an inborn language-generating mechanism. He asserts that the human brain has evolved neuropsychological patterns that facilitate the learning and use of language, and this distinguishes us from lower animals (we will return to Chomsky's language theory later in the book).

Spotlight

What is ethology?

Several researchers have suggested that certain human behavior patterns and features have undergone evolutionary adaptation and have endured because of their survival value. For example, Lorenz (1965) proposed that physical features in the young of many animal species stimulate mothering behaviors in the adults. Crying may serve this same purpose. Another researcher has confirmed Lorenz's findings in humans. Hess (1962), reports that the pupils of adult women enlarge significantly when they are shown pictures of babies. Pupillary dilation is a reflex that indicates interest in and curiosity about an object. Hess concludes that women, unlike men, may have a biological predisposition to respond to babies in ways that help to ensure the babies' survival.

The process by which a human infant becomes attached to its parents through emotional bonds is similar to the imprinting process found among some bird and animal species. Imprinting is an irreversible learning process that occurs within a relatively short time after the birth or hatching of the young. During this critical period, the young will attach themselves psychologically to anything that moves within their vision field. Researchers have found that the process of imprinting differs from other types of learning. It is influenced by genetic factors, and appears to have the function of ensuring the survival of the young.

Some developmentalists suggest that there are other critical (or sensitive) periods in other areas of human development. They have hypothesized that these periods exist at each stage of an individual's life. During these optimal times for learning, an individual is especially sensitive to mastering tasks that are necessary to healthy developmental progress (Colombo, 1982; Crain, 2005). The presence of such critical or sensitive periods at any stage of the life span is highly speculative and an area of active research.

One of the current lines of research on evolutionary psychology examines the basis of many gender differences as a function of evolutionary mechanisms (Buss, 1989). In a series of fascinating studies Buss suggests that many gender specific behaviors often exhibited during dating and mating are a function of the differing gender specific adaptations developed throughout evolutionary history.

## Attachment Theory and Socioemotional Selectivity Theory

Two other theories that are of increasing interest in human development are attachment theory and socioemotional selectivity theory. We will discuss these theories at length when we discuss socioemotional development later in the text. For now, we just want to introduce these two theories.

**Attachment theory**

Intense emotional tie between two individuals, such as an infant and a parent.

John Bowlby developed **attachment theory** by integrating the psychodynamic, evolutionary, and ethological perspectives (Dixon, 2003). Mary Ainsworth greatly extended the theory through developing methodology to assess attachment and further research on the implications of attachment on development. This theory views the need for attachment as real as the need for food or water. Early in life, we develop mental models of attachment based upon caregiver behavior. As we shall see, these attachment models have life-long consequences.

Many times, older people are viewed as lonely because they do not seem to have as extensive of friend networks as adolescents or young adults do. Research, however, shows that older people are simply choosier in selecting relationships that are rewarding, and letting negative relationships fall to the wayside. **Socioemotional selectivity theory**, developed by Laura Carstensen, discusses this process and the developmental outcomes associated with social networks (Carstensen, Mikels, Mather, 2006).

**Socioemotional selectivity theory**

A theory that as age increases, so does the desire to be more selective in one's social relationships, optimizing positive interactions.

## Implications

Evolutionary theory, sociobiology, and ethology have proved helpful in filling out our understanding of the causes of developmental changes. Although these approaches raise many interesting issues for contemplation, critics point to a number of problems with each approach.

Sociobiology's main premise—that biological heritage shapes and limits human nature—is reminiscent of Freud's statement that "biology is destiny." Essentially, the theory proposes that what one is today is the result of past ancestral evolution. One's current developmental status has not been determined by intellect, social process, free choice, self-determination, learning, or other environmental factors. Some ethologists insist there are critical or sensitive periods for optimal development. They believe that it is next to impossible for someone who has a developmental deficit to "catch up" at a later time (White, 1975). We will soon read about other theories that allow for flexibility in developmental milestones.

# THE LIFESPAN THEORY

In an effort to synthesize developmental theory a consortiums of developmental scientists have suggested a new orientation to the study of development. This orientation termed *the lifespan theory* emphasizes the need to approach the study of development in a more complex and eclectic fashion. To clarify how this new study of development should be approached the consortium produced a collaborative statement emphasizing the complexity of this orientation:

Developmental science is an interdisciplinary approach. It emphasizes the dynamic interplay of process across time frame, levels of analysis, and contexts. Time frame is central & relative to the lifetime of the phenomena studied. Individual functioning is viewed at multiple levels. Recognizing the complexity of development is the first step toward understanding its coherence and simplicity. Patterns of adaptation represent interactions across levels within and without the person. Relative weights of contributions to behavior vary across ontogeny and domain: longitudinal analysis in needed to understand how they are coalesced over development. The pathways of development are relative to time and place. They contribute to and reflect temporal changes in cultures and society. Developmental investigation focuses on the ontogenies of embryos and ancestors and on the process by which pathways may be repeated or redirected across successive generations. Thus, comparative, cross-cultural, and intergenerational research strategies are needed along with standard experimental methods. (The Carolina Consortium on Human Development, 1996, p. 1)

Development within a person can be conceptualized as occurring within different domains. A human undergoes biological changes (e.g., puberty or brain development), cognitive changes (e.g., memory development or language development), and socioemotional changes (e.g., personality development or identity development) throughout life. Although nearly every human activity encompasses all three of these processes simultaneously, it is sometimes useful to separate these activities into their component parts to understand developmental changes more easily. It is important to keep in mind that the biological, cognitive, and socioemotional processes of development are intertwined and influence each other across the life span. Each broad domain has many subdomains within it.

## *Principles of Developmental Change*

The lifespan orientation suggests several principles that characterize developmental change (Baltes, Lindenberger & Staudinger, 1998). Many of these principles are a synthesis of ideas suggested by theorists already discussed in this chapter.

- *Lifelong* Development is a lifelong process, from conception until death in old age.

- *Multidimensional* Development occurs within the physical, cognitive, and socioemotional domains across the life span.

- *Multidirectional* Human development does not simply involve growth. It also involves the processes of maintenance and decline. For example, bone density increases early in life, is (hopefully) maintained for a while in adulthood, and then shows decline in later adulthood. The rate of decline can depend upon diet and exercise. The principle of multidirectionality applies to all the domains of development, and the timetable for growth, maintenance, and decline can vary.

- *Multidisciplinary* As mentioned at the beginning of this chapter, information from many fields is used to gain a comprehensive understanding of human development. Understanding human development takes more than just psychology. The field of human development is a rich and diverse field that incorporates the

*The stages of experience between conception and death seem to be culture bound. (iStock)*

research and theories of many disciplines (National Research Council & Institute of Medicine, 2000). Some of the disciplines that have greatly contributed to our understanding of human development include genetics, molecular biology, neuroscience, nutrition, embryology, medicine, computer science, cognitive science, psychology, sociology, gerontology, epidemiology, cultural studies, anthropology, philosophy, theology, linguistics, economics, and history. Although there is significant overlap between some of these fields, each has made unique contributions to our understanding of human development. Throughout the book research and theories from each of these disciplines, and more, will be woven into our discussion about human development.

- *Continuity* Early development is influential for later development; however, the connection is not always perfectly predictive. Although early development makes later outcomes more or less likely, development is way too complex to allow for a crystal ball vision of one's future.

- *Dance between nature, nurturing, and the individual* Human development involves complex interactions between biological components, environmental influences, and individual actions. For example, a person may have the genetic propensity for developing schizophrenia. However, she can choose to avoid environmental triggers, which can prevent initiating the onset of the disease.

- *Context* Development is embedded in an environment. These settings can be micro in nature, such as one's family, or macro in nature, such as one's culture or historical time period. We will discuss Bronfenbrenner's bioecological theory later in the chapter, which will explain one conceptualization of the levels in which development occurs. On a more general level than Bronfenbrenner's theory, developmentalists can focus on three specific contexts for influences on development (Baltes, 2003):

- *Normative age-graded influence* These influences include experiences that most people experience around the same age within a given population of interest. For example, most healthy males experience puberty within a certain age range. Most children in the United States start school around the same age.

- *Normative history-graded influences* Individuals born within the same time-frame and location often experience life-influential events unique to their cohort. Some normative history-graded influences include the Great Depression, the JFK assassination, the Challenger Space Shuttle explosion, and the events of 9/11. Although individuals born after September 11, 2001, will be able to watch the Twin Towers destruction on video, it is not the same as having lived through that day.

- *Non-normative life event influences* The above influences include events that most people of a given cohort will experience. They are common experiences that we share with most of our peers. However, nonnormative life event influences are unique because they are events that most people do not experience. For example, it is estimated that more than one million children are currently homeschooled in the United States. Nevertheless, percentage wise, homeschooling is still relatively rare and could be considered a nonnormative life event. A life-threatening illness in childhood, losing a parent in childhood, winning the lottery, or being able to travel the world in eighty days would all be considered nonnormative life event influences.

# COMPARING DEVELOPMENTAL THEORIES

Four broad categories of theories have been discussed in this chapter. Always remember that theories are not facts, but can change and are not all-inclusive. Theories provide a springboard for exploration, discussion, and debate about the many issues involved in explaining a complex process in a complex organism—developmental changes in human beings.

Some of you may feel confused and frustrated by the variety of developmental theories presented here. You may find it helpful to remember that each theory addresses different aspects of human functioning. As yet, we have no grand unifying theory of human development that explains everything in an integrated, concise manner.

Theories that focus on intrapsychic processes vary considerably in their stance of the philosophical issues. Freud's psychodynamic theory viewed humans as animalistic and instinct driven—hence, a negative view of human nature. Conversely, humanistic theory views human nature in a positive light. Most of these theories appreciate the biological propensities with which we are born, as well as the influence of our experiences and environment. Psychodynamic and psychosocial theory both view human development within a discontinuous, or stage-like framework.

Theories that focus on cognitive processes typically view humans as having a positive human nature. These theories also emphasize the active nature of knowledge acquisition.

Some cognitive theories see development as continuous (e.g., information-processing theories), whereas others see development as discontinuous (e.g., Piaget's theory of cognitive development). Piaget's theory of cognitive development and information-processing theories tend to focus on the universal aspects of development, and Vygotsky's social-historical theory emphasized the importance of context.

Theories that focus on the environment or context of development tend to view human nature from the *tabula rasa* perspective. These theories also tend to emphasize the empirical view of human development. Behavioral theories would view learning as largely passive in nature.

Theories that focus on biological processes view us with at least some preprogramming in our genes that will guide our development. Reflecting back on the philosophical issues in the first section, these theories would be seen as largely nativistic in their approach. They also tend to focus on the universal aspects of development.

**Theoretical eclecticism**

The approach of investigating the varied models and concepts and choosing the best to apply to a particular issue.

Although we did not discuss all of the philosophical issues for all of the theories, we did cover the ones most pertinent to each theoretical approach. You may be thinking, "What does all this mean for me? How can I, a student, apply this information?" Perhaps the most useful approach is to study and consider the many different theories and then construct your own explanation of developmental change. Most developmentalists do just this. They investigate the varied models and concepts and choose those they think best apply to each particular issue. This approach is termed **theoretical eclecticism**.

# DEVELOPMENTAL RESEARCH METHODS

Statistically, most of you reading this book will one day be a parent. How will you know how to best raise your children? Will you simply raise your children the same way you were raised? Will you do the exact opposite of what your parents or caregivers did? Will you seek advice? Whose advice will you seek: family, friends, and/or expert opinions?

There are many ways of knowing how to raise a child. There is knowledge based on personal experiences, television shows, folklore, religious beliefs, wisdom from other people's lives, superstitions, and science (Cozby, 2001).

What is science? Science is the marriage of rationalism and empiricism that provides a mechanism allowing for understanding the world within a system of checks and balances (Hergenhahn, 2005). Science uses observations, guided by theory, to test ideas and understand the world. Of course, the scientific method is a little more complicated than that brief definition would allow, but it is a good place to start.

This section will help you to understand some of the more common research methods in human development. Much of the information in the chapters ahead is based upon findings using these research methods. This is why it is critical that you gain a good understanding of research methods early on in this course. You want to be a critical reader of the information that lies ahead. We don't have the time or space to teach you every single research method and technique out there, but you will have a good foundation from which to begin your studies in human development.

# THE FOUNDATION FOR RESEARCH

## *The Scientific Method*

**Scientific method**

A series of steps that scientists from any field use as a process to test theories and gain knowledge within their field.

The **scientific method** is a series of steps that scientists from any field use as a process to test theories and gain knowledge within their field (Cozby, 2001). The general steps in the scientific method include:

1. Making observations about some phenomenon (e.g., people's behavior).

2. Developing a theory to explain your observations.

3. Generating a hypothesis that can test your theory and either support or not support it. You need to identify variables in your hypothesis and operationally define these variables.

4. Selecting a method to test your hypothesis and carry out the research.

5. Review the results of the study.

6. Revise your theory, share your results, and start the cycle over.

What is the scientific method?

An important assumption embedded in the above steps is that the scientist is aware of the research within the field he or she is studying and use this past research as a guide in developing his or her current research (Cozby, 2001).

There are probably quite a few unfamiliar words within our scientific method steps. Hopefully, the next few sections will help clarify some of these terms and provide a better context for understanding these steps.

**THEORY**   Have you ever noticed that parents seem particularly stressed and short-tempered with their children at shopping stores and amusements parks? Why do you think this occurs? Have you ever noticed those individuals who play the radio so loud in their cars that the vibrations tell you something is coming before you can see them? Why do these people feel the need to pollute the air in this way? If you ventured any guesses to explain these behaviors, then you just used theories—in a very generic yet common way.

**Theory**

A collection of ideas used to explain observations.

People use theories everyday. A **theory** can be thought of as a collection of ideas used to explain observations. A good theory must be testable; hence, falsifiable (Cozby, 2001; Hergenhahn, 2005). One of the biggest theories in human development faced its decline because it was largely untestable, at least in its heyday. We will talk about this more when we discuss psychoanalytic theory later in the chapter.

Let's go back to an earlier example. You may have observed that parents seem particularly stressed with their children at amusement parks. You may also have theorized as to why this may occur: heat, crowds, exhaustion, or overly excited kids. Well, in order to make this more manageable (and testable); you may want to break your theory down into smaller parts to test:

- If the weather is hot, then parents experience more stress.

- If the amusement park is crowded, then parents experience more stress.

- If parents are exhausted, then parents experience more stress.

- If children are excited, then parents experience more stress.

What we just did was take our more global theory (or collection of ideas about why parents seem more stressed with children at amusement parks) and broke it down into four testable hypotheses. The generic and ubiquitous definition of a **hypothesis** is that it means an educated guess. A hypothesis should come from a theory, be a statement (preferably in an if-then format), and be testable (Cozby, 2001).

Still, a hypothesis must be narrowed to a **prediction** in order to be tested. Choosing the first hypothesis above, we could develop the following prediction: it is predicted that as temperature increases, parental stress will increase. The difference is slight, nevertheless, we have moved from a general idea of hot weather, to the specific idea of temperature increases.

There is now one final piece of information that we must add to our above prediction in order to be able to test it: **operational definitions** of the **variables**. We have two variables (or things that vary) in our prediction, temperature and stress. The operational definitions will let everyone in the world know exactly how we plan to measure these two variables (Cozby, 2001). Are we going to measure temperature in Celsius or Fahrenheit? How are we going to measure parental stress? We could measure blood pressure, heart rate, self-report, or use some other observational measure.

You may be wondering why we should care if the world knows how we plan to measure temperature and stress. Not all variables in human development are as concrete as temperature. Most reasonable people could guess that you are going to either use Celsius or Fahrenheit when measuring temperature. However, other variables are much more conceptual and abstract in nature, like stress. Americans seem to be constantly talking about stress; we eat, sleep, and breathe stress day in and day out. Yet, what you consider stressful and how you experience stress may be completely different from someone else. Some people thrive on challenges, living on the edge, and standing in hour long lines. Other people prefer quiet, predictable lives. This is why it is so important to be extremely precise in defining what we mean by conceptual, abstract variables, and how we plan to measure them; because, two reasonable people may have completely different conceptual ideas of what stress is and how to measure it—and both could be right. Also, good research must be replicable. A theory must be tested over and over again in order to have confidence in its tenets. Having good operational definitions allows for easy study replication (Cozby, 2001).

**Hypothesis**

Generically, hypothesis means educated guess. A hypothesis should come from a theory, be a statement, and be testable.

**Prediction**

A statement of what somebody thinks will happen in the future.

**Operational definitions**

How a variable is defined in a measurable way.

**Variables**

Anything that can vary.

**THE IMPORTANCE OF THEORY**     Why is theory important to research? Couldn't you just have a question that you want to test? Good questions, if we must say so ourselves. Remember that a theory is an organized collection of ideas developed to help explain observations. Without theory, all you have are random observations without any reasoning or understanding behind these observations. In some ways, to borrow a favorite metaphor, you would see the tree but not the surrounding forest.

You could easily observe: "The baby is crying." However, what good is that observation? Why is the baby crying? Is there something that the baby needs? Is crying developmentally appropriate? What will help the baby stop crying? How long do babies typically cry? Can babies cry too much? What can happen if you don't respond when the baby cries? All of these follow-up questions bridge the gap between a simple observation and the larger, theoretical context in which the observation is embedded. Observations provide the "what," but theory provides the much more interesting "why."

# HOW ARE THEORIES TESTED?

## Types of Questions

The method that a researcher uses is dependent upon the type of question that he or she seeks to address (Cozby, 2001). Some questions focus on describing a situation, some focus on understanding relationships between variables, and still others seek to understand cause-and-effect relationships. Although specific techniques can be used regardless of the type of question asked (e.g., laboratory research could address any of the above questions), each of these different foci requires a different approach.

## Descriptive Research

**Descriptive research**

Research that seeks to describe a phenomenon.

**Naturalistic observation method**

A method of conducting research on human development that usually occurs in the "real" world where behavior happens spontaneously.

Like its name, **descriptive research** seeks to describe human development. The basic tool and method of gathering information regarding descriptive research is observation. This method is useful in making generalizations about individuals, to test a new theory, and to collect data to support or reject hypotheses. Observation is also a method used to help students gain a better understanding of human behavior at various stages of the life span.

Observation may be used in either a natural setting or in a laboratory (Cozby, 2001). A **naturalistic observation** method for conducting research on human development usually occurs in the "real" world where behavior happens spontaneously. There may be no attempt to control the environment of the people being studied and observed. Among the places that can provide rich opportunities for observing people in a natural setting are shopping malls, fast food restaurants, or beaches, for example.

Sometimes, a naturalistic observational study is conducted because it would be impossible or unethical to try to recreate the situation in a more controlled way. For example,

*Observation is the basic tool of descriptive research. This method is useful in making generalizations about individuals. (iStock)*

**Ethnographic research**

A specific type of naturalistic research largely used in anthropology, education, and cultural studies.

**Laboratory studies**

Allow for better variable control and manipulation than naturalistic studies.

**Observer bias**

Different accounts given by people who observe the same event.

riot behavior is an interesting phenomenon to study, but no one would cause a riot for the sole purpose of research. Instead, it must be studied when it spontaneously occurs.

**Ethnographic research** could be considered a specific type of naturalistic research. Ethnographic research is largely used in anthropology, education, and cultural studies; however, other fields can also utilize this strategy. Although ethnographic research can vary in approach, it can broadly be defined as the use of systematic observation in order to understand a particular social or cultural group's way of life. Very often, though not always, the observer will become an active participant in the setting of interest. Such research takes an extended amount of time because the group must come to trust the observer and view them as an insider before trusting them with open access to their group (Vogt, 1993).

Many studies using observation as the primary method of data collection are conducted in a laboratory. In this setting, the researcher can control certain variables or conditions. These may be lighting levels, or excluding distractions such as the conversations of others, traffic sounds, or household noises, for example. **Laboratory studies** allow for better variable control or manipulation than naturalistic studies. However, what is gained in control is lost in generalizability. Although we have laboratory observational research under descriptive research, with enough control and a shift in focus, this type of research can be classified as experimental research (discussed later on in the chapter).

Studies using observation data collection methods may be very valuable and provide the researcher with much information. However, there always is a question about the validity and reliability of the data that are collected by observers. Scientists are careful to use several observers to collect the data they wish to analyze. The observers receive special training to help them recognize behaviors under investigation. Different accounts, however, often are given by people who observe the same event. This is called **observer bias** and constitutes a major disadvantage of this method of data collection.

## *Correlational Research*

**Correlational research**

The study of relationship existence between two or more variables.

**Correlational research** seeks to study if a relationship exists between two or more variables (Cozby, 2001). How is information gathered for correlational research? Lots of ways! Surveys, physiological measurements, interviews, observations, and archival data sources are among the ways data can be collected for correlational research.

Let's work through a few examples in order to gain a better understanding of correlational research and types of correlations.

> **EXAMPLE 1:** Do you think that there is a relationship between the number of hours you spend studying for an exam and the score you earn on the exam? If yes, what is that relationship? Hopefully, you would say that as the number of hours studying increases, your score on the exam increases. This would indicate a **positive correlation**—as one variable increases, the other variable increases.

**Positive correlation**

As one variable increases, the other variable increases.

> **EXAMPLE 2:** Have you ever watched the reality show, *The Biggest Loser?* In this show, individuals that are extremely overweight are taught how to eat healthy and exercise. They then compete for a cash reward for losing the most weight. At the beginning of the competition, each individual is given a comprehensive physical examination. Often, the contestants suffer from high cholesterol, elevated blood pressure, and diabetes. Do you think that there is a relationship between weight loss and bad cholesterol levels? If yes, what is that relationship? Ideally, you would say that as a person's weight decreases, his or her levels of bad cholesterol decreases. What type of correlation would this indicate? If you answered positive correlation you are correct. Say what? How can a positive correlation characterize a relationship in which two variables are decreasing together? Well, the key idea behind a positive correlation is that both variables move in the same direction; that is, both variables increase together and decrease together. Spend some time thinking about this because it is a concept that many students struggle with for some time.

> **EXAMPLE 3:** Let's pretend that you start keeping a journal. In this journal, you keep track of the number of hours that you sleep each night and your level of irritability during the following day. Do you think there will be a relationship between these two variables (hours of sleep and daytime irritability)? It is possible that as hours of sleep increases, level of irritability decreases. What type of correlation would this be? It can't be a positive relationship, because the variables are not going in the same direction. Instead, as one variable increases, the other decreases. This type of correlation is referred to as a **negative correlation**.

**Negative correlation**

As one variable increases, the other decreases.

Positive and negative correlations are the two basic types of correlations examined in research. A correlation coefficient indicates how strong two variables are related (Cozby, 2001). A correlation coefficient of zero indicates that there is absolutely no relationship

**Curvilinear relationship**

In this type of correlation, two variables increase or decrease together up to a point, then switch to a negative correlation where one variable increases while the other decreases.

**Experimental research**

Seeks to establish cause and effect relationships.

**Independent variable**

A variable that is controlled and/or manipulated.

**Dependent variable**

A variable that is measured in an experimental study; the outcome of an experimental study.

**Sample**

A subset of a population.

**Randomly assigned**

Assignment of research participants to groups in an experimental study by chance.

**Experimental group**

The group that receives the experimental treatment.

**Control group**

The group that receives the placebo.

**Placebo**

An inert or innocuous substance used especially in controlled experiments testing the efficacy of another substance (as a drug).

between two variables. A score of +1.00 indicates a perfect, positive correlation between two variables. A score of −1.00 indicates a perfect, negative correlation between two variables. Hence, correlation coefficients can range from −1.00 to +1.00. The closer to -1.00 or +1.00 a correlation coefficient is, the stronger the correlation. The closer to zero a correlation coefficient is, the weaker the correlation.

There are, of course, other types of correlations. When you take a statistics course or a research methods course, you will learn about all the possible types of correlations out there. Nonetheless, it is worth mentioning one other type of correlation—**the curvilinear relationship**. You can visualize this type of correlation as either a U-shaped curve or an upside-down, U-shaped curve. In this type of correlation, two variables increase or decrease together up to a point (i.e., exhibit a positive correlation), then switch to a negative correlation (i.e., as one variable increases, the other decreases). Can you think of something that increases with age up to a certain point, then starts to decrease with continued aging? If you can't think of an example at the moment, you should certainly know some examples by the end of this course.

We cannot complete this section without teaching you the most important mantra within all of research methods: "A correlation does not imply causation!", or something to that effect. What this mantra means is that just because two variables are related does not mean that one variable is causing the other variable. Going back to our *"Biggest Loser"* example, losing weight may very well cause a decrease in bad cholesterol. However, some third variable (such as an increase in exercise or healthy food) may be influencing both the weight loss and cholesterol level. Because correlational research is just measuring variables, and not manipulating or controlling any, we must avoid assuming any cause-effect relationship exists. Only experimental research, discussed in our next section, can hope to establish cause-and-effect relationships.

## Experimental Research

**Experimental research** seeks to establish cause-and-effect relationships (Cozby, 2001). Up until now, we have used the word variables rather globally. However, there are different types of variables. In experimental research, the experimenter hypothesizes that the **independent variable** has a causal effect on the **dependent variable**. The independent variable is controlled and/or manipulated and the dependent variable is measured.

Let's start with a simple example. Dr. Doe has created a brand new drug and she is convinced that it will cure depression. She hypothesizes that if people with depression take her drug, then they will be cured of depression. The independent variable is her new drug and the dependent variable is depression. To test her hypothesis, she will need to find a **sample** of depressed people. The sample should resemble the entire population of depressed individuals in the world—meaning they should have similar ages, percentage of males and females, ethnicity, socioeconomic breakdowns, and other important characteristics. The sample participants should then be **randomly assigned** to one of two groups: the **experimental group** which will receive the new drug, or the **control group** which will

**Double-blind study**

An experiment where neither the researcher nor the participants are aware of who is receiving the actual treatment or who is receiving the placebo.

**Experimenter bias**

The influence of the experimenter's expectations or behavior in an experiment.

**Informed consent**

Providing research participants with enough information about a study that they can knowledgeably agree or disagree to participate.

**Institutional Review Board**

A committee that evaluates whether a research study is ethical and allowed to be conducted.

receive a **placebo**. Neither Dr. Doe nor the participants should be aware of who is receiving the actual drug and who is receiving the placebo; it needs to be a **double-blind study** in order to avoid **experimenter bias**. After a specified amount of time, all of the participants will have their depression measured. If the experimental group shows a statistically higher rate of depression being cured than the control group, then Dr. Doe's hypothesis will have been supported.

That was a pretty dense example. Here are the key points. First, a researcher has a hypothesis that one variable (the independent variable) has an effect on the other variable (the dependent variable). Second, the researcher must be able to control or manipulate the independent variable. Third, the hypothesis must be tested with a sample of participants that resembles the population of interest. In the example above, we needed a sample that resembled all people with depression, not all people with schizophrenia. Fourth, the participants needed to be randomly assigned to either the experimental group or the control group. Fifth, neither the participants nor the researcher should know which group they are in or bias could occur. Finally, after the study and statistical analysis is complete, the hypothesis will either be supported or not supported.

As complicated enough as the preceding two paragraphs sound, true experimental research is usually even more complicated. Researchers must worry about confounding variables, the reliability and validity of measures, and ethical issues (Cozby, 2001). To avoid ethical issues, all participants should receive **informed consent** and be debriefed after the study. Additionally, the benefits of the study must outweigh any costs, deception of participants must be avoided, and the research must be judged as ethical by an **Institutional Review Board** (IRB).

# DEVELOPMENTAL CONSIDERATIONS IN RESEARCH

Because developmentalists are interested in change across time, they must include an additional layer to their research designs. There are three basic developmental designs (cross-sectional, longitudinal, and sequential) that are used by scientists when conducting research into developmental processes. Each of these designs attempts to capture the significance of developmental changes in relation to the passage of time.

## *Cross-Sectional Research*

**Cross-sectional research design**

A research design that compares measurements or observations of some particular trait or behavior between groups of people of different ages at the same time.

A **cross-sectional** research design compares measurements or observations of some particular trait or behavior between groups of people of different ages at the same time (Cozby, 2001). For example, maybe you are interested in how children's understanding of death changes throughout childhood. You could gather a sample of three-year-olds, seven-year-olds, and eleven-year-olds all at once and compare their understanding of death. This one-shot approach would allow you to obtain a broad understanding of how children change between ages three to eleven in their understanding of death. Cross-sectional designs offer the researcher efficient, quick, and economical means to survey the way in which a particular developmental process may occur.

Cross-sectional designs, however, present problems to researchers. First, it is important to use similar groups of people at the different age levels being investigated. In other words, it is essential to keep the people in all of the groups as similar as possible in their common characteristics. For example, these may include racial group membership, income levels, intelligence, and so on. This is a very difficult challenge to accomplish successfully. Second, researchers are challenged to ensure that their measurements are the same for each age group being investigated. It is a difficult problem to ensure that the test used to measure a three-year-old

*Children who were aware of 9/11 have a different perspective of death. (AP)*

child's understanding of death is measuring the same equivalent quality in eleven-year-old children, because language must be simplified for a younger child. Third, these designs can present distorted evidence of the influence of age changes. Each **cohort** of children has experienced a decidedly different environment and it may be cohort differences instead of age differences that you are measuring. For example, children who were alive and aware of the events of 9/11 may have a very different perspective on death, not because of their age but because of the experience of living through that day.

## *Longitudinal Research*

**Longitudinal design**

A study that makes repeated measurements or observations of the same individuals over an extended period of time.

**Microgenetic studies**

A study that only lasts a matter of days or weeks.

A study that makes repeated measurements or observations of the same individuals over an extended period of time uses a **longitudinal design** (Cozby, 2001). In the previous section, we were interested in how children's understanding of death changes across childhood. To study this longitudinally, we could find a sample of three-year-olds and survey them at the ages of three, seven, and eleven. This way, we can see the progression of death understanding as the same group of children develops across time.

How long a longitudinal study lasts can vary significantly. Werner and Smith (2001) have followed the same group of individuals in Kauai, Hawaii for more than forty years. There have been a small number of such studies that have followed a group of individuals across the life span. However, **microgenetic studies** usually last only a matter of days or weeks. What aspect of development you are interested in and the time-frame during which it develops will help determine the length of the longitudinal study.

There are three advantages to the researcher in using this design: (1) direct analysis of changes is allowed in relation to increasing age; because the same people are being studied repeatedly over a period of time, only the time element changes in relation to the same group of individuals, (2) there are fewer problems with the sample of people being studied in that the same individuals are investigated at each age level that changes in relation to the passage of time, (3) the researcher can use powerful statistical tests with this design that reduce the problem of error and large variations in the data over the time period of the study (Nunnally, 1973).

Two major criticisms usually are mentioned about longitudinal studies: (1) there may be a "practice" effect present in the data in that any changes that are found can be traced to the effects of repeated performance on the same tests used over the period of the research study, (2) the feasibility of conducting such studies is limited due to the enormous expenses involved in supporting a group of researchers, keeping in touch with participants, and providing the same research facilities over the time period of the investigation (Nunnally, 1973).

## Sequential Research

**Sequential design**

A compromise that minimizes the disadvantages of both cross-sectional and longitudinal designs.

Studies may be conducted that use a **sequential design** based on the concepts of the cross-sectional and longitudinal designs (Cozby, 2001). The sequential design is a compromise that minimizes the disadvantages of both cross-sectional and longitudinal designs. The sequential design uses cohorts as participant groups. A cohort group represents a particular generation of individuals. Comparisons are made with generational groups rather than with age groups. The cohort sequential design has a strong advantage. It allows the researcher to obtain estimates of developmental changes by using an economized longitudinal strategy. Several different cohort groups are observed over a specified period of time.

This type of design is increasingly popular with researchers. This is due to its ability to provide relatively quick longitudinal results. The design can determine fairly accurate age differences over time rather than cohort differences among participants.

# WIDELY USED STATISTICAL APPROACHES

Up until now, we have covered three basic research approaches (descriptive, correlational, and experimental) and three basic developmental designs (cross-sectional, longitudinal, and sequential). Here, we will briefly introduce you to three statistical approaches that are increasingly used in developmental research. These approaches are complicated; however, if you can grasp the conceptual ideas behind them it will serve you well when discussing specific research findings in future chapters.

**Multiple regression**

A statistical method that allows researchers to predict one variable based on the values of other variables.

**Time-series analysis**

A study of the same variable across time.

**Meta-analysis**

The data from numerous studies on a particular topic are synthesized and analyzed.

**Structural equation modeling**

A model that is developed to explain patterns of relationships among variables.

**Multiple regression** is one statistical method that allows researchers to predict one variable based on the values of other variables (Vogt, 1993). Going back, once again, to our *"Biggest Loser"* example, we could hypothesize that higher levels of exercise and fiber intake will predict lower levels of bad cholesterol. After data collection, a multiple regression could be used to analyze the data. Results would either support or not support our hypothesis. The advantage here is that more than one variable can be used to predict the outcome of another variable. Once again, a cause-and-effect relationship cannot be presupposed unless the experimental method was utilized.

**Time-series analysis** typically studies the same variable across time (Vogt, 1993). Perhaps you are curious as to how ADHD rates have changed over the last fifteen years. A time-series analysis would allow you to track this information. Further, additional variables could be examined in relation to ADHD in order to ascertain if they seem predictive of ADHD rates.

**Meta-analysis** is another statistical method gaining popularity. It was mentioned earlier in this chapter about the importance of replicating studies in science. In meta-analysis, data from numerous studies on a particular topic are synthesized and analyzed (Vogt, 1993). For example, let's say that more than one thousand studies have researched the effect of toxin A on developmental disorder B. Meta-analysis is one statistical way of integrating the findings of these one thousand studies so that data from the studies can be analyzed and overarching outcomes identified.

**Structural equation modeling** (SEM) is the final statistical approach we will discuss here. In SEM, models are developed that help explain patterns of relationships among variables. Typically, multiple models are examined until the best fit (best theoretically and statistically) is found. These models are complex, but are helpful in testing complicated theories (Vogt, 1993).

This section describes a few statistical approaches. Please do not confuse these with research approaches or designs. Statistics are a way of analyzing data collected using a research approach. Said another way, a researcher's question determines the research approach (descriptive, correlational, or experimental). There are many research techniques (e.g., observation, surveys, biological measures, etc.) that can be used for any one research approach. An appropriate technique must be matched to the specific hypothesis. Because we are particularly interested in development across the life span, we have the additional layer of either a cross-sectional, longitudinal, or sequential design. Once data is collected, it must be analyzed using statistics. Once again, the appropriate statistical approach must be matched to the research approach. The results of the statistical analysis will either support the hypothesis or not.

# THE CURRENT BOOK AND STATE OF THE DISCIPLINE

After examining the background behind the study of human development it is now time to discuss how this all relates with the current book and how all of this may translate into a relevant occupation. After all the goals of going to college is having the ability to apply the information in a work setting.

## *The Current Book's Format*

Although development is continuous and the timetable for development is unique to each person, developmentalists like to organize the human life span into distinct phases. Such distinctions allow for ease in discussing broad changes across the life span. We are going to discuss two ways of organizing developmental phases in this section: stages of the life span and conceptualizations of age.

The stages of the life span are a conceptual framework for organizing the transformations human beings experience between conception and death. These stages are necessarily culture bound. For example, the stages presented here (characteristic for the mainstream culture in the United States) is very different than the life span stages for the traditional Navajo culture (Rogoff, 2003).

It should be understood that the stages of the life span are categorized into approximate age ranges. Although most adolescents are between the ages of twelve and eighteen, it is possible to have a thirty-year-old adolescent. This is because that although chronological age is a factor in considering one's stage, each developmental stage of the life span has unique characteristics and tasks, and some individuals are considered developmentally off-time.

**Developmental tasks**

The unique characteristics and tasks that help define each stage of life span.

The unique characteristics and tasks that help define each stage are known as **developmental tasks** (Havinghurst, 1972) and are derived from both maturational and environmental sources. Each stage's characteristics and tasks are the accomplishments that a person is expected to achieve or master at that particular period. These expectations help to ensure that a person will function effectively in the present and be prepared for healthy development in subsequent stages.

Society tempers its expectations of people according to the developmental stage they are currently experiencing. Additionally, social norms are often tied to a person's developmental stage. For example, people typically tolerate young children throwing food at each other in a restaurant and use the occasion as a teachable moment for table manners. Conversely, people would typically stare in wonder if they saw a group of middle-aged women in a restaurant throwing food at each other. It is more likely they would think that the women had too much alcohol instead of seeing the occasion as a good time to enter a discussion on proper etiquette.

Everyone is expected to experience each of the life stages in sequence, though the rate of development in each stage will differ from person to person. Still, many developmentalists contend that a person should resolve and accomplish the major developmental tasks at the appropriate stage in order to be considered healthy.

Eight stages are used in this text to delineate the developmental progress of human beings over the life span. These are described in greater detail in the chapters that follow. Here they are listed with approximate age ranges.

1. Prenatal (conception to birth)

2. Infancy (birth through two years)

3. Early childhood (three to six years)

4. Middle childhood (six to twelve years)

5. Adolescence (puberty to eighteen years)

6. Early adulthood (eighteen to thirty-nine years)
   a. Emerging adulthood is a term sometimes used to describe individuals eighteen to twenty-five years of age.

7. Middle adulthood (forty to retirement)

8. Late adulthood (retirement to near death)
   a. Centenarians are individuals one hundred years of age and older.

When someone asks you how old you are, do you say it depends? Actually, it should depend because you may have more than one answer. Most of us give our chronological age when presented with this question. Our **chronological age** is the number of years that have passed since our birth (or conception in some cultures). You also have a biological age, psychological age, and social age (Hoyer & Roodin, 2003; Rogoff, 2003; Santrock, 2007).

Your **biological age** is how old your body is, based on health. You may be biologically older, younger, or the same as your chronological age based on lifestyle choices and other health factors.

**Psychological age** is based upon your adaptive capacities in relation to your chronological age. A mentally challenged individual may be chronologically twenty years of age; whereas psychologically, he or she may be only five years of age. Like biological age, you may be psychologically older, younger, or the same as your chronological age.

**Social age** is based upon social norms and expectations in relation to what an individual "should" be doing at a specific chronological age. These norms can vary by gender. For example, it is often expected for girls to be more socially mature than boys on the first day of kindergarten or during early adolescence. Although these norms may or may not be accurate, social age expectations can be powerful in guiding peo-

**Chronological age**

The number of years that have passed since an individual's birth (or conception in some cultures).

**Biological age**

How old an individual's body is based on health.

**Psychological age**

Based upon an individual's adaptive capacities in relation to their chronological age.

**Social age**

Based upon social norms and expectations in relation to what an individual "should" be doing at a specific chronological age.

*Age is determined in various ways such as chronological, biological, psychological, and social. (iStock)*

ple's thoughts and behaviors. The comic strip "Cathy" used the main character's violation of the social age norm for marriage for years to engage readers.

## *Careers in Human Development*

Now that you know that human development is interdisciplinary, you may be wondering what type of careers a person can pursue with a degree in human development.

First, approximately 170 colleges and universities in the United States offer a major in either Human Development or Human Development and Family Studies leading to a bachelor's degree (College Board, 2008). A bachelor, master, or doctorate degree in human development can prepare you for a variety of careers. Some of the more obvious career choices include child care work, social work and human services, pre-K–12 teaching, college teaching, university teaching or research, and counseling. However, there are also some less obvious career choices for which a degree in human development can prepare you.

Many branches and departments at all levels of government work engage in work on issues related to human development. For example, the Census Bureau, Department of Education, Department of Health and Human Services, Department of Housing and Urban Development, Department of Justice, and the Department of Labor all have offices that focus on family and/or child issues. In addition to government, many non-profit organizations hire individuals with expertise in human development. Nonprofit organizations include research institutes, professional associations (such as the American Psychological Association), advocacy organizations, and foundations. Finally, a degree in human development could lead to a career in the private sector. Many management consulting firms and survey/evaluation research firms employ individuals from the human development field. If you are considering majoring in human development, consider visiting http://cfp.igpa.uiuc.edu/brseek/learnfields.asp. This website has a wonderful career guide for life span development majors, written by Chase-Lansdale and Gordon that is updated regularly. It is truly amazing the diversity of fields one can work in with a degree in human development. Of course, websites are continually created and dismantled, so a search on "careers in life span development" may lead you to some other insightful career guides available online. Your college counseling center can also provide a wealth of information on careers, not just in human development, but for any number of other majors as well.

Finally, in several places in this book you will find a feature titled "Development in the Real World" which will highlight some careers that are involved in the field of human development. This feature will include interviews with various professionals who in their daily work apply the concepts discussed in the text. The feature will begin with an introduction to the individual interviewed and a description of the work they do, followed by the responses to the questions. The questions presented to these practitioners will include inquires about their work setting, type of work conducted, how they apply developmental psychology in their work and their job satisfaction. This feature will help in understanding how human development is applied in the real world.

# SUMMARY

1. Life span development involves the study of human beings from conception until death in old age. Understanding human development incorporates research and theories from a diversity of disciplines. A degree in human development can lead to a career in education, counseling, the government, nonprofit organizations, or the private sector.

2. There are persistent, philosophical issues that form the foundation of theory and research in human development. Not all theories share the same perspective on these issues. These philosophical issues will be revisited throughout the text.

3. The study of human development is important for several reasons. Social norms and social policy are guided by our understanding of human development. Therapy and intervention must consider development in order to be effective. Understanding the multiple paths that development can take gives perspective to our own development and broadens our awareness of human development across history and culture.

4. Development occurs in three broad domains: physical, cognitive, and socioemotional. Although nearly all human activities involve all three of these domains concurrently, it is sometimes easier to research and understand development by categorizing it into these domains. Each domain consists of numerous smaller subdomains.

5. Principles of developmental changes guide our understanding about the process of development. Development is lifelong, multidimensional, multidirectional, multidisciplinary, contextual, and a dance between nature, nurture, and the individual. The life span can be categorized into eight periods of development: prenatal development, infancy, early childhood, middle childhood, adolescence, early adulthood, middle adulthood, and late adulthood. Age can be conceptualized into four types: chronological, biological, psychological, and social.

6. This chapter introduced you to the scientific method and research designs. Theories are an important part of research and can generate hypotheses. A good theory must be falsifiable; hence, testable.

7. One's research approach should depend upon the type of question being asked. If one wishes to describe behavior, cognitions, or emotions, then a descriptive approach should be taken. If one wishes to explore relationships among variables, then a correlational approach should be utilized. If one wishes to establish cause-and-effect, then an experimental approach should be used.

8. Because developmentalists are interested in change across ages and time, researchers must consider an additional layer in their work. Development may be studied utilizing cross-sectional, longitudinal, or sequential designs.

9. Thanks to advances in statistical theory and computer software, statistical approaches are increasingly discussed in developmental textbooks. It is helpful for students to have a conceptual understanding of multiple regression, time-series analysis, meta-analysis, and structural equation modeling. With such knowledge, students can understand the results of research studies more easily.

10. All research designs have their own strengths and weaknesses. Every theory must be tested and retested. Theories also must be modified based upon the results of research studies.

11. Theories provide a comprehensive framework from which to conduct research. A theory must be testable. Theories tend to focus on one aspect of human development: biological, cognitive, socioemotional, or environmental/contextual. They also differ on their stances on the historical, philosophical issues. There is no one theory that explains every aspect of human development. It can be helpful to select the most useful aspects of a variety of theories for addressing a particular question about developmental changes. This approach is known as theoretical eclecticism.

# SELF-QUIZ

1. Which philosopher believed that humans are born basically good and that it is civilization that corrupts the human race?
2. What are three views of human nature?
3. What are the three domains of human development?
4. What is the principle that development involves growth, maintenance, and decline?
5. What is the principle that development is embedded in an environment?
6. What is the principle that early development is related to later development?
7. What are three specific contexts for influences on development?
8. What is the term used to refer to individuals 100 years of age and older?
9. What is the age range that refers to early adulthood?
10. What are the four conceptualizations of age?
11. What is the scientific method?
12. What is a theory?
13. Why are operational definitions important?
14. The method that a researcher uses is dependent upon the type of _____ that he or she seeks to address.
15. What are the three broad approaches to research?
16. What are two specific types of observational research?
17. What are three general types of correlations?
18. Which correlation is stronger, −.84 or +.62?
19. The _____ variable is controlled and/or manipulated and the _____ variable is measured.
20. What are three developmental designs?
21. What theories discussed in this chapter focus upon biological processes?
22. What theories discussed in this chapter focus upon cognitive processes?
23. What theories discussed in this chapter focus upon socioemotional processes?
24. What theories discussed in this chapter focus upon the environment or context of development?
25. What is ethology?
26. What is cognition?
27. What is a schema (or scheme)?
28. What is personality?
29. What are the three components of Freud's personality structure?
30. What are two main ways learning is believed to occur in behavioral theory?

# TERMS AND CONCEPTS

# The Dawn of Development

(iStock)

## OUTLINE

### GENETICS

- Biological foundations
- Genetic disorders
- Behavior genetics

### PRENATAL DEVELOPMENT

- Stages of prenatal development
- Critical factors in prenatal development
- Complications in pregnancy
- Prenatal care
- Reactions to pregnancy

### BIRTH AND THE NEWBORN

- Labor and delivery
- Complications during delivery and at birth
- The newborn
- Transitions

If I asked you to reflect upon your life and remember your most important moments, what would come to mind? You may recall your high school graduation, birth of a sibling, or other such monumental events. Did you think about your moment of conception? Arguably, this is your most important moment in life, because it is when you became a life. As you will learn in this chapter, the period of prenatal development is a magical time of incredible growth and development. We will also discuss genetics and the birth process.

# GENETICS

**LEARNING OBJECTIVES:**

1. *To have a general knowledge of genetic terminology and processes*
2. *Awareness of some of the different types of genetic disorders*
3. *Appreciation for the field of behavior genetics within the context of studying life span development*

We know, we know—most of you just learned about genetics in your college or high school biology class. That's good! Some of the basic terminology and processes will simply be review for you. However, it is possible that you will learn some new material as well. We will explain some genetic disorders that are of interest to developmentalists in this section. Most of them are heart wrenching. We will also briefly touch upon the field of behavior genetics. In general, we will try to keep the focus on why genetics is important to the field of human development, hopefully providing a new perspective for you.

# BIOLOGICAL FOUNDATIONS

What color are your eyes? How tall are you? What shape is your nose (before any breaks or plastic surgery)? Clearly, genetics play a role in how you answer each of these questions. Are you shy or outgoing? Do any of your relatives have schizophrenia? Are you smarter than a fifth grader? Did you also know that genetics play a role in answering these questions as well? Genetics, in conjunction with the environment, play a role in all aspects of your development: biological, cognitive, and socioemotional. In this section we will discuss some of the basic biological aspects of genetics.

## *The Basics in Genetics*

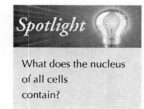

*Spotlight*

What does the nucleus of all cells contain?

At the moment of conception a complex hereditary process is initiated. This allows for a new genetic blueprint of a human being who is similar to others but genetically unique. It has been estimated, for example, that there is the possibility of 17 million different genetic combinations available for the makeup of a human being when conception occurs (Kowles, 1985; Patten, 1976). Genetics can be defined as "the study of how parents pass on characteristics to their offspring" (Jenkins, 1998, p. 16).

## Chromosomes

A collection of genes contained within a cell nucleus; the total number per cell is constant for each species, with humans having forty-six in each cell, except for the gametes, which have twenty-three.

## Autosomes

A single chromosome; any one of the forty-six chromosomes found in the nucleus of a human cell.

## Sex chromosomes

The twenty-third pair of chromosomes, which determines a person's gender.

## Gene

The basic agents of heredity from one generation of humans to the next.

The nucleus of all cells contains **chromosomes**. The number of chromosomes typically found in a cell nucleus is species-dependent. For example, dogs and chickens have seventy-eight chromosomes, chimpanzees have forty-eight chromosomes, goldfish have ninety-four chromosomes, and alligators have thirty-two chromosomes (Jenkins, 1998). For a number of years in the past, humans were thought to have forty-eight chromosomes in each cell of their bodies. Investigations conducted in 1965 determined this to be an error. These reported only forty-six chromosomes per each normal human cell, which is widely accepted today as the accurate chromosome count. Therefore, you have twenty-three pairs of chromosomes, half from your mother and half from your father. Geneticists refer to the first twenty-two pairs of chromosomes as **autosomes**, and the twenty-third pair as your **sex chromosomes**.

Chromosomes are composed of **genes**, which are the basic agents of heredity from one generation of humans to the next. Genes are known today to be composed of chemical molecules. It is through genes that one's biological make-up is passed on to offspring. They also direct the daily functioning of individual cells as well as organ systems. The total genetic makeup of an individual is known as that person's **genotype**. The interactions of genes with one another and with the environment produce the person's **phenotype**. We cannot directly see a person's genotype (it's inside his or her genes); however, we can observe a person's phenotype in certain traits and characteristics such as hair color, skin color, and behavior.

Each gene contained within a chromosome package is a single but uniquely composed molecule of **deoxyribonucleic acid** (DNA). DNA molecules have a special structure called a double helix (see Figure 2-1). It resembles a twisting ladder or a spiral staircase. There are two known functions for DNA: passing genetic material on to the next generation and the instructions for cells to make proteins (Werner, 2007). Any DNA molecule is formed of four basic nucleotides (commonly referred to as A, T, C, and G—see below). These are paired in repeated sequences to form a specific genetic code. These nucleotides

## FIGURE 2-1    A MODEL OF THE DNA MOLECULE

DNA molecules have a special structure called a double helix. DNA passes genetic material to the next generation.

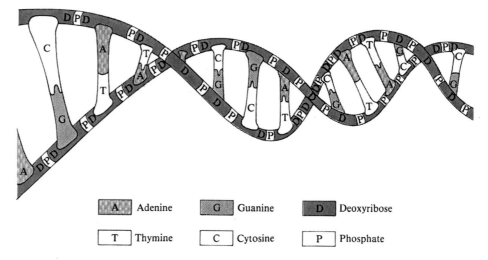

| | | | | | |
|---|---|---|---|---|---|
| A | Adenine | G | Guanine | D | Deoxyribose |
| T | Thymine | C | Cytosine | P | Phosphate |

**Genotype**

The total genetic makeup of an individual.

**Phenotype**

The traits and characteristics such as hair color, skin color, and behavior that can be observed.

**Deoxyribonucleic acid (DNA)**

A complex molecule composed of four basic nucleotides that is the carrier of genetic inheritance.

**Mitosis**

The splitting of each chromosome in the body cell to form a new pair.

**Meiosis**

The process by which the gametes (sperm and ova) are produced in the male testicles and the female ovaries.

**Mutation**

A change in the chemical structure of the gene or genes and can occur during cell division or as a result of environmental influences.

are composed of a carbohydrate (deoxyribose), a phosphate, a purine (adenine or guanine), and a pyrimidine (cystocine or thymine).

It is important to distinguish between the replacement of other body cells and the manufacture of the sex cells responsible for fertilization. The average body cell is eventually replaced by new ones as growth and development occur over the life span. Through a process called **mitosis**, each chromosome in a body cell splits to form a new pair. The result is a new daughter cell containing forty-six chromosomes that are identical with those of the original cell. **Meiosis** is the process by which the gametes (sperm and ova) are produced in the male testicles and the female ovaries. Two cell divisions usually occur when the testicles (or ovaries) produce a new sperm cell (or ovum). The result is that the nucleus of the gamete contains only twenty-three rather than the usual forty-six chromosomes. At conception, the sperm and the ovum (produced via meiosis) join together. The process of mitosis is initiated and the new genetically constituted human being begins to grow.

As most of you know, your biological sex was determined at conception. The female ovum contains twenty-three chromosomes, one of which is known as the X sex chromosome. Every normal ovum contains only an X sex chromosome.

Sperm cells from the male also contain twenty-three chromosomes. Some sperm contain an X sex chromosome, like the one found in the female ovum, whereas other sperm cells contain a Y sex chromosome. When a sperm containing an X chromosome fertilizes an ovum (containing its own X chromosome), a biological female is created. When a sperm containing a Y sex chromosome unites with an ovum (containing its X chromosome), a biological male is created. Males have a genotype of XY and females have a genotype of XX. It is the type of sperm from the father, then, that determines the biological sex of the offspring.

## Gene Mutation

Sometimes one or more genes change as a result of a **mutation**. A mutation changes the chemical structure of the gene or genes and can occur during cell division or as a result of environmental influences. Three types of gene mutations are insertion mutations, deletion mutations, and point mutations. Most mutations cause illness or death; relatively few result in a desirable outcome.

## Genetic Processes

Okay, so half of your genetic material (twenty-three chromosomes) comes from your mother and half (the other twenty-three chromosomes) comes from your father. For each pair of chromosomes, the genes that you inherit may be the same (homozygous) or may be different (heterozygous). This is because the gene may have identical or different alleles (Jenkins, 1998, p.159). This sounds confusing, so maybe the following passage from a developmental biology textbook will help:

"For each kind of a gene there is a position—a locus—where it is found along the length of a chromosome. The locus for most genes is found on two chromosomes—one inherited from our mother and one from our father. That is, we have two copies (alleles) of most genes. These copies may be identical or different. If they are different, they may both be expressed, or one copy (dominant) may mask the other (recessive)" (Dye, 2000, p. 16).

For example, you may have inherited an allele for five fingers from your dad and an allele for six fingers from your mom. Will you end up with five and half fingers? Or is one allele stronger than the other allele? We will see that some genes have a dominant/recessive process to determine how a genotype is expressed as a phenotype. Other genes have a polygenetic process to determine phenotype. Still others work by genetic processes that we are just beginning to understand. Things are much more complicated than Gregor Mendel (often called the father of genetics) may have imagined.

## Dominant/Recessive Processes

Sometimes, one allele is stronger than another allele. For example, look at your fingers. Are they long and slender (let's call this L for its genotype) or are they short and clublike (let's call this S for its genotype)? The allele for short, clublike fingers is **dominant**, whereas the allele for long, slender fingers is **recessive**. This means that if you have long, slender fingers, both of your alleles are recessive (genotype LL). If just one of your alleles was S, you would have short, clublike fingers because it is a dominant allele. This means that people with either genotypes SL or SS have the phenotype of short, clublike fingers.

Gene dominance occurs when any two partner alleles are not identical for a gene. One allele is said to be dominant and the other recessive. The dominant gene of the pair acts to produce the trait this pair of genes is supposed to affect, and the activity of the recessive gene is repressed. However, sometimes there can be **incomplete dominance** (such as when a red flower and a white flower bred together can create a pink flower) and **codominance** or **intermediate inheritance** (such as when a white cow and a red bull will produce a calf with red and white hairs). Occasionally, a specific trait or characteristic may have more than one pair of alleles possible (multiple allelism). Blood type is an example of this (Dye, 2000; Jenkins, 1998).

*A pink flower is an example of incomplete dominance. (iStock)*

**Dominant**

A gene from one parent that controls or suppresses the influence of the complementary (recessive) gene from the other parent in the offspring.

**Recessive**

A gene from one parent whose influence is repressed by the complementary (dominant) gene from the other parent in the offspring

**Incomplete dominance**

Occurs when one allele is not completely dominant over the second allele.

**Codominance**

Occurs when both alleles are fully expressed.

## Sex-Linked Inheritance

As mentioned earlier, there are two sex chromosomes that control the biological sex of a child (XX or XY). The X chromosome is larger than the Y chromosome and seems to carry more genetically rich information (Dye, 2000). Later in this chapter we will briefly discuss some sex-linked chromosome disorders. If a male inherits a recessive gene on his X chromosome, he will exhibit the recessive trait. However, if a female inherits a recessive gene on one of her X chromosomes, she will be a carrier of the gene, but may not exhibit the recessive trait if her other X chromosome has a dominate gene. This is why males are more likely to inherit certain sex-linked traits, characteristics, or disorders such as color-blindness, baldness, or hemophilia.

## *Polygenic Inheritance*

**Polygenic process**

The interaction of alleles from more than one gene.

Although some inherited traits and characteristics follow a dominant/recessive process, others involve a **polygenic process** (or the interaction of several genes). Intelligence, skin color, eye color, and height are just some of the human traits that involve polygenic inheritance (Dye, 2000; Jenkins, 1998). For instance, you may have been taught that eye color is a matter of dominant/recessive alleles; however, eye color is determined by the amount of melanin present in your iris. Light-colored eyes have lower amounts of melanin than dark-colored eyes. Skin color is the same way, and many geneticists believe that at least three genes interact to determine skin color.

**Discontinuous variation**

When a trait or variation can be placed into distinct categories.

Some human traits and characteristics are coded for an either/or presentation (i.e., **discontinuous variation**) driven by dominant/recessive processes. For example, either you have five fingers or six fingers, depending upon your genotype. However, other human traits and characteristics are coded for a **continuous variation** as seen with polygenetic inheritance. For example, an individual's intelligence or height is limited by a range set forth in the genotype, but it is the interaction of genes (and sometimes environmental influences) that ultimately determines that person's phenotype (Dye, 2000; Jenkins, 1998).

**Continuous variation**

When a trait or variation is distributed on a continuum or spectrum.

## *Beyond the Genes*

**Epigenetic information**

A characteristic of developmental changes meaning that changes that are currently observed were determined by those that occurred earlier in time, and changes that follow will be influenced by the ones currently being observed.

A child receives three kinds of information during prenatal development: "genes, maternally derived substances, and differential chemical modification of parental genes" (Dye, 2000, p. 16). The first, the genes, we have already covered. The other two forms of information can be collectively referred to as **epigenetic information**. These mechanisms are still in the process of being understood, but some preliminary information is known.

**Genetic imprinting**

The repression or expression of a gene or chromosome in an offspring that is dependent upon which parent it is inherited from.

**Genetic imprinting** can be considered one form of epigenetic information. It is the fascinating process whereby how genetic material is expressed is dependent upon from which parent it is inherited (Moore & Persaud, 1998). For example, some chromosome disorders will manifest as different syndromes dependent upon whether the chromosome deletion is carried by the mother or the father. Another form of epigenetic information is the cytoplasmic environment during ovum development (Dye, 2000). As stated, epigenetic information is a new area of research; however, some preliminary findings suggest that longevity, metabolism rates, and height may be influenced by epigenetic information from both the parents and possibly the grandparents.

In summary, each of us is endowed with a unique genetic make-up at the moment of conception. Sometimes, however, mistakes can happen in our genes and a genetic disorder is the result. The next section will discuss some ways in which our genetic process can go awry.

*Pause and Process:*

1. Distinguish between genotype and phenotype.

2. Explain the genetic processes of dominant/recessive genes and polygenetic inheritance.

# GENETIC DISORDERS

There are different categories of genetic disorders (ACOG, 2005); we will discuss three broad categories here. Some disorders are caused by a single gene. Other disorders are caused at the chromosomal level (or by many genes). Still others are multifactorial in cause (or caused by genes and environmental factors). Below, we will briefly highlight several genetic disorders and then discuss a few of the more common ones at length.

## *Inherited Disorders*

**Inherited disorder**

A disorder or disease that develops due to a gene mutation, chromosomal problem, or other genetic factor.

As mentioned above, some genetic disorders are initiated by a single gene. These are referred to as **inherited disorders**. They may originate from dominant genes, recessive genes, or sex-linked genes.

If a disorder is inherited from a dominant gene, then it can be given to a child by a single gene from one parent. These disorders can range from life-threatening to nonserious. See Table (2a-1) of some dominant-gene (or autosomal dominant) disorders (ACOG, 2005; Carlson, 1999).

| TABLE 2A-1 | DOMINANT-GENE DISORDERS |
| --- | --- |
| **DOMINANT-GENE DISORDERS** | **BRIEF DESCRIPTION** |
| Anchondroplasia | Dwarfism with short limbs |
| Aniridia | Incomplete iris |
| Crouzon syndrome | Abnormalities to the cranium structure |
| Huntington's disease | Degeneration of the nervous system |
| Neurofibromatosis | Pigmentation abnormalities and tumors on the skin |
| Polycystic kidney disease type III | Having cysts in the kidneys |
| Polydactyly | Having extra fingers or toes |

| TABLE 2A-2 | RECESSIVE-GENE DISORDERS |
|---|---|
| **RECESSIVE-GENE DISORDERS** | **BRIEF DESCRIPTION** |
| Albinism | Reduction or lack of pigmentation in the skin, eyes, and/or hair; eye problems |
| Bloom syndrome | Prenatal and childhood growth problems, cognitive deficits |
| Cystic fibrosis | Mucus build-up in the respiratory system, frequent respiratory infections |
| Polycystic kidney disease type I | Having cysts in the kidneys |
| Phocomelia syndrome | Deformities in the limbs |
| Sickle-cell disease | Misshapen red blood cells that cannot properly carry oxygen to all parts of the body and block white blood cells |
| Tay-Sachs disease | Nervous system degeneration and early childhood death |

If a disorder is inherited from a recessive gene, then both parents must be carriers of the gene in order for the child to have the disorder. If only one parent is a carrier, then the child may be a carrier but will not have the disorder. Many of these disorders have different prevalence rates for different ethnic groups. See Table (2a-2) of some recessive-gene (or autosomal recessive) disorders (ACOG, 2005; Carlson, 1999).

Sex-linked chromosome disorders are carried on the X chromosome; hence, they are sometimes referred to as X-linked recessive disorders. These disorders are much more common in males. This is because males have only one X chromosome; therefore, if there is a recessive gene on it, they will develop the disorder. On the other hand, females have two X chromosomes, so if one has a recessive gene, the other may have a dominant gene that prevents the disorder from materializing or will mitigate the materialization of the disorder. See Table (2a-3) of some sex-linked disorders (ACOG, 2005; Carlson, 1999).

| TABLE 2A-3 | SEX-LINKED DISORDERS |
|---|---|
| **SEX-LINKED DISORDERS** | **BRIEF DESCRIPTION** |
| Fragile X syndrome | Cognitive deficiencies possible, including learning disabilities or mental retardation |
| Hemophilia | Inability to clot blood normally |
| Hydrocephalus | Large cranium |
| Icthyosis | Skin disorder |
| Testicular feminization syndrome | Genetic male with a female phenotype |

## Chromosomal Disorders

**Chromosomal disorder**

A disorder due to a chromosomal abnormality or defect.

**Chromosomal disorders** stem from a missing, duplicate, or damaged chromosome (ACOG, 2005). In this category of disorders, the problem typically originates during fertilization. The risk of having a baby with a chromosome disorder increases with the mother's age. For example, a twenty-five-year-old woman has a 1/476 chance of having a baby with any chromosomal disorder; conversely, a thirty-five-year-old woman has a 1/192 chance and a forty-five-year-old woman has a 1/21 chance of having a baby with such a disorder (as cited by the ACOG, 2005). The two most discussed chromosome disorders are Down syndrome and trisomy 18.

## Multifactorial Disorders

**Multifactorial disorder**

A disorder that results from the interaction of genetics with the environment.

**Multifactorial disorders** come from a combination of genetic and environmental causes. Often, doctors are never quite certain what the specific cause of such disorders is. Some examples of multifactorial disorders include neural tube defects and cleft palates.

## Support for Families Coping with Genetic Disorders

Genetic disorders may be minor in nature or life-threatening. Regardless, the impact of learning that you or your loved one is facing such a disorder cannot be underestimated. Some of these disorders are widely known and have established support networks. Others are so rare, that finding support can be difficult. The genesis of the World Wide Web has offered individuals facing a genetic disorder a new hope in finding support. Information, support groups (online and in person), medical interventions, and research information are now available in an easy-to-use interface. Again, the rarer disorders may still be hard to find support for; however, families can reach out and try to find help in ways never thought possible.

*Pause and Process:*

1. What is the difference between inherited disorders and chromosomal disorders?

2. Why are males more likely to inherit some genetic disorders than females?

# BEHAVIOR GENETICS

The field of behavior genetics seeks to understand how genetic and environmental factors interact to produce particular behaviors, characteristics, and traits. This is not the nature versus nurture argument of old; instead, it is an endeavor to truly understand the interactive dance between nature and nurture and their coactive influence on development. Environmental factors can be broadly conceptualized as external environmental factors and internal environmental factors that influence the expression of genes (National Research

Council, 2000). This section will address some of the research designs used in behavior genetics and some of the ways in which genetics and the environment interact and influence one another.

## Research Designs

Because developmentalists can neither ethically nor practically enact selective breeding programs to study behavioral genetics, they have heavily relied upon twin and adoption research. Both approaches have their strengths and their limitations.

In adoption research, a child's characteristics are compared with his biological and adoptive mothers' characteristics. For example, let's say you are interested in how musical preferences are influenced by genetics and environment. You could compare an adopted child's preference for classical music to his biological mother's like of classical music (where the child and mother share genes, but not the home environment). You could also compare the adopted child's preference for classical music to his adoptive mother's like of classical music (where the child and mother share a home environment, but not genes). What could you assume if the child's preferences closely resemble the adoptive mother's preferences but not the biological mother's preferences? One possible assumption could be that home environment is more important in the development of musical preferences than genetic endowment. This is an overly simplified example of the adoptive research design, but it gives you a general idea of what the approach is like. There are variations on this theme that may focus upon biologically related and unrelated siblings.

There are some potential problems with the adoption research design (National Research Council, 2000). Can you guess what they may be? First, adoption designs can neglect to consider the possibilities that adoption agencies are selective in their placements and how that may bias the research. Second, adoption studies may neglect to consider the impact of prenatal experiences on the child. Finally, a child is not a lump of clay when placed with an adoptive family. He or she comes with their own set of characteristics that may evoke certain responses and interactions from adoptive parents. This can also bias, or at least impact, the outcomes of any study.

Twin studies compare the traits/characteristics/behaviors of monozygotic (genetically identical—identical twins) and dizygotic (genetically similar, but not identical—fraternal twins) twins. What would you suppose if monozygotic twins were more alike in their music preferences than dizygotic twins? It would be easy to assume that music preference is at least somewhat influenced by genetics. Again, this is an overly simplified example, but it gives you the big picture of twin studies. Sometimes, twin studies compare twins that were raised together against those that were separated at birth and reared apart (think *The Parent Trap* here). This allows researchers the additional layer of considering home environment influences.

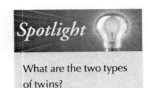

*Spotlight*

What are the two types of twins?

Twin study designs also have some potential problems (National Research Council, 2000). It is possible that monozygotic twins and dizygotic differ in regards to how similar their home environments are. Perhaps parents are more likely to treat monozygotic twins

*Twin studies compares the traits/characteristics/behaviors of monozygotic and dizygotic twins. (iStock)*

more alike than dizygotic twins. If the twin study involves separation at birth and adoption, then we have the same issues mentioned earlier for the adoption studies. Additionally, maybe twin development is not the same as development in individuals who are not twins. In this case, the research findings are applicable only to twins, not people in general. Still, adoption and twin studies within the paradigm of behavior genetics have offered some interesting insights into the co-influence of genetics and environment.

## Genetic/Environment Interactions

How do genes and the environment interact? The answer is that it depends. There are a few different ways that we can see genes and the environment interact (Scarr, 1993). These are largely false categorizations, because in the real world, all of these different interactions are probably happening simultaneously and continuously.

One perspective on gene/environment interactions highlights the dynamic nature of such interactions. A child's genetic endowment may lead to some behavioral propensities, which in turn, evoke certain responses from the environment. For example, a child with impulsive behaviors may elicit impulsive behaviors from the parents. Hence, this type of relationship could be viewed as an **evocative genotype-environment** relationship (or correlation).

Another perspective on gene/environment interactions may focus upon the influence of the environment in activating genes. For example, a person may have the genetic propensity for developing bipolar disorder; however, whether those genes are activated depends upon environmental factors. This type of relationship is viewed as a **passive genotype-environment** relationship (or correlation).

A final perspective on gene/environment interactions may emphasize what is referred to as niche-picking. Within this perspective, attention is paid to the fact that people, influenced by their genetics, seek out environments that are in harmony with their genetic

**Evocative genotype-environment correlation**

An environment in which the child elicits certain environments or behaviors due to his or her genetics.

**Passive genotype-environment correlation**

An environment in which the child passively receives an environment.

**Active genotype-environment correlation**

An environment that the child seeks due to genetic preferences.

propensities. For example, a child who is, by nature, social and active may seek out sports that are social and active. Conversely, a child who is, by nature, quiet and introspective may seek out activities that mesh better with his or her nature. This type of a relationship is viewed as an **active genotype-environment** relationship (or correlation) in which individuals seek environments in tune with their biological preferences.

*Pause and Process:*

1. What is the goal of behavior genetics?

2. Describe adoption and twin studies.

# PRENATAL DEVELOPMENT

*LEARNING OBJECTIVES:*

1. *Understand and describe the nature of developmental changes occurring between conception and birth*

2. *Identify and describe various hazards that may be experienced during a woman's pregnancy*

3. *Discuss complications that may arise during pregnancy*

4. *Relate common prenatal care*

5. *Understand typical reactions to pregnancy*

The period before birth is perhaps the most crucial stage in the life span. During the average 280-day period, the biological foundations are established that are influential for the entire life span.

In earlier times, development before birth was surrounded by mystery. Because it is hidden from direct observation, the beginnings of life were largely misunderstood, even by scientists. In these less-informed times, folklore and superstition governed popular speculation about pregnancy. One folk belief held that everything a pregnant woman experienced affected the developing child within her uterus. Birthmarks on the baby's body, for example, were attributed to the mother's having a frightening or stressful experience, spilling wine at a meal, or eating too many strawberries during pregnancy. A newborn's harelip (a deformation of the upper lip and palate that produces a rodentlike appearance) was attributed to the mother's viewing a rabbit during pregnancy. On a more elevated plane, many women believed that if they listened to classical music, read fine literature, and thought "good" thoughts, their child would be born with an appreciation for music, high intelligence, and a good character.

These folklore beliefs were discarded in modern times as scientists gained information on how life begins, how the process of genetic transmission occurs, and how the internal and external maternal environments influence the individual's development during pregnancy. These advances in knowledge are discussed in this section. Other topics explored are the course by which these changes occur, the factors that critically influence how they occur, and the tools used by modern medical science to provide the kind of prenatal care that will enhance an individual's development.

# STAGES OF PRENATAL DEVELOPMENT

The developmental changes that occur before birth are significant in many ways. Many experts consider this the most important stage of life. The changes an individual experiences during this time have a critical bearing on development in subsequent stages in the life span.

The time before birth is the shortest stage of the life span. The average length of pregnancy is 280 days (about nine calendar months or ten, twenty-eight-day lunar months). Although the length of pregnancy is somewhat variable, there are invariably many remarkable changes between conception and birth. Essentially, an individual develops from a genetically unique, one-celled human into a newborn with more than 200 billion cells during this relatively short time. As we will soon learn, the most rapid rate of growth and development of the entire life span occurs before birth! As we will also soon learn, this is a highly critical period in human development, in which the person is sensitive to many hazards and benefits to its development provided through the maternal environment.

## *Stages Versus Trimesters*

When thinking about pregnancy, most people think about the three trimesters. The first trimester would be the first three months of pregnancy. Many women experience morning

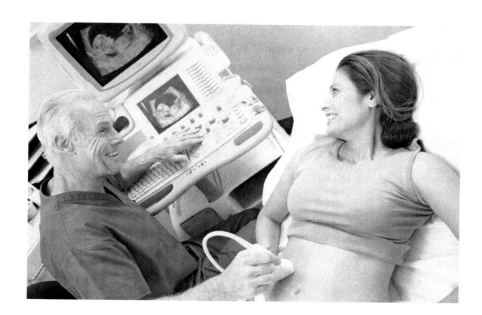

*The average length of pregnancy is 280 days. During this time life begins with one cell and quickly grows into a newborn with more than 200 billion cells. (shutterstock)*

sickness, or all day sickness, during this time. The second trimester would be the second three months of pregnancy. This trimester is sometimes alluded to as the honeymoon trimester because morning sickness subsides for most women and the woman is still comfortable physically. The third trimester would be the final three months of pregnancy. This is the trimester when the baby gains weight rapidly and the woman can begin to have aches and pains due to the weight of the baby and shift in her center of gravity.

Developmentalists, however, view prenatal development as occurring in three periods that do *not* correspond with the three trimesters. These periods are based on biological milestones and are not broken into equivalent lengths. The germinal period is from conception to two weeks. The embryonic period is from three to eight weeks. The fetal period is from nine weeks until birth. As you will see, each of these periods is highlighted by unique developmental milestones during this prenatal stage of life.

## Conception

**Fertilization**

The penetration of the ovum by a sperm cell.

**Conception**

The fertilization of an ovum by a sperm cell.

The development of an individual begins with **fertilization** of an ovum by a sperm cell. This is called **conception**. The sperm contained in the semen from the male are deposited by ejaculation into the vaginal tract. One ejaculation—about a teaspoon of fluid—normally contains about 300 million to 500 million sperm cells. Of this vast number, only several hundred survive to reach the fallopian tube that harbors the ovum.

Sperm cells are propelled on the journey by their long, whipping tails, which move them up the vaginal tract to the cervix. From this point, sperm are assisted through the uterus and fallopian tubes by small, weak contractions of these organs. The great majority of sperm fail to survive the journey to the ovum because of the highly acidic condition of the female reproductive tract, the immaturity of some sperm cells, breakage of tails, fatigue, and moving into the wrong fallopian tube.

Conception begins when the surviving sperm encounter the ovum in the upper end of the fallopian tube into which the ovum was deposited after ovulation. The sperm cells gather around the ovum with their head areas pointing toward the surface. The head region of the sperm cells releases an enzyme. A pathway may then be opened through the cellular matter surrounding the ovum.

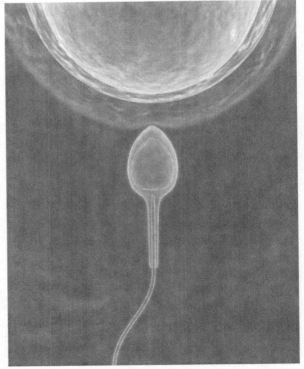

*A sperm cell fertilizes an ovum. This is the point of conception and the beginning of an individual. (iStock)*

When the head of one sperm comes into contact with the ovum's surface, a biochemical change occurs within the ovum that prevents the entry of other sperm cells. This process is not clearly understood. The sperm cell in contact enters the ovum, initiating a complex process leading to the completion of a fully constituted, single-cell human. If normal, this single cell now contains forty-six chromosomes, twenty-three from the sperm cell and twenty-three from the ovum. Hence, from the moment of conception, the human being has a unique, genetic composition (Moore & Persaud, 1998).

## Germinal Period

**Germinal period**

The phase of prenatal developing lasting from conception until implantation in the uterus (around ten to fourteen days).

**Zygote**

The name of the developing individual during the germinal period.

The **germinal period** lasts from conception of the individual until his or her implantation into the uterus (about ten to fourteen days). We refer to the baby as a **zygote** during this period of prenatal development. From the moment of fertilization, the zygote's sex is already determined by the sperm (X-bearing or Y-bearing sperm). Fertilization also initiates cleavage—or cell division—in the zygote (Moore & Persaud, 1998).

The first two weeks following conception constitute a critical period for the developing individual. For the first three or four days after conception, cilia lining the fallopian tube move the zygote on his or her journey to the uterus. Again, the zygote experiences cleavage as he or she moves along the tube.

The one-celled zygote created at conception divides by mitosis into two genetically identical cells within twelve to fifteen hours. These cells reproduce themselves to make four, then eight, then sixteen, and so on. Cell division begins slowly, but then rapidly picks up speed. By the third day following conception, the cells have divided sufficiently through mitotic cleavage to form a small ball that is known as a blastocyst. It is in this form that the zygote enters the uterus. Attachment in the uterus begins about six days after conception, although the process of implantation takes some time to complete (Moore & Persaud, 1998).

The endometrial tissue has been prepared for accepting the zygote by hormones. The outer layer of the blastocyst, called the trophoblast, will develop into the support structures for the individual during prenatal development (e.g., placenta). The inner part of the blastocyst (or inner cell mass) is the part where the zygote resides.

**Implantation**

Occurs when the zygote burrows into the uterus.

**Implantation** occurs when the blastocyst sinks into the endometrium. With this event, an important process begins that serves to ensure the survival of the zygote. Through the action of hormones produced by the blastocyst, an intensive chemical exchange occurs between the blastocyst and the mother's tissue to signal his or her presence in the mother's womb. The exchange temporarily impairs the mother's immune system to prevent antibodies from attaching the blastocyst as foreign matter. Said in plain English, the baby has a unique genetic composition. As such, the mother's immune system would see the baby's body as foreign tissue and attack it. However, implantation triggers biochemical activity that is equivalent to the zygote saying, "I'm here! Please don't reject me!" If this biochemical reaction did not occur, all pregnancies would result in miscarriage due to the woman's body rejecting the baby.

While the blastocyst is implanting itself in the uterine wall, other changes are taking place within. During the second week after conception, the inner cell mass separates into three distinct layers that specialize and give rise to different organ systems and structures of the body.

The outer layer is known as the ectoderm. It gives rise to cells that form skin, hair, sweat glands, tooth enamel, salivary glands, and all the nervous tissue, including the brain. The middle layer, or mesoderm, forms the muscles, bones, blood, circulatory system, teeth, connective tissues, and kidneys. The inner layer, the endoderm, is the one from which most of the internal organs (stomach, intestines, liver, lungs, heart, and so on) are formed. The implantation process is usually completed by the second week after conception.

## Embryonic Period

**Embryonic period**

The two weeks after conception until around eight weeks after conception.

**Embryo**

The name of the developing individual during the embryonic period.

The **embryonic period** spans from two weeks after conception until around eight weeks after conception. The individual is called an **embryo** during this time. Developmental changes during this crucial period are characterized generally by rapid cell growth and differentiation, the formation of the placenta, and initial organ functioning. While all the organs are formed and begin functioning at some level during this period, some organs are not fully mature until the person is in his or her early to mid-twenties.

Several important functional systems of pregnancy appear early in the embryonic period. These are the development of the placenta, the umbilical cord, and the amniotic fluid. Their function is to ensure the survival and proper development of the individual throughout the pregnancy.

The placenta has three primary functions: (1) metabolism; (2) transfer of gases and chemicals between the developing individual and the mother; and (3) hormone production. A wide variety of chemical and nutrient matter is exchanged across the placental tissue between the developing child and its mother. The blood of the two never mixes in this transfer process. Rather, exchanges are made through the chemical process of osmosis. The placenta acts as a barrier to many harmful substances that could enter the developing baby's body. However, it also can expose the child to many adverse environmental influences before birth.

The umbilical cord extends from the center of the placenta into the baby's abdomen. Two major arteries and one vein from the embryo's body lead into the placenta. The structure is twisted in a way that resembles a coiled rope or cord. It has no nerves.

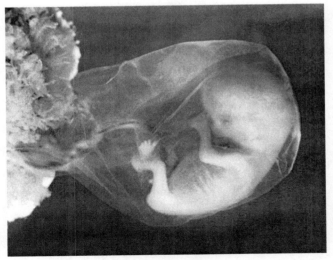

*An individual is called an embryo from two to eight weeks after conception. (Photo courtesy of T. Grayson)*

**Organogenesis**

The formation of organs during the embryonic period.

**Fetus**

The name of the developing individual beginning in the ninth week after conception until birth.

**Fetal period**

The phase of prenatal development that spans from eight weeks after conception to birth (at around forty weeks).

**Quickening**

The first detection by a mother of movements made by a fetus.

**Lanugo**

A fine down-like hair covering the baby's body.

**Vernix caseosa**

A thick, cold cream-like substance covering the baby's skin. It serves to protect the skin and lubricate the fetus for passage through the birth canal.

**Age of viability**

The point in prenatal development where the baby stands a chance of surviving outside of the womb.

The amniotic fluid is saline in nature. This material fills the amniotic sac during pregnancy. It cushions the developing child from jolts and bumps by allowing it to float freely and buoyantly within the cavity. It also maintains a constant temperature environment for the baby. Because it enables freedom of movement, it encourages muscle development. Amniotic fluid is swallowed by the developing child, which serves to prime the intestines and kidneys for functioning after birth. It is also useful in determining the health status of the child in a type of prenatal diagnostic test discussed later in this chapter.

The main body organs make their first appearance during the third week following conception. The central nervous system and the circulatory system are the first primary organ systems to appear. The heart begins to beat and circulate blood during this early time. By the eighth week, all of the organ systems are present in their early forms and functioning at some level. Although human since conception, the embryo now has a human appearance. **Organogenesis** is the term given to organ formation and it is the completion of organogenesis that marks the end of the embryonic period.

## *Fetal Period*

The developing individual is known as the **fetus** from the beginning of the ninth week after conception until birth (around forty weeks). The **fetal period** of prenatal life is characterized by refinements in organs formed earlier, by reflexive actions, and by rapid increases in the weight and length of the developing individual.

Although the fetus has been on the move since conception, the mother will usually feel the fetus move for the first time around the fourth or fifth month of pregnancy, called the **quickening**. The fetus' body also becomes covered with a fine downlike hair called **lanugo**.

Meanwhile, the skin begins to be covered with a substance called the **vernix caseosa** that is much like thick cold cream. It serves to protect the skin from chapping in the liquid environment of the uterus before birth. It also lubricates the fetus's passage through the birth canal and protects the infant from skin infections for a short time after birth.

The **age of viability** is the point in prenatal development where the fetus stands a chance of surviving outside of the womb. This typically happens between the twenty-second and twenty-fourth week. Even though the fetus may survive if born at this point in time, there can be serious complications and difficulties associated with premature birth. We will discuss this in more depth in the next section.

During the seventh, eighth, and ninth months, there are continued refinements in the body and large gains in body weight. The lanugo is shed and the vernix covers the entire body by the end of this last trimester.

*Pause and Process:*

1. What are the three periods of prenatal development? How are they different than the three trimesters of pregnancy?

2. Which period of prenatal development is when the organ systems develop and begin functioning? When is organogenesis complete?

# CRITICAL FACTORS IN PRENATAL DEVELOPMENT

The individual is exposed to many factors before birth that can influence his or her development positively or adversely. In this section, we will learn about some critical factors in prenatal development.

## *General Factors of Concern*

One general risk factor during pregnancy is the age of the mother. Women younger than eighteen and older than thirty-five years of age have a higher probability of having a high-risk pregnancy—one that is characterized by complications that endanger the health and well-being of either the mother or child or both.

Adolescents are more likely to have problems during pregnancy or delivery than women in their twenties. However, proper nutrition and prenatal care can help prevent these problems. Older women seem especially prone both to miscarriage and to bearing children with a genetic disease. For example, the incidence of Down syndrome (a type of mental retardation cased by a genetic disorder) increases significantly among women older than thirty-five. Older women are also more likely to struggle with infertility.

Another general risk factor during pregnancy is poor nutrition. The nutrition of the pregnant woman is an important influence on the quality of development of her child. This factor also strongly affects the mother's well-being and can influence the course of subsequent pregnancies.

One of the most significant aspects of nutrition in pregnancy is the association between adequate weight gains by the mother and the infant's weight (and health) at birth (Brazelton, 1987). Birthweight is related to the baby's ability to survive as well as to his or her susceptibility to certain health risks (Cassady & Strange, 1987). Most women of average weight should gain between 25 and 35 pounds during pregnancy. Underweight women should gain slightly more and overweight women should gain slightly less. Due to an increase in obesity among women of childbearing age, medical professionals are currently researching

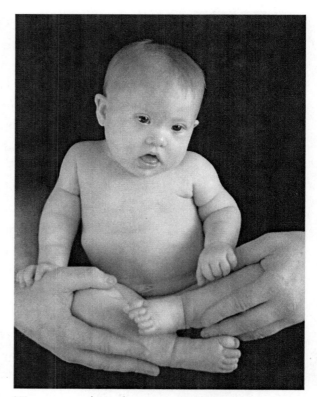

*Women over thirty–five are more likely to have children with Down syndrome. (iStock)*

what a safe weight gain is for them. However, current research indicates that it is never advisable for a woman to diet and/or lose weight during pregnancy.

Beyond just weight gain, the quality of the food a woman eats is reflected in the health and well-being of her child. Adequate folic acid intake is critical early in pregnancy, as it can help prevent neural tube defects such as **spina bifida** (ACOG, 2005). Calcium and iron are also important for health and development. Most doctors recommend that a woman take a prenatal vitamin during pregnancy (if not before) in order to ensure proper levels of vitamins and minerals.

## Teratogens

"**Teratology** is the branch of science that studies the causes, mechanisms, and patterns of abnormal development" (Moore & Persaud, 1998). Therefore, a **teratogen** is anything that can cause abnormal development: drugs, diseases, or environmental hazards. The influence of a teratogen depends upon the following:

- The genetics of the child

- During what stage of prenatal development exposure occurred

    - Germinal period—miscarriage or no effect

    - Embryonic period—major abnormalities in limbs, tissues, and organs

    - Fetal period—functional or morphologic abnormalities (especially in the brain or eyes)

- What the teratogen is

- Amount of teratogen the baby is exposed to in utero

- Impact may be first apparent during prenatal development, at birth, or years later

## Drugs

Physicians generally urge their pregnant patients not to take any drugs without their advice. This warning is based on the knowledge that certain drugs can cause malformations and other related problems in the developing individual (Moore & Persaud, 1998). The effects of drugs vary widely, depending upon the factors listed above.

The list of drugs that can cause abnormal development is long. One of the most common is alcohol. No amount of alcohol consumption during pregnancy can be considered safe (Moore & Persaud, 1998). Alcohol consumption during pregnancy is one of the leading causes of mental retardation and even learning disabilities (ACOG, 2005). Moderate to heavy drinking during pregnancy can lead to **fetal alcohol syndrome** (FAS). FAS results in a baby with characteristic malformations to areas of the face, mild to severe mental retardation or lowered intelligence, severe growth disturbances, and heart malforma-

**Spina bifida**

A birth defect in which the tissue surrounding the spinal cord does not properly close during prenatal development.

**Teratology**

A branch of science that studies the causes, mechanisms, and patterns of abnormal development.

**Teratogen**

Anything that can cause abnormal development.

*Spotlight*

What is a teratogen?

**Fetal alcohol syndrome**

A disorder that may include physical abnormalities and cognitive deficits due to a mother drinking alcohol during pregnancy.

tion. However, even light drinking during pregnancy can cause cognitive deficiencies and behavioral troubles.

Caffeine is widely consumed in the United States and abroad. It is not known, at this time, to cause any birth defects (Moore & Persaud, 1998). Heavy consumption may be associated with miscarriage early in the pregnancy or low birth weight at delivery. More research on the potential effects of caffeine is still needed.

Nicotine and cigarette smoking is a well-known teratogen. Cigarette smoking doubles the risk of premature birth (and all the complications that come with that). It is also a leading cause of low birthweight and the strongest predictor of infant death (Moore & Persaud, 1998). Lowered intelligence, heart defects, and limb defects are also related with smoking in both mom and dad. One of the reasons smoking is so detrimental to the child during prenatal development is that nicotine decreases the amount of oxygen in the blood. No amount of smoking is considered safe during pregnancy, by either mom or dad.

Entire chapters of embryology textbooks are devoted to the teratogenic effects of drugs. Certain antibiotics can lead to teeth discoloration and deafness. Aspirin may lead to cognitive and motor deficiencies. The effects of illegal drugs vary depending upon the type of drug, but common effects include low birthweight, irritability in the newborn, and cognitive and motor deficiencies (Moore & Persaud, 1998). In general, all drugs should be avoided and those needed for medical reasons should be consumed only after consultation with a doctor.

## Diseases

Several types of infectious diseases are transmitted by the mother to the developing child through the placental membrane. The severity of their effects depends on when during the pregnancy the disease is contracted. Other diseases can damage the baby during delivery as it passes through the birth canal.

German measles (rubella) is one of the best known diseases that can harm a developing baby. Infection with this virus can result in deafness, blindness, heart defects, central nervous system damage, and mental deficiencies, or a combination of these, depending on when the virus enters the mother's body (Moore & Persaud, 1998).

Other viral agents that are known to damage the central nervous system during the prenatal period include the cytomegalovirus and toxoplasmosis. The cytomegalovirus is found in the vaginal tracts of many women. This virus enters the nasal and throat passages of the baby during delivery and quickly becomes established in the central nervous system. Infection can cause learning disabilities and related behavior problems in children later in life. Toxoplasmosis is a common parasite in cats and other animals. Women are typically tested for these two agents during pregnancy so that the proper precautions may be taken.

The HIV (human immunodeficiency virus) that causes AIDS (acquired immune deficiency syndrome) can also be passed by an infected pregnant woman to her developing child. Current research suggests that the probability of transmission may be influenced by the method of delivery of the fetus. For example, birth via Cesarean may reduce the risk of transmission of HIV from mother to child (DuBard & Newton, 1999). Other STDs, such as syphilis and gonorrhea, can also cause permanent defects if passed from mother to child. Early detection and treatment is vital.

## *Environmental Hazards*

We are just beginning to understand some of the dangers that environmental factors can pose to prenatal development. For example, pregnant women are now advised to avoid eating certain seafood due to mercury. Mercury can cause cerebral palsy, mental retardation, and growth deficiencies in a developing child. Exposure to lead can lead to miscarriage, growth deficiencies, mental retardation, and other abnormalities. Polychlorinated biphenyls (PCBs), found in some water and fish, can lead to growth deficiencies, skin discoloration, and cognitive deficiencies. X-rays can lead to leukemia, mental retardation, and growth defi-

*Certain fish contain high levels of mercury. (iStock)*

ciencies. Radiation is linked to mental retardation. The list could go on; however, the moral of the story is for pregnant women to stay healthy, avoid toxins, and receive prenatal care. To do otherwise is to risk causing the developing child a lifetime of suffering.

Finally, an additional discovered environmental factor that may contribute to prenatal risk is maternal stress (Gutteling, Weerth, Zandbelt, Mulder, Visser, & Buitelaar, 2006; Huttunen & Niskanen, 1973; Kinney, Hyman, Greetham, & Tramer, 1999). Although preliminary in nature, research on maternal stress during pregnancy indicates a higher likelihood of the child developing emotional and academic difficulties including even higher occurrences of schizophrenia. For example, babies born to women who were in their second month of pregnancy during the height of the 1967 Arab-Israeli Six-Day War were significantly more likely to be diagnosed with schizophrenia as adults (Malaspina, Corcoran, Kleinhaus, Perrin, Fennig, Nahon, et al. 2008). The authors suggest that the maternal stress of being in a war zone may have contributed to the increase in schizophrenia. In addition to revealing a disturbing outcome of maternal stress during pregnancy, this preliminary study also highlights the importance of the examining the timing of the stress. The study found that women who were specifically in their second month of pregnancy during the war had offspring with an increased likelihood of being diagnosed with schizophrenia as adults.

*Pause and Process:*

1. What is a teratogen? What influences how a teratogen will impact a developing child?

2. Which teratogen surprised you the most and why?

# COMPLICATIONS IN PREGNANCY

Most pregnancies proceed with little difficulty for the mother or child. Some, however, are complicated by one or more conditions that threaten the well-being of the mother or child or both. The purpose of prenatal care is to monitor the progress of a pregnancy to enhance the health and well-being of both mother and baby. Proper prenatal care improves the probability of detecting problems and treating them to minimize their effects.

## *Extrauterine Pregnancy*

**Ectopic pregnancy**

A pregnancy that develops in a location outside the uterus.

An **ectopic**, or extrauterine, **pregnancy** is one that develops in a location outside the uterus. The individual may implant in the fallopian tube, on the ovary itself, or on the lining of the intestine. These pregnancies necessitate the surgical removal of the area on which the child has implanted. As of yet, there is no way to save the child and transplant him or her to the uterus for the duration of the pregnancy.

## *Loss of Pregnancy*

**Miscarriage**

The unwanted ending of a pregnancy, usually within the first three months of pregnancy.

A **miscarriage** is the unwanted ending of a pregnancy, usually within the first three months of pregnancy (ACOG, 2005). Up to 15–20 percent of all pregnancies end in miscarriage, so it is far from uncommon. Generally, they are caused by abnormalities in the developing child, most frequently resulting from chromosome errors or acute infectious diseases. In addition to chromosome abnormalities and maternal illness, hormone imbalances, immune system disorders, and uterine problems can all lead to miscarriages. The loss of the child is devastating to most parents. We will discuss coping with the loss of a pregnancy and stillbirth in the last chapter of the textbook.

## *Toxemia*

**Toxemia**

An acute hypertensive disease of pregnancy characterized by high blood pressure, retention of body fluids, and the presence of protein in the urine.

Maternal **toxemia** is an acute hypertensive disease of pregnancy. Typically, it is characterized by high blood pressure, retention of body fluids, and the presence of protein in the urine. It generally appears after the sixth month of pregnancy. Toxemia varies in severity but will become progressively worse if left untreated. This condition is highly dangerous to both the mother and child. It can be treated successfully with medication and diet.

Although these are clearly not all of the complications that can occur during pregnancy, they are some of the more common ones. They point toward the importance of early prenatal care, which is the topic of our next section.

*Pause and Process:*

1. Where in the woman's body can an ectopic pregnancy occur?

2. What are potential causes for a miscarriage? Why do you think that up to one in five pregnancies end in miscarriage?

# PRENATAL CARE

**Perinatology**

Concerned with the detection and treatment of illness in developing individuals before birth.

Prenatal development is important for the health of the child and mother. **Perinatology** is concerned with the detection and treatment of illness in developing individuals before birth. This field was made possible by recent advances in diagnostic methods and intervention techniques in prenatal medical care. However, prenatal care is not simply the detection and treatment of medical problems. Prenatal care includes counseling, education, childbirth and parenting preparation, and identification of necessary community resources (ACOG, 2005).

Prenatal care is very important for preventing abnormalities in children. It includes: being in good health before conception; eating a balanced diet and getting a sufficient amount of the right kinds of exercise during pregnancy; ceasing all alcohol consumption, smoking, or other drug use; avoiding excessive stress while pregnant; and making regular visits to a health-care provider all through the pregnancy. Family health histories should also be given to the health-care provider. Many programs are available to encourage expecting mothers to engage in prenatal care. For example, a relatively recent program offered by www.text4baby.org provides text message reminders of prenatal care milestones and tips.

## Typical Prenatal Care

A woman's first prenatal visit usually takes longer than most of her subsequent visits. On this first visit, a health history will be taken, a physical exam will be conducted, lab work may be completed, an estimated due date is calculated, and the baby's heart beat will be heard for the first time (either by an external Doppler ultrasound device or an internal Doppler ultrasound device—depending on how far along the baby is in development). The fetus' heart begins beating around the time a woman finds out she is pregnant (about eighteen to twenty-four days after conception); however, it takes several weeks to be able to be heard by an external Doppler device. Prior to that, an internal Doppler ultrasound device can detect the heartbeat.

Monthly visits are typically scheduled for the first thirty weeks, unless health concerns necessitate more frequent visits. During most of these visits, the expectant mother's weight and blood pressure is recorded, urine is tested, uterus height is measured (externally), the baby's heart beat is heard, and the woman can ask any questions she may have of her health-care provider.

Typical prenatal tests include various lab tests throughout the pregnancy. The first test a woman will receive will be a pregnancy test. This can be either a blood test or a urine test to check for the human chorionic gonadotropin (HCG) hormone. As mentioned above, urine checks are also conducted regularly to check for various issues such as infection or diabetes. At various points during the pregnancy, blood tests may be conducted to check for anemia, HIV, STDs, Rh factor, or thyroid levels. Additionally, lab tests from pelvic exams can check for various infections. Finally, a glucose screening test to check for gestational diabetes is normally done in the later part of pregnancy.

Beyond these typical prenatal tests, other forms of fetal assessment are possible—some are routine and others are need-based. During the third trimester, expectant mothers may be asked to chart their baby's kicks/movements each day as an easy check on fetal well-being. Ultrasounds are conducted for multiple reasons. The most common reason ultrasounds are conducted is to assess the age and sex of the baby, as well as to identify the placenta's location and baby's position. Ultrasounds can also monitor potential problems such as retarded growth or low amniotic fluid. Amazingly, ultrasounds can sometimes identify birth defects, some of which can be fixed prenatally or shortly after birth.

## Prenatal Diagnostic Methods

**Amniocentesis**

The withdrawal of a sample of amniotic fluid (which includes the baby's sloughed off skin cells) from the mother's uterus.

One of the best known and most widely used prenatal diagnostic tools is **amniocentesis**, or the withdrawal of a sample of amniotic fluid (which includes the baby's sloughed off skin cells) from the mother's uterus. This procedure is done to help determine whether the child has a hereditary disorder. Amniocentesis is usually performed between the fifteenth and twentieth week of pregnancy. The positive part of this test is that if the baby has a disorder, such as hypothyroidism, medication can be provided during pregnancy to help correct the problem. If it is a disorder that cannot be treated or cured, the parents have time to become educated about the disorder prior to birth. Two negative possibilities associated with an amniocentesis are a false positive (i.e., the amniocentesis saying the child has a disorder, when in fact they do not) and an increased risk of miscarriage after the procedure (~0.5 percent) (ACOG, 2005).

**Chorionic villus sampling**

A procedure by which chorionic villi (hair-like structures that are the predecessors of the placenta) are removed and analyzed to determine if genetic disease is present.

Another procedure that is used to diagnose genetic disease is **chorionic villus sampling** (CVS). Chorionic villi are small hairlike structures that are the predecessors of the placenta. Ultrasound is used to locate the tissue, then a small catheter is inserted through the vagina into the cervix and a very small section of chorionic villi is removed from the uterine wall. CVS allows an earlier diagnosis of genetic disease than is possible with amniocentesis because it is typically performed between the tenth and twelfth week of pregnancy. CVS carries the same potential benefits and costs as an amniocentesis; except, the risk of miscarriage after the procedure is slightly higher (~ 1 percent) (ACOG, 2005). Both the CVS and the amniocentesis are offered or recommended

**FIGURE 2-2    AMNIOCENTESIS PROCEDURE**

This procedure consists of inserting a needle through the woman's abdominal wall into the uterine cavity to draw out a sample of amniotic fluid (fluid surrounding the fetus). Fetal cells from the fluid are cultured for chromosomal analysis.

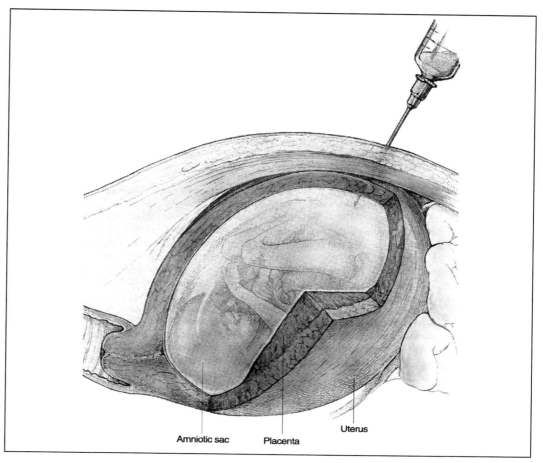

Amniotic sac    Placenta    Uterus

based upon the parents' genetic profiles and the mother's age. Women who conceive after the age of thirty-five have a higher probability of having a child with genetic abnormalities than younger women.

These diagnostic methods have been used in the past for several reasons. The knowledge of the impending birth of a child with genetic abnormalities can help in preparing parents for the difficulties inherent in raising a child with disabilities. Other parents may use this knowledge as part of the decision-making process to keep the child or undergo an abortion. It is estimated that 88–92 percent of babies identified as having Down syndrome by these tests are aborted (Bristow, 2008).

**Fetal medicine**

Any medical intervention or care directed at the developing, in utero individual.

## Fetal Medicine

Any medical intervention or care directed at the developing, in utero individual could be considered **fetal medicine**. For example, if an amniocentesis indicates a hormonal deficiency, medication may be able to be administered prenatally to help reduce or eliminate the consequences of such a deficiency.

**Fetal surgery**

Surgery that is conducted while the child is still developing prenatally.

**Fetal surgery** is also a growing, although still experimental, field. Fetal surgeries have been successful in correcting or lessening certain heart defects, spinal cord abnormalities, vascular lung issues, and other organ problems. However, this is still a field in its infancy. Just as there are potential risks with any surgery, there are severe potential costs to fetal surgery. First, both the mother and fetus must be given pain medication and face the potential side effects inherent in such drug administration. Second, the mother could face such complications as infection, blood clots, or early labor. Third, the fetus could be accidentally injured by surgical instruments, be born prematurely, or die. Clearly, the potential benefits for such a potentially dangerous procedure must outweigh the costs. Still, these surgeries have already been credited with saving lives and reducing the need for surgery and drugs after birth for those in which the surgery was successful (Kalb, 2005).

*Pause and Process:*

1. What is prenatal care? Why is it important?

2. Compare and contrast amniocentesis and CVS.

# REACTIONS TO PREGNANCY

There is a wise old saying that the reason pregnancy lasts nine months is to allow the expectant parents plenty of time to get used to the idea of being parents and to prepare. The initiation of a pregnancy can produce several reactions in a couple. Although the pregnancy has an impact on the mother and father, each may react differently.

Holmes and Rahe (1967) report that pregnancy is the twelfth most stressful life event during adulthood. The initiation of a pregnancy causes many reactions in the expectant

*Couples experience different reactions to the idea of being a parent. Pregnancy is the twelfth most stressful life event during adulthood. (iStock)*

mother. Among these are changes in her body image and a sense of physical and psychological well-being, feelings of uncertainty about what it is like to be pregnant (if this is her first pregnancy), and alterations in her mood. Many women and their partners react with excitement to the confirmation of pregnancy, especially if the pregnancy was planned and desired.

Pregnancy is a common human experience, but it carries many different meanings for couples. For some, it validates their sexuality. The woman proves her femininity by conceiving, and the man proves his masculinity by impregnating. For others, impending parenthood revives memories of childhood and anticipation of a happy future as a parent. For still others, expecting a child fulfills an expectation laid when they took their marriage vows. They now can share the excitement of bringing a life into the world that they created together.

However, not everyone reacts with pleasure to the confirmation of a pregnancy, however. Less positive emotional reactions are often attributed to feelings of ambivalence about becoming a parent, marital difficulties, and lack of an adequate social network to provide emotional support during the pregnancy (Flemming et al., 1988). Pregnancy crisis centers are wonderful places to turn to in such circumstances. They can help an expectant couple prepare emotionally for the child's arrival, as well as provide social and financial support. Many can even provide support after the birth of the child, or help find additional sources of support in the local community. We live in a society where no woman needs to face a pregnancy alone; there is always help to be found. Complicating the decision about the future after having an unplanned pregnancy is the considerable political debate about abortion. Ultimately, educating oneself abut all the options available can help in reducing the difficulties associated with this process (Major, Appelbaum, Beckman, Dutton, Russo, & West, 2009). Several websites with different political approaches to this question, which may be a good starting place are www.plannedparenthood.org, www.pregnancycenters.org and www.care-net.org.

Pregnancy, especially a first one, focuses a couple's thinking on many new issues. They ponder what it will be like to be a parent or what kind of parent they will make. Some prepare for the immense change a baby will make in their lives—at least intellectually. Pregnancy lasts long enough to allow couples to do some preparation for parenthood—to begin transforming their identity from a couple without children to parents. Many couples prepare for first-time parenthood by attending childbirth preparation classes, reading books and articles about child development, and arranging for prenatal and birth care. They equip a nursery and enjoy getting gifts at baby showers. They may spend some time caring for babies and young children of relatives and friends. In all these ways, couples begin the process of accepting a radical change in their identities and lifestyles.

## *"In Their Own Words"*

**Jessica, a 19-year-old Caucasian, describes her initial reaction to pregnancy and the ambivalence surrounding many aspects of the experience:**

*"At first I was in shock, I took a second pregnancy test just to make sure. I couldn't believe I was pregnant! I mean come on … I was on birth control! Even after the second pregnancy test came out*

*positive I scheduled an appointment with my doctor, I thought for sure it had to be a mistake because I almost never missed a (birth control) pill. He tested my urine and told me I was definitely pregnant, I felt sick the entire day. I was absolutely terrified ... I decided to tell my mom first and I made sure my younger sister was there. I wanted my sister there for emotional support and to help calm my mom down if she freaked out. I can't remember exactly what I said but when I told my mom I swear she was dead silent for two minutes just staring at me. My mom has never looked at me like that before. I could have sworn she was going to scream or slap me across the face or even kick me out of the house. But she just started saying that it was my choice whether or not to keep the child. I told her I was going to keep it. She immediately started talking about prenatal vitamins, dropping out of school, a secretarial job at her office I could apply for, exercise ... I was totally shocked. Once I had my mom's support I knew telling my stepdad would be so much easier. And it was! It turned out my mom already told him before I did and he acted fine with it ... Well at first I thought about abortion, but my boyfriend (now ex-boyfriend) literally screamed at me to abort the child. That got me so angry, so then I thought I would keep the child but give it up for adoption so I could go back to school. So that was the plan for a while, but I recently found out I'm having twins and that's when I knew I couldn't give up my children. When I saw the ultrasound with two heartbeats my mom and I both were crying so hard, it's not even a question anymore. God gave me these two beautiful children and there is no way I'm giving them up! ... My ex and I used condoms, he pulled out, and I was on the pill. I believe everything happens for a reason, I think I'm supposed to have twins at this age, it was just meant to be. Maybe one of my children will grow up and help find the cure for cancer, or maybe one of them will have a beautiful voice and become a vocal artist ... ya' never know! I never really thought of myself as becoming a mom or a 'kid type of person', but after getting pregnant I found that my attitude towards children and life is changing. My sisters and I are fighting less, when I have a shift at the grocery store I'm more patient, and I'm starting to love kids! It's so weird; I think this pregnancy has really changed me for the better."*

*Pause and Process:*

1. What are some common reactions to pregnancy?

2. What are the contributing factors to a negative reaction to pregnancy? What can be done to help in these circumstances?

# BIRTH AND THE NEWBORN

**LEARNING OBJECTIVES:**

1. *Understand and describe the process by which birth occurs as well as the different types of birth experiences*

2. *Identify complications associated with the birth process*

3. *Describe the characteristics of newborns*

4. *Describe the transition that newborns and parents go through during this period*

Birth is obviously a major event in the life of an individual and the family into which he or she is born. This section will discuss the birth process, complications that can arise during birth, characteristics of the newborn, and the transitions that the newborn and family go through the first couple of weeks after birth.

# THE BIRTH PROCESS

As you learned in the previous section, a pregnant woman waits around forty weeks to meet her baby face to face for the first time. Late in the third trimester, the expectant mother is probably both excited for this first meeting and a bit anxious about the birth process. First time mothers often wonder what this birth process will be like. How long will labor and delivery last? How painful is labor really? What are the options for medicated pain control? What techniques work best to control pain that do not involve medication? What can go wrong during labor and delivery? What will the little bundle of joy be like immediately after birth? How will life change after the baby is born?

**How many stages of labor are there?**

This section will address all of these questions. Even if you (or your partner) never have a child, chances are that you will experience the birth of a child of a relative or close friend at some point in your life. The information you learn in this chapter will help you to know, at least somewhat, what to expect. It will also help you to be able to critically evaluate television shows and movies that depict birth and newborns. After all, you must have wondered at some point in time why shows that depict a person assisting a woman giving birth outside of a hospital are always in need of water, towels, and string of some sort.

**Labor**

The process by which the cervix is opened prior to birth and the fetus is moved from the uterus through the birth canal; accomplished by means of contractions of the uterus, which increase in strength, duration, and frequency as delivery nears.

**Braxton-Hicks contraction**

Practice contractions by the uterus.

**Lightening**

Occurs when the fetus' head drops down into the pelvis.

## Labor and Delivery

It's called **labor** for a reason, as we will see. Women often know that labor is getting close due to several preceding events. The woman will be visiting her doctor or midwife frequently toward the end of pregnancy. If the doctor or midwife believes that labor may be starting soon, he or she can check the condition of the woman's cervix. Certain physical changes to the cervix can let the doctor or midwife know that the body is preparing for labor. Other events can also occur as labor nears. **Braxton-Hicks contractions** will often increase in frequency and strength as the uterus starts practicing for the big event. Vaginal discharge may also increase and/or change in color as the body prepares for labor. Finally, the fetus may become less active and may drop into the pelvic cavity of the woman (**lightening**). Experts are still uncertain as to what actually initiates labor, but most believe it is the fetus that triggers its start (Hrdy 1999).

If you remember, prenatal development occurs in three stages. Well, labor occurs in three stages as well. Just like the periods of prenatal development, the stages of labor are not equal in length of time.

*When a pulse can no longer be detected in the umbilical cord it can then be cut. The husband or support person may cut the cord if they wish. (Photo courtesy of T. Grayson)*

During the first stage of labor, the Braxton-Hicks contractions give way to real contractions. These real contractions typically come at regular intervals and increase in intensity, length, and frequency. The contractions help efface and dilate the cervix, and push the baby down. If the membranes did not rupture (i.e., water break) at the onset of labor, they will break (or be broken) sometime during this stage. Typically, the first stage of labor is the longest, lasting an average of six to twelve hours. The first stage is usually shorter in second and subsequent childbirths. This stage is over when the cervix has dilated to 10 centimeters and the baby is ready to be pushed out.

The contractions during the second stage of labor are paired with the urge to push down. The crowning of the baby's head signals that birth is imminent. Delivery is the actual birth or expulsion of the baby from the uterus and is the highlight of this stage of labor. This part of the birth process typically lasts from twenty minutes to three hours (ACOG, 2005). In a normal delivery, the baby is delivered head first (known as a **cephalic presentation**). Once the head is out, the rest of the body is usually quick to follow. Sometimes the baby is not head down, which can cause complications during the delivery process. **Breech** and **transverse** presentations are often delivered via cesarean-section, which we will discuss later in the chapter.

You may think that labor is over after the birth of the child, but you would be wrong. The final stage of labor is referred to as the **afterbirth** phase. The afterbirth phase involves the expulsion of the placenta and the membranes, as well as any remaining amniotic fluid from a woman's uterus. This part of the birth process usually lasts less than twenty minutes (ACOG, 2005). The uterus continues to contract after the birth of the baby. These contractions and the assistance of a nurse or midwife manipulating the woman's abdomen help the uterus to cleanse itself of the debris of birth. The umbilical cord is cut when the doctor or midwife can no longer detect a pulse in the cord. The baby feels no discomfort because the cord does not contain nerves. The woman's husband or support person may cut the cord if all has gone well.

## Cephalic presentation

Head first delivery.

## Breech

When a child is upside down for delivery, with the bottom being delivered first.

## Transverse

When a child is sideways during labor (requires either that the child is physically moved to the head-down position, or delivered c-section).

## Afterbirth

The final stage of labor which involves the expulsion of the placenta and the membranes as well as any remaining amniotic fluid from a woman's uterus.

## FIGURE 2-3    BIRTH OF A FETUS

Illustration of birth of a fetus showing rotation of the head and trunk through the woman's pelvis.

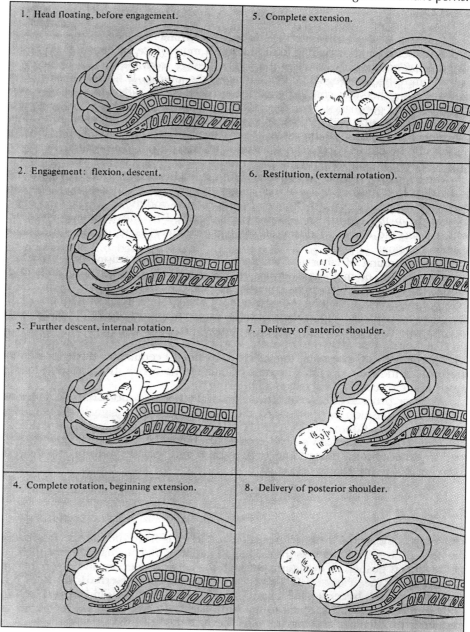

1. Head floating, before engagement.

2. Engagement: flexion, descent.

3. Further descent, internal rotation.

4. Complete rotation, beginning extension.

5. Complete extension.

6. Restitution, (external rotation).

7. Delivery of anterior shoulder.

8. Delivery of posterior shoulder.

## *Approaches to Labor and Delivery*

Now that we know the nuts and bolts of labor and delivery, we can take time to examine some of the finer details. Let's start with the well-known saying that "misery loves company." Now, of course, no one should consider giving birth to a beautiful child misery. Nonetheless, the fact of the matter is that labor is physically—well—uncomfortable to say the least. Pain is a very subjective experience, and the degree of discomfort or pain endured during labor and delivery varies greatly across women. However, research shows that women experience less pain and discomfort when they have a support person during the birth process (ACOG, 2005).

The customary choice of a support person is the expectant woman's partner; except, this is not always possible for a number of reasons. A friend or relative can also be an excellent support person. Ideally, any support person should attend childbirth classes with the expectant mother in order to be best prepared to be a labor coach. An expectant mother may also want or need a professional support person. In that case, she may want to consider a **doula**. A doula is a professional labor coach. He or she can offer emotional, psychological, and physical support during the birth process; however, a doula cannot assist in any medical care. The doula can offer support to the woman alone or can work in partnership with the woman's support person to offer a support network.

**Doula**

A professional labor coach.

Regardless of whom an expectant mother's support person is, this labor partner can be invaluable. According to the American College of Obstetricians and Gynecologists (2005), a support person can assist in many ways, including: timing contractions and talking the woman through them, monitoring room conditions (such as lighting), giving massages or assisting in various labor positions, coaching the woman through breathing techniques, and offering general encouragement and assistance.

Thus, one approach to lessen pain during the birth process is to have a support person. Another approach is commonly referred to as prepared childbirth. Although there are a few different, specific strategies that fall under this general umbrella (e.g., Bradley, Lamaze, Read, etc.), the general idea is the same. Prepared childbirth asserts that expectant mothers being educated as to what to expect during the birth process will lessen anxiety, and in turn, lessen pain. Specific strategies may include breathing techniques, labor postures, and other relaxation techniques. Having a support person is usually instrumental in prepared childbirth. Successful implementation of prepared childbirth includes minimal (if any) use of pain medication during labor, active participation of both the

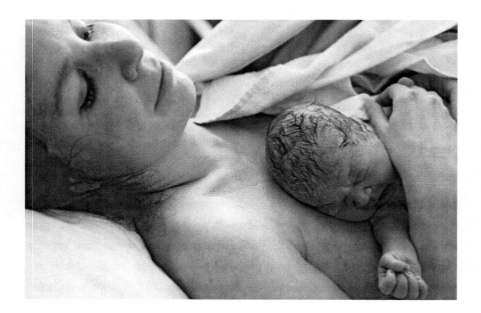

*The pain and discomfort that is experienced during labor varies between women. However, studies show that the pain experienced is lessened when there is a support person present. (iStock)*

mother and support person in the birth process, and a reduction of fear and anxiety about labor and delivery.

Even with support and preparation, some women opt for the use of pain medication during labor and delivery. There are two general classes of pain medications: analgesics and anesthetics. Systemic analgesics lessen pain by working on the entire nervous system. The woman will maintain consciousness, but may be tired. Regional analgesia numbs a specific area. Epidurals and spinal blocks are two examples of regional analgesics. After insertion of the epidural tube by an anesthesiologist, some hospitals now allow women to self-administer pain medication via their epidural using a hand held button control. There are pros and cons to using pain medication during labor and delivery, and these issues should be considered prior to the onset of labor.

There are numerous alternative or supplemental strategies for pain control not yet mentioned. For example, hypnosis is sometimes used in place of drugs to reduce pain during delivery. The technique is somewhat limited by the fact that not every mother can be trained to enter a hypnotic state. Also, it requires special training that not many physicians have. The use of birthing tubs is also increasing in popularity. Massages, acupuncture, and music therapy are also possible choices for pain management during the birth process. The thing to keep in mind is that all women will experience pain differently during labor and delivery, and there are a variety of options for pain management.

## Settings for Labor and Delivery

For a healthy and uncomplicated vaginal birth, there are some options for labor and delivery (ACOG, 2005). Some women give birth at home with the assistance of a doctor or midwife. As long as the pregnancy has been healthy and there are no risk factors or complications, this is a viable choice for many women. There are also birthing centers. These are free-standing centers that are devoted to labor and delivery. Again, as long as the pregnancy has been healthy and there are no risk factors or complications, this is a viable choice. Birthing centers may offer labor options, such as tubs and massages, which a typical hospital may not offer. However, if complications arise during labor or delivery, precious time may be lost in transit to a hospital. Most American women choose to give birth in a hospital.

Many modern hospitals have entire wings devoted to labor and delivery. These wings can offer separate entrances (so women in labor do not need to come in through the emergency room), birthing rooms, and easy access to operating rooms in case an emergency cesarean-section is needed. Modern birthing rooms typically have a homelike atmosphere, with a sleeper sofa for dad, room for the baby after birth, soft lighting, and personal bathrooms with showers. The beds can be transformed from a typical bed one can sleep in, into a delivery bed, and back into a typical bed with a few easy maneuvers. This means that labor, delivery, and recovery can all occur in the same room. Most of the medical equipment can be strategically hidden from view until needed.

Of course, around one out of four births are not vaginal, but cesarean-sections (ACOG, 2005). What can cause a woman to need a C-section? Is it more dangerous than a vaginal birth? Our next section will address this topic.

### *Cesarean Deliveries*

C-sections are performed when delivery through the vaginal birth canal may be hazardous to the baby, the mother, or both. Possible reasons for a C-section include (ACOG, 2005):

1. A small pelvis or large baby (cephalopelvic disproportion)

2. Transmittable infections (such as an active herpes outbreak)

3. Insufficient dilation of the cervix, making it likely that passage of the fetus from the uterus to the birth canal would perforate or tear this structure

4. Placenta previa in which the placenta is at least partially blocking the cervix

5. Multiple births or an irregular presentation (e.g., breech or transverse presentation) that makes vaginal delivery difficult

C-sections can be planned ahead of time (such as when it is known that the baby is breech or that there is placenta previa) or done when an emergency arises (such as when the cervix ceases to dilate or the umbilical cord becomes pinched). It is performed by making an incision into the woman's abdominal wall and uterus to remove the baby and placenta. This surgical procedure requires the use of general or regional anesthetic. By now close to 30 percent of births in the U.S. are done via a C-section. Many believe that this procedure is overused and that C-sections should be done only when medically essential. Like all surgeries, a C-section carries an increased risk for complications including infection, blood loss, and blood clots. Aside from the physical risks, C-sections may entail attachment related ramifications for the child (DiMatteo, Morton, Lepper, Damush, Carney, Pearson, & Kahn, 1996). As discussed in the section on attachment development there are several critical periods in infancy during which the child is in a greater position to benefit from maternal attachment formation. One of those periods is during the first few hours after birth. However, in C-section cases, the newborn is often separated from the mother after birth which may interfere with early attachment processes.

*Pause and Process:*

1. Describe the three stages of labor.

2. What are some reasons that a C-section may be needed?

# COMPLICATIONS

Most pregnancies and deliveries cause little difficulty to the mother or baby. Some, however, are complicated by one or more conditions. The purpose of prenatal care is to monitor the progress of a pregnancy to ensure the good health and well-being of both mother and baby. Proper medical attention during the course of a pregnancy can detect problems. Treatment during pregnancy, or delivery, can minimize the effects of the complications discussed in this section.

## Complications During Delivery

The previous section already mentioned two complications that can happen during delivery: cephalopelvic disproportion and irregular presentation. A prolapsed umbilical cord is another complication. Sometimes, the umbilical cord will get pinched in the birth canal as the baby is being delivered. This can cut off the baby's vital oxygen supply. If this occurs, and doctors are aware of it, an emergency C-section may be necessary.

## Anoxia

**Anoxia**

Oxygen starvation of tissues.

Oxygen starvation of tissues, or **anoxia**, is a major concern in the delivery of a baby. A baby who is normal and has not experienced complications during delivery can be expected to establish respiration on his or her own within one minute after birth—usually spontaneously. Some babies, however, have difficulty initiating respiration, and this can quickly lead to anoxia. Brain tissue is especially sensitive to oxygen starvation, and the damage is irreversible. Anoxia may be caused by several factors including hemorrhages, prolonged labor, and placenta previa.

A variety of problems can affect the baby, depending on the degree of anoxia experienced. Cerebral palsy, mild to severe mental retardation, hearing and speech impairments, mild to severe learning disabilities of various types in later years, and related behavioral disturbances are the most common problems. Fetal monitoring during labor and delivery can help to minimize the risk of birth traumas resulting in anoxia.

## Low-Birthweight and Prematurity

**Premature baby**

A baby who weighs five and one half pounds or less at birth and has a gestational age of less than thirty-seven weeks.

A low-birthweight or **premature baby** is one who weighs five and one half pounds or less at birth and has a gestational age of less than thirty-seven weeks. In the United States, approximately 12 percent of all babies are born prematurely (ACOG, 2005). Although babies at or past the age of viability stand the best chance of survival, long-term problems are less likely in those who make it past thirty-two weeks. Many preterm babies experience learning or attention disorders later in life. Preterm babies are also at risk for breathing problems, infections, and feeding problems (ACOG, 2005).

When babies are born too soon, their lungs and brains are particularly vulnerable. If a woman is experiencing preterm labor, she may be given shots to help mature the baby's lungs ahead of schedule. Recent research also suggests that preterm babies' brains also lack the ability to filter out the multitude of information it will be bombarded with in the world. This means that the blaring lights and beeping sounds of a typical NICU (neonatal intensive care unit) may overwhelm the preterm infant's brain and contribute to future learning and attention difficulties. Based on recent research, the care of preterm infants is changing. Sounds and sights are now muted, infant massages are given, and kangaroo care is promoted. The outcomes of such interventions seem encouraging. For example, pre-term babies provided with massages and kangaroo care demonstrate

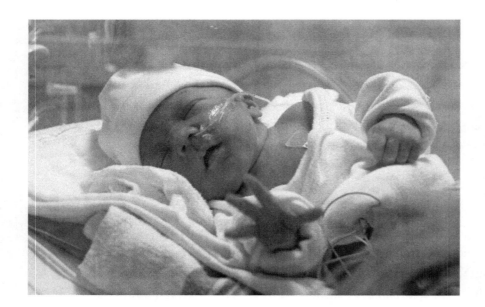

*Premature babies weigh five and one half pounds or less at birth. Because they are pre-term they are at risk for breathing problems, infections, and feeding problems. (iStock)*

better growth and earlier release dates from hospitals than pre-term babies not provided with such care (Field, Hernandez-Reif & Freedman, 2004; Hill, Brooks-Gu & Waldfogel, 2003; Ludington-Hoe et al., 2006; Teti, 2005). It is hopeful that these early interventions will prevent the learning and attention disabilities that traditionally plague preterm babies throughout childhood.

## *"Development in the Real World"*

Marie Baugh is a neonatal nurse at St. Joseph's Medical Center in Pennsylvania. She earned a bachelor's degree in Nursing and is charged with infant assessment, recording vital signs, monitoring intake and output including feedings, diaper weights, and lab work. She also teaches families how to care for their critically ill newborn and promotes breast-feeding when needed.

### What type of work do you conduct?

*"I am a registered nurse specializing in neonatology. As a neonatal nurse, I take care of critically ill infants as well as infants born less than thirty-six weeks gestation. I also attend high-risk deliveries and cesarean sections. My job is to evaluate the infant and I also assist resuscitation if necessary, and help transport the infant to the NICU also known as the neonatal intensive care unit."*

### Describe your general work setting.

*"I work in a six-bed intensive care unit for critical ill newborns and infants. These are private rooms, which can hold a glider rocker, footstool, and an armchair for the comfort of the parents. The babies are in a radiant warmer, isolated, or a crib. Each room also has its own sink to encourage hand washing and decrease infection. There is also a window overlooking a pasture."*

**What do you like and dislike about your job?**

*"I enjoy the challenge of caring for the critical ill infants and their families. I also enjoy attending the high-risk deliveries with the thrill of the unknown and jumping in to assist resuscitation. The miracle of birth is a beautiful thing. Teaching is a big part of my job, and can be a big challenge, but is very rewarding when the parents are comfortable and finally able to take their babies home. I dislike working the twelve-hour shift from 7:00 p.m. to 7:00 a.m., because it disrupts your entire sleep and eating cycles. It tends to make me cranky."*

**In what way do you apply child/adolescent psychology in your work?**

*"Many of the parents I work with are teenagers. They are still dealing with their own adolescent needs while trying to learn how to care for their newborn. You have to recognize their limited life experience and immaturity, while trying to encourage them to take on a parental role. Also for infants we use many development techniques to foster growth and development. Examples being swaddling, positioning on developmental cushions, encouraging skin-to-skin contact with the parents, also known as kangaroo care to decrease the stress of the baby and promote family bonding."*

**What are some talents and abilities that would be required to do well in this occupation?**

*"In order to do well as a neonatal nurse, you need excellent clinical skills such as starting IVs, drawing lab work, and assisting in resuscitations. You need critical assessment skills to evaluate the neurological, cardiac, and respiratory conditions of the infant. You must be a patient advocate and an effective communicator with the physician. A neonatology nurse also needs to be an educator who can guide the families on how to care for their infant's needs and encourage family bonding."*

**To your knowledge what are the job prospects in this field?**

*"The job prospects for the nursing field are good after a registered nurse has at least one year of experience in a well newborn or maternal child health center. Many strides are being made to save even the smallest infants, therefore there will always be a need for neonatal nurses."*

**Tell me about your job satisfaction.**

*"I have worked as a neonatal intensive care unit nurse for eighteen years and took a six year hiatus to care for ill elderly parents, and then returned to neonatal intensive care unit nursing for the past two years and have really enjoyed being back in the field. I love my job in regards to taking care of the critically ill infants. I enjoy working with the parents and teaching them. I work with a supportive staff and competent physicians. On the downside, I do not enjoy working nights or weekends."*

**Baby blues**

Feelings of sadness and exhaustion that over seventy percent of women experience the first week or two after birth.

## *Postpartum Depression and Psychosis*

Many of you have probably heard of the baby blues. The **baby blues** are feelings of sadness and exhaustion that more than 70 percent of women experience the first week or two after birth (ACOG, 2005). With rest, support, and time, these feelings pass

**Postpartum depression**

The feelings of sadness and exhaustion persist or even worsen past the two week mark.

**Postpartum psychosis**

When a woman is afraid to be left alone with the baby and has thoughts of hurting herself or the baby.

quickly for most women. However, for around 10 percent of women, the feelings persist or even worsen past the two week mark. **Postpartum depression** interferes with a woman's ability to function in everyday life, including caring properly for her newborn. Medical help should be sought when postpartum depression is suspected. Rarely, symptoms may go beyond postpartum depression and instead be **postpartum psychosis**. If a woman is afraid to be left alone with the baby and has thoughts of hurting herself or the baby, postpartum psychosis may be the cause and immediate medical intervention is needed.

*Pause and process:*

1. What are some complications that can occur during birth?

2. What is the difference between the baby blues and postpartum depression?

# THE NEWBORN

## *Physical Appearance*

Newborns usually weigh between five and one-half and nine and one-half pounds with an average weight of seven and one-half pounds (ACOG, 2005). Average length is between eighteen and twenty-two inches. During the first several days following birth, newborns usually lose a small amount of weight before beginning to gain weight.

Unlike the diaper commercials you have probably seen on TV (which usually use infants a couple of months old); newborns are not very attractive physically. Because they have spent nine months in the wet environment of the uterus, their skin is exceptionally wrinkled. It is also covered with **vernix**, the lubricating, creamlike substance that was formed during the fetal period. The skin is loose and lies in folds on the neonate's body. This is because newborns have little fat in the cells that lie immediately under their skin. The skin is very soft to the touch, however, and is sometimes covered with fine, downlike hair called lanugo.

**Vernix**

The lubricating, creamlike substance that has formed during the fetal period.

The eyes of a newborn are always striking. They are quite large because of their advanced maturation. Newborns squint their eyes a great deal, probably because of the initially unpleasant task of adjusting to a bright environment after months of being in the mother's uterus.

The newborn's head occupies almost one-fourth of its total body length. In adulthood, its head will be about one-seventh of its total body length. The trunk of a newborn also occupies a large proportion of its body length. The extremities are short in comparison with other body features.

In summary, the newborn is wrinkly and looks scrunched up. However, they will quickly lose the newborn appearance and look more like the adorable babies on commercials.

## Assessment of the Newborn

*Spotlight*

What quick assessment is made of the newborn to determine the presence and/or extent of any injury?

**Apgar score**

An evaluation method for assessing the health status of a newborn.

**Colostrum**

The first liquid secreted by the mammary glands, full of antibodies and nutrition.

**Meconium**

A newborn's first bowel movement.

**Reflexes**

A response controlled by the autonomic nervous system, over which an individual has no willful control.

**Sucking reflex**

The sucking reflex is closely associated with both the rooting and swallowing reflexes. It is produced when the soft palate in the baby's mouth is stimulated.

The health status of the newborn is assessed immediately to determine the presence and/or extent of any injury. Several factors are observed and evaluated: (1) heart rate, (2) respiratory effort, (3) reflex irritability (ease of elicitation), (4) color (indicative of oxygenation of blood and lung functioning), and (5) muscle tone (see Table 2-4). The baby is assessed usually at one minute and then again at five minutes following its birth. Each factor is given a rating of zero (absence of observed effect), one (average functioning of the factor), or two (excellent functioning of the factor). These ratings are summed to obtain a total score that may range from zero to ten. Scores below five indicate difficult health status; those above five indicate a more optimistic health status. The total score is known as the **Apgar score**. It is named for Dr. Virginia Apgar, the pediatrician who devised this assessment method.

There are also two widely used assessments for newborns that are more comprehensive than the Apgar in assessing neurological development and problems: the Brazelton Neonatal Behavioral Assessment Scale (NBAS) and the Neonatal Intensive Care Unit Network Neurobehavioral Scale (NNNS). Typically, these assessments are given only if problems are expected or in research. Reflexes and reactions to stimuli are some newborn behaviors measured with these scales.

So far, we have learned that the Apgar is administered to nearly all newborn babies as a quick assessment of newborn health. The NBAS and NNNS may be given if neurological problems are suspected. In addition to these assessments, nearly all newborns are given a routine hearing test at the hospital and have a blood test for certain genetic or congenital disorders (specific tests can vary by state).

## Physical Adjustments

In order to survive outside the uterus, the newborn must make adjustments—some of them rather quickly. The most important adjustments are: (1) establishing the ability to breathe, (2) regulating its own body temperature, and (3) initiating the functioning of its digestive system.

| TABLE 2-4 | THE APGAR RATING SCALE | | |
|---|---|---|---|
| **FACTOR** | **ASSIGNED VALUE** | | |
| | **0** | **1** | **2** |
| Heart rate | Absent | Slow (<100) | Rapid (>100) |
| Respiratory effort | Absent | Slow | Good; crying |
| Reflex irritability | Absent | Grimace | Cough; sneeze |
| Color | Blue, pink | Body pink; extremities blue | Completely pink |
| Muscle tone | Flaccid | Weak | Strong |

Source: Adapted from Apgar, V. A. (1954). A proposal for a new method of evaluation of the newborn infant. Current Research in Anesthesia and Analgesics, 4, 105–116.

Independent breathing begins as soon as the baby is born. This is one of the most dramatic aspects of birth. Most newborns begin respiration without assistance. Help may be provided by the medical staff by suctioning the mouth and nasal passages to clear them of fluid and mucous.

The newborn emerges warm and wet from the uterus into the cooler environment of the delivery room. The processes of evaporation and radiation work to produce a drop in the baby's body temperature. Newborns are usually wrapped in towels or receiving blankets immediately after birth and placed in the mother's arms. A newborn struggles to maintain body temperature and will need to be kept comfortably warm.

Usually within a day after birth, a baby will have his or her first bowel movement. **Colostrum** primes the newborn's digestive track for digestion of more complex nutritional substances contained in human milk or formula. **Meconium** is eliminated from the intestines for several days following birth. This material is composed of metabolized bile and other digestive juices, cellular material, and mucous built up in the intestinal tract during the final days of prenatal development.

## Newborn Behavior

Developmentalists have determined through observation and study that newborns show distinctive behavioral patterns at birth. This research has changed our ideas about human development in the first weeks following birth. Newborns are born with the capacity to adapt and selectively choose among stimuli to respond to in the environment.

## Reflexes

Newborns are thought to have more than two dozen distinct reflexes that are functional either before birth or at birth (Illingworth, 1975). **Reflexes** are involuntary actions that occur in response to particular stimulation. Eye blinking is an example of a reflex. Some reflexes disappear in the months after birth; others are with us our entire lives.

Reflexes are useful indicators of neurological functioning at birth. Tests of reflexes allow assessment of the newborn's health status (e.g., Apgar ratings). Some reflexes have immediate survival value, such as the **sucking reflex** and **rooting reflex**, which is when a baby turns his head toward a finger that touches his cheek. These are called **adaptive reflexes.** Many reflexes serve as the foundation of future behaviors. Others are possibly remnants of behaviors that apparently had survival value earlier in evolutionary history, but are no longer useful in humans. These are called **vestigial reflexes.** Some examples of vestigial reflexes are the **moro reflex, startle reflex, palmar grasping reflex,** and **plantar reflex.** Reflexes that tend to defy categorization include the **Babinski reflex, tonic neck reflex, walking reflex,** and **swimming reflex.** You can probably tell what most of these reflexes are by their name. For unfamiliar ones, they are defined in the glossary.

**Rooting reflex**

This is a searching reflex motion that helps the neonate to locate a breast or bottle nipple. It occurs when the baby's cheeks are stroked or the corner of its mouth is touched. The response is "rooting," in which the baby turns its head in the direction of the stimulation, and as it does so, opens its mouth. The baby's tongue begins to move forward and backward in its mouth.

**Adaptive reflexes**

This group of reflexes aids the neonate to locate and obtain food, thus helping to ensure its survival.

**Vestigial reflexes**

Several reflexes present at birth that seem to be relics of adaptive experiences sometime in our vast evolutionary past.

**Moro reflex**

This reflex is associated with a sudden change in movement or support of the newborn. If a neonate is raised or lowered suddenly or if support of its head is released, the baby responds by raising its arms upward very quickly and curling its fingers. Moving of the legs accompanies these reflex motions.

**Palmar (hand) and plantar (foot) grasping reflex**

These reflex movements are produced by touching or stroking the palm of the newborn's hands or the soles of its feet. Both fingers and toes curl in the grasping manner in response. The strength of these reflexes is remarkable.

**Babinski reflex**

Named for its discoverer, this reflex occurs when the sole of the baby's foot is stroked along the outer edge. In response, the neonate's toes spread wide in a fanning action, relax somewhat, curl forward tightly closed, and return to their original position.

**Tonic neck reflex**

This reflex usually occurs when the neonate is placed on its back. The arms, legs, and head move to a characteristic "fencing" position in which the arm and leg on one side are extended, while those on the other side are flexed. The baby's head turns to one side, usually in the direction of its extended limbs.

# *The Senses at Birth*

As mentioned in the previous section, the senses become functional during prenatal development. However, vision is the sense that takes the longest to reach mature levels during the first year after birth.

Newborns are sensitive to brightness. Their pupils contract and dilate in response to changes in degrees of light. Their ability to focus on an object is rather rudimentary, however. This is because the muscles that control this function are immature. It is estimated that a typical newborn can focus clearly on objects only within seven to ten inches from his or her face. **Visual acuity** is about 20/600, compared to about 20/20 for an adult with normal vision (Banks & Salpatek, 1983; Maurer & Maurer, 1988).

Given the newborns' visual abilities and restrictions, things apparently look blurry to them. What is it in the environment that interests them? What do they like to look at and how do they see these things? It seems newborns are selective in their visual explorations (Fantz, 1958, 1963; Fantz, Fagan & Miranda, 1975; Haith, 1980). They are attracted to the human face and like to explore its features. They also apparently enjoy looking at objects that have patterns rather than solid colors, especially bold patterns. Newborns tend to gaze at the edges of an object for a period of time rather than attempting to explore it in more detail (as they will when they are a bit older).

Babies are born with the ability to imitate the facial gestures and features of other people (Maltzoff & Moore, 1977, 1979, 1983). For example, sticking out the tongue and opening and closing the mouth are imitated by newborns shortly after birth. Apparently, newborns can integrate various senses to match their own behavior with that of someone they observe.

We already know that a baby can hear sounds (and remember these sounds) within his or her mother's uterus during at least the last three months before birth. However, hearing is not quite at adult levels at birth. Newborns cannot hear soft sounds or low-pitched sounds as well as adults. These abilities will develop within the first couple of years after birth.

The senses of smell, taste, and touch are well-developed at birth. Newborns can recognize the smell of their own amniotic fluid and mother's milk. They prefer some smells, such as vanilla, over other smells, such as fish. Newborns also prefer the taste of sweet foods, over bitter or sour foods. Finally, newborns are sensitive to touch and pain. The American College of Obstetricians and Gynecologists (2005) advises parents to be certain that their sons receive pain medication prior to circumcision.

*Pause and process:*

1. In what ways are newborns' health assessed?

2. Which senses are fairly well-developed by birth? What sense is the least-developed at birth?

# TRANSITIONS

### Walking reflex

Step-like motions of the legs occur reflexively when the neonate is held in an upright position and allowed to touch a flat surface with its feet. The legs respond by flexing alternately as if the child is walking.

### Swimming reflex

This unusual reflex occurs when the neonate is submerged on its abdomen in water. The baby holds its breath and makes swimming motions with both arms and legs.

### Visual acuity

Sharpness or clarity of vision.

### Individual difference

Any quality, trait, or characteristic that distinguishes one person from others..

Every human being is unique in many ways. Any quality, trait, or characteristic that distinguishes one person from others is referred to as an **individual difference**. These individual differences are present from birth (and some prenatally). Just look through the window of a newborn nursery, some babies are quiet and content. Other babies cry a lot. All babies are born with mini-personalities. Some research suggests that activity level in the womb is predictive of activity level after birth.

One individual difference proposed in newborns is **temperament**. A temperament can be thought of as a baby's general approach to the world and behavioral orientation. Some see temperament as the foundation from which personality will grow. Because temperament is apparent so early in life, it is assumed that it is at least somewhat genetic in origin (Paludi, 2002).

Thomas and Chess (1987) suggest a temperament classification scheme in which neonates are described as **difficult** (resisting physical handling, crying inconsolably, showing irregular sleeping and eating patterns), **slow-to-warm-up** (quiet activity levels, somewhat fussy, wary around others and situations), and **easy** (adaptable, cheerful and happy, responsive to others and situations), or a mixture of these.

A critical issue is what effect these individual differences are likely to have on the adults who care for newborns. For example, a newborn classified as difficult is probably frustrating for his parents. This child may even be abused if his parents' frustration limits are exceeded. A newborn described as quiet or slow-to-warm-up may be equally frustrating to parents, but for different reasons. Caregivers may have to try hard to stimulate any type of response in a newborn with this type of temperament. An easy newborn has the type of temperament that most American parents want.

Thomas (1986) proposes that there is such a thing as "goodness of fit" between the personality of the parents and the temperament of the child at birth. This fit may enhance

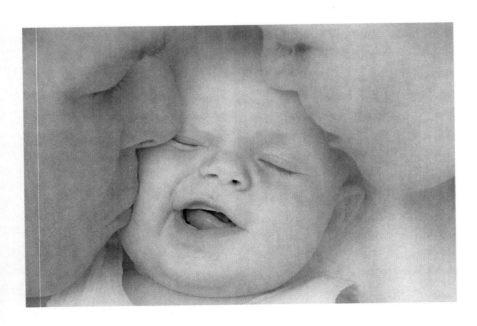

*Thomas and Chess suggested a temperament classification. Thomas proposed the "goodness of fit" idea that exists between the personality of the parents and baby. (iStock)*

development and growth among all family members. Conversely, lack of fit may make interactions in the family difficult.

All parents should realize that their offspring will be different in many respects from one or both of them. Furthermore, individual differences make using a "standard" child-drearing style for all one's children questionable (Bigner, 1989). The best approach is for family members to acquire an empathic understanding of the individual differences of each new member.

The birth of a couple's first child moves the family into a new stage of the family life-cycle. The couple must redefine their roles and develop new behaviors. This transitional period can take time and may be difficult. The adjustments that couples make at this time constitute a transition to being parents as well as redefining their role in the marriage, if married. It is important to still make time for each other during the hectic period of caring for a newborn.

The hospital will try to provide educational materials to new parents prior to discharge. New parents may be required to watch videos or attend short classes on newborn care. A lactation consultant will probably visit the mother to give tips on breastfeeding. Nurses or doctors will provide instructions on the first bath, belly-button care, diapering, feeding, and possible problems for which to watch. Nurses are also usually taught to watch for signs of bonding between the newborn and parents. Parents will also be provided with resource information for the road ahead.

**Temperament**

A baby's general approach to the world and behavioral orientation

**Difficult temperament**

The resisting of physical handling, crying inconsolably, and showing irregular sleeping and eating patterns.

**Slow-to-warm-up temperament**

The display of quiet activity levels, somewhat fussy, and wary around others and situations.

**Easy temperament**

A baby who is adaptable, cheerful and happy, and responsive to others and situations.

*Pause and process:*

1. What are the three basic temperaments that newborns may be classified as?

2. How can a hospital help to prepare parents for taking home and caring for their newborn?

# SUMMARY

1. Genetic information contained in the male and female gametes intermingles at conception, resulting in a new combination of chromosomes (and genes). The chemical basis of genetic inheritance is DNA. The genetic blueprint determined at conception will be identical in all cells that are produced during the individual's life span. Most cells reproduce themselves through a process known as mitosis. The production of sex cells, however, occurs through a process called meiosis.

2. Genetic processes include the dominant/recessive process, polygenetic inheritance, and epigenetic information. Some traits and characteristics behave according to the either/or nature of dominant/recessive genes, whereas others behave according to the continuous variation nature of the polygenetic process. Epigenetic information, such as the cytoplasmic environment during ovum development and genetic imprinting are new areas of research that are just beginning to be understood.

3. One category of genetic disorders may be inherited by a single gene that may be dominant, recessive, or sex-linked. A second category of genetic disorders may be inherited at the chromosomal level. A third category of genetic disorders are multifactorial. Although it is often unknown what specifically causes a multifactorial genetic disorder, it is thought that an interaction of genetics and environmental issues give rise to the problem. An increasing number of organizations are available to offer support and information to individuals with genetic disorders and their loved ones.

4. The field of behavioral genetics investigates how interactions between genetic and environmental factors influence cognitive and behavioral processes. Research designs in behavioral genetics have typically included adoption studies and twin studies. Gene/environment relationships can be viewed as passive, active, or dynamic in nature.

5. The prenatal stage is thought to be the most crucial stage of the life span. Changes experienced during this time have a critical bearing on development throughout the rest of the individual's life.

6. The individual can be exposed to many factors before birth that could positively or negatively affect his or her development. These include the age of the mother, maternal nutrition, and exposure to teratogens. The effects of teratogens depend upon genetics, dose, timing of exposure, and specific teratogen. Different teratogens target different parts of the body at different stages of prenatal development. In general, the embryonic period is the most vulnerable stage.

7. There are several common complications that can occur during pregnancy. Three include miscarriage, ectopic pregnancy, and toxemia. A miscarriage usually occurs during the first three months of pregnancy as a result of chromosomal abnormalities or other health factors. An ectopic pregnancy is a pregnancy that occurs outside the uterus. Toxemia can be life-threatening to the mother and child, but is treatable.

8. Adequate prenatal care is vital for preventing and/or treating birth defects and related problems of pregnancy. Prenatal tests provide a means for diagnosis of potential genetic and metabolic disease before birth. Fetal medicine offers hope for treating some medical disorders or diseases prior to birth.

9. Both partners react to the initiation of a pregnancy in the woman. Validation of one's sexuality, marriage vow fulfillment, changes in body image, and reassessment of personal well-being are among the more common reactions. Reactions may be largely positive or negative. Negative reactions are typically due to a lack of social support or marital difficulties. Pregnancy crisis centers are a wonderful place to receive emotional, social, and financial support throughout the pregnancy or even after the birth. Pregnancy provides time for couples to adjust to impending changes in their identities and lifestyles. A couple's preparation during their first pregnancy assists them to move to a new stage in their family life-cycle.

10. This chapter discussed birth, delivery, and the newborn. The birth process has three distinct phases of labor: stage one involves the effacement and dilation of the cervix; stage two involves the delivery of the baby from the uterus; stage three involves the expulsion of the placenta and other matter from the uterus. The length of time each phase lasts is variable. It usually depends partly upon whether or not the woman is having her first baby.

11. Birth can occur vaginally or via C-section. Pain management during a vaginal birth can include a support coach, prepared childbirth techniques, medication, or strategies such as hypnosis or massage. A C-section requires the use of general or regional anesthesia. A healthy woman who has had a healthy pregnancy with no risk factors can sometimes choose to give birth at home, in a

birthing center, or in a hospital. A C-section should always be done in a hospital. Modern hospitals often have entire wings devoted to labor and delivery with birthing rooms that accommodate labor, delivery, and recovery.

12. Delivery and birth may be complicated by one or more conditions. Anoxia, or oxygen starvation, to the baby during delivery may occur for a variety of reasons. Low-birthweight and prematurity may give rise to many complications. Postpartum depression of the new mother may affect her ability to function adequately.

13. The average weight of a newborn is between five and one-half and nine and one-half pounds, and the average length is between eighteen and twenty-two inches. The appearance of the newborn reflects the nature of their existence before birth—their skin is very wrinkled and is covered with vernix. The eyes are a prominent feature, and the head is large in proportion to total body length. Overall health of the newborn is assessed with the Apgar at birth.

14. Newborns must make some physical adjustments to ensure their survival following birth. They must establish independent respiration, regulate their body temperature, and initiate the process of digestion and elimination of body wastes. Newborns are also born ready to interact with the world with reflexes and senses functioning. They are also born with mini-personalities commonly referred to as temperaments. Babies typically have one of three types of temperaments: difficult, slow-to-warm-up, or easy.

15. The period after birth is a period of adjustment for both newborn and parents. New parents will need to redefine their roles within the marriage. This adjustment period can be stressful, but at the risk of sounding like a hippy, this too shall pass. The hospital provides basic care information prior to discharge.

## SELF-QUIZ

1. What does the nucleus of all cells contain?
2. How many chromosomes do humans have?
3. What do geneticists sometimes refer to as the first twenty-two pairs of chromosomes?
4. What is the process by which the gametes are produced?
5. What genetic process involves the interaction of two or more genes?
6. What is the term used to describe information passed on to offspring that is not genetic in nature?
7. What are the three different categories of genetic disorders?
8. What are two types of research designs in behavioral genetics?
9. What are the two types of twins?
10. What are three possible relationships between genotypes and the environment?
11. Are the three stages of prenatal development and the three trimesters of pregnancy the same?
12. What are the three stages of prenatal development?
13. By what week after conception are all the organs present and functioning at some level?
14. What is the age of viability?
15. How much weight should the average woman gain during pregnancy?
16. What is a teratogen?
17. What is it called when a pregnancy develops in a location outside the uterus?
18. About what percentage of known pregnancies end in a miscarriage?

19. What prenatal diagnostic tool involves the withdrawal and testing of amniotic fluid?

20. What is fetal surgery currently used to correct?

21. What is it called late in pregnancy when the fetus becomes less active and drops into the pelvic cavity?

22. How many stages of labor are there?

23. How long does the first stage of labor typically last?

24. During which stage of labor is the baby delivered?

25. What is delivered during the third stage of labor?

26. What are the two general classes of pain medications that can be administered during labor?

27. What are some possible reasons for a C-section?

28. What complications do pre-term infants possibly face?

29. What percentage of women experience the baby blues? What percentage of women experience postpartum depression?

30. What quick assessment is made of the newborn to determine the presence and/or extent of any injury?

## TERMS AND CONCEPTS

# Infancy

——— ❧ ———

(iStock)

## OUTLINE

**PHYSICAL DEVELOPMENT DURING INFANCY**

- Physical growth
- Motor development
- Perceptual development
- Health issues

**COGNITIVE DEVELOPMENT DURING INFANCY**

- Piaget's cognitive development theory and the sensorimotor stage
- Information-processing in infancy
- Language development in infancy

**SOCIOEMOTIONAL DEVELOPMENT DURING INFANCY**

- Psychosocial development
- Emotional development
- Self and others

They come out scrunched up and pink and spend most of their hours sleeping, and within no time at all they are running around full of energy. Infancy (birth through the second year) is a time of remarkable growth and change. In this chapter, we will see some of the amazing physical, cognitive, and socioemotional feats infants achieve during this short period of time.

# PHYSICAL DEVELOPMENT DURING INFANCY

*LEARNING OBJECTIVES:*

1. *To have a general knowledge of genetic terminology and processes*
2. *Awareness of some of the different types of genetic disorders*
3. *Appreciation for the field of behavior genetics within the context of studying life span development*

# PHYSICAL GROWTH

Physical changes in infancy are dramatic and rapid. We gain a stark impression of the drama of these changes when we compare the abilities and functioning of a newborn with those of the same child at the end of the infancy stage. Significant physical changes are observed in all aspects of the body. In this section, we will describe these dramatic physical changes during infancy.

## Growth Patterns

Many significant physical milestones are reached before a child's third birthday. These include mastery of the basic motor competencies shared by all human beings: locomotor (movement) and manual (hand) skills, perceptual skills, and coordination of sensory and motor activities. These basic competencies allow the individual to interact actively with the environment. They stimulate development in other areas as well.

Growth in infancy follows two basic patterns that began with the physical changes observed during the prenatal stage. The progression of these basic patterns can be observed in many physical changes that happen during infancy, especially in those associated with motor skill development and physical development. These patterns will continue throughout the growing years until the individual achieves full maturity.

**Cephalocaudal growth pattern**

Changes occur in the head region of the body, both internally and externally in advance of those occurring toward the abdominal region.

The first basic pattern is that changes are **cephalocaudal** in direction. This means that changes in the head region of the body, both internally and externally, are in advance of those occurring toward the abdominal region. Maturation takes place in a head-to-foot direction. For example, developmental changes in motor performance and functioning occur first in the head region and last in the foot region of the body. The spinal cord, nerves, and muscles experience maturational changes in the head region earlier than in the

*The physical changes and abilities of a newborn through the end of the infancy stage is dramatic. (iStock)*

pelvic region. For this reason, infants are able to rotate their heads from side to side long before they can sit up without support or walk.

The second basic pattern is that maturational and developmental changes occur in a **proximodistal** manner. This means that changes happen first in the center, innermost area of the body and then move outward to the ends of the extremities. This proximodistal pattern is also observed in prenatal development. For example, during the embryonic period, arms and legs appear containing finger and toe buds at their ends. Eventually, these buds give rise to the digits of the hands and feet.

**Proximodistal growth pattern**

Changes happen first in the center, innermost area of the body and then move outward to the ends of extremities.

| FIGURE 3-1 | **CHANGES ARE CEPHALOCAUDAL IN DIRECTION** |
| --- | --- |

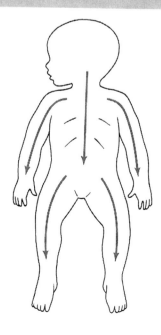

Generally, function follows form in growth trends throughout infancy (Timiras, 1972). The pattern of proximodistal changes predicts, for example, that infants will use their arms before they are able to use their hands or fingers to grasp an object accurately.

For the first six months following birth, growth is a continuation of the rapid changes begun during the prenatal stage. Thereafter, the rate of changes declines slowly for the remainder of infancy.

## Weight and Height Changes

Weight changes are much more dramatic than height changes during the first year. A normally developing baby doubles his or her birth weight by the fourth month and triples it by his or her first birthday. Newborns grow to about one and a half times taller by their first birthday. By the second year, an individual has reached about 50 percent of his or her potential adult height and 20 percent their adult weight (Tanner, 1990).

## Brain Development

Before specifically discussing brain development during infancy, it is important to lay the foundation by describing some basic features of the brain. The brain of an infant develops in two arenas; the neurological and the overall structure of the brain. First, the neuron is the information-processing cell of the nervous system (Bransford, Brown & Cocking, 2000). Nearly all of your neurons were generated during your prenatal life and will continue to function into old age. In fact, neurons started being created within ten weeks after conception and production was pretty much complete by twenty-eight weeks after conception. These neurons were created at the astonishing rate of about 1,000 neurons per second, resulting in somewhere around 100 billion neurons.

Each individual **neuron** has several important parts (Bransford, Brown & Cocking, 2000). The **cell body** containing the nucleus is the part of the cell that keeps the entire cell alive and functioning. On the opposite side of the cell are the **dendrites** which receive information from other neurons. Connecting the cell body and the dendrites is the **axon**, which takes the information from the dendrites, through the axon and the cell body, and transmits this information away to other neurons. The axon is surrounded by a layer of fat, or the **myelin sheath**, which insulates the axon and speeds up message transmission. Although each neuron transmits information to the next, the neurons are not actually connected. There is a small microscopic gap between each neuron called the **synaptic gap**. The way messages transfer from one neuron to the other through this gap is via chemicals called the **neurotransmitters**.

Next is the overall structure of the brain. The outer surface of the brain (the wrinkled part) is called the cerebral cortex (called cortex for short). The cortex is where the magic called "human qualities or traits" occurs. Personality, problem-solving, language, purposeful movement, and emotional control are just some examples of important human behavior that are at least partially controlled by the cortex (Siegler, 1998). Areas of the cortex can be specialized for special processes—we will learn more about this with language development.

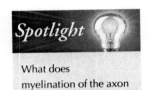

**Spotlight**

What does myelination of the axon accomplish?

**Neuron**

The information processing cell of the nervous system.

**Cell body**

Contains the parts of the cell to keep it alive and functioning (such as the nucleus).

**Dendrites**

Receives information from other neurons.

**Axon**

Takes information from the neuron away to be sent to other neurons.

**Myelin sheath**

A layer of fat that can surround the axon.

**Synaptic gap**

The tiny gaps between neurons.

**Neurotransmitters**

Chemical messengers that carry information to other neurons.

There are two hemispheres to the brain, the left and the right. Language ability is specialized in certain areas of the left cerebral cortex for most individuals (Siegler, 1998; Tanner, 1990). This specialization is evident in newborns as measured by brain activity in response to speech. It is theorized that such specialization may help prime the brain to learn language quickly in infancy. Spatial processing seems to be specialized in certain areas of the right cerebral cortex for most individuals. This specialization is evident during infancy.

Sometimes, babies are born with (or develop after birth) severe forms of epilepsy which necessitate removal of the left hemisphere of the brain. If this is done during infancy, language function is moved to the remaining right hemisphere with relatively little problem. Interestingly, when language processing moves in, spatial processing moves out (at least somewhat). It appears that it is within our genetic code to give language processing preference for any available healthy brain tissue over spatial processing. It is important to note that the earlier in life that such brain surgery is done, the better. The brain appears to lose some of its plasticity with development, resulting in less optimal recovery at later ages (Siegler, 1998).

An adult brain is about three pounds. The brain achieves 25 percent of its weight by birth and 75 percent by the first birthday. Although the newborn is born with most of the neurons he or she will ever have, the number of dendrites (with corresponding synapses) increases significantly during infancy. No experience is lost on a newborn, as experiences build connections in the brain. Research shows that animals and humans reared in stimulating environments have bigger brains and more connections than animals and humans reared in barren or neglectful environments (National Research Council and Institute of Medicine, 2000).

Different areas of the brain develop at different times. Many are not complete until well into adolescence. In terms of infants, areas important for language, visual, motor, emotions, and planning all show development during infancy (National Research Council and Institute of Medicine, 2000).

## *Other Physical Changes*

Three major areas of physical development would include muscle development, fat development, and bone development. Although nearly all of a person's muscle fiber is present at birth it continues to grow, strengthen, thicken, and band together during infancy and throughout childhood. During the end of prenatal development, a layer of fat begins to be deposited below the skin.

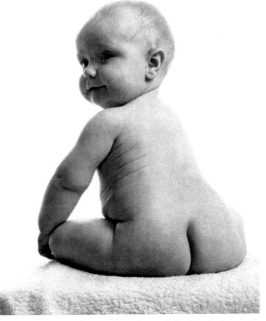

*The layer of fat that is developed during infancy is important for body temperature control. (iStock)*

This layer of fat continues to develop during infancy and is important for body temperature control. Finally, bones begin as cartilage during prenatal development. It slowly hardens to bone in the center core during prenatal development and the outer ends (epiphyses) harden to bone near birth. The rest of the cartilage turns to bone slowly and, when complete, finishes growth of the skeleton (Tanner, 1990).

*Pause and Process:*

1. Describe the physical growth patterns discussed in this section.

2. In which hemisphere of the brain is language localized for most people? Why may the brain have such a specialized area?

# MOTOR DEVELOPMENT

Basic motor, or movement, skills are developed in infancy. Changes or refinements in these skills are based on (1) maturation of structures such as nerves and muscles, (2) exercise of existing reflexes present at birth, and (3) experiences in practicing and refining the skills as they appear and change. In many respects, motor skill development reflects the interaction between genetic programming and environmental experiences more dramatically than any other developmental pattern.

The pattern of motor skill development in infancy illustrates many of Gesell's ideas regarding maturation (that development unfolds according to a preprogrammed, biological sequence). Gesell stressed that motor skills emerge in accordance with a predictable, inborn sequence that is highly organized and common to all humans. Babies do not acquire them before they are developmentally ready. Individual differences in the rate at which these skills emerge and become refined are apparent among infants.

## *Motor Skills*

The achievement of upright locomotion is a milestone in human development. An infant's first steps reflect much developmental progress in motor skills from the time of birth. They set the stage for many related developmental events later in the life span.

Walking is a highly complex behavior. It involves the coordination of a large number of muscle groups working in association with sensory perception to maintain balance. Reflex activity in the neonatal period and movement behaviors in the early months of infancy prepare the individual to walk. Upright locomotion develops as a sequence of events that follows the cephalocaudal pattern. It is accompanied by maturation of muscle groups and nerve fibers involving the spinal cord and lower brain structures. Please note that although we are heavily emphasizing the importance of biological maturation in this section, keep in mind the importance of caregiving behaviors and infant experiences in promoting infant motor development. As always, nature and nurture both play a role in this developmental feat.

The sequence of events that culminates in walking illustrates the principle that changes in motor skills proceed from the general to the specific. The diffuse, largely uncoordinated behaviors of early infancy are brought under the control of the specific body parts involved in walking. The process involves orderly changes as an infant experiences the maturational preprogrammed responses that partially compose motor skill development.

The sequencing begins in association with the behavior of early infancy. The child first acquires the ability to lift its head and then its chest from a prone position. The ability to sit up with, and then without, support is attained next. This illustrates an infant's increasing control over the muscles and nerves of the trunk region of its body. By about seven months of age, most infants show the rapid increase in motor skill activity and changes that permit **crawling** (locomotion with the abdomen on a surface). This is followed by **creeping** (locomotion by moving the hands and knees with the abdomen off the surface). A variation in locomotion is **hitching**, or crawling or creeping backward using the buttocks rather than the hands and knees. Using various body parts in numerous combinations produces movement in all directions.

*By their first birthday many infants are able to pull themselves into a standing position by using the sides of their cribs. (iStock)*

### Crawling

Locomotion with the abdomen on a surface.

### Creeping

Locomotion by moving the hands and knees with the abdomen off the surface.

### Hitching

Crawling or creeping backward using the buttocks rather than the hands and knees.

### Cruising

Walking using the assistance of objects or people.

Toward their first birthday, many infants are able to pull to a standing position using crib sides, furniture, or walls for support. **Cruising**, or walking using the assistance of objects or people leads to upright, independent walking. Walking occurs for most American infants around the first birthday. Although we are giving approximate ages for these motor milestones, remember that infants can vary and have their own timetable.

One of Gesell's principle conclusions about the role of maturation was that none of these events will occur until an individual is ready developmentally. In other words, neither the appearance of these events nor their rate of development can be altered. His conclusion is questionable, however, because infants who have received special training have been shown to walk earlier than usual (Zelazo, 1983). What is controversial is the *purpose* of accomplishing this achievement earlier than typically expected.

### Hand Skills

**Hand skills**

The ability to explore and manipulate a wide variety of objects with the hands.

The human hand is an engineering marvel. Composed of several dozen bones, the hands provide the means for exploring and manipulating a wide variety of objects. **Hand skills** let the developing infant take in rich sensory input from the environment and participate in much instrumental or goal-oriented behavior. They are as significant for active exploration as walking or locomotion.

Much of our understanding of the developmental changes in hand or manual skills come from observing the grasping activities and behaviors of infants (Frankenburg et al., 1981; Halverson, 1931; von Hofsten, 1983). The emergence and refinement of the ability to handle objects and use the hands with agility follows the proximodistal pattern and conforms to the trend of general to specific responses. Essentially, there is an orderly sequence of steps and refinements in this type of motor skill.

At birth, grasping is governed by reflexive action. By the second month, this behavior is random and clumsy as the infant attempts to reach and retain objects. Initially, a baby uses the entire hand to grasp or pick up something. Later an infant uses only the palm and the fourth and fifth fingers. This is referred to as the ulnar grasp.

By six months of age, a different problem emerges. The infant is able to grasp an object in a primitive manner, but is unable to let go of it. Willful letting go of objects is not possible until about eight months of age. At this age, the ulnar grasp is modified to include the middle fingers and the center of the palm (the palmar grasp). Next it is refined to include the index finger and the side of the palm (the radial grasp). The final refinement involves the use of the thumb with the forefinger, known as the pincer grasp. The pincer grasp becomes the preferred method of picking up all objects, large as well as very small in size. This final ability is achieved at twelve to fourteen months of age. From this point forward, an infant experiences great delight in this new mastery and becomes absorbed in searching for all kinds of objects to successfully transfer to its mouth.

*Pause and Process:*

1. How does walking develop?

2. How do hand skills develop in infancy?

# PERCEPTUAL DEVELOPMENT

### Perceptual Development

**Perceptual skill** development is closely associated with changes in motor skills development. This association is clearly observed in the emerging abilities of infants to use visual-motor skills in many activities. Infants learn to guide their movements and make adjustments in motor actions based on what they see.

**Perceptual skill**

The ability to perceive through sight and sound; especially those skills related to motor skill development, such as depth perception and pattern perception, that emerge in infancy.

Much of the change that takes place in grasping behavior reflects the increasing ability of an infant's brain to organize and interpret visual feedback. Up until they are four to five months of age, infants devote a great deal of their time to gazing at their hands. Even while reaching for an object, an infant will become fascinated with watching his own hand. In fact, he will often lose sight of the object because he is so intent on examining the movements his hand is making (Bower, 1977; von Hofsten & Fazel-Zandy, 1984).

By the time a baby is about five to six months old her hand movements are more controlled by visual feedback (Hatwell, 1987). The infant is now more motivated to grasp and manipulate objects and less fascinated by her own hand movements. This important achievement results from continual practice in hand gazing. Hand gazing apparently establishes neural circuits in the brain, and these provide information about where the hand is in space, which way the arms and legs are moving in space, and what happens as a result of such actions. The development of kinesthetic sense, or knowledge of where one's body is in space, how it performs when making certain movements, and what happens as a result—will become significant in learning to walk.

In learning about visual-motor coordination, researchers have studied two other related areas: the acquisition of depth perception and pattern perception.

## *Depth Perception*

The ability to detect differences in surface depths and three-dimensional perception seems to be inborn in many animal species. These skills in depth perception are not innate in human beings but emerge very early in their development. Their early emergence may serve to protect infants from falling and injuring themselves.

Psychologists Eleanor Gibson and Richard Walk (1960) conducted a famous investigation called the visual cliff experiment to study depth perception in infancy. An apparatus was constructed using checkerboard patterns. One pattern was part of one end of the surface of the apparatus; the other was on the floor but could be seen through glass that extended across the apparatus' surface. This gave the appearance of a change in surface depth. A group of infants from six and one-half to

*The differences in surface depths and three-dimensional perception protects infants from falling and injuring themselves. (iStock)*

fourteen months of age were placed individually at the shallow end of the apparatus and encouraged to crawl to their mother, who was at the other end. The reactions of the majority of infants showed that they detected the apparent change in depth of the surface. Some would approach the edge, touch the glass, and retreat back to the shallow end. Others cried in frustration at not being able to reach their mother. All of these infants clearly demonstrated avoidance of the apparent deep zone.

This experiment cleverly showed that stereoscopic or binocular vision appears by the time an infant is ready to begin actively exploring its environment by crawling and creeping. This is usually at about six months of age. Several studies have revealed that a rapid increase in this ability to perceive the world in a three-dimensional manner occurs between the age of three and six months as a result of the establishment of neural circuitry in the brain (Bertenthal & Camos, 1987; Yonas, Granrud & Pettersen, 1985). Other work has shown the importance of early visual experiences in the development of binocular vision (Hubel & Wiesel, 1970). The cells in the brain that are responsible for this ability apparently disappear if they are not stimulated with sensory signals from both eyes during the first few months of life. In effect, the brain will not establish the appropriate neural circuitry for this necessary visual ability unless the infant has adequate experience visually exploring his or her environment. This is a good argument in favor of providing visual experiences to infants during their alert periods.

*Pause and Process:*

1. Describe what is meant by perceptual skills.

2. What do we know about infant depth perception?

# HEALTH ISSUES

## *Nutritional Needs*

"Breast is best." Surely you have heard this mantra before. Overwhelming research indicates that breast milk provides the best nutrition for infants; it offers the perfect combination of carbohydrates, fats, and proteins. Breast milk also contains the mother's antibodies to help fight infections. In comparison to formula-fed babies, breastfed babies have lower childhood obesity rates, lower rates of illnesses and infections, lower rates of SIDS (sudden infant death syndrome), lower childhood cancer rates, lower rates of diabetes II, lower rates of allergies, and denser bones. Additionally, breastfeeding may be correlated to better cognitive development and visual acuity. Breastfeeding also provides benefits to the mother; including, lower stress levels, weight loss, and a sense of peace and bonding (thanks to hormones).

However, there are reasons as to why breastfeeding should be avoided. If the mother has a disease that can be transmitted through the breast milk (such as AIDS), breastfeed-

*Research has shown that breast milk has many benefits for infants. For example, breastfed babies have lower childhood obesity rates, lower rates of SIDS and denser bones. Breast milk also contains the mother's antibodies which helps fight infections. (iStock)*

ing should be avoided. Additionally, certain medications that may harm the baby may prevent a woman from breastfeeding.

Approximately two-thirds of women breastfeed while in the hospital, with about a third still breastfeeding six months later. Most medical professionals recommend breastfeeding for at least the first year. Women with social support are more likely to continue breastfeeding than women without such support.

Baby foods (special infant cereal is usually first) are introduced typically between four and six months. The practice of mixing formula with cereal in a bottle before this time with the thought of helping the infant sleep through the night is discouraged because the infant's digestive system is not yet developed enough to handle the cereal and the parents may cause some serious health issues. By the first birthday, the infant is usually ready to eat some finely cut or mashed table food. Pediatricians often assist parents in knowing when it is appropriate to introduce certain foods. If certain foods are introduced too soon, parents can risk triggering allergic reactions that may create sensitivities that will last a lifetime.

## *Safety Concerns*

As motor skills advance from crawling and creeping to upright walking, the infant's perspective of the world changes. Now an infant can move about with increasing speed and has more freedom to explore the physical surroundings. To grow and develop adequately, they need these experiences. They need to learn they are distinct persons, separate from other people and things, yet also a part of their surroundings. As children act upon their environment, they discover how their environment acts.

Naturally, parents are concerned about the infant's physical safety at this time. It soon becomes obvious that a child's quest to discover the environment can lead to danger. Parents generally react by **childproofing** their home—that is, they adapt it to the needs and

**Childproofing**

Arranging and adapting housing and physical space (e.g., by capping electrical outlets) to meet safety concerns for infants.

behavior of a small child (Duvall & Miller, 1985). Cleaning solutions are placed out of reach, accessories are moved from tables, tablecloths are put away, protective gates are placed across doorways, and electrical outlets are plugged with specially designed caps. Often the entire family's lifestyle must be modified to protect an infant's safety.

In recent years, numerous baby products and toys have been recalled because of lead paint or other toxins. Because babies have the tendency to put everything in their mouth, it is especially important to avoid anything that may have lead or lead paint. Although steps have been taken to ensure the safety of infant and child products, safety should not be taken for granted. It is important for parents to stay up to date on product recalls.

## Promoting Wellness

Health should be closely monitored during infancy. Periodic visits to health-care professionals help to promote well-being and normal growth patterns during this stage.

## Immunizations

Making sure that an infant is immunized against a variety of communicable diseases is an important aspect of health care. Most of the diseases that once killed people in infancy are now preventable by immunization. Although there is some debate in the general public as to whether a preservative in vaccinations may have triggered autism in children, medical professionals vehemently deny this assertion (Miller & Reynolds, 2009). Sadly, some once erad-icated childhood illnesses are making a comeback because

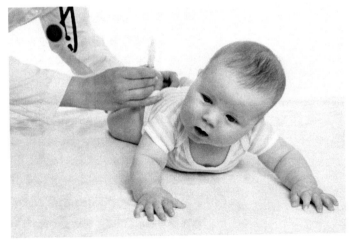

*Immunizations protect infants against a variety of communica-ble diseases. (shutterstock)*

of parents not vaccinating their children. Parents who are concerned about vaccinations and potential health hazards should talk to their pediatrician.

## Sleep

Labor is not just hard on the mother; it is stressful for the baby as well. Newborns are often alert for a while after birth and then sleepy for the next several hours or days. All babies are born with their own unique personalities. Some babies like to sleep more than other babies. Some babies are more predictable in their sleep patterns than other babies. In general, newborns will sleep an average of fourteen to eighteen hours a day, in small stretches at a time (ACOG, 2005).

Newborn sleep cycles are different than adult sleep cycles. Interestingly, newborns will often begin their sleep cycle in the REM (rapid eye movement) stage. This is thought to be a stage where dreaming occurs. Adults begin sleep in a state of non-REM sleep. Additionally, newborns will spend around 50 percent of their sleeping hours in REM sleep, whereas adults spend only 20 percent of their sleep time in this stage. It is speculated that newborns, and infants in general, spend so much time in REM sleep due to the brain's need for stimulation, brain development, or learning.

Although babies differ as to when they will actually start sleeping through the night, parents can rest assured that it should happen sometime before the first birthday. However, in some cases sleep becomes more complicated when infants suffer from **baby colic**, a condition in which a healthy baby cries or screams frequently for extended periods of time for no apparent reason. The condition typically appears a few weeks after birth and eventually disappears by about four months of age. The cause is not established and the amount of crying differs between babies, and hence a child is deemed "colicky" if he or she cries intensely most evenings for about three hours.

**Sudden Infant Death Syndrome** (SIDS) is a worry for parents of infants. What is SIDS? It is when an infant stops breathing during sleep and suffocates to death. SIDS claims approximately five thousand infant lives in the United States each year. The peak age for SIDS deaths is between two and four months of age.

Doctors and researchers are not sure what causes SIDS. A genetic predisposition and brain defect are likely candidates; however, there are known environmental factors that can place infants at risk. For example, exposure to maternal smoking in the womb, second-hand smoke, low-birthweight, premature birth, co-sleeping, heavy blankets/sleepwear, and a sibling death due to SIDS increase the risk of SIDS. Breastfeeding, sleeping in the parents' bedroom (but in a separate bed), sleeping with a fan on, and sleeping on one's back seem to help prevent SIDS.

Co-sleeping is a controversial issue in the United States. **Co-sleeping** is when parents and children sleep in the same bed. Many cultures accept co-sleeping as a natural way of life. Many parents enjoy the time of closeness with their infant and it facilitates breastfeeding. However, many U.S. medical professionals advise against co-sleeping because of the risk of rolling over on the infant and suffocating them. Some American parents are opting to have an infant room-in with them—the infant sleeps in the same room (making breastfeeding easier), but a separate bed.

## *Baby Exercise*

Infants are typically active on their own. They work very hard, almost nonstop, toward reaching their next motor milestone (e.g., rolling, crawling, or walking). Free movement and playtime, while being supervised, is encouraged for infants. Structured exercise, however, is largely unnecessary and potentially dangerous. Because infants cannot directly

---

**Baby colic**

A condition in which a healthy baby cries or screams frequently for extended periods of time for no apparent reason.

**Sudden infant death syndrome (SIDS)**

A condition of unknown cause resulting in the sudden and unexpected death of an infant.

**Co-sleeping**

Parents and children sleep in the same bed.

communicate if a parent is going too far in helping them exercise, it is usually recommended that parents hold off on the structured exercise classes until the child is older. An obvious exception to this general rule is if the infant has a developmental disability that requires physical therapy.

*Pause and Process:*

1. Do vaccines cause autism?

2. What are risk factors for SIDS? What can help prevent SIDS?

# COGNITIVE DEVELOPMENT DURING INFANCY

### LEARNING OBJECTIVES:

1. *Understand the general progression of cognitive development during the sensorimotor stage*
2. *Describe infant information-processing skills*
3. *Identify milestones in infant language development*

We are going to begin this section by discussing Piaget's first stage of cognitive development: the sensorimotor stage. This stage lasts from birth until around the age of twenty-four months. Remember, Piaget posited that individuals go through four stages of cognitive development, each qualitatively different from one another. The stages must be gone through in order, and no stage may be skipped. However, in Piagetian theory, not all individuals reach the fourth stage of cognitive development, which we will discuss later in the book.

If you remember back to Chapter 1, Piaget's cognitive developmental theory saw assimilation and accommodation as two processes that help individuals adapt or change their schemas based upon their experiences in the world. This means that we can view cognitive development as driven by intellectual adaptation to the world.

This would be a good time to introduce two other key concepts in Piagetian theory: equilibrium and disequilibrium. There was probably a time back in your childhood when you believed in Santa Claus, the Easter Bunny, and the Tooth Fairy. When you accepted their existence without question, you were in a state of equilibrium. However, as you grew, you started to have some questions. Santa has a sleigh, but how does the Easter Bunny get around the world in one night? What does the Tooth Fairy do with all these teeth? Why does Tommy down the street keep saying that there is no Santa Claus? These, and many other doubts, started entering your mind. You entered a state of disequilibrium, an uncomfortable cognitive state in which your experiences and beliefs are no longer perfectly aligned. When this happened, you were forced to seek out answers and go through a process of equilibration, until your beliefs and experiences/observations were once again aligned.

Therefore, cognitive development is driven by adapting our thinking to our experiences in the world. When our thoughts and beliefs are no longer in equilibrium with our experiences, we are thrown into a state of disequilibrium. As we go through the equilibration process, we use the processes of assimilation and accommodation to adapt our schemas; hence, we grow cognitively.

After we finish discussing Piaget's sensorimotor stage, we will highlight information-processing and language development during infancy. Although the infancy period lasts from only about two weeks after birth until the age of two, cognitive development is astronomically quick. When you compare the cognitive abilities of a two-year-old child with a two-week-old child, the amount of growth seems incomprehensible. Yet, it is a task that occurs in all cognitively healthy infants and toddlers.

# PIAGET'S COGNITIVE DEVELOPMENT THEORY AND THE SENSORIMOTOR STAGE

Piaget uses the term sensorimotor to describe the integration of sensory input (perceptions of sound, sight, taste, smell, and touch) with motor behavior during infancy. Motor skills that are quickly developed in infancy, such as walking, grasping, and manipulating objects, are increasingly guided by sensory input as the infant matures. In Piaget's view, self-differentiation is accomplished through sensory and motor activities. With adequate brain maturation, an infant can learn about the world, discover how to react to it, and develop schemes to solve problems in interactions with it. At first, the child is able to do this only through such sensory means as taste and touch and through motor actions. An infant's understanding of the world is therefore limited. However, it is through such means and level of functioning that lifetime mental development begins.

One of the infant's major accomplishments is learning that objects, people, and things are permanent. This enables an infant to realize that she or he is a distinct and separate entity from the things and people that populate the environment. This realization requires the construction of a concept known as **object permanence**—the understanding that something continues to exist even though it is hidden or removed from sight. The reason the game of peek-a-boo is so fascinating to young infants is that they do not yet understand this principle. As they develop and discover that things can be moved and manipulated, they master this cognitive skill.

One other accomplishment during this time of the life span is the elementary ability to represent the external world by internal, mental images. An infant takes the first step in this rather complicated process (which is not mastered until later in life) by understanding the world through sensory means. Things are known by how they feel, taste, look, and smell, as well as by how they can be manipulated. If it were possible for an infant to use language effectively and she was asked to define a ball, her likely answer would be in words noting sensory and motor characteristics: "It's something that's slick on my tongue, and rolls across the floor when I hit it." This is probably the only way a ball can be understood at this stage in life.

**Object permanence**

The understanding that something exists even though it is not in sight or has been removed from the field of vision; accomplished between 18 and 24 months of age.

The cognitive changes during this period happen in a sequence Piaget describes as beginning with reflexes at birth and culminating in symbolic reasoning at eighteen to twenty-four months of age (see Table 3-1). They are facilitated by the acquisition of the ability to use language in communication with others. The next section discusses the order of this sequence.

## Substages of the Sensorimotor Stage:

1. *Use of existing reflexes* to progress toward developing sensorimotor schemas occurs between birth and one month of age. Reflexes present at birth provide much of the basis for motor behavior at this time. The infant performs these reflex actions more efficiently with practice. As the infant's brain structures mature, the same actions come more under willful control. Searching for a nipple, for example, is first guided by the rooting reflex. Such behavior becomes learned rather than automatic as the reflex is replaced by willful action by virtue of the maturation process. In adapting from automatic to willful acts, infants gain more control over their interactions with the world.

**Circular reactions**

Actions that occur by chance and then are repeated and modified through practice.

2. *Primary circular reactions* are formed between one and four months of age. **Circular reactions** are actions that occur by chance and then are repeated and modified through practice. We will use the act of sucking to illustrate how primary circular reactions are formed. An infant accidentally happens to put a finger in her mouth. This stimulates sucking, an action based on a strong reflex present before birth. Because this is a pleasurable act, the baby repeats it. The repetition leads to learning how to suck on a thumb. As maturation proceeds, anything the baby grasps is brought to her mouth to be sucked

| TABLE 3-1 | SUMMARY OF THE SUBSTAGES OF THE SENSORIMOTOR STAGE |
|---|---|
| **SUBSTAGE** | **DESCRIPTION** |
| 1.   Use of reflexes (birth to one month) | Use of reflexes present at birth to adapt to the environment. |
| 2.   Primary circular reactions (one to four months) | Repetition of pleasurable acts that happen first by body acts; object permanence not yet developed. |
| 3.   Secondary circular reactions (four to nine months) | Focus shifts to environment as infant learns that chance, then deliberate, actions produce certain results. |
| 4.   Coordination of secondary schemas (nine to 12 months) | Coordination and integration of secondary schemas to achieve goals; increasing awareness of object permanence. |
| 5.   Tertiary circular reactions (12 to 18 months) | Purposive variation of behavior to experiment and vary schemas; trial-and-error used in solving problems and reaching goals. |
| 6.   Symbolic logic (18 to 24 months) | Primitive reasoning system used; object permanence achieved, symbol user. |

upon. These actions involve hand-eye and hand-mouth coordination. They are called primary because they occur first in reference to the infant's body. They are called circular because they are habitual actions based on continual repetition.

3. *Secondary circular reactions* are formed between four and nine months of age. In forming secondary circular reactions, the infant's reference shifts from the body (primary reactions) to the physical environment. The baby observes that random chance movements produce specific results and outcomes—for example, a particular kicking motion in his crib produces wild, swinging movements of the mobile hanging overhead. This pleases, delights, and fascinates the infant. He rapidly learns that willfully controlled actions of his body produce results in the physical environment. As this

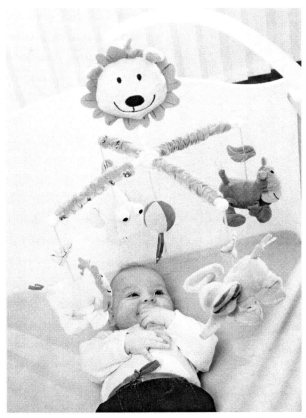

*An example of secondary circular reaction is when a baby is able to make a mobile move by kicking his legs. (iStock)*

type of association between a personal action and its environmental result is repeated, a secondary circular reaction is formed. Later in the infancy stage, a baby may modify his physical actions to produce similar results with different objects. For example, the baby who formed a secondary circular reaction to make his crib mobile move learns to modify basic movements to make a similar piece of equipment move when placed in his playpen. It is in such simple ways that an infant learns to act in certain ways to make certain things happen. This is a very significant advance. The ability to make a connection between action and result (cause and effect) is the very foundation of human learning ability.

Object permanence, as far as we know, is not understood this early in infancy. Infants are mastering this skill, however, as they recognize and recover objects only partially hidden from their view. But they still will not try to discover an object's whereabouts if it is hidden from their view.

4. *Coordination of secondary schemas* occurs between nine and twelve months of age. If you can remember from Chapter 1, schemas (or schemes) are the basic building blocks of mental life. They are consistent, reliable patterns or plans for processing information, experiences, or perceptions of the world. Individuals change or modify their schemas with experience throughout life. Piaget suggests that the numerous schemas formed in interaction with the physical environment earlier are combined and coordinated at this particular

time in infancy. New behavior patterns emerge from existing ones as an infant learns new ways to solve problems and interact with the surroundings. An infant may learn, for example, to search for an object that she saw hidden. She will grasp the object once she has located it. Piaget describes this as intentional behavior. The infant established a goal before acting and purposely tailored her physical actions to enable her to reach that goal. The infant can adapt behavior to attain goals effectively in the social and physical environment.

*An example of tertiary circular reaction is when a baby repeatedly throws or drops a toy. (iStock)*

5. *Tertiary circular reactions* are formed between twelve and eighteen months of age. Piaget describes infants as true scientists now because of their incessant motivation to explore their environment, to discover new understandings, and to experiment with new approaches to solving problems and attaining goals. A new skill learned by the infant is the ability to make new events happen. These refinements in cognition are shown by the baby's first efforts to learn the cause-and-effect nature of bodily movements and physical acts. Toys are dropped or thrown repeatedly. This is because the infant observes that they always fall, make certain sounds, or produce particular actions when treated in this manner.

Infants' exploration of their environment is largely by trial-and-error. This is the hallmark of the type of change taking place in their mental functioning at this time. It explains their fascination with banging pots and pans, investigating waste cans, playing in the toilet, splashing water in the bath, and exploring everything in detail with their fingers. Childproofing the home is a necessity at this time.

6. *Symbolic (or elementary) logic* emerges between eighteen and twenty-four months of age. There are first indications of simple internalization as infants gradually develop mental images of objects and actions. Object permanence usually becomes fully established now. The first sign of symbolic thought processes is that infants require little or no experimentation to reach solutions to their problems. For instance, an infant at this age may try to wake her father by placing eyeglasses on his face because she associates this feature with his being awake and seeing to her needs.

Infants this age engage in much imitation of others' actions and pretend play. As they learn to incorporate others' actions into their own range of behaviors, they learn other ways to solve problems and reach goals. Ways to solve future problems and reach goals are anticipated.

## Characteristics of Sensorimotor Thought

In summary, sensorimotor thought is based largely on motor actions. Two important milestones are reached during this stage: object permanence and symbolic thought. During this stage, the infant already actively explores the environment and adapts his or her schemas based upon these experiences. By the end of the sensorimotor stage, the child is capable of symbolic thought, meaning he or she can use mental representations when thinking.

## Critiques of Piaget's Theory

The critiques to Piaget's theory will seem familiar to issues discussed in Chapter 1. Piaget's theory allowed us to view infant thought as unique, not as simply a rudimentary form of adult thought. Indeed, infants do not think less than adults, they think differently (hence, the idea of qualitative changes).

Current research indicates that Piaget underestimated the cognitive abilities of infants. As developmentalists have created amazing research techniques that allow us a glimpse into an infant's mental world, it has become apparent that infants are far more cognitively capable than we previously thought. For example, there is some evidence that they achieve object permanence and deferred imitation earlier than Piaget thought (Crain, 2005). As we continue to progress in our research abilities it should be interesting to see what cognitive skills infants achieve far earlier than we ever dreamed.

*Pause and Process:*

1. What is object permanence? What would your life be like if you thought people and objects ceased to exist if they left your view?

2. Describe what sensorimotor thought is like.

# INFORMATION-PROCESSING IN INFANCY

**Basic processes**

"Frequently used, rapidly executed, memory activities such as association, generalization, recognition, and recall. They are among the building blocks of cognition, in the sense that all more complex cognitive activities are built by combining them in different ways."

Although Piaget viewed cognitive development as occurring through qualitatively distinct stages, information-processing theories view cognitive development as a continuous process during which specific processes increase in efficiency to a certain point, and then, perhaps, decline.

Within the information-processing paradigm, **basic processes** are defined as "frequently used, rapidly executed, memory activities such as association, generalization, recognition, and recall. They are among the building blocks of cognition, in the sense that all more complex cognitive activities are built by combining them in different ways" (Siegler, 1998, p. 180). Basic processes are functional at birth, with some functioning prenatally. Although infants lack knowledge structures, memory strategies, and such, their ability to use basic processes allow them to form and access memories.

## Explicit memories

Conscious memories that can be visualized as well as provide a verbal account.

## Implicit memories

Unconscious memories that influence our behavior.

## Association

The ability to form a connection between a stimuli and a response.

## Recognition

Awareness or recollection of having seen something before.

## Habituation/ dishabituation

An experimental technique that allows researchers to measure recognition in babies.

## Imitation

The basic process of a newborn being capable of immediately imitating your behavior.

## Recall

The basic process of a newborn being capable of recalling observed behavior experiences.

First, we should distinguish between the basic processes of explicit and implicit memories. **Explicit memories** are memories of which we are conscious. We can typically visualize these memories and provide a verbal account. **Implicit memories** are unconscious memories that influence our behavior. For example, most of you have probably been driving for a while. You do not need to (hopefully) consciously try to remember which pedal is for the gas and which is for the brake. You implicitly know this and this knowledge directs your behavior. This is an example of an implicit memory. However, if I asked you to recount your scariest driving moment, you would verbally relate the story to me as you consciously extricate it from your memory. This would be an example of an explicit memory. Both types of memory are important; yet, they have their own developmental timetable.

It appears that infants are capable of forming implicit memories from birth, if not prenatally. However, it is not until around six to eight months that infants seem able to form explicit memories. Evidently, implicit and explicit memories utilize different parts of the brain that mature at different times (Siegler, 1998).

**Association** is the most fundamental of basic processes and it is the ability to form a connection between a stimuli and a response. **Recognition** is another basic process. Once again, both of these are certainly present at birth and are most likely present prenatally. Association can be tested through the classical conditioning process discussed in Chapter 1. Recognition has been tested in preterm and full term infants using the **habituation/dishabituation** process. For example, newborns like to gaze at novel visual stimuli. Once a stimulus becomes familiar, their gazing time decreases. However, if you present a new, novel stimulus, gazing time increases again. This basic knowledge allows us to test both visual preferences and recognition. Using habituation/dishabituation, we know that two-month-olds recognize old visual stimuli for more than two weeks after initial exposure.

Have you ever stuck your tongue out at a newborn? I suppose most of you haven't, but guess what would happen if you did? The newborn would stick his or her tongue out at you in reply. The newborn isn't being rude; instead, they are imitating observed behavior. **Imitation** and **recall** are also basic processes present at birth. Not only is the newborn capable of immediately imitating your behavior, but they still recall the experience twenty-four hours later. Newborns that have observed tongue protrusion behavior are more likely to engage in such behavior for the twenty-four hours afterward than newborns who did not observe such behavior. This pattern holds true not just for tongue protrusion behavior, but also for opening and closing of mouth behavior. As infants grow older, the amount of time between observation and imitation/recall increases. Shortly after the first birthday, infants can demonstrate imitation and recall more than four months after the initial observation (Siegler, 1998).

Rovee-Collier (1995) demonstrated the memory capabilities of infants across a series of experiments utilizing infant mobiles (the circular things that hang above cribs with dangling toys that play music). Rovee-Collier would tie a string connected to a mobile to the ankle of an infant. If the infant kicked, the mobile would make sounds. The studies showed that three-month-olds would experience an "aha" moment in which they would learn that their kicking behavior caused the mobile's noise. Infants were able to recall and

*Spotlight*

What are the two basic types of memories discussed in this chapter?

generalize their learning across similar situations if comparable experiences were provided within three days of each other.

In summary, infants are born with basic processes that allow for quick learning about the surrounding world. These basic processes provide the foundation for all information-processing throughout life. Future chapters will discuss the specifics of intelligence, attention, memory, and problem-solving development.

## *Infantile Amnesia*

**Infantile amnesia**

The inability to remember much about the first two or so years of life after birth.

What is your earliest memory? How old are you in this earliest memory? Most of us do not remember much about the first two or so years of our life after birth. This is referred to as **infantile amnesia**. It used to be assumed that infants could not form long-term memories; however, we now know that is false. Experiences at the age of eleven months can sometimes be recalled a year later and some three-year-olds can remember experiences from when they were one. So why is it that we cannot remember our own birth? Why can't we remember our first steps, walks, or piece of birthday cake? These seem like worthwhile memories to keep, so where have they gone?

There are three leading theories in regard to the causes of infantile amnesia. The first theory is that the parts of the brain instrumental in storing long-term, explicit, retrievable memories continue to mature well past infancy. The frontal lobes seem to be particularly important for these memories (Siegler, 1998).

The second theory highlights the importance of practicing information in order to retain information (and access to that information) in long-term memory. For example, the more young children hear stories about their first birthday—and relate stories about their first birthday—the more likely it is that they will form enduring memories about their first birthday. Parents seem to naturally begin having these dialogues with their children around the age of three, which may be why some of our earliest memories are around that age (Siegler, 1998).

The third theory is in regard to how infants and older individuals may encode information differently. For example, when you try to remember something, how do you do it? Do you use words (verbal codes)? Do you use mental images (visual codes)? It has been theorized that infants are more likely to encode their memories using smells, tastes, and touches rather than our preferred verbal and visual codes. However, as children acquire language and begin using verbal codes to encode and retrieve information, they may lose the ability to access memories encoded in different modalities (Siegler, 1998).

In all likelihood, it is a combination of these three theories, and perhaps some other theories not considered here, that will eventually explain the phenomenon of infantile amnesia. But honestly, even if you could remember your own birth, would you really want to?

*Pause and Process:*

1. Give a description of information-processing abilities in infancy.

2. In your own words, explain the three explanations for infantile amnesia discussed above. Which explanation seems the most plausible to you?

# LANGUAGE DEVELOPMENT IN INFANCY

### Language

"A system of abstract symbols and rule-governed structures, the specific conventions of which are learned."

### Speech

Orally expressed language.

### Phonemes

The simplest and most elementary sounds in speech, or the building blocks of speech.

### Morphemes

Meaningful units of speech.

### Syntax

The rules for making grammatical sentences.

### Semantics

The ability to express meaning through language.

One characteristic that is uniquely human emerges during infancy. This is the ability to use language to communicate information, ideas, feelings, and thoughts to others. Before individuals emerge from infancy, they are expected to be able to pronounce words so that others can understand them. They are also expected to learn meanings associated with words, so that they can understand others.

An infant's acquisition of communication skills is a very complex process and one that is not completely understood. Our human brain structure is extremely important to language development and seems to hint that aspects of language acquisition are innate with proper exposure. This means that humans are hardwired with the ability to learn language with proper social interaction. Two basic areas of the brain appear to be responsible for speech and language skills. They are located deep within the left hemisphere.

Hulit and Howard (1997) define **language** as "a system of abstract symbols and rule-governed structures, the specific conventions of which are learned" (p. 3). Although language is related to speech, they are not one and the same. **Speech** is orally expressing language; however, language can be conveyed through modalities other than verbal speech. Both speech and language are important processes for communication.

Language has some basic components. **Phonemes** are the simplest and most elementary sounds in speech, or the building blocks of speech, such as "ah", "ma", and "ba". **Morphemes** are meaningful units of speech, such as "mama", "cup", and "book". **Syntax** comprises the rules for making grammatical sentences. **Semantics** is the ability to express meaning through language. **Pragmatics** is the ability to adjust speech in socially and culturally appropriate ways. Each of these components is mastered at different points in development. They are typically understood before they are fully able to be mastered in speech production (Dixon, 2003; Hulit & Howard, 1997; Piper, 2003).

*Babies try to mimic the sounds of their caregivers, and by their first birthday they say their first word. (Photo courtesy of J. James)*

**Pragmatics**

The ability to adjust speech in socially and culturally appropriate ways.

Mastering the complexities of language is important for several reasons. First, language permits communication. It is through the medium of language that an infant is given information about many things. Cognitive changes, which allow the developing individual to understand the world in which he lives, are motivated and based on language. Words are the means by which the individual is educated, not only about facts of the world, but also about the rules by which his family operates, what his parents expect of his behavior, how people in his community live, and how society, in general, functions on a daily basis.

Second, language permits individual expression. By using language, an individual is able to express her inner feelings, attitudes, and thoughts and to connect her personal experiences with those of others. That is why language is often viewed as the observable expression and extension of inner thought processes and seen as reflective of the individual's level of cognitive development (Galatzer-Levy & Cohler, 1993; Kolata, 1987; Piper, 2003).

## Theories of Language Acquisition

In the first year following birth, an infant comes to understand others' speech and to use some speech in an elementary and limited fashion. The change from uttering incomprehensible sounds to making sounds that are given meaning by others happens dramatically. There are some basic avenues to this dramatic change, according to developmental researchers.

**Language Acquisition Device (LAD)**

An innate brain structure proposed by Chomsky that regulates the means by which an individual learns language.

Some developmentalists believe that there is an innate language structure, or **language acquisition device (LAD)**, within the brain that regulates the means by which an individual learns language (Chomsky, 1959). This is a very nativistic theory, focusing on the biological innateness to language acquisition.

The LAD is theorized to be a deep brain structure which is identical in all human beings, and allows any infant to acquire the language of the family and culture into which she or he is born. The human brain appears to be sensitive to the sound of language. The LAD organizes these sounds into meaningful understandings according to the grammatical structure of the particular language the child is exposed to daily. This explanation rests on the proposition that humans are born with a predetermined ability to learn any language, and that this is what makes them distinctly different from every other species. It does not completely explain just how language acquisition takes place, however.

**Infant-directed speech**

Speech that is more accentuated and of a higher pitch.

Language acquisition is also thought to be influenced by environmental factors (Hulit & Howard, 1997). Imitation, caretaker speech (i.e., **motherese** or **infant-directed speech**), and reinforcement appear to play some role in speech development. However, the behavioral principles of reinforcement and imitation are not enough to explain language acquisition entirely. For example, we will learn soon that the vocabulary explosion that occurs in early childhood happens too quickly to be explained by imitation and reinforcement alone.

Linguists currently seem to favor an interactionist approach to understanding language development. This approach appreciates both biological endowments and social interactions in the acquisition of speech (Hulit and Howard, 1997). Over time, research may clarify what aspects of speech are primarily genetically preprogrammed (or primed) and which are highly dependent upon social interaction.

## *The General Sequence*

There is a general sequence to language learning during infancy. First, infants cry at birth to communicate with their caregivers. Around one to two months of age, infants begin to coo. Next, around three months of age, infants enjoy making consonant sounds. It is around six months of age that babbling begins. Babbling involves combining consonant and vowel sounds and repeating them. Typically, babies will mimic the intonation that their caregiver is using in communicating with them. Babies appear to understand their first word around eight months of age. Finally, around the first birthday, infants say their first word (Siegler, 1998).

The typical age range for generating their first word is between ten and thirteen months. First words are usually focused upon people, objects, and actions. Vehicles and food are among their favorite objects to speak about.

After achieving their first word, infants quickly progress to speaking in one-word phrases, commonly referred to as **holophrases**. Speaking seems to tax their cognitive resources, so infants use the least amount of words (and simplest words) possible to get their message across (Siegler, 1998).

Between the ages of eighteen and twenty-four months, the average toddler will begin speaking in two-word sentences. These sentences, again, leave out the niceties of speech (e.g., adjectives, adverbs, prepositions, etc.), and focus on conveying meaning. There are some common errors that occur during this time in regards to word meanings.

Toddlers will often commit errors of underextensions, overextensions, and overlaps (Siegler, 1998). An **underextension** is when a child limits the meaning of the word too narrowly. For example, a child may think that the word chair can refer only to a dinner table chair, not to office chairs, recliners, rocking chairs, or other forms of chairs. An **overextension** is when a child applies the meaning of a word too broadly. For example, all flying insects may be called a fly, including butterflies, bees, hornets, and mosquitoes. **Overlaps** occur when a word is underextended on some occasions and overextended on other occasions. For example, the word dress may not be appropriately used to refer to a wedding gown (underextension), but may be used to refer to a bathrobe (overextension).

Vocabulary development begins slowly in early infancy and then speeds up substantially during toddlerhood. For example, it is estimated that a child has a vocabulary of three words at his or her first birthday. However, a vocabulary explosion begins between eighteen months (with a vocabulary of 22 words) and twenty-one months (with a vocabulary of 118 words). Then there is another major jump by twenty-four months (with a vocabulary of 272 words). Such **fast-mapping** of words continues through early childhood with five-year-olds having a vocabulary of more than two thousand words and ten-year-olds having a vocabulary of more than forty thousand words. Mathematically, this works out that between the ages of eighteen months and ten years of age, a child learns

**Holophrases**

An early speech form used by infants in which single words convey a wide number of meanings.

**Underextension**

When a child limits the meaning of the word too narrowly.

**Overextension**

When a child applies the meaning of a word too broadly.

**Overlaps**

When a word is underextended on some occasions and overextended on other occasions.

**Fast-mapping**

A language skill used by young children; the meaning of a new word is acquired by comparing it with one that is familiar.

about ten words a day (Siegler, 1998). Can you imagine trying to achieve this at your current age? Flashcards, anyone? Yet, these children achieve this with little or no effort through basic, everyday social interactions and educational experiences. Amazing!

Sentence structure and grammar is understood before it is produced by children. Grammatical knowledge is connected with vocabulary development. Typical two-word sentences will typically follow basic grammar rules (e.g., subject/verb). We will discuss how grammar, semantic, and pragmatic skills continue to develop across childhood in future chapters. The important thing to realize is that by the end of the second year, children can effectively communicate their intentions and messages. The children also enter the early childhood period with a basic grasp of the language rule systems.

*Pause and Process:*

1. What is the difference between language and speech?

2. Summarize language development between birth and two years of age.

# SOCIOEMOTIONAL DEVELOPMENT DURING INFANCY

### LEARNING OBJECTIVES:

1. *Describe emotional development during infancy*
2. *Explain infants self-understanding, family influences, and societal influences*
3. *Understand psychosocial development during infancy*

Social and emotional development during infancy is a fascinating topic. What emotions can an infant feel? What purpose do these emotions serve? When does an infant realize that he or she is a person? How does an infant develop psychosocially? This section will attempt to answer these questions as we take a peek into socioemotional development from birth through the second year.

# PSYCHOSOCIAL DEVELOPMENT

In chapter one, we were introduced to Erikson's psychosocial theory. We will discuss the first two stages of psychosocial development in this section.

### *Establishing Basic Trust*

**Basic trust**

The sense that others are predictable and can be relied on.

Erikson (1950, 1964) describes the development of an attitude of **basic trust** as a primary task of psychosocial development in infancy. This sense usually is established between birth and eighteen months of age. It is believed to have long-range implications for a person's social and psychological adjustments throughout the life span.

Impressions of infants, gained both from informal observations and empirical study, suggest that the sense of basic trust merges through numerous interactions and activities between the mother and the baby. The father becomes a significant force in the infant's development at a later time, according to Erikson's theory. Feeding situations provide ample opportunities for the infant to explore its caregivers both through vision and touch. Feeding is thought to be a significant event for the infant in encouraging attachment. It also assists to identify the caregiver as a primary source of physical and psychological nurturance.

A consistent caregiver who holds the infant consistently and who has a consistent pattern of behavior toward

*An infant learns to trust the caregiver when held and fed consistently. (iStock)*

the infant in the feeding situation, for example, leads the child to learn to trust the integrity of others. This elementary attitude is based on the infant's discovery that there is predictability in his or her world. The early learning that there is consistency in life and in activities helps an infant to predict how it will be treated. It learns that certain events or sensations will occur if he or she behaves in particular ways. For example, a baby learns that a lusty cry will produce the appearance of the caregiver who attends to his or her needs. Other interactions with the physical environment contribute to an infant's learning that there is predictability or consistency in many things. The baby discovers, for example, that movement in the crib makes a mobile move in response. As babies gain better motor control, they learn that fingers and toes move in accordance with their will. Their behavior becomes instrumental or goal-oriented.

As the body matures, an infant learns that objects can be manipulated and that they can move their bodies from one location to another. In essence, they learn to experience and explore their physical setting. They actively reach out to interact with their environment.

An attitude of mistrust may prevail if an infant learns that routines and the physical and social environment are unpredictable and inconsistent. This is especially true regarding people who are its primary caregivers. Infants who have been deprived of consistent nurturing show such a pervasive sense of mistrust regarding others' integrity. This attitude also is characterized by apathy, delayed developmental progress, poor appetite, and even illness. Such an attitude makes infants less vulnerable to emotional pain. It is devastating, however, in preventing the child from loving and being loved. This can affect progress through other developmental stages adversely.

## *Acquiring a Sense of Autonomy*

**Autonomy**

Refers to establishing personal boundaries and self-differentiation from things and others.

**Shame and doubt**

Refers to the belief that one is unable to be autonomous and that one's inner self is basically flawed and defective.

Erikson proposes that individuals establish a sense of **autonomy** versus **shame and doubt** between eighteen months and three years of age. Parents may view interactions with their infant as a series of troublesome encounters. This is because so much of his or her behavior is directed toward developing an initial identity as a person independent of parents.

What may amaze and confound parents of a child this age is not so much that changes are experienced; rather, it is the rapid nature and intensity by which they occur. Stubborn insistence on having their own way and expressing their own point of view in interactions with parents are common. These are predominant behavioral patterns among many children who are in the process of developing an attitude about their autonomy. An emerging sense of self is shown for the first time in the swings from independent to dependent behavior and back again. The behavior and nature of the infant at these ages appears to be unpredictable in many ways. This relates to their attempts to develop a sense of autonomy.

From a family systems theory perspective, what are occurring for the infant at this period in its life are experiences that teach about personal boundaries. The attachment process in the early period of infancy apparently leads an infant to believe that there is a symbiotic relationship between him or her and the parents. This may be the case especially with the mother as she is very often the principal caregiver. The relationship is described as emotionally enmeshed. Both an infant and the mother may have difficulties in perceiving the personal boundaries that distinguish them as distinct individuals.

Both mothers and infants experience blurred personal boundaries because of the intense closeness and intimacy of their relationship. It is thought that an infant may have difficulty in perceiving that he or she is not an extension of the parent and vice versa. Lack of such distinctions between the self and others cannot continue indefinitely, however, as this is unhealthy psychologically. Self-differentiation from others begins when an infant learns to erect personal boundaries by behaving in ways that establish its autonomy.

For many infants, there is a change in personality at this time of their life span. The smiling, friendly, accepting child is replaced on many occasions by what seems to be a surly, whining, little demon. This child now is obstinate, gets into mischief, refuses to cooperate or obey parents' requests, and has only one apparent and very overworked word in his or her vocabulary: "NO!" This is the terrible two-year-old at his or her very worst, according to many parents. Yet, some parents can be very preoccupied or motivated with using power to gain control over their child's unacceptable actions. Many may be unaware that these difficult interactions are a very necessary part of the child's healthy psychosocial development.

The attitude of feeling ashamed and doubtful occurs when parents restrict or fail to encourage an infant's attempts to be autonomous. This is an unhealthy attitude that may stem in part from many parents' overreaction to negativistic behavior from an infant. However, such behavior is normal at this time in life. Many adults were raised by parents who used strict, rule-oriented methods. It is only to be expected that these methods are likely to be repeated in raising their own children. This is done unthinkingly because our society does so very little to train people to be parents.

Reliance on rules and rigid standards of acceptable behavior becomes imposed on children at this time as appropriate childrearing by such parents. This is likely because of the parents' belief that strict control is called for. It also is implemented because so much of a toddler's behavior appears to be acting out against parental authority. These attempts to control the rebelliousness of a child are seen as necessary and appropriate. However, many parents are apparently too successful and relentless in trying to achieve this end. The result is that many infants emerge from this period of their lives with the basic negative belief about the inner core of their self. This is the part that is basic to the self-concept and their essence as a human being. The belief is that they are bad, flawed, unacceptable, undesirable, and unlovable.

This is what Erikson calls an attitude of shame and doubt. For many children, the overwhelming majority of interactions with parents are corrective in nature. This relates to their behavior that is seen as problematic by parental standards (John-Roger & McWilliams, 1990). The focus of parental attention toward an infant shifts from unconditional and unadulterated adoration prior to this time, to being one of exasperation and punitiveness. Infants are more active now than ever before. They are more liable to do things that are dangerous and disruptive.

The challenge of parents who want to facilitate a child's healthy psychosocial development now is to focus on the behavior rather than on the child's character. Behavior that is appropriate deserves as much or more attention than behavior that is not. A parent may say, for example, "You're just the most rotten kid I've ever seen." This promotes feelings of shame and doubt by labeling the child's inner self negatively. It is more helpful to say, "I'm glad you're so interested in touching the cat but I can't let you pull its tail because it may scratch and you can get hurt." This promotes feelings of autonomy while teaching limits for the child's behavior.

Some biologically-oriented events contribute to preparing and assisting an infant to achieve the psychosocial attitude of autonomy. These include learning to walk and to feed oneself, controlling eliminations, and so on. Toilet training is an especially significant developmental event that assists in this endeavor.

*Pause and Process:*

1. What can assist in the development of basic trust?

2. What can assist in the development of autonomy?

# EMOTIONAL DEVELOPMENT

**Emotions**

Subjective feelings such as love or joy that help to define our existence as human beings.

**Emotions** are subjective feelings such as love or joy that help to define our existence as human beings. Without these feelings and the ability to express them our lives would be impoverished. Emotions are also among the earliest means of communication that infants have with their caregivers, allowing infants to learn about the world, themselves, and others (Galatzer-Levy & Cohler, 1993; Gallese, 2005).

**What neural circuit in the brain seems important for emotional and social understanding?**

Emotional development is dependent upon brain development. As the brain develops, we see emotion expression, emotion recognition, and emotion regulation evolve. One neural circuit in the brain that seems important for emotional and social understanding (among other things) is the mirror neuron system (Gallese, 2005; Keestra, 2008). The mirror neuron system (MNS) seems to allow for early imitation and empathy. The research on the MNS is new and complicated, but it appears that the brain is hardwired in a way that allows us to "feel" what certain motor behaviors and emotions in others feels like to them. Said another way, sports and movies can emotionally move us because we vicariously experience the athletes and actors emotions via these mirror neurons. Our brains mimic the athlete and actor brains, allowing us to empathize with their emotions. Thus, it is currently hypothesized (and actively being researched) that these mirror neurons play a key role in early emotional development. However, let's take a step back and take a slightly broader view of what research in emotions has entailed up to now.

Behavioral scientists have described emotions in various ways. Some descriptions focus on the physiological basis of emotional reactions—for example, the changes that occur in blood vessels, heart rate, kidney, and digestive system function when someone feels angry or frightened. Other descriptions focus on the subjective aspect of emotions— people's own words describing their feelings. Others focus on the ways that emotions are expressed—for example, crying when feeling sad or using physical force when angry. This means that behavioral scientists can focus on the *physiological, cognitive/subjective feeling,* or *behavioral* aspects of emotions.

Just as behavioral scientists can focus on different manifestations of emotion, developmentalists can have different theoretical viewpoints as to the importance and purpose of emotions. One notion is to view *emotion* as *communication.* Darwin was among the first to view human emotion as communication with the potential to provide us with an evolutionary advantage. For example, emotion communication (such as dominance and submission) can allow for the settlement of disputes without fighting to the death (Galatzer-Levy & Cohler, 1993). Such communication, within this viewpoint, greatly facilitates infant/caregiver interactions, allowing for sensitive, responsive, and appropriate caregiving behavior.

Just as the physiological manifestation of emotion can be the focus of

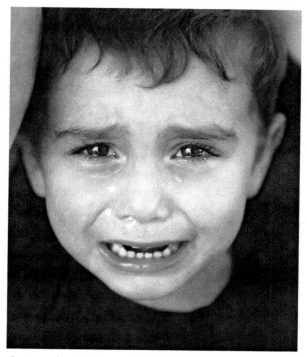

*Crying when feeling sad is one way of expressing emotions. (iStock)*

research, it can also provide an overarching theoretical perspective into the study of emotion (Galatzer-Levy & Cohler, 1993). *Emotion as bodily change* is a perspective with a long and diverse history. One main idea that is of particular importance to emotions in infancy is that children learn to label and monitor their physiological states as emotions via interactions with caregivers. Although an infant may exhibit physiological arousal and accompanying stress, the parent may help label that bodily change as anger or frustration. Hence, it is through a caregiver's response to an infant's bodily change that an infant comes to recognize and label such changes as a particular emotion. It is theorized that if a child is raised by caregivers that are dismissive or repressive of emotional expression, the child may lack the ability to label and express emotions throughout life.

A third viewpoint is *emotion as a means to discharge tension* (Galatzer-Levy & Cohler, 1993). This viewpoint is largely based upon Freud's psychodynamic theory discussed in chapter one. From this perspective, emotion is energy that compels a person to action. In regards to emotion in infancy, caregivers can help infants to understand and channel their emotions into appropriate behaviors, as well as learn emotional control in general.

The fourth perspective that we will discuss here views *emotion as an indicator of importance* (Galatzer-Levy & Cohler, 1993). This position views emotion as a motivating system that is hardwired in all healthy people and allows for communication. Much like some of the other perspectives mentioned previously, this position views emotion as an important mechanism through which infants can hope to educe appropriate caregiving responses.

There are, of course, other perspectives on emotion; however, these four will serve as an excellent basis from which to begin our study of emotional development. Other perspectives will be introduced throughout the book as appropriate. In all likelihood, human emotion is complex enough to allow for all of the above perspectives to provide insight into emotional development. In summary, emotions probably provide humans with an evolutionary advantage by means of providing us with an early and effective communication system. Emotions are correlated with bodily changes that, when labeled correctly, enhance emotion communication. Emotions can motivate us, or distract and impair us. It is important for children to learn to understand, control, and channel emotions in adaptive ways.

As an example of how emotions enable communication, let's examine crying. Crying is one of the infant's most powerful means of communicating with others because it almost invariably brings someone to investigate his or her needs. Four basic patterns have been identified in infant crying. Hunger cries are a rhythmic series of cries associated with feeding needs. Angry cries are a loud series of rhythmic cries associated with distress. Frustration cries involve a long cry and holding the breath. Painful cries are loud, sudden cries that may be prolonged and are associated with injury.

Crying shows the strong effect a small child's behavior can have on adults' behavior. It is an infant's most powerful means of getting a caregiver's nurturing attention. It is never a good idea to ignore a young infant's cry. First, it is their only way of communicating many needs (such as a hurting ear or stomach). Second, when an infant has caregivers that are reliably responsive to his or her cries, the infant will learn to self-soothe sooner and more effectively, cry less, and trust their caregivers more. You will not spoil your child by responding to his or her cries, but you may harm your child by ignoring them.

## *Basics of Emotional Development*

Emotions can be broken into two main categories during infancy, primary (or basic) emotions and secondary (or self-conscious, discrete, or complex) emotions (Izard, 1991; Lewis, 2000; Saarni, Mumme & Campos, 1998). **Primary emotions** are present from birth or are evident shortly thereafter. The emotions appear to be universal, meaning that all healthy infants from anywhere in the world display these emotions early in life. Given the universality of these emotions and the early stage at which they develop, two theories emerge: one, these primary emotions are hardwired into the brain; two, these primary emotions must serve some evolutionary purpose. **Secondary emotions** are dependent upon cognitive development and the internalization of parental/societal standards and expectations. Secondary emotions can vary by culture.

## *Primary Emotions*

Emotions in infancy are largely assessed via facial expressions, vocalizations, and other observable behaviors. Some primary emotions include pleasure, distress, joy, anger, and fear. Pleasure and distress are evident at birth; whereas joy, anger, and fear are measurable within the first six months. It is always important to be mindful that just because we fail to measure something until a certain age (such as a specific emotion), it is not the same as the infant lacking that skill or emotion (Galatzer-Levy & Cohler, 1993). Developmentalists are continually amazed at the emotions and cognitions that infants possess as we develop better ways to assess such emotions and cognitions. Therefore, at the moment, we believe

**Primary emotions**

Emotions which are present at birth or shortly thereafterwards. They are believed to be hardwired into the brain and serve an adaptive purpose.

**Secondary emotions**

Emotions that develop during the second year or so after birth, as cognitive development advances. They can be a blend of two or more primary emotions, culturally-specific, or self-conscious/self-evaluative in nature.

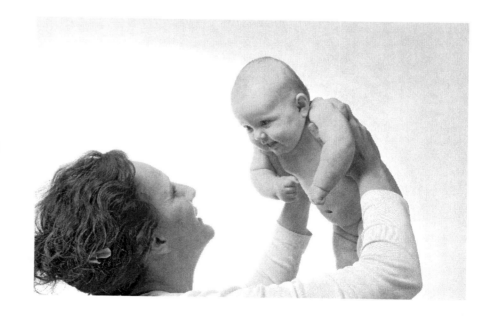

*Infants seem to experience joy by social smiling. They smile in response to social stimulation from others. (iStock)*

that infants develop joy around two or three months of age. However, it is possible that a decade from now some bright young researcher will develop a new technique of assessing joy and find that it is present as early as one month or even one day of age.

One way researchers have ascertained that infants experience joy is by social smiling. The first **social smile**—smiling in response to social stimulation from others—is usually observed at about six weeks of age. Before this time babies smile as well, but researchers assume that this is either a reflex activity seated in the brain, a random occurrence, such as gas, or by being about to fall asleep (Sroufe & Waters, 1976). Of course, many parents disagree with researchers on this particular issue.

**Social smile**

Smiling in response to social stimulation from others.

Smiling is a powerful method for eliciting caregiving. It reinforces nurturance from caregivers and forms the basis for positive interactions between the baby and his or her parents (Tautermannova, 1973). At about four months of age, babies begin to laugh to express their delight at positive experiences such as being kissed, or seeing interesting and unfamiliar things (Sroufe & Wunsch, 1972). One of the authors used to elicit the biggest belly laugh from one of their children by walking toward them like a big ogre with a silly face. Another good way of getting a laugh is by pretending to drink or eat the baby's food.

Developmentalists believe that anger emerges around four months of age and fear around six months of age. Anger expression can be provoked by thwarting goal directed behavior, such as preventing a baby from obtaining a desired toy. Fear is easily observable around six months of age because **stranger wariness** (or stranger anxiety) develops around this time. Stranger wariness can serve an adaptive purpose because it emerges around the same time that a child begins creeping or crawling; hence, it can prevent babies from straying too far from parents. Stranger wariness can also be mitigated by the environment (i.e., it is less likely in a familiar versus unfamiliar place) and stranger behavior. If the stranger gives an infant some space and interacts with the adults first, the infant will usually initiate some interaction in a few moments (after he or she has had a chance to see how mom or dad is interacting with the stranger). This means that Aunt Lucy from Omaha, who sees the baby only once a year, should wait for the baby to initiate contact instead of entering the room and swooping the fear-struck infant up immediately.

**Stranger wariness**

Or stranger anxiety, which is observable around six months of age.

**Social referencing**, when infants look at their parents' faces and behavior for information about something, emerges around the first birthday (Dickson & Parke, 1988; Klinnert et al., 1986; Sorce et al., 1985). This is a valuable way for infants to obtain knowledge about the world. They use it to make decisions about acting as well as reacting. Apparently, the emotional reactions of our parents condition many of our own reactions in the early years.

**Social referencing**

When infants look at their parents' faces and behavior for information about something.

## Secondary Emotions

As mentioned earlier, secondary emotions are dependent upon cognitive development and the internalization of at least some parental expectations and/or societal norms. These emotions may vary by culture and may involve a blend of two or more primary emotions. Examples of secondary emotions include embarrassment, pride, guilt, and contempt. Secondary emotions begin to emerge around eighteen to twenty-four months, at the end of Piaget's sensorimotor stage of cognitive development. If you try to recall your earliest memory, there is a good chance that it will involve a secondary emotion (such as embarrassment over not making it to the potty in time or pride over writing your name correctly).

## *Emotion Regulation*

Emotion regulation is also evident in infancy, although with limited strategies (Galatzer-Levy & Cohler, 1993; Saarni, Mumme & Campos, 1998). For a moment, imagine that you are lying in your bed, trying to catch some shut eye, and some strange giant keeps shaking a noisy rattle in your face. Also assume that you do not have very good control of your speech, hands, arms, or legs at the moment. What would you do? What would you be feeling? Infants can become overstimulated when adults fail to read their body language. One way infants deal with their annoyance (i.e., regulate their emotion) is by withdrawing. Clearly, a young infant can't up and move away from the imbecile, so they use basic strategies such as closing the eyes or looking away. Infants also learn to regulate fear by moving close to loved ones when feeling afraid.

## *Revisiting Temperament and Goodness-of-Fit*

Differences in temperament are an aspect of emotional and personality development in infancy (Thomas & Chess, 1984). About two-thirds of infants studied can be classified into one of three categories: easy, difficult, or slow-to-warm-up. Infants and children can be placed into these classifications based upon their behavior on nine dimensions: activity level, adaptability, approach/withdrawal, attention span/persistence, distractibility, intensity of reaction, quality of mood, rhythmicity, and threshold of responsiveness.

In general, easy babies are happy, have rhythmic bodily functioning, and are accepting of new experiences. These are the babies that have a predictable bodily schedule for when they will be hungry, tired, or in need of a diaper change. These are the babies that can go anywhere and will allow themselves to be admired and cuddled by just about anyone. These are the typical American parents' dream baby.

Difficult babies are generally irritable, have irregular bodily function, and show more intense emotional expressions. These are the babies that, biologically, struggle with feeding or sleeping schedules. It is best to feed them on demand (when their body tells them they are hungry) and be flexible with their other body functions.

Slow-to-warm-up babies have generally mild emotional expressions and are slow to adapt to new experiences. Although both the difficult and slow-to-warm-up infants have negative reactions to new experiences, the slow-to-warm-up infants' emotional reactions are lower in intensity and they will eventually accept the situation.

Temperament is assumed to have a genetic component, because it is observable so early in life. Interestingly, literature given to expectant mothers often suggests that an active baby in the womb will be an active infant, whereas a quiet baby in the womb will be a quiet infant. Talk about setting up parent expectations! Temperament also shows some stability during early childhood. However, temperament is not carved in stone.

Thomas, Chess, and Birch spent more than two decades studying temperament (among other developmental issues) in a longitudinal study known as the New York Longitudinal Study. One concept which they presented was that of goodness-of-fit. **Goodness-of-fit** can be defined as how adaptable a child's environment is to his or her temperament. For example, a difficult temperament child with a difficult-type parent would often clash heads and may result in adjustment problems. However, a difficult temperament child with an easy-going-type parent would be in a more flexible and responsive environment, allowing for optimal development. Hence, a good fit between child and parent can lead to good developmental outcomes. Alternatively, a poor fit can place a child at risk for poor developmental outcomes, such as behavioral disturbances (Dixon, 2003). Future chapters will discuss the relationship between temperament and cognitive and socioemotional development in early and middle childhood. We will also see what aspects of temperament appear most likely to remain stable, and which are more malleable.

## *Attachment*

What is attachment? Every healthy infant develops an **attachment** to someone. According to Bowlby (1969) forming an attachment to a primary caregiver is a key developmental task of infancy. Infant attachment is an evolutionary response to the vulnerabilities of early life. In order for infants to survive the difficulties inherent in early development, they must attach to a capable caregiver who will protect and nurture them. In order to accomplish attachment, infants elicit proximity from caregivers through attachment behaviors such as crying and grasping. These infant attachment behaviors elicit a protective response from caregivers. Hence, attachment behaviors are manifested in order to maximize the infant's chances of survival by connecting to a shielding caregiver. Consequently, specific attachment behaviors are activated when the infant feels vulnerable such as when the caregiver is distant or separated from the infant or when a stranger is present. Furthermore, the attachment process must be present and solidified in order for the infant to have the necessary sense of security to explore his or her surroundings. By serving as a "secure base" for an infant, caregivers help in developing within the infant a sense of confidence. This security is used as a base from which to go out and explore the world. As this security is established the infant feels safe to explore his or her surroundings more widely and retreat less often to the caregiver (Ainsworth & Wittig, 1969). It is thus the task of an infant to develop a balance between exploration and proximity. An infant who is able to develop this balance is identified as having a **secure attachment**. According to Ainsworth, Blehar, Waters, and Wall (1978), if a child is consistently replied to when he or she is in distress in early infancy, over time the infant internalizes this sense of security with the caregiver. Once a sense of security is developed toward the caregiver the infant is able to generalize the sense of security to society as a whole. This creates an "internal working model" of relationships serving as the example for the quality of all future relationships. In the long

### Goodness-of-fit

How adaptable a child's environment is to his or her temperament.

### Attachment

A strong affectional tie or emotional bond between two individuals.

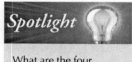

*Spotlight*

What are the four developmental phases of attachment?

### Secure attachment style

An infant misses their mother when she leaves the room and greets her upon returning.

run, successful attachment in infancy generates greater competence throughout life. This is shown in a greater capacity to cope with novelty, handle failure, persist in problem-solving, participate in loving relationships, and maintain a healthy self-esteem (Sroufe, 1985; Galatzer-Levy & Cohler, 1993).

## Attachment Styles

Hence, it is the early dynamics between the mother and child that determines the ability of an individual to develop an adaptive attachment pattern. Patterns of early mother-child interactions may produce various styles of attachment. In an attempt to understand the differing attachment types, Ainsworth et al., (1978) developed an observation protocol called the "Strange Situation." The procedure entailed examining an infant's response to his or her mother after a period of being in an unfamiliar surrounding in the presence of a stranger. The original work by Ainsworth yielded three attachment categories: **secure**, **insecure-avoidant**, and **insecure-ambivalent**. A secure attachment is characterized by an infant using the mother as a secure base from which to freely explore new surroundings. When the infant who is securely attached encounters his or her caregiver after a strange situation the infant may continue to explore the surroundings after a brief period of seeking comfort from the caregiver. In contrast, the infant with an insecure-avoidant attachment is likely to have no proximity-seeking behavior after a strange situation, representing a "deactivated" attachment. An insecure-ambivalent child is identified when after encountering a strange situation the infant stays extremely close to the mother, becomes upset at separation, and cannot be easily comforted. This ambivalent type is considered to have a "hyperactivated" or vigilant attachment.

In terms of the maternal behaviors associated with specific attachment types, Ainsworth et al. (1978) found that caregivers of securely attached children were more available and psychologically accessible to their children and were accepting and cooperative when the infants were in distress compared to caregivers of insecurely attached children. In contrast, the caregivers of avoidant infants were found to be more rejecting of their infants and became more angry and irritated with their infants than caregivers of securely attached infants. Additionally, they were found to be emotionally rigid and showed aversion to close bodily contact with their infants. Ainsworth continued to report that caregivers of ambivalent children tended to be inconsistently responsive to their children. These caregivers were at some times accepting of their children and at other times rejecting. When these caregivers came in bodily contact with their infants it was seen as more of a daily routine than an affectionate gesture.

Several studies have pointed to the long-term ramifications of attachment development in infancy (Ainsworth, 1973, 1977; Ainsworth et al., 1978; Fraley & Shaver, 2000; Hazan & Shaver, 1994; Waters, Merrick, Treboux, Crowell, & Albersheim, 2000). As noted, the attachment type developed during those early infant-mother interactions serves as a model for all future relationships. As a result of repeated interactions with primary attachment figures, internal representational models are formed. Also referred to as a

**Secure attachment style**

An infant who misses his/her mother when she leaves the room and greets her upon returning.

**Avoidant attachment style**

An infant who does not seek out his/her mother and exhibits a detached pattern of closeness

**Ambivalent attachment style**

An infant who seeks proximity to his/her mother with extreme distress and hyperactivity of closeness "working model", this schema of rules, expectations, perceptions, and beliefs about the self and others becomes established over time as a heuristic base for future relationships (Bowlby, 1980). Working models are increasingly resistant to change over time, as new information not fitting into the schema is difficult to assimilate and is often disregarded. For example, if a child after repeated positive interactions with a caregiver establishes a model of security and comfort then even when specific instances in childhood invoke a temporary sense of insecurity and hostility the original secure base remains the default orientation. The beliefs developed in infancy and early childhood about the self in relation to others set the foundation for the child's interpersonal style, which tends to be automatic, generalized, and inflexible. Attachment classifications in infancy tend to be stable, except in economically disadvantaged families, or those who have experienced stressful life events or both (Sroufe, Egeland, & Kreutzer, 1990). This stability or continuity of attachment style is not suggested to be an invariant determinant of adult relationship styles, but more like a structural pattern, that if confirmed throughout childhood, becomes fixed by adolescence and therein increasingly resistant to change.

In a longitudinal study seeking to assess the stability of attachment styles from infancy to adulthood Waters et al. (2000) observed 60 infants at 12 months of age subjected to Ainsworth's "Strange Situation." Twenty years later 50 of the original 60 subjects were administered the Berkeley Adult Attachment Interview (as sited in Waters et al., 2000). Seventy-two percent of the adult sample had the identical attachment classification as they had in infancy. However, several events were shown to alter the original attachment classification. Negative life events such as a loss of a parent, divorce of parents, life-threatening illness of a parent, parental psychiatric disorder, or physical or sexual abuse by a family member caused a change in the subject's attachment classification. This finding supports Bowlby's (1980, 1982) assertion about the stability of attachment throughout development and the openness to change based on life experiences.

## Attachment and Mental Models

Early parent-child interactions provide the early environment in which infants begin to develop mental models regarding themselves and others (Dixon, 2003; Galatzer-Levy & Cohler, 1993). If a caregiver is dependable, warm, and responsive, an infant will come to trust that the caregiver will be there when needed. The infant will also come to believe that they must be worthy of such care and attention and learn to love and trust him or herself. If, on the other hand, the caregiver is undependable, emotionally inept, and unresponsive, an infant will come to believe that the caregiver cannot be trusted to be there when needed. The infant may also begin to question whether they have any self-worth, and/or if he or she can trust him or herself. Of course, an infant neither verbally encodes this information, nor consciously has these thoughts. Nonetheless, these early experiences set mental expectations that can last a lifetime if not challenged or questioned. Future chapters devoted to social and emotional development will discuss how attachment impacts development.

*Pause and Process:*

1. What is the difference between primary and secondary emotions?

2. How does attachment develop?

# SELF AND OTHERS

In this section, we will highlight the development of self-awareness, play behavior, and daycare.

## *Understanding of Self and Others*

When does a baby know that they are a person, separate from the rest of the world? One way of figuring this out is with the famous experiment involving a baby, a mirror, and some make-up (rouge). First, place the baby in front of the mirror and observe her behavior. Next, place some rouge on her nose (or other face location) without her noticing what you are doing. Then, place her back in front of the mirror and observe? Does she seem to notice the make-up on her nose? Does she touch her face as she views her reflection in the mirror? The mirror test is one research technique that has been used to assess when self-recognition emerges in infancy. Self-recognition is measurable around fifteen months of age.

Between fifteen months and two years of age, a child's growing sense of **self-awareness** is evident in their use of self-referencing pronouns (i.e., me or I), using their own name, and occasionally labeling themselves by sex and age. Toddlers seem to have some awareness of how others see them and strive to please their caregivers (Galatzer-Levy & Cohler, 1993).

**Self-awareness**

A child's use of self-referencing pronouns, using their own name, and occasionally labeling themselves by sex and age.

*The mirror test is a technique used to assess when self-recognition emerges. (iStock)*

Not only do toddlers have a growing sense of self, but they also have a growing sense of others. Toddlers often spontaneously display **prosocial behavior**. They will try to offer comfort to others that seem to be sad or worried. Toddlers will often pat or hug someone or say in their telegraphic speech something like "It okay." Such early prosocial behaviors demonstrate early emotion recognition in others and empathy.

## Play

Play is another behavior that emerges during the toddler period. Between twelve and fifteen months, parallel play appears. **Parallel play** entails two toddlers playing side by side, occasionally observing each other, but not interacting with each other. It is not until around the age of two that children learn to **play cooperatively**. Parents with children this age will often arrange "play dates" so that their child can play with others and learn early social skills with peers.

Some research has examined mother-child play. Mother's who engage in exploratory play (object-oriented play) tend to have children who engage in **exploratory play**. Mother's who engage in **symbolic play** (using objects in a pretend fashion—like tea parties) tend to have children who engage in symbolic play. Hence, children seem to imitate the type of play modeled by their parents. That said, boys are more likely to engage in exploratory play, whereas girls are more likely to engage in symbolic play (Bornstein et al., 1999). Parent-child play interactions facilitate social and cognitive development in children.

## The Outside World

The United States is one of only a few industrialized societies that do not offer paid parental leave after the birth of a child. At least partly for this reason, the majority of American infants are placed into some form of child care before their first birthday.

The developmental consequences of daycare depend upon the quality of the daycare, the number of hours spent there, and parent-child interaction when at home. High quality daycare on a part-time basis, coupled with sensitive parenting at home will either have no negative consequences for the child or even lead to positive cognitive and socioemotional outcomes for the child. Unfortunately, the majority of daycare is of low quality (NICHD Early Child Care Research Network, 2001). Low quality daycare, long hours, and inadequate parent-child interactions are all predictive of poor cognitive and/or socioemotional outcomes. Can daycare be harmful to infants? Yes. Is daycare always harmful for infants? No. However, many children do suffer suboptimal developmental outcomes because quality daycare is the exception in this country, instead of the rule.

*Pause and Process:*

1. How do researchers test for self-recognition in infants?

2. What is the difference between exploratory and symbolic play?

---

**Prosocial behavior**

A growing sense of others (e.g. comforting other children who seem sad or worried).

**Parallel play**

The side by side playing of two toddlers who occasionally observe each other, but do not interact with each other.

**Cooperatively play**

The willingness to play with one another.

**Exploratory play**

Object oriented play.

**Symbolic play**

Using objects in a pretend fashion (e.g., tea parties).

# SUMMARY

1. Many physical changes occur during infancy. First, there is a continuation of growth patterns established before birth, in that changes occur in cephalocaudal (head-to-foot) and proximodistal (inner-to-outermost) directions. Second there are significant increases in weight and height. The birthweight is doubled by four months of age, and tripled by the infant's first birthday. Height increases by about 50 percent the first year. The brain shows a rapid increase in connections during infancy. Fat, muscle, and bones all show growth during infancy as well.

2. Basic motor skills occur sequentially. Use of the hands in manipulating objects also progresses sequentially. It begins with use of the full hand in grasping objects, then proceeds to use of various combinations of fingers, and culminates in the ability to use the forefinger and thumb with accuracy in picking up objects.

3. Perceptual skills advance with motor skill development. Perceptual changes at this stage primarily involve the ability to use eyesight to guide and make adjustments in motor behaviors. They may be observed in the ways infants use their eyesight in learning to judge depth or surface changes.

4. Health concerns for infants include meeting their nutritional needs, protecting them from diseases, and taking steps to prevent SIDS. Breastfeeding provides the best nutrition for infants. Vaccinations help prevent many childhood diseases and do not appear to cause autism. Infants should be kept away from second-hand smoke and put to sleep on their back in order to prevent SIDS.

5. A major stage in cognitive development, the sensorimotor period, is experienced during infancy. This period primarily involves changes that result in the integration of sensory input and perceptions with motor behaviors. Infants acquire an understanding of their environment through these means. A major accomplishment at this stage is understanding object permanence, or the notion that something continues to exist even though it has been removed from the child's field of vision. This understanding is part of the process of self-differentiation, according to cognitive development theory.

6. The changes observed during the sensorimotor period occur in a graduated sequence. It begins with an infant's use of reflexes present at birth and progresses to more complex circular reactions. These are habitual actions that are constructed through continual repetition. The process culminates in the use of symbolic logic and reasoning at the end of infancy. Sensorimotor schemas are rudimentary ideas about the nature of the world. They are constructed and modified through experience in interacting with the environment by sensory and motor actions.

7. Infants are born with some basic processes that allow for learning and information-processing. Many of these processes are evident prenatally, but we can test them more definitively after birth. Infants are capable of forming memories, association, recognition, imitation, and recall. These early basic processes pave the way for future problem-solving, memory strategies, and other information-processing development.

8. The ability to use language to communicate with others emerges in infancy in a series of gradual advancements. Infants are born with the ability to cry, then progress through cooing, babbling, understanding words, and producing their first word. Speech begins with one-word sentences, then progresses to two-word sentences. Infants typically understand the rules of language prior to being able to fully utilize these rules.

9. Developmental changes are observed in the emerging emotional expression of infants. Infants become gradually capable of expressing a wide

range of feelings through facial gestures, vocalizations, and other behaviors.

10. An infant develops an emotional attachment to his or her primary caregivers. This attachment provides the infant with a sense of security and promotes his or her exploration of the environment. Attachment is believed to occur in four distinct phases: undiscriminating social responsiveness, discrimination in social responsiveness, active seeking of physical proximity and contact, and goal-corrected partnership.

11. Attachment can be assessed in infants by utilizing the strange situation paradigm. There are three main patterns of attachment: secure, avoidant, and ambivalent. Each attachment style has distinct mental models of self and others. Although a person may have a predominant attachment style, attachment is a process between two people and can vary by relationship.

12. Self-awareness increases during the toddler period. Prosocial behavior and play behavior also emerge during this time. Parents can influence type of play behavior in infants and gender differences are apparent. Daycare can be correlated to positive or negative developmental outcomes, dependent upon quality of daycare, hours spent in daycare, and parent-child interactions.

13. Establishing a sense of basic trust as opposed to mistrust is the first of a series of psychosocial tasks the individual experiences during the life span. The optimal time for acquiring the healthy attitude of trust is between birth and eighteen months of age. It is derived principally from consistent, positive interactions with the maternal caregiver, according to Erikson. Favorable interactions with the physical environment also contribute to this attitude. According to psychosocial theory, the accomplishment of basic trust significantly improves the chances of healthy development at subsequent stages of the life span.

14. Acquiring a healthy sense of personal autonomy as opposed to an unhealthy attitude of shame and doubt is the principal psychosocial challenge for the individual between eighteen and thirty-six months of age. The behaviors leading to the acquisition of a healthy sense of autonomy are often quite troublesome to parents. They are necessary, however, if the infant is to accomplish self-differentiation and establish personal boundaries. An infant who feels comfortable in separating from primary caregivers is able to explore his or her environment. Certain developmental tasks of infancy, such as toilet-training, contribute to this healthy attitude. An unhealthy attitude of personal shame and doubt is promoted when infants are discouraged from becoming autonomous and made to feel that exploratory behaviors are inappropriate.

# SELF-QUIZ

1. What are the two basic growth patterns?
2. How much do weight and height increase between birth and the first birthday?
3. What is the information-processing cell of the nervous system called?
4. What does myelination of the axon accomplish?
5. Which hemisphere of the brain is language localized in for most people?
6. What influences motor skill development in infancy?
7. When do most infants achieve walking?
8. What purpose do hand skills serve in infancy?
9. How do hand skills progress during infancy?
10. What classic study allowed for the investigation of depth perception in infancy?
11. Within Piaget's cognitive developmental theory, what two processes help individuals adapt or

change their schemas based upon their experiences in the world?

12. When your thoughts and beliefs are no longer in equilibrium with your experiences, what cognitive state are you thrown into?

13. What is the term for Piaget's first stage of cognitive development?

14. How many substages are there within Piaget's first stage of cognitive development?

15. What are the two basic types of memories discussed in this chapter?

16. What are three theories about why we have infantile amnesia?

17. Is language the same as speech?

18. What are the five basic components of language discussed in this chapter?

19. What innate language structure is hypothesized to help us learn language?

20. What are three common errors toddlers make in word use?

21. What are emotions?

22. What neural circuit in the brain seems important for emotional and social understanding?

23. What are three aspects of emotion?

24. What are four viewpoints as to the importance or purpose of emotion?

25. What are the two main categories of emotions during infancy?

26. What is attachment?

27. What are the four developmental phases of attachment?

28. What are the three attachment styles?

29. What type of play emerges during infancy?

30. What two stages of psychosocial development are important during infancy and toddlerhood?

---

## TERMS AND CONCEPTS

| TERM | PAGE | TERM | PAGE |
|---|---|---|---|
| Cephalocaudal growth pattern | 102 | Co-sleeping | 113 |
| Proximodistal growth pattern | 103 | Sudden infant death syndrome (SIDS) | 113 |
| Neuron | 104 | Object permanence | 115 |
| Cell body | 104 | Circular reactions | 116 |
| Dendrites | 104 | Basic processes | 119 |
| Axon | 104 | Explicit memories | 120 |
| Myelin sheath | 104 | Implicit memories | 120 |
| Synaptic gap | 104 | Association | 120 |
| Neurotransmitters | 104 | Recognition | 120 |
| Crawling | 107 | Habituation/dishabituation | 120 |
| Creeping | 107 | Imitation | 120 |
| Hitching | 107 | Recall | 120 |
| Cruising | 107 | Infantile amnesia | 121 |
| Hand skills | 108 | Language | 122 |
| Perceptual skill | 109 | Speech | 122 |
| Childproofing | 111 | Phonemes | 122 |
| Baby colic | 113 | Morphemes | 122 |

# CHAPTER 4

# Early Childhood

(iStock)

## OUTLINE

### PHYSICAL DEVELOPMENT DURING EARLY CHILDHOOD

- Physical growth
- Motor development
- Health issues

### COGNITIVE DEVELOPMENT DURING EARLY CHILDHOOD

- Piaget's theory and the preoperational stage
- Information-processing during early childhood
- Other cognitive development theories
- Language development during early childhood

### SOCIOEMOTIONAL DEVELOPMENT DURING EARLY CHILDHOOD

- Psychosocial development
- Emotional development
- Self and others

143

Early childhood is a time of refinements in physical abilities. These not only allow greater personal freedom but facilitate mental and social changes as well. In fact, the interrelationship among physical, socioemotional, and cognitive skills is very evident at this time of the life span. There is a close relationship between these changes and the type of environmental experiences to which a child is exposed.

# PHYSICAL DEVELOPMENT DURING EARLY CHILDHOOD

### LEARNING OBJECTIVES:

1. *Describe physical growth during early childhood*
2. *Explain motor skill development during early childhood*
3. *Awareness of the unique health issues faced in early childhood*

Physical changes occur rapidly in early childhood (ages three to six years), but not at the rate seen in infancy. Generally, the physical changes in early childhood are also less dramatic than those observed in infancy. Yet, they are impressive. The changes in hand skills, for example, allow a child to explore objects more easily, and new body skills permit greater investigation of the environment.

# PHYSICAL GROWTH

## *Height and Weight Changes*

Preschool-age children grow at half the rate they did during infancy. Height gains exceed weight gains. A typical preschool child grows about three inches each year. At age three, the average child is about thirty-eight inches tall, and by age five, has reached a height of about forty-three inches (Cratty, 1986; Tanner, 1978, 1990; WHO, 2007).

Weight increases follow a similar pattern of deceleration in early childhood. Children gain about four pounds a year during this stage. The average child weighs approximately thirty-one pounds at three years of age and forty pounds by age five (WHO, 2007). A rule of thumb is that children should be about seven times their birthweight by age six (Bloom, 1964).

There are individual differences in these trends related to sex, genetics, medical history, eating habits, and general nutrition (Eveleth & Tanner, 1976; Tanner, 1990). Height and weight changes during this stage are closely followed by health-care professionals to determine if the child falls within normal limits. Very slow or very rapid changes can signal the presence of certain abnormal conditions. Most of these conditions can be treated effectively if detected early.

## Other Body Changes

The changes in body proportions and appearance in early childhood are very noticeable. As bone and muscle growth occur, there is a gradual lengthening of the body. A preschooler looks less like an infant and more like a child. At age four, most begin to lose the chubby appearance of a baby (Tanner, 1978, 1990). A child's abdomen is quite prominent at this age—almost a "pot belly"—and the head and face are still large in comparison to other body parts. But with continued growth in the extremities and trunk areas, a young child becomes leaner-looking. This change to a spindly appearance is also attributed to the metabolism of fatty tissue acquired in infancy. This material is consumed as a source of energy by the constantly active child.

Weight gains in infancy resulted from increases in fatty material deposited into adipose tissue. In early childhood, weight gains come more from increases in muscle and bone tissue. Muscle tissue is composed 72 percent of water and 28 percent of solids in early childhood (Timiras, 1972). Muscle fatigue occurs more easily among young children because of this high ratio of water to solids, as well as because muscles are not yet strongly attached to bone and skeletal material. A young child needs frequent rests and naps (although they may fight a nap every step of the way).

Ossification of bony tissue continues throughout this period. The long bones grow faster than the other bones of the body, accounting for the lengthening in arms and legs that gives the young child a lanky appearance by age six. Because the ossification process is not yet complete, the bones, joints, ligaments, and tendons are flexible. Injury and infection can result in severe damage to these tissues.

## Teeth

**Deciduous teeth**

The primary or first set of sixteen teeth that erupt when an infant is between five and seven and one half months of age.

Most of the primary or **deciduous teeth** have erupted by a child's third birthday. These teeth will remain in the gums until about age six or seven, when they are shed as part of the natural growth process.

Many parents and caregivers tend to overlook young children's need for dental care. Only 76 percent of children in the United States visit the dentist at least once a year (Federal Interagency Forum on Child and Family Statistics, 2008). Regular dental care (along with adequate nutrition and other factors) improves the quality of the secondary (permanent) teeth that are developing in the gums.

## The Brain

The brain and central nervous system experience perhaps the most significant changes of any body system during early childhood. These follow the cephalocaudal trend that began during prenatal development and continued during infancy.

Most brain growth during early childhood takes the form of weight gain. By age three, the brain has attained about 75 percent of its total adult weight; by age six, it has reached

*Primary or deciduous teeth come in by the age of three. At about six or seven they will begin to be replaced by adult teeth. (iStock)*

almost 90 percent of adult weight. Because nearly no new neurons appear in the brain after birth, most of these increases come from growth in neuron size, from slight increases in glial cells (which support the neurons), and from myelination of the axons.

Brain circuitry is established in early childhood in something like the manner in which a sculptor produces a final image from stone (Kolb, 1989). Excess neurons and unnecessary connections between millions of neuron cells are eliminated over time. This is referred to as **pruning**. In addition, brain circuit patterns governing particular functions become established in graduated sequences as myelination is accomplished in various areas of the brain between infancy and adolescence.

As noted earlier, myelination involves the deposit of fatty material called **myelin** around axons. Myelin facilitates the transmission of electrical impulses between neurons. Advancing myelination makes certain brain functions possible, rapid, and/or more efficient, such as speech, sensory perception, and logical thought. The myelination process will continue throughout childhood and adolescence. For example, the areas of the brain that are responsible for hand-eye coordination become fully functional (myelinated) by age four. Those that facilitate focused attention are fully functional by age ten, and those that regulate skilled language use mature by age fifteen (Tanner, 1978, 1990). Improvements in all these abilities, however, can be observed in early childhood as myelination progresses in the areas of the brain that govern them (Higgins & Turnure, 1984). Because of these improvements, most young children are ready for formal educational instruction around the age of six.

There are two other significant changes in the brain and central nervous system in early childhood. First, the brain continues to coordinate its parts to specialize in particular functions. The human brain has two sides, or hemispheres, that work together to control the functions of each side of the body. The organization format is unusual in that it is the right hemisphere of the brain that controls the left side of the body and the left hemisphere that controls the right side. The process that leads to hemispheric specialization begins early in life and continues for years, but marked changes are evident during early

**Pruning**

The elimination of unnecessary excess neuron connections between millions of neuron cells over time.

**Myelin**

A fatty material deposited around axons.

childhood. When the process is completed, the right hemisphere will govern a variety of visual and creative skills, as well as spatial perception, and the left hemisphere will govern language abilities and logical thought processes (Tanner, 1978, 1990). A channel for neural communication known as the corpus callosum connects both hemispheres, facilitating coordination of the various functions. Myelination in this structure is also significantly advanced during early childhood, which explains the improvements in mental and motor skill functioning observed in young children.

Second, the definitive preferential use of one hand over the other emerges during early childhood as another indication of brain specialization. As mentioned in the last chapter, the first hint of this appears very early in life. Fetuses that suck their right thumb in utero are more likely to become right-handed than those that suck their left thumb. Most infants orient their heads to the right, and these infants usually become right-handed (Gesell & Ames, 1947). As infants grow older, most tend to reach with their right hand, though there is much experimentation in manipulating objects with both hands throughout infancy and into early childhood. By age four, however, the majority of children have developed a preference for using one hand over the other (Tan, 1985).

## Perceptual Skills

Visual and hearing abilities are firmly established by six months of age, but subtle refinements continue to unfold as a child progresses through early childhood (Siegler, 1986). Maturation of the brain accounts for some of these refinements.

Because the eyeball does not complete its growth until puberty, young children tend to be farsighted (Roberts & Rowland, 1978). The ability of the eye to accommodate or focus accurately improves during early childhood, but not enough to produce accurate vision. By age six, the visual acuity of most young children measures 20/30 rather than 20/20. So although their vision has vastly improved since infancy, young children still do not see things quite clearly. Corrective lenses or glasses may be needed, particularly if the child constantly squints when looking intently at something. About 5 percent of children begin to use glasses in early childhood (Siegler, 1986).

*Pause and Process:*

1. How do height and weight change during early childhood?

2. Describe two ways that the brain continues to develop during early childhood.

*By the age of six a child may need to have corrective lenses or glasses. (shutterstock)*

# MOTOR DEVELOPMENT

**Spotlight**

Define bilateral coordination.

**Bilateral coordination**

The coordinated, integrated use of both sides of the body in performing motor acts.

**Gross motor skills**

Those motor acts that require the use of large muscle groups.

**Fine motor skills**

Those motor acts that require the use of small muscle groups and hand-eye coordination.

Developmental changes in motor skills in early childhood follow the proximodistal and general-to-specific patterns that emerged earlier in life. Motor skills now become more refined. Activity and energy levels remain high during this period as well.

In many respects, the changes observed in motor skills in early childhood reflect maturation and changes in body metabolism. Parents often remark that young children are constantly on the move. This restlessness reflects a desire to learn about the environment and a quest for novel stimulation. Restlessness declines by the end of this period, however. Researchers note that children change their activities and physical location less and less as they grow older (Eaton & Ennis, 1986; Routh, Schroeder, & O'Tauma, 1974).

Maturation and environmental influences on motor skill improvement are also evident in the child's **bilateral coordination** (Williams, 1983). Bilateral coordination (e.g., symmetrical gait pattern) refers to the coordinated, integrated use of both sides of the body to smoothly and efficiently perform numerous actions. In early childhood, improvements are seen in climbing stairs, tying shoelaces, running, and using a tricycle—all skills that require use of both hands, both feet, or the arms and legs, and both sides of the body. Opportunity is an important environmental factor in these improvements. Young children not only profit from practicing these skills but also appear to gain much pleasure from doing so. Most children put a lot of effort into mastering these skills until they can perform them smoothly and efficiently (Bertenhal & Clifton, 1998).

There are significant improvements in both **gross motor skills** (those involving the large muscle groups of the body) and **fine motor skills** (those involving the small muscle groups) in this stage. Elementary motor skills that allowed for locomotion of the body and manipulation of objects emerged during infancy. Now children expand these basic skills into more specific actions (Bertenhal & Clifton, 1998). For example, the ability to run, hop, climb, and jump are specific gross motor skills that are mastered in early childhood. Cutting with scissors, drawing, turning pages in books, and manipulating small toys are among the fine motor skills that emerge at this stage.

Gender differences in motor skill performance show up in early childhood. Boys are generally more advanced than girls in performing quick and agile gross motor activities. Girls generally outshine boys at activities involving fine motor skills. Girls also perform better than boys at gross motor activities that require coordination, such as skipping, hopping, and balancing on one foot (Cratty, 1986). These differences are probably due to both inherent biological factors and socialization. For example, most parents still steer their children into sex-appropriate play activities—expecting boys, for instance, to be more physically active, especially outdoors, and girls to be less active and to play more indoors (Harper & Sanders, 1978).

## Gross Motor Skills

Gross or large-muscle skills involve many muscle groups. These are the skills that are used in throwing objects, walking, running, climbing, and so on. By age four, children's level of performance at these skills resembles that of adults. Young children perform these skills awkwardly. But with the establishment of the necessary nerve circuitry and much practice, speed improves, balance becomes more automatic, and stride lengthens (Bertenhal & Clifton, 1998).

To illustrate how gross motor skills advance at this time of the life span, we will use the ability to catch a ball as an example. Three-year-old children typically have their arms outstretched when trying to catch a ball. Four-year-olds continue to use this approach, but also open their hands. Neither of these approaches results in many successful catches. Five-year-olds typically hold their arms to the sides of the body and open their hands. This gives them greater flexibility, and they make many successful catches.

## Fine Motor Skills

Fine motor skills relate to the use of the hands and fingers to manipulate objects. They are also known as hand-eye skills because they involve the integration of visual and manual abilities. Fine motor skills are required for self-feeding, dressing, and many play activities.

Visual feedback plays an important role in the mastery of these skills. For example, drawing with crayons depends on a constant interchange between seen results and modifications and adjustments in hand and finger movements (Fraiberg, 1977). Manual dexterity is improved through this interchange. The child becomes more efficient at cutting with scissors, brushing teeth, washing hands, and playing with toys. Again, practice and maturation are both important for fine motor skill development (Kellogg, 1970).

## Hand Skills

We already discussed handedness in the section pertaining to brain development. Therefore, we will devote this section to discuss the young child's development of art skills. Although adults often dismiss children's art as little more than play, we will soon learn that art skills provide an early foundation for later skills that are vital to academic success.

Preschoolers show an interest in creative expression through drawing with a variety of media. Their drawings may seem primitive to adults, but they are evidence of the integration of visual perception, cognitive skills, and fine motor skills. These early artistic efforts provide the foundation for the acquisition of other skills, such as printing and writing.

Researchers have traced the origins and developmental patterns of artistic abilities in early childhood (Cratty, 1979; Goodnow, 1977; Kellogg & O'Dell, 1967; Taylor & Bacharach, 1981). The sequences they found occur in a general-to-specific manner. A young child does not see the world as an adult does; by preschool, children's artistic endeavors have a freshness and directness that adult artists often try to recapture. When you look at art by modern abstractionists, you can see certain similarities with the productions of young children.

Scribbling is the foundation of artistic abilities. This is the experimentation that children make with some drawing instrument (pencil, crayon, etc.) when they are about two

*Consistent practice performing manual dexterity movements enables a child to improve tasks such as brushing their teeth. (iStock)*

years old. Young children have a propensity to scribble on just about any surface. Most adults are not aware that these scribbling experiences are the beginnings of self-expression. Instead, they see the scribbles as disorganized chaos and fail to value and validate the child's efforts.

About twenty basic patterns of scribbling have been catalogued and described (Kellogg & O'Dell, 1967). Compositions range from vertical, horizontal, diagonal, circular, and curving lines to waves and dots. Placement patterns of scribbling also vary. Even at this early age, a child's artwork reflects primitive organization and planning. A child makes progress in scribbling; shapes are implied in the patterns that are produced. These are hints at what will be outlined as circles, squares, crosses, and X's when children are about age three. Young children outline these shapes and learn to recognize and distinguish among them.

*Pause and Process:*

1. How do males and females differ in their motor skill development?

2. Why are art skills important for development?

# HEALTH ISSUES

## *Nutritional Needs*

Nutrition, physical changes, and psychosocial development are closely associated. In infancy, this was evident in the feeding experiences that facilitated a sense of trust. In early childhood, this association is seen in the formation of eating habits, food preferences, and social interaction patterns. It is also evident in the ways that preschoolers explore food and food choices.

Because of their declining growth rates, young children have less demanding appetites than infants (Hamilton & Whitney, 1982). Caregivers usually describe preschoolers as being "picky" about food. This refers not only to what they will and will not eat, but also to the amounts of food they consume.

Preschoolers often will not eat any food that is unfamiliar to them (Birch, 1987). At this stage of life, children are acquiring food preferences. This sometimes causes friction with their parents. For example, some children want only foods that are salty (pretzels, pickles, nuts, chips) or sweet (candy, pastries, cookies) (Birch, McPhee, & Sullivan, 1989). These foods tend to have "empty" calories, so parents may worry whether the preschooler is getting adequate nutrition. They may constantly offer food and even encourage the child to overeat. This can lead to further problems, such as obesity (see subsection below), that exacerbate the original eating problem.

Nutritionists suggest other ways to compensate for poor eating habits (Williams & Caliendo, 1984). First, serving sizes should be smaller than those for adults and older children. Children this age will not be harmed if they eat small amounts of food. Most children, even young infants, regulate their food intake quite satisfactorily (Hamilton & Whitney, 1982). Second, nagging children to eat food they don't want invites a power struggle. Vegetables may be good for children, but if they hate them, it's better to find nutritious substitutes that appeal to them. Third, snacks don't have to be high in sugar and salt. Examples of snack foods that are both nutritional and tasty to most children are celery stuffed with peanut butter or cheese spread, yogurt, puddings, fruit and cheese kabobs, and popcorn.

Although many American children can afford to be picky eaters, approximately twenty million children throughout the world suffer from malnutrition (WHO, 2007). Malnutrition places children at risk for illness, death, and cognitive delays and/or deficits. The World Health Organization postulates that nearly 75 percent of these children could be helped if ready-to-use foods that are specially fortified with nutrients were made available to them.

## *Obesity*

**Obesity**

A body weight that exceeds by 20 percent what is considered to be appropriate for one's age.

Childhood obesity is of growing concern in the United States, as evidenced by shows such as *Honey, We're Killing the Kids*. **Obesity** is defined as a body mass index (BMI) two standard deviations above the average BMI (WHO, 2007). This condition is believed to affect about 12.4 percent of all preschool-age children in the United States (CDC, 2009).

Being overweight or obese poses many social and psychological consequences to children in early and middle childhood, and beyond (CDC, 2009). Obese children have negative self and body-images. They are also likely to be unpopular. Peers often exclude them from play activities and sometimes reject them altogether (Mendelson & White, 1985; Williams & Stith, 1980). In addition, because eating patterns that are established in childhood usually last a lifetime, children who are overweight or obese are at an increased risk of being overweight or obese as adults (Rolfes & DeBruyne, 1990). Obesity poses serious health risks. It is associated with numerous health issues such as cardiovascular disease, hepatic steatosis (fatty liver), asthma, sleep apnea, and type 2 diabetes (CDC, 2009).

Scientists speculate that obesity is caused by a combination of genetic, behavioral, and environmental factors (CDC, 2009). Some individuals may have a *genetic* predisposition for obesity; however, except for rare genetic disorders, environmental and behavioral factors must come into play for obesity to occur. *Behavioral factors* include caloric intake and physical activity. Television, video games, and computer use seem to contribute to a sedentary lifestyle that precludes physical activity. *Environmental factors* include the influence of family, childcare, and school in helping establish healthy eating and exercise habits.

There are several steps families can take to prevent obesity (CDC, 2009). First, be aware of caloric intake. Avoid sugary drinks and high-calorie/low-nutrient snacks. Eat at home, sitting at the table. Avoid eating in front of the television where it is easy to lose track of what you are eating. Second, lead an active lifestyle. Limit television and other media time. Third, provide healthy role models for eating and exercise to young children. Educate children early about healthy habits. Provide quick, easy, healthy snacks and meals. All of these steps can help prevent obesity.

## *Illness, Disorders, and Other Concerns*

**Pediatric psychology**

The area of psychology that studies the interactions and relationships among health, illness, physical development, cognitive development, and socioemotional development across the life-span.

**Phenomenism**

The first stage for understanding of illness "as an external concrete phenomenon that is spatially and temporally remote from the condition of illness."

**Contagion**

The second stage for understanding of illness as "caused by people or objects that are proximate to, but not touching, the child."

The interactions and relationships among health, illness, physical development, cognitive development, and socioemotional development across the life span are studied in **pediatric psychology** (Bearison, 1998). Researchers in this interdisciplinary field study many important issues in health, including how children understand and cope with illness.

How a child understands illness is dependent upon cognitive development (Bearison, 1998). Bibace and Walsh (1979, 1980, and 1981) conducted a series of classic studies into the stages children go through in understanding illness. During early childhood, understanding of illness is very limited. Two stages of understanding of illness predominate this time period: phenomenism and contagion. **Phenomenism** is the first stage and is described as understanding illness "as an external concrete phenomenon that is spatially and temporally remote from the condition of illness" (Bearison, 1998, p. 679). For example, a young child may say that you can catch the chicken pox from the space shuttle in space. I know that this example seems like nonsense, but such is the reasoning at this stage.

The second stage for understanding illness is called **contagion**. Contagion thinking can be described as understanding illness as "caused by people or objects that are proximate to, but not touching, the child" (Bearison, 1998, p. 679). This means that children believe that you can get sick by being around other sick people, no contact needed. Such thinking applies to all types of illness—colds, flu, or even headaches and heart attacks. About 50 percent of four year olds display this type of thinking.

Although these stages predominate the early childhood years, such thinking may continue into the early school-age years. Additionally, some preschoolers may think at stages beyond these first two. Again, understanding of illness is highly dependent upon cognitive development; hence, as thinking in general develops, so to does an understanding of illness.

## *Physical Illnesses During Early Childhood*

Most of the serious communicable diseases that used to plague childhood are preventable today through immunization. Diphtheria and whooping cough, for instance, were once fatal to many young children but are almost unheard of now in the United States. Most infants are placed on immunization schedules that continue through early childhood. About 80 percent of all American children are fully immunized by their third birthday (Federal Interagency Forum on Child and Family Statistics, 2008).

Although most of the serious diseases are now preventable, young children can still get a variety of illnesses, including upper respiratory diseases such as colds, influenza, and infectious diseases (U.S. Bureau of the Census, 1990a, 1991; WHO, 2007). Preschoolers don't have much resistance to these kinds of diseases because they still lack natural antibody protection and because their organ systems are still maturing. In developing countries, diseases that cause diarrhea, malaria, and pneumonia are of major concern for children (WHO, 2007). Vaccinations, antibiotics, antimalarial medication, clean air and water, breastfeeding, proper nutrition, and insecticide-treated nets for sleeping areas are all needed to help decrease childhood deaths due to these illnesses.

Chronic diseases that are likely to result in death decrease during this time of the life span, although pediatric AIDS is one chronic disease that is advancing rapidly as a leading cause of death among young children (National Center for Health Statistics, 1990). According to the World Health Organization (2007), approximately 2.3 million children worldwide (under the age of fifteen) are infected with HIV. Approximately 1400 more children are infected everyday. Most of these children contact HIV in utero or through breastfeeding; hence, many of these new cases can be prevented through safer delivery and feeding practices and/or antiviral medication.

In the United States, approximately 88 percent of all children have some form of health insurance coverage (Federal Interagency Forum on Child and Family Statistics, 2008). Younger children are more likely to participate in public health insurance programs than older children. Uninsured children are 14 times more likely to lack a primary care physician or clinic than those with health insurance. Regular check-ups and preventative care are important steps in avoiding illness at all stages of development.

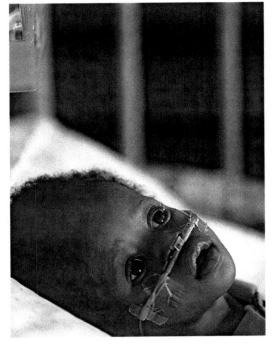

*Pediatric AIDS is quickly becoming the leading cause of death among young children. (AP)*

# Mental Disorders During Early Childhood

**Mental health**

A state of psychological well-being in which an individual is able to behave according to cultural standards.

**Mental health** is a global aspect to an individual's functioning (SAMHSA, 2003). It has behavioral, cognitive, and socioemotional components and influences on how we function in our daily life. A mental disorder can include harmful behavior, unrealistic thoughts and perceptions, inappropriate emotions, and unpredictable behavior (Hergenhahn, 2005). Mental disorders can range from mild to severe (SAMHSA, 2003). Additionally, mental disorders are often co-morbid, meaning that a person typically suffers from more than one (U.S. Department of Health and Human Services, 1999).

It is estimated that one out of every five children and adolescents suffer from a mental disorder (SAMHSA, 2003 and 2005). Further, approximately 10 percent of all children and adolescents suffer from a serious emotional disturbance that interferes and disrupts their ability to function in everyday life. If you do the math, this means that six million children and adolescents in the United States suffer from a mental disorder. Mental disorders can lead to school struggles, substance abuse, family tension and stress, aggressive behavior, or suicide if untreated.

Mental disorders are diverse and have different causes, symptoms, and treatments (SAMHSA, 2003). Sometimes, we are unaware of the cause. Genetics, injury, viruses, chemical imbalances, and toxins are all biological factors that can cause or trigger a mental disorder. Abuse, stress, or loss of loved ones due to death, divorce, or otherwise are environmental factors that can cause or trigger a mental disorder.

There are many categories of mental disorders. These categories include anxiety disorders, attention deficit/hyperactivity disorder (ADHD), disruptive behavior disorders, eating disorders, learning and communication disorders, affective mood disorders, schizophrenia, and tic disorders. We will highlight different disorders at different stages of the life span. In this chapter, we will focus on ADHD.

**Attention deficit/hyperactivity disorder**

A disorder that causes children to be highly distractible and energetic. It is caused by a chemical imbalance in the brain leading to difficulties in regulating attention, impulsivity, and hyperactivity.

**Attention deficit/hyperactivity disorder**, or ADHD, is predominantly thought to be due to a chemical imbalance in the brain leading to difficulties in regulating attention, impulsivity, and hyperactivity (Fewell & Deutscher, 2002). These children are highly distractible and energetic. They struggle to sit, be still, or behave in the way we expect in a typical school classroom.

Most people do not begin to discuss ADHD until the school-age years. However, there is a push for earlier identification and intervention of ADHD during the preschool years (Fewell & Deutscher, 2002). Perhaps with earlier, accurate identification and intervention, the disorder can come under control prior to entering school. Hence, children will be prepared to learn from day one of kindergarten.

Approximately 5 percent of all children suffer from ADHD (U.S. Department of Health and Human Services, 1999). There are some early signs that parents, child care providers, and preschool teachers can watch for in early childhood: "acts before thinking, changes activities frequently, has a short attention span, fails to focus and follow directions, distracts easily, has difficulty staying on task" (Fewell & Deutscher, 2002, p. 186). Of course all children display these behaviors occasionally. You would want to consider having the child evaluated if the behavior is consistent for at least six months, occurs in multiple settings (e.g., home and daycare), interferes with learning or ability to function, affects relationships and development, is uncontrollable by the child, and cannot be otherwise explained. ADHD can be treated in various ways. Medication and psychosocial interventions can be helpful (Fewell & Deutscher, 2002).

**Psychotropic medication**

Any medication capable of altering cognition, or behavior.

More and more children are being prescribed **psychotropic medication** for mental disorders (Brown, 2003). However, many of these medications have not been approved by the FDA for use in children due to a lack of research (Brown, 2003; NIMH, 2000). Children's bodies have a different composition than adults and metabolize medication differently than adult bodies. Further, children's brains are developing rapidly, and the affect of psychotropic drugs on these brains is unknown. For this reason, the National Institute of Mental Health (2000) states that children should be prescribed these unapproved medications only when the potential benefits clearly outweigh the potential risks. Medication should always be used in conjunction with psychosocial interventions and be carefully monitored.

## Safety Concerns

Accidents claim more lives and cause more injuries to children in the United State between one and four years of age than any other factor (National Center for Health Statistics, 1991, 2007). Most accidental deaths involve a motor vehicle, fires and burns, drowning, or poisoning. Many accidents occur within the home. This indicates that preschoolers need supervision to protect their well-being.

Many home-based injuries are due to the ingestion of harmful substances. Preschoolers are curious and tend to put a lot of substances they are curious about in their mouths. They are also prone to imitate adults who take medicines and pills. Aspirin, pesticides, lead found in paint chips, and petroleum products such as gasoline are common chemical agents that lead to injury and death in young children. Most of these injuries and deaths are preventable.

Children must also be taught to be careful with pets and to avoid wild animals. The Center for Disease Control (2009) urges parents to not allow young children to kiss pets or place animal toys in their mouth because children younger than five are more susceptible to contracting animal diseases than older children. Further, young children should not be allowed to come into contact with cat litters or other areas where pets use the bathroom. Finally, children should be routinely checked for ticks after playing outside. Ticks can carry Lyme disease and Rocky Mountain spotted fever, so they should be removed as soon as possible.

The physical environment must also be considered. Approximately 55 percent of children in the United States live in counties with polluted air (Federal Interagency Forum on Child and Family Statistics, 2008). Ozone and particulate matter that pollute the air can aggravate respiratory systems and increase respiratory problems and symptoms, such as asthma. Clean drinking water can also be of concern, with 10 percent of children in the United States living in communities that fail to meet drinking water health standards.

Substandard housing and lead can also be safety concerns and must be considered. Paint with lead should be removed from walls and homes should be checked for safety.

## *Promoting Wellness*

There are many aspects to consider when promoting the wellness of young children. Child care is one area that must be considered. More than 60 percent of all children age six and younger are in child care (Federal Interagency Forum on Child and Family Statistics, 2008). It is important to make certain that this child care is of good quality.

Child abuse is another area of concern. The consequences of abuse can be severe and life-long. Out of every one thousand there are twelve documented cases of child abuse (Federal Interagency Forum on Child and Family Statistics, 2008). Younger children are more likely to be abused than older children. Early detection and intervention is critical for optimal child development.

Economic issues should also be considered when promoting wellness. Approximately 20 percent of all children in the United States, younger than the age of six, live in poverty (Federal Interagency Forum on Child and Family Statistics, 2008). Poverty is especially prevalent among female-householder families (families with an unmarried female as head), with 42 percent of such children living in poverty (compared to only 8 percent of children living with two parents that are married). Additionally, about 12.6 million children (or 17 percent) live in a home where there is a shortage of food. Such economic issues must be addressed in order to promote optimal child development.

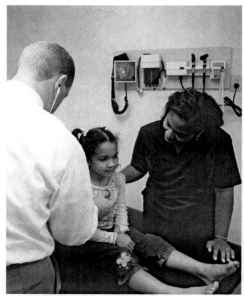

*Regular medical check-ups is one way to promote wellness of young children. (shutterstock)*

Finally, health and safety should be promoted through vaccinations, regular dental and medical check-ups, proper adult supervision, and cleanliness (CDC, 2009). Furthermore, utilizing developmental research more in the creation of public policy, education programs, and intervention programs will help enhance early childhood development across our nation (National Research Council and Institute of Medicine, 2000).

*Pause and Process:*

1. How is illness understood during early childhood?

2. What issues must be addressed in order to promote health and well-being during early childhood?

# COGNITIVE DEVELOPMENT DURING EARLY CHILDHOOD

> ### *LEARNING OBJECTIVES:*
>
> *1. Characterize the preoperational stage of cognitive development*
> *2. Describe information-processing during early childhood*
> *3. Apply Vygotsky's theory to early childhood cognitive development*
> *4. Explain language development during early childhood*

Early childhood is a time when children expand their knowledge of the world and develop an attitude of accomplishment. Changes in these years will be the foundation for many future learning experiences. This stage is an exciting time when a child learns to explore the environment in many ways.

This section explores cognitive changes during early childhood, a period that occurs between three to six years after birth. Developmental researchers have concentrated more on this life stage than on any other.

# PIAGET'S COGNITIVE DEVELOPMENT THEORY AND THE PREOPERATIONAL STAGE

**Preoperational**

The kind of thinking young children do when they begin to use mental imagery but are not yet able to use logic; intuition is often used in reaching decisions.

There is a shift in the nature of mental changes at three years of age. Piaget (1967) calls this a change to the **preoperational** mode of thinking. Parents and other caregivers readily recognize that a preschooler thinks differently when compared to an infant. This different way of thinking becomes more noticeable as young children solve problems in their play and daily activities. Their memory and information-processing skills are also more noticeable. Additionally, they show indications of the ability to use elementary logic.

Thought during this new period of mental change focuses on internalizing the environment. Children accomplish this by an increasing use of symbols and mental imagery. They come to rely on representational thought more frequently as they progress through the early childhood stage. Between four and six years of age, children are in transition to the next stage of cognition. They use intuition or hypothesizing to reach decisions. They are increasingly preoccupied with classification and the beginnings of more ordered, logical processing of information.

Preschoolers make judgments and reach conclusions based on their limited understanding of operations and rules. They use a minimal amount of cues and information in doing so. Piaget refers to this as the *intuitive* period of preoperational thought. It is a time when young children are acquiring a knowledge base about things, people, and their environment. Later cognitive functioning will make use of this information.

Mental changes are facilitated by new language skills and perceptual abilities and the changes in brain functioning that occur during early childhood. The preoperational label implies that the child's thought processes are *prelogical* in nature. These prelogical skills lay the foundation for many other, more complex mental changes at later stages of the life span.

## Characteristics of Preoperational Thought

Preoperational thought is relatively inflexible. This means that once young children adopt a particular point of view, they have difficulty understanding another one. It also means that young children's thought is dynamically tied to their perception. Preschoolers use sensory information extensively in forming conceptions and reaching conclusions. The maxim "What you see is what you get," is a good way to remember how preschoolers form their ideas of the world. A thing's appearance is often the only means preschoolers use for making judgments or evaluations about that thing.

Piaget uses several concepts to describe the relative rigidity of preschoolers' thought: equation of appearance with reality, egocentrism, centering, irreversibility, inability to solve problems of conservation, preoccupation with classification, animism, and precausal thinking.

## Appearance and Reality

Young children define reality almost exclusively as what they see. This characteristic of preoperational thought influences many other aspects of preschool-age cognition. It is generally recognized that preschoolers' thought is bound by their perceptions. They have almost no ability to generalize beyond the obvious or the information at hand (Flavell, 1986; Wadsworth, 2004).

Judgments, decisions, and conclusions are based on what is seen in the world. For example, a young child is shown a car that is colored red. The car is then covered with a special filter that changes its color to black. The filter is then removed to show the red color again. The car is again placed under the filter. When asked to name the color of the car, the child will say that it is black, totally disregarding the reality that the car is actually red and only appears to be black because of the filter. He will do this even though he just saw confirmation that the car is red when the filter was removed. The filter was put back on, and now the car looks black, so it is black as far as he is concerned.

## Egocentrism

**Egocentrism**

A cognitive trait that limits a child's understanding of the world to their own perceptions.

Piaget (1967) believes that the preoperational thought of young children is limited in part by their **egocentrism**. Piaget did not use this word in our usual sense of "selfish" or "conceited." Rather, he used it to describe how young children focus on their own viewpoint and are unable to consider other alternatives. From their perspective, their own vantage point is all that is possible.

Piaget demonstrated the egocentric nature of young children's thoughts in what is now known as the "three mountains experiment" (Piaget & Inhelder, 1967). Preschool-age children were shown a three-dimensional model of three mountains that differed in size and color. The model was placed on a table at which a young child sat on one side. A doll was placed in a chair on an adjacent side of the table. The child was asked to show, by using cardboard cutouts of the mountains models, how the mountains looked to the doll. None of the young children who were the subjects of this experiment were able to do so. They all depicted their own view of the mountains rather than the doll's because they could not understand that an event, object, or situation has a different perspective for someone else.

Young children typically believe that they are the center of their own universe, that things function and happen for their benefit. Appearances fuel this conclusion. For example, a young child on a walk at night might be asked what the moon does. The child will likely explain that the moon follows her everywhere—after all, that is what it appears to be doing. Likewise, a ball does not roll down a hill because it is round or because gravity pulls it. A young child believes it acts this way because he kicked it. This is reason enough for the ball's movement downhill.

Piaget discovered how difficult it is for a child to develop the ability to be knowingly empathic. In early childhood, the individual first learns that each of us has our own interpretation of reality. What must be learned next is that our personal views are not the only representations of reality possible, and certainly not the absolute truth. It is usually a challenge to understand that others have their own views, opinions, problems, perspectives, and knowledge. This understanding will not be completely accomplished by most people until the end of adolescence. In others, it may take even longer to gain an empathic perspective.

Young children begin to overcome their egocentrism and gain a degree of the empathic perspective by the end of early childhood. They start to realize that others see things differently from them and also know or like different things (Flavell, 1985; Hart & Goldin-Meadow, 1984; Taylor, 1988; Wadsworth, 2004).

Critics of Piaget's descriptions of early childhood egocentrism question the conclusiveness of his three mountains experiment (Borke, 1975; Hay et al., 1985). Others have observed that the prosocial behaviors young children demonstrate—such as altruism and sharing—indicate that empathy and responsiveness to others arise earlier than Piaget's schema allows (Leung & Rheingold, 1981; Zahn-Waxler, Radke-Yarrow & Brady-Smith, 1977). Researchers are continually refining our understanding of childhood egocentrism and illuminating how children make adaptations as they become more self-differentiated and socially oriented to others.

**Centering**

A cognitive trait in early childhood that limits information processing to only one aspect or characteristic rather than several simultaneously.

## Centering

Piaget calls another aspect of preoperational thought **centering** (Piaget & Inhelder, 1969). Young children concentrate on only one aspect of an object they see or an activity they do. They have difficulty in perceiving other aspects or elements simultaneously. When young children are attracted to the color of something, for example, they usually can't consider its size or shape at the same time. They can separate all the yellow buttons, from a large pile of assorted buttons, but the task of separating the yellow wooden round ones is too difficult for them. Because they can handle only one dimension of something at a time, they are capable of making only broad discriminations. The ability to make fine discriminations develops later in the life span.

## Irreversibility

**Irreversibility**

The inability of young children to comprehend that some processes and operations can be reversed in sequence.

Young children typically cannot understand that some operations or processes can be reversed. To a young child, things operate in only one way and that way is irreversible (Piaget, 1967). Some examples will illustrate the **irreversibility** of preschoolers' thinking.

When asked if he has a sister, a preschool-age boy can be expected to reply, "Yes. Her name is Julie." However, when asked if his sister has a brother, the boy replies, "No." A preschooler is shown a blue ball being placed in a cylinder, followed by a green and a yellow one. The child can accurately predict that they will appear from the bottom in that order. However, if the cylinder is rotated to its opposite end, the child cannot understand that the order of appearance will be

*Reversibility of thought, such as in subtraction, is difficult for young children to comprehend. (iStock)*

reversed as the balls appear from this end. Sequential, or serial, reasoning is difficult for young children because they are unable to trace their thought processes backward. Many young children can add or count upward. However, they find subtraction hard to comprehend. This is because subtraction is the reverse of addition and involves reversibility of thought. Similarly, they usually have difficulty understanding how water can be frozen into ice and then melted back into its liquid state.

## Conservation Problems

**Conservation**

The understanding that the essential characteristics of something are preserved even though it is rearranged in different ways.

Young children cannot understand that something retains the same properties when it is rearranged or reshaped. It is not until middle childhood that they comprehend that its essential properties are preserved, thus mastering the problem of **conservation**.

A trip to the supermarket reveals the prevalence of the problem of conservation even for adults. Manufacturers package similar products in differently shaped containers. A gal-

What is conservation?

lon in one type of container may not be recognized as a gallon in another. With the help of labels and an understanding of conservation, adults and older children understand that they can purchase equivalent amounts of a substance in these different containers.

Conservation problems illustrate how preschoolers' perceptions are governed largely by appearances. A classic Piagetian experiment shows that they do not understand that the volume of water is conserved (preserved) when it is poured into a container shaped differently from the original one. The preschooler usually concludes that there is a different amount of water in the new container because the physical appearance of the water has changed owing to the container's different shape. The understanding that the volume is the same is mastered in middle childhood. Comprehending problems of conservation among school-age children is facilitated by their developing abilities to decenter.

## Classification

**Classification**

The cognitive ability to group objects according to traits of similarity or likeness.

The mastery of **classification** skills is a challenge that is accomplished by age six. Centering and egocentrism account for the inflexibility of thinking that prevents younger children from being able to group things according to shared likeness. For example, when young children are given an assortment of plastic shapes (circles, squares, triangles) of different colors and asked to sort them according to likeness, they are unable to do so. Any sorting they do is usually by color rather than shape, especially among older preschool children (Ault, 1983). Similarly, irreversible thinking hampers the ability of young children to move back and forth between various groups to sort them correctly (Siegler, 1998; Wadsworth, 2004).

*Sorting different colored shapes according to likeness is a challenge for younger children. (iStock)*

## Animism

**Animism**

The belief of young children that all things, including objects are alive.

Young children believe that all things, including inanimate objects, are alive (Bullock, 1985). This **animism** is a charming aspect of preschool-age thinking. It is often observed when young children are involved in solitary play and talk to their toys using private speech.

When young children bump into a chair, it is not unusual to hear them scold it for being in their way. They believe things fall because they have a life of their own and can move to a different place. In many respects, animism is an extension of egocentrism and prelogical thinking. Young children may use animistic thought to develop hypotheses about a complicated world.

## *Precausal Thinking*

Preschoolers often jump to conclusions. They base their decisions on a limited amount of information or knowledge of circumstances, or on how close one event follows another (Pines, 1983; Pulaski, 1980; Wadsworth, 2004). Young children seem to reason in this manner: If event A causes event B to happen, then whenever event B is observed, event A will follow. For example, a young child may notice that when her mother is asleep (event A), she doesn't wear her glasses (event B). When her mother removes her glasses (event B) during the day to clean them, the child asks, "Is it time for you to go night-night (event A), Mom?" Removing the glasses is associated with going to sleep by the young child, and vice versa. This appears to be an understanding of reversibility. However, it is a type of reasoning based on what is known as **transductive reasoning**, or reasoning from one event to another.

Adults are often amazed at the tall tales and fanciful statements made with certainty by young children. Piaget and Inhelder (1969) describe two aspects of thought that account for **precausal thinking** among preschoolers; their inability to distinguish physical from psychological events, and their belief in an ultimate cause of events—that is, their conviction that there is a reason or explanation for everything. As we have seen, young children have problems differentiating the real from the imagined. For this reason, nightmares are real and fantasy is confused with reality. Intuitive thinking characterizes precausal thinking processes.

**Transductive reasoning**

Seeing a relationship between two objects or events, when in fact no relationship exists.

**Precausal thinking**

A type of logic unique to young children based on intuition rather than fact.

## *Revising Piaget's Findings*

Contemporary developmental researchers have found that the children they study do not always behave in the ways reported by Piaget. Many of Piaget's findings have been confirmed when the researchers replicated his methods of studying children (Gelman & Baillargeon, 1983). However, Piaget's approaches are not the only possible for studying changes in individuals' thinking processes over the life span. Contemporary academics have found other ways to study cognitive changes in childhood, and these methods have sometimes yielded results that contradict Piaget's findings (Crain, 2005; Wadsworth, 2004).

One such result is that young children are not as egocentric as Piaget reported. They do understand that an object having a variety of sides (like a house) looks different from various angles than one having similar sides (like a ball) (Flavell et al., 1981). Preschoolers also can classify objects if they have had experience with the task and it is not too complicated (Brown et al., 1983). These findings suggest that young children's abilities are not as limited as Piaget believed.

*Pause and Process:*

1. How would you describe preoperational thought?

2. How is the preoperational stage different from the sensorimotor stage we learned about in chapter three?

# INFORMATION-PROCESSING IN EARLY CHILDHOOD

## Attention

Attention is selective, involves constructive processing, and has limited capacity (Flavell & Miller, 1998). Infants display the beginnings of understanding attention through shared gazes. Although preschool children have some understanding of attention, it is limited. They often fail to understand that attention is selective. Instead, they often assume that adults will be able to attend to and process any information in the vicinity.

## Memory

The ability to process information received from the external environment is an important aspect of cognition. The use of memory is paramount in this process as children gain more experiences with a complex environment. Memory skills improve considerably during early childhood, partly because of the increasing efficiency of the cerebral cortex in storing information. Young children also show improvements in the strategies they use to place such information into their memory (Chance & Fischman, 1987; Schneider & Bjork-lund, 1998; Siegler, 1998).

**Classification and categorization skills**

The ability to use salient features to place objects or constructs into distinct groups.

**Rehearsal**

Practicing something over and over again.

Two strategies are used increasingly and more efficiently by young children to help them place information into their memories. First, they strive to master **classification and categorization skills** to facilitate learning and the use of memory in information-processing. In recalling words, for example, young children may associate words that rhyme ("sun-fun" and "fat-hat") (Rossi & Wittrock, 1971; Schneider & Bjorklund, 1998; Siegler, 1998). Second, young children learn by **rehearsal**—by doing or saying something repeatedly. For example, when three-year-olds are directed to remember where something is hidden, they look more intently, touch the area, and point to it repeatedly (Wellman, Ritter & Flavell, 1975). Naming objects repeatedly may also assist in the process of memory formation. Parents may quiz a child about what she sees, help her to name it, and ask the child to recall it later (Rosinski, Pellegrini & Siegel, 1977). Preschoolers especially rely on this method of learning when they receive approval for remembering. They become aware that rehearsal improves their ability to use recall (Fabricius & Cavalier, 1989).

## Emerging Academic Skills

Although some children learn foundations for academic skills at daycare or preschool, many others learn such skills from their parents or even older siblings. Early academic skills can also be acquired from educational programming (such as *Sesame Street, Between the Lions, or Sid the Science Kid*) or computer programs (such as mathisfun.com, brain-pop.com, or specific software programs). Academic skill development is intertwined with cognitive development and language development (Piper, 2003).

## *Early Mathematic Skills*

Culture is very important in determining what mathematical skills are important and need to be learned (Ginsburg, Klein, & Starkey, 1998). Learning the number words and using them to count begins around the age of two. For a while, adult (or older child) help is needed to count things with any accuracy. In fact, the average three-year-old will make a counting mistake 33 percent of the time. A conceptual understanding of what counting means takes longer than simply memorizing the order of the number words.

Counting with conceptual understanding progresses so that by the age of four children have a general conceptual understanding of adding objects or subtracting objects in relation to a group (Ginsburg, Klein & Starkey, 1998). This does not mean that the average four-year-old can do addition and subtraction problems. Instead you can show them an original picture with three cows. You can then show them two other pictures: a picture that still has three cows, and a picture with only two cows. If you asked the child, "Which picture shows that one of the cows left?" he or she would be able to choose the picture with only two cows.

Most three-year-olds do not display a strategy when asked a mathematical question (Ginsburg, Klein & Starkey, 1998). However, across the preschool years, some rudimentary mathematical strategies emerge. An early strategy to emerge is counting. For example, when asked which of two pictures has more tomatoes, most four-year-olds will use counting to answer the question. Another early strategy to emerge is learning to start counting from the larger of two addends. For example, consider the following word problem:

> Amy picks four apples from a tree. Then Amy picks three more apples from the tree.
> How many apples does she have altogether?

A younger child would start counting from one, all the way up to seven. However, an older preschool child would start with the four in mind, and count up three from there. Older preschool children also acquire finger counting for addition and subtraction problems. Surprisingly, older preschool children have two strategies for division problems: consecutive and overlapping (Ginsburg, Klein & Starkey, 1998). For example, consider the following word problem:

> Leonardo has five friends. He has ten pencils that he would like to give to them, making sure that each has the same number of pencils. How many pencils will each friend receive?

This division problem could be solved by a young child using either a consecutive strategy or an overlapping strategy (Ginsburg, Klein & Starkey, 1998). In the overlapping strategy, a child could draw five boxes representing the five friends. He or she would then place a tally mark in each box (representing a pencil) until they counted up to ten. In this way, the child could learn that each friend would receive two pencils. The alternative would be the consecutive strategy. With this strategy, the child would distribute the pencils to each friend completely before moving on to the next friend. Early on, this strategy could involve a lot of trial-and-error while trying to figure out how to distribute the total number of pencils equally among the friends.

## *Early Language Arts Skills*

To be successful in our society, a child must learn to read and write. However, how do children come to learn that the strange shapes and lines they see on paper stand for letters? Further, how do they come to know that these letters represent specific sounds in their language? Finally, how do they come to know how to share their thoughts, memories, feelings, or imaginations with the written word? All of these skills typically begin in early childhood.

**Phonics** can be defined as a system "designed to help children use the correspondences between letters and sounds to learn to read and write" (Adams, Treiman & Pressley, 1998). The first step in phonics is to teach that the letters of the alphabet stand for specific sounds. Some letters have only one sound (e.g., the letter B), whereas other letters have more than one sound (e.g., the letter G). Once children know the sounds that letters can make, they can begin sounding out words. Of course, they must learn the language-specific rules during the school-age years (e.g., when "le" is at the end of a two-syllable word, the consonant before the "le" joins it in forming the last syllable, like "candle"). Although phonics is very important for reading development, context is also important in helping young readers decode words that are neither familiar, nor easily sounded out. Additionally, some words must be taught that are neither phonetic nor easily learned through contextual clues. Many of these words, along with high frequency words, are taught in preschool as "sight words."

Writing skills are limited in early childhood. Writing is both a cognitive and motor skill task. Simply holding the pencil (or crayon) and working to make the hand make the desired marks on the paper uses much of the young child's cognitive resources. If a child

**Phonics**

An approach to teaching reading and spelling based upon phonetics, or the sound of letters.

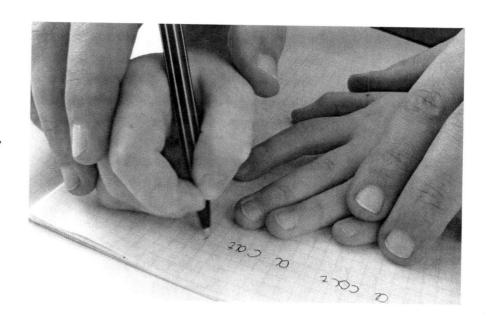

*The act of writing is an example of both a cognitive and a motor skill. The child works to make his hand hold and move the pencil to create marks on the paper. (iStock)*

has to write a story himself, it will be limited and sketchy. However, if a teacher or parent writes a story that the child dictates, the story will be filled with much more information and details.

### Metacognition

**Metacognition**

The ability to be aware of and understand the changes occurring in one's own cognitive processes.

Knowing how to place information into memory and how to retrieve that information are new skills for preschoolers. Many researchers believe that children do not master this basic skill until they are older (Siegler, 1998; Wellman, 1985). It depends on **metacognition**, or the ability to be aware of, understand, and take note of changes in one's own cognitive processes. Metacognition includes knowing how to pay attention to things to remember them later; what interferes with making one's attention work properly to perform memory storage; and what works well to facilitate the use of one's memory. There is some controversy about whether young children are aware that they can use memory in information-processing. It is clear, however, that in early childhood improvements occur in acquiring skills that help children control what they learn and remember (Brown, 1982; Siegler, 1998).

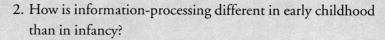

*Pause and Process:*

1. How does information-processing develop during early childhood?

2. How is information-processing different in early childhood than in infancy?

# OTHER COGNITIVE DEVELOPMENT THEORIES

### Vygotsky's Theory

In the first chapter, we learned the foundational concepts for Vygotsky's social-historical theory of cognitive development. The concepts of psychological tools, social-historical context, zone of proximal development, and scaffolding were all introduced. What is important to keep in mind for this chapter is that both Piaget and Vygotsky saw children as active agents in their cognitive development. One of the key distinctive features of Vygotsky's theory is the importance placed upon the social-historical context. Although Piaget is typically portrayed as viewing children as independent agents out in the world, constructing their own development, Vygotsky viewed children as active yet highly guided by more mature mentors in the environment.

**Zone of proximal development**

A range of what a child is capable of achieving.

It is also worth revisiting the key concepts of zone of proximal development and scaffolding from Chapter 1. The **zone of proximal development** is a range of what a child is capable of achieving. At the low end of the range is what the child is capable of achieving independently, whereas the high end represents what the child can achieve with guidance

**Scaffolding**

An instructional strategy in which a learning task is structured whereby a lot of support is offered early on, but as the student begins to learn, less and less support is given.

from a mentor. Scaffolding seems to be inherent across cultures. Parents, caregivers, and teachers seem to know to structure tasks in a way that best facilitates learning. With **scaffolding**, intensive help and guidance is given when a new skill is being taught to a child. As the child begins to understand the task and learn the skill, less and less help is given. Ultimately, the child is able to perform the task completely independently. Vygotsky's theory is an area of continued research and will probably continue to impact educational practices for some time.

## *Theory of Mind*

**Theory of mind**

The ability to understand your own mental state, as well as the mental state of others.

A **theory of mind** is the ability to understand your own mental state, as well as the mental state of others (Dixon, 2003). Furthermore, a theory of mind allows you to understand the connection between mental states and behavior. Mental state refers to your thoughts, knowledge, beliefs, and desires. For example, you know that you do not believe in Santa Claus. However, you may know that your three-year-old niece does believe in Santa Claus. Further, because you know about her beliefs, you may also be able to conjecture her thoughts about Christmas morning. However, a theory of mind takes time to develop.

Henry Wellman has completed a series of studies examining the development of theory of mind. He has also written numerous articles and chapters describing this phenomenon (e.g., Wellman, 1993; Wellman, Cross & Watson, 2001; Wellman & Gellman, 1998; Wellman, Lopez-Duran, LaBounty & Hamilton, 2008). Around the age of two, children begin to understand that people have wants and desires. By the third birthday, this understanding grows to include other mental states, such as thoughts and beliefs. It is at the age of four that children really begin to understand the connection between mental states and behaviors. Children are unable to deceive others until they have a theory of mind. Although most children fully achieve it by the age of four or five, children with older siblings achieve it earlier.

*Pause and Process:*

1. Give an example of how a teacher can scaffold learning for children.

2. Why do you think children with older siblings achieve a theory of mind sooner than children without older siblings?

# LANGUAGE DEVELOPMENT

In Chapter 3, we discussed language development in infancy. We learned the components of language, theories of language acquisition, and received an overview of language development in these early years. But why do we have language? What function does it serve?

There are various perspectives as to what functions language serves (Piper, 2003). In her book on language development, Piper (2003) integrates the perspectives of several researchers to identify some of the primary functions of language. Some early functions of language include: satisfy needs, direct the behaviors of others, describe self, facilitate social interactions, information gathering and sharing, and play, and imagination. Later functions of language include: interpretation and integration of experiences, expression of cognitive and socioemotional processes, and organizing communication.

These important functions of language necessitate the ability to converse skillfully with others. What makes one individual a good conversationalist and another a boring or inept conversationalist? There are some basic guidelines that allow one to be a competent conversationalist and they begin developing early in childhood.

One important skill to be a competent conversationalist is to be sensitive and empathic to the listener (Piper, 2003). What is the listener's viewpoint? Do they seem to comprehend what you are saying? Is the person even paying attention? Sensitivity to listener needs is a key component to conversational skills. This skill is closely intertwined with cognitive development, and one sees great improvements in this area during the school-age years.

Another important skill is learning to take turns during a conversation (Piper, 2003). Without turn taking, you don't have a conversation, but a monologue. Again, although this skill begins development during infancy (with caretakers taking turns responding to coos), development continues throughout childhood.

There are many other important skills for being a competent conversationalist (Piper, 2003). These skills include use and response to indirect requests, awareness and understanding of relevance, ability to make conversational repairs, and pragmatic adjustments for gender.

Now that we have considered some of the broader, foundational issues of language use, let's consider some specific areas of speech development during early childhood.

## *Private Speech*

**Private speech**

A speech form prevalent in early childhood in which children talk to themselves or continue to talk even when no one is listening to what they are saying.

One characteristic of language acquisition in early childhood is the use of **private speech**. Piaget (1926) first noted this as a language form in early childhood. He observed that young children frequently talk even when no one is listening to them. He believed that this shows egocentrism in young children—their inability to see things from another's viewpoint. Piaget believed that this type of speech pattern became replaced by other means of self-expression as children developed.

Another interpretation of private speech has been suggested by Vygotsky (1962). Rather than being an indication of egocentrism, private speech, in Vygotsky's view, is used by preschoolers to direct their actions, make plans, and maintain a psychological focus on the present. Again, rather than disappearing, as Piaget suggested, Vygotsky theorized that private speech becomes merely unspoken or sometimes subconscious thought (Berk, 1986; Crain, 2005; Frauenglass & Dias, 1985; Kohlberg, Yaeger & Hjertholm, 1968). Private speech is often observed among preschoolers when they are involved in solitary play. It is also observed when they think "out loud" as they work through situations and learn problem-solving strategies (Crain, 2005; Harris, 1990; Manning, 1990).

## *Vocabulary*

Vocabulary continues to expand rapidly during early childhood (Siegler, 1998). The average three-year-old has a vocabulary of 896 words. By the age of four, vocabulary size increases to an average of 1,540 words. Another jump is seen in vocabulary by the age of five, with an average vocabulary of 2,072 words. Words acquired during this time become more complex with more of the derivatives and inflections acquired (Piper, 2003).

The use of private speech is believed to show egocentrism in young children. (iStock)

## *Grammar*

Young children learning English as their primary language experience many challenges because English has rather difficult grammar. Parts of speech must be learned, as well as the rules for forming correct sentence structures. This involves comprehending, at an elementary level, such rules as (1) the subject precedes the verb; (2) verbs have different tenses to reflect past, present, and future action; (3) words have different forms in the possessive case; and (4) verbs change form with plural subjects. However, there are many exceptions to these basic rules and they take years to master. Young children are able to place the subject before a verb and the object after it (Clark, 1982). This is the grammatical structure commonly used in English. Infant usage such as "Baby go sleep" is refined into "I'm sleepy, and I want to take a nap." There is limited use of possessive words such as "my" and "mine" at age three, and understanding of the possessive case increases during this period. Verb tenses are learned. Negatives are learned as well. For example, a two-year-old would say when told it is bedtime, "No go!" whereas a four-year-old might say, "I don't wanna go night-night!" Prepositions are difficult and may not be mastered at this time.

Preschoolers often resort to inventing words when forming sentences (Clark, 1982; Piper, 2003). Although they lack the vast vocabulary and cognitive abilities of older individuals, young children strongly desire to communicate so they create words according to their limited knowledge of grammatical structure. For example, they will add an s to a verb, as in "I gots to use the potty," and an er to a noun for a doer, as in "My mom is a good cooker." This type of error is known as overgeneralizing the rules of grammar. Speech in early childhood is abundant with mistakes, but trial-and-error is the means by which young children learn the complexities of language.

## Bilingualism

The ability to speak more than one language is a cognitive advantage (Piper, 2003). The earlier a child learns a second language, the easier it is for him or her to master it. When a child is raised in a home where two languages are spoken, some confusion may occur between the two languages during early childhood. However, this confusion typically subsides by the end of early childhood. Interestingly, a child raised in a bilingual home will eventually favor one language over the other. It is rare to find balanced bilingualism. Which language dominates is typically determined by which language is dominant in the surrounding environment.

**Communicative disorders**

Any disorder that impairs one's ability to communicate.

**Voice disorders**

Persistent difficulties with the quality of voice.

**Fluency disorders**

Disorders in which a person struggles to communicate smoothly.

**Articulation disorders**

Disorders in which a person struggles to produce appropriate speech.

## Communicative Disorders

**Communicative disorders** can range from mild to severe and make either learning or using the language difficult (Piper, 2003). Three of the most common communicative disorders in children involve voice, fluency, and articulation of particular sounds.

**Voice disorders** are persistent difficulties with the quality of voice (Piper, 2003). They may simply be a nuisance (such as a nasal tone or breathiness) or may make speech unintelligible. **Fluency disorders** disrupt the ability to speak continuously or at a normal rate. Stuttering is one example of a fluency disorder. **Articulation disorders** range from difficulty with specific sounds to severe impairment in the phonological system. Lisping is one example of a mild articulation disorder.

The cause of these communicative disorders varies (Piper, 2003). Sometimes they are due to anatomical abnormalities. Other times they are due to brain injuries. In many cases, however, the cause is unknown. In general, the sooner a communicative disorder is identified and intervention begins, the better the chance of communicative improvement.

*Pause and Process:*

1. How do Piaget and Vygotsky differ in explaining private speech?

2. How does language develop during early childhood?

# SOCIOEMOTIONAL DEVELOPMENT DURING EARLY CHILDHOOD

**LEARNING OBJECTIVES:**

1. *Characterize emotional development during early childhood*
2. *Describe understanding of self and others during early childhood*
3. *Explain psychosocial development during early childhood*

**Socialization**

The process by which individuals are taught to conform to social rules, to acquire personal values, and to develop attitudes typical of their culture.

Early childhood is a time when socialization efforts begin in earnest. **Socialization** is the process by which individuals are taught to conform to social rules, to acquire personal values, and to develop attitudes typical of their culture. A preschooler experiences growing pressures to conform to expectations of "good" behavior. Early childhood is the time when parents start to explore styles of child rearing in earnest. They experiment to find patterns they feel comfortable with and that succeed in achieving the desired results. They encourage their preschooler to develop routines and habits of everyday living. Children at this stage typically must also learn to separate easily and frequently from their parents, especially if they are placed into daycare or a preschool program.

This phase of the life span is also a time when social roles and interaction patterns are first learned and shaped. Children learn to play with others their age in early childhood. As they do so, they experiment in how to relate to others. Most preschoolers like participating with other children in play activities. Several social and mental changes occur in the types of play children engage in at this stage. Play facilitates learning about the social roles found in the child's culture, including appropriate sex-role behaviors. Children experience some conflicts as they learn what is acceptable to both parents and peers.

# PSYCHOSOCIAL DEVELOPMENT

## *Developing a Sense of Initiative*

Describe psychosocial development during early childhood.

According to Erikson's theory of psychosocial development, many social changes occur during early childhood. These changes relate to the shift in psychosocial focus that takes place at this time of life. In early childhood, an individual's challenge is to develop a healthy sense of *initiative* versus an unhealthy *sense of guilt*. This attitude represents children's further adaptation to their now-enlarging world of experiences and people and reflects their self-confidence in their abilities and powers. The motivation of children this age is to master whatever they encounter—whether that is relationships, objects, or activities.

**Attitude of initiative**

A feeling of confidence.

The **attitude of initiative** translates behaviorally into a focus on action. The curiosity of young children shows an initiative orientation to life. They explore, ask questions, and are constantly active. Initiative is boosted by the attitude of personal autonomy a child acquired during the previous stage of psychosocial development. Now the pervasive psychological attitude of "I can!" fully emerges.

Young children's behavior becomes directed toward what Erikson termed "making and making like." This behavioral theme shows up in children's awareness of social roles. Their interest centers on learning the patterns within their family system that regulate behaviors. The circle of significant others now widens to include the entire family group, rather than just the child's parents. These people have a great impact on whether a child learns the healthy or unhealthy attitude for this stage.

**Shame**

The feeling that one's inner self is exposed as being flawed in some manner.

**Guilt**

Feeling shame and remorse.

If the psychosocial focus becomes centered on guilt rather than initiative, there will be an inhibition of action. Guilt differs from shame, the unhealthy attitude that may have flourished in late infancy. **Shame** is the feeling that one's inner self is exposed as being flawed in some manner. This results in loss of self-esteem. **Guilt** focuses on the pervasive negative aspects of one's behavior. Essentially, guilt is the feeling that one's actions are somehow wrong or bad. This "bad" behavior adds further proof to the conviction that one's inner self is indeed shameful (Burns, 1980/1989).

An attitude of initiative is enforced when children learn that their behavior is appropriate. (iStock)

In Erikson's framework, then, young children develop the attitude of initiative when they learn that their behavior is appropriate. This makes them believe that their inner self is good. They acquire the attitude of guilt when they learn that their behavior is inappropriate. In that case, they perceive their inner self as bad.

These lessons about behavior and self-concept originate from parents, family members, and other caregivers (Erikson, 1950). The unhealthy, inhibiting attitude of feeling guilty about oneself and one's behavior is acquired in several ways. For instance, parents commonly scold children this age when their behavior exceeds established limits. This is not necessarily harmful. Children this age need to know when they have crossed a parentally established boundary or violated a family rule. However, the feeling of guilt is promoted when parents confuse the child's behavior with his or her inner character. If a parent tells a young child "*You're* absolutely the most rotten kid in the world when you hit your brother!" it is only logical for that child to fuse his act with his self-image. When an adult makes this type of negative evaluation, a young child may conclude, "*I* am bad *because* I act this way."

The attitude of guilt becomes deeply ingrained when young children consistently receive negative reinforcement or punishment from adults. This can happen simply because they are behaving with initiative. Parents who seek to restrain their children's active behavior by constantly scolding them for it can encourage guilt rather than initiative. Guilt tends to inhibit learning the value of taking calculated risks, inquisitiveness, and other valuable traits. A child who acquires an attitude of guilt may be hindered in developing to his or her fullest potential in later stages of the life span.

*Pause and Process:*

1. Why is an attitude of initiative important for optimal development?

2. What is the difference between guilt and shame? Give an example of each.

# EMOTIONAL DEVELOPMENT

## *Key Emotional Development Highlights*

Emotional development is intertwined with cognitive development (Siegel, 1999). As we learned in the last chapter, preschool children enter the preoperational stage of cognitive development. Although preschool children experience increases in attention and memory, they also experience egocentric thought, appearance as reality, animism, and precausal thinking. Hence, this is a period where fears peak and aggression is common. Conversely, it is also a period of increased empathy and gratification delay.

## *Emotion Regulation*

Learning to control one's emotions is a slow and sometimes painful process. During early childhood, controlling emotions is observable in displays of prosocial behavior. Failed attempts at controlling emotions are observable in displays of aggression. Coping with fears is another area that children work with emotion regulation during this phase of the life span. It is these three areas that we will touch upon in this section.

## *Prosocial Behaviors*

**Prosocial behaviors**

Those behaviors that promote helpfulness and show concern for others, such as altruism or empathy.

**Empathy**

The ability to comprehend accurately the thoughts, feelings, and actions of others.

**Sympathy**

The ability to feel the same way that others do; learning to sympathize is the first step toward developing empathy.

Most young children are taught to show some social interest in others. **Prosocial behaviors** are those that promote helpfulness and concern for others. These altruistic behaviors involve an awareness of others' feelings and appropriate reactions to those feelings. Prosocial behavior requires **empathy**, or the ability to comprehend accurately the thoughts, feelings, and actions of others (Burns, 1980; Eisenberg & Fabes, 1998). Empathy differs from **sympathy**, which is the ability to feel the same way that others do, but learning to sympathize is the first step toward developing empathy.

As mentioned in our discussion of emotional development in infancy, early empathy may be possible because of the mirror neuron system. Toddlers are also capable of early, if ineffective, attempts at prosocial behavior when trying to comfort an upset loved one. It is common in early childhood to observe empathic responsiveness when children share, comfort, and help each other.

It is unclear what role a parental model plays in facilitating these behaviors

*Trying to comfort an upset loved one is prosocial behavior. (iStock)*

in young children. It does appear that when children have opportunities to observe sympathetic behaviors, they tend to behave sympathetically more frequently themselves (Eisenberg & Fabes, 1998; Yarrow, Scott, & Waxler, 1973). Researchers note, however, that sympathetic behaviors are observed throughout infancy and childhood regardless of parental modeling.

## Aggression

**Aggression**

Any hostile act that causes fear in others and leads to forceful contact; may be verbal or physical and directed at people as well as objects.

Psychologists define **aggression** as any hostile action that causes fear and leads to forceful contact with another (Coie & Dodge, 1998; Parke & Slaby, 1983). Aggression can be either verbal or physical or both, and can be directed at people or things. Aggressive behaviors can also be either positive or negative.

During early childhood, verbal aggression increases while physical aggression decreases (Coie & Dodge, 1998). Increases in language ability and the ability to delay gratification may contribute to the decline in physical aggression. Across cultures and socioeconomic groups, boys are more physically and verbally aggressive than girls during the preschool years.

Theorists believe that a wide variety of factors may contribute to aggression (Coie & Dodge, 1998). Genetics, psychobiology, and cognitive processes have all been implicated as contributors to aggression. Other researchers focus on the role of the family environment. They note that children who are treated in harsh, aggressive ways by parents act aggressively toward others. Some attribute the tendency toward aggressive behavior in these children to genetic factors (Ghodsian-Carpey & Baker, 1987). Others stress that an aggressive parent promotes similar behavior in children through modeling (Bandura, 1973; Bandura & Walters, 1963), just as children frequently imitate the violent behavior they see on television (Singer & Singer, 1981). One explanation emphasizes that physical punishment by parents increases a child's aggressiveness (Eron, 1987).

Despite the partial merit of these explanations, it is clear that all young children act aggressively at times. Parents and other caregivers are challenged to teach children to control their aggressive impulses. Research points to the powerful role of reinforcement in helping children learn to act in other ways. Adults give children a confusing message when they spank them for hitting others. If, instead, they positively reinforce prosocial behaviors that are incompatible with aggression, children are likely to learn more beneficial ways to express themselves. Another less damaging way to discourage aggression is to briefly isolate the aggressive child from others. Social learning theory suggests still other alternatives. One is to expose children to models who show appropriate ways for handling the feelings that motivate aggression.

*Spotlight*

Define aggression.

## Coping with Fears

**Fear**

A reaction that involves physical and/or psychological agitation and dreadful anticipation of real or imagined danger to one's safety.

**Fear** is an emotional response marked by psychological or physical agitation and a dreadful anticipation of actual or imagined danger. We develop fears both by learning and by using our imagination to cope with anxiety. Fears resemble phobias, but are different in nature. A fear may be based on reality, on something that has actually occurred, or stands a good chance of occurring. A phobia, on the other hand, is a compulsive, maladaptive response to relatively harmless and poorly defined stimuli. A fear may serve as the basis of a phobia. For example, a child may be frightened by a large snarling dog. This is a realistic response. But if the child develops a fear of all dogs, even after repeated exposure to the harmless variety, that child has a phobia. Most young children do not develop serious phobias. Those who do may need professional assistance if their reactions interfere with normal functioning.

Most fears of young children relate to the stressfulness of encountering unfamiliar situations and people. Preschoolers have a vivid imagination that fuels an active fantasy life. Their immature level of cognitive functioning does not permit them to easily distinguish between reality and fantasy. Although their interactions with the world are increasing dramatically, they lack the experience to make predictions about the future based on what has occurred in the past. Therefore, they commonly make gross overgeneralizations and jump to conclusions.

Children's fears change as they advance through the preschool stage. One of the most comprehensive examinations of this subject ever conducted was done by Arthur Jersild and Francis Holmes in 1935 (Jersild, 1960). Their findings have been confirmed repeatedly by contemporary investigators (Baurer, 1976; Poznansky, 1973). Young children's fears focus on unpredictable and unknown situations, objects, and events over which they feel they have little control. Studies report that preschoolers show the greatest fear reactions to animals, snakes, the dark, falling, loud noises, and high places. As they gain more experience with the world and advance in cognitive maturation, their fears become more manageable. It is common, however, for early fearful reactions to recur at later stages in the life span, usually in association with major transitions and crises.

*A child frightened by a large dog may be the basis of a phobia. (shutterstock)*

When parents hear children voice their fears and act them out by withdrawing, crying, or trembling, their response is often to regard the fears as irrational (which they are) and to scold the children or become impatient with them. This behavior may promote a sense of guilt rather than alleviate the child's fearfulness.

Children can learn how to overcome their fears (Alexander & Malouf, 1983). Parents and other caregivers can best respond by encouraging children to work through their thoughts about the fearful situation. This helps them to learn to cope successfully, rather than feel guilt about being afraid (Graziano, DeGiovanni & Garcia, 1979). Parents should also encourage children to talk about their fears. This lets them know that they are being taken seriously and have their parents' support. With support, they will learn how to reduce anxiety and gain some degree of mastery over fear-producing stimuli (Eisenberg, 1998). Their self-esteem is heightened in the process.

## *Delaying Gratification*

**Delay gratification**

The ability to put off something pleasurable and rewarding and work hard in the here and now.

Adults often ask preschoolers to wait for what they want to have right now. The ability to **delay gratification** is desirable to many families. They expect their children to put aside a smaller need satisfied now in exchange for receiving a greater benefit later. This is an important lesson in self-control.

People are able to cope more successfully with difficult situations later in life if they learned to delay immediate gratification in early childhood (Mischel, Shoda & Rodriguez, 1989). For example, researchers identified young children who were highly self-controlled at four years of age. These children were more competent and better able to cope with frustration during middle childhood and adolescence than those who had lower levels of self-control in early childhood. Modeling appears to help preschoolers learn this valuable behavior (Mischel, 1974). Teaching young children to say, "It is good if I wait," also helps them to control their impulsiveness (Toner & Smith, 1977).

## *Temperament*

In earlier chapters, we discussed Thomas and Chess' conceptualization of temperament. If you remember, Thomas and Chess' years of research suggested that there were three basic types of temperament: easy, difficult, and slow-to-warm-up. Although not all infants fit into one of these three categories, most could. However, other conceptualizations of temperament have been proposed (Rothbart & Bates, 1998). In fact, the idea of temperament "types" has been questioned, with a shift toward looking at temperament groups or profiles instead (e.g., Aksan et al., 1999). The idea behind temperament groups emphasizes that although these groups are distinct from one another, there is also great variability within each group.

Regardless of which perspective on temperament you focus on, a clear pattern has emerged showing correlations between specific temperament dimensions and behaviors (Rothbart & Bates, 2006). Some dimensions of temperament are seen as protective factors against suboptimal behavioral outcomes, whereas others are seen as risk factors for problem behaviors (e.g., Buss & Plomin, 1984; Prior, 1999). For example, a child who is high in negative emotionality is at risk of both internalizing and externalizing behavioral problems. Conversely, low negative emotionality seems to act as a protective factor against internalizing and externalizing behavioral problems.

## *Attachment*

If you remember from Chapter 3, attachment is a strong affectional tie or emotional bond between two individuals (Ainsworth, 1973). Attachment develops from early caregiving interactions and impacts the development of expectations of what to expect in relationships and mental models about self and others (Thomson, 1998). Attachment can be secure, insecure-avoidant, and insecure-ambivalent.

Numerous studies have examined the impact of infant temperament on early childhood behavior (see Thomson, 1998, for a review of this research). In general, when you compare a secure child to an insecure child, the secure child is more likely to display the following behaviors and characteristics: lower dependency on preschool teachers, higher empathy, higher ego resiliency, higher self-esteem, better emotional health, more positive mood, higher social competence, higher compliance, and better social skills.

Hence, secure attachment in infancy is predictive of better outcomes during the preschool years than insecure attachment. We will return to attachment and overall adjustment in Chapter 5.

*Pause and Process:*

1. Describe aggression and prosocial behavior during early childhood.

2. Given what you have learned about temperament so far in this book, why do you think it would be related to behavioral outcomes such as depression or aggression?

# SELF AND OTHERS

## *Understanding of Self and Others*

**Self-concept**

One's basic ideas about one's inner self.

The process of developing a **self-concept** that began in infancy continues in early childhood. If you remember, the self-concept is a person's ideas about his or her inner self. In late infancy, individuals learn to establish personal boundaries and to differentiate themselves from their parents. In early childhood, they continue to construct elementary notions about their personal identity. Increasingly, young children use their physical characteristics, possessions, and abilities as the basis for constructing their self-concept (Elder, 1989; Harter, 1983, 1998). More importantly, they learn to evaluate their inner selves

*Self-concept such as gender identity classifies whether a child feels that they are either male or female. Cues such as hairstyle and clothing help children determine gender. (iStock)*

according to what others tell them about themselves. Children this age see their parents as omnipotent. Parents have the answers to the questions they ask, the power to make things happen that they cannot accomplish, and the ability to protect them from harm. The lessons parents teach a young child about the world and how to act are powerful and lasting. They also deeply affect the child's self-concept.

## Gender Identity

**Gender identity**

One's knowledge of being either male or female.

An important aspect of an individual's self-concept is **gender identity**. This is the knowledge that one is classified as either male or female.

Children first learn gender or sex roles through their parents' and culture's interpretations of masculinity and femininity. In early childhood, reinforcement is used to shape such behaviors. However, innate tendencies also help guide behavior development. Said another way, some sex-role behavior seems largely shaped by the society a child is raised in—such as whether women and girls eat only after the males in the family have been fed. Conversely, some sex-role behavior seems to cut across cultures (and sometimes even species), which hints at an underlying biological tendency—such as males tending to be more physically aggressive than females.

Young children go through a period of rigid stereotypes and ideas about what it means to be male or female. It is helpful to recognize that preschoolers make rigid interpretations of sex-role behaviors because this helps them to understand their own social roles and to organize their behavior accordingly. This rigidity is partly due to the constraints in thought processes that are typical at this age. Young children's reasoning can be primitive and rather inflexible. They base a lot of their notions on concrete cues. Preschoolers typically use visible physical cues to recognize others as either male or female (Bem, 1989). Such cues usually are hairstyles, clothing, and accessories such as hair barrettes. Such limited reasoning means that gender can be changed if the physical cues change. For example, if a preschool child sees a boy dressed like a boy, the preschooler will call him a boy. However, if that same boy is then dressed in girl's clothing, then it is likely that the young preschool child will call him a girl. It is not until around age six that many children have realized that sex roles usually conform to external genitalia. Children with younger, opposite sex siblings will sometimes realize this sooner if they paid attention during diaper changes or baby baths.

The behavioral aspect of children's sex-role development begins at birth when parents are told, "It's a boy!" or "It's a girl!" This immediate classification is made more public by naming a child. Names generally conform to one's biological sex, although in our culture androgynous names can sometimes be given. At any rate, from birth onward, children are channeled into one sex role or the other. They are dressed in clothing and given hairstyles that will help others know whether to treat them as a male or female (Fagot et al., 1985). Girl babies are cuddled more and spoken to softly; boy babies are handled more energetically.

A preschool-age child's knowledge of sex-appropriate role behaviors comes from several sources. The family system is particularly important here. Adults and others in the family system model and reinforce what they consider to be sex-appropriate behavior (Maccoby & Jacklin, 1974). Reinforcement from other same-sex children also promotes sex-appropriate behaviors, especially among boys (Fagot, 1985; Maccoby & Jacklin, 1987).

With time, preschool children will outgrow their rigid ascription to sex-role behaviors and realize that males can cook and be great chefs and females can be firefighters. Sex-role rigid outlooks can be viewed as developmentally appropriate in early childhood and not equivalent with the gender stereotypes adults sometimes hold.

## *"In Their Own Words"*

Carly, a 5-year-old girl, answers some questions about gender which highlights the unique perspective on gender taken in early childhood.

**What are some girl games?**
*Barbies they're my favorite, baby dolls like Lucy, dress up, and play house.*

**What are some boy games?**
*Boys are gross, they play tag at school during recess and they get all dirty. And they chase Megan and I around all the time. They try to catch us but we are so fast, like lightning and they never do. We just go pshh around the swings.*

**Do you think there is anything that boys can do but girls can't?**
*Boys can fart and burp. It's funny when Daddy burps after dinner and Mommy yells at him. But I don't burp like Daddy does. I even tried to once but I couldn't do it.*

**Do you think it's better to be a boy or a girl?**
*It's better to be a girl, duh.*

**What are some things that Mommy does but Daddy doesn't?**
*Mommy cooks and cleans the bathroom. Sometimes she has to clean the toilet and the tub and she gets really mad 'cause its dirty. Mommy stays home when I'm sick too. She calls off of work because she likes to take care of me and make sure I'm okay. Daddy still goes to work but it's ok 'cause he has to get money to buy stuff.*

**What are some things that Daddy does but Mommy doesn't?**
*Daddy goes to work in the morning and he doesn't come back until right before dinner. But Mommy goes to work after she takes me to school and she is home when I get home from school. She gets me off the bus everyday. Then when Daddy comes home from work he has to do more work after dinner on the desk. It doesn't take him long but Mommy never has to do work when she gets home.*

## Play

Play, like language, is a primary means by which young children experience socialization. Play is especially pertinent to developing social skills such as prosocial behaviors. It is through play activities with others that young children construct the culture of childhood. Play is usually seen by adults as recreational, something to keep children busy. But play is much more constructive than most adults realize (Galatzer-Levy & Choler, 1993; Garvey, 1977; Sutton-Smith, 1985; Vandenberg, 1978).

First, play helps children to learn problem-solving skills such as sharing, taking turns, and cooperating. Second, play encourages self-discovery and self-concept formation. The discovery of one's capabilities and limitations, and others' reactions to those capabilities and limitations, during play helps to develop self-definition. Third, repetitive play advances skill mastery and exploration. Fourth, play encourages creativity. Children investigate different approaches as they interact with others and manipulate toys in different ways.

The classic study of children's play was conducted by Parten (1932). Her findings have been confirmed by other investigators who have studied developmental changes in play activities (Barnes, 1971; Harper & Huie, 1985). Parten discovered six categories of play activities in early childhood. They show a progression from general to specific types. A couple of these types were alluded to in chapter three.

An early form of play activity is called **unoccupied play**. A child watches others or engages in seemingly aimless activity such as wandering about. **Solitary play** takes place when children are alone or are playing independently of others. A child makes little attempt to interact with others. **Onlooker play** involves observing others playing. A child asks questions, makes comments, or carries on conversations with others who are actively playing. **Parallel play** is playing alongside others who are doing the same or a different activity. **Associative play** is engaging in a common activity and interacting with others. A

**Unoccupied play**

Play that seems random and without purpose.

**Solitary play**

Children are alone or are playing independently of others.

**Onlooker play**

Observing others at play.

**Parallel play**

Playing alongside others who are doing the same or a different activity.

**Associative play**

Engaging in a common activity and interacting with others.

**Cooperative play**

The integration of several children into group play where different roles are assumed.

child may borrow, lend, share, or influence others' behavior by suggestions. Finally, **cooperative play** is the integration of several children into group play where different roles are assumed. This type of play has an agreed-upon goal or outcome, as when children work together to build a fort.

This progression shows how children's play activities can be expected to change as they grow older (Harper & Huie, 1985). Parallel play dominates among two and three-year-olds. It persists as a primary play form throughout early childhood. Associative play is increasingly observed among three-year-olds. This type of play continues to increase in frequency during early childhood to levels comparable to parallel play. Cooperative play emerges during the third and fourth years and slowly increases thereafter.

It is not uncommon for a child to favor one type of play activity over others. For example, some five-year-olds prefer solitary play activities to associative play activities (Smith, 1978). These children can play at something for hours and be perfectly happy. When playing with other children, they also enjoy the companionship and what they are doing. Piaget (1967) proposes that play changes in conjunction to refinements occurring in cognitive skills.

Dramatic play is another type of activity frequently observed in children at this age. In this form of play, also known as *pretend* or *fantasy play*, children use their imaginations to create characters and project themselves into the activities they fantasize for those characters. Dramatic play begins in late infancy when a child pretends to feed a stuffed animal or doll, for example. In early childhood, dramatic play becomes more complex because young children can create complicated plots and fanciful characters (Rubin et al., 1983).

Dramatic play is used by young children to explore behavioral alternatives and options. It may serve as a rehearsal of roles they will assume at some point in their future (Roskos, 1990). Empathy—the ability to project oneself into another's role and approximate what that person feels, perceives, and says—is facilitated by dramatic play.

One of the most common scripts in dramatic play by young children has a simple domestic theme (Garvey, 1977). Young children enjoy playing out scenarios that duplicate home life. By experimenting with playing mother, father, grandmother, or grandfather, children can enhance their empathy skills and further develop their schemas for these roles.

Dramatic play is also a helpful diagnostic tool for therapists. In this context, it is called **play therapy**. Play provides a medium in which children can communicate more easily with professionals, because they lack sophisticated verbal communication skills. Feelings, fears, and fantasies are explored in play therapy and events are replicated from the past.

**Play therapy**

The use of play to assist a child with psychological, behavioral, or emotional problems.

**Rough-and-tumble play**

Physically active play.

Another predominant type of play in early childhood, especially among boys, is **rough-and-tumble play** (Humphreys & Smith, 1987). This kind of play involves much physical contact, such as pretend fighting, chasing, pushing, and wrestling. Some adults don't like to see this type of play among children because they equate it with aggressiveness and hostility. Actually, rough-and-tumble play requires more social competence than aggressiveness (Pellegrini, 1987) and it has some benefits. One is that it facilitates use of physical skills. Another is that it may be a variation of cooperative play, which requires negotiation between participants and continual redefinition of rules. Finally, it can teach children problem-solving skills.

Adults often fear that this type of play will escalate into real aggression. Usually, children understand that rough-and-tumble play is just fun. Those who find it hard to relate to others, however, may well see this kind of activity as true aggression rather than a form of fun with no harm intended to anyone (Coie & Kuperschmidt, 1983; Dodge & Frame, 1982).

## Family Influences

As mentioned in the introduction to this section, socialization is a process that begins in earnest during early childhood. Parents and significant others in a child's life take an active role in teaching these lessons. The lessons are not usually given by formal instruction. More often they are taught by **modeling**, by allowing a child to observe others' behavior, and by providing directions and interpretations.

Children are expected to adopt the rules, behavioral expectations, and boundaries established by their family. They are expected to learn the patterns by which their family system operates. Some psychologists call this kind of learning internalizing behavioral standards promoted by parents and other caregivers. When internalization is completed, a child has the information to judge any action as appropriate and acceptable or inappropriate and unacceptable. Parents must understand that transgression and mistakes are to be expected from young children as they are learning.

We live in a diverse society and different families promote different standards of behavior. Despite the diversity of families today, almost all families teach certain kinds of behaviors and values to children—among them prosocial behaviors, limiting aggression through self-control, delaying gratification, and coping with fears—topics all previously discussed in this chapter.

Divorce is quite prevalent in our society. Although divorce is difficult for all children, age plays a factor as to how the divorce will affect children. Preschoolers are often confused by the changes caused by their parents' divorce. It is difficult for children this age to understand why their father is no longer living with their family. Their reactions include general restlessness, sleep problems, increased aggression, fretfulness/anxiety, regressive behaviors (e.g., bed-wetting), and irritability (Hetherington, Cox & Cox, 1976;

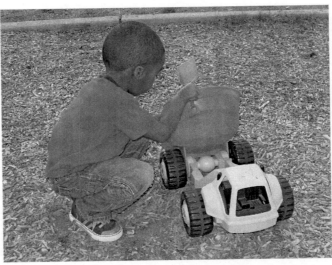

*A child learns the socialization process by observing the behavior of others. (iStock)*

**Modeling**

The process by which behavior is acquired and modified through observing and replicating behavior of others.

Parke & Buriel, 1998; Wallerstein & Kelly, 1975). We will discuss divorce in more detail in Chapter 5.

## *Parenting Strategies*

There are many factors that influence how someone behaves as a parent (Bigner, 1989; Parke & Buriel, 1998). Some factors come from past experiences, whereas others come from more contemporary sources. One of the strongest from the past is a social script for parenting behavior that is formed when we are growing up. This is usually unconscious until parenting is assumed in adulthood. Other factors also are thought to predispose one's future parenting behavior and include (1) cultural influences such as the social group of our family of origin, (2) personality patterns of ourselves and our parents, (3) attitudes about how to behave as a parent, and (4) the model of parenting behavior demonstrated by parents and others that are observed. Factors coming from currently experienced sources include (1) situational influences that occur in the present such as the time of day, the sex of a child, the sex of a parent, and so on; and (2) the goals that are established for childrearing. All of these influence parental behaviors that contribute to the nature of a child's character.

The adults in a family system have much to discuss in defining standards for their parenting behavior patterns. This serves to outline the acceptable patterns in a particular family system for parenting. The central mission is to reach agreement on the significant issues that regulate adults' behavior as parents of young children. For example, these may include (1) what kinds of behaviors are acceptable from young children, (2) what rules and limits should be established, (3) how these can be enforced, (4) what are the consequences of transgressions to rules, (5) what can and cannot be said to communicate with young children, (6) what kinds of equipment do children need to stimulate their development, (7) how can resources be allocated to provide for these, (8) what are acceptable behaviors from both adults and children in a variety of circumstances, (9) how much television should young children watch, or (10) should children be punished for misbehavior and in what ways?

Most mothers and fathers appear to hold similar goals for children (Chilman, 1980). These represent long-term aims that result directly from what parents want to accomplish in their child rearing efforts. Even more global goals are the desires voiced by many parents

| TABLE 4-1 | DIFFERENT PARENTING STYLES |
|-----------|---------------------------|

|        |      | STRUCTURE | |
|--------|------|-----------|---|
|        |      | **High**  | **Low** |
| **WARMTH** | **High** | Authoritative | Permissive |
|        | **Low**  | Authoritarian | Rejecting/neglecting (or uninvolved) |

that their children (1) have a happy and fulfilling life, (2) become a person who functions independently but gets along well with others, and (3) possess skills and competencies that allow effective functioning as an adult in society (Bigner, 1989).

The values, attitudes, and beliefs about goals of child rearing work in association to shape the type of child rearing style parents adopt. Four basic types of child rearing styles have been identified by Baumrind (1967, 1971, and 1991) that are briefly outlined here. It may be helpful to visualize these patterns as lying on a continuum for structure and a continuum for warmth (see Table 4-1 below). The table shows how different parenting styles are classified based upon the degree to which structure and warmth are evident. The parenting styles are described below.

It is helpful to remember that these are dynamic. They may be adapted in response to situations, age and sex of a child, and so on. It is with such adaptability that a family system maintains equilibrium and homeostasis in parenting patterns.

An adult who believes that parents should be strict with children most likely uses an **authoritarian style**. Adults who practice this approach place a high premium on gaining both immediate and long-range obedience. These parents value "keeping the child in his place … restricting his autonomy, and … assigning household responsibilities to inculcate respect for work" (Baumrind, 1966).

**Authoritarian style**

Parents that display discipline, but show little affection.

The focus of this parenting style is on controlling a child's behavior. Structure is high, whereas warmth is low. The adult decides what is appropriate child behavior, what rules are to be followed, and enforces consequences to transgressions. Obedience of children is valued highly and obtained in a variety of ways. Frequently, this is accomplished by using physical punishment (such as spanking) and other forceful methods. Little effort is expended by an authoritarian parent to explain the reasoning that underlies rules and regulations. A parent's typical response to a child's questioning of rules may be, "Because I said so." This illustrates the origin of the authoritarian label for this style. The adult is the sole authority in regulating a child's life.

Usually an authoritarian parent evaluates and shapes the behavior of a child according to an absolute standard of appropriate behavior. In many respects, this appears to be based on a perfectionistic notion about acceptable child behavior (Bradshaw, 1988; Miller, 1990). The authoritarian parent's word is law for a child. A parent's actions are always thought to be in the child's best interests.

*Authoritarian style of parenting is where the parent is the sole authority in regulating a child's life. (iStock)*

Parents who practice this style, like all others, firmly believe that their actions express their love and concern for their child. Their goal, like other parents, is to make sure that children are equipped with the abilities to succeed in life and function effectively as adults. This parenting style, however, is not believed to benefit children in the long-run as parents anticipate.

A classic review of the research on child rearing (Becker, 1964) evaluates the effects of various parenting behaviors on children. It was demonstrated that parental hostility and control, as observed in authoritarian styles, tended to disrupt conscience development. It encouraged hostility, aggressiveness, and resistance to authority in children. More recent research supports this initial research, finding that children with authoritarian parents are indeed aggressive, and that they frequently have low self-esteem and are unhappy (e.g., Silk, et al., 2003).

Currently, some observers suggest that overreliance on this style of parenting equates to psychological and emotional abandonment of children. This approach to raising children may plant the seeds for a variety of adulthood addictions in individuals who are raised in this manner. Manifestations of this parenting style in adulthood are seen in other ways. These range from difficulties in intimate relationships and work roles to emotional disturbances such as chronic depression and difficulty in making decisions (Forward, 1989; Friel & Friel, 1988; Garbarino, Guttman & Seeley, 1986; Whitfield, 1987).

**Permissive style**

Parents that are affectionate, but display little discipline.

Adults who approach their parenting behavior using a **permissive style** have different ideas about raising children. With this style, structure is low, whereas warmth is high. They believe that they should respond to their children as individuals. They encourage children's autonomy and help them to learn how to make their own decisions. Parents who adopt this style typically rely on reasoning and manipulation in working with children. They do not usually use overt expressions of parent power to work with children. For example, permissively-oriented parents are not interested in being viewed by a child as an authority figure. Instead, they prefer to be seen as a resource for the child to use in learning to make decisions.

This type of style does not pit adult against child in power struggles and conflicts. Instead, children are given much of the responsibility to learn from their own mistakes. Policies, rules, or limits to a child's behavior are determined by negotiation and consultation. The child's opinion has equal weight with that of the adult. Essentially, a permissively-oriented parent "allows the child to regulate his own activities as much as possible, avoids the exercise of control, and does not encourage him to obey externally defined standards" (Baumrind, 1966).

This style of parenting has received perhaps the same negative review by the public as authoritarian approaches. Children raised by permissive parents are seen as spoiled, unruly, and inconsiderate of others' needs. This approach was popular during the late 1940s through the early 1970s (Bigner, 1972a). It gained popularity as a means that was thought to counteract the negative aspects of authoritarianism. It was promoted by many experts in childrearing including Sigmund Freud, whose theory of personality development was widely adopted in the United States (Bigner, 1989). Research has found, however, that this form of parenting can lead to some problematic outcomes. Children of permissive parents are reported to lack self-control and to be impulsive (Dixon, 2003).

The **rejecting-neglecting parenting style** is the saddest of the parenting styles. With this parenting style, parents are low in both structure and warmth. Children with rejecting-neglecting parents are likely to be aggressive and suffer academic failure (Dixon, 2003).

The **authoritative parenting style** is a compromise between authoritarian and permissive approaches and is seen as the best parenting style for optimal developmental outcomes. With this parenting style, both structure and warmth are high. The authoritative-oriented style emphasizes ways to help children in becoming more autonomous as they grow older. Children are allowed a reasonable degree of latitude in their behavior but are not completely restricted by their parents' authority. When parents enforce limits, they typically resort to whatever lies within their grasp. They use a variety of methods to achieve control over their children's behavior. These may include reasoning, using overt power, or shaping desired behavior by using positive reinforcement.

Limits are used with children but they are labeled as reasonable in what is expected of children. Age of the child often is used in deciding the reasonableness of limits. Baumrind (1966) describes this type of parenting style as when the adult "encourages verbal give and take, sharing with a child the reasoning behind a policy, and soliciting his objections when he refuses to conform."

The benefits of having parents that use an authoritative parenting style are numerous (e.g., Amato & Fowler, 2002; Aunola, Stattin & Nurmi, 2000). For example, children with authoritative parents typically have high academic achievement. They also tend to be self-reliant and responsible.

## Learning to Be a Sibling

There is a cultural belief that the role and status of children within a family system should be separate from those of adults. This separation frequently is maintained by social power in the relationship between parents and children. Most families establish boundaries and patterns that maintain distance between children's and adults' worlds. A major family developmental task of young children is to learn the sibling roles of a brother or sister.

Being a brother or sister is an important relationship pattern in a family system. The significance of this relationship to individuals often lasts a lifetime (Goetting, 1986; Parke & Buriel, 1998). Positive sibling relations have been associated with enhanced cognitive, emotional, and social abilities in childhood (Bryant & Crockenberg, 1980; Dunn, Brown, Slomkowski, Telsa, & Youngblade, 1991; Howe & Ross, 1990; Milevsky, 2003; Smith, 1993). The significance of siblings in the lives of children can also be seen in studies assessing the negative influence siblings can have on each other. Younger siblings have been found to be at an elevated risk of drug use, risky sexual behavior, and delinquency when their older sibling was engaged in these activities (Duncan, Duncan, & Hops, 1996; East & Khoo, 2005; Pomery, Gibbons, Gerrard, Cleveland, Brody, & Wills, 2005; Snyder, Bank, & Burraston, 2005; Windle, 2000). More significantly, Rende, Slomkowski, Lloyd-

---

**Rejecting-neglecting parenting style**

Parents that display little affection or discipline.

**Authoritative parenting style**

Parents that display both affection and discipline.

*A hierarchy is established within a sibling relationship. This is usually determined by birth order. (iStock)*

Richardson, and Niaura (2005) found that the elevated risk for adolescent drug use due to sibling use was evident even when genetic relatedness was controlled.

Furthermore, this relationship may provide many opportunities for learning social skills not available through other means. Researchers also believe that what children learn within their sibling relationships generalizes to interactions with others outside their family system.

Children learn what it means to be a brother or sister through interactions and from instruction provided by parents. The emergence of this role between children creates another microenvironment within a family system. This microenvironment is analogous to other relationship patterns in a family system. Thus, by the end of this family stage, there are at least three distinct microenvironments within a family system. These are based on the relationship between (1) the adults as marriage partners, (2) each adult and each child (the parent-child relationship), and (3) each child and his or her sibling. Each microenvironment is distinct but an integral part of a family system. There are rules that govern the conduct of a sibling relationship, and consequences outline infractions.

**Birth order**

The order in which children are born in a family.

A hierarchy becomes established in sibling relationships based on who holds the greatest social power. This is usually determined by **birth order**, or whether a child is the first, second, or last-born child. Beginning at this stage, siblings establish social positions based on their order of birth in a family. Parents may contribute to this hierarchy by consciously or unconsciously treating children differently (Sutton-Smith & Rosenberg, 1970). For instance, the oldest child may be assigned more responsibilities than the youngest child.

Researchers have conducted many studies about birth order effects on children's personality development (Goetting, 1986). Researchers consistently find that distinctive personality traits are associated with each birth order position of children in a family system (e.g., Herrera et al. 2003; Sulloway, 2005; Sutton-Smith & Rosenberg, 1970). For example, first-borns are more achievement-oriented and show more responsible behavior traits than later-born children. Middle-born children are found to have lower self-esteem than other children. Last-born children are noted to have charming natures and more advanced social skills than other siblings.

Birth order, however, plays a different role in the relationship between siblings than in individual personality development. Children who have brothers or sisters learn how family relationships are based on social power (Bigner, 1974a,b; Koch, 1956). First-born preschoolers learn to use high-power tactics to achieve social goals with younger siblings. These tactics typically include bossing, making verbal threats, using physical force, and so on. Younger children are not completely at the mercy of an older sibling, however. These children learn to manipulate situations in their favor with other power tactics. These may include sulking, teasing, tattling, harassing, and using verbal or physical aggression. By observing their older sibling, young preschoolers learn how age operates as a factor in social power. Greater age (and implicitly greater experience) is recognized as giving people more social power in relationships.

This knowledge about social power also is used to learn the patterns and boundaries that regulate family sex-roles (Bigner, 1972b; Bigner & Jacobsen, 1980; Koch, 1956). An older sibling frequently serves as a model of behavior for younger siblings. Siblings attribute greater social power to brothers. Sisters are characterized as facilitating social interactions, whereas brothers are noted to be socially disruptive. Sex-role behaviors also are modeled by siblings for each other. Cross-sex and same-sex sibling arrangements facilitate learning and understanding of sex-appropriate behaviors by children.

Having an older sibling helps a preschooler acquire initial meanings and interpretations of family roles. This is seen in preschoolers' descriptions of a "good" or "bad" sibling (Bigner & Jacobsen, 1980). Second-born children use phrases that describe a "good" sibling in positive terms and a "bad" sibling in negative ones. For example, these children describe a "good" brother as someone who helps with chores, plays with the younger sibling, and does not tattle to parents. A "bad" brother is bossy, a pest, uncooperative, and a nuisance in play activities. They describe a "good" sister as nice, loving, and helpful. A "bad" sister destroys toys, talks too much, and doesn't clean up her messes.

Brothers and sisters, then, serve various social functions for individuals. These initial ideas may equip children with a social-psychological template. This serves as a guide for regulating a significant aspect of a family system in which the relationships between children are the principle focus. It also may guide interaction patterns with others from outside the family system (Parke & Buriel, 1998).

# THE OUTSIDE WORLD

## Friendship and Peers

During early childhood, peer interaction increases in frequency and becomes more multifaceted (Rubin, Bukowski & Parker, 1998). Play is the main domain in which peer interactions have been researched. In general, play during the preschool years provides young children with a venue in which to learn about social roles and rules. Peer relationships during the preschool years are also characterized by increased prosocial interactions and increased verbal exchanges.

Friendships also begin to emerge during the preschool years. There are developmental changes in how people perceive friendship. Early in childhood, friends are often referred to as momentary playmates (Selman, 1981). Although the title doesn't sound promising, preschool children do treat friends differently from nonfriends (Rubin, Buikowski & Parker, 1998). The focus of the friendship is upon physical objects or activities. Little thought is given to sharing thoughts or feelings. Additionally, children usually choose friends that are similar in physical appearance and behavioral tendencies. This stage in friendship perception is referred to as stage zero, or **momentary playmates**. In Chapter 5, we will learn about stages one through three in friendship perception development.

**Momentary playmates**

Temporary playmates, typically because they happen to be in the same physical location.

## *The Electronic World*

The National Research Council and Institute of Medicine (2000) states that "today's children spend more time with media (e.g., television, VCRs, CD players, game systems, computers, among others) than any generation before them" (p. 221). It is estimated that children between the ages of two and four watch an average of three to four hours of television everyday. Even more disturbing is that many parents use the television as an electronic babysitter, leaving young children to watch it alone.

Television provides a medium in which observational learning can occur (Ruble & Martin, 1998). Although some programming, such as *Sesame Street*, may help children learn pre-academic skills, other programming can expose children to harmful images and information. For example, many shows geared toward young children expose children to gender stereotypes. Additionally, children exposed to violence on television tend to behave more aggressively (Attar et al., 1994). Hence, television consumption, along with other media use, should be carefully monitored by caregivers.

## *Preschool*

The benefit of preschool is an area of research that has received a lot of attention lately. Would it be worth the cost to our taxpayers to fund public preschool? It appears that most research says yes, at least for children living in poverty. It appears that the potential benefits of preschool outweigh the costs (Barnett & Hustedt, 2003; Bracey & Stellar, 2003).

Preschool education is correlated with better school readiness for kindergarten, better reading and math skills, higher graduation rates from high school, higher college attendance, and lower delinquency rates (e.g., Bracey & Stellar, 2003). However, to achieve these outcomes a preschool must be of high quality. A high quality preschool should start at age three, have small class sizes and highly qualified teachers, have involved and supportive parents, and have a strong curriculum. Additionally, preschool programs should promote social skills, positive attitudes toward learning, emotional well-being, mental health, and physical health (Stipek, 2006).

*Pause and Process:*

1. Describe the four parenting styles discussed in this chapter and the developmental outcomes associated with each.

2. How can sibling relationships impact development?

# SUMMARY

1. Growth rates slow during early childhood compared to infancy, and increases in body length and weight are less dramatic. There are characteristic changes in body proportions and appearance. As body fat diminishes, the child's body becomes leaner in appearance.

2. The brain and central nervous system experience the fastest rate of growth among the major body systems in early childhood. The process of myelination of neural tissue accounts for the many advanced abilities observed in young children. Other significant changes include continued hemisphere specialization and hand preference.

3. Muscle and bone growth account for much of the weight gains observed in early childhood. The process of bone ossification continues during this time as well. The primary set of teeth has already erupted by the beginning of this period. Adequate dental care is necessary to maintain their health and that of the developing permanent teeth within the gums.

4. Refinements continue to occur in vision and hearing abilities in early childhood. Advances in motor skills are manifested in the high energy and activity levels of children this age. Refinements also occur in gross motor and fine motor skills.

These refinements are attributed to both maturation and environmental influences.

5. Maintaining adequate nutrition for preschool-age children is difficult because they often have a poor appetite and strange, nonnutritious, food preferences. Offering small portions of food and seeing that snacks are nutritious will help young children to eat healthy. Obesity is also on the rise in early childhood and parents should help instill good eating and exercise habits in their children.

6. Understanding of illness during early childhood is limited. During this phase of the life span, they are in the first two stages of understanding illness: phenomenism and contagion. Understanding of illness is dependent upon cognitive development.

7. Most potentially fatal illnesses among young children have been eliminated by immunization in the United States. Less serious illnesses are still common, especially upper respiratory diseases. Mental health is good for the majority of children. However, up to 20 percent of children suffer from a mental disorder. Accidents are the leading cause of death among young children. The majority of these deaths involve a motor vehicle or happen in the home. Ade-

quate supervision may prevent most of these injuries and deaths.

8. The preoperational stage of cognitive development is experienced during early childhood. Cognitive skills are focused on internalizing the environment by an increasing use of mental imagery. Thought during this time of the life span is characterized as inflexible, egocentric, and centered. Children make decisions based on appearances rather than on reality. Preschoolers also have difficulty understanding the principles of conservation and reversibility. Classification skills begin to emerge, as well as precausal thinking, in the later part of this stage. Young children are beginning to master learning skills and to develop strategies for using their memories.

9. Information-processing skills increase during early childhood. Memory strategies improve and early academic skills emerge. The degree to which children have metacognitive skills in early childhood is still open to debate. Vygotsky's social-historical theory and theory of mind are other cognitive theories discussed in the chapter.

10. Language serves several functions. One function is to facilitate social interactions. Conversational skills begin to improve during early childhood. Private speech is often observed in preschoolers, which will eventually become internalized as thought. Three communicative disorders that may emerge during early childhood are voice disorders, fluency disorders, and articulation disorders.

11. Socialization into appropriate behavioral patterns begins in earnest during early childhood. Parents and other caregivers initiate expectations for behavior, attitudes, and values they wish children to acquire to become effectively functioning future adults. Young children respond best to this instruction when they are reinforced positively in acquiring these behaviors and when adults demonstrate such behaviors for children to model and imitate. Most families in the United States expect children to learn to use prosocial behaviors in interactions such as sharing and being kind; to control their impulses to act aggressively; and to learn to cope with fears and anxieties. These behaviors assist the young child to become an effectively functioning member of the family and society.

12. Young children use play as a tool for learning many important socialization experiences. A developmental sequence is observed in the nature of play activities during early childhood. Play changes from unoccupied and solitary activities that dominate in infancy to associative and cooperative activities that involve more complex social interactions as children get older. Two other types of play are popular among young children: dramatic and rough-and-tumble play. Both involve refinements in social and mental abilities.

13. Parents evolve a parenting style when their oldest child enters this stage. Four styles are commonly found: authoritarian, permissive, rejecting-neglecting, and authoritative. The authoritative parenting style is associated with the best developmental outcomes in children. This style is high in both structure and warmth.

14. Young children may experience the family developmental task of learning to be a sibling. Sibling relationships help children learn social skills that may be transferred to future peer relations. Birth order may influence sibling behavior and personality development.

15. Young children may acquire either a healthy attitude of initiative (a feeling that promotes self-confidence and learning) or an unhealthy attitude of guilt (a feeling that inhibits self-growth), according to Erikson. Either of these attitudes may be promoted by significant others in the family because they are the ones who teach young children about the appropriateness or inappropriateness of their behavior.

# SELF-QUIZ

1. What factors impact height and weight increases during early childhood?
2. Describe bone growth during early childhood.
3. What is myelination and why is it important?
4. Define bilateral coordination.
5. Describe eating habits during the preschool years.
6. How prevalent is obesity in early childhood?
7. What are the potential consequences of obesity?
8. What causes obesity and how can we prevent it?
9. What is pediatric psychology?
10. Explain what ADHD is and how a child with the disorder behaves.
11. What stage of Piaget's stages of cognitive development are children in during early childhood?
12. What is egocentrism? How does it limit a child's thinking?
13. What is conservation?
14. Define transductive reasoning and provide an original example.
15. What two memory strategies are prevalent during early childhood?
16. Compare and contrast the overlapping and consecutive math strategies.
17. Why is a solid foundation in phonics important for reading ability?
18. Define theory of mind in your own words.
19. What are some of the functions of language?
20. What makes someone a good conversationalist?
21. What is the difference between sympathy and empathy?
22. Define aggression.
23. Describe early childhood fears.
24. Why is it important for children to learn to delay gratification?
25. What are some positive outcomes associated with secure attachment to parents?
26. What is gender identity?
27. Why is play important?
28. Describe each of Parten's types of play.
29. Explain what factors influence parenting strategies.
30. Describe psychosocial development during early childhood.

# TERMS AND CONCEPTS

# CHAPTER 5

# Middle Childhood

(iStock)

## OUTLINE

### PHYSICAL DEVELOPMENT DURING MIDDLE CHILDHOOD

- Physical growth
- Motor development
- Health issues

### COGNITIVE DEVELOPMENT DURING MIDDLE CHILDHOOD

- Piaget's theory and the concrete operational stage
- Information-processing during middle childhood
- Language development during middle childhood

### SOCIOEMOTIONAL DEVELOPMENT DURING MIDDLE CHILDHOOD

- Psychosocial development
- Emotional development
- Self and others

195

**The tempo of developmental changes slows in the period of middle childhood.** This stage begins at age six and continues through an individual's twelfth birthday. Motor development becomes more refined and sports become an increasing part of many children's lives during middle childhood. Significant changes occur in cognitive processes and socioemotional skills during this period.

# PHYSICAL DEVELOPMENT DURING MIDDLE CHILDHOOD

### LEARNING OBJECTIVES:

1. *Describe physical growth during middle childhood*
2. *Explain motor skill development during middle childhood*
3. *Awareness of the unique health issues faced in middle childhood*

# PHYSICAL GROWTH

## Patterns of Growth

Middle childhood is a quiet period for physical growth and changes. The decline in growth rates noted in early childhood becomes even more evident. Growth in middle childhood is often considered the least dramatic and slowest of any stage in the life span.

An average six-year-old weighs about forty-five pounds and is about forty-five inches tall (WHO, 2006). At age ten, this child will weigh about sixty-nine pounds and stand about fifty-four inches tall. There is one exception to this general trend: the growth spurt that occurs about two years before the initiation of puberty. For many children, this prepubertal, or preadolescent, growth spurt takes place between the ages of ten and twelve (Williams & Stith, 1980). Children grow taller and heavier very quickly in middle childhood compared to earlier.

Girls and boys are about the same height during most of middle childhood though girls begin to weigh more than boys at about age nine. Because girls begin puberty earlier than boys, the **prepubertal growth spurt** also begins earlier for them. Thus girls are usually both taller and heavier than boys for about two years toward the end of middle childhood (Tanner, 1978, 1990).

**Prepubertal growth spurt**

A rapid increase in height and weight preceding puberty (at about age 10 to 12).

## Other Body Changes

There is a genetic tendency for females to have a greater proportion of body fat to muscle than males. This difference becomes more noticeable during the latter part of middle childhood. In the first half of this stage, however, there are a few differences in the body contour and proportions of boys and girls.

Body configuration in middle childhood is distinguished by the loss of the prominent "pot belly" of early childhood. There is a general slimming of the body figure in both boys and girls during this time, though toward the end of this stage, girls start to develop a more rounded figure. This comes from the growth of adipose and muscle tissue associated with their approaching puberty.

There are great individual differences in height, weight, and body shape during this time. The differences are so great, in fact, that it is misleading to think in terms of averages for children this age. These physical differences create problems when adults equate them with social or emotional maturity. For example, a child who is much taller and heavier than others the same age might be expected by adults to also act much older (Ames, 1986; Tanner, 1990). This is an example of adult thinking based on appearances instead of reality.

Body configuration and physical changes strongly affect a child's acceptance by peers. School-age children typically select their friends on the bases of external appearance and physical competence (Hartup, 1983; Rubin, Bukowski & Parker, 1998; Williams & Stith, 1980). For example, boys often use such criteria as body size and shape, muscular strength, and athletic ability in choosing their friends. Girls use similar criteria, often, choosing those who are developmentally mature for their age as leaders of groups (Williams & Stith, 1980).

## Bone Development

Bone growth and development in middle childhood involve changes in size and composition (Tanner, 1990; Williams & Stith, 1980). These changes are slow in comparison with the rate experienced in infancy and early childhood. Growth slows even more at the end of middle childhood because of the initiation of puberty.

Bones grow at their tips or ends, called epiphyses. This is the type of growth that produces changes in length. They also grow at their outermost edge, known as the perisoteum. This type of growth produces changes in width. As children advance from infancy

*The body configuration changes in middle childhood. A general slimming of the body is seen in both boys and girls, and toward the end of this stage girls start to develop a rounded figure. (iStock)*

through adolescence, the soft cartilage at the epiphyses is replaced by hard bone tissue in a process called ossification.

As sex hormone levels increase to prepare the body for puberty, bone development slows. It eventually halts, after the completion of puberty in adolescence. This process occurs at different rates in the various bone groups. For example, most of the bone development of the extremities occurs during the latter part of middle childhood and early adolescence. This development is observed earlier in girls than in boys, in keeping with the earlier ages at which girls begin puberty.

Bone changes during middle childhood are also related to nutrition. Inadequate nutrition delays the ossification process and can even result in bone malformations. Certain physical activities also endanger bone development. For example, ballet dancing to excess and wearing poor-fitting shoes contribute to problems with foot bones.

## Muscle Development

A school-age child's strength and greater endurance reflect changes in muscle development. Children this age are able to participate in more strenuous activities for longer periods than younger children. Because they usually enjoy this kind of physical activity, they become more physically fit (Krogman, 1980).

Greater physical activity, then, is associated with advances in muscle development during middle childhood. However, if the muscles of children this age are overused, there may be damage (Williams & Stith, 1980). A condition known as "Little League elbow," for example, can occur from the overuse of the connective tissues involved in throwing objects. Similarly, it is common for children this age to complain of muscular aches and pains around the joints because tendons are stretching to attach muscles to bones.

Changes are observed in the degree and types of physical activity children pursue during this period. The typical six-year-old has a high energy level that translates into much random activity. Children this age apparently move about for the sheer enjoyment of moving. By age twelve, there is less random movement and more control over the body. These and other social and mental changes permit more graceful and coordinated movements (Williams & Stith, 1980).

Physical fitness has many benefits for school-age children. It provides opportunities for social experiences with peers (Williams & Stith, 1980). It stimulates bone growth and ossification (Bailey, 1977). It also seems to improve academic performance (Bailey, 1977) and contributes to a healthy self-concept (Ferguson et al., 1989).

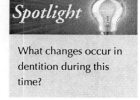

**Spotlight**

What changes occur in dentition during this time?

## Teeth

**Dentition**

The shedding of one set of teeth and the eruption of another.

**Dentition** is one of the most apparent physical changes of middle childhood. This is the process of shedding existing teeth and erupting new ones. The sixteen primary, or deciduous, teeth that erupted during infancy are lost during the school-age years and twenty-eight permanent teeth erupt to replace them. The first permanent teeth erupt around age

## Bilateral coordination

The cooperative, integrated use of both sides of the body in performing motor acts.

## Strength

The ability to exert force.

## Flexibility

The freedom to bend or move the body in various directions.

six or seven. These are the molars. They do not replace deciduous teeth (there are no molars in the deciduous set), but signal that these are about to be shed. Except for the sets of third molars, or "wisdom teeth", which appear in adolescence or early adulthood, a child should have a complete set of permanent teeth by the end of middle childhood.

Many parents use the folklore of the Tooth Fairy to help children cope with the fears and anxieties of losing teeth. This imaginary figure visits children while they sleep. She collects the lost tooth, which has been placed underneath a pillow, and replaces it with some reward, such as a small amount of money or a special treat. Losing teeth in the first half of middle childhood is often a status symbol for children. It communicates their more mature stature to friends and family. The fanfare associated with losing teeth is diminished by the end of this stage. It is looked upon more as a painful nuisance than a status symbol.

*Pause and Process:*

1. What is the prepubertal growth spurt?

2. How do bones and muscles develop during middle childhood?

# MOTOR DEVELOPMENT

## Impulsion

The rate at which body movement begins from a stationary position.

## Speed

The rate of movement once the body is in action.

## Precision

The dexterity and accuracy of movements.

## Coordination

The ability to use various muscle groups together to accomplish specific actions.

## Balance

The ability to maintain equilibrium and stability.

Muscular ability and coordination improve considerably during middle childhood. Although physical changes slow down, these changes are important because they lead to more advanced motor skills. School-age children become more adept at activities requiring **bilateral coordination**. This is the ability to use sets of muscles on both sides of the body to perform complex physical acts. Bilateral coordination is observed especially in activities that involve large muscle groups such as those in the arms, legs, and back. The increasing maturation of these muscle groups help children to function more efficiently. The complex skills required for bike riding, for example, are now more easily accomplished.

Changes in motor skills during middle childhood are characterized by steady improvements in coordination and performance. Improvements are particularly noticeable in the following motor skills (Cratty, 1986; Smoll &Schutz, 1990; Williams & Stith, 1980): (1) **strength**, or the ability to exert force, with boys showing greater gripping ability than girls; (2) **flexibility**, or the freedom to bend or move the body in various directions, with girls showing greater flexibility than boys at the trunk, wrists, and legs; (3) **impulsion**, or the rate at which body movement begins from a stationary position, with all school-age children showing steady improvements in reaction time; (4) **speed**, or the rate of movement once the body is in action, with boys improving at the rate of one foot per second faster than girls each year during this stage; (5) **precision**, or dexterity and accuracy of movements, with girls showing greater advances than boys; (6) **coordination**, or the ability to use various muscle groups together to accomplish specific actions (this factor is associated with precision to produce advances in impulsion); (7) **balance**, or the

*Muscular ability and coordination improves during this stage. Riding a bike is now more easily accomplished. (iStock)*

**Rhythm**

Regular body movements.

**Competence**

An individual's skills, abilities, and proficiency within a specific domain, such as school, relationships, or sports.

**Confidence**

Having certainty in one's ability.

**Connections**

An individual's relationships with others and feelings as though one belongs.

**Character**

Having a moral compass and integrity.

**Caring**

Having empathy and concern for others.

ability to maintain equilibrium and stability in performing the kind of motor acts typical at this stage (e.g., skating), with girls showing improvements earlier than boys; (8) **rhythm**, or regular body movements, with girls exceeding boys throughout this stage, especially in rhythmic movements involving the feet (e.g., dancing).

It is easy to observe common motor skills in children. Common motor skills that involve the upper body region include printing and writing, playing musical instruments, performing household chores, and using tools. Common motor skills that involve the lower body region include running, skipping, and jumping. Common motor skills that involve the entire body include skating, certain sports, swimming, and bicycle riding. The particular motor abilities and skills that children are expected to acquire in middle childhood generally involve gross- and fine-motor skills that are more complex than those of early childhood.

## Sports

A sport can be described as "structured activities with certain rules of engagement" (Theokas, 2009). Although individual sports vary in nature, most provide an opportunity to learn both skills specific to that sport, as well as life skills that can be applied to everyday life (Baron, 2007). Hence, it is widely thought that sport participation can promote healthy development in children and adolescents.

Optimal development can be conceptualized within five categories referred to as the five Cs: **competence, confidence, connections, character,** and **caring** (Lerner et al., 2005; Lerner, Fisher & Weinberg, 2000; Linver, Roth & Brooks-Gunn, 2009). Competence can be described as an individual's skills, abilities, and proficiency within a specific domain, such as school, relationships, or sports. Confidence can be described as having certainty in one's ability. Connections involve an individual's relationships with others and feeling as though one belongs. Character can be thought of as having a moral compass and integrity. Caring can be conceptualized as having empathy and concern for others. Sports can help develop these five domains of healthy development through skill development, adult mentorship, modeling of good sportsmanship, and belonging to a team.

Although sport participation has been associated with positive developmental outcomes, there is also some research that shows that there can be a negative side to sport participation (Gaudreau, Amiot & Vallerand, 2009; Scanlan, 1984; Scanlan, Babkes & Scanlan, 2005). Parents and coaches can place children under extreme stress to perform well. Additionally, injuries, burnout, and delinquency can sometimes plague sport participants.

Despite these potential negative outcomes, sport participation is capable of promoting healthy development if the program is of good quality, the parents and coach are supportive, the coach structures the activity well and provides appropriate praise and direction, and the individual is motivated (Danish, Taylor & Faxio, 2003; Gano-Overway et al., 2009). Further, structured activities besides sports, such as school clubs or religious groups, can offer the same psychological benefits as sport participation. One recent study found that children and adolescents who participated in sports along with other activities achieve better outcomes than children and adolescents who participated only in sports (Linver, Roth & Brooks-Gunn, 2009). Hence, engaging in a broad range of activities appears to offer the best context for development.

*Pause and Process:*

1. What improvements in motor development are seen during middle childhood?

2. What are the five Cs to healthy development and how are they influenced by sport participation?

# HEALTH ISSUES

## Nutritional Needs

Nutrition is important to physical well-being in middle childhood. Most of the physical changes we have described so far are affected by nutrition. Children's eating habits and appetites improve as they take up the more demanding physical activities of middle childhood. As their appetites sharpen, their food intake increases. Although most children maintain a healthy weight, obesity is increasing in school-age children (CDC, 2009). Currently, 17 percent of school-age children are considered obese.

Television advertising affects school-age children's nutrition because children pressure parents to buy the products they see on television (Condry, Bence & Scheibe, 1988; Taras et al., 1989). Children this age watch a lot of television. Advertisers design commercials that appeal to children and influence food choices. The food products designed to appeal to children are usually high in sugar, fat, and salt content. Many are snacks that children

*Children tend to watch a lot of television in middle childhood, and advertisers seem to target this age group which influences their food choices. (iStock)*

will eat while watching television. Few offer much true nutrition. Once again, it is imperative for parents to educate their children about proper nutrition and exercise, and to limit the couch time.

## Illness, Disorders, and Other Concerns

In Chapter 4, we learned about Bibace and Walsh's (1979, 1980, and 1981) first two stages for understanding illness: phenomenism and contagion. During middle childhood, stages three and four predominate children's thinking. Stage three is called contamination. Contamination can be described as understanding illness as "caused by people, objects, or actions that are external to the child, and it is transmitted by physical contact or harmful action" (Bearison, 1998, p. 679). Although children now have some understanding that their behavior can directly influence whether they get ill or not, they still lack an understanding of the role of bacteria or viruses.

Stage four is called internalization. With internalization thinking, children understand that actions such as breathing in a virus or ingesting food with salmonella can lead to illness. It goes a step beyond contamination thinking because the cause of the illness is seen as internalized inside one's body (Bearison, 1998).

Children typically progress through these two stages during the middle childhood years. Around 60 percent of children display contamination thinking at the age of seven (Bearison, 1998). By the age of eleven, approximately 50 percent of children display internalization thinking. We will discuss the final two stages of understanding illness in Chapter 6.

## Physical Illness During Middle Childhood

School-age children generally enjoy better health than preschoolers. Most of the communicable diseases they get are not serious, with the common cold and upper respiratory conditions being most common (Avery, 1989; Starfield et al., 1984). These diseases are spread by contact with other children at school. Immunizations protect most school-age children against the more serious infectious diseases.

Children can also get some infectious diseases because they have not been immunized against them or because no effective vaccine is available. They can also get other minor disorders that affect well-being and school attendance, such as allergies, asthma, or lice.

Accidents are of serious concern during the school-age years, and accidents are the leading cause of death for this age group (Federal Interagency Forum on Child and Family Statistics, 2008; Health United States, 2008). Boys have far more accidents than girls at each stage of development in childhood and adolescence. Accidents can be prevented by adequate supervision and safety restrictions on activities. School-age children are more capable of self-direction than preschoolers, but their judgment is far from adultlike. They still need some supervision.

## *Mental Health During Middle Childhood*

As discussed in Chapter 4, mental health problems plague one in every five children and adolescents (SAMHSA, 2003). Further, one in every ten children suffers from a serious emotional disturbance. Table 5-1 describes some of the mental disorders experienced during childhood (National Institutes of Health, 1997, 1999; SAMHSA, 2003; U.S. Department of Health and Human Services, 1999).

**Oppositional defiant disorder** (ODD) is a disorder that may lead to conduct disorder if left untreated (AACAP, 1999). ODD is a pattern of behavior in which a child is uncooperative and hostile with authority figures. This behavior is so extreme that it interferes with the child's ability to function in his or her daily life. It is estimated that up to 15 percent of all school-age children struggle with ODD. Its cause is unknown, although it is

**Oppositional defiant disorder**

A mental disorder characterized by a pattern of disobedience, hostility, and deviant behavior.

| TABLE 5-1 | DISORDERS EXPERIENCED DURING CHILDHOOD | |
|---|---|---|
| **DISORDER** | **PREVALENCE** | **DESCRIPTION** |
| Anxiety disorders | 13 out of every 100 children & adolescents | Includes phobias, generalized anxiety disorder, obsessive-compulsive disorder, and post-traumatic stress disorder |
| Severe depression | 2 out of every 100 children | Includes negative emotions and thoughts, lack of motivation, and a general sense of ill-being |
| Attention deficit/ hyperactivity disorder | 5 out of every 100 children | Includes an inability to sit still, impulsivity, and distractibility |
| Schizophrenia | 5 out of every 1,000 children | Includes delusions, hallucinations, and inappropriate emotions |
| Conduct disorder | Estimates range from 1 to 4 out of every 100 children and adolescents | Externalizing behavior including verbal assaults, physical aggression, impulsivity, and destructiveness |

speculated that both biological and environmental factors influence its onset. ODD is often co-morbid with other mental disorders, such as ADHD, learning disabilities, anxiety disorders, and mood disorders. ODD is often treated with therapy and parent training. Most children show improvement when parents learn and utilize positive parenting techniques.

*ODD may lead to conduct disorder. (iStock)*

### *Promoting Wellness*

It is important to continue to monitor children during middle childhood. Many accidents and injuries can be prevented by adult supervision. Additionally, proper nutrition and exercise can promote wellness and prevent obesity. Regular doctor and dental exams can further promote wellness.

*Pause and Process:*

1. How do children understand illness during middle childhood?

2. What is oppositional defiant disorder and how can it be treated?

# COGNITIVE DEVELOPMENT DURING MIDDLE CHILDHOOD

**Concrete operations**

The stage of cognitive development experienced in middle childhood in which thought becomes more logical and based on immediate physical realities and mental imagery abilities become more refined.

### *LEARNING OBJECTIVES:*

1. *Characterize the concrete operational stage of cognitive development*
2. *Describe information-processing during middle childhood*
3. *Explain language development during middle childhood*

Although physical changes slow down during middle childhood, cognitive and social changes quicken. The cognitive changes are as significant as the social changes experienced in middle childhood. A new stage of thinking emerges as children experience the formal education process. Piaget (1967) refers to this as the period of **concrete operations**. They now base decisions more on fact and logic as they learn to reason. Refinements of mental abilities allow for more advanced functioning. Information-processing skills and language skills also continue to develop during middle childhood.

# PIAGET'S COGNITIVE DEVELOPMENTAL THEORY AND THE CONCRETE OPERATIONAL STAGE

**5-to-7 shift**

A transition period in cognitive develop-ment between the pre-operational and concrete operations stages; thinking is based more on intu-ition than logic.

School-age children become more sophisticated in their thought processes. Their advanced cognition is obvious when their ways of thinking are contrasted with those of preschoolers. The trend is toward greater use of logic and reasoning based on advanced information-processing skills (Miller, 1986).

Before they enter the stage of cognition that follows preoperational thought, children experience what Piaget (1967) termed the **5-to-7 shift**. This is a transition to what he called prelogical thought. Between five and seven years of age, children use intuition to guess the answers to problems. They do not fully understand the reasoning process behind a solution.

At about age seven or eight, children enter the stage of cognition known as concrete operations. Concrete means children's understanding of their environment is limited to the present and to immediate physical realities. Because of these thought limitations, school-age children have problems with the concepts of past and future. Abstract hypo-thetical problems are difficult for them to understand and solve.

One of the major cognitive accomplishments in middle childhood is the increasing ability to use mental imagery to solve problems. As they acquire this ability, school-age children begin to perform complex operations. These include basic mathematical opera-tions, such as addition, subtraction, multiplication, and division, and classification and grouping. Declining egocentrism throughout this period aids cognitive growth. These advances in cognition are outlined here.

# CHARACTERISTICS OF CONCRETE OPERATIONAL THOUGHT

## *Classification*

**Decentering**

The cognitive ability that allows a school-age child to attend to more than one aspect simultaneously in per-forming classification operations.

An early aspect of a school-age child's application of operations is the ability to classify objects and events. Children become increasingly adept at employing a mental process known as **decentering**, perhaps because the egocentrism so noticeable in early childhood is weakening (Harter, 1983). Decentering allows a child to attend to more than one detail of an object or event simultaneously. It shows a flexible approach to reasoning.

Preschoolers have difficulty with classification problems because they center on only one attribute of an object or event at a time. They usually sort objects according to their color. School-age children are able to apply more specific classification schemes to sorting tasks. For example, they recognize that trucks have some of the same attributes as other gasoline-powered vehicles. But they also know that trucks have special features that allow them to perform certain functions other gasoline-powered vehicles cannot do. They can easily distinguish a cow from other four legged animals with tails. They now may group animals according to whether they provide milk or meat. This ability to decenter—to handle several aspects of something simultaneously—allows school-age children to lead more complex mental lives.

Children this age come to enjoy classification problems. They form collections of objects ranging from stamps and coins to bottle caps, mugs, dolls, rocks, seashells, and sport cards. Initially, collections are general and may appear to be worthless junk. A six-year-old is prone to collect anything and everything. However, collections become more specialized and valuable as children's mental operations grow more sophisticated.

## Class Inclusion

**Class inclusion**

A cognitive ability of middle childhood that allows a child to consider the whole as well as its parts in classification operations.

An additional refinement in classification problem solving during middle childhood is known as **class inclusion**. This is the ability to consider simultaneously the whole as well as the parts in grouping objects (Piaget, 1952a). Preschool children cannot do this. They become confused if they are asked, for example, to separate out all the brown wooden beads from an assortment—an assignment school-age children can handle with ease. Preschoolers cannot recognize larger classes of objects such as wooden in this example. They cannot understand that a bead can have both color and texture attributes and be grouped accordingly.

## Reversibility

**Reversibility**

The cognitive ability of school-age children to understand that certain operations can occur in their reverse order (e.g., subtraction is the reverse of addition).

Grasping the concept of **reversibility** allows a child to understand classification operations like class inclusion problems and subtraction. School-age children are able to reverse several classification schemes to sort objects by larger, more inclusive classes. They comprehend that subtraction is the reverse of addition. Their ability to decenter enables them to understand other phenomena—for example, that the whole can be divided into parts and reconstructed into a whole again. Children this age can see how sunlight can be split into its component colors by a prism and then restored to sunlight.

## Conservation

**Horizontal decalage**

Unevenness in applying an understanding of conservation problems across different contexts.

In contrast to preschoolers, school-age children understand the idea of conservation (Piaget & Inhelder, 1969). However, they apply it unevenly in the early part of this stage. This unevenness of application is known as **horizontal decalage** (Piaget, 1952b). For example, a school-age child may understand conservation of volume but find conservation of number confusing. By the end of middle childhood, most children have resolved the horizontal decalage difficulty.

## Seriation

**Seriation**

A cognitive ability that allows objects to be scaled according to various dimensions (e.g., large to small).

**Seriation** is an extension of classification problems that school-age children easily accomplish (Wadsworth, 1971, 2004). This is the ability to scale objects according to various dimensions, such as height or weight. It requires an understanding of the concepts of greater than (>) and less than (<). For example, school-age children can easily solve this problem:

Doll A is taller than (>) Doll B; Doll B is taller than (>) Doll C. Is Doll A taller than (>) or shorter than (<) Doll C?

## Understanding Time

Time is an important concept in our culture. Americans' lives tend to be oriented around schedules. Therefore, knowing how to tell time and being familiar with other concepts involving time (days of the week, months of the year) are important skills (Taylor, 1989). Middle-class children have an advantage over poorer children here because clocks are important equipment in middle-class homes. Children from poorer families often have a more difficult time adjusting to a school schedule because a strong sense of time is not emphasized in their households.

Preschoolers are poor judges of time, especially of the duration between events (Levin, 1982; Piaget 1969). Judgment of time spans and knowledge of calendar events improve in middle childhood (Levin, Wilkening & Dembo, 1984). School-age children have a much better grasp of the idea of the future. They can state accurately what day will occur three days from now, for example (Friedman, 1986). However, the ability to work backward in time and an accurate understanding of the concept of past time are not acquired until late adolescence for most individuals.

*Understanding the concept of time is an important skill to learn. (iStock)*

## Cognitive Style

School-age children evolve a cognitive style that is distinct from that of preschoolers. As we have said, this style is less bound by the egocentrism that leads preschoolers to judge by appearances rather than reality. This is a major accomplishment in middle childhood that leads to higher-level mental functioning.

School-age children use elementary logic to infer reality from situations. This is demonstrated by their ability to solve some types of conservation problems. This mental accomplishment permits them to function effectively in the classroom.

The cognition of school-age children is still limited, however. Just as thinking in early childhood was bound by egocentrism, thinking in middle childhood is bound by cognitive distortions in reasoning. School-age children make many errors in logic as they attempt to understand how their world functions, why people act as they do, and so on. The all-or-nothing type of reasoning they use is called **cognitive conceit** (Elkind, 1976). It limits their understanding of the complexities of human behavior.

**Cognitive conceit**

A characteristic of thought in middle childhood in which individuals perceive situations and people in black-and-white, all-or-nothing.

Problems of social cognition illustrate this limitation. School-age children eventually observe a teacher making a mistake. Because of cognitive conceit, they incorrectly conclude that the teacher cannot be trusted to provide correct information. If a teacher is not always right, they think, she must often be wrong. Similarly, a child may reason that because she can give the correct answers on several issues, she is an authority on all issues. This is a type of cognitive distortion that may continue throughout the life span, or it may become resolved at a later life-stage (Burns, 1989).

*Pause and Process:*

1. How is thinking in the concrete operational stage different from thinking in the preoperational stage?

2. Why may the development of reversibility and seriation be important for academic success during middle childhood?

# INFORMATION PROCESSING IN MIDDLE CHILDHOOD

School-age children have many learning experiences, especially in the school system. Individuals are expected to acquire the basic skills our society considers essential for effective functioning during middle childhood. They are also expected to absorb much information about the world of people and things.

Some developmental researchers study the ways that children learn (Bransford, Brown & Cocking, 2000; Brown et al., 1983). This involves trying to understand how a child's mind perceives and processes information from the external world. These researchers have amended Piagetian and learning theory according to what is known about how computers process and logically handle information. However, information-processing researchers emphasize that a human brain is far more complex and sophisticated than any existing computer. Attention, memory, and problem solving are three areas addressed by information-processing research that will be discussed below. However, general developments in information processing seen in middle childhood include better strategies for problem solving or academic skills, increased capacity in working memory, faster information processing, more information processed automatically, and greater control of thinking (referred to as executive functioning in many research articles).

## *Attention*

Compared to preschoolers, school-age children have a better understanding of attention (Flavell & Miller, 1998). They understand that attention is selective and requires processing. They are also able to distinguish between attention and comprehension.

Beyond understanding attention, school-age children possess better attention skills. It is difficult to process information and store it in memory without paying adequate attention. Young children have short attention spans, partly because they are easily distracted (Kaplan, 1990). School-age children show considerable improvement in this area (Flavell, 1985; Flavell & Miller, 1998). Their greater ability to differentiate their attention—that is, to determine the relevance of something—comes partially from instruction by parents and teachers (Small, 1990) and partially from brain development, including myelination.

To perform learning activities, school-age children show improvements in another important cognitive skill: **selective attention** (Enns & Girgus, 1985; Maccoby & Hagen, 1965). This involves tuning out distracting stimulations when performing a particular task. For example, second-grade children find it hard to concentrate on a task while music is playing (Higgins & Turnure, 1984). Sixth-grade children are not so bothered by music in performing the same task. Adolescents may be able to handle even more complex distractions.

## *Memory*

The use of memory to process information has been intensively studied among children. Memory is critical to cognition. Recall allows individuals to compare information newly received with information gained from past experiences.

Researchers know that storage of information in the brain's memory occurs in three phases. First, information is temporarily stored in the **sensory register** (or sensory memory) as it is received from the external world (Hoving et al., 1978; Siegler, 1998). This storage is only for a very brief time, often for less than a second. This form of memory functions at adult levels by the age of five. Second, information is passed into **short-term memory** storage. It remains here for about one minute. It may then be processed into **long-term memory**, where it may remain indefinitely.

It is well recognized that memory in general improves significantly through middle childhood (Siegler, 1998; Williams & Stith, 1980). Memory improvement probably occurs for several reasons, including improvements in attention span, brain development, maturation, and strategies for processing information (Siegler, 1998; Wingfield & Byrnes,

**Selective attention**

A cognitive ability to tune out distracting stimulation while performing a task.

**Sensory register**

The first memory storage location where sensory information is stored in the brain before becoming short- or long-term memory.

**Short-term memory**

An initial memory storage location in the brain where information remains for about one minute before being erased or placed into long-term memory; recall of information, events, and so on that are relatively recent.

**Long-term memory**

The final memory location in the brain where information is stored indefinitely; recall of events in the distant past.

1981). In any case, it is known that children discover that verbal strategies assist them to process information into memory (Flavell, Beach & Chinsky, 1966). Through trial-and-error, they find some strategies work better than others (Justice, 1985).

School-age children typically use repetition and rehearsal to place information into memory (Fabricius & Wellman, 1983). They also use chunking, or grouping into one category items that share some attribute. For example, a long list of American presidents may be remembered by grouping all whose last names begin with B, M, and S. Various other mnemonic devices are used by school-age children to help in memory storage. Learning to spell words in English is a challenge. There are many tried-and-true rules to negotiate the spelling irregularities of English. For example, children find this rhyme very helpful for spelling certain words: "i before e except after c, or when sounding like a as in neighbor and weigh."

## Scripts

Researchers have discovered that one reason school-age children become better at memory retrieval is because of improvements they experience in memory organization. One of the more notable organization methods is to develop **scripts**.

**Scripts**

An organized series of acts committed to memory (e.g., getting dressed, brushing the teeth).

A script is formed out of a series of things that occur repeatedly. Frequently, these are routine events in one's daily life. For example, most people develop a repetitious way for brushing their teeth. Instead of intentionally selecting each step in the process every day, they form a "tooth-brushing script" and use it almost automatically. The steps in the process become unconscious—stored in long-term memory for repeated recall (Nelson & Gruendel, 1981; Slackman & Nelson, 1984).

Many scripts are developed during middle childhood because of children's improved memory and more extensive experiences. These range from the mundane, such as "getting

*Scripts help children with memory retrieval. An example is a "getting dressed script". (iStock)*

dressed scripts," to those that have social significance, such as "parenting scripts" and "spouse scripts." The latter scripts are formed through observation of adults in a family system and are not initiated by an individual until needed later in life. Because all scripts are based on learning, they may be modified and changed in any way at any point in the life span. Before changes can be made, however, a script must be dredged up from the unconscious (Harris & Harris, 1985; Hendrix, 1988; James & Jongeward, 1971).

## Metacognition and Metamemory

**Metacognition**

The ability to be aware of and understand the changes occurring in one's own cognitive processes.

**Metamemory**

An awareness of the extent of one's memory.

**Metacognition** is the awareness of the extent of one's knowledge. In middle childhood, many individuals improve in metamemory as well as metacognition. **Metamemory** is the awareness of the extent of what is in one's memory. The degree to which children can comprehend their particular capacity of knowledge and memory has important implications for their academic performance (Holt, 1964; National Research Council, 2000).

School-age children who have high levels of metacognition and metamemory may express more misunderstanding about concepts than others. This is because they are more aware of the extent of their knowledge than children who have lower levels of such awareness. Because they know what information they lack, they understand how to go about getting that information. These children are better students than others. Researchers are discovering ways to help school-age children develop better metacognition and metamemory skills (Cross & Paris, 1988).

## Intelligence

**Multiple intelligences**

A theory in which there are various domains or abilities in which a person can be intelligent.

**Linguistic intelligence**

Involves the mental abilities in the semantics, syntax, and overall expression of language.

**Logical-mathematical intelligence**

Involves mental abilities in pattern recognition, relationships, reasoning, and mathematical operations.

Traditionally, intelligence is defined as "the ability to solve problems and to adapt and learn from experiences" (Santrock, 2008, p. 312). In this traditionalist view, intelligence is conceptualized as a general mental ability. However, not all psychologists or developmentalists conceptualize intelligence in the traditional way. Some view intelligence occurring with various mental abilities (Ferrari & Sternberg, 1998), and these more domain-specific abilities may or may not impact academic success or standardized testing success. Howard Gardner is one such theorist who has developed a theory of **multiple intelligences** (e.g., 1983, 1991 & 1998) or multiple abilities.

Gardner sees intelligence manifested as particular mental abilities (Ferrari & Sternberg, 1998; Gardner, 1993). In other words, you can be smart in different ways. Although his theory is always evolving, eight types of intelligences have been proposed. These types of intelligence are logical, linguistic, spatial, musical, bodily-kinesthetic, naturalistic, interpersonal, and intrapersonal (Bransford, Brown & Cocking, 2000; Hoerr, 2003). A type of intelligence focused upon existential or religious intelligence has also been tentatively proposed.

Linguistic, logical-mathematical, and spatial intelligences most closely resemble the abilities measured by traditional IQ tests. **Linguistic intelligence** involves mental abilities in the semantics, syntax, and overall expression of language (Ferrari & Sternberg, 1998; Gardner, 1983, 1999; Hoerr, 2003; Kail, 2007). **Logical-mathematical intelligence**

**Spatial intelligence**

Involves mental abilities in perception of objects and the ability to mentally transform and manipulate these objects.

**Interpersonal intelligence**

The mental ability to understand one's own emotional self.

**Musical intelligence**

The mental ability to understand the components of music, such as tone, melody, pitch, and rhythm.

**Bodily-kinesthetic intelligence**

The mental ability to control one's body in a purposeful way.

involves mental abilities in pattern recognition, relationships, reasoning, and mathematical operations. **Spatial intelligence** involves mental abilities in perception of objects and the ability to mentally transform and manipulate these objects.

Interpersonal and intrapersonal intelligences encompass communicative and emotional properties. **Interpersonal intelligence** involves having a really good theory of mind. People high in interpersonal intelligence understand others emotions, intentions, and motivations (Ferrari & Sternberg, 1998; Gardner, 1983, 1999; Hoerr, 2003; Kail, 2007). Additionally, people high in interpersonal intelligence understand how to function well in social relationships. Intrapersonal intelligence involves the mental ability to understand one's own emotional self.

Musical, bodily-kinesthetic, and naturalistic intelligences encompass a variety of mental abilities. **Musical intelligence** involves the mental ability to understand the components of music, such as tone, melody, pitch, and rhythm (Ferrari & Sternberg, 1998; Gardner, 1983, 1999; Hoerr, 2003; Kail, 2007). It also involves understanding the ability of music to convey emotion and mood. **Bodily-kinesthetic intelligence** involves the mental ability to control one's body in a purposeful way. For example, dancers are able to tell a story and convey emotions through manipulating their body in dance. **Naturalist intelligence** involves the mental ability to recognize plant and animal life in the environment and the relationships and interconnections between these species. As mentioned above, Gardner has recently proposed the idea of an **existential intelligence**. This type of intelligence involves the mental ability to contemplate the purpose and meaning of life and issues surrounding death and what comes after death.

Traditionally, educational success has measured only a limited number of mental abilities. Further, teaching typically involves strategies that are geared toward a limited number of mental abilities. For the last fifteen years, there has been a push in the educational system to teach and assess using a multiple intelligences framework. Preliminary research seems to

*Tone, melody, pitch, and rhythm are the components of music. Music intelligence involves the mental ability to understand these components. (iStock)*

indicate that students taught using a nontraditional curriculum within the multiple intelligences framework allows students to score well on standardized tests (Hoerr, 2003).

## Academic Skills

In the last chapter, we learned about some early academic skills acquired during the preschool years. Some mathematical strategies developed in early childhood include counting, use of fingers in counting, counting on from the higher addend, and the use of overlapping and consecutive strategies in division. Some language arts skills in early childhood include the ability to identify letters of the alphabet, beginning phonics, and early writing.

## Mathematical Skills

You are probably not surprised that some basic academic skills are either acquired or further developed during middle childhood. Mathematics is one such area. School-age children are expected to master the basic operations of addition, subtraction, multiplication, and division. Although variations on counting were the predominant strategy for early childhood, more sophisticated skills emerge during middle childhood (Ginsburg, Klein & Starkey, 1998).

The math taught in school is **codified**. Codified can be defined as math that is written, systematically arranged, and guided by explicit rules (Ginsburg, Klein & Starkey, 1998). Such math cannot be learned through exploratory learning; instead it must be taught by formal instruction (sometimes called direct instruction). Once again, what mathematical knowledge is taught depends upon the culture.

As we learned in chapter four, counting strategies continue to evolve so that the early school-age child consistently adds on from the larger addend (Ginsburg, Klein & Starkey, 1998). However, through frequent drills, children eventually store basic number facts into long-term memory (e.g., they will learn that $8 - 5 = 3$ without having to do the counting each time). Drills are often useful in learning addition, subtraction, multiplication, and division facts. They can also be useful in learning conversion facts (e.g., converting inches to centimeters). However, a conceptual understanding should be the foundation upon which to drill.

Much of math is too complicated to be committed to memory via the drill method (Ginsburg, Klein & Starkey, 1998). For these areas of math, algorithms and invented strategies can be useful. An algorithm has been "developed and codified over the course of centuries, {and} produce correct results. When used properly, the algorithm always work" (Ginsburg, Klein & Starkey, 1998, p. 419). For example, $A2 + B2 = C2$ is an algorithm that will always work. **Inventive strategies** are different, however, from algorithms. Inventive strategies make use of one's knowledge and current strategies for help in answering novel problems. For example, a child may know that $5 + 5 = 10$. When faced with the problem $5 + 6 = ?$, she may choose to add $5 + 5$ (which she knows the answer to) and count up one, instead of counting up five from the number six. Exploiting the base 10 system is a very popular inventive strategy.

**Naturalist intelligence**

The mental ability to recognize plant and animal life in the environment and the relationships and interconnections between these species.

**Existential intelligence**

The mental ability to contemplate the purpose and meaning of life and issues surrounding death and what comes after death.

**Codified**

Math that is written.

*Spotlight*

What is meant by math being codified?

**Inventive strategies**

Making use of one's own knowledge and current strategies in answering a novel problem.

American children do poorly in these skills compared to children in other countries (Stigler, Lee & Stevenson, 1987). Newer instruction methods are based on what we know about how children in the concrete operations stage of cognitive development learn (Resnick, 1989). They stress cognitive processes rather than memorization and calculation skills. By the end of this period, children should understand fractions, decimals, pre-geometry and pre-algebra knowledge, and conversion between the decimal and standard systems of measurement.

## *Language Arts Skills*

Reading also shows great development during middle childhood. It involves integration of perceptual, attention, and memory skills. Teachers consider many factors in reading instruction: for example, letter size, readability of text material, and the child's knowledge base (Athey, 1983; National Research Council, 2000). Most children enter the first grade knowing the alphabet; some may already know how to sound out words and read easy books. By the end of this period, children should be able to read most books with ease and fluency. When first learning to read, simply sounding out and identifying the words uses most of working memory. It takes time to be able to read and comprehend what one is reading. Reading instruction is based on teaching different reading skills, use of phonics, and different types of comprehension (Jones, 1986; National Research Council, 2000). Phonics is especially important for reading development. Also, the more a child is read to early in childhood, and the more they read independently and with others during middle childhood, the earlier a child is able to read efficiently and for knowledge.

Finally, writing develops by leaps and bounds during middle childhood. Writing also involves the integration of several cognitive skills. Like reading, it is used in many contexts of classroom learning. Classroom writing is less a communication device than a means of evaluating what children have learned. Early during the school-age years, children will often just list everything they have learned in response to an essay question with little organization or coherence. Across middle childhood, children learn to write with thesis statements, introductions, topic sentences, transitional sentences, summaries, coherence, and organization. Children also learn how to write informational

*At this age the skill of reading is greatly developed. (iStock)*

reports, persuasive arguments, research reports, and other such formats during this time. Of course, these skills continue to be improved upon during adolescence and beyond.

*Pause and Process:*

1. How does information processing improve during middle childhood?

2. What are sensory memory, short-term memory, and long-term memory?

# LANGUAGE DEVELOPMENT

### *Growing Language Skills*

**Metalinguistic-awareness**

The capacity to use language to analyze, study, and understand language.

Although children are competent communicators with language in early childhood, language skills continue to develop during the school years (Piper, 2003). During the school years, children achieve **metalinguistic-awareness**. Metalinguistic-awareness (or metalinguistic ability) is defined as "the capacity to use language to analyze, study, and understand language" (Hulit & Howard, 1997, p. 247).

During middle childhood, vocabulary continues to grow, though at a slower rate than in early childhood (Hulit & Howard, 1997). Understanding slight variations between words and word choice skills improve. The meaning and definitions of words grow during this time. Children also improve in their ability to understand and use **figurative language** forms, such as similies, proverbs, idioms, and metaphors.

**Figurative language**

The use of similies, proverbs, idioms, and metaphors.

Language learning during middle childhood often focuses upon mastering the intricacies and rules of the language. Syntax and morphology understanding and use continue to develop (Hulit & Howard, 1997). Early in middle childhood, children are still working to master the exceptions to the general rules of language. For example, they may still occasionally say "childs" instead of "children" or "gooses" instead of "geese." They also begin to learn about rules regarding double negatives in sentences and parts of speech.

Conversational skills, including mastery of pragmatics, continue to improve in middle childhood (Hulit & Howard, 1997). The ability to repair sentences and maintain relevance grows during the school years. The ability to understand the conversational partner's perspective also improves. Finally, the concept of indirect requests, or hinting, in conversation emerges.

### *Second-Language Acquisition*

**School bilingualism**

The offering of courses in a secondary language in the elementary schools.

In Chapter 4, we discussed bilingualism in early childhood. Most children who are bilingual early in childhood learn the second language in the home. However, many elementary schools offer courses in second language, which is referred to as **school bilingualism** (Piper, 2003). School bilingualism differs from home bilingualism in several ways. For example, language in the home is practical, context-based, and sequential. Language learning in schools is considered "formal, abstract language that is largely decontextualized, logical, and expository" (Piper, 2003, p. 132). Hence, it is more difficult to become bilingual in the school than in the home.

Second-language acquisition is best prior to middle childhood. Research has shown that immigrants to the United States master English grammar as well as natives if they arrive before the age of seven (Siegler, 1998). Children who arrive between the ages of eight and eleven show slight decrements in grammar ability. The downward trend in grammar ability in a second language continues as age increases. By the age of fifteen, grammar ability shows significant negative impacts in comparison to the younger children's mastery.

*Pause and Process:*

1. What is metalinguistic awareness?

2. How do language skills improve during middle childhood?

# SOCIOEMOTIONAL DEVELOPMENT DURING MIDDLE CHILDHOOD

**LEARNING OBJECTIVES:**

*1. Characterize emotional development during middle childhood*

*2. Describe understanding of self and others during middle childhood*

*3. Explain psychosocial development during middle childhood*

Developmental tasks during this stage center on mastering the basic skills outlined by society for adequate functioning. These include learning to read, write, and calculate (discussed in the last chapter). Other institutions and people now work in association with parents to teach these skills to children. The school becomes a significant cultural world for individuals at this time.

Beyond academic skills, the school environment also encourages children to master personal and social skills. These reflect what Erikson (1950) calls the skills of duty and accomplishment. They play an important role in helping school-age children acquire a healthy sense of industry. Being punctual with assignments, attending meetings, completing projects, and learning behavior routines are examples of these personal and social skills. In addition, school-age children are expected to be more accomplished in relations with peers. This involves learning to function adequately in groups of other children of similar ages. These are the years when society offers opportunities for learning group politics.

School-age children are expected to become more responsible. Families and schools work together to train them to become workers. They learn the work ethic, which stresses personal responsibility, completion of tasks, and initiating work with little direction. By performing work chores at home and at school, school-age children learn the basics of this ethic.

Other activities help school-age children to learn work roles. Participation in youth groups such as Scouts, 4-H, or church organizations fosters social skills. School-age children may also acquire the feeling of accomplishment through instruction in dance, music, art, drama, athletics, or other clubs. These help to foster feelings of self-worth and a positive self-image.

A dramatic developmental change is the increase in social interactions outside the family system. Peer groups become prominent in individual development during middle childhood. A best friend and a group of friends are desired for play activities and interaction. Having the respect of one's peers is a need that increases significantly during this stage.

School is where many developmental challenges of middle childhood take place. Here children learn to work with an authority figure who is not a member of their family system. The school introduces a child to many different peer groups. A child encounters these groups not only in the classroom and on the playground, but also outside the school world. The experiences provided by this environment and culture operate along with the family system in instilling an attitude of industry or inferiority.

Forces in a family system influence an individual's development at this time. Adults adapt their parenting styles to their child's changing nature. The principal adaptation is that they change from being physical to psychological helpers of their child.

A school-age child encounters pressures not previously experienced. These come from peer groups, from the need to learn new skills, from evaluations by teachers and peers, and from very different parental expectations. A child begins to rely on parents in different ways than in early childhood.

# PSYCHOSOCIAL DEVELOPMENT

**Sense of industry**

A positive, healthy attitude toward work and the need to master certain basic skills.

## *Developing a Sense of Industry*

School-age children focus on resolving a psychosocial conflict in acquiring a sense of industry versus inferiority. A **sense of industry** is a positive, healthy attitude toward work

*Youth programs such as Cub Scouts help children to learn about work roles. They help foster the feeling of self-worth and to have a positive self-image. (iStock)*

*A child can learn a sense of industry by performing household chores such as washing the dishes. (iStock)*

and the need to master certain basic skills. A healthy attitude toward work means learning to apply oneself to an assigned task. It is an extension of the attitude of initiative acquired in the previous stage, but with this difference: it is expected that what is started will be completed satisfactorily. The family and school systems work together to help children learn this attitude. At home, industry is learned by school-age children as they perform household chores assigned to them by their parents. Parents now enforce higher standards of performance because of the child's advanced abilities. At school, a child acquires industry by completing assigned learning tasks. Children are expected to finish their homework assignments, classroom problems, and more extensive projects.

School-age children learn the work ethic by doing all these things. They learn the association between performance and reward as they are evaluated by parents and teachers. Children may be rewarded with money, privileges, or material goods for performing household chores to standards set by parents.

Essentially, industry is a feeling of pride in one's abilities to do what is expected adequately. This is the basis of the work ethic and an important element of adult success. Our culture expects school-age children to begin learning the principles of right and good conduct in preparation for their future roles as workers and contributors to society.

**Sense of inferiority**

A pervasive attitude of worthlessness.

The **sense of inferiority** is a pervasive attitude of worthlessness. It is based on negative assessments of oneself, particularly in comparison with others. School-age children adopt this attitude when they conclude they cannot do anything well. This attitude affects their interactions with other children. School-age children who feel inferior tend to shy away from opportunities to interact with their peers and thus can fail to learn social skills. This is a time of life when others' approval is vastly important. An individual's self-worth is validated by the approval and acceptance of peers. When this is not forthcoming for whatever reasons, school-age children believe that rejection means they are of lesser value than others. This sense of inferiority can have long term ramifications. Older students who are convinced that they do not have abilities in specific disciplines, such as when a female says "I can't do math", may be responding to a sense of inferiority developed during this stage.

In Erikson's framework, the theme of psychosocial developmental changes in middle childhood is "making things together." This refers to the more intensive involvement of school-age children with their peers. It is in the group experience that children master many social and mental skills and learn to be productive within their family system, the school, and their peer groups.

Many toys, video and computer games, and youth programs are geared to help children acquire a healthy sense of industry. Dolls or actions figures help children act out themes. Arts, crafts, and hobby kits help kids learn that they can accomplish something if they try. Many educationally-geared computer and video games allow children to collect tokens as individual competencies are mastered. Programs such as the Cub and Boy Scouts, Brownie and Girl Scouts, 4-H, Boys' and Girls' Clubs, and others teach the work ethic by offering merit badges for completing tasks successfully. The uniforms they provide give children a cherished group identity. The family system is involved to help children perform tasks and in activities that promote family interaction. Hence, childhood culture seems geared to assist children in the development of an attitude of industry.

*Pause and Process:*

1. How does a sense of industry help a child throughout life?

2. How does a sense of inferiority hinder a child throughout life?

# EMOTIONAL DEVELOPMENT

## *Key Emotional Development Highlights*

Emotional communication is an area of amazing development during middle childhood. It is during the school-age years that children first understand that it is their cognitive appraisal of experiences or the environment that directly influences what they are feeling (Saarni, Mumme & Campos, 1998). Furthermore, children at this phase of life begin to understand that the same experience or environment may trigger different emotions in different people. Hence, understanding emotions becomes more mature at this time.

Middle childhood also appears to be a time that children experience an increase in their ability to reflect upon subjective experiences, which is directly related to the ability to extrapolate as to the intensity and duration of emotions (Saarni, Mumme & Campos, 1998). The awareness that multiple emotions may be experienced at the same time may develop as early as the preschool years, or in middle childhood. The ability to integrate conflicting emotions probably does not develop until the end of middle childhood.

In summary, the ability to understand one's own emotions, as well as emotions in others, grows during middle childhood. By the end of middle childhood, children are able to navigate emotional communication because they better grasp the cognitive component of emotions, reflect upon emotion-triggering experiences, and understand that emotions may conflict.

## Temperament

In Chapter 4, we discussed that temperament can be conceptualized in various ways. A recent study by Janson and Mathiesen (2008) investigated four dimensions of temperament: Sociability, activity level, emotionality, and shyness. They then used statistical modeling to examine how the temperament dimensions cluster together. They found support for five temperament profiles (see Table 5-2).

This study included 921 children and longitudinally studied them from the age of eighteen months until the age of nine. Below are some interesting bits of information that came out of this study.

- At the age of eight or nine, gender differences emerge in temperament profiles.

- Boys are more likely than girls to be classified as confident.

- Girls are more likely than boys to be classified as unremarkable.

- Age impacts which temperament profile is most prevalent.

- Eighteen months: confident profile most prevalent

- Thirty months: uneasy profile most prevalent

- Four to five years: uneasy profile most prevalent

- Eight to nine years: unremarkable profile most prevalent

- There was moderate stability in temperament across childhood.

| TABLE 5-2 | TEMPERAMENT PROFILES | |
|---|---|---|
| **TEMPERAMENT PROFILE** | **DESCRIPTION** | **PERCENTAGE WITH TEMPERAMENT PROFILE** |
| Undercontrolled | High sociability, high activity level, high emotionality, and low shyness | 20% |
| Confident | Low shyness, low emotionality, high activity level, and moderate sociability | 23% |
| Unremarkable | Moderately low levels of sociability, activity level, emotionality, and shyness | 22% |
| Inhibited | Low activity level, low sociability, high shyness, and moderately low levels of emotionality | 12% |
| Uneasy | Moderately high shyness, moderately high emotionality, moderate sociability, and moderate activity level | 23% |

- The undercontrolled profile showed the highest degree of externalizing behavior problems.

- The undercontrolled profile, inhibited profile, and uneasy profile showed the highest levels of internalizing behavior problems.

In summary, this study found that temperament is fairly stable from infancy into middle childhood. Further, different profiles are most prevalent at different ages. Finally, certain profiles are more likely to exhibit behavior problems than other profiles.

## *Attachment*

Attachment security in infancy continues to be predictive of behavioral outcomes in middle childhood (Thompson, 1998). A series of studies by Sroufe and colleagues (reviewed by Thompson, 1998) found attachment classification in infancy for boys was predictive of ratings of aggression and passive withdrawal behavior by teachers in elementary school. Additionally, summer camp personnel rated children who were securely attached as infants higher than children who were insecurely attached as infants on the following dimensions:

- Social skills

- Ego resiliency

- Self-esteem

- Self-confidence

- Emotional health

- Social competence

- Friendship development

- Independence

*Pause and Process:*

1. Describe emotional development during middle childhood.

2. Compare and contrast the temperament "types" discussed in Chapter 3 with the temperament "profiles" in this chapter.

# SELF AND OTHERS

## *Understanding of Self and Others*

Many developmental changes in middle childhood are social and mental in nature. As physical changes diminish, social and mental growth accelerates. The central aspect of social

**Spotlight**

Define social cognition in your own words.

**Social cognition**

The skills involved in understanding the dynamics of human social interaction patterns. Self-understanding is also related these skills.

changes among school-age children is a shift to a new psychosocial focus that is both more mature and more self-aware. During this period, individuals refine their self-concept.

Among the skills school-age children are expected to become proficient at are those that involve a basic understanding of interaction patterns and human psychology. Children this age are more and more exposed to people outside their family system for instruction and learning. To cope successfully with many confusing circumstances, they must become adept at **social cognition**.

Social cognition is knowledge of the dynamics of human interaction. This important social skill vastly improves during middle childhood. Social cognition assists school-age children to make sense out of the often chaotic behavior of their peer groups, helps them to understand basic human nature, and promotes self-awareness leading to self-esteem.

## Self-Understanding

School-age children advance in self-understanding. This is a significant milestone in helping a child reach decisions about how to behave. It is especially significant in influencing self-concept formation in middle childhood (Damon & Hart, 1982).

Because of their more advanced cognitive abilities, school-age children are more capable than preschoolers of thinking about what kind of person they are (Harter, 1982). As children advance through this stage, they realize that their personalities are composed of different aspects (Harter, 1983). They are able to acknowledge the negative as well as the positive aspects. For example, they know that they are good at spelling, excellent in reading, but weak in math. Admitting faults, areas of weakness, or negative traits is still difficult.

The ability to see their own negative attributes causes school-age children to become increasingly self-critical. This causes a gradual deterioration in positive feelings about the self as they progress through middle childhood (Harter, 1983; Savin-Williams & Demo, 1984). It is common to hear children this age make such self-derogatory comments as "I'm just no good," "I can't do anything right," "Nobody likes me," or "I'm just plain ugly." Most of these critical self-assessments result from comparisons with others their age.

School-age children come to internalize their problems by blaming themselves. Girls, especially, take personal responsibility for their difficulties (Stipek, 1984). This tendency to be so harsh on themselves goes with children's developing ability to take responsibility for their behavior. Another contributing factor is the increasing number of interactions with peers, who are such an important source of self-esteem in middle childhood.

## Understanding of Others

In more specific ways, social cognition is the knowledge that other people have thoughts and feelings, personality traits, and reaction styles (Flavell & Ross, 1981). The beginnings of social cognition can be seen in social referencing (discussed in Chapter 3). This is the skill infants use when they look to a parent's emotional expressions (e.g., facial expression) to determine how they should react to something. In early childhood, individuals con-

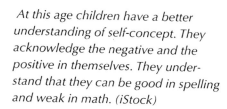

*At this age children have a better understanding of self-concept. They acknowledge the negative and the positive in themselves. They understand that they can be good in spelling and weak in math. (iStock)*

tinue to use these cues—especially facial expressions and voice tone—to determine another's emotional state.

In middle childhood, however, individuals learn that facial expressions are not always reliable indicators of others' emotional states (Bugental, 1986; Flavell, 1985). Children learn around age eight or nine that not only are they expected to control their emotions, but that older people are also very skilled at doing so (Bugental, 1986). At the same time they grasp that people can feign emotional states, they begin to understand teasing, though this behavior is still confusing to children to some extent.

Perhaps the most dramatic insight children learn in middle childhood is that other people are different inside as well as outside. Children begin to comprehend at about age eight that people have personality traits (Schantz, 1983). However, school-age children think in an all-or-nothing manner. Something is either 100 percent one way or another. A person is either all-good or all-bad. They conclude that some personality traits make a person completely good and some traits make a person completely bad.

Once school-age children decide a person has certain traits, they will think about that person almost exclusively in these terms. In many respects, this is similar to the process of stereotyping seen in adults. It is inconceivable to children this age that people possess a mixture of positive and negative traits (Donaldson & Westerman, 1986). It confuses them that personality traits are sometimes contradictory. They have difficulty acknowledging that people do not always behave consistently.

## Play and Leisure Time

The power of play is pervasive during middle childhood (Kaplan & Kaplan, 1973). The richness and extensiveness of play reach a zenith during these years. Developmental changes in the types of activities that appeal to school-age children also are observed.

To the uninformed adult, children's play is a useless, time-wasting, attention-consuming activity. To those who have studied children's play, this assumption is inaccurate. Four important contributions of play to development in middle childhood have been identified: (1) it enhances and encourages a child's creativity, (2) it assists a child to learn developmental tasks, (3) it fosters interpersonal relationships with peers, and (4) it bolsters a child's personality and self-concept. Play is a vehicle for modulating stress and reducing tension for school-age children. It enhances their physical development and fosters their social skills. Play provides a context for children's self-exploration as they interact with their environment.

A sequence of changes is seen in middle childhood play activities (Baumeister & Senders, 1989). This is a continuation of the changes that began in early childhood. Generally, there are strong parallels between the types of play children engage in and their increasing orientation to peers during this stage. The ability to interact effectively within a group emerges between ages five and eight. Children these ages demonstrate an increasing ability to tolerate and follow rules, take turns, and share equipment. Between eight and twelve, children pursue more specialized interests and activities. Some frequently observed types of play activities are outlined in Table 5-3.

Other trends are observed in school-age play. First, there is a decline in the types of play involving imagination or fantasy and in those involving action or rough-and-tumble (Baumeister & Senders, 1989). These types of play do not disappear completely in middle childhood, however.

Second, there is a dramatic increase in the types of play involving rules. School-age children enjoy games like tag that allow them to switch roles frequently. At one time a child is "It," and at another time a child is one of those who are chased. This kind of play may help to dismantle the strong egocentrism of early childhood because switching roles promotes the ability to take others' viewpoints (Piaget, 1967).

| TABLE 5-3 | TYPES OF PLAY ACTIVITIES IN MIDDLE CHILDHOOD | |
|---|---|---|
| **ACTIVITY** | **VALUES FOR CHILDREN** | **EXAMPLES** |
| Games<br>  Quiet<br>  Competitive<br>  Tags, relays<br><br>  Team | Intellectual stimulation; problem solving<br>Social skills; problem solving<br>Energy release; fun; excitement; physical fitness<br>Group skills; physical fitness | Hangman; 20 Questions<br>Four-square ball<br>Chain tag; hide and seek<br><br>Football; soccer; baseball |
| Crafts | Creativity; problem solving; personality enrichment | Art; models; weaving; printing |
| Tricks, puzzles | Problem solving; intellectual skills; curiosity | Connect-the-dots; work searches |
| Collections | Classification skills; knowledge; information | Stamps; coins; rocks; dolls; models |
| Symbolic | Communication; imagination; social interaction "Star Wars"; "house" | Superman; Batman; Wonder Women |

Third, play becomes increasingly competitive in middle childhood. Many school-age children come to prefer sports activities where there are clear winners and losers. These activities introduce them to complex rules. Television watching and recreational computer-use also become primary recreations. The average child spends around three hours a day watching the television or using the computer for reasons other than school work.

## *Family Influences*

The nature and style of parenting change during middle childhood. One major source that motivates these changes is the child. The developmental tasks and challenges that school-age children experience are entirely different. These are more complex than those of infancy and early childhood. The developmental changes of middle childhood are more social and psychological than physical in nature. Physical skills that are acquired in this period, however, play a significant role in shaping children's self-concepts.

Parenting in middle childhood, as in earlier stages, focuses on helping children to accomplish their essential developmental tasks. However, the tone of interaction and caregiving styles changes. This centers increasingly on parents providing psychological assistance and guidance. Because children change during these years, there are corresponding changes in the ways that parents respond to children's needs. Parents learn that they must respond to or interact with the school-age child differently. Methods and parenting styles that were effective with preschoolers are ineffective with school-age children. Children have new accomplishments and emerging abilities during middle childhood. They may not permit parents to continue a response style or interaction pattern that was appropriate when they were younger. Parents essentially learn that they must now become psychological rather than physical helpers for their school-age children.

Changes in the ways that school-age children are disciplined by parents illustrate this process. Parents of preschoolers typically use a variety of control methods. These include isolation, having a child sit in a corner, mild spanking, and so on. These techniques become ineffective in middle childhood. Taking privileges away and reasoning replace the methods used earlier. The methods that are successful with older children place a greater responsibility for behavior management on the child.

**Co-regulation**

The shift to greater sharing and balance of social power between parents and children during the Family and School-age Children stage of the family life career.

Parents begin training children for greater self-control in early childhood. In middle childhood, there is a greater sharing of social power between parents and children. This results in **co-regulation** in which parents exercise general supervision, whereas children gain in moment-to-moment self-regulation (Maccoby, 1984). Parents of school-age children tend to exercise their power mostly when children misbehave in their presence.

Parents of school-age children increasingly use psychological methods of guidance to help children achieve a higher level of self-control. Psychological guidance consists of reassuring children, helping them to recover from social blunders, and giving positive reinforcement for efforts to learn new skills. School-age children continue to need their parents but in ways that are very different from preschoolers.

*Parents help their children with developmental tasks such as tying their shoes. (iStock)*

Increased involvement with peers and the school system calls for parents to release increasing amounts of control over children. School-age children are absent from the home increasingly for longer periods of time. Parents from healthy family systems encourage this as a means of helping children gain independence from the family.

Letting go of school-age children means that parents can be more accepting of the increasing value placed on peers, best friends, and other significant adults. Children this age learn to relate to adults outside the family system. These include teachers, youth group leaders, or religious leaders, for example. Letting go of school-age children means that parents allow children opportunities to interact with other family systems. Children enjoy spending the night at friends' homes, taking weekend camping trips with youth groups, attending summer camp sessions, visiting with grandparents, and so on.

The expectations that parents hold for school-age children change. This also reflects the shift to co-regulation. For example, a group of parents rank-ordered a series of eight behavior traits in degree of importance for school-age children to have or acquire (Bigner, 1980). The ranking resulted in these traits being considered the most important for children this age: (1) developing social cooperation skills such as being considerate, sharing, or cooperative; (2) being open to experience such as curiosity, creativity, or information gathering skills; and (3) being self-directed by expressing needs, starting activities without being directed, or getting help when needed. These traits may be ideals that parents wish children to have to ensure success in adulthood. These may form the foundation of child rearing goals parents may adopt during this stage of the family life career. Such goals can guide and shape parenting behaviors.

To help children acquire a healthy sense of industry versus inferiority, parents can focus on several aspects in their relationship with children this age: (1) focusing on children's accomplishments, (2) avoiding excessive attention that highlights weaknesses and limitations, and (3) promoting increasing abilities for children to develop self-control.

## *Divorce Impacts*

More than 50 percent of all children in the United States are expected to have a single-parent family experience at some time (Stickle, 2008; Kitson & Morgan, 1990). How this will affect children is a major concern of parents who consider divorce.

Most research regarding divorce addresses two central factors that seem to influence children's adjustment to parents' divorce. These include (1) the age of children at the time of the divorce, and (2) use of available social networks to help children adjust to changes related to their parents' divorce.

Many research studies have focused on the age of children when parents divorce. Findings point to different reactions and adjustment challenges based on this factor alone. Most children, no matter their age at the time of the parents' divorce, find this to be a painful experience. Short-term reactions can be considered as symptoms of grief and mourning. Children experience feelings ranging from anger to depression and guilt. Behavior problems become more common such as noncompliance, aggression, regressive behavior, sleep disturbances, and fearful reactions (Hetherington, Stanley-Hagan & Anders, 1989; Wallerstein, 1983). Apparently, short-term effects are mediated according to the stability of the child's home and school environment following divorce. It is also affected by using social supports available to children to help them cope (Kurdek, 1981).

School-age children react to parents' divorce by feeling hurt, rejected by the absent parent, helpless to make the situation better, and lonely (Wallerstein & Kelly, 1976). Anger also is a common reaction. This is most often directed at one parent in blaming them for causing the divorce and disruption to family life. A common fear among children this age is that they will be abandoned just as their custodial parent has been (Wallerstein, 1987). It is not unusual for children this age to become aligned with one parent or the other following the divorce. When this occurs, anger becomes more intensely directed at the nonaligned parent causing difficulties in their relationship.

The first year is a particularly stressful one for children and adults. Parents are less effective parents (Parke & Buriel, 1998). For example, parents require less mature behavior of their children, show less affection, and are less consistent with discipline during this time. Children's grades and school performance suffer, their behavior becomes more noncompliant, and relationships with both custodial and noncustodial parents become more strained (e.g., Fine, Moreland & Schwebel, 1983; Minuchin & Shapiro, 1983; Parke & Buriel, 1998; Wallerstein, Corbin & Lewis, 1988).

Divorce can have some long-term effects on children (Hetherington, 1989; Parke & Buriel, 1998). Girls whose mothers remain single appear well-adjusted two years after the divorce. They are typically close to their mother and thrive with the added responsibilities of living in a single-parent household. Sons, however, struggle in their relationship with their mother. They are monitored less than boys from intact homes, spend more time with peers, and execute more antisocial behavior. We will learn more about the long-term effects of divorce in Chapter 6.

Children recover more quickly and permanently if parents minimize their interpersonal conflict after the divorce (Wallerstein, 1983). Long-term effects are diminished also when both parents remain involved and try to nurture their relationship with their children (Hetherington, Cox & Cox, 1979; Parke & Buriel, 1998).

## Sibling Relationships

Sibling relationships provide a context for learning how to interact with others (Parke & Buriel, 1998). These relationships help children develop social understanding, interpersonal skills, and conflict resolution skills (Eisenberg & Fabes, 1998; Parke & Buriel, 1998). Further, positive sibling relationships may help compensate for negative peer relationships and help prevent problematic outcomes typically associated with negative peer relationships. However, when examining the outcomes associated with sibling compensatory support the research differentiates between the ability of the compensatory support to provide full compensation and the ability of the compensatory support to provide only partial compensation. Partial compensation is achieved when an individual receiving compensatory support is better adjusted than someone who is not receiving the needed compensatory support. However, full compensation is achieved when an individual receiving compensatory support is as adjusted as someone who is receiving the needed support from his or her primary providers and is not relying on compensatory support. Using the sibling-peer dyad as an example, partial compensation is achieved when an individual under a low peer-high sibling support condition is better adjusted than an individual under a low peer-low sibling support condition. Alternatively, full compensation is achieved when an individual under a low peer-high sibling support condition is not found to differ in adjustment compared to an individual under a high peer-high sibling support condition. Sibling compensation at this stage in life may only compensate

*Social understanding, interpersonal skills, and conflict resolution skills can be learned through sibling relationships. (iStock)*

partially for low peer support considering the integral part friends play in the lives of children (Milevsky & Levitt, 2005).

Sibling relationships may provide a context for developing prosocial behavior (Eisenberg & Fabes, 1998). Older siblings sometimes play a caregiver role in monitoring younger sibling behavior and well-being. Such caregiving behavior assists both older and younger children in developing prosocial behavior. Older siblings often display warmth, concern, and kindness when caring for younger siblings. Younger siblings learn to comply with older sibling direction and model the prosocial behavior of their older sibling. Additionally, sibling caregiving relationships provide a context for developing perspective-taking, further assisting in the development of prosocial behavior.

Finally, sibling relationships influence a child's development of self. Older siblings who help care for younger siblings may develop a self-representation of being nurturing or dominating (Harter, 1998). Younger siblings cared for by older siblings may develop a self-representation of being dominated or nurtured.

## The Outside World

**Peer group**

A (usually) same-sex group of children of similar ages and developmental abilities that significantly influences social changes in middle childhood.

**Group politics**

Those social skills that facilitate a child's participation in peer groups.

Describe the social hierarchy of peer groups.

Entrance into the school signals many changes for a child, the parents, and the family system. The **peer group** becomes an additional socialization agent as children learn the mechanics of **group politics**. This group is also a major source of information children use in constructing their self-concept.

## Peers

An individual is a member of several social systems during middle childhood: the family, school, and peer groups. Each is distinct, with its own patterns, rules, and roles. School-age children participate in two separate cultural worlds: that of adults and that of children (Asher & Gottman, 1981; Galzter-Levy & Cohler, 1993).

A peer group consists of children who are of approximately the same age and developmental abilities. Peer groups may be formed spontaneously by children or artificially by adults for children. Children spontaneously form peer groups when they play together on the playground during school recess, for example, or when those who live near each other play together in their neighborhood. Adults artificially form peer groups when they group children together in a classroom, for example. Our schools commonly use age and associated developmental abilities as guides in assigning children to grades (Williams & Stith, 1980).

Peer groups are important agents of socialization. Children learn significant lessons through membership in these groups—lessons that siblings, parents, and teachers cannot teach. These are lessons in group politics, or skills that facilitate successful functioning as a group member. These lessons can last a lifetime.

A peer group functions like any other social system. Patterns and rules of interaction form a code for appropriate behavior. Infractions of rules and patterns result in consequences meant to enforce conformity to the code. A peer group may have its own lan-

*Peer groups provide important socialization lessons that can last a lifetime. (iStock)*

**Social hierarchy**

An organizational ranking of peers based on how much a child is liked or disliked by others.

**Average**

A child with a small group of friends, who is neither greatly disliked nor considered popular.

**Popular**

Children who are liked by many peers.

**Neglected**

Children who are neglected by peers describe themselves as having no friends.

**Rejected**

Children who are rejected by peers are disliked and are at risk of many serious problems that include clinical depression.

guage and dress styles to promote group identification. During middle childhood, peer groups are often sex-divided. This means that school-age children only include children of the same-sex in their peer group. This tendency decreases in adolescence.

School-age children begin to establish a degree of organizational order in their peer groups through a **social hierarchy**. This ranking is based on how much a child is liked or disliked by others. This forms the basis of popularity ratings children make of one another. It is important because some children will be well-liked and others will be unpopular. This can determine who the child plays with, how the play occurs, and under what circumstances. School-age children can be expected to construct their self-image and concept on how they are treated by peers.

Most school-age children are considered as **average** in these ratings by others. The greatest concern relates to children who are neglected or rejected by peers (Kupersmidt, 1989; Rubin, Bukowski & Parker, 1998). The proportion of these children is similar to those who are **popular**.

Children who are **neglected** by peers describe themselves as having no friends (Rubin, Bukowski & Parker, 1998). They have an ambiguous status within a peer group because no one likes nor dislikes them. These children may be described as isolated from others. This may or may not be disturbing to them. In many respects, they resemble children who are average in popularity ratings.

Children who are **rejected** by peers are of much greater concern. They are at risk of many serious problems that include clinical depression (Kennedy, Spence & Hensley, 1989; Rubin, Bukowski & Parker, 1998). These children are disliked, sometimes passionately, by peers. If a child is rejected at one grade, there is a high probability that this continues throughout a child's academic career.

A child is rejected by peers usually for behaving in hostile and aggressive ways. The rejected child resembles the stereotype of the class bully. This is a child who picks on other children, preying on those who are weaker physically (French, 1988; MacNeil & Newell, 2004).

**Controversial**

Children who are liked by many peers, and disliked by many peers.

However, aggressive behavior alone does not result in rejection by peers. Another group of children is seen as **controversial**. These children, although acting aggressively also have positive traits that are valued by a peer group. Because of the positive traits, these children are not rejected but are liked by some of their peers. The children who are rejected are seen by their peers as lacking any positive traits and acting aggressively.

Rejected children may have difficulties in social cognition not observed in other children. For example, they may act aggressively and are not liked by peers because they lack social skills (Putallaz & Gottman, 1981; Rubin, Bukowski & Parker, 1998). They may interpret accidental behavior of others as intentional, a characteristic of social cognition among much younger children (Dodge & Frame, 1982). This interpretation is thought to provoke their hostility toward others.

More recent research suggests that rejected children lack such important social skills because their rejection deprives them of peer group learning experiences (Kuperschmidt, 1989; Rubin, Bukowski & Parker, 1998). Additionally, rejected children's interpretation of others' aggressiveness as intentional may be correct. Some rejected children are indeed the victims of peers' aggressiveness. These children often are the scapegoats within peer groups but do not usually act aggressively themselves. Other rejected children are victimized but also act aggressively to others. These children are called provocative victims. They seem to provoke hostility from peers that is used to justify their aggressive retaliation.

A child's external physical appearances also can contribute to ratings of likability by peers (Kennedy, 1989; Rubin, Bukowski & Parker, 1998). Children who look differently are likely to be rejected by peers as determined by ratings made both from videotapes and still photographs. These factors may operate to define a child's reputation among peers in middle childhood. School-age children tend to think in an all-or-nothing manner. This is based on global assessments of someone's attributes. A child who is rejected, neglected, or controversial may acquire a label as "difficult," "mean," or "temperamental." A rejected child will learn to expect that others will think of him or her in these terms. Similarly, children who are popular also acquire reputations that are positive. The popular child will learn to expect others to view him or her positively (Waas, 1988). Frequently, a child's reputation remains intact for many years thereafter.

## *Friendship*

In Chapter 4 we were introduced to developmental changes in friendship perception. We learned about stage zero in which friends are considered little more than momentary playmates (Selman, 1981). During the school-age years, children progress through stages one, two, and three. It should be noted here that same-sex friendships are the norm among school-age children (Hartup, 1983).

**One-way assistance**

The first stage in friendship perception that occurs early in middle childhood where friends must match a child's personal standard.

Stage one of friendship perception is referred to as **one-way assistance** (Selman, 1981). This stage occurs early in middle childhood. In this stage, friends must match a child's personal standard. For example, if a child believes that a friend should be a girl who is the same age, height, and likes soccer, then a person must meet these criteria in order to

*A "best friend" is considered a stage one friendship. This person is usually the same gender, age, and height, and has the same likes and dislikes. (iStock)*

be considered a friend. A "best friend" would be the person that a child knows the most or is most familiar with, including likes and dislikes.

**Fair-weather cooperation**

The second stage of friendship perception that typically occurs between the ages of eight to ten where ideas of reciprocity and adapting to friends' likes and dislikes govern the early friendship.

Stage two of friendship perception is referred to as **fair-weather cooperation** (Selman, 1981). This stage typically occurs between the ages eight to ten. Ideas of reciprocity and adapting to friends' likes and dislikes govern these early friendships. However, these friendships are fragile. There is no sense of long-term commitment and an argument often ends the friendship.

**Intimate and mutually shared relationships**

The third stage of friendship perception that typically occurs at the end of middle childhood, between the ages of ten to twelve where children value the continuity and longevity of friendship.

Stage three of friendship perception is referred to as **intimate and mutually shared relationships** (Selman, 1981). This stage typically occurs at the end of middle childhood, between the ages of ten to twelve. Here, children value the continuity and longevity of friendship. Hence, arguments and conflicts are no longer seen as the end to a friendship, but an obstacle to be overcome. Friendships are also viewed as a valuable source of social and emotional support. However, possessiveness and exclusiveness can plague friendships at this stage. These attributes arise from the realization that friendships are complex and challenging to develop and maintain.

## School Experiences

Entrance into the school system is a significant event that influences many social and cognitive changes in middle childhood. It is in this setting that a child is introduced to peer groups and exposed to other nonrelated adults who assist in their growth process. Expectations for behavior change yearly as children progress through the school system.

## "Development in the Real World"

Dr. Joseph Kristobak, Jr., is the superintendent of the Cornwall-Lebanon School District in Pennsylvania. He is charged with making all administrative and educational decisions in the district. Dr. Kristobak earned a bachelor's degree in history and political science, a teaching certificate, a master's degree in history and education, and a doctorate.

### What type of work do you conduct?

*"Well, right now I'm basically in charge of the entire school district, which includes anything from curriculum instruction, personnel; I also work with the classified staff, transportation, just about anything that is part of the school district. I have some responsibility, usually in a lot of the final decisions. I have to work with the school board, which is a little different than past positions, and of course, work close with the community."*

### Describe your work setting.

*"That's a good question, since this is new to me. I just started my superintendence in July and my work setting right now is ... I actually do a lot of work in my office or in the district office in with the other directors, with the special education personnel. I do a lot of meetings at night with the board members and members of the community. I do have opportunities at times to go into buildings and meet with teachers and students but not as frequently as I would like to. That's probably been the biggest change. So right now, it's a lot more of meetings, I get to go to Harrisburg a lot for different issues as well as the IU, which is the Intermediate Unit in Lancaster."*

### What do you like and dislike about your job?

*"I do like what I'm doing. It's kind of nice to be in this position now. I've been part of this district for 24 years, so I have some idea of what's important here. I enjoy it, I believe in this school district, I believe in the staff and the students and the parents and the community. I enjoy making decisions based on facts, based on discussion, and trying to come up with the best possible solution to whatever the problem or situation might be. I don't know if I'd say there's anything I don't like about it. The one thing that does bother me is that I'm not in the buildings, which I would like to be at this time, because I do enjoy being around students in particular and teachers. And the other thing that sometimes bothers me is there are a lot of what I would call miscellaneous things that I have to be involved in, things that really don't have a big impact on education. For students, it might be bus stops, or it might be people who are, you know, upset with the play, or sporting events. Not that those things aren't important, but I'd rather focus on the educational issues because that's what we're here for. So getting used to the miscellaneous has not been easy for me."*

### In what way do you apply child/adolescent psychology in your work?

*"It's been a long time since I had those courses. I guess what I learned through those courses I even apply in these situations, where I'm not always working with children, but I am working with adults, and you know, the vast spectrum of their needs and their concerns. I learned back then that you have to listen to people, you have to be patient, you have to do your best to make people believe that you really care about them and that you're concerned and yet at the same time, hopefully, respect you and the final decision that is made. I think that, even though I'm not working with children as much as I am with adults, I still believe that I'm applying those same types of philosophies as I meet and work with parents."*

**What are some talents and abilities that would be required to do well in this occupation?**

*"I think with abilities, I do believe you have to be a good listener. I do believe you have to be sincere and give people the time that they desire. I think you have to have the ability to calm people down when they are upset or have a major concern, and I think people skills are critical. You want people to trust in you, to believe in you, and that, hopefully, they'll accept, you know, whatever the decision might be made in regards to an issue. So I think people skills are critical. I think you have to have some knowledge of the course of education and what's happening around you. What I mean by that is the community, the state, and even more in the regard to educational issues and how you could possibly apply those here at Cornwall-Lebanon School District. So I think a knowledge base is important, I think the people skills, I think also, I don't know if this is a talent, but you have to have a passion for what you do. You have to believe in children. That still has to be the number one criteria, at least in my book. And it is, because I was a teacher first, that's where it all started. And even though I don't teach in the classroom now, I still consider myself an educator and a teacher, it's just at a different stage now than standing in a classroom. But I think the passion has to be there, for believing in children and believing in public education."*

**To your knowledge, what are the job prospects in this field?**

*"I think they're still good. I think that coming out of the elementary area now, I know that we still have a lot of applicants for elementary teachers, more so than we have for, say, the secondary level. So from my perspective, there are still a lot of people who have an interest in being a teacher, I'm a little concerned now because in the last few years I've seen a lot of changes in how educating has changed. Let's face it, with online courses, with cyber charter schools, with those kind of things, I do think the face of education is going to change, and I don't know what kind of impact that's going to have on people that are coming out of four year schools trained as an elementary or secondary teacher. I think there are going to be some changes there. I also believe that finances and budget could have an impact on where public education goes in the next three to five years, which again could have an impact on the actual teaching act. I mean it's still thriving, but the people that are coming out had better be able to adapt and change and accept how things are going to change in the next few years."*

**Tell me about your job satisfaction.**

*"I would say that most of the time I feel pretty good in what I do. I mean, I've always loved education, and that's why this is my 30th year. I hope that alone says that I am satisfied in what I do. Sometimes when you're in the position I am in right now you don't always know what impact your decision has made on a lot of people, and you don't always get a lot of feedback. And unfortunately, some of the feedback I do get isn't always the most positive (chuckles), but I keep that in perspective. I think that's just part of being a leader; you have to deal with those things. Every day that I leave here, I feel pretty good, and I look forward to the next day, coming back."*

Once the responsibility of the family, children's education is now institutionalized. The school system has gained significance as our culture has become more technologically oriented. Children today are expected to become proficient in basic skills such as reading, writing, and calculation during middle childhood. They are also expected to learn many facts and absorb much information about the world. Parents assume that children will succeed in their learning experiences if they have properly trained teachers who conduct effective educational programs. Of course, parental involvement is key to student success, as is student motivation.

The school system teaches important lessons other than those involving cognition. Because a school is a social system, it has patterns, rules, boundaries, and other factors designed to promote its effectiveness. Children learn many different social lessons within this context, including group politics and prosocial behaviors as taught by peers.

## *"In Their Own Words"*

**Adam, a 12-year-old seventh grader, talks about his experiences in school.**

*"I don't like going to school. There aren't a lot of activities for us to do. It's not fun. All we do is sit around and listen to our teachers. It's boring. I do like middle school better than elementary school, I like it a lot more than elementary school. We're so much more independent and we have a lot of freedom. We also do more projects ... I feel like I'm treated differently by my friends and family now that I've been in middle school for two years. I know I'm learning a lot of important things about life ... Eighth graders used to scare me in sixth grade. They seemed really scary because they were older and mean to kids. But now a lot of them are my friends so I'm not scared of them anymore ... I also now like having different teachers because some make class more fun than others. I also like having different kids in my classes. I feel like I've made more friends that way ... I'd say I have a lot of friends. I met most of them through school and my classes. Not really even in the sports I play. I have a lot in common with most of my friends, so it was easy to get to know each other ... But I see bullying kind of often. It's mostly name calling. Kids get made fun of a lot because of how they're dressed or how they act ... I also sometimes make fun of kids in school, but it's only when I'm with my friends. We make fun of boys more than girls, mostly for what they're wearing or if they say or do something weird ... I always feel bad for the kids who get made fun of in class, like the mentally challenged kids. If they act up or make a sound, sometimes kids will laugh at them or say mean things ... I sometimes feel overwhelmed by homework. Sometimes my teachers pile on work at the same time. I get it done, though. I do it right when I get home from school, but after I play my Xbox... I am kind of nervous about going to high school ... It's a bigger school and I don't know how the kids will act. I feel like they'll be meaner than the eighth graders were when I was in sixth grade ... I'm not really scared about getting lost. I know there'll be teachers there to help us find our way. I'm mostly just scared about the kids, like the seniors. They're so much older and they know more than I do."*

## *The Electronic World*

Television, video games, computers, all these and other forms of media are impacting human development like never before in the history of humankind. Media can be good or bad in terms of human development. For example, computers and the internet can help school-age children complete research papers without ever needing to enter a brick-and-mortar library. Often public libraries offer free, online homework help so that any child struggling with their studies has a virtual tutor. However, media can also have detrimental effects.

The impact of television on development is the type of media most researched. Often, research in this area offers conflicting results (see Huston & Wright, 1998, for a review of the research). Most studies find a correlation between watching television in childhood and obesity in adolescence. Although most studies infer that television leads to a sedentary lifestyle—hence the increase in obesity—other studies implicate television ads that promote fattening or sugary foods or graze eating while viewing television. Further, although some studies have found that television viewing has no impact on sport or leisure activity participation in middle childhood or adolescence, others have found that heavy television watching decreases participation in such activities.

Whether television viewing impacts academic skills and achievement is also an area of conflicting research (see Huston & Wright, 1998, for a review of the research). Most research indicates that heavy television viewing is correlated with lower levels of time spent reading. Interestingly, children who watch educational programs are more likely to spend time reading, whereas children who watch adult programs or cartoons are less likely to spend time reading. Research seems to indicate that television viewing has little or no impact on homework completion; however, having the television on while doing homework may result in less concentration and lower learning. In terms of overall academic achievement, it appears that television viewing may interfere with school success when children watch more than four hours a day or thirty hours per week.

Educational programming has been shown to have positive outcomes for children. Shows such as *Sesame Street, Reading Rainbow, Ghostwriter, Barney and Friends,* and *Square One* appear to assist children in learning pre-academic and academic skills (see Huston & Wright, 1998, for a review of the research). For example, counting, reading, writing, math strategies, and prosocial behavior all seem to be promoted by educational programming.

Despite the positive outcomes associated with educational programming, most shows on television fall short of this noble cause. Many shows promote gender stereotypes and the sexualization of girls and women (which we will discuss in our module on adolescence) (APA, 2007; Huston & Wright, 1998; Ruble & Martin, 1998). Violent shows also seem to increase aggression in children and decrease sensitivity toward victims of violence. It is extremely important that parents monitor children's television viewing and watch television with them.

*Pause and Process:*

1. How does divorce impact school-age children?

2. What is the difference between peer groups and friends?

# SUMMARY

1. Middle childhood is a quiet period as far as physical changes are concerned. Body configuration becomes leaner; primary teeth are shed and permanent teeth erupt; bone growth slows; muscle development advances, resulting in greater strength and endurance; and there are steady improvements in coordination and motor skill performance.

2. Sports provide students with the opportunity to learn life skills and maintain physical health. Sports provide an environment in which competence, confidence, connections, character, and caring can all be fostered and developed. Stress from coaches can lead to suboptimal outcomes.

3. Eating habits and appetite improve, and children at this stage have better health than young children. Middle-childhood is also a time where parents must monitor children in order to avoid and prevent accidental injuries.

4. School-age children enter a new stage of cognitive development called concrete operations. Before entering this stage at about seven or eight, they go through a transition period (the five-to-seven shift) when their thinking is based on intuition. The concrete operations stage is characterized by limitation of thought to present physical realities and the increasing ability to use mental imagery in problem solving. Several important cognitive changes take place during middle childhood: (1) classification skills improve because of decentering; (2) class inclusion, or how to consider a whole in relation to its part, is learned; (3) reversible operations such as subtraction are accomplished; (4) most kinds of conservation problems are mastered; (5) seriation tasks, or the scaling of objects according to various dimensions are performed; (6) time is better understood; and (7) a cognitive style that is less bound by egocentrism is formed. Individuals in middle childhood use elementary logic to make inferences, but their reasoning is limited by cognitive conceit, or all-or-nothing thinking.

5. School-age children process information in ways that facilitate the learning experiences required by school systems. They demonstrate their improved abilities to process information in their use of attention and use of memory. School-age children become better at selective attention in gathering information from the environment. Their memory improves significantly and they are better able to recall information when performing cognitive tasks. School-age children use various methods and strategies for memory storage. Many different scripts are formed during this stage to facilitate routines. Other scripts are based on understanding social roles. School-age children show great improvements in metacognition and metamemory. Those who have higher levels of these kinds of awareness perform better in school.

6. Language development includes the emergence of metalinguistic awareness. Children also develop an awareness and use of figurative language. Additionally, conversational skills improve. Finally, children fine-tune their knowledge of the morphology, syntax, and pragmatics during the school years.

7. Emotional communication improves during middle childhood. Temperament profiles and attachment influence developmental outcomes. Five temperament profiles proposed by Janson and Mathiesen (2008) are undercontrolled, confident, unremarkable, inhibited, and uneasy.

8. Social cognition is knowledge of the dynamics of human interaction. It is founded on several skills that improve in middle childhood: understanding of others based on advanced social referencing, self-understanding based on knowledge of one's strengths and weaknesses; greater willingness to

accept responsibility for personal actions, and a positive self-concept based on acquiring a healthy sense of industry that acknowledges both positive and negative aspects of the self.

9. Play serves various functions for school-age children. Play activities in middle childhood follow developmental changes that reflect a child's increasing orientation to peers. Fantasy and rough-and-tumble play declines and activities that use rules and involve competition increase. Television watching takes up much recreational time. Families, siblings, friends, and peers all play a role in socializing children. Divorce has serious short-and long-term effects on children.

10. The fourth stage of psychosocial development proposed by Erikson is experienced in middle childhood. This involves the establishment of a sense of industry versus inferiority. A healthy sense of industry involves a positive attitude toward work, duty, and responsibility. It also requires mastery of the social mental skills considered essential for effective functioning in society. School-age children are influenced by family and school systems, but even more by peer groups in acquiring this attitude. A sense of inferiority is a pervasive attitude of worthlessness, especially in comparison with peers. Either of these attitudes has a profound effect on an individual's perceptions of personal competence.

## SELF-QUIZ

1. When does the prepubertal growth spurt occur for most children?
2. How do boys and girls differ in body composition?
3. What changes occur in dentition during this time?
4. What improvements in motor skills are seen during middle childhood?
5. Give an example for each of the five Cs.
6. What are some positive outcomes related to sport participation?
7. What are some negative outcomes related to sport participation?
8. Explain contamination and internalization in understanding illness.
9. Describe the mental disorders discussed in this chapter.
10. How can health in middle childhood be promoted?
11. Describe concrete-operational thought.
12. How is attention understood during middle childhood?
13. Explain the three phases of memory discussed in this chapter.
14. How does chunking help with memory?
15. Define metamemory.
16. How is intelligence traditionally defined?
17. What are Howard Gardner's proposed areas of multiple intelligences? Define each intelligence in your own words.
18. What is meant by math being codified?
19. What are some math strategies in middle childhood?
20. How is school bilingual education different from home bilingual education?
21. Summarize emotional development during middle childhood.
22. Describe the five temperament profiles proposed by Janson & Mathiesen (2008).
23. What are some positive outcomes in middle childhood associated with having a secure attachment?
24. Define social cognition in your own words.
25. How does self-understanding improve during middle childhood?
26. What are the benefits of play in middle childhood?
27. What are the short-term and long-term impacts of divorce on children?
28. Explain how sibling relationships influence development.
29. Describe the social hierarchy of peer groups.
30. How does the electronic world affect development?

# TERMS AND CONCEPTS

| TERM | PAGE | TERM | PAGE |
|------|------|------|------|
| Prepubertal growth spurt | 194 | Linguistic intelligence | 209 |
| Dentition | 196 | Logical-mathematical intelligence | 209 |
| Impulsion | 197 | Metamemory | 209 |
| Speed | 197 | Metacognition | 209 |
| Precision | 197 | Spatial intelligence | 210 |
| Coordination | 197 | Interpersonal intelligence | 210 |
| Balance | 197 | Musical intelligence | 210 |
| Bilateral coordination | 197 | Bodily-kinesthetic intelligence | 210 |
| Strength | 197 | Inventive strategies | 211 |
| Flexibility | 197 | Codified | 211 |
| Competence | 198 | Naturalist intelligence | 211 |
| Confidence | 198 | Existential intelligence | 211 |
| Connections | 198 | School bilingualism | 213 |
| Character | 198 | Figurative language | 213 |
| Caring | 198 | Metalinguistic-awareness | 213 |
| Rhythm | 198 | Sense of industry | 215 |
| Oppositional defiant disorder | 201 | Sense of inferiority | 216 |
| Concrete operations | 202 | Social cognition | 220 |
| Decentering | 203 | Co-regulation | 223 |
| 5-to-7 shift | 203 | Peer group | 227 |
| Horizontal decalage | 204 | Group politics | 227 |
| Reversibility | 204 | Social hierarchy | 228 |
| Class inclusion | 204 | Average | 228 |
| Seriation | 205 | Popular | 228 |
| Cognitive conceit | 206 | Neglected | 228 |
| Selective attention | 207 | Rejected | 228 |
| Sensory register | 207 | One-way assistance | 229 |
| Short-term memory | 207 | Controversial | 229 |
| Long-term memory | 207 | Fair-weather cooperation | 230 |
| Scripts | 208 | Intimate and mutually shared relationships | 230 |
| Multiple intelligences | 209 | | |

# CHAPTER 6

## Adolescence

(iStock)

## OUTLINE

### PHYSICAL DEVELOPMENT DURING ADOLESCENCE

- Physical growth
- Health issues

### COGNITIVE DEVELOPMENT DURING ADOLESCENCE

- Piaget's theory and the formal operational stage
- Other areas of cognitive development during adolescence

### SOCIOEMOTIONAL DEVELOPMENT DURING ADOLESCENCE

- Psychosocial development
- Emotional development
- Self and others

**Adolescence as a life stage is known only in the United States and other developed countries around the world.** It is so accepted here today, however, that it may be surprising to learn that the period between thirteen and eighteen years of age has been recognized as a unique time in the life span merely for the last hundred years.

G. Stanley Hall (1882, 1904) is credited with formalizing the concept of **adolescence** as a developmental stage with its own characteristics and challenges. He was an early proponent of **maturationism,** or the belief that changes in development are due only to heredity; changes result from the execution of genetic programming. Hall based many of his ideas about adolescence on the Darwinian theory of evolution. His global philosophy of developmental change emphasized the concept of *recapitulation*: the idea that the individual's progress through specific stages reflects the social evolution of the human species. Thus he believed that change throughout the life span followed a primitive-to-civilized pattern.

Hall felt that the time between childhood and adulthood was a cultural invention of Western civilization. He characterized this period as one of "storm and stress" that reflected the turbulent growth and rapid change found in modern societies. Hall coined the name for this stage from a Latin word, *adolescere*, meaning "a state of emancipation." This term was applied to slaves in ancient Rome who were not quite freemen but were no longer in servitude.

Most cultures in the world recognize the physical event of puberty as the developmental landmark dividing childhood from full adulthood. Puberty, the process that initiates sexual maturation in humans, begins at about age twelve or thirteen. Many cultures mark this event with ceremonies and initiation rites. Western cultures rarely do so because they see these practices as somewhat primitive.

The anthropologist Margaret Mead investigated adolescence in the South Pacific island cultures of Samoa and New Guinea (1928, 1935). She was particularly interested in the impact of cultural factors on the transition between childhood and adulthood. Mead's studies significantly challenged the universality of Hall's description of adolescence as a time of "storm and stress." In these South Pacific island cultures, Mead found a smooth peaceful transition to adolescence, which she attributed to young people's greater exposure to everyday life. Mead's own work has since been challenged by others, who assert that adolescence in these cultures is, indeed, a stressful experience (Freeman, 1983; Holmes, 1987). This may be a moot point, however, because the notion that adolescence is always stressful in Western cultures is no longer widely accepted.

Nevertheless, several coincidental factors do make these years a distinct period in the life span (Demos & Demos, 1969; Troen, 1985). First, our society has changed from an agrarian one, to one that is technological and urban. This change precipitated many changes in family structure and organization as people moved to cities, adults worked away from home, and children became more involved with others outside their families.

Second, the public school system created institutions in which children were grouped with others of similar ages and segregated from adults. Out of this system a totally new culture of childhood emerged, which eventually led to a new "youth culture" (Kenniston, 1971). The contemporary signs of this youth culture are rock 'n roll and rap music, adolescent dress codes, gang membership, and certain behaviors and attitudes. Instead of a rite of passage into adulthood, our society gives young people the identity of "teenager," with its license to experiment with roles and limits.

Third, technology has changed the outer boundary of adolescence. The period still has its traditional beginning coinciding with the individual's puberty. But when does it end? Originally, Hall envisioned adolescence as a stage of preparation for adulthood. In his day, most people were finished with their education and entering the workforce by age eighteen. But technology has prolonged the educational process in our society. It is common now for people to continue their education well into their twenties or even thirties.

Adolescence today is seen in contradictory terms. On the one hand, it is portrayed as a special time of increased freedom from adult supervision; a time when one comes into one's own as an autonomous person, life is fun, and energy is abundant. On the other hand, it is described as a difficult period marked by conflict with adults, wide swings in emotions, confusion about one's place in the scheme of things, stressful in terms of self-esteem, and rife with dangerous hazards such as pregnancy and substance use. No stage in the life span is without problems and challenges, of course, but adolescence may present more acute challenges than any other stage of the life span for individuals and family systems.

# PHYSICAL DEVELOPMENT DURING ADOLESCENCE

> ## LEARNING OBJECTIVES:
>
> 1. Describe physical growth during adolescence
> 2. Awareness of the unique health issues faced in adolescence

# PHYSICAL GROWTH

### Adolescence

The fifth stage of the life span, occurring between thirteen and eighteen years of age.

### Maturationism

The belief that changes in development are due only to heredity; changes result from the execution of genetic programming.

### Puberty

The developmental event occurring in early adolescence in which the sexual organs become functional. It is associated with other significant physical changes in the body.

Describe the adolescent growth spurt.

In contrast with middle childhood, adolescence is a time of physical changes. These changes produce a metamorphosis: an individual goes from child to physical adult. For most individuals, this transformation is completed by age sixteen.

**ADOLESCENT GROWTH SPURT**    Most of the physical changes commonly associated with adolescence take place in the early part of this stage. During the first four years of adolescence, there is a rapid spurt in growth that is noticeable in almost every aspect of the body, but especially in height and weight. The rate at which these changes occur is comparable to rates seen in the prenatal and infancy stages (Tanner, 1978, 1990). Girls begin their growth spurt typically between the ages of ten and twelve, whereas boys do not generally begin theirs until somewhere between the ages of twelve and fourteen.

*Height and Weight Changes*    The initiation of **puberty**, the process by which the reproductive organs become functionally mature, signals the beginning of numerous physical and psychological changes. Girls, during their average pubertal period between the ages of ten and fourteen, gain about thirty-eight pounds and ten inches. Boys between twelve and sixteen typically gain about forty-two pounds and also about ten inches (Tanner, 1978, 1990). These changes in height and weight occur sporadically during this four-year period—that is, periods of rapid change are followed by slower periods. The term *spurt* is applied to the periods of most rapid change. During a one-year period, many girls gain about twenty pounds and three inches and many boys gain twenty-six pounds and four inches (Tanner, 1978, 1990).

*Body Proportions*    Growth is asynchronous in adolescence (Katchadourian, 1977). This means that advances in different organ systems take place at different times and at different rates. The extremities (the hands and feet) grow earlier and more rapidly than other areas, giving the young adolescent the appearance of being "all hands and feet." Next the calves of the legs and the forearms begin increasing. This is followed by the trunk area (hips, chest, and shoulders). Most of the gains in height come from growth of the trunk area rather than of the legs.

*Internal Organ Systems*    Internal organ systems respond to the adolescent growth spurt (Katchadourian, 1977; Thornburg & Aras, 1986). The cardiovascular system—heart, lungs, and blood vessels—increases in capacity. The number of red blood cells increases also, especially in boys, probably because of increasing levels of a male hormone (testosterone) in the blood.

The brain shows significant structural changes right before and during adolescence (NIMH, 2001). If you remember back to brain development during infancy, we learned about how synapses (or connections) are overproduced and then later pruned back. The pruning occurs according to the use-it-or-lose-it principle and helps strengthen used connections while eliminating unused connections. Right before the onset of adolescence, there is a second period of overproduction of gray matter in the prefrontal cortex (Giedd et al., 1999; NIMH, 2001; Rapoport et al., 1999). The prefrontal cortex area of the brain is responsible for many of our higher thinking abilities such as reasoning, organization, planning, working memory, and emotional regulation. For girls, this period of thickening tends to peak at the age of eleven; for boys, it peaks around the age of twelve. After this peak, pruning begins.

There appears to be differing patterns of brain development for gray and white matter. The gray matter is considered our thinking part of our brain, whereas the white matter connects various parts of the brain and nervous system (NIMH, 2001). Research shows that there is a wave of white matter growth flowing from the front of the brain to the back of the brain during childhood. Particularly, connections flourish in the temporal and parietal lobes, which are important for language development and spatial relations. This wave wanes around the age of twelve. It appears that the ability to learn a first or second language is easier during this wave of white matter growth than after it subsides.

Gray matter maturation appears to occur in the opposite direction, beginning at the back of the brain and moving forward (NIMH, 2001). It appears that the frontal lobes are not fully developed until early adulthood. Different processes shift location as these structural developments occur. For example, some forms of emotional processing seem to occur in the amygdala during early adolescence, although adults utilize the frontal lobe. Many developmentalists feel that some of the risky behavior and emotional issues seen during adolescence may be partly contributed to the relatively late development of the frontal cortex.

Skin problems are also associated with adolescence. Facial acne is the most prevalent skin problem, and its incidence increases rapidly during this period. **Acne** is a chronic inflammation of the oil glands and hair follicles located in the facial area. Acne can be triggered by stress and nervousness (AMA, 2006). Some adolescents are more prone to acne (it tends to run in families) and more resistant to treatment than others. Many teenagers get very upset about their acne, some to the point of obsessiveness. They experience loss of self-esteem that can interfere with their social confidence (Roberts & Ludford, 1976).

The one major organ system that decreases in size during adolescence is the lymphoid system, especially the tonsils and adenoids. This may account for the improvement seen in asthma among affected individuals (Katchadourian, 1977). It also may be a contributing factor as to why adolescents experience fewer upper respiratory diseases than school-age children.

**Acne**

A chronic inflammation of the oil glands and hair follicles located in the facial area.

*Sexual Maturation*    Puberty, the developmental process by which an individual becomes sexually mature and capable of reproduction, is the physical event most prominently associated with adolescence. The physical changes that take place during puberty are orchestrated by interactions between the central nervous system and the glands of the endocrine system, which produce hormones that regulate the functioning of the body. The *pituitary* is the central gland that coordinates the endocrine system. Its hormone secretions stimulate many other glands in the body to function in particular ways.

When puberty begins, the pituitary stimulates the production of hormones that produce changes in the physical size of the body and its organs. Simultaneously, its hormones stimulate the sex glands to begin producing increasing amounts of hormones. In females, these hormones are estrogen and progesterone (produced by the ovaries). In males, the primary hormone is testosterone (produced within the testicles). These hormones bring sexual organs into mature functioning and produce primary and secondary sexual characteristics.

When does puberty occur? Puberty is experienced by boys and girls in a different maturational sequence and at different ages. Individual differences are also very noticeable in the ages at which this process begins and ends. Both genetics and the environment play a role in the timing of puberty (Mustanki et al., 2004).

**FIGURE 6-1    THE MAJOR GLANDS OF THE ENDOCRINE SYSTEM**

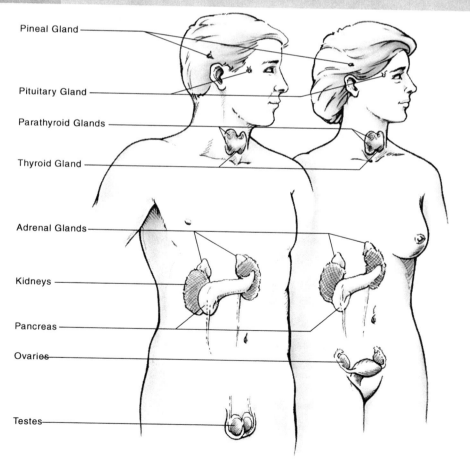

Pineal Gland

Pituitary Gland

Parathyroid Glands

Thyroid Gland

Adrenal Glands

Kidneys

Pancreas

Ovaries

Testes

**Secular trend**

The trend, inferred from observation of several generations, toward achieving sexual maturity at earlier ages than in the past.

**Menarche**

The first menstrual period experienced by a girl, marking the beginning of puberty.

There is a worldwide trend known as the **secular trend**, toward earlier puberty. For example, the average age at **menarche** (first period) in Norway in 1840 was seventeen; in 1950, it was thirteen years and four months (Roche, 1979). The secular trend, which has been noted in many other countries, is thought to be due to a few different factors. First, better health due to better nutrition, lower rates of communicable disease infections (due to immunizations), and greater access to health care may contribute to an earlier onset of puberty. Second, lifestyle changes may be leading to earlier puberty. For example, research has shown that a girl that lives in a home with a nonbiological male (such as a stepfather or boyfriend of the mother) tends to have an earlier onset of puberty (Ellis, 2004; Ellis & Garber, 2000; Mustanski et al., 2004). Some recent research has found this to occur in boys as well (Mustanski et al., 2004). Researchers speculate that pheromones may play a part in this phenomenon (Colmenares & Gomendio, 1988; Ellis, 2004). Third, drinking water contaminated by oral contraceptives and other sources of synthetic estrogen may lead to an earlier onset of puberty in females. Because oral contraceptives are designed to not be broken down by the liver, it is excreted in a woman's urine. Waste water treatment plants are not sufficiently designed to remove these synthetic hormones; hence, traces have been found in drinking water throughout the world. In fact, these synthetic hormones have wrecked havoc on fish, reptile, and amphibian populations throughout the world (Guillette, R., 1994; Gyllenhammar, Holm, Eklund & Berg, 2008; Kidd et al., 2007; Todorov et al., 2002; Xu et al., 2008). Finally, a stressful family environment (which includes poverty, family conflict, inadequate parenting, and absence of the biological father) has been linked to early puberty in girls (Doughty & Rodgers, 2000; Kim & Smith, 1998; Moffitt, Caspi, Belsky & Silva, 1992). Later in this chapter we will learn about the risks associated with early puberty.

In the United States, the average girl begins to experience the changes associated with puberty at about ten years of age (Chumlea, 1982; Tanner, 1990). Individual variations are great, however, and the range is typically from eight to eleven years of age (AMA, 2006). Boys begin the process at about age twelve, and their range is from nine to sixteen years of age. Primary and secondary sexual characteristics typically are fully in evidence within two years of the beginning of puberty in both sexes. Besides an individual's sex, puberty is influenced by a person's genetic background and body weight. The age at which menarche occurs differs considerably between unrelated females, but the average time difference between sisters is only about thirteen months, although that between identical twin sisters is a mere three months (Thornburg & Aras, 1986).

Both males and females who are heavier than age-mates tend to begin puberty at earlier ages than those who are thin. The timing of menarche appears to be sensitive to the proportion of fat present in a girl's body. Girls with athletic figures and little body fat menstruate at later ages and more irregularly than others. Girls who are inactive and weigh more begin menstruation earlier (Frisch, 1983).

How do males experience puberty? Body proportions and size generally undergo a rapid increase during adolescence. Puberty also produces rapid changes in the size and functioning of the reproductive organs. There is a sequence that is followed by most males as they become sexually mature. The initial physical changes associated with puberty are very noticeable in boys because the male reproductive organs are visible.

Growth of the testicles usually signals the beginning of puberty for boys. This change precedes growth of the penis, which usually begins at about age twelve. The testicles begin preparations for producing sperm about this same time, though the prostate gland, which produces seminal fluid to convey sperm outside the body, does not function until about age fourteen. Mature, viable sperm are typically produced at about age fifteen (Richardson & Short, 1978). It should be noted that there are considerable variations in the ages at which these events occur.

Pubic hair growth often begins up to two years before the testicles start to increase in size. Hair begins to appear on the chest and in the armpits after the pubic hair has been established. Facial hair changes in texture and growth rate at about this same time, prompting the need for daily shaving. The change to a more masculine deep voice occurs shortly after the completion of pubic hair growth. The characteristic breaks in tone and pitch as this is happening are due to rapid growth of the larynx and thickening of the vocal cords. Boys experience their first ejaculation of semen typically at about age fourteen or fifteen. This typically happens involuntarily during sleep.

During puberty, boys gain much body weight, primarily in their muscles. This gives them a different body definition than is observed in girls. Other male body configurations resulting from puberty are a widening of the shoulders, growth of the upper body muscles, and expansion of the rib cage. These give mature males a V-shaped torso above the waist (Chumlea, 1982).

How do females experience puberty? Although growth of the reproductive organs in girls is less observable than it is in boys because these organs are mostly internal, the appearance of certain secondary sex characteristics signals the beginning of puberty in a girl's body (Thornburg & Aras, 1986; AMA, 2006). One of the first indications is enlargement and widening of the hips. As this is happening, the breasts begin to develop. The nipples grow larger and darker before mammary tissue starts to develop. Soon after the initiation of hip and breast enlargement, pubic hair appears.

Hair growth at other locations on the body is associated with the first

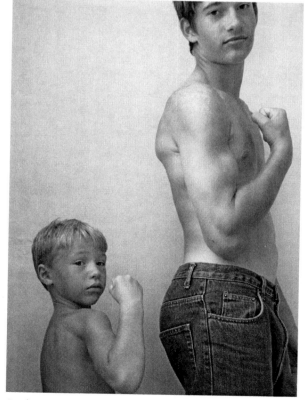

*Body weight and muscle is gained during puberty. (iStock)*

menstrual period. Hair is lighter in pigmentation and softer in texture than in males, except at the armpits and on the legs (because of the practice of shaving these areas). Voice changes are noticeable at this time, but breaks in tone and pitch are uncommon in girls. In both boys and girls, the glands located in the armpits become active at this time, resulting in the production of perspiration and changes in body odor. Similar glands located on the face also begin functioning, sometimes accompanied by acne.

The first indication of sexual maturation is the menarche, or first menstrual period, at about age thirteen (Thornburg & Aras, 1986). The peak of the adolescent growth spurt for girls is associated with the menarche. Menstruation is highly variable in duration and length for about the first year. It is known as *anovulatory* menstruation because regular ovulation, or the production of a viable egg cell during each twenty-eight-day cycle, is not yet occurring. Conception is possible during this time, however, because viable egg cells are sometimes produced.

Menstruation among adolescent girls is sometimes uncomfortable because of cramps. This *dysmenorrhea* may require medical attention if the cramps are painful and limit the girl's activities (Spence & Mason, 1987).

Menarche is a significant physical event for females. It signifies emerging womanhood. However, timing, as our next section will show, is very important.

EARLY VERSUS LATE PUBERTY    As we noted earlier, there is considerable variation in the ages at which puberty begins and when the various physical changes associated with it appear. Imagine your reaction if all of your friends have begun the process of sexual maturing, but you have not. Or, imagine that you are well on your way to sexual maturity when most of your friends are still clearly children. When a person experiences puberty earlier or later than most of his or her same-age peers, it is considered **off-time** puberty (as opposed to on-time puberty). Although variations in the rate and timing of puberty are normal, individuals at both extremes experience both advantages and disadvantages from their position.

Sexual maturity brings other changes in addition to the physical. This developmental event transforms an individual socially and psychologically as well. For example, a youth group coordinator once told one of the authors a story about her granddaughter. The youth group was having a dance, and the youth group coordinator brought her then ten-year-old granddaughter (let's call her Adele) to the dance. Adele matured early and had the physical attributes of the average fourteen-year-old girl. Not knowing her age, an older teen boy asked Adele to dance. How do you think she responded? Do you think she did what the typical teenage girl would do and say either "yes," or "no, thank you"? No. Instead, she covered her face and ran into the bathroom crying. The boy was completely confused. Later, when the youth group coordinator explained that Adele was ten, the boy said that he had no idea how young she was and apologized.

What the above story illustrates is that puberty is far more than just physical and that timing is important. Adele had the body of a teenager, but still had the mind and emotional maturity of a child. However, the rest of the world began treating Adele as though she were socially and psychologically older than her age; and, this would impact Adele's

**Off-time**

When a person experiences puberty earlier or later than most of his or her same-age peers.

development. A year later, Adele was no longer hanging around with the other eleven-year-olds in youth group, but instead with the high school students. Her social circle had changed and she was psychologically more mature than her age-mates. As we will soon see, this can lead to devastating outcomes.

There is a plethora of research on the influence of off-time puberty on developmental outcomes in boys and girls (e.g., Adair & Gordon-Larsen, 2001; Blyth, Simmons & Zakin, 1985; Caspi & Moffitt, 1991; Dick, Rose, Viken & Kaprio, 2000; Duncan et al., 1985; Ge, Conger & Elder, 1996; Ge et al., 2006; Graber, Lewinsohn, Seeley & Brooks-Gunn, 1997; Graber et al., 1998; Jones 1957 and 1965; Kelsey, Gammon & John, 1993; Marshall et al., 1998; McPherson, Sellers, Potter, Bostick & Folsom, 1996; Petersen, 1988; Rudolph, 2008; Sellers et al., 1992; Steinberg, 1987; Susman et al., 2007; Weichold, Silbereisen & Schmitt-Rodermund, 2003; Wellens et al., 1992; Williams & Dunlop, 1999; Wiesner & Ittel, 2002; Wu et al., 1988). Across these studies, the outcomes discussed below were discovered.

Compared to on-time and/or later maturing girls, early maturing girls can experience many problems. The following outcomes have been correlated with early puberty in girls: lower self-esteem, depression, lower coping skills, missing school, risky sexual behavior, eating disorders, substance abuse, body dissatisfaction, and obesity. When compared to on-time and/or early maturing girls, late maturing girls are more likely to experience the following: increased self-consciousness, thinness, and increased future academic goals.

When compared to on-time or late maturing boys, early maturing boys are more likely to experience the following: early alcohol use, increased depression rates, more emotional reliance on others than on-time maturing boys, increased popularity, increased self-image and body satisfaction, and increased substance abuse.

When compared to on-time or early maturing boys, late maturing boys are more likely to experience the following: lower self-esteem, immature behavior, feelings of inferiority, poorer athletic ability and psychopathology.

As the above demonstrates, there are a multitude of problems associated with early or late maturation for both boys and girls. Interestingly, looking at the aggregate, the most severe outcomes are found in early maturing girls. Several possibilities exist to account for this finding. However, keeping the multi-dimensional nature of development in mind, one must examine the social consequences for early maturing girls. Often, they draw the attention of older boys who in turn may introduce these young girls to delinquency inappropriate for this age. This association may be contributing to the found negative effects of early maturation. Of course, steps can be taken to help avoid these outcomes. For example, parental monitoring and social support can help prevent many of these adjustment problems.

*Pause and Process:*

1. How do males and females physically develop during adolescence?

2. What influences the timing of puberty? What are some potential consequences for off-time puberty?

# HEALTH ISSUES

## *Nutritional Needs*

Adults are often amazed at a teenager's capacity for food, especially in contrast to how the same individual ate just a few years earlier. However, the increased need for calories is often met by teenagers eating foods that consist of "empty" calories. The notorious American teenage diet features fast foods and snack foods such as doughnuts, pizza, fries, chips, candies, and burgers. These foods are high in sugar and fat, but deficient in such nutrients as iron, protein, calcium, and zinc. Serious deficiencies in these substances can lead to delayed sexual maturation, stunted growth, and poor skeletal development and organ functioning. They can also adversely affect psychological mood (Steiner, 1990). Nutritional deficiencies are even more serious when a teenage girl becomes pregnant. Improper eating habits can endanger the health and well-being not only of the infant but also of the young mother (Strobino, 1987). Obesity is also a growing concern with 17.6 percent of all adolescents considered obese (CDC, 2009).

The World Health Organization (2008) reports that many individuals are malnourished when they begin adolescence. They may be malnourished due to a lack of food or due to poor eating habits. In fact, it is possible to be overweight or even obese and be mal-nourished. As mentioned above, lack of nutrition can lead to many physical and psychological issues. At the extreme, malnutrition can lead to serious illness and death. Adolescence is a key time for proper nutrition and exercise, as it acts as the springboard into adulthood. We will discuss eating disorders in the mental health section of this chapter.

Some teenagers decide to adopt a vegetarian diet. Because of the physical changes that occur during adolescence, the elimination of an entire food group from one's diet can be dangerous (AMA, 2006). It is often helpful for teenagers to meet with a dietitian when beginning a vegetarian diet in order to ensure proper nutrition and learn about possible food combinations. However, research seems to indicate that vegetarian adolescents do a better job of meeting dietary recommendations than nonvegetarian adolescents (Perry et. al, 2002).

*Teenagers tend to consume nutrient deficient foods such as hamburgers and fries. (iStock)*

**ILLNESS, DISORDERS, AND OTHER CONCERNS**   In earlier chapters we learned about Bibace and Walsh's (1979, 1980, and 1981) developmental stages for understanding illness. We learned that phenomenism and contagion are how illness is understood in early childhood. We also learned that contamination and internalization are how illness is understood in middle childhood. During adolescence, the final two stages of understanding illness typically emerge.

Physiologic is the fifth stage for understanding illness. **Physiologic** thinking can be described as understanding illness "as the malfunctioning of an internal physiologic organ or process and is explained as a step-by-step sequence of events" (Bearison, 1998). This thinking goes a step beyond the internalization stage by a deeper understanding about the physiological process of illness.

The sixth and final stage is called psychophysiologic. In **psychophysiologic** thinking "illness is understood physiologically, but the child also can consider the influence of psychological factors" (Bearison, 1998). An adolescent at this stage of reasoning will understand that stress can trigger heart attacks, as well as the physiological aspects of a heart attack. It is at this point that a person can begin to approach health and well-being holistically.

*Mental Health During Adolescence*   Approximately 20 percent of adolescents have a mental disorder of some type (WHO, 2008). Eating disorders are of particular concern during this phase of the life span. Many adolescents are highly self-critical of their bodies. Frantic to achieve a desired body image, they may diet to the point of malnutrition. Some have such a distorted body image that they convince themselves they are obese when objectively they are not (Mellendick, 1983). They feel such low self-esteem in relation to their perceived weight problem that they become vulnerable to serious eating disorders (Button, 1990).

The most common serious eating disorders in adolescence are anorexia nervosa and bulimia nervosa. Both conditions are seen more in teenage girls than in boys. These conditions have serious consequences for the health, well-being, and even the lives of teenagers (Dukes & Lorch, 1989; Phelps & Bajorek, 1991).

**Anorexia nervosa** is an abnormal fear of obesity that is manifested by distortions of body image and "the relentless pursuit of thinness" (American Psychiatric Association, 1980; Bruch, 1978; SAMHSA, 2003). Its symptoms are excessive weight loss (25 percent of total body weight or more); the cessation of menstruation; a distorted body image—that is, believing that one is seriously overweight when this is not so; obsessive-compulsive preoccupation with dieting; social withdrawal; depression; and feelings of insecurity, loneliness, inadequacy, and helplessness. The typical anorexic is a girl between twelve and twenty years of age who comes from a stable, well-educated, and socially competent family and who is herself bright, well-behaved, and physically attractive (Gilbert & DeBlassie, 1984).

This condition is one of the few psychological disorders that can have fatal consequences if left untreated (SAMHSA, 2003). It begins with dieting to achieve a certain weight level. However, once that level is achieved, an anorexic continues to diet obsessively. Controlling her weight and what she eats has become her central life focus.

---

**Physiologic**

The fifth stage for understanding illness; described as the malfunctioning of an internal physiologic organ or process and is explained as a step-by-step sequence of events.

**Psychophysiologic**

The sixth stage for understanding illness; illness is understood physiologically, but the child also can consider the influence of psychological factors.

**Anorexia nervosa**

An eating disorder involving complex emotional and body image disturbances that lead to an obsession with limiting dietary intake in order to control body weight. The condition is life-threatening if left untreated.

The causes of this condition are not clear, although several explanations have been proposed. One is that heavy cultural conditioning convinces adolescent girls that slim figures are essential to attract males (Carruth & Goldberg, 1990). Another explanation is that anorexia is a means to avoid or delay dealing with the many changes associated with puberty. Extreme thinness often stops menstruation and prevents the development of a female body configuration. Finally, some have seen anorexia as a means of rebelling in a passive-aggressive way against strict, overprotective parents. Unable to establish adequate personal boundaries combined with an inability to individuate or attain personal autonomy in normal ways because of parental over-involvement, the anorexic resorts to proving her control of herself by severely controlling her weight (Bruch, 1978; Romeo, 1984).

If left untreated, anorexia can result in death due to starvation. Therapy can involve hospitalization to treat the malnutrition and individual therapy to help the young woman become autonomous in less damaging ways (Beresin, Gordon & Herzog, 1989). Family therapy may be needed to end the extreme enmeshment of the girl with her parents, to improve communication, and to help the family system acquire healthy ways of resolving conflict (Muuss, 1985; Waller, Calam & Slade, 1988). Approximately one out of every one hundred to two hundred adolescent females suffers from anorexia (National Institute of Health, 1999).

**Bulimia nervosa** involves consuming huge amounts of food and then purging the body by vomiting, using laxatives or enemas, or excessive exercise (Hudson, Pope & Jonas, 1983; Pope et al., 1983, SAMHSA, 2003). The consumption is done in binges, usually to cope with some stressful situation. Like anorexics, bulimics have a distorted body image that leads to an obsession with weight control. Unlike anorexics, however, bulimics know that their behavior is not appropriate. They usually binge and purge in secret to avoid discovery, but they feel much shame and guilt nevertheless.

Bulimia is a common method of achieving weight control among contemporary adolescent girls. Approximately one to three out of every one hundred adolescents suffers from bulimia (National Institute of Health, 1999). It can lead to severe depression, which can result in suicide (Kandel, Raveis & Davies, 1991). Many bulimics are perfectionists with an obsessive desire to control and manage their own and others' lives. They are heavily dependent on others' approval for their self-worth (Pike, 1991).

**Bulimia Nervosa**

An eating disorder involving emotional and body image disturbances that lead to intake of large amounts of food that are then purged by vomiting or use of laxatives to control body weight.

*Bulimia can sometimes be used to cope with stress. (iStock)*

This condition, like anorexia, responds to psychotherapy and treatment with antidepressant medications. These help bulimics to achieve a better understanding of femininity and healthy ways of dealing with stressful situations (Muuss, 1986; Yager, 1988).

*Risky Behavior*    The use of drugs among adolescents is one of the greatest health concerns for this age group. Globally, tobacco is used by more than one 150 million adolescents (WHO, 2008). In the United States, 26 percent of all twelfth graders engage in heavy drinking (Federal Interagency Forum on Child and Family Statistics, 2008). Further, 22 percent of twelfth graders report using illegal drugs (Federal Interagency Forum on Child and Family Statistics, 2008). Why would so many adolescents want to use such mood-altering substances when they are at a period of life that our society sees as the best of times? Perhaps there is no simple explanation. Some teenagers seem predisposed to drug use because they observe their parents doing so (Brown, 1989; Kline, Canter & Robin, 1987). Others are susceptible to peer pressure to experiment with drugs (Newcomb, McCarthy & Bentler, 1989; Swaim et al., 1989). Drug use may also have something to do with a lack of adequate parental supervision before and after school (Richardson & Dwyer, 1989) and the nature of relationships within the family system (Brook et al., 1986; Newcomb & Bentler, 1988a, 1988b).

Adolescents do not always perceive drugs as harmful. In reality, teenagers experience harmful effects from drug use in both the short and the long term. Self-destructive behaviors associated with chronic use of these substances include addiction, lack of motivation, and suicide (Sommer, 1984). Drug use begun in adolescence usually continues into adulthood (Kandel et al., 1986; Newcomb & Bentler, 1988). Teenagers who use drugs regularly tend to be in poorer health than their age-mates and to have unstable job and financial conditions, troublesome relationship histories, and emotional depression. Like adults, teenagers use drugs to cope with unhappiness, stress, loneliness, and physical as well as psychological pain. Recent research finds rather serious consequences for even moderate drug use by teenagers. One is that it is highly associated with sexual behaviors that place adolescents at high risk of HIV infection (Keller et al., 1991).

*Alcohol*    Use of drugs for medicating physical and psychological discomforts is endemic in American culture (Nobles, 1984; Rowe & Rodgers, 1991). Many drugs, in fact, are so widely used that people are surprised to learn they *are* drugs. For example, coffee contains a powerful stimulant, caffeine, which is an addictive drug. Likewise alcohol is a drug that has mood-altering and addictive properties.

Alcohol use among teenagers is so common that some consider it normal, although our society officially defines drinking by those younger than twenty-one as illegal (Newcomb & Bentler, 1989). Nearly 45 percent of high school students have had an alcoholic drink within the past month, according to a comprehensive survey (CDC, 2007). Peer pressure evidently plays a significant role in this behavior.

*Tobacco*    Although many people don't think of tobacco as a drug, cigarette smoke contains nicotine which is one of the most addictive substances. Smoking is regarded by

*The use of marijuana can have adverse affects on the reproductive system. It also impairs motor abilities. (iStock)*

medical authorities as a serious health hazard (Adeyanju, 1989). Around 20 percent of high school students smoke, although nearly 8 percent use smokeless tobacco (CDC, 2007). Teenagers who use other drugs such as alcohol also tend to smoke cigarettes. Other risk factors are having at least one parent who smokes, a greater tendency than the norm for risk-taking behaviors, and a rebellious personality (Ary & Biglan, 1988; Windle, 1991).

*Marijuana*    Marijuana ("pot") may symbolize adolescent rebellion against authority and control more than other drugs. Many more adolescents experiment with this drug than use it regularly (Newcomb & Bentler, 1989). For example, a national survey found that although 38 percent of high school students had tried marijuana, 19.7 percent had used it within the last month (CDC, 2007). Those who use marijuana regularly resemble adolescents who use cigarettes and alcohol: they tend to have parents who use drugs as coping mechanisms and who are somewhat rebellious in nature.

There are both short- and long-term effects of marijuana use on the user's health. The chemical components in marijuana smoke temporarily impair motor abilities and lung functioning, decrease sperm counts in males and interfere with ovulation in females, diminish the responsiveness of the immune system, and contribute to the risk of lung cancer (National Academy of Sciences, 1982). Chronic pot smokers tend to have low motivation and energy, and teenage users may be expected to have problems with school and job performance (Rainone et al., 1987). In addition, violent delinquent behavior is associated with heavy use of marijuana and other illicit drugs among boys (Watts & Wright, 1990).

*Sexual Activity*    Slightly less than half (47.8 percent) of all U.S. high school students have engaged in sexual intercourse (CDC, 2007). Such early sexual behavior is worrisome for several reasons. First, adolescents are not yet emotionally mature enough to handle the aftermath of sexual activity. Second, less than two-thirds of sexually active teens use a condom to prevent sexually transmitted diseases. Third, teenage pregnancy may result from this behavior.

Early sexual behavior is responsible for some scary statistics. Worldwide, adolescents and people in their early twenties account for 45 percent of all new HIV infections (CDC, 2007). Additionally, approximately 11 percent of all births (or sixteen million births) worldwide are to teenage mothers. Furthermore, sexually transmitted disease (STD) rates have increased for adolescents in recent years. According to the Center for Disease Control, "while representing 25 percent of the ever sexually active population, fifteen- to twenty-four-year-olds acquire nearly half of all new STDs." Although condoms can help prevent infections and pregnancy, the one sure way to avoid these outcomes is abstinence (AMA, 2006).

*Promoting Wellness*    The American Psychological Association (APA) recently had a task force convene to investigate the sexualization of girls in the United States. They released their findings in 2007 in a troublesome report. The APA (2007) defines **sexualization** as the following: "a person's value comes only from his or her sexual appeal or behavior, to the exclusion of other characteristics; a person is held to a standard that equates physical attractiveness (narrowly defined) with being sexy; a person is sexually objectified—that is, made into a thing for others' sexual use, rather than seen as a person with the capacity for independent action and decision making; and/or sexuality is inappropriately imposed upon a person" (p. 1).

In our society, girls are especially inundated with messages from every form of media that they are first and foremost sexual beings (APA, 2007). It isn't hard for girls to begin to base their self-worth on their identity as a sexual being. Parents and peers can further contribute to the sexualization of girls by emphasizing physical appearance and conformity to media messages. Girls can internalize all of these messages and begin to think of themselves as sexual objects to be presented to others for their desires.

Sexualization of girls can lead to serious consequences across various domains (APA, 2007). Obsession with one's appearance can prevent concentrating on academic matters. Mathematical ability and logical reasoning are two areas that research has found are impacted by sexualization. Shame is a common emotion experienced by girls and women who have been sexualized. Low self-esteem, eating disorders, and depression are three mental health concerns that research has found to be linked to sexualization. Finally, sexualization can lead to sexual problems in adulthood due to unrealistic expectations or shame.

The impact of sexualization extends beyond the girls who experience it (APA, 2007). Rigid sexual stereotypes are propagated through sexualization. Men may be unable to find a female they consider acceptable (due to unrealistic physical expectations) and establish a healthy relationship (due to treating women as objects). Sexualization contributes to the devaluing of older women who do not meet the young, attractive ideal idolized by our media. Finally, sexualization increases sexism, which is linked to increased rates of sexual harassment and sexual violence, decreased rates of women going into math and science fields, and increased viewership of child pornography.

The sexualization of girls, and society in general, must be fought if health and well-being are to be supported in our adolescents. The APA (2008) has developed specific advice for parents to assist in fighting sexualization of their children. Parents should be

**Sexualization**

A person's value comes only from his or her sexual appeal or behavior, to the exclusion of other characteristics; a person is held to a standard that equates physical attractiveness (narrowly defined) with being sexy; a person is sexually objectified—that is, made into a thing for others' sexual use, rather than seen as a person with the capacity for independent action and decision making; and/or sexuality is inappropriately imposed upon a person.

aware of what their adolescents are watching and listening to on television and in other forms of media. If their favorite show depicts women as sexual objects, talk about it with them. Increase their awareness of how this is wrong and that both females and males must be valued for traits beyond their physical appearance. Parents should encourage their adolescents to be interested in activities that focus on areas beyond appearance. Sports, religious groups, school clubs, and other extracurricular activities can help youth develop identities that focus on qualities beyond their appearance. Finally, educate adolescents. Appropriate sexual behavior and inappropriate sexual behaviors should be discussed. Ideally, adolescents should feel comfortable discussing sexuality with their parents.

Beyond combating sexualization, there are some other issues to consider in promoting the health and well-being of adolescents. Only 34.7 percent of all adolescents engage in the recommended amount of physical activity each week (CDC, 2007). Further, nearly 25 percent of teens play video games or use a computer for reasons other than schoolwork for more than three hours each day, and 35.4 percent watch television for three or more hours each day. Clearly, steps should be taken to encourage teenagers to spend less time in sedentary activities and more time engaging in physical activities.

Sleep is another area of concern. Adequate sleep is necessary for motivation, mood, attention, learning, and mental health (Dahl, 1999). However, only 31.1 percent of all teenagers regularly obtain the recommended eight hours of sleep each night (CDC, 2007).

The World Health Organization (2008) states that "nearly two thirds of premature deaths and one third of the total disease burden in adults are associated with conditions or behaviors that began in youth, including tobacco use, a lack of physical activity, unprotected sex or exposure to violence." Educating youth about healthy behavior will not only assist achieving a healthy and safe adolescence, but lead to a longer and healthier adult life as well.

*Pause and Process:*

1. What are some health and behavior concerns during adolescence?

2. What are some consequences of the sexualization of girls?

## *"Development in the Real World"*

Wendy Bentzoni is a detective for the district judge of Monroe County, PA. She works at the Monroe County District Attorney's office.

**What type of work do you conduct?**

*"I am a police officer dealing with central assault and dating violence investigations."*

**Describe your general work setting?**

*"I sometimes have to go to court. I have interviews with teen victims of sexual assault. I have to do reports and typing. Mostly interviewing and meeting with people. Like today I had court and later I'm going to be interviewing a victim of sexual assault."*

**What do you like and dislike about your job?**

*"I like when I can work with someone and help them get some assistance or justice or help them find resources to help themselves when they are in a situation that they can't fix. I don't like when we lose a trial and the victim feels like it's their own fault. I really hate when that happens."*

**In what way do you apply child/adolescence psychology in your work?**

*"I have to meet with each victim and each one is different and I have to get on their level. According to their personality and their issues and I change the way I interview or the questions I ask. I have to adapt my technique to their problems such as self esteem issues or health issues or whatever it may be."*

**What are some talents and abilities that would be required to do well in this occupation?**

*"To relate to people. People from all different places and backgrounds you have to deal with. It's hard to do but I can relate with my own kids and from the background I come from and how I was raised and brought up that makes it easier for me to be able to relate with all different kinds of people."*

**To your knowledge what are the job prospects in this field?**

*"There is a lot of need for females in law enforcement, I feel, as females can relate better to people and I don't get a lot of people that are in a good place and are happy and there's a great need for people with the ability to do what I do."*

**Tell me about your job satisfaction.**

*"I worked with a lot of people who I don't mind working with. I like helping them or finding resources and agencies to make them better and get them out of the situation that there in whether it's a bad relationship or family issue. Knowing I can help them and get to a better place is extremely rewarding and self-fulfilling."*

# COGNITIVE DEVELOPMENT DURING ADOLESCENCE

### *LEARNING OBJECTIVES:*

*1. Characterize the formal operational stage of cognitive development*

*2. Describe other ways cognitive abilities develop during adolescence*

During adolescence, important changes take place in an individual's cognitive abilities. Thinking and comprehension during early and middle childhood are governed by perceptions. Children use their perceptions of the environment to develop hypotheses about their worlds that they believe are borne out by factual experiences. In adolescence, individuals' understanding of people, events, and circumstances becomes more flexible and abstract reasoning becomes possible.

# PIAGET'S COGNITIVE DEVELOPMENTAL THEORY AND THE FORMAL OPERATIONAL STAGE

**Formal operations**

The fourth stage of cognitive development proposed by Piaget that commences in adolescence; thought is characterized as less rigid, more flexible, and less dependent on perceptions and past experiences.

**Deductive reasoning**

Beginning with the big picture and developing conclusions.

**Inductive reasoning**

Reasoning from specific facts to general conclusions.

**Hypothetical reasoning**

The ability to think and reason about ideas in the abstract.

*Spotlight*

Define inductive and deductive reasoning in your own words and provide an example for each.

**Scientific-inductive reasoning**

Starting with an observation or thought that generates a hypothesis about something.

Piaget (1967) labels adolescence as the period of **formal operations**. Cognitive skills advance during this time as adolescents become increasingly able to use logic and reasoning. They are capable of thinking hypothetically, of using deductive and inductive reasoning to reach conclusions and to solve a variety of problems (Wadsworth, 2004). **Deductive reasoning** is when you begin with the big picture and develop conclusions. Said another way, you move from the general to the specific with deductive reasoning. **Inductive reasoning** can be defined as "reasoning from specific facts to general conclusions" (Wadsworth, 2004, p. 113). **Hypothetical reasoning** or thought is the ability to think and reason about ideas in the abstract.

The egocentrism that colored an individual's perceptions through childhood lessens. By late adolescence, an individual shows much more flexibility. Thinking is less absolute as teens discover that there are gray areas in many situations where rigid rules fail to apply.

## *Characteristics of Formal Operational Thought*

Formal operations thinking is characterized by hypothetical-deductive reasoning and scientific-inductive reasoning (Piaget, 1972; Wadsworth, 2004). Hypothetical-deductive reasoning allows individuals to work through mathematical and other such problems abstractly. For example, consider the following word problem:

> Representatives from eight nations have decided to meet to discuss an international standardized test for graduating college students. The eight nations are China, France, Germany, Italy, Japan, Singapore, Sweden, and the United States. You are the administrative assistant and must develop the seating chart for the meeting. The table is long and rectangular. China must NOT sit across or next to Japan. France must sit next to Germany. Sweden must sit next to Italy and across from Singapore. The United States must be across from Japan. Draw the seating chart.

Hypothetical-deductive reasoning would allow a person to deduce the seating chart from the premises of the problem. Additionally, use of hypothetical-deductive reasoning would allow a person to start with a false premise, yet reason a logical conclusion (Wadsworth, 2004).

In contrast to hypothetical-deductive reasoning, **scientific-inductive reasoning** starts with an observation or thought that generates a hypothesis about something. The person then logically works through the alternatives that are implied as outcomes or conclusions of the hypothesis.

A classic experiment by Inhelder and Piaget (1958) reveals how individuals change their reasoning about the laws of physics by manipulating objects. Shifts in the manner by which hypotheses are generated to explain the physical actions and reactions of objects show how scientific reasoning develops during adolescence. Children and adolescents were given a variety of objects. They were asked to place some in water and explain why certain objects sank while others floated. They were also given different weights to place on a scale or on a pendulum held by a string and challenged to determine what accounted for the speed of the pendulum's swing. Marbles were given to the individuals that they were to roll down an incline and estimate the distance the marbles would roll when reaching a flat surface.

When experimenting with the weights placed on a string pendulum, for example, individuals at all ages were challenged to determine which factor accounts for the pendulum's speed (Ginsburg & Opper, 1979). Several factors must be considered in reaching a solution to this problem:

*Marbles rolling down an incline is an example of a scientific-inductive reasoning test. (iStock)*

(1) the length of the string, (2) the object's weight, (3) the degree of force used to place the pendulum in motion, and (4) the height from which the object is released.

Children at the preoperational stage were perplexed by this problem. They tended to experiment in a trial-and-error fashion with the various factors. They haphazardly experimented with the different factors. They usually concluded (incorrectly) that it is the force by which an object is pushed on the pendulum that determines its speed because this *appears* to be the case.

Children at the concrete operations level approached the problem in similar ways. They did not experiment with the various factors systematically, but rather impulsively. However, because thinking at this level of cognitive development involves more mental imagery, they were able to consider several possible solutions before they began experimenting. When experimenting with the different factors, these children were likely to conclude (again, incorrectly) that more than one factor influenced the speed of the pendulum because they varied two factors simultaneously (e.g., the length of the string and the object's weight).

Adolescents of fourteen or fifteen, the age at which one enters the formal operations stage, realized that the solution to the problem could be determined systematically. By experimenting with changes in factors one at a time, these teenagers discovered that only one factor or one combination of factors could affect the pendulum's speed. They generated hypotheses before they began experimenting with making changes in each factor. By reasoning in a scientific manner, they could change one factor, such as the length of the string, while keeping the other factors constant. By methodically experimenting in this fashion, teenagers were able to conclude (correctly) that the string's length is the key factor in determining the speed of a pendulum.

The increasing flexibility in thinking that occurs during adolescence can be seen in other ways. For example, Flavell (1985) proposes that individuals in late adolescence can participate in what is called the **game of thinking**. This requires divorcing oneself from reality and playfully considering various hypothetical possibilities in certain situations. For instance, it is possible for an eighteen-year-old to play the role of "devil's advocate" in discussions of moral issues. In this role, the person suspends his own personal beliefs and assumes, for the sake of argument or to make a conversation more interesting, a position that may be diametrically opposed to what he actually believes. A school-age child would be unable to do this because individuals at the concrete operations level are bound by their perceptions of reality and have great difficulty seeing situations from other vantage points.

Individuals who are developing cognitive skills characteristics at the formal operations level apply these advanced thinking skills to many different types of problems—moral decisions, understanding others, and developing a philosophy of life or a belief system, for example. They first consider all the possible options, alternatives, or avenues for solving a problem or deriving the explanation of a situation. Then they examine each independently and in relation to others to arrive at an acceptable solution.

## Cognitive Traits

We gain a better appreciation of adolescents' social behavior when we take their level of cognitive ability into consideration. Like most developmental changes, mature thinking is achieved gradually rather than abruptly. For many individuals, the process continues throughout adulthood (Kohlberg & Gilligan, 1971). For example, only 57 percent of adults forty-five to fifty years old who were presented with the pendulum problem just discussed were successful at solving it. This compares with slightly more than half of the adolescents studied.

Mature thinking styles give people greater freedom to explore possibilities in considering and solving a variety of problems. They make people more empathic and capable of critically examining the values and beliefs they have been taught by others. The ability to disengage oneself from reality to consider numerous possibilities opens avenues that less mature thinking styles restrict or inhibit. These less mature styles are carried from middle childhood into early adolescence, however, and act as barriers or challenges to acquiring the more mature, flexible style that characterizes late adolescence and early adulthood. One cognitive distortion that hinders achievement of fully mature thinking is adolescent egocentrism.

Psychologist David Elkind (1967, 1978) states that the type of cognitive egocentrism observed in adolescence is the essence of adolescence itself. Cognitive egocentrism was first observed in early childhood. Preschoolers are egocentric in that they regard their own perceptual viewpoint as the only means for understanding the operations of the world. This trait somewhat continues to color interpretations of the world throughout middle child-

**Game of thinking**

Divorcing oneself from reality and playfully considering various hypothetical possibilities in certain situations.

hood, though it weakens during this time. However, school-age children still make judgments and interpretations in absolute terms based on appearances and perceptions. This causes them to think in polar extremes: something is either all right or completely wrong; people are treated either fairly or unfairly; something is either 100 percent good or 100 percent bad. Children this age have difficulty perceiving that there is middle ground between these two extremes.

In adolescence, childhood egocentrism gives way to logical thinking. However, even as this is occurring, egocentrism persists, though it manifests itself in new ways.

**Pseudostupidity**

The tendency of young adolescents to interpret situations in more complex ways than called for.

1. **Pseudostupidity** is the tendency of young adolescents to interpret situations in more complex ways than called for. This has been termed "reading more into situations than what is intended or implied" or "making mountains out of molehills." Teens can become so overwhelmed by the complexity of issues and the numerous alternatives available for action that they are unable to make any decision. Pseudostupidity produces indecisiveness in some adolescents much of the time, and in most adolescents in some circumstances. For some people, this cognitive distortion continues into adulthood.

**Imaginary audience**

The adolescent egocentric belief that other people are obsessed and consumed with his or her appearance and behavior.

2. Young adolescents typically believe that they are the center of everyone's attention or that they are carefully observed by an **imaginary audience**. This belief often makes them overly self-conscious about their appearance. It also convinces them that they can read other people's minds, which leads to another cognitive distortion: *fortune telling* or *jumping to conclusions* (Burns, 1980). This flaw in logical thinking produces negative interpretations based on incomplete or inaccurate information.

**Personal or Invincibility fable**

The belief that one is immune from all harm or injury.

3. Young adolescents believe in the **personal** or **invincibility fable** (Elkind, 1974). This is the belief that one is immune from all harm or injury. It leads young adolescents to believe they are special, that bad things can only happen to others, but not to them. This cognitive distortion helps explain the outrageous, extreme, and high-risk behaviors common among young adolescents (e.g., early sexual behavior, drinking, smoking, riding with drivers under the influence of alcohol, riding a motorcycle without a helmet, etc.).

**Apparent hypocrisy**

The considerable incongruence between what they say they believe and how they behave.

4. Teenagers show a certain degree of **apparent hypocrisy**, meaning there is considerable incongruence between what they say they believe and how they behave. Apparent hypocrisy is often manifested in stubborn arguments with adults, especially parents. For example, young teens can be very critical of parental insensitivity to their needs, yet feel that they do not have to be sensitive to their parents' needs. Their egocentrism leads them to believe they are exempt from rules they believe are valid and important for others to observe.

A major developmental task of adolescence is to overcome the barriers of egocentrism and advance toward more mature ways of reaching decisions (Ginsburg & Opper, 1979). This requires learning to question one's style of thinking. By using more logical thinking processes and gathering information based on fact, an individual achieves more sophisticated levels of formal operations.

*Pause and Process:*

1. How is the formal operations stage of thinking different from thinking in the concrete operations stage?

2. How may the imaginary audience, invincibility fable, and egocentrism impact the behavior of high school students?

# OTHER AREAS OF COGNITIVE DEVELOPMENT IN ADOLESCENCE

Modern cognitive theorists study ways in which cognitive development continues past childhood. Although many areas of information-processing and language skills reach adult-like levels by the end of middle childhood, other areas of cognition continue to develop.

## *Dialectical Reasoning*

**Dialectical reasoning**

The deliberate coordination of inferences for the purpose of making cognitive progress.

One area that continues to develop is dialectical reasoning. **Dialectical reasoning** can be defined as "the deliberate coordination of inferences for the purpose of making cognitive progress" (Moshman, 1998, p. 961). In plain English, it involves integrating one's assumptions to assist when reasoning through a problem. Argumentation may involve the use of dialectical reasoning. When debating an issue with another, one will often use their beliefs and observations to make a point.

## *Problem Solving*

**Problem solving**

The development of strategies to overcome an obstacle in order to achieve a goal.

**Problem solving** is another area that shows continued development across childhood into adolescence (Deloache, Miller & Pierroutsakos, 1998; Siegler, 1998). Problem solving involves developing a strategy to overcome an obstacle in order to achieve a goal. Problem solving involves many aspects of cognitive processes, such as memory, reasoning, metacognition, and perception.

**Task analysis**

The careful examination of a problem and consideration of what steps will be necessary in order to solve it.

One key component to problem solving is task analysis. **Task analysis** requires you to carefully examine the problem and consider what steps will be necessary in order to solve it (Deloache, Miller & Pierroutsakos, 1998; Siegler, 1998). After task analysis, you must encode. **Encoding** allows you to develop an internal, mental representation of the situation. Finally, your knowledge should be used to assist in addressing the problem and reconciling it.

**Encoding**

Developing an internal, mental representation of the situation.

There are developmental differences in problem solving strategies and abilities (Deloache, Miller & Pierroutsakos, 1998; Siegler, 1998). Rudimentary forms of problem

What is meant by problem solving?

solving are evident in infancy. Across childhood, the ability to plan a strategy for solving a problem improves. As age increases, the ability to develop and achieve subgoals in assistance to solving the larger problem improves. The ability to choose or develop the most appropriate strategy also improves with age. Finally, with formal operational thought, sophisticated forms of reasoning emerge. Such reasoning allows for better problem solving.

## Moral Reasoning

Up until now, we really haven't discussed moral reasoning. Hence, we will need to back up a bit to childhood in order to understand moral reasoning in adolescence.

Kohlberg describes a model of moral reasoning that is widely accepted among developmental researchers. He believes that children are moral philosophers. A series of related stages is experienced by children in learning moral reasoning. These stages parallel those of cognitive growth. Changes are motivated by maturational factors from within a child's psychology.

Three general levels of moral development are proposed, and each has two substages. Children are able to resolve more complex moral issues as they progress through these levels. The first level is experienced in early childhood and continues throughout most of middle childhood. The second level begins in late middle childhood and continues through adolescence.

**Preconventional level**

Moral reasoning based upon physical consequences and the power of those in authority.

Level one (ages four to ten) is called the **preconventional level**. Children generally are well behaved during this period. They recognize the meaning of labels such as "good" and "bad." They behave in relation to the physical consequences and the power of those in authority. *Stage one* of this level is demonstrated when children show concern for being punished for wrongdoing. They show unquestioning obedience to those in authority. Children at *stage two* are concerned with good behavior that is associated with primitive utilitarian needs. They will behave well if they receive some personal profit or reward from doing so.

**Conventional level**

Moral reasoning that consists of conformity to the rules of important groups.

Level two (ages ten and older) is referred to as the **conventional level**. An individual's moral behavior is shown through conformity to rules of important groups, e.g., the family system, peers, the school system. Having allegiances to these are seen as important values for the person. Individuals at *stage three* of this level behave well in order to receive approval from groups. Good behavior is seen as that which helps or pleases others with little attention directed to personal needs. The emphasis is on being "nice." Individuals at *stage four* of this level have a "law and order" orientation. Behaving appropriately is one's duty. Respect is shown for principles or rules that guide appropriate behavior.

The seventh year of life is a watershed period in terms of moral development. Before this time, the ability to reason morally is constrained by a child's egocentrism. After this time, peer group and other social involvements, and a lessening in egocentrism, spur more sophisticated moral reasoning.

**Postconventional level**

Moral reasoning based upon internalized and personalized values.

The last level is referred to as the **postconventional level** of morality and may be experienced first in adolescence by some individuals (although others never achieve it). Moral decision-making is characterized at this stage first by understanding that rules existing in society are for everyone's benefit. These rules are made by consensus. Reasoning at this level disapproves of individuals practicing a personal code of ethics because this is equivalent to social anarchy. Later at this level, the highest and most idealistic moral reasoning becomes based on standards of universal ethics. These standards often are contradictory in relation to the egocentric standards of ethics of lower levels of moral reasoning. Social dictates such as "Act toward others as you wish to be treated," or "Do no harm," are examples of such universally applied standards. It is at this final level that one makes decisions that guide appropriate behavior based on an individual, personal ethic.

Most young adolescents function at the conventional level of moral reasoning that guides their standards

*Cheating on a test challenges moral reasoning. (iStock)*

of appropriate behavior. The strict orientation to peer groups as sources of approval and validation of self-worth indicate this level of functioning. Most individuals remain at this level for the remainder of their lives (Shaver & Strong, 1976). Why is this so?

Because the level of a person's moral reasoning parallels their level of cognitive functioning, it should be expected that changes will take place as development progresses. Teenagers usually make shifts to formal operations cognitive skills by performing more abstract, logical reasoning. Researchers find that a person's level of cognition prepares but does not ensure changes to higher levels of moral reasoning (Sobesky, 1983).

Apparently, each particular situation calling for a decision involving what is right or wrong determines the level of moral reasoning that is applied as a guide. The cognitive skills possessed by a person will frame the limits that outline the format of how logical thinking can occur. This is not enough, however, to guarantee continual use of higher levels of moral reasoning.

Moral decisions may be derived from conflicts or dilemmas in which consequences of each choice must be weighed and considered. When the consequences are heavy, it is likely that a lower level of moral reasoning will be applied. As adolescents experiment with moral decision-making, mistakes and errors will take place that help the teen see the consequences of actions. Because behavior at this life stage is experimental, teenagers can be expected to be inconsistent in their behavioral decisions.

It is this discrepancy between high ideals and lower-level moral reasoning in adolescents that is disconcerting to adults (Kohlberg, 1969). For example, some adolescents might reason that it is perfectly acceptable to cheat on examinations because teachers ask "unfair" questions. Such "unfairness" may be thought to lead to lower grades that can prevent them from being accepted to a university. Teenagers at a different level of moral reasoning would not cheat because they know this is academically and morally dishonest. Some might allow others to cheat from their work in order to gain their approval and acceptance.

The difficulty in establishing a personal standard of moral ethics or values is seen in the dilemmas confronting teenagers today. These can involve conflicts between the conventional and postconventional levels of moral reasoning proposed by Kohlberg. Personal standards and values, which involve the highest level of moral reasoning, may not be fully established, if at all, until well into the adulthood years. They reflect what a person believes to be important ideals to attain in daily living.

Are there gender differences? A major difficulty with Kohlberg's model is that it fails to address gender differences, according to Gilligan (1982). Women in our culture are taught to have an orientation in moral reasoning that differs from males. She believes that women are taught to make moral decisions in terms of how interpersonal relationships would be affected. Men learn to base moral reasoning on individual rights, justice, and self-fulfillment. As such, females determine what is right or wrong on caring and concern for others.

A hypothetical problem posed to school-age children by researchers illustrates her views (Garrod, Beal & Shin, 1989). The children were asked how to resolve this problem:

> A porcupine needed a winter home. The only one he could find was sharing one with a family of moles. The moles, who originally thought this was a good idea, eventually wanted the porcupine to leave. This was because his spines kept pricking all the moles, making them uncomfortable.

No differences were found in solutions given by boys' and girls' between six and nine years old. However, ten and eleven year old boys gave responses that involved aggression of the moles against the porcupine, e.g., "They should shoot him." Much more research is needed to establish if males and females differ in moral reasoning.

*Pause and Process:*

1. What is meant by problem solving?

2. What are Kohlberg's levels of moral reasoning?

# SOCIOEMOTIONAL DEVELOPMENT DURING ADOLESCENCE

*LEARNING OBJECTIVES:*

1. *Characterize emotional development during adolescence*
2. *Describe understanding of self and others during adolescence*
3. *Explain psychosocial development during adolescence*

Socioemotional development in adolescence tends to focus on identity development. Teens wish to know who they are and where their place is in the world. Peers become increasingly important socializers in adolescence, while parents continue to provide social and emotional support.

# PSYCHOSOCIAL DEVELOPMENT

## *How Do Teens Acquire a Sense of Identity?*

**Identity**

The fifth attitude proposed by Erikson. Identity is the notion, acquired in adolescence, that the self is composed of different aspects having distinct boundaries that constitute a whole, integrated personality.

Erikson (1950/1964) refers to **identity** formation as the primary psychosocial focus of adolescence. Identity formation involves the acknowledgement that one assumes many different roles in life that represent different aspects of the self. It includes the awareness that one has strengths and weaknesses and different, but related, selves. Adolescents forge a foundational personal identity by psychologically integrating these various aspects or selves into a composite concept of "me" or "I". Questions about personal identity can be categorized into four overall aspects; political identity, occupational identity, religious identity, and gender identity. Individuals from other cultures in a majority culture environment may also deal with cultural identity issues discussed below.

A helpful analogy for understanding the process of identity formation is the procedure by which a diamond becomes a gemstone. When first brought from the earth, a diamond looks like a jagged, dirty pebble. The gemstone cutter creates facets by cutting and polishing sides into the diamond that admit light at various wavelengths. When working in an integrated manner, the finished diamond has many facets that operate together to create its brilliant appearance. In the course of identity formation, the adolescent's task is to become aware of the different aspects (facets) of the personality. In doing so, the individual reaches a crossroads in psychosocial development that Erikson describes as a crisis. The challenge is to experience continuity between what the individual has learned about the self from childhood experiences and what she or he anticipates being in the future.

The foundations of the adolescent's attempts to develop an integrated self were laid in previous stages of psychosocial development. The process of determining who one is, what values are important to one, what attitudes one should hold, and what directions one should take in life began in childhood. Children are expected by society to establish some idea of who they are and where they will go in life. Adults often ask them, "What do you want to be when you grow up?" During adolescence, the individual rephrases this question as, "Who am I, and what can I become as an adult?"

Socialization experiences have a broad impact on identity formation in adolescence. Adolescents who have a healthy sense of identity have enjoyed nurturing from family members and others that is associated with emotional warmth. Their parents have set limits for them, valued their autonomy, and encouraged their achievement (Newman & Newman, 1991).

Before they can crystallize their personal identity, adolescents need to establish an identity with a group of peers in early adolescence (Newman & Newman, 1991). In effect,

CHAPTER 6 • Adolescence   **267**

identity is drawn first from tribal experiences. These interactions with peers are similar in some ways to peer group experiences among school-age children. However, the peer group takes on additional functions in adolescence

Teenagers, like school-age children, evaluate themselves according to how their peers evaluate them. In adolescence, peers assume an even more powerful influence as the prime source of self-definition. The peer group becomes both an extension and a representation of the self. Adolescents also enmesh their identities with those of public figures they admire—athletes, movie stars, or musicians, for example.

There are strong similarities between establishing one's personal identity in adolescence and establishing personal autonomy in infancy. The psychosocial task at both stages crucially depends on defining psychological boundaries. This push for autonomy reaches its peak in adolescence, as the teenager demands the freedom to test limits, discover areas of abilities and weakness, and commit mistakes while learning adult skills and problem-solving strategies. Boundaries between the self and parents become more distinct as the adolescent struggles to develop a fully autonomous identity. At the beginning of this process, in early adolescence, the individual tends to shift allegiance from parents almost totally to peers. This creates tensions between the individual and the family system. Peer pressures to conform to established or imagined standards are very high at this time, and boundaries between the self and the peer group are blurred. Acceptance and validation from peers bolsters self-confidence, whereas rejection undermines self-esteem and leads to feelings of alienation.

By late adolescence, experiences with peers have provided important lessons in beliefs, attitudes, and notions about the various aspects of the self. Personal identity crystallizes as the individual becomes capable of drawing boundaries between the self and the social group. Experiences within the family, school, and social systems now bring the adolescent into his or her own as an individual, able to make the connections that provide initial answers to the question, "Who am I, with whom do I belong, and where will I go with my life?"

**Role confusion** is a disjointed, fragmented concept of the self resulting from the inability to integrate the various aspects of the personality. Erikson believed that a clear idea of personal identity fails to materialize in certain situations—for example, when a teenager's efforts to establish self-identity are punished, thwarted, diminished, or discounted by parents. Boundaries between aspects of the self are blended and blurred and the individual fails to understand how they all work together to create the self.

Before the outcome of this stage is decided between identity formation and role confusion, adolescents may go through one of two phases (Marcia, 1980; Waterman, 1982). Normally, teenagers experiment with roles and behaviors to test out tentative ideas about careers, personal expression, value, beliefs, and so on. This experimentation usually continues throughout the period, eventually leading to a commitment to those ideas that seem to fit the individual best. The process allows adolescents to truly know and own their values, beliefs, and ambitions. Some adolescents, however, do not experience the process of experimentation fully enough to **individuate** from their parents' values, beliefs, and ambitions. The result is **identity foreclosure**, or an aborted attempt at establishing personal identity. When this happens, individuals may make a premature commitment to a

### Role confusion

The disjointed, fragmented notion of self resulting from an inability to integrate the various aspects of personality into a unified whole.

### Individuation

The process by which an adolescent recognizes and develops his or her personal identity as an individual who is distinct from other family members. It is characterized by developing one's own values and belief systems and having the courage to make decisions and live by these.

### Identity foreclosure

The inability to commit to any role or idea of direction for their lives.

lifestyle, occupation, or type of education more to please parents than to fulfill themselves. Identity foreclosure may merely delay identity formation.

The other phase that may delay identity formation is identity moratorium. Some individuals are unable to make a commitment to any role or idea of direction for their lives. Instead, they continually experiment. If they delay making any decision for too long, role confusion may be deeply established.

Waterman (1982) proposes that the sequence of identity formation moves in this fashion: first, young adolescents experience some role confusion as they experiment and discover various aspects of their personalities. Then, they move into identity foreclosure or moratorium. Finally, by the end of adolescence, they achieve an identity. Most individuals achieve an initial outline of their personal identity by the end of adolescence, but others need several more years to complete this process.

After reading this section, you may think that the personal identity that is established by the completion of adolescence is rigidly fixed for life. It is not. Personality and identity can certainly be refined, even redefined, at later stages of the life span. What we mean by the notion of personal identity formation is that a core self-concept is established during adolescence. Other roles and aspects of self are discovered, developed, recognized, and refined, throughout the remainder of the life span, and these become incorporated into the person's core identity. Marriage, parenthood, and career changes are all life-altering events that could further mold an individual's identity during later life stages.

## Ethnic Identity

Ethnicity is an aspect of self that must be integrated into one's identity (Stickle, 2008). Although some adolescents embrace their ethnic heritage, others resent it. Those that value their ethnic identity and incorporate it as part of their identity often feel an emotional connection to their group. In general, these individuals have an easier time integrating the values of their minority culture and dominant culture than those who struggle to achieve an ethic identity.

*There are those that feel an emotional connection to their heritage when they incorporate their ethnic identity into their lives. (iStock)*

*Pause and Process:*

1. Explain the process of identity formation.

2. Why is identity development important?

# EMOTIONAL DEVELOPMENT

## *Key Emotional Development Highlights*

Emotions during adolescence is a topic of common discussion. Are adolescents extra moody? Do they return to the temper tantrums seen during the terrible twos?

Emotions do appear to fluctuate more during adolescence, possibly due to hormones (Rosenblum & Lewis, 2003). When hormones stabilize in adulthood, these fluctuations subside. In adolescence, the intensity of positive and negative emotions is not always in proportion to the event triggering the emotion (Steinberg & Levine, 1997). Again, this subsides with time. Emotional regulation improves with development of the frontal lobe of the brain (NIMH, 2001); hence, emotional regulation continues to improve beyond the teenage years. Finally, emotion vocabulary and scripts also show development during adolescence (Saarni, Mumme & Campos, 1998).

Adolescents are able to understand the causes of emotions in others. They are also able to understand that individuals can experience more than one emotion at a time. Finally, they understand that individuals may not always display what emotions they are feeling.

**TEMPERAMENT/PERSONALITY**   Temperament in infancy is moderately correlated with temperament in adolescence (Wachs & Bates, 2001). Hence, a shy infant is likely to be a shy teenager—though, not always. Parenting behaviors may either assist in the stability of temperament dimensions, or modify them. For example, a difficult temperament infant may display less negative affect and more adaptability if parenting was responsive.

Although we tend to discuss temperament in infancy and childhood, we shift to discussing personality in adulthood. It appears that some aspects of temperament are related to some aspects of adult personality (Caspi et al., 2005; Costa & McCrae, 2001). We will be learning about personality in early adulthood.

**ATTACHMENT**   Attachment continues to be important to development in adolescence. Adolescents that are securely attached to their parents experience better physical and mental health in comparison to insecurely attached teens (Cooper, Shaver & Collin, 1998). Other studies have found that in comparison to insecurely attached teens, securely attached teens experience higher self-esteem, better peer relationships, higher social competence, and lower levels of psychopathology (e.g., see Thompson, 1998, for a review).

You may be wondering how attachment to parents would impact peer relationships. It all goes back to those mental models we talked about in Chapter 3. If a person believes that he cannot trust others, but that he is competent (i.e., avoidant attachment style), then he may be controlling and bossy in friendships. If a person believes that she is untrustworthy, but that others are competent (i.e., preoccupied attachment style), then she may be clingy and jealous in friendships. Securely attached individuals believe in their self-worth and trust others; hence, they are able to function well, alone or in relationships.

*Pause and Process:*

1. Why may emotions fluctuate more during adolescence?

2. What are some outcomes associated with secure attachment in adolescence?

# SELF AND OTHERS

## *Understanding of Self and Others*

Teenagers become increasingly aware that physical or external attributes are not reliable bases for constructing a self-concept or for judging one's own worth or that of another (O'Mahony, 1989). By adolescence, the self-concept comes to include attitudes, beliefs, roles, and goals (Harter, 1990, 2005; Harter & Monsour, 1992). Adolescents also come to understand that their "self" may vary depending on who they are with and the setting they are in. Because adolescents are now capable of formal operational thought, they are able to think abstractly about their current self and hypothetically about their future self.

Just as self-understanding becomes more abstract in adolescence, understanding of others does as well. By late adolescence, they are generally aware that inner, psychological characteristics are more reliable descriptors for understanding others.

**FAMILY INFLUENCES** Parent-child relationships during middle childhood are predictive of parent-child relationships during adolescence (Stickle, 2008). If the relationship has been warm and harmonious during childhood, it will largely continue to be so during adolescence. However, relationships that were conflict-ridden during childhood will most likely be conflict ridden during adolescence. Parents are often a source of support and guidance during adolescence, while allowing adolescents more freedom (Galatzer-Levy & Cohler, 1993).

There really is no "typical" American family. We learned in Chapter 5 that more than 50 percent of all children will live in a single-parent household at some point in time. A little more than 20 percent of all children

*Parents can offer support and freedom to adolescents. (iStock)*

**Blended family**

A family unit consisting of an adult male and female couple, one of whom has remarried, and the children of one or both from a previous marriage; a new term for stepfamily.

live in a blended family (Stickle, 2008). A **blended family** is one which includes a step-parent and possibly step-siblings. Additionally, a growing number of children are being raised by grandparents. As you can see, children and adolescents live in a variety of family structures. The next section will discuss what the impact of divorce is on adolescents.

**DIVORCE IMPACTS ON ADOLESCENTS**    In Chapter 5 we learned about some of the long-term impacts of divorce on children. Although school-age girls appear to adjust to divorce relatively well if their mothers remain single, this does not remain true during adolescence (Parke & Buriel, 1998). Teenage girls from divorced homes are at increased risk for the following outcomes:

- Mother-daughter conflict
- Noncompliance
- Low self-esteem
- Emotional problems
- Antisocial behavior
- Early sexual behavior and other sexual problems
- Teenage pregnancy (three times more likely)

These difficulties continue into adulthood (Parke & Buriel, 1998). Young women who come from divorced homes are more likely to get pregnant before marriage, marry young, marry unstable husbands, and are more likely to experience divorce themselves. It appears that there is a long-term sleeper effect for the impact of divorce, so although younger girls appear to be coping with the divorce well, the impacts, in fact, lie in wait for the onset of adolescence.

There is further bad news about the long-term impacts of divorce on adolescents—both males and females. Adolescents from divorced homes are more than twice as likely to drop out of high school than high school students from intact homes (Parke & Buriel, 1998). Dropping out of high school has long-term impacts in terms of job prospects and earning potential. However, current work in the area cautions against placing a causal link between divorce and the negative outcomes. A possible mediating variable in this relationship may be parental conflict. It is possible that it is the conflict in the marriage that may be causing the long term negative effects. This possibility calls into question the approach of staying in a bad marriage "for the sake of the children".

# THE OUTSIDE WORLD

## *Peers*

An adolescent's first steps toward independence from the family system are explored more thoroughly in the peer group. Peer-orientation is higher in adolescence than in any other

*Peer groups help teens become more independent. They also help in the identity formation process. (iStock)*

time in life (Stickle, 2008). Although parents are still the most important influence on adolescent adjustment, peers are highly influential in daily life. During early adolescence, peers play an increasingly important role in influencing behavior and attitudes. This can be seen, for example, in the styles of dress, musical tastes, use of slang vocabulary, and acceptable behavior patterns promoted among groups.

Peer groups in adolescence serve as a laboratory setting for teens to experiment with behaviors, attitudes, and values. This assists in the identity formation process. As groups shift and change in composition, teens explore their abilities to be leader, follower, activist, rebel, clown, or athlete, for example. The fear that underlies much of the teenager's concern about acceptance by peers is of being labeled as different from others in some way. Self-confidence is boosted by acceptance by others in early adolescence.

During this time there is an increasing reliance on peers for emotional support. Until recently, it was thought that the peer group increasingly replaced the family system as a source of social and emotional support in adolescence. However, both friends and family offer emotional support. Although psychological closeness to friends grows in adolescence, the family still provides the secure base from which adolescents can venture out into the world with increasing autonomy (Galatzer-Levy & Cohler, 1993).

Parents frequently worry that their child will become more influenced and controlled by friends than by adults during adolescence. However, adolescents typically maintain similar views to their parents in regards to politics, religion, morals, and education (Stickle, 2008).

Peer groups become organized differently in adolescence than in middle childhood. Peer group membership in middle childhood was largely segregated by sex. In adolescence, this characteristic changes as groups become integrated to include both sexes.

Peer groups become major agents of socialization, particularly in early adolescence. It is in the peer group environment that much of the experimentation and exploration occurs that help in identity formation.

Acceptance by others in a group is different in adolescence than in middle childhood. This is a crucial aspect of psychological growth and health for teens. Teenagers look to peers as the major source of validation of their self-worth. Positive self-esteem is evaluated in terms of being accepted by others. Negative self-worth and a sense of alienation is concluded when rejection, lack of acceptance, and being ignored or discounted by others occurs (East, Hess, and Lerner, 1987; Rubin, Bukowski & Parker, 1998).

Most young teens have a high degree of concern, then, about their popularity among friends. This is seen as a gauge that indicates the relative degree of their self-worth. The desire to be recognized by a peer group often is of paramount importance. Although conformity peaks in middle childhood, it is still valued early in adolescence (Galatzer-Levy & Cohler, 1993). Young adolescents often must be willing to forfeit any significant demonstrations of individualism as the price of being accepted by peers.

**Crowds**

A large mixed-sex group of older children or adolescents who have similar values and attitudes and are known by a common label.

Young teens gravitate toward others whom they perceive as being like themselves (Clasen & Brown, 1985). In this way, various **crowds** form and become labeled and categorized. A crowd can be defined as a large "mixed-sex group of older children or adolescents who have similar values and attitudes and are known by a common label" (Kail, 2007, p. 471). For example, those sharing athletic interests and who participate in sports would make up the "jocks." Although specific categories of cliques vary regionally, typical ones include the populars, nerds, grunges, goths, delinquents, and brains (Stickle, 2008).

**Clique**

A smaller group of friends that are similar in appearance, demographics, and activities.

A crowd is different from a clique. A crowd is large and all of the individuals may not know each other, whereas a **clique** is a smaller group of friends that are similar in appearance, demographics, and activities (Kail, 2007). Hence, any given crowd may have smaller segments of cliques.

By middle and late adolescence, the qualities used to construct and maintain peer groups become less valued among adolescents. The emphasis shifts from identity formation via experiences within groups to that attained through expressions as an individual. This reflects the developmental changes a teen experiences in reaching self-definition during this stage of the life span.

Dating often begins during adolescence. In general, males and females have different motivations for dating. Females are looking for a companion with which to be psychologically close, whereas males are looking for someone attractive with which to have fun experiences. Of course, there are exceptions to this generality, but it holds for most. Given these different motivations, expectations for the relationship and its longevity are probably different; however, few teens would think to discuss this up front. That said, when a dating relationship ends, lines of communication can become crossed because there is little understanding of the other person's perspective. Despite the confusion and hurt sometimes experienced in teen dating relationships, these relationships do provide a mechanism for learning about what one wants to look for in a future significant other. Additionally, dating relationships help individuals develop dating schemas and scripts that will be used (and continually modified) until marriage.

## "In Their Own Words"

**Erica, a 14-year-old girl, talks about her early dating experience.**

"My first real boyfriend was when I was in seventh grade; I used to go to see him play base-ball and go to his house to watch T.V. and stuff. We kissed on the cheek and then on the lips but it wasn't like making out or anything. We would sit together on the bus and hold hands, it was so cute now that I think about it … My first make-out kiss was in eighth grade. I was at a school dance and I had met the boy I liked at the time there. He asked me to slow dance with him and so I said yes, during the dance we were talking and then we looked at each other and just kissed … I want a boyfriend who is fun, likes to do things with me and my friends, plays sports and is very cute … My boyfriend likes to skateboard and sometimes my friends and I hang out and watch him and his friends. Before it got cold out this year we were all hanging out and my boyfriend was skateboarding towards me, but I didn't see him. He told me to move at the last second but it was too late and he knocked me over onto the ground by running into me with his skateboard. He tried to help me up but I pulled him down with me. We both just laughed at each other for a good five minutes … My dream date is going out to dinner as a double date and then going back to someone's house to hang out and maybe watch a movie or something? I like to be with friends and if I can have my friends and boyfriend at the same time that's even better … I think being in love with someone means that you can't live a day without them. The person is your best friend and you like to do everything together. The person you are in love with would do anything for you and you would do anything for them too … I think that sex is not that big of a deal as long as you are in a long relationship with the other person. I want to wait until I am in a longer relationship and a little older … A lot of my friends have boyfriends or girl-friends, but some of them don't … I would break up with a boyfriend if he cheated on me or if he was talking about me in a bad way to his friends and I found out … Being in school with my boyfriend is awesome! I get to see him in between classes and sometimes he even walks me to my class, even though I tell him he'll be late to his if he does."

## The Electronic World

Computers and the internet are an ever increasing part of our lives. In fact, it is estimated that 97 percent of high school students and 95 percent of middle school students used computers in 2003 (National Center for Education Statistics, 2005).

Although computers and the internet offer the world at our fingertips, there is some concern about the impact of computers on development. Some educators and develop-mentalists voice concern that the power of such technology is introduced before students develop the moral fortitude to handle such power responsibly (Monke, 2006). For exam-ple, students are purchasing entire research papers online and turning them in as their own work. Cutting and pasting information from websites into one's own paper without quot-ing the source is rampant. Yet, when students are caught, their typical response is that they

*Computers are now a part of life. It remains to be seen how this technology will influence lives in the long term. (iStock)*

didn't know buying papers or cutting and pasting the work of others into their paper was wrong (Chaker, 2003). Clearly, these students learned to use a wonderful and powerful technology before they learned the difference between right and wrong.

Beyond students lacking the morals to use technology responsibly, research indicates that computer use may negatively impact academic achievement (Monke, 2006). Studies have found that as access to home computers increases, standardized test scores decrease (Fuchs & Woessmann, 2004). It is theorized that computers more often distract children and adolescents from studies, rather than facilitating school work.

Because computer technology and the internet is relatively new, it will take time and longitudinal studies in order to ascertain the long-term effects such technology may have on development. However, adolescents, and people in general, may do well to find a balance between living life in the world and life online.

## Schools

During early adolescence, most teens make the transition from elementary school to middle school or junior high. This is a significant transition and can be stressful. Middle schools tend to be larger than elementary schools with more students. Crowding may be an issue. Students no longer have one primary teacher, but instead must learn the structure and format required by multiple teachers. Sometimes students may not have books to bring home to study from, or they must learn to utilize teacher online forums for their homework. Finally, adolescents must learn to navigate the world of adolescent peers, classroom changes, more complex lunchrooms, and lockers. Adolescents should be monitored for adjustment struggles during this transitional period so that stressors may be addressed and intervention or help provided if necessary. The same is true for when the teen transitions to high school.

**Bullying**

An aggressive behavior (words, actions, or social exclusion) which intentionally hurts or harms another person; the behavior occurs repetitiously and creates a power imbalance such that it is difficult for the victim to defend him or herself.

**Hostile attributional bias**

The thinking that bullies are always suspect of the intentions of others and see hostility where there is none.

Define hostile attributional bias in your own words.

Bullying can also be of concern in school. **Bullying** can be defined as "an aggressive behavior (words, actions, or social exclusion) which intentionally hurts or harms another person; the behavior occurs repetitiously and creates a power imbalance such that it is difficult for the victim to defend him or herself" (MacNeil & Newell, 2004, p. 174). Often, others silently witness these acts of bullying; hence, enabling the perpetrator to continue this evil. Although most children experience bullying occasionally, 10 percent of U.S. and European children are chronically bullied (Kochenderfer & Ladd, 1996; Olweus, 1994).

Although bullying used to occur primarily in or around schools, an increasing number of adolescents are bullied via media (e.g., text messages, social networking sites, etc.). This means that children and adolescent victims that used to be able to find comfort and solace in their homes are now bullied at any time with no reprieve.

Brutus in *Popeye,* Lucy in *Charlie Brown,* Draco Malfoy or Dudley in *Harry Potter,* and Sharpay in *High School Musical* are all famous bullies in cartoons or literature. What are the characteristics of bullies in real life? Research has found that bullies typically come from homes in which some form of abuse occurs (MacNeil & Newell, 2004). Further, bullies tend to have low self-concepts and feel unconnected to their loved ones. Often, the aggressiveness is generational, with parents using aggressive and hostile parenting. Bullies may also have a **hostile attributional bias** in which they are always suspect of the intentions of others and see hostility where there is none. Additionally, they often miss the prosocial overtures of others, while being hypersensitive to hostile and aggressive cues. Male bullies tend to be physically strong and use physical aggression and dominance. Female bullies come in any size and tend to use relational aggression and social dominance (e.g., verbal assaults, gossiping, social exclusion, etc.). In general, physical bullying is more common in elementary and middle school, whereas relational and social bullying is more prevalent in high school (Harris, 2004).

Now that we have a picture of what bullies are like, what are the characteristics of victims? Victims tend to lack social and interpersonal skills (Harris, 2004; MacNeil & Newell, 2004). Further, they are often younger and physically smaller than their aggressors. The lack of friends often makes them lack the social support that could help ward off or buffer the effects of bullies. Victims experience physical and emotional scars. They often withdraw socially, suffer academically, develop anxiety, and experience mental and physical health problems.

Programs aimed at preventing bullying or providing interventions must take a multi-faceted approach (Harris, 2004; MacNeil & Newell, 2004). Schools must have a zero-tolerance policy for bullying. Supervision and monitoring at schools must be increased. Witnesses to bullying must be encouraged to report such abuse, as must the victims. Bullies must be taught conflict management skills, whereas victims must be given assertiveness training. Finally, both bullies and victims will probably need psychological counseling.

## *Work*

Many adolescents work part-time. Working can have a positive influence on adolescents (Stickle, 2008). For example, working allows adolescents to develop a sense of the value of money. Additionally, working can help adolescents learn about the work culture, responsibility, and the importance of punctuality. However, there can be too much of a good thing. Adolescents who work more than twenty hours a week appear to experience negative outcomes. These negative outcomes include academic struggles, increased substance use, increased delinquency, and increased physical and psychological health issues. Hence, adolescents should consider working part-time, but limit the number of hours.

*Pause and Process:*

1. Describe peer relations during adolescence.

2. What are the characteristics of bullies and victims?

*Work provides for many positive influences such as learning the value of money. (iStock)*

# SUMMARY

1. Adjusting to the many physical changes associated with puberty is a major developmental task of adolescence. Boys experience this process differently and at later ages than girls. Psychological changes are intertwined with physical maturation. Problems can arise when individuals begin puberty either sooner or later than most of their peers.

2. Nutrition is important during adolescence. Obesity and eating disorders are areas of concern during adolescence. Some teenagers decide to adopt a vegetarian diet. Most research indicates that vegetarian teens eat healthier than the average, meat-eating teen.

3. Teenagers develop a complex understanding of illness. Although teens, in general, experience good physical health, risky behaviors may contribute to a premature death down the road. The early sexualization of girls by the media has far reaching negative consequences for girls and society as a whole. In order to promote wellness in teens, we must educate them about the risks of substance use and early sexual behavior. Further, we must educate teens about the importance of sleep, nutrition, and exercise.

4. Some adolescents move from concrete operational thought into formal operational thought during the teen years. Formal operational thought is characterized by hypothetical, deductive, and inductive reasoning. Additionally, egocentrism, pseudostupidity, the imaginary audience, the

invincibility fable, and apparent hypocrisy characterize thought at this stage.

5. Dialectical reasoning and problem solving show developmental improvements during adolescence. Further, moral reasoning typically continues to show advancement during the teenage years.

6. Emotional development can be challenging during adolescence. Fluctuations in hormones can lead to intense moods and mood swings. Luckily, these issues subside toward the end of this period.

7. Temperament in adolescence is moderately related to temperament from infancy and childhood. Parenting behaviors either assisted in the continuity of temperament or contributed to its change. Attachment in adolescence is related to numerous areas of well-being and functioning, including psychopathology and peer relations.

8. Understanding of self and others becomes more complex and abstract during adolescence. Parent-child relations continue to be warm and supportive, if they were so during childhood. Divorce increases the risk for numerous problems in adolescence, including teenage pregnancy and antisocial behavior.

9. Peer relationships become more important during the teenage years. Crowds and cliques are common and form based upon similarities between group members. Dating may begin during adolescence, but is complicated due to differing motivations between males and females. Bullying is an area of growing concern in schools and now occurs 24/7 due to online social networking sites and text messaging.

10. The establishment of a sense of personal identity is a major developmental task of adolescence. Identity is based on an understanding that one's self, or personality, is composed of many related aspects. Teens learn about these aspects through experimentation and exploration in a variety of experiences. Role confusion, the diametrical opposite of identity formation, is a fragmented idea of the self that results from the inability to integrate the various aspects of the self into a unified personality.

# SELF-QUIZ

1. Describe the adolescent growth spurt.
2. Explain brain development during adolescence.
3. What is the secular trend? What may be contributing to it?
4. Why is the timing of puberty important to development?
5. Explain, in your own words, physiologic and psychophysiologic thinking.
6. Describe anorexia nervosa.
7. What is bulimia and how is it different from anorexia?
8. Characterize substance use (alcohol, tobacco, and drugs) among adolescents.

9. Define the sexualization of girls.
10. What areas of health are of concern in adolescence?
11. Define hypothetical thought in your own words and give an example.
12. Define inductive and deductive reasoning in your own words and provide an example for each.
13. How are hypothetical-deductive reasoning and scientific-inductive reasoning different?
14. What is meant by the game of thinking?
15. How may the imaginary audience impact a teenager's everyday behavior?
16. Define the invincibility fable and describe how it may contribute to risky behavior.

17. Give an example of dialectical reasoning.

18. Provide an example of a time you used dialectical reasoning in an argument or debate.

19. What is meant by problem solving?

20. Describe the levels of moral reasoning development.

21. Describe emotional development in adolescence.

22. How is attachment related to peer relationships?

23. What are some family structures children and adolescents may experience?

24. What are some outcomes related to divorce for adolescents?

25. Explain the differences between crowds and cliques.

26. Why are researchers concerned about computer and internet use by youth?

27. Define hostile attributional bias in your own words.

28. What are some of the effects of being bullied?

29. What are the positive and negative outcomes for working during adolescence?

30. How may identity formation impact the family system?

## TERMS AND CONCEPTS

# CHAPTER 7

# Early Adulthood

(iStock)

## OUTLINE

**PHYSICAL DEVELOPMENT DURING EARLY ADULTHOOD**

- Physical growth
- Health issues

**COGNITIVE DEVELOPMENT DURING EARLY ADULTHOOD**

- Beyond Piaget's theory
- Information-processing during early adulthood

**SOCIOEMOTIONAL DEVELOPMENT DURING EARLY ADULTHOOD**

- Psychosocial development
- Emotional development
- Self and others

The period of the life span that we call adulthood has been considered the pinnacle of individual development for many years. To be an adult means that one has arrived at a respected and competent station in life, that one has attained the characteristic we call maturity. The cultural meaning of maturity is completed development. Traditionally, it has been thought that developmental changes cease when one becomes an adult.

This notion is an artifact of past Western civilizations. Until recent historical times, there were two stages in the life span: childhood and adulthood. Childhood was a time of preparing for adulthood that lasted only until an individual reached six or seven years of age. At this age, individuals assumed adult status in their family systems. With this status came new responsibilities, expected behaviors, and appropriate traits. Just attaining adulthood was a significant achievement before the advent of antibiotics, advanced medical care, and advanced sanitation in modern times. Earlier, great numbers of infants and their mothers died of disease and unsanitary living conditions. Artistic works of former periods show adulthood as the more valued and important era in the life span. Even today adulthood is associated with greater social power, influence, and position more so than earlier stages in the life span.

*Adulthood was important in former periods. (iStock)*

Philosophical and theoretical changes in the last several decades have prompted a reconsideration of the notion that developmental changes cease at the closure of adolescence. Actually, we know little about changes during this period of the life span, compared to what we know about changes during the stages leading to adulthood.

Because adulthood is the longest period in the typical person's life, it is more easily studied by dividing it into three separate but related stages: early adulthood (eighteen to thirty-nine years), middle adulthood (forty to sixty-five years), and late adulthood (sixty-five years +). We know more about development during late adulthood, than development during early and middle adulthood.

# PHYSICAL DEVELOPMENT DURING EARLY ADULTHOOD

### LEARNING OBJECTIVES:

1. *Describe physical development during early adulthood*
2. *Awareness of health issues in early adulthood*

# PHYSICAL DEVELOPMENT

**Adulthood**

The period of the life span following adolescence.

We reach our peak of physical well-being in early adulthood. This is the period of greatest strength and good health. Physical **maturity** in height and weight has been reached—in fact, most physical growth ceases before early adulthood begins. Yet there are many physical changes in appearance and in physiology during this stage of the life span.

## Maturity

Completion of all growth and developmental changes; associated with attaining adulthood in the past.

## Accommodation

Changes made in a personal scheme in order to bring about a better match with reality; in vision, the ability of the eyes to focus quickly and efficiently on objects both near and far away.

## Visual acuity

Sharpness of vision.

## Presbyopia

Difficulty in accurately perceiving objects that are close.

## Presbycusis

The loss of hearing of high-frequency tones.

**Spotlight**

What is periodontal disease?

## Periodontal disease

Disease of the gums caused by improper hygiene; it can lead to significant tooth loss.

# *Body Changes*

**THE SENSES**    The ability of the eyes to accommodate begins changing in this stage. **Accommodation** refers to the dilation and constriction of the pupils to see things at different distances, as well as to the ability of the eyes to focus properly and quickly. There is a gradual loss in accommodation throughout the years of early adulthood (Fozard et al., 1977).

**Visual acuity**, or sharpness of vision, is at its peak for most people in early adulthood (Spence & Mason, 1987). Men generally have better acuity than women. However, both sexes begin to notice deficiencies in distance perception between ages thirty-five and forty. This results in a condition known as **presbyopia**, meaning difficulty in accurately perceiving objects that are close. People notice this when they find they must hold books and newspapers far away in order to read them. The condition is corrected with reading glasses.

Most young adults who need general vision correction choose contact lenses rather than eyeglasses. Those who need glasses generally begin wearing them by about age twenty-nine. Even people who wear contact lenses develop presbyopia, making reading glasses necessary.

Hearing loss also becomes apparent during this life stage. Typically, it becomes noticeable after age twenty-five, although most adults in their thirties can still hear a whisper (National Center for Health Statistics, 1980). The loss of hearing is most noticeable at high-frequency tones. This results in a condition known as **presbycusis**. Most men experience greater loss of hearing sensitivity than women during adulthood. This may be because greater numbers of them work in noisy occupations for prolonged periods of time.

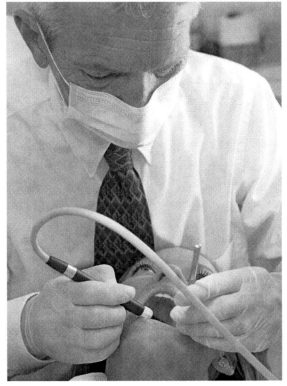

**THE TEETH**    Most people retain all their permanent teeth through early adulthood. A small percentage loses all of their upper or lower teeth (Kelly & Harvey, 1979). Tooth loss is more likely among women, partly due to calcium loss during pregnancy. There is a steady increase in filled teeth during early adulthood. The probability of **periodontal disease** also increases. Periodontal disease is an inflammation of the gums and bone tissue surrounding teeth. It results from poor or improper dental hygiene, and genetics may also play a role. If left untreated, this condition can lead to significant tooth loss.

*Cavities and periodontal disease increase at this age. (iStock)*

**THE CARDIOVASCULAR SYSTEM**   As people age, their hearts become more sluggish at pumping blood. This partially explains why people are unable to sustain large work loads for long periods as they get older.

The risk of getting diseases that affect the heart and circulatory system rises throughout early adulthood. Blood pressure rises as part of the natural aging process that begins during this stage. People become more susceptible to **hypertension**, or high blood pressure, at this time (Spence & Mason, 1987). Hypertension is a condition in which the blood vessels become constricted, raising the level of pressure necessary for circulating blood through the body. If untreated, it can lead to heart failure, cerebral hemorrhage (stroke), and related disorders. Hypertension is more common among African Americans and among men of all racial groups.

**Hypertension**

Abnormally high blood pressure caused by constriction of arteries; it increases the likelihood of kidney damage, heart failure, and brain damage via strokes.

Hypertension is a silent disease, meaning it has no signs that can be readily observed. Diagnosis requires accurate measurements taken with special equipment. By being aware of the need to have their blood pressure monitored periodically, young adults can begin treatment of the condition long before it becomes serious. Hypertension may be treated by drug therapy, although dietary changes are frequently used as well.

**THE LUNGS**   The lungs play an important part in the body's ability to sustain exercise and work. They begin to function less efficiently toward the end of early adulthood. Young adults are able to absorb about four and a half times as much oxygen as older adults. The decline in oxygen absorption is partly due to a lowering of the amount of blood pumped to the lungs and partly to losses in the mechanical efficiency of these organs as people age (Timiras, 1972). Throughout adulthood, there is a decline in the amount of air breathed into the lungs. Many people notice this difference at about age forty.

Smoking was long associated with adult status in our culture. This is less so today after multitudes of reports that smoking cigarettes and other tobacco products is associated with heart and lung disease, cancer, and related health disorders (U.S. Department of Health and Human Services, 1987). **Passive smoking**—inhaling air in an area where someone has been smoking—is also hazardous to health.

**Passive smoking**

Inhaling air in an area where someone has been smoking.

Since the 1950s, the percentage of adults who smoke has been declining. Today, approximately 21.6 percent of adults smoke (CDC, 2005).

Many people who smoke try to quit. Young adults have greater success than older adults in quitting. Most people stop on their own, although there are many drugs and programs available for those who need help.

**THE SKIN**   The skin begins to show some signs of aging in early adulthood. Wrinkles appear in the facial area, particularly around the eyes and on the hands. The skin begins to lose its fine texture toward the end of this stage. In early adulthood, most people recover from the acne and related skin disorders that are common in adolescence. The more usual types of skin disorders in young adults are fungal infections (dermatophytosis), especially in the feet, and malignant or benign tumors. Both conditions affect men more than women, perhaps because of differences in working conditions and standards of hygiene (Johnson & Roberts, 1977; Spence & Mason, 1987).

MUSCULAR STRENGTH AND PHYSICAL PERFORMANCE    People are at their peak muscular strength between ages twenty and thirty. After that, there is a gradual decline until old age, when the decline becomes rapid. Muscular strength differs from work rate. Although muscle strength does not change very noticeable in early adulthood, power output declines after forty, and considerably during middle adulthood (Shock & Norris, 1970; Spence & Mason, 1987).

*Pause and Process:*

1. How do the heart and lungs change in early adulthood?

2. What problems may occur with the skin in early adulthood?

# HEALTH ISSUES

Health in early adulthood is generally very good, though subject to certain hazards. Accidents are a leading cause of death among young adults, but diseases cause numerous health problems (U.S. Bureau of the Census, 1990b). These include upper respiratory infections, flu, and sexually transmitted diseases. Among the last, AIDS is of particular concern among young adults. Other factors that affect health in early adulthood are outlined here.

**Stressors**

Events that can cause stress reactions.

**Stress**

The physiological and psychological reactions of an organism to demands placed upon it.

**"Type A" personality**

Highly competitive, restless, and achievement oriented.

**"Type B" personality**

A personality that is low in hostility and aggression, and moderately ambitious.

**"Type C" personality**

Associated with an increased risk for cancer, this personality type tends to be introverted and eager to please.

STRESS    A harsh reality of life is stress. Stress refers to the physiological and psychological reactions of an individual to demands made on him or her. **Stressors** are events that can cause stress. **Stress** in and of itself is not necessarily harmful—in fact, some stress is helpful for motivation (Kobasa, Maddi & Kahn, 1982). However, prolonged severe stress is associated with many negative effects on health and well-being (Selye, 1956). Some of the disorders associated with excessive levels of stress are heart disease, hypertension, migraine headaches, lowered immune system responsiveness, ulcers, gastroenteritis, and asthma (Aldwin, 1994; Denollet et al., 2008; Goleman & Gurin, 1993; Weg, 1983).

Why do some people react more negatively to stress than others? First, personality configuration appears to play a role. People with a **"Type A" personality** seem to be more prone to excessive levels of stress (Rosenman, 1974). These individuals are highly competitive, restless, and achievement-oriented. They often perceive that others are attacking them, and react hostilely. Other people have what is called a **"Type B" personality**, which is diametrically opposite to Type A. **"Type C" personalities** describe individuals that repress their emotions and stress (Cooper & Faragher, 1993). Type A individuals have levels of heart attacks and coronary heart disease that are twice as high as those found in the more easygoing Type Bs. Type A individuals also have higher blood cholesterol levels and higher levels of stress hormones in their blood. Type C personalities show poorer coping with cancer.

Second, stressful life events that occur cumulatively influence reactions (Holmes & Rahe, 1967). Taken singly, many of these events, such as the death of a spouse or divorce, are highly traumatic. When several occur in succession, stressful reactions become much more severe. However, recent research calls in to question whether multiple stressful events in close proximity to each other have a cumulative effect (linear), multiplicative effect, or asymptotic effect (where there is a maximum level that can't be exceeded) (Aldwin, 1994).

Third, the way someone interprets life events influences the reactions. What is distressing to one person may have little effect on another (Chiriboga & Cutler, 1980; Folkman & Lazarus, 1980). How people cope with various levels and sources of stress may, in fact, be the key to modulating the first two factors (personality style and cumulative stressful life events). Regaining a personal sense of control is an important element in coping with stress (Taveris, 1983). Many young adults today are exploring new techniques for regaining this sense of control, such as meditation, blogging, massage, exercise, and diet.

**STRESS AMONG COLLEGE STUDENTS**    Approximately 30 percent of American college freshman report experiencing substantial stress (National Health Ministries, 2006). Chronic stress can contribute to depression, which we will discuss later in this chapter. Many factors can contribute to stress during college. Lack of regular exercise, substance use, poor diet, weight gain, and use of stimulants (such as caffeine or nicotine) are all unhealthy behaviors that can contribute to stress. Additionally, a lack of social support or failure to establish relatedness in the college environment can contribute to stress. Finally, procrastination, perfectionistic tendencies, becoming a workaholic, and losing one's sense of humor contribute to stress. In the "Promoting Wellness" section of this chapter, we will discuss ways to combat stress.

**NUTRITIONAL NEEDS**    The number of calories required for normal functioning reaches a plateau in early adulthood. Because physical growth is generally completed in adolescence, the bulk of calories in an adult's diet are used to perform the tasks of daily life and work. Those in excess of what are required for this purpose are metabolized into fat and stored in

*Many factors can contribute to stress such as lack of regular exercise, substance use, and a poor diet. (iStock)*

the body. In both men and women, certain areas of fat storage become more prominent as weight is gained in early adulthood. In men, fat tends to accumulate in the abdominal area, whereas in women it accumulates in the abdomen, hips, and thighs.

Contemporary young adults are more health conscious than their predecessors. They recognize the role of diet in promoting well-being. We now know that many health problems that develop in later stages of adulthood can be traced to a poor diet in early adulthood (American Heart Association, 1984). A healthy diet can lower blood serum cholesterol, thus protecting against heart and kidney disease in the later stages of adulthood.

## Health and Risky Behavior

**Healthy behavior**

Any behavior that reduces the susceptibility to disease and enhances physical and psychological function and well-being.

**Risky behavior**

Any behavior that detrimentally effects health or increases the likelihood of disease, although they typically increase an individual's sense of well-being at the moment.

RISKY BEHAVIOR    What are healthy and risky behaviors? A **healthy behavior** can be defined as any behavior that "can enhance physical and psychological function and well-being, and in some cases, reduce vulnerability to disease and/or slow disease progression" (Leventhal et al., 2001, p. 188). A **risky behavior** can be defined as any behavior that detrimentally effects health or increases the likelihood of disease, although they typically increase an individual's sense of well-being at the moment.

The risky behavior we discussed in the chapter on adolescent physical development continues in early adulthood. In 1995, the CDC sponsored the National College Health Risk Behavior Survey. Results indicated that:

- 27.4 percent drove after drinking alcohol in the last month

- 10.2 percent rarely, if ever, used seat belts

- 10.2 percent had engaged in a physical fight in the last year

- 8.0 percent carried a weapon not related to work in the last month

- 14.0 percent had used marijuana in the last month

- 14.4 percent had used cocaine during their life

- 34.5 percent had six or more sexual partners during their life

- 29.6 percent had used a condom during their last sexual intercourse

- 20.5 percent were overweight

- 26.3 percent ate five or more servings of vegetables and fruits daily

As if the above statistics are not disturbing enough, the CDC (2000) has written a report stating that the United States is experiencing a multiple sexually transmitted disease (STD) epidemic. More than twenty-five diseases are now spread through sexual activity. In the United States, more than sixty-five million people have an STD that is incurable. Each year, more than fifteen million people contract at least one STD, of which 50 percent will be a lifelong infection (Cates, 1999).

Different STDs have different incidence (number of new cases each year) and prevalence (number of people infected) rates (CDC, 2000). More than forty-five million people are infected with herpes, and there are around one million new cases each year. There is no cure for herpes. More than three million people are infected with chlamydia each year in the United States. This disease is highly curable with antibiotics; however, many people do not show any symptoms and fail to receive treatment. Long-term infection can lead to pelvic inflammatory disease and infertility. Gonorrhea, syphilis, HPV, hepatitis B, and trichomoniasis are other STDs that impact the lives of millions of Americans each year. Because STDs can be caught only through risky behavior, these diseases are entirely preventable by making healthy choices.

**MENTAL HEALTH**    Depression is a mental disorder of serious concern in early adulthood, and throughout the life span. Approximately 9.5 percent of all American adults, or twenty million adults, suffer with depression (NIMH, 2004). In fact, depression is so prevalent that one out of every ten college students has been diagnosed with depression (National Health Ministries, 2006). The median age at which depression manifests is thirty years (NIMH, 2004).

**Depression**

A disease that involves a person's thoughts, emotions, and feelings.

What is depression? **Depression** is a disease that involves a person's thoughts, emotions, and feelings (NIMH, 2004). Although it is unknown what specifically causes depression, there is evidence that genetic, biochemical, psychological, and environmental factors all may play a role (NIMH, 2009). Signs and symptoms of depression include a persistently sad mood; feelings of helplessness, emptiness, worthlessness, and hopelessness; and loss of interest in engaging in activities that one used to find interesting and enjoyable. In essence, it's a feeling like you are circling down a deep spiral into a bottomless, dark pit from which you can never see yourself escaping.

Although medication and therapy can help most individuals with depression, some suffer so severely and persistently that they consider suicide (Vitiello et al., 2009). In fact, 10.3 percent of all college students have seriously considered attempting suicide (CDC, 1995), and suicide is the second leading cause of death for college students (National

*Depression, if left untreated, can lead to suicide. Suicide is the second leading cause of death for college students. (iStock)*

Health Ministries, 2006). In 73 percent of suicide events (suicide ideation or attempt), some interpersonally stressful event had just occurred—such as family conflict or relationship troubles. Most importantly, the sooner an individual seeks help for depression, the better the prognosis for a full recovery.

**HEALTH ISSUES**    By and large, young adults are quite healthy. One health problem that may be encountered during early adulthood is infertility. **Infertility** can be defined as "the failure to conceive after a year of regular intercourse without contraception" (www .medterms.com, 2009). Approximately one-third of infertility cases are due to problems with the wife, one-third are due to problems with the husband, and one-third are due to either problems with both spouses or the cause is unknown (NIH, 2009).

Approximately 11.8 percent of married couples in the United States struggle to conceive, whereas 7.4 percent are considered infertile (CDC, 2002). There are several physical reasons why a couple may experience infertility; however, we are going to focus upon the role of stress in the struggle to conceive. Stress in and of itself cannot cause infertility, but its impact can be great in reducing fertility.

When a couple is trying to conceive a child and is unsuccessful, emotional stress can become high (Seibel & McCarthy, 1993). Emotions such as anger, guilt, and isolation can be experienced. Over time, this emotional stress can impact the reproductive system, including causing ovulation problems, fallopian tube spasms, decreased sperm production, or sexual dysfunction resulting in less opportunity for intercourse. Research indicates that stress reduction techniques and therapy can help couples struggling with fertility to conceive. One study found that 34 percent of women previously struggling to conceive a child became pregnant within six months of receiving stress reduction therapy. However, the longer a woman has struggled with fertility, the less likely stress reduction will help in conceiving a child. Beyond stress reduction therapy, support groups also appear to be an effective method in helping couples reduce stress and achieve pregnancy.

**PROMOTING WELLNESS**    As discussed throughout this chapter, stress and emotions can have serious impacts on all aspects of physical and mental health (Aldwin, 1994; Goleman & Gurin, 1993). What are some ways individuals can decrease and/or manage stress in their lives? Exercise, a healthy diet, avoiding stimulants and drugs, and getting at least seven hours of sleep each night are important steps in managing and limiting stress (National Health Ministries, 2006). Further, time management skills, relaxation techniques, and a healthy social support system can aid in managing stress. If these behaviors are not enough, then counseling can help teach an individual specific techniques for managing daily stress.

## Infertility

The inability to conceive a child after consistently having intercourse without contraception for at least a year.

*Pause and Process:*

1. What is stress?

2. Describe the risky behaviors prevalent in early adulthood.

# COGNITIVE DEVELOPMENT DURING EARLY ADULTHOOD

> *LEARNING OBJECTIVES:*
>
> 1. *Characterize the cognitive development during early adulthood*
> 2. *Describe information-processing during early adulthood*

In many ways, writing a chapter on cognitive development in early adulthood is difficult. Everything in terms of cognitive processes that was developing throughout childhood is achieved during early adulthood, after which many of these processes decline. Hence, it would be easy to simply say that speed of processing, attention skills, memory, problem-solving, metacognition, and language are all at peak performance during this stage of the life. However, such a view would be far too simplistic. In this section, we will discuss post-formal thought, intelligence, and language/communication in terms of technology use.

# BEYOND PIAGET'S THEORY: COGNITIVE DEVELOPMENT DURING EARLY ADULTHOOD

## *Postformal Operational Thought*

**Postformal operational thought**

A possible fifth stage of cognitive development, in early adulthood.

A topic of much debate in cognitive development is whether thinking is basically different among adults than among older adolescents. Even though many adults never achieve the stage of formal operations described by Piaget for adolescence, some researchers suggest that others attain a fifth stage of cognition called **postformal operational thought**.

A classic study illustrates how thought processes change in early adulthood (Perry, 1970). A group of Harvard undergraduates was interviewed during each year of their four-year college career. At their first interview as freshmen, the students expressed the belief that there is only one correct answer to a problem or question. They firmly believed that professors had the duty either to provide the correct answers or assign projects that would lead students to deduce the correct answers. As the students were exposed to classes and learning experiences that provided competing and contradictory opinions, they came to understand that knowledge is relative. No authority figure can provide all the "right" answers on any topic. After discovering this diversity of realities and opinions, the students felt overwhelmed. However, they came to understand that some realities are more credible than others. By the end of their college careers, they saw that they must make choices among the many differing opinions and "right" answers available, and they understood that their choice of "right" answer might apply only to themselves. In comprehending this, they grasped the complexity of decision-making that adults face.

**Dialectical thinking**

A style of thinking in adulthood in which individuals appear to accept and may even relish contradictions and conflicts in values.

**Acquisition period**

A shift in cognition seen in childhood and adolescence.

To function as a mature adult may require a shift to what is known as **dialectical thinking** (Riegel, 1973, 1975). This means accepting, and even relishing, contradictions and conflicts in viewpoints. Sorting through these contradictions and considering alternative courses produce intellectual and moral growth.

Not all researchers subscribe to this fifth stage of cognition in adulthood (Schaie & Willis, 1986). The shifts in cognition seen in childhood and adolescence, referred to as the **acquisition period**, are believed to lay the foundation for all the changes in thinking that take place in early adulthood. These thinking abilities assist young adults to choose a career during the achieving period. When individuals make choices from an immense array of possibilities, they gain personal autonomy. This prepares them to move to the next phase—social responsibility—during the middle adult years.

Perhaps the greatest intellectual challenge during early adulthood is learning to accept the uncertainties of life. The choices that must be made in adulthood are sometimes overwhelming, particularly ethical decisions. Young adults may long for the old childhood assurance that life is simple, that right and wrong are obvious. But, after all, the freedom and power to think for one's self, to make one's own choices, and to live with the consequences, was what we all looked forward to as children.

*Pause and Process:*

1. What is postformal thought?

2. Describe dialectical thinking.

# INFORMATION-PROCESSING IN EARLY ADULTHOOD

In general information-processing skills peak during early adulthood. Attention skills are strong, memory is robust, metacognitive skills are solid, and language skills are fully developed. In this section, we will examine some specific developmental aspects of information-processing in early adulthood.

Define cognitive style.

**COGNITIVE STYLE**  Cognitive style can be defined as "the intellectual aspects of learning style that represent culturally attuned ways of perceiving, organizing and evaluating information" (Jackson et al., 2003, p. 4). For the purposes of our chapter, you can consider cognitive style as a person's preferred way of learning. In general, people learn better when information is presented to them in the modality (or cognitive style) that they prefer. There are different theories and measures of cognitive style, and there is little consensus as to which constructs of cognitive style are most accurate or how to apply this in the classroom (Reid, 1995). A person's cognitive style may include a preference to perceive and learn information through visual, auditory, haptic (touch and kinesthetic), global/relational (meaningful context), or analytical modalities (Jackson et al., 2003).

**Intrinsic motivation**

A person's internally generated drive to learn because it is inherently enjoyable.

**Extrinsic motivation**

A person's drive to learn because of what he or she will receive in doing so.

**Self-regulated learning**

When a person keeps track of what they have learned, what they still need to learn, and have a strategy for how to learn it.

**Planning phase**

A person sets goals and considers what they already know and what they need to still learn.

**Monitoring phase**

Maintaining awareness of what is being learned and thinking.

**MOTIVATION AND LEARNING**    Motivation is very important for learning in college, as throughout childhood. Motivation is important because it "affects the amount of time that people are willing to devote to learning" (National Research Council, 2000). An environment that promotes motivation for learning provides challenges that incorporate the following:

- Material and assignments are appropriate for the level of knowledge and skills of the learner

- Incorporates social opportunities in which an individual can contribute knowledge

- Learners can see the usefulness and applicability of the material they are being asked to learn

Some motivation is intrinsic, whereas other motivation is extrinsic (for example, see Boggiano & Pittman, 1992; Deci, Koestner & Ryan, 2001; Wigfield & Eccles, 2002). **Intrinsic motivation** is internally generated—a person is driven to learn because learning is inherently enjoyable to him or her. **Extrinsic motivation** is externally generated—a person is driven to learn because of what he or she will receive in doing so (e.g., good grades, stickers, money, avoidance of punishment, etc.). In general, researchers stress the superiority of intrinsic motivation for academic achievement.

Beyond motivation, the ability to regulate what one is learning is also important for academic achievement and life-long learning (Pintrich & Zusho, 2001). **Self-regulated learning** can be defined as "an active, constructive process whereby learners set goals for their learning and then attempt to monitor, regulate, and control their cognition, motivation, and behavior in the service of those goals, guided and constrained by both personal characteristics and the contextual features of the environment (Pintrich & Zusho, 2001, p. 250). Working memory, prior content knowledge, and metacognitive abilities are all important for self-regulation. Theories on self-regulated learning differ in their specifics,

*The reward of receiving a good grade is an example of extrinsic motivation. (iStock)*

## Control phase

The period where necessary changes and or adaptations are made in the approach to the learning task.

## Reflection phase

The time to judge one's own work, make attributions in regards to the quality of the work, and evaluate the outcomes within the given context.

## Crystallized intelligence

Skills acquired through education and socialization such as verbal skills, mathematical skills, inductive reasoning, and interpersonal skills; the ability to recall and use information.

## Cognitive flexibility

The ability to shift from one thinking style to another.

## Visuomotor flexibility

The ability to shift from familiar to unfamiliar tasks involving hand-eye coordination.

## Visualization

The ability to organize and process visual materials.

## Fluid intelligence

The ability to perceive relationships, reason logically and abstractly, and form concepts and interpretations.

but most acknowledge four general areas or phases important to this process: planning, monitoring, control, and reflection.

During the **planning phase**, a person sets goals and considers what they already know and what they need to still learn (Pintrich & Zusho, 2001). This is a time of effortful planning, keeping in mind goals, knowledge, and context. The **monitoring phase** involves an individual maintaining awareness of what they are learning and thinking. A person is mindful of time management and decides what help may be needed. During the **control phase**, a person decides if changes need to be made in their approach to the learning task and makes necessary adaptations. This can be a phase where a person decides to seek help, renegotiate the task, or give up. A person may also come to realize that they need to increase effort. Finally, the **reflection phase** is a time to judge one's own work, make attributions in regards to the quality of the work, and evaluate the outcomes within the given context.

**INTELLIGENCE**    Psychologists disagree about the nature of intellectual development in adulthood. There is some evidence that intelligence increases during these years (Bayley & Oden, 1955). Other evidence indicates that intellectual growth peaks in early adulthood and declines thereafter (Bayley, 1970; Baltes & Scahie, 1974). Developmental psychologists suggest that intellectual functioning changes in four areas during early adulthood: (1) **crystallized intelligence**, or skills acquired through education and socialization (e.g., verbal and mathematical skills, inductive reasoning, and interpersonal skills), becomes more refined; (2) **cognitive flexibility**, or the ability to shift from one thinking style to another, improves; (3) **visuomotor flexibility**, or the ability to shift from familiar to unfamiliar tasks involving hand-eye coordination, improves; and (4) **visualization**, or the ability to organize and process visual materials, improves (Baltes & Schaie, 1974).

Researchers report that fluid intelligence reaches its peak between twenty and thirty and declines thereafter (Horn & Donaldson, 1980). **Fluid intelligence** refers to the ability to process information and to make interpretations of events. It differs from crystallized intelligence in being dependent on the functioning and integrity of the nervous system and on one's heredity. It is manifested in speed of thinking, problem-solving ability, and information recall.

**LANGUAGE AND COMMUNICATION**    Compared to childhood or old age, there is very little research focusing on language development during early adulthood. Instead, most research focusing on language development in relation to young adulthood involves aspects of adult speech and behavior that promote language development in children. The use of direct instruction, modeling, and scaffolding by adults appears to assist in the development of language in childhood (Cazden, 1983). Further, adult use of questions, extending utterances (adding on to what the child has said), and directives appear to assist in language development (Barnes et al., 1983).

*Communication via Text-Messaging*    Text-messaging is an area of communication that has blossomed in recent years; research on this type of communication is only beginning to catch up. Within this realm of research, older teenagers and young adults are sometimes referred to as the "net generation" (Thurlow, 2003). People text-message for various communicative reasons. Research has categorized these reasons in order to better understand text-messaging (Thurlow, 2003).

As you can see, friendship maintenance is the most common type of text-message (Thurlow, 2003). When you group the above types of messages into two general categories of low intimacy/high transaction orientation and high intimacy/high relational orientation, more than 60 percent of text-messages are of the high intimacy/high relational orientation variety. This means that text-messaging is being used for social interactions as opposed to being used simply as a tool to exchange necessary information.

**Ostracism**

A social control mechanism used by peer groups to enforce group rules and conformity to behavior standards; it is seen, for example, when children are ignored and rejected on the school playground.

Social communication can be positive or negative. **Ostracism**, or the purposeful ignoring and exclusion of others, can be extremely hurtful to the person being ostracized (Smith & Williams, 2004). Ostracism is associated with lower self-esteem, sense of belongingness, and self-control.

Most ostracism occurs via face-to-face interactions; however, social internet sites such as chat rooms and personal pages can also provide a forum for ostracism. Smith and Williams (2004) recently conducted a study to ascertain whether text-messaging can be used to produce feelings of ostracism. Through a controlled study, participants were either included in a three-way cell phone text-messaging interchange, or excluded after an initial period (the ostracized condition). In comparison with the participants in the controlled condition, participants in the ostracized condition reported a more negative mood, decreased sense of a meaningful existence, and lower self-esteem, self-control, and sense of belonging. Further, they also wrote more provoking text-messages in response to the exclusion. This study shows the power of text-messaging communication.

Beyond the harm that text-messaging can cause through ostracism, provocation, or harassment, a new area of alarm has emerged. Sexting, or text-messaging sexually explicit messages or pictures, is an area of growing concern (www.cyh.com, 2009). Sexting communication can easily become shared communication with the community at large due to the ease of passing the information electronically along or posting it to the internet. When such private communications become public, embarrassment, shame, distress, and humiliation can result. Once this information is public, it can never become private again, and the socioemotional damage can have long-term, devastating effects. Schools, parents, and law enforcement are scrambling to deal with this new form of communication.

*Communication via Social Networking Sites*    Online social networks can serve a multitude of purposes, and social network theory in relation to the internet is an area of increasing research (Ethier, 2009). "The study of social networks is important because it helps us to better understand how and why we interact with each other, as well as how technology can alter this interaction" (Ethier, 2009, pg. 1). Social networks can be used to help form and persuade opinions, market products or services, influence the reputation of people or companies, and provide a forum for groups to meet and share information.

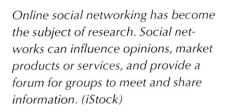

*Online social networking has become the subject of research. Social networks can influence opinions, market products or services, and provide a forum for groups to meet and share information. (iStock)*

Many colleges are beginning to provide social network forums for their students (Ethier, 2009). Much like the text-messaging research discussed previously, social network forums can be used for positive or negative communication. The use of buddy lists can increase feelings of exclusion and allow people to estimate how popular (or unpopular) they are. That said, social network communities can be used to create a sense of cohesion and identity among student clubs and majors. They can also be used to decrease one's sense of isolation and provide entertainment.

A recent study by Kramer and Winter (2008) examined the relationship of extraversion (or outgoingness), self-esteem, self-efficacy, and self-presentation in regards to social networking sites. First, let's explore some of the general information they found in regards to the "typical" social networker. In the study, they found that the average social networker has nearly ninety-two virtual friends and belongs to around twenty-eight groups. Additionally, the typical social networker posts forty-five pictures and will complete 59 percent of available profile fields. On social networking sites, the most popular group categories in order are entertainment, personal data, geography, hobbies and interests, and social life and relationships. More than 98.3 percent of social networkers register with their real name and post their real photo. The majority of photos show the individual's face with either a posing or serious facial expression. Social networkers are also not shy in posting personal information with nearly 33 percent posting their political orientation and 62 percent posting their relationship status.

Now that we have a general description of social networkers, we can see what the Kramer and Winter (2008) study discovered in regards to personality, and other personal characteristics, and social networking. Individuals with a medium score on the extraversion measure participated in the greatest number of groups. Additionally, the higher a person's extraversion score, the more likely they were to post an experimental photo (such as a black and white photo). Self-esteem was not related to the content or style of the social networker's profile, although other studies have found such an association (Banczyk et al.,

2008). Participants did display high-efficacy in terms of being able to create a positive impression through self-presentation.

What does all this information mean? Individuals feel that they can control how others perceive them by how they present themselves on social networking sites. That said, most individuals are honest and use real information when creating their profiles. Hence, although social networking sites are often perceived as a virtual world where people can create alternative versions of themselves, most individuals keep it real and enjoy social interaction that is based on reality.

*General internet communication*    Are there any relationships between internet use, personality, and cognitive style? Well, research in this area of communication is relatively new and more longitudinal studies are needed; however, an initial picture has begun to emerge. Personality does appear to have some relationship to online communication. Extroverted individuals tend to spend more time online and communicate more with e-mail than more introverted individuals (Jackson et al., 2003). The higher an individual is in neuroticism (or emotional instability and high anxiety), the less time they spend online.

Cognitive style, which we discussed earlier in this chapter, also appears to be related to online communication (Jackson et al., 2003). A visual cognitive style is associated with less time spent on the internet. A global/relational cognitive style is associated with more time spent on the internet and more e-mail communications.

Internet use appears to be related to certain demographic characteristics (Jackson et al., 2003). African Americans spend less time online and visit fewer sites than European Americans. In general, the more educated a person is, the more time they spend online. Single adults spend less time online than currently married adults. One study using path analysis (a statistical technique) found that socioeconomic factors and personality factors best predict internet use, cognitive style was not as strongly related.

*Pause and Process:*

1. What is motivation and why is it important in learning?

2. How is technology influencing communication?

# SOCIOEMOTIONAL DEVELOPMENT DURING EARLY ADULTHOOD

**LEARNING OBJECTIVES:**

1. *Characterize emotional development during early adulthood*

2. *Describe the self in relation to others during early adulthood*

3. *Explain psychosocial development during early adulthood*

## Intimacy versus isolation

The sixth psychosocial attitude described by Erikson; it is developed optimally between eighteen and twenty-four years of age. Intimacy is the ability to have a close and loving relationship with another. Isolation is the refusal to allow oneself to become vulnerable enough to establish intimate relationships.

Developmentalists have begun to research the many changes that take place in early adulthood. Not everyone experiences these changes at the same rate, but most people between the ages of eighteen and twenty-five follow a predictable pattern.

Like other stages of the life span, adulthood poses unique challenges and tasks. These tasks focus primarily on individuating completely from one's family of origin and creating an independent lifestyle. Social expectations are that individuals at this stage will develop and refine skills and abilities that promote competency or mastery of work related roles; use interpersonal skills to choose a mate and develop a lifestyle based on responsible adult-like behavior; and make the necessary effort to maintain a committed relationship that may include children.

Psychopathology has increased for young adults in recent years. It is speculated that this is partly due to their inability to achieve the expected roles for this phase of life, such as moving out of the parents' home, establishing a career, marriage, and parenthood (Compass, Hinden & Gerhardt, 1995; Seiffge-Krenke, 1998; Seiffge-Krenke, 2006).

# PSYCHOSOCIAL DEVELOPMENT

## *Intimacy Versus Isolation*

## Generativity versus stagnation

The seventh psychosocial attitude described by Erikson; It is developed optimally between twenty-four and fifty-four years of age. Generativity is an interest in caring for others and sharing one's knowledge, skills, and information. Stagnation (self-absorption) is directing all one's interest inward to oneself.

Erikson proposed a normative-crisis model of human development that depicts emotional and social changes as taking place in a sequence. Two stages of psychosocial development are observed in early adulthood, according to Erikson (1950, 1964): (1) a sense of **intimacy versus isolation** is established between eighteen and twenty-four years of age, and (2) a sense of **generativity versus stagnation** (sometimes called generativity versus self-absorption) is established between twenty-four and fifty-four years of age. Because the generativity versus stagnation stage lasts most of middle adulthood, we will discuss this stage in Chapter 8. In this section, we will focus on intimacy versus isolation.

During adolescence, an individual establishes a basic idea of personal identity and settles on an initial direction in life. By accomplishing this central task of adolescence, a person prepares for the next stage in psychosocial development. This occurs in the first years of early adulthood, when an individual is concerned with "losing and finding himself in another," according to Erikson.

During this period of young adulthood, between eighteen and twenty-four, the individual is challenged to learn the skills that will facilitate having an intimate relationship with another person. This is one of the most pressing concerns of young adults. They need to go through a series of experiences in order to learn how to conduct a meaningful adult love relationship. These skills are often learned by observing parental behavior and trial and error.

Through time, individuals learn about themselves and others. They discover what is attractive in others, how and to what degree they should lower barriers to intimacy, when and how they should disclose personal information to another, and how to go about placing trust in another person. The lessons of trust that were learned in infancy

Why is it important for a person to achieve intimacy instead of social isolation?

are transferred to relationship experiences in adulthood in ways that facilitate the development of intimacy skills.

Social isolation is the principle hazard of inadequate psychosocial development in early adulthood, according to Erikson. It results from an inability to develop a close relationship with another. This can happen because an individual withdraws too soon from his or her peer group, before having opportunities to development close associations. It may also stem from negative relationship experiences that convince the individual that it is emotionally safer not to break down personal boundaries and allow one's self to become vulnerable.

Those who do acquire the skills of intimacy eventually choose a partner for a long-term committed relationship. This relationship serves as the basis for forming a new family system for many people. It is with this partner that an individual now shifts his or her psychosocial focus of the next stage: generativity versus stagnation.

*Pause and Process:*

1. What is the psychosocial task that should be accomplished in early adulthood? Said another way, which of Erikson's conflicts should be resolved in early adulthood?

2. What can cause social isolation?

# EMOTIONAL DEVELOPMENT

The areas of the brain responsible for emotional regulation reach maturity in early adulthood. This allows for greater control of emotions. Such emotional control is important, as early adulthood is typically a time for establishing a life-long marriage and beginning a family. In this section of the chapter we will focus upon personality and attachment, both of which play key roles in emotion-related behavior.

**Trait**

A distinguishing feature or characteristic.

**Big five factors personality theory**

A theory that posits that there are five super-traits that are the foundation of personality.

**Openness**

The degree to which a person is comfortable with variety, autonomy, and change.

PERSONALITY    There are many theories of personality. In this chapter, we are going to focus on a trait theory of personality, called the big five factors personality theory (for example, see Costa & McCrae, 1995; McCrae & Costa, 2006). A **trait** is a disposition or characteristic that has some heritability and produces certain behaviors that are displayed across diverse settings. The **big five factors personality theory** posits that five supertraits lay the foundation for all of our personality possibilities. These five traits are openness, conscientiousness, extraversion, agreeableness, and neuroticism.

**Openness** can be conceptualized as the degree to which a person is comfortable with variety, autonomy, and change (for example, see Costa & McCrae, 1995; McCrae & Costa, 2006). **Conscientiousness** can be conceptualized as the degree to which a person values and/or needs organization, precision, and self-discipline. **Extroversion** can be conceptualized as the degree to which a person is outgoing, demonstrative, and fun-loving.

**Conscientiousness**

The degree to which a person values and/or needs organization, precision, and self-discipline.

**Extroversion**

The degree to which a person is outgoing.

**Agreeableness**

The degree to which a person is trusting, giving, and kind.

**Neuroticism**

The degree to which a person is insecure, emotional, and anxious.

**Agreeableness** can be conceptualized as the degree to which a person is trusting, giving, and kind. Finally, **neuroticism** can be conceptualized as the degree to which a person is insecure, emotional, and anxious.

Trait theories, in general, have been criticized for overemphasizing traits and under-emphasizing the role of the environment in personality development. Most developmentalists believe that personality is the result of complex interactions that include both traits and the environment (Cervone & Mischel, 2002; Mischel, 2004). In chapter eight, we will see which traits tend to change with age, and which tend to stay the same.

**ATTACHMENT** Attachment styles play an important role in adult relationships. These attachment styles have their foundations in infancy, where mental models were built based upon parental caregiving and parent/child interaction (Dixon, 2003; Galatzer-Levy & Cohler, 1993). In fact "a central notion of attachment theory is that attachment representation once formed in early childhood, continue to function as a relatively durable template for later relationships throughout adolescence and into adulthood" (Seiffge-Krenke, 2006, p. 865).

Attachment to romantic partners is likely to resemble attachment to parents (Hazen & Shaver, 1987; Steele et al., 1998). Much of the information discussed in this section is based upon the initial research by Bowlby and Ainsworth, and more recent research by Hazen, Shaver, and their colleagues. Let's review the attachment styles introduced in chapter three, with an expanded description of each one's mental model of self and others and their approach to relationships.

Secure attachment:

- Secure attachment style: Trusts self and others and is comfortable in a relationship or out of a relationship. Having parents that were responsive and dependable is related to the development of this attachment style.

*Attachment styles are important in adult relationships such as having a romantic partner. (iStock)*

Insecure attachment:

- Ambivalent style (a.k.a., resistant attachment style): Has trouble trusting self, and is dependent upon others. This attachment style feels the need to constantly be in a relationship and may display possessiveness and jealousy. Having parents that were inconsistent is related to the development of this attachment style.

- Avoidant attachment style (a.k.a., dismissive attachment style): Trusts self, but has trouble trusting others. Is generally avoidant of close relationships and can be emotionally distant when in a relationship. Having parents that were emotionally dismissive, psychologically distant, or physically unavailable is related to the development of this attachment style.

- Disorganized/disoriented attachment style (a.k.a., unresolved attachment style): Has trouble trusting self and others. Generally struggles in relationships and is at risk for being a victim of domestic violence. Having parents that were neglectful or abusive is related to the development of this attachment style.

*Spotlight*

Explain the four patterns for leaving home and launching an independent life.

The transition from adolescence to complete independence in adulthood can be difficult. Young adults with a secure attachment to their parents typically report a more emotionally positive transition from adolescence to adulthood than young adults with insecure attachment (for a review see Seiffge-Krenke, 2006). Securely attached individuals seem able to achieve independence in early adulthood more easily, whereas insecure and anxious young adults display lower adjustment and greater distress (Grossman, Grossman & Zimmermann, 1999). More positive interactions are seen in the relationships between securely attached young adults and their parents than in the relationships between insecurely attached young adults and their parents. Adults with a secure attachment to their parents typically value these relationships and believe that this relationship has influenced their life course.

Attachment style greatly impacts one's ability to adjust to the expected tasks in young adulthood, like developing a romantic relationship that will grow into a life-long marriage (Scharf et al., 2004). Securely attached individuals tend to be in longer lasting and more satisfying relationships that exhibit greater trust and commitment than the relationships of insecurely attached individuals (Feeney & Collins, 2007). Further, the romantic relationships of securely attached adults are close and intimate, yet the individuals can maintain a healthy degree of individuality (Shaver, Belsky & Brennan, 2000). When in need of a secure base, individuals with a secure attachment style tend to rely on their romantic partners in adulthood, whereas individuals with an insecure attachment style tend to rely on their parents (Cox et al., 2008). During periods of separation due to work travel, insecurely attached individuals experience greater separation anxiety as exhibited in self-reported stress, cortisol levels (related to physiological stress), and sleeping problems, than securely attached individuals (Diamond, Hicks & Otter-Henderson, 2008). Also, securely attached individuals are more skilled in providing emotional support to their partners than insecurely attached individuals (Rholes & Simpson, 2007).

Beyond romantic relationships, attachment in adulthood is related to numerous other aspects of development and adjustment. For example, adults with insecure attachment tendencies exhibit greater physiological stress and lower levels of self-reported love when listening to an infant cry than adults with secure attachment tendencies (Groh & Roisman, 2009). Such reactions could impact parenting behavior. Attachment also seems to be related to one's religiosity and belief in a loving God (Cassibba et al., 2008). Catholic priests have higher rates of secure attachment than the general population. Additionally, priests and lay Catholics have lower rates of disorganized/disoriented attachment styles than the general population. Several studies have indicated that a secure attachment style and the ability to trust parents in childhood is predictive of the ability to trust and believe in a loving God during adulthood (for example, see Birgegard & Granqvist, 2004; Cassibba et al. 2008). In general, compared to individuals with an insecure attachment style, secure individuals have greater resiliency, self-esteem, emotional control, mental health, coping skills, self-efficacy, and overall positive adaptation (Berman & Sperling, 1991; Hankin, Kassel & Abela, 2005; Miklincer & Shaver, 2007; Scharf et al., 2004).

*Pause and Process:*

1. What are the big five personality traits?

2. How do the four attachment styles differ in the mental representations of self and others?

# SELF WITH OTHERS

Early adulthood is a time of achieving independence from one's parents. It is also a time of establishing a life-long partnership and establishing a family. In this section, we will discuss how young adults go about leaving the parents' home, cohabitation, marriage, career development, and parenthood.

## *Living Arrangements*

**LEAVING THE NEST** In the chapter on socioemotional development during adolescence, we learned that this period of time can be difficult because adolescents and their parents must strike a new balance between autonomy and relatedness, control and freedom. During the emergence of early adulthood, young adults and their parents must once again seek this balance (O'Conner et al., 1996; Seiffge-Krenke, 2006).

One developmental task that is expected to be completed during early adulthood is moving out of one's parents' home and living independently. Many young adults move out, move back in, and then move back out of their parents' homes (Goldscheider & Goldscheider, 1994; Seiffge-Krenke, 2006; Settersten, 1998). The percentage can vary greatly across ethnicities, cultures, religions, socioeconomic status, and sociohistorical and economic times. Young adults who return home to live with their parents are typically referred to as **incompletely launched young adults**.

Research has indicated four patterns for leaving home and launching an independent life in early adulthood (Seiffge-Krenke, 2006). **In-time leavers** are individuals that move out of their parents homes permanently before the age of twenty-five. Approximately 55 percent of all young adults fall into this category. The average age for a female to move out is twenty-one years, whereas the average age for a male to move out is twenty-three years. Approximately 14 percent of all adults are considered **still in the nest**. These are individuals who are still living at home between the ages of twenty-one to twenty-five years, but are actively working toward moving out, and are out by the end of this age-range. **Late leavers** are those individuals that are still living at home after the age of twenty-five. Approximately 20 percent of young adults fall into the late leavers category. **Returners** are young adults who had ventured out to independent living, but subsequently returned to live with their parents at some point between the ages of twenty-one and twenty-five years of age. Approximately 11 percent of young adults fall into the returner category.

In a study examining these patterns of leaving the nest by Seiffge-Krenke (2006), participants categorized as late leavers and returners shared key demographic characteristics; hence, these two categories were combined into one general category (late leavers/returners) for statistical analysis. Analysis revealed that there are virtually no differences between in-time leavers, still in the nesters, and late leavers/returners in terms of education level, parents' marital status, number of siblings, socioeconomic status, or gender. Only two participants were unemployed and both were in the late leavers/returners category. Across categories, approximately half of the participants were in an apprenticeship or profession, while the other half was attending college.

So how do individuals in these various patterns of leaving home differ? What predicts how a young adult will time leaving home? One robust finding by Seiffge-Krenke (2006) was the impact of marriage and romantic relationships in terms of leaving the nest. All of the participants in the study that were married were in-time leavers. Further, in-time leavers were more likely to be in a long-term committed relationship than those individuals still at home. In-time leavers predominately had a secure attachment style, whereas late leavers/returners predominately had an avoidant attachment style. Individuals still in the nest were divided in regards to attachment style, with 46 percent classified as secure, 31 percent classified as avoidant, and 23 percent classified as preoccupied.

Another predictor of leaving the home in-time was conflict in the home during adolescence, although this conflict gave way to negotiation in terms of establishing a new balance between autonomy and relatedness. Individuals still in the nest had lower levels of independence during early adulthood, when compared with those that leave in time. Adults that are late leavers/returners have higher levels of mental illness symptoms (as reported by their parents) than in-time or still in the nest individuals. It is speculated that especially rough transitions to independent living may lead to psychopathology.

## Cohabitation

Living with a romantic partner prior to marriage.

## Cohabitation effect

The increased risk for divorce associated with cohabitation.

**COHABITATION**    Involvement in a long-term, romantic relationship increases across early adulthood, with 62 percent in such a relationship by age twenty-five (Seiffge-Krenke, 2006). Living with a romantic partner prior to marriage, referred to as **cohabitation**, is an increasingly popular choice among young adults. It is estimated that up to 70 percent of young couples cohabitate in the United States (Bumpass & Lu, 2000; Stanley, Whitton & Markman, 2004). Unfortunately, there are some serious negative consequences to cohabitation.

Couples that cohabitate prior to engagement or marriage report lower marital quality than those that marry prior to living together (Cohan & Kleinbaum, 2002; Stanley et al., 2002). Additionally, couples that cohabitate and then marry are at an increased risk for divorce (Kamp Dush, Cohan & Amato, 2003). In fact, this finding is so robust in the research literature, that it has been coined the **cohabitation effect** (Rhoades, Stanley & Markman, 2009). In comparison to couples that engage or marry prior to living together, cohabiting couples exhibit the following problems: lower marital satisfaction, lower relationship quality, lower dedication to the spouse and marriage, increased rates of infidelity, greater potential for divorce and poorer outcomes for children (abuse, problem behavior, poverty, overall welfare).

The above findings are based on numerous research studies (for example see: Kline et al., 2004; Rhoades, Staley & Markman, 2006, 2009; Stanton, 2009; Stets, 1991; Stets & Straus, 1989; Waite & Gallagher, 2000; Wing, 2009; Yllo & Straus, 1981). However, studies conducted on this issue have been correlational in nature. As you can remember for chapter 1, correlational research does not infer causality. A third variable may be contributing to the association between the predictor and outcome variables. In this case a hypothetical third variable influencing both cohabitation and the negative outcomes may be religiosity. Religious individuals may be less likely to cohabitate and they also may be less likely to experience the outcomes associated with cohabitation. Hence it may not be the cohabitation that is causing the negative outcomes but rather it may be the third variable, religiosity, influencing both the cohabitation and the negative outcomes.

*There are a variety of beliefs for the purpose of marriage. (iStock)*

**MARRIAGE**    Why do people marry? Well, the answer is dependent upon one's religion, ethnicity, culture, and overall socialization. For Christians, the purpose of marriage is to help guide your partner to be closer to God, to be open to procreation, and to use the marriage to glorify God everyday. In a more American, secular sense, marriage is usually based upon love, fulfillment of psychological and financial needs, and parenthood (Brehm, 1992; Cherlin, 1999; Cox, 1990; Steinmetz, Clavan & Stein, 1990). Marriage is correlated with happiness, better health, and increased longevity (Brehm, 1992).

How does one achieve a happy and life-long marriage? First, one should marry someone that they have dated for at least six months and who shares the view that marriage is a life-long commitment. Second, one must shift his or her self-concept from one of "me" to one of "we." Everyday, efforts should be made to show selflessness and appreciation for your spouse. Third, healthy communication styles must be developed and conflict must be handled in a productive way (Brehm, 1992). Fourth, the marriage must be the primary relationship. Friendships and other family relationships (like sibling or parent relationships) must take a back seat if a marriage is to stay strong and healthy.

Men and women can differ in their communication styles (Brehm, 1992). Women tend to use more self-disclosure in emotional matters. Additionally, women tend to be more expressive (warm and responsive) in their communication style, whereas males are more instrumental (practical). Spouses must come to appreciate and understand each others communication style. Premarital classes can help with this. In general, to improve communication, decrease conflict, and improve marital satisfaction, spouses should do the following (Brehm, 1992; Gottman and colleagues, 1976, 1979, 1994, 1998, 1999):

- Clearly understand the intent and impact of communication

- Validate each others feelings and thoughts

- Discuss problems openly

- Focus on the solvable problems and negotiate agreements and compromise

- Don't assume that the spouse can read your mind

- Avoid mind-reading your spouses intentions, as you may assume more negative intentions

- Turn toward each other in times of distress and nurture affectional ties

- Create a life-story together with shared meaning and history

**BECOMING PARENTS**    Becoming a parent is a life-altering experience. Once again, one's self-concept must switch from one of "we" (self and spouse), to one of "three" (self, spouse, and child). The transition to parenthood can be both exciting and stressful. The committed marital relationship is the foundation for the new family system.

## The Outside World

**FRIENDSHIP**    The nature and importance of friendships change in early adulthood. Now friends are frequently chosen for the congeniality. The need for group experiences that was declining in late adolescence decreases even more in early adulthood. As individuals focus on developing skills that promote intimate relationships, their social interactions tend to center on one person. As they become involved in a committed relationship, their friendships tend to be with other couples of similar ages and social situations. In the later years of early adulthood, friendships are formed in more complex ways. Regardless, friendships provide a source of support, security, and love (Brehm, 1992).

**LEISURE TIME**    Leisure activities can provide an opportunity for socialization (Hansen, Dik & Zhou, 2008). During early adulthood, particularly the college-age years, leisure provides a forum for establishing social status, cultivating relationships, and forming a peer reference group (Hansen, Dik & Zhou, 2008; Kleiber & Kelly, 1980). During the college-age years, leisure activities can be completely social in nature (e.g., partying for the sake of hanging out together and having fun). Conversely, leisure time becomes more constricted during the mid and latter part of early adulthood as family and work obligations grow. Hence, a party at work may serve multiple purposes such as social networking with the intention of making career contacts, making a good impression on colleagues, and hanging out with your work friends.

**Generation Y**

Individuals born after the year 1980.

**CAREERS IN EARLY ADULTHOOD**    Many young adults today are considered to be part of **Generation Y** (i.e., individuals born after 1980) (Schultz & Schultz, 2010). Within the next couple of years, Generation Y individuals will comprise approximately 50 percent of those who work in the United States. Interestingly, these young adults differ from the preceding generations in what they want and expect in a career.

**Silent generation**

Individuals born between 1922 and 1945.

Before we discuss what young adults today seek in a career, it would be helpful to describe previous generations' expectations and behaviors. The **Silent Generation** includes individuals born between 1922 and 1945 (Schultz & Schultz, 2010). Most of these individuals have either retired from the workforce or plan to do so in the near future.

*What is wanted in a career depends upon ones expectations. These expectations vary from one generation to the next. (iStock)*

The Silent Generation valued loyalty, hard work, and respect for authority. Loyalty was seen as a two-way street: employees were loyal to their employers and employers were loyal to their employees. Many individuals in the Silent Generation had only one or two employers, largely because of the importance of loyalty.

**Baby boomer generation**

Individuals born between 1946 and 1964.

The **Baby Boomer Generation** includes individuals born between 1946 and 1964 (Schultz & Schultz, 2010). Due to the large number of individuals born to this generation, competition for jobs was intense in their early adulthood. Unfortunately, two related outcomes of this competition were individuals choosing to become workaholics and a decline in time spent with the family.

**Generation X**

Individuals born between 1965 and 1979.

**Generation X** includes individuals born between 1965 and 1979 (Schultz & Schultz, 2010). These are the children of the Baby Boomer Generation, and as such, were committed to not becoming workaholics like their parents. This generation values their independence, questions authority, and is skilled in technology.

Now that we know about previous generations of young adults we can learn about Generation Y with a comparative eye. This is a generation that grew up during the big "self-esteem" push in the 1980s. During this time, many school children were shielded from competition and praised for simply trying their hardest. One outcome of this non-competitive, full-of-praise environment is that many Generation Y individuals are self-centered, narcissistic, and expect constant positive feedback from supervisors regardless of actual work produced (McCormack, 2007; Schultz & Schultz, 2010; Zaslow, 2007). These individuals shun the idea of starting at the bottom and working their way up the corporate ladder. Instead, they want to be involved in meaningful, high-end jobs immediately upon graduating from college (Rexrode, 2007; Schultz & Schultz, 2010). Despite all this negative information, Generation Y individuals are enthusiastic and entrepreneurial in the workplace. In contrast to the previous generations discussed, they value leisure time more than money, wish for a flexible schedule, guard against long work hours, disvalue loyalty to their employer, seek creative opportunities, and tend to change jobs every few years. They also seek a career that will allow them to change the world.

Do career interests change substantially between adolescence and middle adulthood? This was a question asked by Low and colleagues (2005) in a review of longitudinal studies. In general, vocational interests in physical, hands-on, or artistic careers are more stable than vocational interests in more clerical, scientific, or social careers. Hence, childhood dreams of certain careers usually do not lead to that career in adulthood, but may for some.

*Pause and Process:*

1. What are the dangers associated with cohabitation?

2. Compare and contrast the four generations discussed in terms of work expectations and behaviors.

# SUMMARY

1. Although physical growth was nearly completed in adolescence, individuals experience a variety of physical changes in early adulthood. The eyes gradually lose their ability to focus after about age thirty-five. The likelihood of periodontal disease increases. The heart gradually loses its ability to pump blood efficiently and the risk of cardiovascular disease rises. The lungs begin to work less efficiently as well. The skin begins to show signs of aging. Muscular strength reaches its peak during this period.

2. Health during adulthood is generally very good, though subject to certain hazards. These include high levels of stress over long periods of time, poor diets, and inadequate exercise. Risky behaviors seen in adolescence continue to plague some individuals in early adulthood. According to the CDC (2000), some STDs are at epidemic levels in the United States. Depression and suicide are issues to be aware of and addressed during this phase of life.

3. Intellectual functioning changes in several areas during adulthood. Crystallized intelligence increases, while fluid intelligence declines. Developmental researchers disagree about whether there is a fifth stage of cognitive development called postformal operational thought. Thinking as a mature adult may require a shift to dialectical thinking, or the ability to tolerate uncertainty, contradictions, and conflicts in logic.

4. Motivation and self-regulation are important for learning and academic achievement in college. Extrinsic motivation is dependent upon reward and punishment, whereas intrinsic motivation is internally generated and more powerful. Self-regulated learning allows an individual to keep track of what they are learning and adjust behaviors as needed.

5. Language and communication have been forever altered by the dawn of technology. Text-messaging, social networking sites, and general internet use are increasingly used for social interactions and communications. Although research in this domain is in its infancy, it appears that technology use differs by demographic characteristics, personality, and cognitive style. Further, social and communication interactions using technology may be positive or negative.

6. Personality in early adulthood can be conceptualized as being comprised of five supertraits: openness, conscientiousness, extroversion, agreeableness, and neuroticism. Attachment style in early adulthood is important for overall adjustment to adulthood and the establishment of healthy romantic relationships.

7. Researchers have identified four patterns for young adults to leave their parents' home and establish independent living: in-time leavers, still in the nest leavers, late leavers, and returners. Essentially, individuals in all four categories have similar educational levels, parental marital status, and number of siblings. Factors that impact launching into independent living include committed romantic relationships, support for independence during early adolescence, and conflict in the home during adolescence.

8. Cohabitation prior to engagement or marriage is associated with numerous negative outcomes; including, higher divorce rates, domestic violence, infidelity, and overall lower relationship quality. Marriage is associated with happiness, better health, and longevity. Healthy communication is

important for a marriage to be successful. Becoming parents is a transitional period that may be both exciting and stressful.

9. Generation Y individuals, the majority of which are either in early adulthood or quickly approaching it, will comprise 50 percent of the U.S. workforce within the next couple of years. These individuals tend to be egocentric and expect positive praise regardless of work performance. Further, they desire flexible, limited work hours, and display little employer loyalty. In fact, many Generation Y individuals seek to change jobs/careers every few years in search of personal growth opportunities and creative outlets.

10. The two major psychosocial changes in early adulthood are acquiring a sense of intimacy versus isolation; and beginning efforts to establish a sense of generativity versus stagnation. Acquiring a healthy sense of intimacy between eighteen and twenty-four years equips people with the skills needed to establish and maintain a committed relationship—leading to a happier and more satisfying life.

# SELF-QUIZ

1. What is the cultural meaning of maturity?
2. What is the age-range for early adulthood?
3. When do deficiencies in distance perception first become noticeable?
4. What is periodontal disease?
5. Describe changes in muscular strength and physical performance in early adulthood.
6. Describe the three "types" of personalities discussed in the stress section of the chapter and explain how they relate to health.
7. What factors contribute to stress in college students?
8. How do men and women differ in their weight and height changes during early adulthood?
9. Explain what depression is and what are its symptoms?
10. How may stress be related to fertility issues?
11. What is an example of postformal operational thought?
12. How is postformal operational thought different from formal operational thought (discussed in Chapter 6)?
13. Define cognitive style.
14. What do you believe is your predominant cognitive style and why?
15. How are extrinsic motivation and intrinsic motivation different?
16. Why do you think intrinsic motivation is associated with better academic outcomes than extrinsic motivation?
17. Describe the four general phases to self-regulated learning. Provide an example for each phase.
18. What is the nature of intelligence in adulthood?
19. What are the main purposes of communication when text-messaging?
20. Describe the typical person who uses social networking sites.
21. What are some speculations as to why psychopathology in young adults has increased in recent years?
22. What is a trait?
23. Compare and contrast the big five factors of personality discussed in this chapter with the characteristics of temperament discussed in previous chapters.
24. Why is adult attachment predicted by childhood attachment?
25. What are some ways adult attachment style is related to romantic relationships and general well-being?

26. Explain the four patterns for leaving home and launching an independent life.
27. What factors impact when a person moves out of their parents' home?
28. What is the cohabitation effect and why do you think it exists?
29. What are some strategies to make a marriage work?
30. Why is it important for a person to achieve intimacy instead of social isolation?

## TERMS AND CONCEPTS

# CHAPTER 8

# Middle Adulthood

(iStock)

## OUTLINE

### PHYSICAL DEVELOPMENT DURING MIDDLE ADULTHOOD

- Theories of biological aging
- Physical growth
- Health issues

### COGNITIVE DEVELOPMENT DURING MIDDLE ADULTHOOD

- Beyond Piaget's theory
- Information-processing during middle adulthood

### SOCIOEMOTIONAL DEVELOPMENT DURING MIDDLE ADULTHOOD

- Psychosocial development
- Emotional development
- Self and others

311

**The middle adulthood stage is a transitional period.** This stage in the life span takes place when people are approximately between the ages forty and sixty-five. During this time, individuals experience both continuity and change in many aspects of their lives. Physical changes signal approaching old age. Roles that have occupied so much of adult life come to a close by the end of this period. These range from reproductive to parenting and work roles. Individuals are challenged to adjust to these and other significant changes in order to make new adaptations of life. Middle age can bring about new perceptions, redefinitions of roles, and different means for achieving personal happiness.

**Middle age** may be a prime time of life in many respects, but physical changes indicate that the aging process is accelerating. Our culture is prone to **ageism**, or unreasonable and irrational beliefs about aging and older individuals (Neugarten, 1970). When people reach middle age, they notice physical signs of aging in themselves and fear the end of their physical attractiveness. Many go to great expense to forestall this. Middle-aged Americans sometimes turn to cosmetic surgery to stave off the waning of exterior beauty.

The first physical signs of aging appear during early adulthood. They are not dramatic, however, so people often overlook them. In middle age, the signs multiply rapidly. It is not unusual to find an occasional gray hair in early adulthood, for example. In middle age, people notice many more of these, along with more wrinkled skin, bags under the eyes, a larger waistline, and less attractive muscle tone. Rather than accepting such signs as part of the normal process of getting older, many people determine to hide or reduce them.

Longer life expectancy may also contribute to people's desire to deny the aging process. In earlier eras, people in their fifties and early sixties were considered elderly. Today that is considered relatively young in relation to the amount of time left to live (Perdue & Gurtman, 1990).

# PHYSICAL DEVELOPMENT DURING MIDDLE ADULTHOOD

## Middle adulthood

The seventh stage of the life span, occurring between 45 and 65 years of age.

### LEARNING OBJECTIVES:

1. *Explain the theories of why we age*
2. *Describe physical development during middle adulthood*
3. *Awareness of health issues in middle adulthood*

# THEORIES OF BIOLOGICAL AGING

## Middle age

A term synonymous with middle adulthood. Middle age can bring about new perceptions, redefinitions of roles, and different means for achieving personal happiness.

**Aging** is a process that is not well understood (Busse, 1987), though we know it involves a series of complex and interrelated changes. Although this process is largely biological in nature, it also affects psychological and social functioning. With recent advances in the biological sciences, scientists are beginning to unravel this complex process. Some of these questions are being addressed by research: Can aging be prevented? Can the effects of aging be reversed? How far can we push the life expectancy of humans beyond current biological barriers?

Although we do not know why, exactly, the body ages, we do have some theories. In the following paragraphs, we discuss some current theories of why the body ages.

**Ageism**

Unreasonable or irrational beliefs about aging and older individuals.

**Aging**

A complex process involving a decline in physiological competence that inevitably increases the incidence and intensifies the effects of accidents, disease, and other forms of environmental stress.

**Cellular clock theory**

When biological errors in the DNA genetic code accumulate, the cells are unable to function at all and die.

**Stochastic processes**

The probability of random accidental injury to cellular DNA.

**CELLULAR CLOCK THEORY**    Some research suggests that aging results from cells becoming defective because of errors in the DNA genetic code (the cellular command molecule located in the nucleus of cells). As cells experience greater numbers of reproductions over time, errors within the DNA chain are inevitable. Thus, aging may result from an accumulation of errors at the cellular level. Ultimately, the **cellular clock theory** asserts that when these biological errors accumulate, the cells are unable to function at all and die (Hayflick, 1980; Lumpkin et al., 1986; Orgel, 1970; Shay & Wright, 2007; Vinters, 2001; Wareham et al., 1987).

Cells are also vulnerable to **stochastic processes**, or the probability of random accidental injury to cellular DNA (from radiation, for example). The likelihood of accidental injury increases with the passage of time, and these mutations are passed on through subsequent cellular reproductions, eventually leading to the death of cells (Comfort, 1970).

**FREE-RADICAL THEORY**    **Free-radicals** are unstable oxygen molecules that are released when cells metabolize energy (Chandel & Budinger, 2007). These react with other chemicals within cells, interfering with normal cell functioning and damaging DNA (Liu et al., 2007). Cells are usually able to repair the damage that results. However, their ability to repair themselves may be hampered by the aging process itself or by the lack of adequate chemicals to initiate healing. Free-radical damage could lead to numerous diseases, including cancer and neurodegenerative diseases (Katakura, 2006; Vinters, 2001).

**MITOCHONDRIAL THEORY**    The **mitochondrial theory** is closely related to the free-radical theory. When free-radicals are released in a cell, they can damage the mitochondria (which are responsible for providing energy for cellular growth and repair). When mitochondria cannot properly function, more free-radicals are released, which then further damage the

*Aging may be the result of errors in the DNA genetic code, an accumulation of errors at the cellular level. (iStock)*

**Free-radicals**

Unstable oxygen molecules that are released when cells metabolize energy.

**Mitochondrial theory**

The inability of the mitochondria to properly function as the cell's powerhouse and failure to provide enough energy for the cell to function. Damage to the mitochondria is caused by free-radicals released into the cell.

**Autoimmune responsiveness theory**

As people grow older their immune system begins to attack the body's own tissues.

**Hormonal stress theory**

As the hormone system ages, it is less effective at managing stress.

mitochondria. Eventually, mitochondria are unable to perform their jobs as the cell's powerhouse and fail to provide enough energy for the cell to function properly (Lee & Wei, 2007). Mitochondria defects have been linked to liver problems, dementia, metabolic disorders, and cardiovascular disease (Armstrong, 2007; Davidson & Duchen, 2007; Vinters, 2001).

AUTOIMMUNE RESPONSIVENESS    The efficiency of the body's defense system in protecting tissues against disease declines as people grow older. In young children, the body is protected by the thymus, a gland that is a prime component of the child's immune system. This gland shrinks as a child approaches puberty. The **autoimmune responsiveness theory** suggests that as people grow older their immune system begins to attack the body's own tissues. Aging results from this immune response gone awry. People become more susceptible to conditions such as cancer as they grow older because their immune systems are less efficient at producing antibodies and cells that can destroy cancerous and other abnormal cells (Makinodan, 1977). The autoimmune responsiveness may also explain why death in old age usually comes from internal diseases such as cancer and cardiovascular disorders such as heart attack and stroke. In contrast, death in childhood is usually associated with infectious disease (Timiras, 1972).

HORMONAL STRESS THEORY    When you are stressed, your body releases stress hormones that allow your body to cope with the stressful event. Then, these hormone levels decrease as the stress diminishes. **Hormonal stress theory** posits that as the hormone system ages, it is less effective at managing stress. Indeed, as we age our stress hormones stay elevated for longer periods of time, which weakens the body's immune system. The weakened immune system leaves the body susceptible to illnesses that could normally have been kept at bay (Aldwin, 1994; Epel et al., 2006; Finch & Seeman, 1999; Goleman & Gurin, 1993; Magri et al., 2006).

*Pause and Process:*

1. What is the cellular clock theory of aging?

2. What are free-radicals? How may they cause aging?

# PHYSICAL DEVELOPMENT

## *Changes in Weight and Height*

The trends in physical change that relate to aging first appeared in early adulthood. These continue throughout middle adulthood, with differences between men and women becoming more pronounced, especially regarding weight and height. Men show an average decrease in weight, whereas women add pounds during middle age. These weight change differences between the sexes reflect differences in biological functioning. They also reflect differences in lifestyle (Abraham, 1979).

Most of the internal organs—skeletal muscles, liver, kidneys, and adrenal glands for example—decrease in weight starting in the fifties. The heart is the exception. This organ generally enlarges with age in an attempt to compensate for its declining efficiency (Timiras, 1972).

The trend to declining height that began in early adulthood continues, more rapidly in women than in men. It is caused by shrinkage of the disk material in the spinal column. Height decreases are quite small—almost unnoticeable—during middle adulthood.

## Changes in Bodily Systems

What changes does the skin experience during middle adulthood?

**CHANGES IN SKIN TISSUE**    The body organ most often associated with aging is the skin. Its texture, composition, and appearance all change noticeably in middle age (Spence & Mason, 1987). The skin becomes dryer and loses its ability to retain moisture. Therefore, it feels rougher to the touch.

The loss of skin elasticity results in wrinkles, particularly on the neck, face, and hands. There is also a loss of subcutaneous fat, which exacerbates the skin's tendency to fold and wrinkle. One of the most popular types of cosmetic surgery among middle-aged people involves removing wrinkles and skin blemishes associated with aging.

The hair continues to thin and lose its natural pigmentation during middle adulthood. Hairlines of both men and women recede further during these years. Graying and thinning of the hair occurs over the entire body, including the armpits and pubic areas of both men and women, although men tend to become hairier in certain body areas during middle age. The nails, which are actually skin cells, also show signs of aging. Their growth rate declines and they thicken and show color changes.

The incidence of skin conditions and diseases increases throughout middle adulthood. Although fungus diseases are still the most common skin problem, skin tumors increase dramatically during this period (U.S. Bureau of the Census, 1990a, b). These tumors can be benign, precancerous, or cancerous. They are indicative of the aging process as well as environmental conditions such as prolonged and severe exposure to sunlight earlier in life.

*Hair thins and hair lines recede during this age. (iStock)*

## Osteoporosis

Inflammation of bone tissue causing softness and porous structure; the condition can lead to bone breakage and tooth loss.

**THE TEETH AND SKELETAL SYSTEM**    The principal change affecting teeth and skeletal system during middle adulthood is osteoporosis. **Osteoporosis** is an inflammation and loss of the bone tissue throughout the body. In the mouth, it causes the bone tissue surrounding the teeth to soften and become more porous. As a result, teeth loosen in their sockets and eventually are lost unless there is intervention (Kart, Metress & Metress, 1978; Spence & Mason, 1987).

Osteoporosis throughout the skeletal system becomes more noticeable during middle adulthood, especially in women. There is a gradual decrease in the rate which new bone tissue forms, but bone absorption continues at a normal rate. Deficiencies in calcium and vitamin D contribute to osteoporosis. When calcium intake is inadequate to supply its needs, the body leaches calcium from bones, which weakens bone structures throughout the body. That is why bone breakage and incomplete healing plague people in old age. Beyond calcium and vitamin D, a decline in estrogen can exacerbate osteoporosis. Increasing weight bearing exercise and ensuring adequate intake of calcium and vitamin D can help slow down bone tissue loss. Hormone replacement therapy (HRT) has come under scrutiny in recent years for links to serious health problems. Such therapy should be carefully considered under the guidance of a competent physician, in which the costs and benefits of HRT are weighed with your personal health history in mind.

People typically experience the first signs of arthritis and rheumatism during middle adulthood. These conditions can occur at earlier stages, but they are generally associated with the aging process. **Arthritis** is an inflammation of a joint area between bone junctions. The two basic types are osteoarthritis and rheumatoid arthritis (Spence & Mason, 1987). Trauma to a joint, chronic obesity, infections, and metabolic disorders are thought to contribute significantly to most forms of osteoarthritis. Rheumatoid arthritis is believed to be some kind of autoimmune response by the body to inflammation in joint areas. As white blood cells invade these areas in overwhelmingly large numbers, the body reacts by forming fibrous tissue around joints. This causes stiffness and soreness and disforms the joints, restricting movement.

## Arthritis

Inflammation of the joint area between bone junctions.

## Rheumatism

A variety of conditions resulting in stiffness and soreness in tissues associated with bone joints.

**Rheumatism** describes a variety of conditions that cause stiffness and soreness in the connective tissue associated with the bone joints. Upon rising from bed in the morning, many middle-aged people feel some stiffness in the muscles and joints, making it harder to move about.

Arthritis and rheumatism tend to run in families. Treatment commonly involves use of various anti-inflammatory drugs to reduce swelling and pain.

## Atherosclerosis

A cardiovascular disease in which plaques of fatty material form along arterial walls in the body and especially in the heart. This leads to blockage of blood flow and the possibility of clots, increasing the likelihood of heart attack and stroke.

**THE CARDIOVASCULAR SYSTEM**    The cardiovascular system, which includes the heart and the circulatory system, begins to show the effects of diet, lifestyle, and aging during middle adulthood. Three basic changes may be observed: (1) a decline in the elasticity of the arteries, (2) an increasing accumulation of fatty deposits in the arterial tissues, and (3) a general decline in the ability of the heart to pump blood efficiently.

Two major abnormalities of the cardiovascular system appear with increasing frequency during middle age. They result from the interaction of the aging process with diets that are high in fat and cholesterol (Spence & Mason, 1987). In **atherosclerosis**, plaques of fatty material form along the walls of arteries, blocking and slowing down the flow of blood. As a result, blood clots may form, further contributing to restricted blood flow. In **arteriosclerosis**, commonly called "hardening of the arteries," there is a gradual loss of elasticity in arterial walls throughout the body.

Both of these conditions lead to a reduced blood flow throughout the body, raising the blood pressure. Some increase in blood pressure is natural with age, but these cardiovascular diseases lead to **hypertension**, or abnormally high levels of blood pressure. Hypertension increases the probability of kidney damage, heart attacks, and strokes.

These cardiovascular conditions can be largely controlled through diet, exercise, and drug therapy. Although dietary contributions to cardiovascular diseases begin early in life, the effects do not show up until middle or late adulthood. Diets that are low in fat and sodium and high in fiber appear to give some protection against these conditions, as well as against cancers of the colon and reproductive organs and diabetes (Hausman, 1983; Hausman & Hurley, 1989).

**THE DIGESTIVE SYSTEM**    The digestive system shows fewer signs of aging than the other organ systems in middle adulthood. Common digestive disturbances in middle age are intestinal obstructions due to ulcerative colitis, absorption problems, gallstones, ulcers in the stomach and duodenum, and hemorrhoids of the lower rectum and anal region.

Gallstones, ulcers, and hemorrhoids result more from poor diet and stress than from the aging process. People who consume a diet high in fat and cholesterol are prone to gallstones. Hemorrhoids can result from a diet high in fat and low in fiber. People subjected to chronically high levels of stress are susceptible to ulcers as well as hemorrhoids (Spence & Mason, 1987). Ulcers are a leading digestive disorder in middle adulthood (U.S. Bureau of the Census, 1990a, b; 1991a, b).

The incidence of **diabetes** increases dramatically during middle age. This condition involves the failure of the pancreas gland cells to secrete an adequate amount of an enzyme (insulin) that is essential for metabolizing sugars. The tendency for diabetes is genetics, but the disease is closely associated with obesity in middle-aged and elderly people (Spence & Mason, 1987).

**THE REPRODUCTIVE SYSTEM**    Both men and women experience changes in their reproductive organs and sexual functioning during middle adulthood. The changes are perhaps more pronounced among women, because their reproductive functioning ceases at some point during middle age.

**Menopause** is the term applied to the cessation of reproductive functioning in women (Kelly & Byrne, 1992; Spence & Mason, 1987). This is a gradual process that is completed when ovulation and menstruation cease and hormone levels drop. Most women begin to notice irregular menstrual periods between forty-five and forty-eight years of age. The process is completed by about age fifty-five for most women (Ansbacher, 1983).

The major characteristics of menopause are the cessation of ovulation and menstruation, and a decrease in the production of estrogen. While hormone levels begin to decline,

---

**Arteriosclerosis**

A condition usually occurring in advanced cases of atherosclerosis in which there is a gradual loss of elasticity in arterial vessels. The end result is high blood pressure or hypertension.

**Hypertension**

Abnormally high blood pressure caused by constriction of arteries; it increases the likelihood of kidney damage, heart failure, and brain damage via strokes.

**Diabetes**

The failure of the pancreas gland cells to secrete an adequate amount of an enzyme (insulin) that is essential for metabolizing sugars.

**Menopause**

The climacteric in females; cessation of all reproductive functions that begins at about age forty-five to forty-eight and is completed by about age fifty-five.

women may experience palpitations, insomnia, hot flashes, chills, headaches, irritability, and anxiety (Burnside, 1976). During menopause, the uterus decreases in weight and the walls of the vaginal tract become thinner (Masters & Johnson, 1966).

Middle-aged men experience changes in sexual functioning more so than in reproductive capacity (Mulligan & Moss, 1991). These changes constitute the **climacteric**. Sperm continue to be produced, but in smaller numbers. There is a gradual degeneration of the reproductive organs and a decline in sexual abilities. The prostate gland enlarges and becomes increasingly coarse as men age. This leads to slower urination. Testosterone levels also diminish with age and are associated with physical changes in the external genitalia.

**CHANGES IN SENSATION AND PERCEPTION**   Several changes in vision and hearing can be expected during middle age. Common eye symptoms of aging are further loss of accommodation (focusing ability), depigmentation of the iris, declining retinal reflexes, and changes in the lens and cornea (Spence & Mason, 1987). People who did not require reading glasses during the latter part of early adulthood will probably need them sometime during middle adulthood.

**Cataracts** and **glaucoma** increase in frequency during this stage. Cataracts involve a change in the lens of the eye that renders it opaque to entering light (Fujikado et al., 2004). The condition can be treated with surgery and special glasses or contact lenses (Stifer et al., 2004). Glaucoma is a group of diseases characterized by increases in pressure from within the eyeball (Mok, Lee & So, 2004; Molteno et al., 2006). This condition often damages the optic nerve, causing blindness. It can be controlled by medication and other medical treatment. Because the tendency to both conditions increases in middle age, people should have regular eye examinations when they reach this stage of life.

Hearing loss may become more noticeable during middle adulthood. People often notice a decline in their ability to hear high-frequency sounds or those at the lower ranges.

**Climacteric**

Decline in sexual functioning among middle-aged men.

**Cataracts**

A change in the lens of the eye causing it to become opaque to entering light, which reduces vision considerably.

**Glaucoma**

A group of diseases resulting in increased pressure within the eyeball and leading to blindness if left untreated.

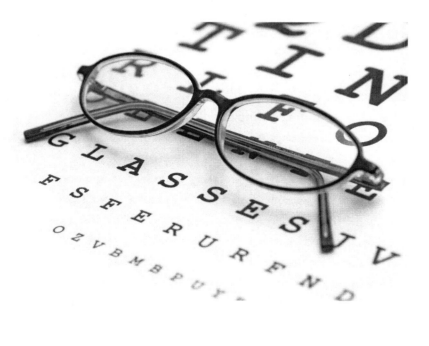

*A decline in vision is common at this stage. For example, focusing ability, retinal reflexes, changes in the lens and cornea all are diminished. (iStock)*

This hearing loss may be more a product of living in a noisy environment for many years than a natural part of the aging process. The threshold at which people can easily detect and understand speech and other sounds also declines throughout this stage (Rowland, 1980).

*Pause and Process:*

1. How does the body change during middle adulthood?

2. What are some of the changes in the sensory system in middle adulthood?

# HEALTH ISSUES

## *Nutritional Needs*

As muscle mass decreases and metabolism slows, middle-aged adults need fewer calories each day. A balanced diet rich in fruits, vegetables, and fiber helps enhance health during this phase of the life span.

**PHYSICAL AND MENTAL HEALTH**    Most people enjoy a satisfactory state of health during middle adulthood and a general sense of well-being. They adjust to the fact that their bodies are older and function differently and learn how to make compensations.

Health inevitably becomes more compromised, though, as the effects of chronic stress, careless diet and lifestyle, and the wear and tear of life accumulate. To illustrate, among the leading reasons middle-aged people visit a physician are stomach pains and cramps, lower back pain, and hypertension—all of which are symptoms of chronic stress (DeLozier & Gagnon, 1991). Doctor visits increase considerably during middle age as people become more worried about their health and decide to monitor it by having annual examinations.

*Mental Health*    Post-traumatic stress disorder (PTSD) can be experienced at any stage of the life span. It is an anxiety disorder triggered by witnessing or experiencing a traumatic and terrifying event (NIMH, 2009). Traumatic events can include a sexual assault, an acute life-threatening illness, witnessing a murder, or experiencing an accident. Approximately 8 percent of people in the United States will experience PTSD at some point in their life (U.S. Department of Veteran Affairs, 2009). PTSD is different from acute stress disorder (ASD). ASD is a temporary state of hypervigilance and stress following a traumatic experience, which subsides within a short period of time (NIMH, 2009). PTSD is a disorder that may not appear immediately after a traumatic experience, but once it manifests, it lasts for an extended period of time and interferes with one's ability to function in daily life.

The symptoms of PTSD fall into three general categories: re-experiencing the event, avoidance, and hyperarousal (NIMH, 2009). Re-experiencing the event can occur through nightmares and flashbacks. Avoidance involves social withdrawal and avoiding situations and locations where the traumatic event occurred. Hyperarousal is the experience of always being on alert and waiting for the event to reoccur. An individual may not experience all of these symptoms, but some unique combination of them.

Although any traumatic event can cause PTSD, most of the research has focused on soldiers returning from war. In the general population, 8 percent of men and 20 percent of women will develop PTSD after a traumatic event (U.S. Department of Veteran Affairs, 2009). In any given year, approximately 5.2 million adults in the United States are struggling with PTSD. Different wars have seen different rates of PTSD in soldiers:

- Vietnam soldiers: 30 percent

- Desert Storm soldiers: 10 percent

- Enduring Freedom (Afghanistan) soldiers: 6–11 percent

- Operation Iraqi Freedom soldiers: 12–20 percent

The military is working hard to provide psychological support services to returning soldiers. Recent research has indicated that soldiers who feel that their unit is highly cohesive and has a good leader perceive less stigma and barriers in seeking PTSD care (Wright et al., 2009). Providing PTSD care, working to remove the stigma attached to having a mental disorder, and eliminating barriers will help struggling soldiers heal from their traumatic experiences.

*Promoting Wellness*    People tend to become more sedentary as they grow older (Sidney, 1981; Timiras, 1972). During middle adulthood, participation in exercise, sports, and general physical activity decreases. A program of mild to moderate exercise in middle age maintains endurance and physical stamina (Schoenborn & Danchik, 1980), prevents excessive weight gain, keeps joints and muscles limber, and aids cardiovascular response.

As throughout the life span, sleep is important to health and well-being in middle adulthood. Sleep problems may begin to manifest during middle adulthood. These problems include difficulties falling asleep, wakeful periods during the night, and decreased

*Problems arise such as the inability to fall asleep or to stay asleep throughout the night. (iStock)*

amounts of the deepest stage of sleep—all resulting in feeling tired the next day (Abbott, 2003; Alessi, 2007; Ingelsson et al., 2007). Sleep deprivation can also decrease cognitive processes, mental health, and physical health. Although changes in sleep may be linked to the brain aging, limiting caffeine and alcohol consumption near bedtime, daily exercise, and managing stress can help improve one's chances of getting a good night sleep.

*Pause and Process:*

1. Describe health in middle adulthood.

2. What is PTSD?

# COGNITIVE DEVELOPMENT DURING MIDDLE ADULTHOOD

### LEARNING OBJECTIVES:

*1. Characterize cognitive strategies and specialization of knowledge during middle adulthood*

*2. Describe information-processing during middle adulthood*

In this section, we will discuss how there is a shift in middle adulthood from cognitive development to the maintenance of cognitive process and its eventual decline. The idea of experts and how they differ from novices in their cognitive strategies is also discussed. Finally, examples of attention, memory, and intelligence in middle adulthood will be examined.

# BEYOND PIAGET'S THEORY: COGNITIVE DEVELOPMENT DURING MIDDLE ADULTHOOD

**Selection, optimization, and compensation (SOC) theory**

A theory that examines how selection, optimization, and compensation assist individuals in coping with the declines associated with aging. It is often considered a theory of successful aging.

## *Optimization and Compensation*

We will learn in this chapter that during middle adulthood, some aspects of cognitive processes continue to develop, others are maintained, and still others decline. **Selection, optimization, and compensation theory (SOC theory)** stresses that adaptive aging involves maximizing gains and minimizing losses (Baltes, Lindenberger & Staudinger, 1998). With aging, resources shift from promoting growth toward maintenance and the regulation of loss. Behaviors associated with selection include goal specification and identifying new goals when faced with loss. Behaviors associated with optimization include focusing attention, persistence, energy, and effort toward goal obtainment. Behaviors associated with compensation include use of external resources and support, learning new skills, and increasing time and effort in the obtainment of goals.

**Growth**

Behaviors meant to increase functioning and adaptation.

**Maintenance**

Behaviors striving to keep functioning at current levels despite declines in processes or ability.

**Regulation of loss**

Behaviors that allow for reorganization or functioning at lower levels because maintenance is no longer possible.

Within SOC theory, describe a behavior or strategy for optimization.

**Expertise**

Having extensive experience, knowledge, and understanding within a specific area of interest.

Within SOC theory, **growth** is defined as behaviors meant to increase functioning and adaptation (Baltes, Lindenberger & Staudinger, 1998). **Maintenance** is defined as behaviors striving to keep functioning at current levels despite declines in processes or ability. **Regulation of loss** is defined as behaviors that allow for reorganization of functioning at lower levels because maintenance is no longer possible.

There are four foundational rationales in SOC theory (Baltes, Lindenberger & Staudinger, 1998). First, biological resources decline in quality and amount as people age. For example, our mitochondria become less functional with aging increasing the risk for certain illnesses. Second, the need for culture increases in quality and amount as age increases. For example, as one gets older they may need access to better health care more often. Third, as age increases the efficiency of culture decreases. This means that as a person gets older, the effectiveness of cultural interventions decreases. For example, although we can treat many medical conditions associated with old age, we cannot ultimately stop the aging process or prevent death. Fourth, there is a general lack of cultural support structures for the elderly. Said another way, available cultural resources and support decreases as age increases.

Research has focused on how well the SOC theory can be applied to help promote successful aging (Freund & Baltes, 1998). Findings indicate that use of selection, optimization, and compensation strategies and behaviors is associated with satisfaction with age, decreased emotional loneliness, decreased social loneliness, lack of agitation, and positive emotions.

Personality and subjective assessments are related to one's selection, optimization, and compensation (SOC) scores (Freund & Baltes, 1998). Individuals high in neuroticism have lower SOC scores. Individuals who are highly invested in their life and rate their subjective health highly have high SOC scores. General intelligence is positively correlated with optimization and compensation, but showed no relationships with selection. Hence, certain personal characteristics may influence one's propensity to employ SOC strategies to optimize aging.

**EXPERT VERSUS NOVICE KNOWLEDGE**  During middle adulthood, many individuals develop expertise within their area of work or hobby. **Expertise** can be defined as having

*Expert knowledge and experience is usually obtained by middle adulthood. (iStock)*

**Novice**

A person with limited experience, knowledge, or understanding within a specific area of interest.

**Conditionalized knowledge**

The skill experts have in retrieving the specific information that they need for any given problem.

**Merely skilled experts**

Expertise that functions largely on routine.

**Highly competent experts**

Experts who exhibit great adaptability, flexibility, and creativity in utilizing their expertise across a variety of situations.

**Adaptive expertise**

An approach to problems that is characterized by flexibility and promotes life-long learning.

extensive experience, knowledge, and understanding within a specific area of interest (National Research Council, 2000). A **novice** would be someone with limited experience, knowledge, or understanding within a specific area of interest. Experts and novices in a given realm differ in their abilities to problem-solve, remember, and reason in this domain.

Experts differ from novices in their ability to detect meaningful patterns of information (National Research Council, 2000). The detection of these meaningful patterns activates knowledge of corresponding problem-solving strategies and the implications of these strategies. Experts are also better able to "chunk" or group individual pieces of information into meaningful units, and fit this information into a vast network of knowledge. From doctors to chess players, this ability to detect meaningful patterns of information allows experts to outperform novices consistently.

The organization of knowledge is another area that experts differ from novices (National Research Council, 2000). It's not just that experts know more, it is that they structure and store the information in a better organizational framework. Novices typically approach learning new information as a series of facts and information, whereas experts organize specific facts within a web that is organized around major orienting (or core) concepts. Hence, when new facts or information is learned, experts can easily link this new information into the greater web of knowledge. "Within this picture of expertise, 'knowing more' means having more conceptual chunks in memory, more relations or features defining each chunk, more interrelations among the chunks, and efficient methods for retrieving related chunks and procedures for applying these informational units in problem-solving contexts" (National Research Council, 2000, p. 38).

Context and access to knowledge is another realm in which experts differ from novices (National Research Council, 2000). For any given problem, a small part of an expert's knowledge is applicable. For example, an oncologist has an immense amount of knowledge about cancer. However, for any given patient a comparatively small amount of this knowledge is utilized. Hence, experts not only have more knowledge, but they are skilled in accessing the specific information that they need for any given problem. This aspect of expert knowledge and retrieval is referred to as **conditionalized knowledge**.

Novices sometimes struggle to retrieve information from memory that is needed to solve a problem. Experts have achieved automatic and fluent retrieval of information from memory (National Research Council, 2000). So not only are they better at retrieving relevant information, they can retrieve this information with great speed and little effort.

We have just discussed some of the general differences in cognitive processes between novices and experts. Interestingly, there are at least two very different types of experts (National Research Council, 2000). **Merely skilled experts** have expertise that function largely on routine. **Highly competent experts** exhibit great adaptability, flexibility, and creativity in utilizing their expertise across a variety of situations. Merely skilled experts display extensive skills when solving problems and focus on using these skills as quickly and efficiently as possible. Highly competent experts capitalize on solving problems as an opportunity to be creative in their strategies and develop new skills. Highly competent experts are sometimes said to possess **adaptive expertise**, which is an approach to problems that is characterized by flexibility and promotes life-long learning. Both types of experts monitor their understanding and problem-solving approach and make adjustments as needed.

*Pause and Process:*

1. What is SOC theory?

2. How do experts and novices differ in their approach to problems?

# INFORMATION-PROCESSING IN MIDDLE ADULTHOOD

**Crystallized intelligence**

Skills acquired through education and socialization such as verbal skills, mathematical skills, inductive reasoning, and interpersonal skills; the ability to recall and use information.

**Fluid intelligence**

The ability to perceive relationships, reason logically and abstractly, and form concepts and interpretations.

Various researchers have demonstrated an age-related decline in intellectual functioning (Botwinick, 1977). This is attributed to significant declines in information-processing abilities and other skills involving the central nervous system. People appear to learn new things more slowly as they age. This slowdown begins to be noticeable at middle age and continues for the duration of the life span.

Other research suggests that some aspects of intellectual functioning decline, whereas others are maintained or improve (Schaie, 1983). Increases continue to occur in **crystallized intelligence** through the years of middle adulthood. Crystallized intelligence, you may recall, involves cognitive skills, such as verbal reasoning and comprehension and spatial relations, which are acquired through educational experiences. **Fluid intelligence** involves information-processing skills, such as those involved in memory, speed of learning, and mathematical calculation. These skills decline through middle adulthood (Knox, 1977).

There are, however, considerable individual differences in the rates at which both of the processes occur—which suggests that more than the aging process is at work here. An individual's "life complexity" appears to affect how quickly these changes in cognitive functioning take place. Such factors as having an intact marriage and engaging in many social interactions can determine the rate of these processes (Schaie, 1983).

Cognitive style may also change during middle adulthood (Knox, 1977; Labouvie-Vief, 1985, 1986). The style of thinking that emerges during early adulthood emphasizes exploration of options in solving problems. According to Riegel (1973, 1975), mature thinking involves a tolerance of contradictions and conflicts out of the realization that this is how the world functions. In middle adulthood, people rely more on subjectivity and intuition in contrast to the strict logical processing that characterizes earlier adult cognitive style. Middle-aged people incorporate lessons learned from past mistakes into their problem-solving strategies. The ability is especially valuable in ambiguous situations.

We will now turn our attention to some of the specific aspects of information-processing in middle adulthood. We will highlight the areas of attention and memory.

**ATTENTION**    Selective and divided attention skills peak in adulthood and begin to show decline toward the latter part of middle adulthood. One area that has increased in research

*Selective and divided attention skills both peak and decline during middle adulthood. The use of cells phones while driving challenges these skills. (iStock)*

interest is the influence of cell phone use on attention and ability to drive effectively. This research has typically included both young adults and middle-aged adults as participants. One interesting question has been: is there a difference in attention and driving ability if a conversation is occurring between two people in the vehicle (passenger conversations) or if a conversation is occurring on a cell phone (cell phone conversations) (Drews, Pasupathi & Strayer, 2008)? Research findings indicate that driving errors are lower for those engaged in passenger conversations than for those in cell phone conversations. The proposed explanation for this is that when two conversing individuals are in the same vehicle, they have a shared attention and awareness for the traffic and road conditions. This allows for conversation to ebb and flow as needed for the driver. This research helps explain why cell phone conversations quadruple the risk of driving accidents (McEvoy et al., 2005), while the risk of an accident decreases when there is another adult in the vehicle besides the driver (Rueda-Domingo et al., 2004).

**Working memory**

The workbench of memory where simultaneous cognitive processes can be attended to and handled.

**MEMORY** **Working memory** is typically conceptualized as the workbench of memory where simultaneous cognitive processes can be attended to and handled (Baddeley, 1986, 1996; Kemper & Mitzner, 2001). Working memory improves across the life span and peaks during middle adulthood—around age forty-five (Swanson, 1999). Declines in working memory begin toward the latter part of middle adulthood—around age fifty-seven—and continue to decline in late adulthood (Kemper & Mitzner, 2001; Swanson, 1999). Part of the decline in working memory experienced in middle adulthood is attributed to a general decline in information-processing speed (Chaytor & Schmitter-Edgecombe, 2004).

Research investigating the impact of hormones on memory is a growing field. The vast majority of this research has focused upon rodent hormones, brain changes, and memory (Galea et al., 2008). The emerging picture is complex, with level of hormones being an important factor, as well as the observation that hormones impact different parts of the brain and different memory processes in diverse ways. To further complicate matters, hormones have differing influences on males and females. There are two interesting findings worth mentioning here. First, the extended use of oral estrogen (like that in birth control pills and hormone replacement therapy) may negatively impact memory. In research on mice, a medium dose of estrogen decreased **spatial reference memory** (or memory for location and space) (Fernandez & Frick, 2004). Conversely, testosterone has been found to increase memory in castrated rats, including reversing spatial reference memory deficits (Khalil, King & Soliman, 2005). Although this research utilized rodents as research subjects, it is clear that hormones may play an important role in memory—or at least some aspects of memory—in humans. Future research will try to tease apart the complex nature of hormone, brain, and memory interactions.

**Spatial reference memory**

The aspect of memory that stores information about one's environment and spatial orientation.

**Emotional intelligence**

The ability to recognize the emotions of others and regulate one's own emotions while effectively utilizing emotions in adaptive and skillful ways.

**INTELLIGENCE**    One proposed type of intelligence is **emotional intelligence**, which was first proposed by Salovey and Mayer in 1990. The idea never really became popular until Goleman wrote the book *Emotional Intelligence* in 1995. Emotional intelligence can be thought of as the ability to recognize others' emotions, regulate one's own emotions, and effectively utilize emotions in adaptive and skillful ways (Chapman & Hayslip, 2006). Hence, emotional intelligence is an important and distinct mental ability that allows for smooth interpersonal relationships and social functioning.

There is some question as to whether emotional intelligence should be conceptualized as a "type" of intelligence, a cognitive style, or a personality trait (Chapman & Hayslip, 2006). Schaie (2001) has commented that emotional intelligence is a concept that is "somewhere at the intersection between the domains of intelligence and personality" (p. 202). Despite the ambiguity as to what domain emotional intelligence should be categorized, the general theory hypothesizes that emotional intelligence is an ability that increases across childhood, as do other cognitive processes and socioemotional skills (Mayer et al., 2001). What was less known, until recently, was how emotional intelligence develops in adulthood.

A recent study by Chapman and Hayslip (2006) investigated emotional intelligence in young and middle adulthood. Three factors of emotional intelligence were examined: appraising others' emotions (i.e., emotional recognition), optimistic mood regulation (i.e., emotion regulation), and emotion utilization (i.e., emotion use in problem-solving, motivation, and other behaviors). The study found that young and middle-aged adults have similar levels of emotional intelligence in the areas of appraising others' emotions and emotion utilization; however, optimistic mood regulation showed significant increases in middle-aged adults in comparison to younger adults. This means that although some aspects of emotional intelligence appear to be fully developed and stable across early and middle adulthood (emotional recognition and emotion utilization), optimistic mood regulation continues to develop into middle adulthood.

You may recall from earlier in the chapter that crystallized intelligence continues to increase across middle adulthood, whereas fluid intelligence shows decline. Chapman and Hayslip (2006) investigated whether the three components of emotional intelligence were related to crystallized and fluid intelligence. Analysis indicated that crystallized and fluid intelligence are positively correlated, meaning that as crystallized intelligence scores increase, fluid intelligence scores increase. However, there were no correlations between fluid or crystallized intelligence and the three components of emotional intelligence. Based on this study, it appears that a person's emotional intelligence is in no way related to a person's fluid intelligence or crystallized intelligence, further supporting the idea that emotional intelligence is a distinct mental ability.

In summary, emotional intelligence is the ability to function adaptively in interpersonal and social relationships. Emotional intelligence appears to be a distinct mental ability that develops across childhood. Two aspects of emotional intelligence (emotion recognition and emotion utilization) appear to reach maturity in early adulthood, whereas optimistic mood regulation shows increased development into middle adulthood.

*Pause and Process:*

1. What affect might hormones have on memory?

2. What are the three components of emotional intelligence?

# SOCIAL AND EMOTIONAL DEVELOPMENT DURING MIDDLE ADULTHOOD

### LEARNING OBJECTIVES:

1. *Characterize emotional development during middle adulthood*
2. *Describe family and social influences during middle adulthood*
3. *Explain psychosocial development during middle adulthood*

What does the term sandwich generation mean?

**Sandwich generation**

The term sometimes used to describe middle-aged individuals, referring to their divided loyalties and responsibilities toward the younger and the older generation within their family systems.

As in all other stages in the life span, middle adulthood has its own unique challenges. These developmental tasks result from physical changes that occur in association with the aging process, environmental pressures, and new obligations prompted by the person's own changes in values and aspirations (Erikson, 1982; Erikson, Erikson & Kivnick, 1986). Developmental tasks in middle adulthood include achieving adult civic and social responsibility, establishing and maintaining an economic standard of living, assisting teenage children to become responsible and happy adults, and developing adult leisure-time activities (Havighurst, 1970). Middle adulthood also includes the tasks of accepting and adjusting to the physiological changes of middle age and adjusting to aging parents.

Middle adulthood can be a particularly challenging time in terms of socioemotional development. Some researchers refer to middle-aged people as the **sandwich generation** because they are often responsible for the care of aging parents while still having some parenting responsibilities for their children. This is a generation "caught" between two others. For some people, reaching middle age brings the new perspective of acting as a bridge between the older and younger generations in an extended family system.

The developmental tasks of middle age not only help people to adjust to this stage of the life span but also prepare them to meet the challenges of old age. Not all these tasks are mastered simultaneously. There are individual differences in the rate of mastery. Some tasks are even put off to the next stage of the life span.

The age at marriage, birth of children, and other life events may determine when individuals confront the developmental tasks of middle age. Because today's young adults are delaying marriage and parenthood, they may confront these tasks at later ages than those given in this chapter.

# PSYCHOSOCIAL DEVELOPMENT

## *Generativity Versus Stagnation*

As mentioned in Chapter 7, Erikson proposed that the generativity versus stagnation stage begins in early adulthood (around age twenty-four). However, it lasts well into middle adulthood (around age fifty-four), so we are discussing it in this chapter. Most modern psychologists refer to this stage as the generativity versus stagnation stage; however, it is also known as the generativity versus self-absorption stage—as you will see why.

Once a person is in an established relationship, they can begin the process of facing the psychosocial task of generativity versus stagnation. In the productive years of adulthood, people center on establishing a new family system, on achieving progress in their work, on creative efforts, and on community involvement. Parenting and family experiences provide the principal opportunities for most people to explore generativity.

Erikson describes the sense of generativity as "the interest in establishing and guiding the next generation … the absorbing object of a parental kind of responsibility." The central component of generativity is the desire to care for others, by teaching them the skills and knowledge one has learned and passing on to them one's culture and values. Generativity need not be restricted to parenting. It can also be explored by sharing one's self intimately with others in work roles, mentorships (such as Big Brothers or Big Sisters), spiritual parenthood (such as nuns or godparents), or in creative efforts.

The attitude of self-absorption develops when an individual is unwilling or unable to care for others. To be self-absorbed is to treat oneself as one's own infant and pet, according to Erikson. Instead of directing social interest to others, self-absorbed people direct their interest exclusively toward themselves. The self-absorbed person becomes unhealthy and ceases to grow, like a stagnant lake that has no outlet.

**PECK'S PSYCHOSOCIAL DEVELOPMENT IN MIDDLE ADULTHOOD**    Psychologist Robert Peck (1968) elaborated on Erikson's (1950, 1964) concept of generativity as it is developed during middle adulthood. Erikson proposes that individuals start to explore ways to achieve a sense of generativity in their mid-twenties and continue this task until their mid-fifties. A growing, dynamic individual seeks ways to focus on others, especially those who are younger and may profit from the knowledge the older person has gained in life skills. Peck proposes that during middle age, people focus more on achieving a sense of well-being than on what Erikson labels generativity. This focus includes:

- Valuing wisdom versus valuing physical powers: Physical endurance and stamina begin to decline as individuals experience the aging process more intensely during middle adulthood. Physical attractiveness and abilities were highly valued earlier in life, and people judged others as well as themselves first on these attributes. Now these attributes no longer seem valid as measures of competence. Instead, individuals learn to value knowledge gained from experience in dealing with many different complex problems. This gives them an advantage over younger people.

- Socializing versus sexualizing in human relationships: After experiencing menopause or the climacteric, people come to devalue sexuality as a basis of interpersonal relations. Social skills now take on a greater importance as the focus shifts to relating to others as personalities rather than as sex objects.

- Cathectic flexibility versus cathectic improverishment: Middle-aged people discover the importance of emotional flexibility. Instead of making a heavy emotional investment in one person or one activity, they learn that it is to one's advantage to invest emotion in many people or activities. As parents and friends die, as children leave home, and as they themselves retire from work roles, middle-aged people widen their social support network. Thus they obtain social insurance for times of need.

- Mental flexibility versus mental rigidity: One hazard of growing older is becoming closed-minded to new ideas or solutions. Surviving to this point in the life span often gives people the illusion that their knowledge is complete. However, this attitude stifles growth and promotes stagnation. By remaining open and receptive, people can continue to foster their mental and personal development.

*Pause and Process:*

1. How can a person express generativity?

2. Compare and contrast Erikson's and Peck's theories about psychosocial development in middle adulthood.

# EMOTIONAL DEVELOPMENT

## *Transition to Middle Adulthood*

Middle age is a transition period between early and late adulthood. It is a time for reassessment and redefinition as changes take place both within the individual and within the family system in which she or he participates. Most people experience a kind of dualism at this time (Chilman, 1968; Chiriboga, 1981; Sherman, 1987). From one viewpoint, this period produces a crisis. People often feel their family is deteriorating because their children are maturing and leaving the home and their own parents are declining. At the same time, they are experiencing initial declines in their own physical well-being and functioning, and witnessing the death of friends and family members in significantly greater numbers than in earlier periods of the life span. There are also significant shifts in parenting, occupation, and family roles. All of these changes are felt as losses, so middle age can be a stressful period.

All these changes force people to reexamine the meaning of their lives, their state of happiness, and the progress they have made toward personal goals. Some researchers believe that this constitutes a midlife transition or crisis (Gould, 1978; Levinson, 1978). Perspectives on life, time, personal happiness, relationships with others, and other important issues change. Many people see middle adulthood as the beginning of the end of life. The future looks more finite. Physical declines that show the signs of aging reinforce these notions. More importantly, however, the change in time perspective spurs people to let go of inefficient or ineffectual ways of coping with stress, solving problems, and interpreting behavior—their own as well as other people's. Thus, the midlife transition can bring about meaningful changes and refinements in aspects of personality that people just discover in themselves or create through new experiences.

From another viewpoint, middle age is the prime of life. People are finally experienced enough to affect change rather than be affected by it. They can take command of their lives. Physical changes are taken in stride as part of the seasoning process. People with this attitude see aging as a positive experience. Like wine, they believe they become better with the passage of time.

Midlife crisis or midlife transition? Popular U.S. culture depicts men as experiencing a midlife crisis in middle adulthood. Some developmental theorists agree with this view, while others do not. First, we will discuss the view that men do experience a midlife crisis; then, we will discuss the criticisms of this view.

Both Levinson (1978) and Gould (1978) regard middle adulthood as a turbulent time that churns up many confusing, conflicting, and contradictory feelings. These researchers

*New experiences are brought about by midlife transitions. Being middle-aged is considered by some to be the prime of life. (Corbis)*

believe, however, that the disturbing questioning that characterizes middle age will produce developmental growth—provided the individuals meet these challenges rather than retreat from them because they feel so threatened.

Levinson and Gould describe early adulthood as the period when people develop initial goals for their lives and determine actions that they hope will secure these goals. Gould believes that individuals must come to terms with their own mortality by the end of middle adulthood. In doing so, they recognize their limitations and weaknesses—which is to say, they fully accept their humanity. They also learn to relinquish the desire to control situations and other people in order to achieve outcomes they wish for strongly. With this comes serenity and acceptance of the nature of life. They learn to go with the flow of life rather than struggling to manipulate what happens and under what circumstances. Ultimately, this leads to a greater acceptance of the certain inevitability of aging and death.

Levinson (1980, 1986) describes middle age as a time when many people start to seriously question the meaning and direction of their lives. Beginning at about age forty, the majority of men in his study had a crucial struggle within themselves and with their environment because of this question. Levinson sees this questioning as a healthy sign of developmental progress. The person undergoing it, however, is more likely to view it as threatening. First reactions may be decisions that others label irrational. From the outside, the decisions do look extreme. From the inside, however, they are seen as necessary to secure desired changes before it is too late. Such decisions can include positive choices such as making a radical occupational change, taking dream vacations, or moving off to some exotic location. Some decisions can be frivolous choices such as dying hair, buying a sports car or motorcycle, or dressing inappropriately for one's age. Finally, some decisions can be emotionally devastating to the self and/or others, such as divorcing after many years of marriage or participating in extramarital sexual affairs. The colloquial expression for such behavior is the middle-age crazies.

Levinson describes a series of transitions that he observed in the men he studied. The midlife crisis involves examining one's own needs in relation to those of others. In early adulthood, needs were prioritized. The men chose either to meet their own needs then or to delay gratification. Most gave certain personal needs low priority. At midlife, they reexamined this ordering. When the reexamination coincided with physical and social changes in their lives, the men often felt pressured to try to accomplish important objectives while they still could. This made them feel conflicted because it was hard to accomplish their personal objectives without compromising the needs of others they loved and valued.

Other developmental researchers question the universality of the midlife crisis (Neugarten & Neugarten, 1987; Rossi, 1980; Schlossberg, 1987). Although not everyone experiences a midlife transition as a crisis, many researchers agree that people do have serious adjustment challenges at some time during this stage of life. Moreover, the changes described by Levinson and Gould can occur earlier in life. The reaction to midlife also seems to differ according to socioeconomic situations (Farrell & Rosenberg, 1981). Midlife may be more stressful for blue-collar workers than for more advantaged middle-class professionals.

Some have critiqued Levinson's idea of a midlife crisis because it ignores "variations in social structure and culture over historical time. Psychosocial transitions were affixed to age as if immutable to institutional change …" (Elder, 1998, p. 944). Some research implies that the midlife transition is a cultural phenomenon specific to societies that recognize middle age as a stage in the life span (Levine, 1980; Rogoff, 2003). One African culture, the Gusii of Kenya, hold a different idea of middle age than Western societies. The men experience only one stage in adult life, that of "warrior," which may last from twenty-five to forty years. Women similarly experience only one stage in adult life, that of "married woman," in recognition of the importance of marriage and procreation for females in this culture. This society apparently has no words for "adolescence," "early adulthood," or "middle age." Transitions in the life span are geared to events rather than to chronological age. Instead of experiencing what our culture labels a midlife transition, Gusii men and women may undergo a spiritual enlightenment in which they recognize their physical limitation for performing work as well as the temporal limits of life. This experience causes them to seek spiritual powers in witchcraft and ritualism to provide help for themselves and their family members against illness or death.

Hence, the idea of a midlife crisis is debatable, whereas the idea of a midlife transition is more palatable to most researchers. However, the midlife transition is far from universal. Instead, a midlife transition is influenced by socioeconomic, cultural, and historical factors.

**PERSONALITY AND SELF-CONCEPT**    Is personality set by middle adulthood or does it continue to change during this phase of the life span? This is an intriguing question that researchers are still actively researching today. The answer is impacted by which theoretical approach to personality the researcher is utilizing (Srivasta et al., 2003). At present, it appears that some aspects remain stable and others change (Finn, 1986). Those aspects that generally remain stable over the life span are intellectual, cognitive, and self-concept traits. Those that appear to be most subject to alteration are attitudes and interpersonal relationship factors.

In Chapter 7, we learned about the big five factors personality theory. Which factors show change with development and which tend to stay the same? Conscientiousness and agreeableness have been found to increase during early and middle adulthood (Srivasta et al., 2003). Neuroticism decreases during this time frame, most significantly in women. There is a slight decline in openness during adulthood. Extroversion appears to increase slightly in men and decrease slightly in women.

Humans manifest a strong desire to master their environment and achieve self-satisfaction or happiness from infancy, and this desire does not appear to lessen with age. As mentioned previously, middle adulthood is a major period of transition that is self-examination, self-evaluation, and restructuring of self-image. There is a consolidation of the various components of the self at midlife. Both continuity and change in self-concept and personality can be observed as individuals address self-acceptance and self-knowledge during middle adulthood.

Kimmel (1980) describes personality during middle age as more balanced and stable than it was earlier in life. The expansion of the self and interpersonal relations are less demanding and shifting because people have gained experience in coping with stress and dealing with problems. Self-knowledge allows them to deal more effectively with the changes they encounter as part of middle adulthood. However, inflexibility, rigidity, and resistance to creative solutions are equally likely to appear at midlife. Kimmel's conclusions differ considerably from Levinson's research findings about how men react to reaching middle age.

**ATTACHMENT** Sometimes when discussing adult attachment, the category we have labeled disorganized/disoriented is called unresolved attachment. If you recall from our previous discussion of attachment styles, the disorganized/disoriented attachment style consists of a mental model in which a person lacks self-worth and struggles to trust others. This attachment style can experience significant difficulties in middle adulthood.

A recent study by Alexander (2009) investigated the relationship between attachment and abuse by multiple partners in adulthood. The study found that women with an unresolved attachment style were more likely to be victimized by multiple partners in adulthood than women with a different attachment classification. Post hoc analysis revealed that women with the unresolved attachment style reported a childhood plagued with parent-child role reversals and exposure to domestic violence.

Although abuse and neglect in childhood are common predictors of unresolved attachment style in children and adults, researchers have begun to investigate if genetics play a role in this particular attachment style (Caspers et al., 2009). A recent study by Caspers and colleagues has discovered that a short 5-HTTLPR allele is correlated with an increased risk for an unresolved attachment style. This research is exciting because attachment has been primarily conceptualized as a process largely social in nature. By demonstrating that genetics may play a role in attachment disposition, researchers will now need to broaden their perspective to study the influence of both relationship experiences and biology.

*Pause and Process:*

1. Describe Levinson's idea of a midlife crisis.

2. What aspects of personality are likely to change throughout adulthood?

# SELF AND OTHERS

## *Family Influences*

**PARENTING IN MIDDLE ADULTHOOD** One of the most prominent, as well as early, indications of entrance into this stage of the family life career is when the adult children become completely emancipated. It is this event that can serve as a significant stressor in many family systems causing important shifts in roles, adjustment problems, and emotional crisis.

Family sociologists often refer to this situation as the **empty nest** phase of the family life career that introduces the system into the postparental aspect of family life.

Researchers describe this as a transition period for parents as they redefine their image and identity away from parenthood. Their behavior as parents also is redefined in line with the process that began during the previous family life stage (Harkins, 1978).

It is not clear if mothers are more affected than fathers by the empty nest transition. Early studies focused on the adjustments of women to loss of their primary parenting responsibilities. The more frequent finding was that many experienced negative reactions (Bart, 1971, 1975; Spence & Lonner, 1971). The women who were studied usually had been full-time mothers who were not nor had not been employed outside the home. Parenting had been a major responsibility within their family systems. When children became grown and left the home, many reacted by becoming depressed emotionally, feeling lost and unneeded.

Bart (1971) found also that women who rechanneled their activities and energies into new roles made better adjustments than those who did not. These women reacted to the role shift during this stage by entering the work force, enrolling in college, assuming new volunteer activities, or refocusing on their marriages. Subsequent studies have substantiated this finding (Glenn, 1975; Harkins, 1978; Robertson, 1978). Apparently, many women view the experience of the empty nest as a positive time in life. The completion of full-time childrearing responsibilities is seen as liberating. Those who prepare, plan, and anticipate that adjustments will be required also make more positive adjustments to the role shift (Targ, 1979).

Relatively little is known about the reactions of fathers to the empty nest phase. Some fathers seem to have few adjustments to the shift in their parenting responsibilities whereas others find the experience to be painful emotionally (Barber, 1980; Lewis, Feneau & Roberts, 1979; Robinson & Barret, 1986). Men's reactions may depend on how emotionally involved they have been in their role as fathers and with their children. It is possible that some men may be more vulnerable to negative reactions than women. The principal reason cited by many fathers that is negative in nature is the perception that they have lost an opportunity to be involved in their children's lives. This is in direct contrast to negative reasons cited by women who react to a loss of personal identity when parenting ends.

Most individuals make a successful shift to a lifestyle that does not include children or parenting as a principal focus during middle-age (Kerckhoff, 1976). This adjustment offers opportunities for personal

*Enrolling in college is one way that women can rechannel their activities and energies. (iStock)*

growth and for placing greater emphasis on the committed relationship that may have been neglected in many respects.

**THE MARRIAGE IN MIDDLE ADULTHOOD**    Marital satisfaction increases considerably during this stage. As their children become more autonomous during adolescence and early adulthood, many couples begin to find greater satisfaction within their marriage (Olson, 1986). Marital satisfaction at this time of life is as high as among newlyweds. Couples still have disagreements and conflicts, but these are more manageable than earlier, when children absorbed so much attention.

*Spotlight*

What are some roles that grandparents may play in the family system?

**BECOMING A GRANDPARENT**    Many people assume the new family role of grandparent during this stage of the family life career. It is increasingly common that many will assume this role during their middle-age years (Cherlin & Furstenberg, 1986; Hagestad, 1985; U.S. Bureau of the Census, 1990, 1991). Today, it is increasingly unlikely that this role will overlap with the parenting role as often as it occurred in the past.

The contemporary grandparenting role is ambiguous regarding what this role means and how it functions in a family system (Bengston, 1985; Cherlin & Furstenberg, 1986). This differs considerably from the past when grandparents are thought to have played a vital, active role within a family system. This is thought to have included functions as mentor, role model, caretaker, and repository of wisdom for younger family members.

Today, there is considerable variation as to what this role means and how it is enacted. The popular image of a contemporary grandparent is passive in nature where the companionship characteristics of the role are emphasized (Cherlin & Furstenberg, 1985). This individual is seen to be a loving older person who does not interfere with the functioning of adult children in their parental role. This person sees grandchildren frequently and acts as a "reserve parent" in times of need, crisis, or emergency. Grandparents are seen to be

*Becoming a grandparent is a new family role for some. (iStock)*

more actively involved with grandchildren during their infancy and childhood years as caretakers. As children grow older, they are expected to provide more of a recreational or fun-oriented, leisure role in interacting with grandchildren.

A variety of meanings is given to this role by the individuals who assume it. Symbolically, grandparents may attribute several dimensions to their role that include (1) "being there" to act as an element of stability during change and transition for the extended family system, (2) acting as the "family watchdog" to provide care when necessary, (3) serving as family arbitrator during times of family conflict, and (4) serving as the family historian as a bridge between the past, the present, and the future (Bengston, 1985). Other meanings can be attributed to this role as well (see Figure 8-1).

Because this role has no clear guidelines for behavior, individuals usually adapt and create behavioral styles that fit their situation and that of their family system. Three basic grandparenting styles have been identified. These include (1) the **remote relationship**, characterized by infrequent contact with grandchildren governed by behavior that is ritualistic and highly symbolic; (2) the **companionate relationship**, described as an easy-going, friendly relationship that involves emotionally-satisfying leisure-time relationships with grandchildren; and (3) the **involved relationship** that focuses on an active role in raising grandchildren and conducting the role as an active caretaker much like a parent (Cherlin & Furstenberg, 1986).

When researchers have examined the activities of grandparents with grandchildren, a pattern emerges that illustrates the companionate style as one that is practiced more frequently (Cherlin & Furstenberg, 1986) (see Figure 8-2). Pleasurable activities that emphasize expressions of affection toward grandchildren occur more frequently than those involving active caretaking responsibilities such as disciplining children.

Certain factors appear to influence how this role functions. For example, middle-class individuals often assume more active grandparenting roles than others (Clavan, 1978). Liv-

## Sidebar definitions

**Remote relationship**

A grandparent-grandchildren relationship characterized by infrequent contact governed by behavior that is ritualistic and highly symbolic.

**Companionate relationship**

A grandparent-grandchildren relationship described as an easy-going, friendly relationship that involves emotionally-satisfying leisure-time.

**Involved relationship**

A grandparent-grandchildren relationship that focuses on an active role of raising grandchildren and conducting the role as an active caretaker much like a parent.

---

| **FIGURE 8-1** | **MEANINGS GIVEN TO THE GRANDPARENT ROLE** |
| --- | --- |

**Biological Renewal**   "It is through my grandchildren that I feel young again."

**Biological Continuity with the Future**   "It is through these children that I see my life going on in the future." "It's carrying on the family name."

**Emotional Self-Fulfillment**   "I can be and I can do for my grandchildren things I could never do for my own kids. I was too busy with my business to enjoy my kids but my grandchildren are different. Now I have time to be with them."

**Resource Person**   "I take my grandson down to the factory and show him how the business operates—and then, too, I set aside money especially for him."

**Extension of Self**   "She's a beautiful child, and she'll grow up to be a beautiful woman. Maybe I shouldn't, but I can't help feeling proud of that."

**Sense of Remoteness from Kin (geographical, age difference)**   "My grand-daughter is just a baby, and I don't even feel like a grandfather yet."

Source: Adapted from B. L. Neugarten, & K. K. Weinstein (1968). The changing American grandparent. In B. L. Neugarten (Ed.) *Middle age and aging*. Chicago: University of Chicago Press.

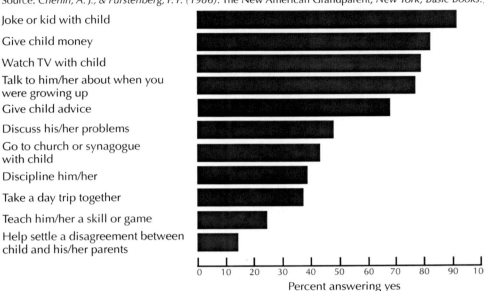

**FIGURE 8-2    THE ACTIVITIES OF GRANDPARENTS WITH GRANDCHILDREN**

Source: *Cherlin, A. J., & Furstenberg, F. F. (1986). The New American Grandparent, New York; Basic Books.)*

Joke or kid with child
Give child money
Watch TV with child
Talk to him/her about when you were growing up
Give child advice
Discuss his/her problems
Go to church or synagogue with child
Discipline him/her
Take a day trip together
Teach him/her a skill or game
Help settle a disagreement between child and his/her parents

0  10  20  30  40  50  60  70  80  90  100
Percent answering yes

ing within close physical distance to one's grandchildren also increases the likelihood of a more active grandparenting role (Cherlin & Furstenberg, 1986). More frequent interactions occur when distances are small. A more remote style is enhanced when distances are great.

Despite the ambiguous nature of this role and sometimes infrequent contact with grandchildren, grandparents appear to influence their grandchildren and the extended family system in several ways (Barranti, 1985) (see Figure 8-3). This can be jeopardized when parents divorce. Grandparental rights are not typically specified when parents divorce, and contact with grandchildren can cease. This is especially the case among paternal grandparents because fathers often have limited visitation and custody rights following divorce (Derdeyn, 1985). However, when parents remarry, children often have access to even more grandparents than before the parental divorce. Little is known about step-grandparent/step-grandchild relationships at this time, however.

**CARING FOR AGING PARENTS**    A longer life expectancy and other social factors, such as delayed age at first marriage and childbearing, have reshaped the nature of family life. By middle age, parents may have promoted their children into adulthood. However, the expectation continues that they will provide emotional and even financial support for adult children (Aldous, 1987; Troll, 1986).

Caregiving, however, is not restricted to providing support for adult children by middle-aged parents. These individuals also provide care, either through direct means or giving financial support, to aging parents. This is why middle-aged parents are referred to as the "sandwich" or "caught" generation (Hagestad, 1986; Vincent, 1972). Middle-aged parents continue to have ties to the younger and older generations. One of the hazards of

| FIGURE 8-3 | INFLUENCES OF GRANDPARENTS ON FAMILY SYSTEMS |
| --- | --- |

- Accepting behaviors and traits that parents may not be able to tolerate.
- Providing nurturance that parents may not be able to provide.
- Providing instruction in values, ethics, and morals.
- Providing backup support for parents in raising children.
- Providing parents with options for solving interaction problems and conflicts with grandchildren.
- Acting as an equalizer to provide balance within a family system.

Source: Adapted from C. C. R. Barranti (1985). The grandparent/grandchild relationship: Family resource in an era of voluntary bonds. *Family Relations, 34,* 343–352.

being a member of the sandwich or "caught" generation is experiencing a division of one's loyalties. The middle-aged parent is confronted with the dilemma of coping with simultaneous demands from adult children and from aging parents.

Interactions between middle-aged children and their parents are a mixture of problems, benefits, rewards, and difficulties (Alam, 1978). Problems frequently mentioned involve (1) generation gap issues (differences in values, attitudes, and behavior, (2) interference issues (conflicts where both generations attempt to dominate the lives of each other), (3) issues of impatience with the parents' age (health concerns, slower reaction times, and so on), and (4) communication issues (power and dominance concerns). Benefits and rewards of having older parents include (1) the value of having the benefit of their greater experience, wisdom, and knowledge; (2) the reciprocal nature of help available between the two generations; and (3) the value of both younger and older generations to family continuity and effective system functioning.

The arrangements between middle-aged adult children and their parents in providing care and assistance can be stressful and can lead to depression (Cicirelli, 1983). This is especially the situation when role-reversal occurs that accentuates the dependency of elderly parents upon middle-aged adult children. The stressfulness of this situation is manifested in feelings of exhaustion and negativity toward the aging parent. Although the levels of stress are not often excessive, middle-aged children cite feelings of frustration, impatience, and guilt in relation to the elderly parent.

## *The Outside World*

**Friendship and Peers**  Friendship patterns change in middle adulthood. Lowenthal and associates (1977) find that friendships among middle-aged people are more complex than those among adolescents and young adults. People at middle age continue to value the same qualities in friendships that they did at earlier ages—namely, reciprocity (sharing), helping, having similar experiences, and ease of communication. Women tend more to choose friends on the basis of reciprocity, whereas men consider similarity with others of prime importance (Johnson, 1989).

*While friendships at this stage are more complex the same qualities that were important in adolescence still remain. (iStock)*

Friendships at middle age may reflect some of the personality changes that occur in midlife. People grow more introspective and appreciative of differences in themselves and others by this time of life. Friendships may be especially important to single people as a support system in place of family ties (Lowenthal et al., 1977). Although the frequency of contact with friends diminishes with age, the quality of associations improves considerably (Antonucci, 2001; Cartensen, 1992, 1995). People maintain friendships longer and on a more intimate basis.

Describe leisure time in middle adulthood.

**LEISURE TIME**    Leisure activities are important for mental and physical health (Hansen, Dik & Zhou, 2008). Engagement in leisure activities is correlated with increased self-esteem, marital satisfaction, life satisfaction, and career involvement. During middle adulthood, leisure is limited due to work and family obligations (Kleiber & Kelly, 1980; Hansen, Dik & Zhou, 2008). Therefore, leisure and socializing are often incorporated into other activities. For example, part of an adults' parenting duties may include taking their children to soccer practices and games, which then also becomes a time to socialize and relax with other parents.

**CAREERS IN MIDDLE ADULTHOOD**    Middle adulthood is sometimes likened to adolescence because of the interpersonal conflict and inner turmoil that can sometimes occur in both of these periods. These are important processes, however, in stimulating personal growth and integration of various aspects of the individual's self-concept. Vocational development at midlife is characterized by the dual processes of stability and change seen in other areas of development. Career and work roles are examined as part of the midlife transition. Goals are reevaluated in terms of progress made toward vocational objectives determined in early adulthood.

**MIDLIFE CAREER CHANGE**    It is not uncommon for people to make a career change near the end of early adulthood or the beginning of middle adulthood. Some of these career changes are due to a desire for change; others are due to being forced out of a job (Schultz & Schultz, 2010). For some individuals disenchantment with their work sets in between their mid-forties and mid-fifties (Doering & Rhodes, 1989; Mergenhagen, 1991). Various factors may increase the likelihood of job dissatisfaction occurring.

**Job simplification**

Work that is repetitive, simplified, and fragmented.

**Gender harassment**

A workplace environment that is hostile, degrading, or insulting toward one particular gender.

**Sexual harassment**

Unwanted sexual attention.

**Ethnic harassment**

A workplace environment where verbal assaults are targeted toward individuals because of their ethnicity.

**Job simplification**—work that is repetitive, simplified, and fragmented—can lead to job dissatisfaction (Schultz & Schultz, 2010). With job simplification, boredom, monotony, and fatigue can quickly develop. Job dissatisfaction can also occur due to ethnic, gender, or sexual harassment. You may be wondering what the difference is between gender harassment and sexual harassment. **Gender harassment** involves a workplace environment that is hostile, degrading, or insulting toward one particular gender. **Sexual harassment** involves a workplace environment where unwanted sexual attention occurs. **Ethnic harassment** involves a workplace environment where verbal assaults are targeted toward individuals because of their ethnicity. These may include ethnic jokes, slurs, or other offensive comments. Finally, job dissatisfaction may be linked to having an awful supervisor. In fact, surveys have found that 75 percent of employees point to their boss as the worst and most stressful part of their job.

Although some individuals seek a midlife career change due to job dissatisfaction, others do so for more positive reasons. Perhaps they are seeking new challenges or opportunities for growth. Maybe they had always dreamed of owning their own business and now they have the financial ability to do so. This is a period in the life span where individuals focus less on how many years have passed since their birth, and instead focus on how many years are left until their death (Neugarten & Neugarten, 1987). This may explain why middle-aged people feel more pressured to make critical life changes, like career changes, than earlier in adulthood.

*A change in career is common. The reasons vary, for example, a desire for change or being forced out of a job. (iStock)*

*Pause and Process:*

1. What are some grandparenting styles?

2. What are some reasons individuals may change careers in middle adulthood?

# SUMMARY

1. It is interesting to ponder that although we accept aging as a part of life, we do not really understand what causes the body to age. Some theories are focusing upon aging at the cellular level—such as the cellular clock theory and free-radical theory, whereas others focus on a body system, like the hormonal stress theory.

2. Physical changes in middle adulthood focus on the initial effects of aging. Many organ systems show general declines in function and efficiency. The major physical changes at this time of life are a decline in body weight among men and increase among women; various changes in skin tissue, such as increased wrinkling and dryness; gradual declines in visual abilities; increasing occurrence of a variety of conditions such as arthritis, atherosclerosis, arteriosclerosis, hypertension, and minor digestive disturbances.

3. Post-traumatic stress disorder is an anxiety disorder that can develop after experiencing or witnessing a traumatic event. Symptoms of PTSD include hypervigilance, avoidance, and re-experiencing the event. Approximately 8 percent of adults in the United States will experience PTSD at some point during their life.

4. Selection, optimization, and compensation theory strives to assist individuals in aging optimally by teaching strategies that minimize losses and maxi-

mize gains. By modifying goal selection, optimizing current functioning levels, and compensating with external support when needed, adults can continue to live happily throughout life.

5. Experts and novices differ in their cognitive abilities. In comparison to novices, experts have a broader knowledge base, organize their knowledge better, and have better retrieval of knowledge. There are two main types of experts with varying degrees of adaptive expertise.

6. Some aspects of information-processing improve while others decline during this stage. Crystallized intelligence continues to grow, whereas fluid intelligence declines. Cognitive style is adapted to involve past experiences and intuition in making decisions.

7. Emotional intelligence is comprised of three main components: emotion recognition, optimistic mood regulation, and emotion utilization. Optimistic mood regulation continues to develop into middle adulthood.

8. Middle adulthood is a transition period in the life span that takes place between forty and sixty-five years of age. Socioemotionally, this stage is characterized by changes in personal and family roles, and intensive self-examination and assessment of personal progress toward life goals.

9. Socioemotional changes at midlife feature shifts in personality and self-concept. The midlife tran-

sition offers people the opportunity to reassess their progress toward personal happiness and to change in necessary ways to achieve this. Friendship patterns become more complex during this period. People often examine their work roles in conjunction with the midlife transition. Frequently this results in a career change.

10. Parents have to adjust to the end of their parenting careers with an empty nest. Both men and women may experience difficulties with this change in their role status, but the end of parenting permits couples to refocus their energies on their marriage. Marital satisfaction usually increases when this is done.

11. The new family role of grandparent is often initiated during this stage. The contemporary version of this role is ambiguous, allowing wide differences in structuring. The most commonly observed grandparenting style is companionate: an easygoing, nurturant relationship with grandchildren.

12. Many middle-aged people feel caught between their responsibilities for the younger and the older generations of their family system. Hence, they are known as the sandwich generation.

13. Generativity is an interest in caring for others and sharing one's knowledge, skills, and information. As individuals master these psychosocial attitudes, they acquire the ability to respond to life situations and events in mature ways. This leads to greater personal happiness and adjustment, satisfaction with work, and physical health.

## SELF-QUIZ

1. What age-range characterizes middle adulthood?

2. What is meant by ageism? What is an example of ageism you have seen?

3. Which theory of aging makes the most sense to you? Provide a reason for your answer.

4. Which theory of aging do you find the least plausible? Provide a reason for your answer.

5. How do height and weight change during middle adulthood?

6. What changes does the skin experience during middle adulthood?

7. Explain what osteoporosis is and how to prevent it.

8. What are the two basic types of arthritis?

9. Explain the difference between atherosclerosis and arteriosclerosis? How do they both contribute to hypertension?

10. What can individuals do during middle adulthood to promote wellness?

11. Within SOC theory, describe a behavior or strategy for selection.

12. Within SOC theory, describe a behavior or strategy for optimization.

13. Within SOC theory, describe a behavior or strategy for compensation.

14. Provide an example of a cognitive process that shows growth, maintenance, and regulation of loss throughout the life span.

15. Explain and provide a unique example for each of the four foundational rationales in SOC theory.

16. How could the ability to detect meaningful patterns of information assist an expert teacher?

17. In what area or activity would you consider yourself an expert (or on your way to becoming an expert)?

18. Which type of surgeon would you want to operate on you: a merely skilled expert or a highly competent expert? Provide reasons for your choice.

19. How does intelligence change in middle adulthood?

20. Explain changes in attention and memory during middle adulthood.

21. What does the term sandwich generation mean?

22. Why is middle adulthood considered a time of transition?

23. What are some criticisms of the idea of a midlife crisis?

24. What new information did you learn about attachment in this chapter?

25. Describe how marriage may change during middle adulthood.

26. What are some roles that grandparents may play in the family system?

27. How does friendship change during middle adulthood? How does it stay the same?

28. Describe leisure time in middle adulthood.

29. What is the difference between gender harassment and sexual harassment?

30. Describe behavioral differences between a person who has achieved generativity versus a person who has fallen into stagnation.

## TERMS AND CONCEPTS

| TERM | PAGE | TERM | PAGE |
|---|---|---|---|
| Middle age | 306 | Expertise | 316 |
| Middle adulthood | 306 | Regulation of loss | 316 |
| Ageism | 307 | Maintenance | 316 |
| Aging | 307 | Growth | 316 |
| Cellular clock theory | 307 | Adaptive expertise | 317 |
| Stochastic processes | 307 | Highly competent experts | 317 |
| Free-radicals | 308 | Merely skilled experts | 317 |
| Mitochondrial theory | 308 | Conditionalized knowledge | 317 |
| Autoimmune responsiveness theory | 308 | Novice | 317 |
| Hormonal stress theory | 308 | Fluid intelligence | 318 |
| Atherosclerosis | 310 | Crystallized intelligence | 318 |
| Rheumatism | 310 | Working memory | 319 |
| Arthritis | 310 | Emotional intelligence | 320 |
| Osteoporosis | 310 | Spatial reference memory | 320 |
| Menopause | 311 | Sandwich generation | 321 |
| Diabetes | 311 | Remote relationship | 330 |
| Hypertension | 311 | Companionate relationship | 330 |
| Arteriosclerosis | 311 | Involved relationship | 330 |
| Glaucoma | 312 | Job simplification | 334 |
| Cataracts | 312 | Gender harassment | 334 |
| Climacteric | 312 | Sexual harassment | 334 |
| Selection, optimization, and compensation (SOC) theory | 315 | Ethnic harassment | 334 |

# CHAPTER 9

# Late Adulthood

(iStock)

## OUTLINE

### PHYSICAL DEVELOPMENT DURING LATE ADULTHOOD

- Physical development
- Health issues

### COGNITIVE DEVELOPMENT DURING LATE ADULTHOOD

- Beyond Piaget's theory
- Information-processing during late adulthood

### SOCIOEMOTIONAL DEVELOPMENT DURING LATE ADULTHOOD

- Psychosocial development
- Emotional development
- Self and others

**When does old age begin?** Should this depend on chronological age or a life event such as retirement from work? Although many people maintain that old age is a state of mind, there are several life events that signal the beginning of late adulthood. These are tied to chronology, just as other life events are in previous stages of the life span.

Age sixty-five is considered a milestone and the beginning of late adulthood. Reaching this age generally brings about retirement from work, eligibility for Social Security and Medicare benefits, income tax advantages, reduced fares and admission prices to leisure events, and special purchase or discount privileges. It is projected that by the year 2020, approximately 16.5 percent of the population will be sixty-five years of age or older (up from 4.1 percent in 1900, 8.1 percent in 1950, and 12.4 percent in 2000) (Himes, 2001). This percentage is expected to increase to 20.8 percent by 2060.

Advances in modern medical care, better health practices, improved nutrition, and other factors keep people in better health and living longer today (Himes, 2001). For these and other reasons, the period of late adulthood can be divided into five subcategories based on age by decade (Burnside, Ebersole & Monea, 1979). Please note that originally there were only four subcategories; however, the category of centenarians has been added due to an increasing number of people living past one hundred. These subcategories are described below. Neugarten (1978) was among the first to recognize that not all individuals in late adulthood are disabled or feeble. These age divisions help to create a more realistic and positive impression of the elderly. Upon reading about them, you may conclude correctly that late adulthood comprises a diverse group of individuals. In this respect, it is like every other stage discussed in this text.

The young-old (sixty to sixty-nine years): Society expects people in their sixties to have less energy, responsibility, and independence in adulthood. This expectation demoralizes people and serves as a self-fulfilling prophecy. True, physical strength declines from earlier periods of the life span. Despite this limitation, many individuals in this age bracket are energetic, active in volunteer work, pursue hobbies and interests, lead vigorous lifestyles, and are in a state of good health (Kovar, 1986a, b; Kovar & LaCroix, 1987; Ries & Brown, 1991). Release from work and financial responsibilities gives them the chance to redirect their energies to activities that please them. Self-improvement, sometimes even in the form of entrance into college degree programs, is actively pursued by many people this age.

The middle-aged old (seventy to seventy-nine years): Losses characterize this decade. Deaths of spouses and friends occur more frequently. Health problems become a preoccupation and restrict activities within and outside the home, which can further shrink a person's social world. A significant challenge for people in their seventies is to retain the reintegration of personality accomplished following retirement.

The old-old (eighty to eighty-nine years): People in this age bracket find it increasingly difficult to adapt to the effects of the advanced aging process. Housing and physical space are often obstacles to effective living. People in their eighties become more preoccupied with their memories and interested in relating their past living experiences to others. Health problems become more frequent, severe, and of longer duration. Some people need to be cared for by others, which could be within a family member's home, a nursing home, or some other supervised living situation.

The very old-old (ninety to ninety-nine years): There are far fewer people in this age bracket, so we have very little accurate information about them. Obviously, health problems play a central role in their lifestyles. People in their nineties have very limited physical and social activity, but they appear to be happy, serene, and fulfilled (Bretschneider & McCoy, 1988).

Centenarians (one hundred years and older): Centenarians are a particularly hardy and diverse group of individuals (Duenwald, 2003). They are known for their positive dispositions and lower rates of chronic illness and age-related disabilities that plague their younger, elderly peers. More women than men live to be one hundred; however, men tend to maintain greater health and mental capacity. Although many centenarians avoided smoking and obesity throughout life, others live to be one hundred or more despite suboptimal nutrition, little exercise, environmental toxins, and poor lifestyle choices (such as smoking). A few common themes among centenarians include remaining emotionally close and involved with loved ones throughout life, achieving financial security, and staying mentally active (e.g., reading, writing, and cross word puzzles). Such extreme longevity seems to run in families, hinting that genetics may play a role. Researchers hope to identify the genetic factors that promote such longevity in order to develop drugs that will mimic these genetic effects in others.

There are more women than men in all of the subcategories of late adulthood (Himes, 2001). This difference is because men have higher mortality rates than women throughout life. In general, for every one hundred girls born, one hundred and five boys are born (of course, sex-selection during IVF or abortion can skew these numbers). However, by the age of eighty-five there is a 41:100 ratio—that is for every one hundred women, there are only forty-one men. In general, women can expect to outlive their husbands.

There are also some ethnic differences in terms of the elderly population (Himes, 2001). During the 2000 census, 84 percent of all elderly people were white, non-Hispanic. However, it is projected that the elderly population will become more ethnically diverse over the next fifty years, with 64 percent of the elderly population being considered white, non-Hispanic. It has been speculated that barriers to health care have contributed to earlier mortality rates for African American and Hispanic individuals. Improved access to health care, fertility rates, and immigration will all play a role in the increased diversity of the elderly population in the years to come.

# PHYSICAL DEVELOPMENT DURING LATE ADULTHOOD

> **LEARNING OBJECTIVES:**
>
> 1. *Describe physical development during late adulthood*
> 2. *Awareness of health issues in late adulthood*

# PHYSICAL DEVELOPMENT

**Senescence**

The process of aging.

**Collagen**

A fibrous protein that is a basic component of connective tissue.

The vast majority of physical changes observed during late adulthood are closely related to the process of advanced aging. Physical functioning and daily activities are curtailed as the organ systems degenerate. Many of the symptoms of organ degeneration appear prominently in middle adulthood, but they become even more pronounced as people progress through late adulthood.

The aging process in late adulthood is termed **senescence**. The general effects of aging combine to make the body's organ systems work less efficiently. For quite a while, people can compensate for the declining efficiency of their organs and the body in general, but the decline becomes dramatic later in this stage.

The discussion of theories of aging in Chapter 8 indicated that various causes have been proposed for aging in human beings. Although no one factor has been identified as being solely responsible for the aging process, researchers note that changes in **collagen** closely parallel changes throughout the body and are associated with the aging process (Spence & Mason, 1987; Timiras, 1972). Collagen, a fibrous protein that is a basic component of connective tissue, is found throughout the body. It is characterized as a large molecule having elastic properties. The flexible nature of collagen allows muscles, blood vessels, tendons, and other organs to transmit tension and experience compression without becoming deformed. We would not be able to move about in a normal way without this important molecule.

The effects of aging may be closely related to the loss of collagen's elastic properties. This can be observed throughout the body. Calcium salts, for example, begin to be deposited in tissues as people advance in age during middle and late adulthood. This

**What does senescence mean?**

substance contributes to arteriosclerosis or "hardening of the arteries," a condition that causes hypertension, related circulatory system disorders, and eventually death. Collagen changes in heart muscle tissue reduce the ability of this organ to perform properly.

## Changes in Weight and Height

The loss of weight in men that begins in middle adulthood continues through late adulthood. Elderly women begin to lose weight in gradual increments during this stage. Decreasing physical activity, less food consumption, lower metabolism, poorer health, and related factors result in a reduction of muscle and tissue mass and hence weight.

Reductions in height also continue into late adulthood for both men and women (Abraham, 1979; Hegner, 1991). This loss in height is caused by compression of the spinal column and the softening of muscle and bone tissue. The changes also result in the characteristically stooped posture, with the head held forward and down from the body, seen in older people.

## Changes in Bodily Systems

As the body declines in physical functioning, numerous changes are occurring in bodily systems.

**THE TEETH**    Total loss of teeth occurs in a sizable minority of people between the ages of sixty-five and seventy-four (Cassel, 1990; Kelly & Harvey, 1979). Advanced age is associated with a higher incidence of periodontal disease and **gingivitis**, inflammations of gum tissue that contribute highly to tooth loss. Many of the dental problems of old age, however, are the result of earlier neglect.

Dental problems contribute to poor eating habits that lead to malnutrition. Some elderly people do not get dentures to replace missing teeth for financial reasons; others have poorly fitting dentures. As a result, they may eat only foods that are easy to chew, eliminating many vegetables, fruits, and meats from their diet.

**THE MUSCULAR AND SKELETAL SYSTEMS**    The ability to move about becomes more restricted as aging advances because of changes in muscle and bone functioning. Muscles atrophy, reducing strength and restricting movement. Loss of elasticity in muscle tissue reduces flexibility, causing stiffness. Osteoporosis leads to easier bone breakage, **kyphosis** ("humpback" posture), and **scoliosis** (S-curved spinal column). Back pain increases in frequency and intensity, reflecting deterioration of the vertebrae (Hazard, 1990; Meuleman, 1989; Spence & Mason, 1987).

Arthritis and rheumatism are the most prevalent musculoskeletal disorders among the elderly. Other conditions that often cause disability or discomfort at this stage are muscle cramps, bursitis in the shoulder or elbow, and **gout** (a metabolic disorder that results from uric acid crystals forming at joint areas, especially in the feet).

**Gingivitis**

Inflammation of gum tissue that contributes highly to tooth loss.

**Kyphosis**

A "humpback" posture.

**Scoliosis**

S-curved spinal column.

**Gout**

A metabolic disorder that results from uric acid crystals forming at joint areas, especially in the feet.

**THE CARDIOVASCULAR SYSTEM**
The effects of aging on the heart and blood vessels that became increasingly apparent in middle adulthood worsen in late adulthood. There is further accumulation of fatty material in the heart muscle and in the arteries (atherosclerosis), the heart valves thicken, and arteriosclerosis (hardening of the arteries) becomes more pronounced (Schrier, 1990; Spence & Mason, 1987). These conditions cause higher blood pressure, extra stress on the heart, and related cardiovascular problems, although regular exercise has been found to be beneficial in maintaining cardiovascular responsiveness (Thompson, Crist & Osborn, 1990; Van camp & Boyer, 1989).

*Muscular and skeletal systems become more restricted. (iStock)*

Decreased cardiac output further jeopardizes the health and well-being of the elderly (Spence & Mason, 1987). The slower heart rate of older people results in a decreased level of oxygen in the blood, which is why elderly people tire more easily and cannot endure stress as well as younger people.

Coronary heart disease increases steadily during late adulthood. It is a leading cause of death at this stage of life. Coronary heart disease stems from a diminished supply of oxygen to the heart muscle through the blood caused by hypertension, atherosclerosis, or coronary aneurysm (ruptured blood vessel in the heart muscle). Over a long period of time, it can lead to heart attack or congestive heart failure.

**THE RESPIRATORY SYSTEM**    The lungs have lowered capacity for inhaling and exhaling air in late adulthood (Horan & Brouwer, 1990; Spence & Mason, 1987). There are three causes of this reduced capacity. First, a change in collagen composition of the lungs causes them to become less elastic and thus less capable of expanding and contracting. Second, the diaphragm and chest muscles that help expand and contract the chest weaken. Third, age-related conditions such as scoliosis reduce chest capacity.

Among the most common serious respiratory conditions among the elderly are cancer of the lungs, **emphysema**, and **pneumonia**. Lung cancer increases considerably during late adulthood; it is associated with chronic conditions such as smoking, pollution, and occupational hazards. Emphysema is a condition involving destruction of lung tissue that results in lowered lung elasticity. People with emphysema have difficulty breathing and moving about freely. Pneumonia is an inflammation of the lungs. It increases in incidence in old age because of decreased lung efficiency, poor circulation, and lowered

**Emphysema**

A condition involving destruction of lung tissue that results in lowered lung elasticity.

**Pneumonia**

An inflammation of the lungs.

resistance to infection. Pneumonia is a particular risk for an elderly person who is bedridden for an extended period of time because physical inactivity prevents the lungs from clearing themselves.

**THE DIGESTIVE SYSTEM** Digestive problems generally increase through adulthood (Spence & Mason, 1987). In old age, the most commonly reported digestive disorders are constipation, hernia, gallbladder conditions, gastritis (heartburn), and diverticulitis (Drury & Howie, 1979; Whitehead, Drinkwater & Cheskin, 1989).

Constipation and hemorrhoids are frequent complaints of the elderly. Their concern with not having a regular daily bowel movement may be more of a matter of socialization than a true effect of aging, however. Of greater concern for many elderly individuals is the high rate of hemorrhoids and the reliance on laxatives to produce regular bowel movements. This often is related more to dietary practices than to the aging process as well. These conditions may be controlled by adding more fiber to the diet in the form of grain bran, fresh fruits, vegetables, and nuts or by taking dietary supplements containing fiber (Hazard, 1990). In general, between twenty and thirty grams of dietary fiber should be consumed by adults daily for effective control of constipation and hemorrhoids.

**Hiatal hernia**, a condition in which a portion of the stomach slides up next to the esophagus, is common among the elderly, especially among overweight or obese individuals. Hiatal hernia causes indigestion, gastritis, chest pain, and difficulty in swallowing. It can be treated with therapeutic methods or surgery if severe.

**Diverticulitis** is an inflammation of a portion of an intestine that causes pain, nausea, and a change in bowel habits. It is usually treated without surgery, unless the affected area of the intestine perforates or ruptures.

Gallbladder problems in old age usually involve gallstones or inflammation of the gallbladder. The gallbladder stores bile from the liver. Gallstones sometimes form from insoluble substances in the bile. They don't cause serious problems unless they block the duct leading from the gallbladder to the intestine. "Gallbladder attacks" are very painful, however, and may be accompanied by nausea and vomiting.

**THE GENITOURINARY SYSTEM** Elderly people are susceptible to a variety of disorders in the reproductive organs and the urinary system (kidneys, bladder, and urethra) (Schrier, 1990; Spence & Mason, 1987). As people age, there is a decrease in the blood flow through the kidneys as well as a gradual decrease in the kidneys' efficiency to remove wastes from the blood. Among people of advanced age, urinary **incontinence** (the inability to retain urine in the bladder until voluntarily released) is a very real and embarrassing problem (Ruff & Reaves, 1989).

These changes bring on certain conditions that affect the functioning of the urinary system. Men commonly experience enlargement of the prostate gland, which causes blockage of the urine flow. This encourages bladder infections and other complications. The most common types of cancer affecting this system in elderly men are cancer of the bladder and of the prostate gland.

**Hiatal hernia**

A condition in which a portion of the stomach slides up next to the esophagus.

**Diverticulitis**

An inflammation of a portion of an intestine that causes pain, nausea, and a change in bowel habits.

**Incontinence**

The inability to retain urine in the bladder until voluntarily released.

Women have more urinary system problems than men throughout life. Bladder infections, such as cystitis, are frequent. In late adulthood, women are at increased risk for problems of the vaginal area, prolapsed uterus, and cancer of the cervix, vulva, and breasts. Breast cancer is a leading cause of death among elderly women (U.S. Bureau of the Census, 2000).

**THE BRAIN AND CENTRAL NERVOUS SYSTEM**   Several developmental changes in the brain and central nervous system are related to advanced aging (Albert & Killiany, 2001; Spence & Mason, 1987; Vinters, 2001). First, the speed of nerve cell transmission slows with age. Second, brain and nerve cells diminish in number. These two factors, plus decreased transmission of oxygen to the brain, produce the slowing in reaction time that is commonly observed among elderly individuals.

Reaction time affects perception and memory as well as the soundness of various reflexes. Progressively slower reaction times endanger the safety of the elderly people, especially when they are driving. Many states now require extra testing for issuance of driver's licenses to the elderly.

| FIGURE 9-1 | LOCALIZATION OF CORTICAL FUNCTIONS IN THE FOUR LOBES OF THE LEFT CEREBRAL CORTEX |
| --- | --- |

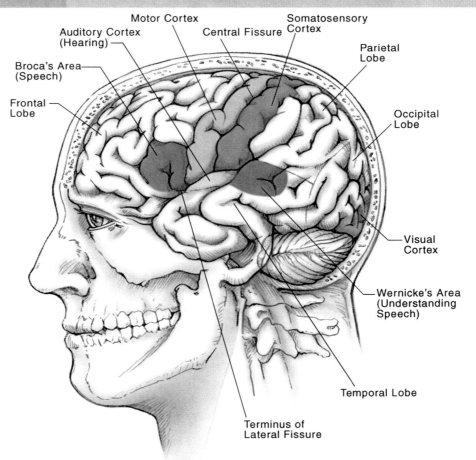

Reduced availability of oxygen to the brain can contribute to other conditions that are troublesome to elderly individuals. Sleep disturbances, memory difficulties, and general irritability are related to decreased cerebral blood flow and to changes in the biochemical functioning of the brain in old age (Pollak, Perlick & Linsner, 1990). Insomnia is a frequent complaint among the elderly (Cassel, 1990). There is a general trend to need less sleep as age increases. A newborn infant may sleep about sixteen hours daily, whereas school-age children sleep about ten hours, and adults about eight. Elderly people may be able to sleep only five hours or so a night.

**CHANGES IN SENSATION, PERCEPTION, AND MOTOR SKILLS**    The ability to adjust and adapt in late adulthood partly depends on the capacity to receive and process information gained through the senses. Elderly people experience sensory deprivation as the sensory organs and the area of the brain that regulate them decline in efficiency. This deprivation has enormous implications for mental alertness and contact with reality.

*Vision*    Age-related changes in vision during late adulthood include an increase in the threshold of light needed to stimulate retinal cells; a decrease in acuity (sharpness of vision) due to changes in the lens, pupil size, and accommodation (focusing ability); and a decrease in adaptation to dark and light environments (Fozard & Gordon-Salant, 2001; Saxon & Etten, 1978; Spence & Mason, 1987).

Elderly people can expect to experience several eye disorders that can limit visual ability: "specks" in a visual field due to loose cells floating within the vitreous humor of the eyeballs; cataracts; glaucoma; **macular degeneration**, or a decreased blood supply to the retina, causing loss of visual sharpness when looking directly ahead but not in the peripheral vision areas; and drooping eyelids. The risk of blindness increases considerably after age sixty, often because of glaucoma.

**Macular degeneration**

A decreased blood supply to the retina, causing loss of visual sharpness when looking directly ahead but not in the peripheral vision areas.

*Hearing loss is the most significant sensory change during late adulthood. (iStock)*

*Hearing*   Perhaps the most significant sensory change during late adulthood is hearing loss. It sometimes leads to a complete withdrawal from social interaction. Hearing handicaps increase considerably with age (Rowland, 1980; Spence & Mason, 1987). About half of all people older than sixty-five have some hearing loss. These losses occur earlier in men than women, perhaps because men were more likely to be exposed to hazardous noise on the job.

The loss of hearing for high-frequency sounds that was first noticed during middle adulthood continues. Loss of hearing in the mid- to low-range frequencies becomes more likely with age. Many elderly people become deaf because of damage to the cochlea hair cells, hardening of the bones, and nerve damage to the structures of the inner ear that transmit sound waves to the brain (Fozard & Gordon-Salant, 2001).

*Taste and Smell*   Taste and smell perception decline in old age. Many elderly people remark that food tastes bland, and season it heavily with salt, pepper, and other condiments to improve its flavor. This loss of taste is attributed to a decrease in the number of taste buds and to the need for stronger stimulation to taste receptors in the mouth.

People do not smell odors as well in late adulthood. This is because of a decrease in the number of nerve fibers in the nose (Saxon & Etten, 1978; Spence & Mason, 1987). This decline has important safety implications. Elderly people sometimes cannot easily smell food that has burned during cooking or smoke from a house fire.

*Pause and Process:*

1. Why do people see a decrease in height in late adulthood?

2. How do the senses decline in late adulthood?

# HEALTH ISSUES

The majority of elderly people are in relatively good health (Kovar, 1986a); although they usually have one or more chronic conditions that require medical attention (DeLozier & Gagnon, 1991). The most common complaints are cardiovascular disease, hypertension, arthritis, hearing impairment, cataracts, glaucoma, and lower back problems.

Elderly people also experience acute illnesses, but less frequently than younger people (U.S. Bureau of the Census, 2000). However, when they do get an acute illness such as influenza, it tends to be more severe and of longer duration than it is among younger people. Elderly people are hospitalized for illness more frequently than younger individuals. Medical expenses play a major role in elderly people's budgets.

## *Nutritional Needs*

The relationship between diet, exercise, and health continues to be strong in late adulthood (Goodwin, 1989; Leventhal et al., 2001). Nutritionists note that many health problems are related to the diets and eating habits of elderly people. These include a lower resistance to disease (Chavance, Herbeth & Fournier, 1989), poor absorption of nutrients (Knox, Kassarkian & Dawson-Hughes, 1991), elevated blood pressure (Lowik, Hoffman & Kok, 1991), and dehydration (Post, 1990). Additionally, diets that are high in fat and protein increase a person's risk for several types of cancer, including colon, uterus, breast, prostate, kidney, and pancreas (Perls, 1999). To decrease a person's risk for developing cancer or heart disease, a diet should emphasize fruit and vegetable consumption.

**A NUMBER OF FACTORS WORK AGAINST ADEQUATE NOURISHMENT OF THE ELDERLY:** Declining health and general well-being; tooth loss that affects the ability to chew many foods; declines in the senses of taste and smell that affect the enjoyment of food; inadequate fixed incomes that force people to lower food expenditures; physical disabilities that limit shopping and meal preparation; forgetting to eat meals; and loss of appetite (Cain, Reid & Stevens, 1990; Goodwin, 1989; Horwath, 1989; Zheng & Rosenberg, 1989).

Many elderly people erroneously believe they are eating a balanced diet (Fischer, Crockett & Heller, 1991) because they have many misconceptions about nutrition. Malnutrition is not uncommon in late adulthood for this reason (Davies & Carr, 1991). Community nutrition programs promote improved nutrition among the elderly. These services, such as Meals on Wheels, are particularly helpful for the disabled elderly (Manning & Lieux, 1991).

Vitamin and mineral supplements alleviate some nutritional problems among the elderly and improve health (Daly & Sobal, 1990; Perls, 1999). For example, vitamin E is an antioxidant and is believed to impede the development of stroke, heart disease, and Alzheimer's. Selenium is believed to inhibit some forms of cancer. Fiber is thought to have numerous benefits including lower rates of colon cancer and high cholesterol.

## *Common Illnesses and Disorders*

We have already covered many of the common illnesses previously in the chapter in regards to the decline and deterioration in the functioning of physical systems. However, we have yet to discuss cerebrovascular accidents, or strokes. **Strokes** are a leading cause of death among elderly people (Spence & Mason, 1987). A stroke occurs when a blood clot forms and causes a blockage in the amount of blood reaching the brain (Lewis, 1990; Spence & Mason, 1987). The clot can form in an artery of the neck or in the brain. When it does, brain tissue dies from lack of oxygen. An **aneurysm**, or rupture of an artery wall within the brain, can also cause a stroke. In this case, the blood clot forms within the brain.

The severity and damage to the stroke victim's brain varies according to where the hemorrhage or blockage occurred. Some people are only minimally affected; others experience various degrees of paralysis, loss of motor functioning, speech, or combinations of these effects. These effects may or may not last for a lengthy period depending on the severity of injury to brain tissue.

**Strokes**

A cerebrovascular accident occurring when a blood vessel in the brain ruptures or is obstructed by a blood clot.

**Aneurysm**

A rupture of an artery wall within the brain.

There are some early warning signs for a stroke (Saxon & Etten, 1978). A person may experience sudden, temporary weakness or numbness in the face, arm, or leg. He or she may temporarily have difficulty in speech or vision. Further, a person may experience unexplained headaches, dizziness, or a change in personality or mental ability. Most people who have had a stroke in the initial years of late adulthood can expect a limited recovery through occupation, physical, and other kinds of therapy (Lewis, 1990). Occupational therapy is helpful, for example, in assisting stroke patients to develop new patterns of functioning within living environments.

**MENTAL HEALTH**    One of the greatest fears people have about growing older is that they will lose their mental capacities—in popular terms, become senile. **Senility** is a catch-all term for what many believe are the inevitabilities of old age: loss of mental and emotional abilities to relate to reality, helplessness, and incontinence (Cook & Miller, 1985). Senility is technically referred to as dementia. There are numerous non-Alzheimer dementias that vary in cause and symptoms (Vinters, 2001).

**Dementia** is a global term for a variety of organic brain disorders related to brain cell impairment (Vinters, 2001). The symptoms of these disorders can include disorientation to time, place, and/or people; memory loss; disturbances in thinking, especially in abstract thinking and reasoning; impairment of judgment; or inappropriate emotional responses (Saxon & Etten, 1978). Symptoms may appear slowly or rather suddenly.

These symptoms are often regarded as idiosyncrasies of the elderly. Actually, people showing these signs are experiencing a type of mental illness that until recently was thought to always be irreversible. Organic brain syndrome occurs in two forms: (1) **acute**, which is reversible in many cases; and (2) **chronic**, which is not reversible. Acute brain syndrome responds to treatment that is directed toward correcting malnutrition, inflammations and infections, and various chemical imbalances in the body. Chronic

### Senility

Marked deterioration in mental organization characterized by confusion, memory loss, information-processing difficulties, and disorientation.

### Dementia

A type of organic brain syndrome that is a neuropsychiatric disorder related to brain cell impairment.

### Acute

A form of organic brain syndrome that is reversible in many cases.

### Chronic

A form of organic brain syndrome that is not reversible.

*Alzheimer's disease can begin in middle adulthood but is much more common after the age of sixty-five. (Getty)*

brain syndrome is permanent and is responsible for many of the mental disorders associated with late adulthood.

One of the more commonly known chronic organic brain disorders is **Alzheimer's disease**. This degenerative disease is an area of active research (Vinters, 2001). Although symptoms can appear during middle adulthood, this condition is much more common after age sixty-five. Although genetics play a role, many other factors may also influence the onset of Alzheimer's disease.

People with Alzheimer's disease seem to follow a certain course. The first sign of the condition is usually forgetfulness. Individuals cannot easily remember where objects are and their short-term memory of recent events is impaired. The next phase is characterized by impaired cognitive functioning. The person is confused, makes inappropriate and irrational decisions, and displays bizarre or eccentric behavior. The final phase is characterized by dementia. The person shows severe disorientation, behavior problems are recurrent, and rage reactions can be common. People in this phase can wander off and become lost or are unable to recognize where they are. Eventually, physical functions diminish so much that people with Alzheimer's disease are unable to provide for their own care and need constant supervision. Death may result from an infection such as pneumonia.

Although Alzheimer's disease is currently considered irreversible, researchers continue to test new drugs and methods to help people cope with its symptoms (Cassel, 1990; Cohen, 1987). Treatments to improve memory include drugs. Researchers are also studying the levels and types of neurotransmitters in the brain and experimenting with ways to alter or improve these.

Many elderly people with Alzheimer's disease eventually need around the clock care. This care can be either provided in the home by loved ones and/or hired nursing staff, or the care can take place in a convalescent home. Care in a twenty-four hour nursing home is costly to families both emotionally and financially. Alzheimer's disease has a devastating effect on the individual experiencing it, but it is also extremely difficult for family members who must watch this physical and psychological deterioration in a loved relative. Religiosity can help family members cope, as they believe that suffering is a process that unites them to Christ and brings them closer to God. There are also support groups devoted to helping family members cope with a loved one's Alzheimer's disease.

Another degenerative brain condition commonly observed in late adulthood is **Parkinson's disease** (National Parkinson Foundation, 2009; Spence & Mason, 1987). It occurs nearly equally in men and women. Like Alzheimer's disease, Parkinson's disease involves brain cell impairment or death over a long period of time that eventually results in the person's death. More specifically, Parkinson's disease is the result of cell impairment and death in the substantia nigra area of the brain. These cells produce the neurotransmitter **dopamine**, which is responsible for smooth and coordinated movement of the muscles in the body. Surprisingly, it is not until 80 percent of these cells have become impaired or died that an individual begins to show the symptoms of Parkinson's disease.

Parkinson's disease is characterized by tremors (shaking) that spread slowly throughout the entire body, sluggish movement, muscle weakness, rigidity, and a peculiar walking gait

## Alzheimer's disease

A degenerative chronic brain disorder occurring commonly in late adulthood. It is characterized initially by forgetfulness, later by serious cognitive dysfunction; and eventually by complete loss of mental functioning and death.

## Parkinson's disease

A chronic degenerative brain disorder commonly occurring in late adulthood. It is characterized initially by tremors, muscle weakness, and a peculiar gait; then speech becomes slurred; death eventually results from severe brain cell damage.

## Dopamine

A neurotransmitter that is responsible for smooth and coordinated movement of the muscles in the body.

**Where are somatic stem cells obtained from?**

**Embryonic stem cells**

Stem cells obtained from human embryos that result in the death of the embryo.

**Adult stem cells**

Stem cells obtained from patients or donors found in numerous tissues and organ systems, even fat.

**Umbilical cord blood and placental stem cells**

Stem cells found in the umbilical cord blood and placenta after birth.

**Amniotic fluid stem cells**

Stem cells found in amniotic fluid.

**Somatic stem cells**

Another term for adult stem cells.

**Equipotentiality**

The ability for a cell to develop into any type of cell in the body.

(National Parkinson Foundation, 2009; Spence & Mason, 1987). Speech becomes slurred and muffled as the disease progresses. Facial expressions may become stiff and handwriting is small and restricted. Depression is also sometimes experienced by individuals with Parkinson's disease.

Currently, it is estimated that 1.5 million Americans suffer from Parkinson's disease (National Parkinson Foundation, 2009). There are nearly sixty thousand new cases diagnosed each year. Around 85 percent of diagnosed cases are in individuals older than the age of sixty-five. There is no cure for Parkinson's disease; however, medications that replace or mimic dopamine can be helpful in decreasing the symptoms.

It is difficult to discuss Parkinson's disease and not discuss the issue of stem cell research. This is a topic of much controversy in America today. Sadly, most people engaged in the debate are poorly educated about the types of stem cells and what has been accomplished with this research so far.

A stem cell can be defined as a cell "capable of becoming another more differentiated cell type in the body … they can be used to replace or even heal damaged tissues and cells in the body" (stemcellresearchfacts.com, 2009). There are **embryonic stem cells**, umbilical cord blood stem cells, amniotic fluid stem cells, and **adult stem cells**. The controversy involves embryonic stem cells from which a human embryo must die in order to obtain the initial cells (Elizabeth Johnson, MD, personal communication, 2008). They can also be obtained from miscarried or aborted fetuses. Alternatively, adult stem cells can be obtained from bone marrow, fat, the olfactory bulb, or reprogrammed skin cells without causing any harm to the donor. **Umbilical cord blood and placental stem cells** can be obtained after the birth of a child; and **amniotic fluid stem cells** can be obtained through methods similar to amniocentesis. Stem cells from adults, umbilical cord blood, and amniotic fluid can be grouped under the umbrella term of **somatic stem cells**—allowing them to be easily differentiated from embryonic stem cells (stemcellresearchfacts.com, 2009). Hence, there are many ways to obtain stem cells, of which one is controversial and morally reprehensible to a sizable segment of society.

Some researchers have zeroed in on the use of embryonic stem cells in the development of treatments due to their ability to proliferate and differentiate into many types of cells—referred to as **equipotentiality** (Perin, Geng, & Willerson, 2003). However, in recent years, adult stem cells from the skin have been reprogrammed to have the same equipotentiality. Additionally, some stem cell types in the bone marrow and umbilical cord also show this flexibility (stemcellresearchfacts.org, 2009). Hence, it may be possible to avoid the whole moral and ethical controversy of embryonic stem cells by utilizing certain somatic stem cells instead.

Beyond the ethical/moral debate, there are other reasons that somatic stem cells may be preferable to embryonic stem cells (Elizabeth Johnson, MD, personal communication, 2008; stemcellresearchfacts.com, 2009; The Coalition for Research Ethics, 2008). These are highlighted in Table 9–1 below:

Given the recent breakthroughs using somatic stem cells, it is the hope of many researchers that the debate and controversy of embryonic stem cell research can subside,

| TABLE 9-1 | TWO TYPES OF STEM CELLS |
| --- | --- |
| **EMBRYONIC STEM CELLS** | **SOMATIC STEM CELLS** |
| Difficult to induce growth into the desired cell type or tissue | Some have already begun specialization, so inducing growth into the desired cell type or tissue can be easier |
| Immunogenic—because the cells come from embryos or fetuses with their own unique DNA, rejection of this donor tissue by the recipient is likely | Not immunogenic—if the stem cells are harvested from the recipients own body (e.g., skin, fat, bone marrow, etc.), rejection is not an issue. |
| Tumorigenic—tend to produce or promote growth of tumors due to difficulty in controlling their proliferation and growth | Nontumorigenic—Tend not to produce or promote growth of tumors because it is easier to control their growth |
| No current disease treatments or cures have been developed using embryonic stem cells | Several dozen diseases have been treated or cured using somatic stem cells, including certain cancers, autoimmune diseases, cardio-vascular diseases, ocular disorders, immuno-deficiencies, neural degenerative diseases and injuries, blood disorders, metabolic disorders, liver disease, and other wounds and injuries. |

and more energy and money can be spent on the more fruitful research with somatic stem cells. The question is if taxpayer dollars will indeed be spent funding the research that has produced results in treatments and cures, or if the money will be given to research that has (as of press time) produced only tumors and tissue rejection.

One final aspect of mental health in late adulthood that must be mentioned is suicide. When people think of suicide, it is typically the image of a teenager tragically taking their own life. Statistically, however, elderly white males have a higher suicide rate than any other age group (Sahyoun, et al, 2001). This rate has increased dramatically in recent years, with a 25 percent jump between 1981 and 1997. Mental health professionals are working to address this growing problem among the elderly.

**PROMOTING WELLNESS**   Although health behaviors earlier in life have set an elderly person on a certain course, there are still some behaviors that older adults can adopt to improve health and increase longevity. Although sleep becomes difficult in older adulthood, sleeping an average of seven to eight hours can improve mental health and ability (Shoenborn & Danchik, 1980). Not skipping breakfast, controlling weight, and exercising are other activities that improve health. In general, the same health behaviors that are recommended throughout life still apply in late adulthood.

*Pause and Process:*

1. What causes a stroke?

2. Compare and contrast embryonic stem cells and somatic stem cells.

# COGNITIVE DEVELOPMENT DURING LATE ADULTHOOD

*LEARNING OBJECTIVES:*

*1. Characterize the cognitive development during late adulthood*

*2. Describe information-processing during late adulthood*

*3. Explain changes in language during late adulthood*

**Elderly**

The term describing individuals in late adulthood who are sixty-five years of age or older.

**Late adulthood**

The eighth stage of the life span and final stage of adulthood; traditionally, the stage begins at age 65 or retirement from the work force and continues until near-death.

**Ageism**

Unreasonable or irrational beliefs about aging and older individuals.

**Gerontophobia**

The unreasonable and irrational fear of the elderly; related to ageism.

Late adulthood is the stage of life in which people are known as the **elderly**. This period of the life span is characterized by declines that occur in association with advanced aging in almost all aspects of development. Old age, or **late adulthood**, extends from age sixty-five until the processes of dying and near-death are initiated. Surprisingly, to many, this stage of the life span is a dynamic period with unique challenges and problems.

Our culture generally promotes youthfulness. No one, we are told, really looks forward to old age or wants to grow old; instead, it is an unfortunate consequence of being human. Our impressions of aging and the aged are based on misleading information and are largely negative, and often times, false. In fact, many individuals look forward to growing old with their spouse and seeing their grandchildren and great-grandchildren born.

Social scientists refer to this negativism about aging and the elderly as **ageism** (Neugarten, 1970) or **gerontophobia** (Kuhn, 1978). Both terms describe an attitude toward the elderly and the aging process that is at best indifferent and at worst unreasonable and filled with irrational fear. This attitude is due in part to historical influences, segregation of the elderly, and lack of positive in-depth experiences with them.

*In Asian cultures it is common to have three or more generations living together in a household. (iStock)*

Asian cultures have had decidedly different beliefs about this part of the life span (Martin, 1988). In many of these cultures, such as Japan and Korea, the extended family was the traditional family form, with three or more generations living together in a household. Today, however, the Western model seems to be infiltrating these cultures. Many elderly people no longer expect to live with their children. The Western practice of putting infirm elderly people into nursing homes is no longer unthinkable in many Asian cultures. Most are grappling with the same issues Western cultures face. The elderly group is growing, both numerically and as a percentage of the population, in most advanced societies of the world.

Nevertheless, attitudes about aging and the elderly may be becoming more positive because longevity statistics have convinced younger people that they are likely to survive to an advanced age themselves. Certain structural changes are contributing to this change in thinking. We are no longer a "frontier" society where youth is valued for providing the strength, energy, and force needed to build civilization and industry. We are an advanced society, and thus more ready to appreciate the leadership and wisdom of older people.

Late adulthood presents some formidable challenges to maintaining an active, stimulating mental life. Change in the ability to process information place people of advanced age at a disadvantage, though most are able to compensate for these losses in functioning. Moreover, most elderly people do not suffer from an organic brain condition, which is the prime factor limiting or terminating developmental progress.

# BEYOND PIAGET'S THEORY: COGNITIVE DEVELOPMENT DURING LATE ADULTHOOD

**Selection, optimization, and compensation (SOC) theory**

A theory that examines how selection, optimization, and compensation assist individuals in coping with the declines associated with aging. It is often considered a theory of successful aging.

## *Optimization and Compensation*

In Chapter 8 we learned about **selection, optimization, and compensation theory (SOC theory)**, which stresses that adaptive aging involves maximizing gains and minimizing losses (Baltes, Lindenberger & Staudinger, 1998). Selection refers to the process of choosing appropriate goals. These goals can be behavioral, cognitive, or socioemotional in orientation. Optimization refers to the attention, energy, effort, and persistence given to achieving the selected goal. In optimal conditions, the goal is to achieve one's highest level of ability. Compensation involves mobilizing necessary resources to achieve the goal, particularly in the face of losses or decline. As an individual ages, there is a shift in energy from growth to maintenance and regulation of decline in abilities.

Research using the SOC theoretical framework has found that the focus of goals shifts with age (Freund, 2006). Freund (2006) conducted a study to compare the performance of young adults and older adults in regards to commitment and achievement when performing a sensorimotor task on a computer. The sensorimotor task had two conditions: an optimization condition and a compensation condition. In the optimization condition the stated goal was to perform the task as well as possible. In the compensation condition the stated goal was to prevent losses/decline in the task. Young adults showed greater persistence and motivation in the optimization task, whereas older adults showed greater persistence and motivation in the compensation task. This study supports the idea that goal focus and motivation shift with aging.

## *Wisdom*

Wisdom is not a well-defined or well-understood concept. In fact, until recent years it was a topic that was considered more in the realm of philosophy or theology than psychology. However, wisdom is an area of research that is gaining popularity in human development. Although there is no agreed upon definition of wisdom in human development, a leading theorist in the field conceptualizes it as involving "some balance of intelligence and creativity" (Sternberg & Lubart, 2001, p. 515).

There are three broad categories for approaches to studying and understanding wisdom in human development: **philosophical approaches**, implicit-theoretical approaches, and explicit-theoretical approaches (Sternberg & Lubart, 2001). The philosophical approaches value the history of wisdom discourse in philosophy. They look to the ancient philosophers and analyze their conceptualizations of wisdom.

**Implicit-theoretical approaches** "search for an understanding of people's folk conceptions of what wisdom is" (Sternberg & Lubart, 2001, p. 501). Here, the goal is to develop a concept of wisdom that is seen as true by the average person, as opposed to some objective, quantifiable construct.

The **explicit-theoretical approaches** largely seek to empirically study wisdom in an objective and scientific way (Sternberg & Lubart, 2001). However, the individual perspectives within this broad category vary in their methodology and conceptualizations of wisdom.

Overall, wisdom is viewed as an important asset in constructing integrity in late adulthood. Wisdom is the perspective the elderly need to understand their own reality and make sense of their lives. It is the product of introspection, and goes far beyond what people learn through education and reading.

**Philosophical approaches**

Values the history of wisdom discourse in philosophy.

**Implicit-theoretical approaches**

Approach to the study of wisdom that investigates people's common understanding of wisdom

**Explicit-theoretical approaches**

Seek to empirically study wisdom in an objective and scientific way.

*Pause and Process:*

1. How does motivation differ between younger and older adults?

2. What is wisdom?

# INFORMATION-PROCESSING IN LATE ADULTHOOD

In middle adulthood we saw that many aspects of information-processing begin to decline. This trend continues in late adulthood. Declines in the speed of cognitive processing are similar to the slowdown in physical development in late adulthood (Birren, Woods & Williams, 1980). These declines parallel the changes taking place in the brain and central nervous system at this time of life. Speed in the ability to process information and in reaction time gradually declines, for example, because of less efficient functioning of the neurological and sensory bases of cognition as well as the desire of elderly people to be accurate (Madden, 2001; Salthouse, 1985).

## Attention

Speed of processing and the ability to control what one pays attention to are vital for daily functioning (Rogers & Fisk, 2001; Tun & Lachman, 2008). We already know that processing speed declines as the brain ages, but what about attention? When attention is assessed globally, attention for complex tasks appears to decline over time. However, college-educated adults perform complex attention tasks at levels for individuals who are ten years younger than them, but uneducated. Let us restate this. Have you ever seen the TLC show How to Look *10 Years Younger*? In this show, people who look rather tired and worn for their age are given a complete makeover. By the end of the show, they look ten years younger. Back to attention, the people who went to college have the attention ability of people ten years younger. Pretty cool, huh? This college-effect persists up to the age of seventy-five (Tun & Lackman, 2008). However, this was a study focusing on complex attention measured in a global fashion. Is there a way to tease apart aspects of attention, much like there are different aspects of memory? If so, would these different aspects show the same effects with aging, or differ?

There is evidence to suggest that there are at least two systems devoted to attention in the brain: the **posterior attention system** and the **anterior attention system** (Posner & Peterson, 1990). The posterior attention system includes brain areas such as the posterior parietal cortex and the thalamus (Posner, 1995). This attention system appears to be important for being able to pay attention to visual information, particularly visual space. The anterior attention system includes brain areas such as the prefrontal cortex. This attention system appears to be important for being able to direct and choose what a person wants to pay attention to among a multitude of stimuli. Research using both cognitive tasks and electroencephalogram (EEG) recordings seems to indicate that the aging process affects the anterior attention system more than the posterior attention system (West & Bell, 1997). This would mean that older adults maintain their ability to pay attention to and cognitively process visual information, whereas the ability to focus attention on one particular aspect of a task would show decline.

Not all news is bad news, however, when discussing attention in old age. **Parallel processing** refers to the ability to cognitively process and complete two or more tasks at a time. One study found that older adults outperform young adults in parallel processing when at least one task is automatic (Lien et al., 2006). For example, word recognition is automatic in elderly adults—who have been reading for decades. Older adults are able to complete a word recognition task and another visual or auditory task better than young adults. However, it must be kept in mind that this superior parallel processing in older adults is "restricted to processes for which older adults have greater cumulative experience" (Lien et al., 2006, p. 443). In other words, for older adults to excel in parallel processing, they must be completing tasks that they have been doing for years.

## Memory

Among the most striking mental changes are those that affect memory (Poon, 1985). Undoubtedly, these changes are frustrating for both older people and those with whom they interact. A slowing, shrinking brain plays a large role in memory decline.

**Posterior attention system**

Includes the brain areas such as the posterior parietal cortex and the thalamus.

**Anterior attention system**

Includes the brain areas such as the prefrontal cortex.

**Parallel processing**

Refers to the ability to cognitively process and complete two or more tasks at a time.

As individuals progress through late adulthood, they have a harder time recalling more recent events in memory, although maintaining the ability to recall information in the distant past. As they advance in age, elderly people may find that they can describe in intricate detail a high school prom attended sixty years ago, but have difficulty remembering what they had for breakfast that morning.

There may be increasing difficulties with the steps required for processing memory. Usually, three steps are involved in this process: (1) encoding information, (2) storing the information into long-term memory, and (3) retrieving the information for use at a later time. Older people appear to be less efficient in the first step. Encoding is organizing information so that it can be stored in a particular way in the brain (e.g., associating a person's name with an object). Elderly people are also much slower than younger people at retrieving information. Their memory searches take up longer periods of time as they generate and think about alternatives and options. This slowdown is influenced by a person's level of mental activity (Craik, Byrd & Swanson, 1987), for those who remain intellectually stimulated seem to have fewer problems with retrieving information. Hence, if you want to slow down your own memory decline in old age, stay mentally active (e.g., read, do puzzles, write, etc.). The contributions of an enriched lifestyle to maintaining the neurological aspects of mental functioning cannot be overestimated (Hopson, 1984).

Beyond decline in the process of memory, the picture is complex for what specific aspects of memory decline during adulthood. **Episodic memory**, working memory, source memory, and explicit memory all show decline in late adulthood (Backman, Small & Wahlin, 2001). Episodic memory is memory of specific life events. **Working memory** is the workbench where simultaneous cognitive processes can be attended to and handled (Baddeley, 1986, 1996; Kemper & Mitzner, 2001). **Source memory** is the ability to remember where you heard, saw, or learned something. **Explicit memory** is the information that you purposely try to recall, such as when you tell a friend about a movie you just watched.

**Semantic memory**, or your general knowledge, appears to remain intact. However, it appears that it becomes more difficult to retrieve semantic knowledge in late adulthood (Backman, Small & Wahlin, 2001). **Procedural memory** is knowledge about how to perform certain tasks, like riding a bike, driving a car, or even walking. This type of memory remains largely unchanged with aging (Backman, Small & Wahlin, 2001). **Implicit memory**, or unconscious memory that guides your behavior, thoughts, and feelings, also appears to remain intact. **Primary short-term memory** is the conscious process of keeping information in short-term memory. This aspect of short-term memory appears to remain stable in late adulthood (Backman, Small & Wahlin, 2001).

## Intelligence

The aged person is often pictured as forgetful, intellectually slow, and indecisive. IQ scores among people of very advanced age (older than eighty) do show a constant decrease closely associated with the aging process. Scores on the portions of tests that measure problem-solving and speed of performance show a greater decline than scores on the parts that measure verbal skills (Salthouse, 1985). Other information suggests that the lower level of

**Episodic memory**

Specific life event memories.

**Working memory**

The workbench where simultaneous cognitive processes can be attended to and handled.

**Source memory**

The ability to remember where you heard, saw, or learned something.

**Explicit memory**

The information that you purposely try to recall, such as when you tell a friend about a movie you just watched.

**Semantic memory**

General knowledge.

**Procedural memory**

Knowledge about how to perform certain tasks, like riding a bike or driving a car, or even walking.

**Implicit memory**

Unconscious memory that guides your behavior, thoughts, and feelings.

**Primary short-term memory**

The conscious process of keeping information in short-term memory.

functioning in late adulthood is due more to encountering problems that are new and unfamiliar than to a general diminishment in problem-solving abilities (Labouvie-Vief & Schell, 1982).

A dual-process model of intellectual changes has been proposed to explain what happens to mental functioning in late adulthood (Dixon & Baltes, 1986). This model describes two aspects of intelligence: (1) the mechanics dimension, which resembles fluid intelligence; and (2) the pragmatics dimension, which relates to practical thinking, applying knowledge and skills gained from experience, and wisdom in solving problems of everyday life.

According to this model, elderly people decline in the mechanics dimension because the information that fuels this aspect of intelligence was gained in childhood and has limited usefulness in old age. Pragmatic intelligence, however, is extremely useful at this time of the life span. It can be likened to the wisdom gained from experience. This dimension is much broader in scope than crystallized intelligence. In late adulthood, it enhances the quality of life and may well play an important part in helping elderly individuals achieve the sense of integrity discussed by Erikson.

What about crystallized and fluid intelligence in old age? The trends in cognition that began in middle adulthood continue through the years of late adulthood. Crystallized intelligence skills remain stable or even increase during this stage. As you will recall, these are skills acquired through education, such as verbal comprehension. However, fluid intelligence (involved in processing information) declines during this stage.

*Pause and Process:*

1. How does attention change in late adulthood?

2. Describe intelligence and the aging process.

# LANGUAGE

## *Changes in Language Skills*

One aspect of our language ability is reading. In fact, reading can be quite demanding on our information-processing skills, for we must visually make sense of the written symbols we are seeing, comprehend the words that these symbols make up, assess the syntax and semantics of the sentence, integrate the sentences into a cohesive whole, and consider the context and pragmatics of what has been read (Kemper & Mitzner, 2001). Does aging impact our ability to read? If yes, how and why does aging impact our reading skills?

Working memory, processing speed, and inhibition are three areas that decline in older adulthood. It has been widely researched what role these three areas play in contributing to declines in language-processing tasks such as reading (Kemper & Mitzner, 2001). Working memory can be conceptualized as "where active thinking occurs ... Its operation involves combining information coming into sensory memory with information stored in long-term memory and transforming that information into new forms" (Siegler, 1998, p. 67). Working memory is thought to have limited capacity and consists of different components for different types of information and processing (Kemper & Mitzner, 2001; Siegler, 1998). Declines in working memory are correlated with declines in reading (Kemper & Mitzner, 2001). Specifically, declines in working memory appear to impede older adults' ability to keep information in memory for future recall or application.

Beyond declines in working memory, older and younger adults differ in their strategies when reading for comprehension (Kemper & Mitzner, 2001). Although younger and older adults are more similar than different in how they allocate their time when reading a passage, older adults spend less time pausing at sentence boundaries than younger adults. Further, younger adults focus more on new vocabulary words and concepts, whereas older adults rely on the context and connecting new information with old information.

**Inhibitory deficit theory** suggests that a decline in inhibition plays a primary role in reading decline (Kemper & Mitzner, 2001). Inhibition cognitive processes allow a person to focus on relevant information and ignore irrelevant information. Some research supports this idea showing that older adults get distracted by irrelevant information when reading passages of text. However, other research has failed to support this theory. More research is needed to clarify the role of inhibitory processes in reading.

One interesting, yet controversial, area of research focuses on off-target verbosity. **Off-target verbosity** is the tendency for some older adults to drift to irrelevant topics during conversation (Kemper & Mitzner, 2001). Several areas have been found to be correlated with off-target verbosity, including:

- Lower frontal lobe functioning in the brain
- Psychosocial stress
- Extroverted personality
- Smaller social networks
- Lower social support

Although some research supports the above correlations, other research has not found such results (Kemper & Mitzner, 2001). Similarly, inhibitory deficit theory has been offered as one explanation for off-target verbosity; however it is not the only explanation out there. Alternative theories suggest that perhaps older adults misread cues during conversation or speaking tasks, causing them to engage in more off-target verbosity and monologues about their rich and diverse past.

## Elderly-Directed Speech

**Elderspeak** refers to a style of speech used when speaking with older adults. It is similar to infant-directed speech in which speech is simplified, spoken slowly, and higher in pitch

**Inhibitory deficit theory**

A theory that examines what aspects of cognitive processing declines with age, and what aspects of cognitive processing remain stable.

**Off-target verbosity**

The tendency for some older adults to drift to irrelevant topics during conversation.

What is the communicative predicament of aging?

**Elderspeak**

A style of speech used when speaking with older adults. It is similar to infant-directed speech in which speech is simplified, spoken slowly, and higher in pitch and intonation.

and intonation (Kemper & Mitzner, 2001). Elderspeak is tied to negative stereotypes of the elderly, as well as real communication needs (such as reduced hearing ability).

Elderspeak can lead older adults to develop an "old" identity (Kemper & Mitzner, 2001). This has been correlated with lower levels of self-esteem, cognitive decline, and social isolation. These outcomes further increase the use of elderspeak by those around the older person. This nasty downward spiral of communication is referred to as communicative predicament of aging, a term coined by Ryan and colleagues in 1986. Elderspeak is especially noticeable in convalescent homes, where the environment is typically accepting of such speech.

*Pause and Process:*

1. How is memory related to reading?

2. Explain what off-target verbosity is.

# SOCIOEMOTIONAL DEVELOPMENT DURING LATE ADULTHOOD

**LEARNING OBJECTIVES:**

1. *Characterize emotional development and adjustment during late adulthood*
2. *Describe understanding of self with others during late adulthood*
3. *Explain psychosocial development during late adulthood*

Late adulthood can take up a considerable portion of the individual's life span. One does not immediately become elderly upon reaching sixty-five. Aging is a gradual process and the changes come slowly. Nonetheless, late adulthood is a time of continued decline. This general trend is most noticeable in the physical changes that occur with increasing regularity. The role changes that accompany old age are also very noticeable. These are primarily in work and family roles. Although people are often able to compensate for these declines, adjustments are made more slowly and less frequently as aging advances.

The developmental tasks of late adulthood differ from those of earlier stages of the life span in two fundamental ways. First, there is a focus on the maintenance of one's life and quality of lifestyle rather than on discovery and creativity (Havighurst, 1972). Second, the tasks center on happenings in the person's own life rather than on what is occurring in the lives of others (Hurlock, 1980).

The developmental tasks of late adulthood are vast and varied. People at this stage are challenged to adjust to their increasing dependency upon others, shrinking financial resources that lead to changes in lifestyle and living conditions, and the need to develop new interests (Havighurst, 1972). Furthermore, they may need to cope with the death of a spouse and continue to meet social and civic obligations.

Many people find old age a time of contradictions. On the one hand, they experience deterioration in physical skills and functioning. On the other hand, personal and social growth continues through the years of late adulthood. Thus continuity and change rule even in late adulthood.

Adjusting to changes is a central challenge of social development at this time of life. Most people know that limitations can impede development during their lifetime. Some limitations originate from within, others from the environment. In late adulthood, people become aware of more limitations, but as in all other stages of life, successful adjustment and adaptation can lead to healthy development in late adulthood.

*Coping with the death of a spouse and shrinking financial resources is a challenge for some. (iStock)*

# PSYCHOSOCIAL DEVELOPMENT

**Sense of integrity versus a sense of despair**

The final psychosocial attitude proposed by Erikson; it is developed in late adulthood. *Integrity* is characterized by completion of the task of integrating the various aspects of the self-concept and identity and evaluation of one's life as having been a meaningful and fulfilling experience. *Despair* is characterized by a feeling of loss, disappointment, and deep dissatisfaction with the way one's life was lived.

## Integrity Versus Despair

The final stage of psychosocial development during the life span described by Erikson (1950, 1964) is the fulfillment, result, and culmination of all preceding stages. Acquiring a **sense of integrity versus a sense of despair** is the challenge of late adulthood.

One achieves a sense of integrity by identifying with all humanity. An individual who acquires the attitude of integrity has come to understand and accept the meaning of life. This person recognizes and values the uniqueness of his or her existence during a particular historical time in a particular culture. Included in this understanding is an acceptance of the temporal limits of life. This acceptance produces serenity at the end of life.

Healthy psychosocial change in old age allows one to complete the integration of the various aspects of the self that has occupied so much developmental attention during the life span. There is wholeness to the self, characterized by acceptance of who one is, how one's life has been lived, the decisions one has made in guiding and directing life changes, and the consequences of these decisions.

Psychosocial development in late adulthood challenges people to reconcile the realities of life with what they had hoped for, dreamed about, or desired. Elderly people spend time reflecting upon and evaluating the course of their lives. They examine the essentials of the self or personality, no longer preoccupied with how they should act and no longer holding false beliefs about what is right or appropriate behavior.

Those who achieve the attitude of integrity attain a stronger sense of satisfaction than they experienced earlier in their life. They see the future as less urgent and everyday temporal existence as more important. For many people at this stage, life is lived for the self rather than for others, as it was in the past.

This period of life is one of renewal. Individuals continue to grow until they die. This new growth is motivated by the courage to face virtues, strengths, weaknesses, and shortcomings.

The attempt to integrate the self at this time of life can also lead to a sense of despair derived from a feeling of loss, disappointment, and deep dissatisfaction with the way one has lived one's life. Elderly people with this attitude feel regret and apology. They fear and dread death. Disgruntlement marks their psychosocial demeanor rather than serenity. They may have a pervasive sense of "If only …" related to intense feelings of remorse about decisions and choices made at crucial points in their life span: "If only I had gone to college, I might have had a better job and been happier in my life," for example, or "If only I hadn't had an abortion, I would have had a child to love and someone to love me right now."

It is a terrible thing to gain such insights about one's life when there is very little time left to make changes that might lead to personal happiness. Despair is psychologically crippling, producing hopelessness, depression, and even desperation.

Most people apparently establish a sense of integrity rather than a sense of despair at this time in life (Neugarten & Neugarten, 1987). This attitude is derived from a sense of satisfaction, apparently not only with decisions made earlier in life, but also with present circumstances. These can include having a sound enough financial base to live decently following retirement and having reasonably good health (Brubaker, 1990). Satisfaction with life in the present also depends on the measure of control an elderly person has of their daily affairs. This is why those who reside in nursing homes often have less positive self-concepts and feel less satisfaction with their lives than elderly people living in their own homes (Kovar, 1988).

*Pause and Process:*

1. How does a person obtain a sense of integrity?

2. Why might someone obtain a sense of despair?

# EMOTIONAL DEVELOPMENT

## *Emotional Adjustment to Aging*

**Affect intensity**

One's intensity of emotion.

**Affect intensity,** or one's intensity of emotion, is one area of emotional development studied in respect to adulthood and aging (Magai, 2001). Although studies have differed in their results, one rather consistent finding is that older adults report experiencing less intense negative emotions than younger adults. Other studies have found that older adults report lower levels of intensity for both negative and positive emotions. This means that older adults still experience negative and positive emotions, but less intensely.

Beyond intensity, what about frequency of emotions in adulthood? Studies have found that the experience of positive emotions either remain stable or increase across the adult years and remain so until very late adulthood (Magai, 2001). Other studies have found that the experience of negative emotions is highest for younger adults or no difference across adulthood. In summary, older adults are similar to younger adults in their emotional experiences, or experience slightly more positive emotions and less negative emotions.

In comparison with younger adults, older adults appear to be more complex in their emotional experiences (Carstensen et al., 2000; Magai, 2001). This is referred to as **affective complexity**. However, other research indicates that there is an increase in affective complexity between early adulthood and middle adulthood, and then a decline in late adulthood. Affective complexity and emotion regulation has been correlated with healthy coping in adulthood.

**PERSONALITY**    Personality can be defined as "individual differences in diverse human characteristics, such as traits, goals and motives, emotion and moods, self-evaluative processes, coping strategies, and well-being" (Ryff, Kwan & Singer, 2001, p. 477). There are many theories of personality. In previous adulthood chapters, we focused on the big five traits theory of personality. In this chapter, we are going to learn about some classical theories of personality that focus on older adults.

*Peck's Views of Personality Adjustments*    Psychologist Robert Peck (1968) extends Erikson's views about psychosocial adjustments in late adulthood (which we will discuss at the end of the chapter). Peck believes that three main adjustments occur in the personality development of elderly people. First, **ego differentiation versus work-role preoccupation** refers to the adjustments that must be made to retirement from work roles. The person must adapt to shifting the primary personal identity away from a work role to other means of self-identity in other roles.

Second, **body transcendence versus body preoccupation** refers to the necessity of finding happiness and satisfaction in relating to others and in creative or mental endeavors for healthy development to occur. Unhealthy development takes place when a person focuses on their bodily concerns and experiences distress due to the increasing decline in physical functioning.

Third, elderly individuals are challenged to master **ego transcendence versus ego preoccupation**. This involves recognizing and accepting one's impending death by living life as fully as possible and attempting to make life more secure, more satisfying, and more meaningful for those who will survive after one's death. The psychosocial tug at this time in life is to be intensely introspective. Although this is important, it cannot become the

## Affective complexity

The appearance of older adults having more complex emotional experiences compared with younger adults.

## Ego differentiation versus work-role preoccupation

The adjustments that must be made to retirement from work roles.

## Body transcendence versus body preoccupation

The necessity of finding happiness and satisfaction in relating to others and in creative or mental endeavors for healthy development to occur.

## Ego transcendence versus ego preoccupation

Recognizing and accepting one's impending death by living life as fully as possible and attempting to make life more secure, more satisfying, and more meaningful for those who will survive after one's death.

consuming interest and focus of one's psychological attention at the expense of others who are important in one's life.

*Personality Types among the Elderly*    Several researchers propose that successful adjustment in late adulthood relates to an individual's personality type (Neugarten, Havighurst & Tobin, 1968; Reichard, Livson & Peterson, 1962). Four basic types are identified in addition to role activities that describe these.

An **integrated** personality type in late adulthood may be thought to resemble the sense of integrity described by Erikson. These individuals are well-adjusted and flexible in their approach to life. Three basic variations can be observed in this pattern: (1) reorganizers are involved in a wide range of activities and rearrange their lives by substituting new roles for those that are terminated, (2) the focused participate in moderate levels of activity and reserve their attention and energies for only a few roles, and (3) the disengaged maintain low levels of activity but attain a high degree of personal satisfaction.

Others have an **armored-defended** personality type. These individuals strive to maintain control of their lives. This is accomplished by implementing various means to defend against anxiety and other threats to one's well-being. Two variations may be observed among such individuals: (1) those who hold-on cling as long as possible to activities typical of middle-aged people such as continuing employment past the time when many others have retired, and (2) those who are constricted or who become withdrawn from activities and people as a defense against the ravages of advanced age.

Others are seen as **passive-dependent** personality types. Two basic variations may be observed: (1) those that are succorance-seeking, or having strong dependency needs on others, and (2) those who are apathetic or having little or no interest in others or in their surroundings. Others are seen as **unintegrated** in personality. These individuals may be described as experiencing dementia. They have poor control of emotional expression and disorganized thought processes.

**ATTACHMENT**    Compared with other stages of the life span, relatively little research has focused on late adulthood and attachment. What little research is out there seems to indicate that there is a shift in attachment style profiles during late adulthood (Magai, 2001). Although the majority of young adults are secure in their

## Integrated

A personality type in late adulthood that may be thought to resemble the sense of integrity described by Erikson.

## Armored-defended

A personality type where the individual strives to maintain control over their lives.

## Passive-dependent

A personality type with two basic variations that may be observed: (a) those whom are succorance-seeking in having strong dependency needs on others; and (b) those who are apathetic or having little or no interest in others or in their surroundings.

## Unintegrated

A personality type where individuals may be described as experiencing dementia.

*A shift to avoidant attachment is seen at this stage.
(iStock)*

attachment style, there is an increase in the avoidant (a.k.a., dismissive) attachment style with age. The rise in avoidant attachment styles in old age may have something to do with an increase in the number of losses during this period. Many elderly individuals have had to cope with the loss of family and friends; a dismissive attachment style may be an adaptation that attempts to help them prepare for future losses.

*Pause and Process:*

1. Explain how emotions change in late adulthood.

2. Why may attachment change in the elderly?

# SELF WITH OTHERS

## *Leisure Time*

Whereas leisure time is constricted in middle adulthood due to family and work obligations, leisure time increases in late adulthood. Retirees are able to appreciate a party for the pure social aspect of it (Hansen, Dik & Zhou, 2008). Like younger adults, older adults enjoy leisure activities such as entertainment, shopping, and gardening. Older adults do differ in terms of leisure interests for more active forms of leisure. Whereas younger and middle age adults see physical, competitive, and outdoor activities as separate interests, older adults do not make such a distinction. It appears that these types of activities converge into one general category for elderly adults.

## *Moral Development*

Values, spirituality, and religiosity are three terms that typically fall into the category of moral development. Earlier in this textbook, we discussed the stages of moral development proposed by Kohlberg, in this section we will discuss what is known about religiosity across the life span.

**Values** can be defined as a person's belief about what is right and what is wrong. Some values are secularly-based, whereas others are derived from one's religion. For example, Hitler had the secularly-based value that a Jew's life was worth little and should be eliminated and that life should be valued only in specific types of people. In contrast, the Judeo-Christian value in the sanctity of all human life is based on their religion. Hence, values can be vastly different dependent upon what they are based.

**Spirituality** can be conceptualized as a sense of connectedness with God (or some other higher spiritual being). **Religiosity** incorporates this spirituality, but includes the additional dimension of living the faith. Said another way, a spiritual person may feel that they have a close relationship with God, but never go to church. A person high in religiosity, however, has both this close relationship with God and acts on this belief by going to

**Values**

A person's belief about what is right and what is wrong.

**Spirituality**

A sense of connectedness with God (or some other higher spiritual being).

**Religiosity**

Incorporates spirituality, but includes the additional dimension of living the faith.

church and engaging in other sorts of religious activities. Gallup polls consistently find that most Americans consider religion an important part of their lives.

In general, children and adolescents that are raised in families that value social responsibility and compassion internalize these values. These children and adolescents engage in higher levels of volunteerism and show greater compassion for those in need than children not raised in such homes (Flanagan, 2004). Children and adolescents raised by religious parents tend to internalize this belief system (Paloutzian & Park, 2005), especially if the parent-child relationship is good (Dudley, 1999; Ream & Savin-Williams, 2003; Streib, 1999).

*Religion plays an important role for moral development. (iStock)*

Numerous research studies (for example, see Cotton et al., 2006; Fehring et al., 1998; King & Benson, 2005; Oser, Scarlett & Butcher, 2006; Ream & Savin, Williams, 2003; Sinha, Cnaan & Gelles, 2007; Youniss, McLellan & Yates, 1999) have examined the impact of religiosity on youth development. Religiosity in adolescence is associated with many positive outcomes, including:

- Meaning and direction in life

- Healthy coping skills

- Higher levels of community service/volunteer work

- Lower drug use, alcohol use, and smoking rates

- Lower delinquency rates

- Lower risk-taking behavior

- Lower rates of premarital sex

- Less depression

- Better grades and less truancy

- Healthier role models

- Greater empathy for those in need

Religion continues to be important and associated with positive outcomes in adulthood. Although it is important to keep in mind that not all Americans consider religion important in their lives, for more than 70 percent of adults it is an important part of their identity and daily living (Brim, 1999). Religiosity typically increases with aging (Wink & Dillon, 2002). Women usually report higher levels of religiosity than men, and African Americans and Latinos report higher levels than European Americans (Idler, 2006; Taylor, Chatters & Levin, 2004). Religiosity is associated with better physical health, mental health, longevity, and coping skills (for example, see Gillum & Ingram, 2007; Hummer et al., 2004; Krause, 2006; McCullough & Laurenceau, 2005; Yoon & Lee, 2007). Some research indicates that by increasing meaning in life, religiosity results in a greater sense of well-being (Steger & Frazier, 2005).

## *Family Influences*

**Widowhood**

A label applied to both men and women who survive the death of a spouse.

Just as adult children must adjust to the death of a parent, many individuals must adjust to the death of a spouse in middle or late adulthood. **Widowhood** is the label applied to both men and women who survive the death of a spouse. Due to differences in life expectancy and death rates, more women become widows than men. Becoming a widow can change a woman's identity, especially if her role as a wife has been a central aspect of her family role. This usually does not hinder a woman's personal development, however. In our culture, there are many alternatives available to women on becoming widows (Anderson, 1984; Houser & Berkman, 1984; Lopata, 1973). Options include remarriage, retraining or education for jobs, reentry into the work force, participating in voluntary organizations and activities, devoting additional time and effort to parenting and grandparenting roles, and so on.

Some of the more pressing needs of women who become widows include (1) expressing grief and experiencing the bereavement process with family and friends; (2) meeting companionship needs, especially if being alone is occurring for the first time in adulthood; (3) being protected from the "good" intentions of people wanting to give advice that is often contradictory in nature; (4) gaining experiences that build self-confidence, personal skills, and competencies; and (5) gaining assistance in reengaging socially with others (Lopata, 1973).

Men who are widowed appear to have different reactions and adjustment issues (Robinson & Barret, 1986; Marshall, 1986). Loneliness and depression may be central problems for middle-aged men because they are less likely than women to have a close, intimate, confidante relationship with someone other than their spouse. These men may experience other difficulties on becoming single at mid or late life. This suggests that these men are poorly prepared to care for themselves (performing household tasks, for example). When widowhood coincides closely with retirement at the end of middle adulthood, losing a spouse tends to destroy plans that have been made for late adulthood involving a couple rather than a single individual. This devastating change in status and situation can be manifested in the high likelihood of suicide observed among men who are widowed (U. S. Bureau of the Census, 1990). Not all men who are widowed react in this manner, however. Healthy ways of adjustment can occur when men become more invested in their grandparenting role or use the experience as a means for initiating personal growth opportunities.

## Friendship and Social Support

Friendship and social support continues to be important in late adulthood (for example, see Antonucci, 2001; Carstensen, 1991, 1998, 2006). Friendship provides psychological intimacy and camaraderie. Social support can be emotional in nature (such as holding a person's hand while undergoing kidney dialysis), or instrumental in nature (such as driving a person to doctor appointments). However, the structure of social support networks tends to change in late adulthood.

Socioemotional selectivity theory is a theory that has been developed by Laura Carstensen (e.g., 1991, 1998, 2006) during the past couple of decades. This theory emphasizes that older adults optimize their social networks. They allow peripheral relationships to end, actively end negative relationships, and focus attention and energy on happy, fulfilling relationships. So although older adults may have smaller social networks, they are often filled with rewarding relationships that will stand the test of time.

## Adjusting to Retirement

The average person will spend 10–15 percent of their life in retirement. This developmental event that typically occurs in late adulthood is both a process and a significant change in social status (Atchley, 1971, 1976; Dudley, 1991).

What six lifestyle patterns did Cox and colleagues find for older adults?

Cox and colleagues (2001) recently identified six lifestyle patterns in older adults:

- Older adults who continue to work full-time

- Older adults that continue to work part-time

- Older adults that retire and become active in volunteer work

- Older adults that retire and become active in recreational/leisure activities

- Older adults that retire and later return to work full-time

Several factors influence when someone will retire (Kovar & LaCroix, 1987). First, the age at which a person is eligible for receiving Social Security benefits influences when many people are able to retire. This age is slowly being increased to sixty-four for early retirement and sixty-seven to receive full Social Security benefits. Second, economic and social conditions influence the decision to continue working or to retire in late adulthood. Third, the ability to do work-related activities is an important determinant of when people retire. Inability to perform certain physical acts required in some jobs—stooping, kneeling, crouching, lifting, carrying, walking, climbing stairs, standing on the feet for extended periods of time—often hastens the decision to retire.

Traditionally, retirement has been viewed as a debilitating experience that people dread. In this view, the work ethic is strongly ingrained in our culture as the primary means for achieving and maintaining identity in adulthood, that retirement becomes equal to social suicide (Beck, 1982; Brubaker, 1990). It is becoming apparent, however, that what people miss when they retire is the income from work rather than the social status and interaction with others (Anrig, 1988; Kirkpatrick, 1989). When people know they will be financially secure during retirement, they frequently are more willing to leave the work force and to do so at earlier ages (Crone, 1990; Flatermayer, 1991).

*Those that develop hobbies and friendships adjust best to retirement. (iStock)*

Many actually look forward to retirement as a time of renewal and personal growth (Palmore & Maeda, 1985). Individuals that retire of their own free will are happier with the transition than individuals that are forced to retire due to health or occupational age limits (Cox et al., 2001). Additionally, individuals that are healthy, well-educated, married, and with a good social support system typically adjust best to retirement (Elovainio et al., 2001; Price & Joo, 2005). Further, individuals who are flexible and develop hobbies, interests, and friendships that are not work related typically adjust best to retirement (Atchley, 2007; Baehr & Bennett, 2007; Cox et al., 2001; Eisdorfer, 1996; Zarit & Knight, 1996). Volunteer work is also related to greater happiness after retirement (Cox et al., 2001).

It is important to make adequate preparations to ensure a sufficient financial base for retirement. Many people start making plans during the latter part of early adulthood or during early middle age for this life change (Bergstrom, 1990; Kirkpatrick, 1989; Weistein, 1991). In general, men spend more time planning for retirement than women (Jacobs-Lawson, Hershey & Neukam, 2005). One important consideration is whether certain employment benefits such as medical and death insurance, disability coverage, annuities, and investments will continue after retirement.

**RETIREMENT AS A PROCESS**    Although many conceive of retirement as an event (like a birthday party), it is actually a process (Atchley, 1976; Kim & Moen, 2002). According to Atchley (1976), retirement is a process that progresses in stages. Adapting successfully to this significant life event depends on a variety of factors, such as loss of finances, loss of self-esteem, loss

### Pre-retirement

The period preceding retirement during which a person may make plans and arrangements for his or her retirement.

### Honeymoon phase

Immediately following the formal event of retirement, most people feel happy and peaceful initially as they experience the independence of retirement.

### Disenchantment stage

In the aftermath of the honeymoon phase, emotional depression settles in as people come to realize that they have actually fully withdrawn from a constant and fulfilling social role in their lives.

### Reorientation stage

People attempt a more realistic appraisal of their options for the future.

### Stability stage

The routine of established behaviors.

### Termination

The last stage which is marked by a role shift from retiree either to being employed again or to being disabled in advanced age.

of work-related social contacts, loss of meaningful tasks, and loss of a reference group. The stages Atchley describes relate to changes in the retired person's adult social role. The length of time each stage takes and the tasks that need to be accomplished during it differ from person to person. Moreover, not everyone goes through all these stages.

- **Pre-retirement** is composed of two substages. In the first, people have negative attitudes about retirement and see it as an event far into the future. In the second, people realize that retirement is fast approaching and that they must finalize their plans for it if they are to adjust successfully. People may now participate in pre-retirement programs and seminars and seek out others who have already retired for information.

- The **honeymoon phase** immediately follows the formal event marking retirement. Most people feel happy and peaceful initially as they experience the independence of retirement. This is characteristically an active and busy period in which people participate in projects and tasks they have delayed for lack of time.

- The **disenchantment stage** is the aftermath of the honeymoon period. It is a time of emotional depression as people come to realize that they have actually fully withdrawn from a constant and fulfilling social role in their lives. They often feel "at loose ends" with little direction in their lives. They have plumbed the depths of "free time" and are now ready to explore more useful and resourceful ways to spend their days. Many people take up volunteer work, travel, or hobbies as meaningful and enjoyable ways to use their time.

- In the **reorientation stage**, people attempt a more realistic appraisal of their options for the future. Some discover that volunteer activity is too much like actual work, is without meaningful reward, and withdraw from it. Others find that hobbies are boring but find volunteer activity highly rewarding. Finding one's niche and developing routines helps at this time.

- In the **stability stage**, people have a routine of established behaviors. These assist them to cope with other changes taking place in their lives. At this stage of retirement, people have come to accept the new role and personal identity of retiree. In doing so, they acquire a new set of behavioral standards, social norms, and expectations.

- The last stage, **termination**, is marked by a role shift from retiree either to being employed again or to being disabled in advanced age. In the latter instance, people can no longer function independently. However, nearly seven million adults return to work after retirement, with about one-third doing so for financial reasons. This means that two-thirds return to work for reasons that are not financial and they report general happiness about this decision (Putnam Investments, 2006).

*Pause and Process:*

1. What are some adjustments that need to be made when widowed?

2. What are the stages in the retirement process?

# SUMMARY

1. Late adulthood is the final stage of life span development. It begins at age sixty-five or at retirement and continues until death. Five subcategories of late adulthood are recognized: the young-old (sixty to sixty-nine years), the middle-aged old (seventy to seventy-nine years), the old-old (eighty to eighty-nine years), the very old-old (ninety to ninety-nine years), and the centenarians (one hundred or more years). The developmental tasks of late adulthood focus on adjusting to the aging process and to role changes occurring at this stage of life.

2. Major physical changes in late adulthood are continued reductions in height and weight, dramatic changes in sensory functioning, restricted movement owing to changes in muscle and bone functioning, decreased heart output and rising rates of cardiovascular disease and stroke, decreased elasticity of the lungs, a variety of digestive disorders, increased genitourinary disorders, and less efficient functioning of the brain and central nervous system. Quality of life in late adulthood can be affected positively or adversely by diet, health, and exercise.

3. Two major disorders that can develop during late adulthood are Alzheimer's disease and Parkinson's disease. Both diseases are progressive and involve brain cell impairment and death. Currently, there is no cure for these diseases; however, stem cell research is seen as a hopeful field for the eventual development of a cure. There are two main branches of stem cell research: embryonic stem cells and somatic stem cells. As of the writing of this textbook, embryonic stem cell research has produced no treatments or cures, and is prone to tissue rejection and tumor growth. Conversely, somatic stem cell research has developed dozens of treatments and cures without the controversy surrounding embryonic stem cell research. There is great promise in somatic stem cell research in the future development of treatments and cures for late adulthood diseases and disorders.

4. Research within the framework of selection, optimization, and compensation theory has found that goals and motivations shift across adulthood. Older adults show greater persistence on compensation tasks than younger adults.

5. Wisdom is an area that is gaining attention in human development research. Three broad categories of approaches to wisdom are the philosophical approaches, the implicit-theoretical approaches, and the explicit-theoretical approaches.

6. Two principle cognitive changes occur in late adulthood: a decline in general processing speed and significant decline in some areas of memory. Attention shows decline in some areas. Crystallized intelligence continues to increase or remain stable, whereas fluid intelligence continues to decline during this stage.

7. Language skills are dependent upon the brain, processing speed, memory, and other cognitive processes. We see decline in language abilities as other cognitive processes decline. Two interesting topics of research in language and late adulthood are off-target verbosity and elderspeak.

8. Late adulthood is a time of change and adaptation. Developmental tasks during late adulthood include adjusting to retirement and reduced income, death of a spouse, meeting social and civic obligations, and establishing satisfactory physical living arrangements.

9. Emotional development continues in late adulthood, with the intensity of emotions decreasing, and the experience of positive emotions increasing. Peck theorized that personality goes through three developmental adjustments in late adulthood: ego differentiation versus work-role preoccupation, body transcendence versus body preoccupation, and ego transcendence versus ego preoccupation.

There is a shift in attachment style in late adulthood, with more adults developing an avoidant attachment style.

10. Religiosity throughout life is associated with positive outcomes. In adulthood, individuals higher in religiosity seem to have better physical and mental health, longevity, and coping skills.

11. Many individuals will lose a spouse in late adulthood. Men and women typically have different issues that they must deal with during this time of grief. Friendships and social support continue to be important throughout late adulthood, with social networks changing in structure.

12. Retirement is more of a process than a one-time event. Individuals that are financially secure, well-educated, healthy, married, and active in volunteerism or other hobbies adjust best to retirement and experience the greatest satisfaction. After a honeymoon period upon retirement, individuals must seek meaning and validation through volunteer work or hobbies. Eventually, individuals either seek re-employment or complete termination from work activities.

13. Erikson proposes that people develop a sense of integrity versus despair during late adulthood. Integrity is acquired by completing one's personality integration and coming to terms with the way one's life was lived, the decisions that were made, and the consequences of those decisions. Despair may emerge if this evaluation results in feelings of loss, disappointment, and deep dissatisfaction.

## SELF-QUIZ

1. How is the population changing in terms of the percentage of older adults?
2. Describe the age divisions for older adults.
3. What does senescence mean?
4. How does weight and height change in late adulthood?
5. Highlight some changes in the muscular and skeletal systems in late adulthood.
6. What changes do we see in the cardiovascular system in late adulthood?
7. What are some early warning signs for a stroke?
8. Explain the course of Alzheimer's disease.
9. Where are somatic stem cells obtained from?
10. What are some medical reasons why somatic stem cells may be preferable to embryonic stem cells?
11. Define ageism in your own words.
12. How is SOC theory important in understanding cognitive changes in late adulthood?
13. Compare and contrast the three approaches to studying wisdom.
14. What can people do to slow down the decline in attention for complex tasks?
15. How do the posterior attention system and the anterior attention system differ in their attentional processes?
16. Describe parallel processing in late adulthood.
17. List the aspects of memory that show decline and the aspects of memory that remain relatively intact.
18. Compare and contrast the dual-process model of intelligence with the idea of fluid and crystallized intelligence.
19. What are some reasons that reading ability declines in late adulthood?
20. What is the communicative predicament of aging?
21. Describe the developmental tasks of late adulthood.
22. What is meant by affect intensity and how does it relate to late adulthood?
23. How is aging related to affective complexity?

24. Describe the four personality types discussed in the chapter (i.e., integrated, armored-defended, passive-dependent, and unintegrated).
25. Why might attachment change in late adulthood?
26. What are values?
27. Explain the difference between spirituality and religiosity.
28. Discuss the issues that women and men face in widowhood.
29. What six lifestyle patterns did Cox and colleagues find for older adults?
30. What factors help determine if an individual achieves a sense of integrity versus a sense of despair?

## TERMS AND CONCEPTS

# CHAPTER 10

# The Dusk of Life

(iStock)

## OUTLINE

### PHYSICAL ASPECTS OF DYING AND DEATH

- What is death?
- Dying trajectories
- Leading causes of death
- Advanced directives
- End of life care

### COGNITIVE ASPECTS OF DYING AND DEATH

- Development and understanding death
- Communication during the dying process
- Coping with dying

### SOCIOEMOTIONAL ASPECTS OF DYING AND DEATH

- Emotional aspects of death
- Social aspects of death

**What is it like to die?** Will it hurt? Will I know what is happening to me? Will I lose all control of my behavior and ability to react to my surroundings? Will I know what is happening to me after I die?

Many of us have asked ourselves such questions from time to time. One of the authors had the unfortunate experience of viewing a *Tales from the Crypt* episode way too early in life in which a person died, but was still consciously trapped in his body. This person then suffered the humiliation of hearing the coroner comment about his body and "friends" make derogatory remarks about him at the viewing, without anyone being aware of his consciousness and him being unable to communicate his consciousness. Ultimately, he faced cremation and his final demise. This author has often shuddered at the thought of this character's fate if he had been buried instead of cremated.

All kidding aside, although what happens after death is open to religious beliefs, it is possible to describe what it is like to die. Within this chapter, we will discuss the process of dying, especially as it is experienced by those with a terminal illness who know they are dying. Researchers are just beginning to investigate dying phenomena, so our knowledge about the dying process is in the earliest stages. This information is presented here to provide a better understanding of a process that is difficult not only to research, but also to describe to others by those who are experiencing it.

# PHYSICAL ASPECTS OF DYING AND DEATH

*LEARNING OBJECTIVES:*

*1. Gain awareness of the different definitions of death*

*2. Understand the different trajectories of death*

*3. Explain what the leading causes of death are at different stages of life*

*4. Describe what an advanced directive is and why it is important*

*5. Discuss end of life care*

# WHAT IS DEATH?

**Death**

The cessation of all observable or measurable physical signs of life (physical death); related aspects are social and psychological death.

**Death** can occur at any point in the life span. This event is most commonly associated with old age, however, and is an anticipated part of late adulthood. For these reasons, the elderly are more aware of, even preoccupied with, death than younger people (Kalish, 1987; Kalish & Reynolds, 1981). The elderly generally are less anxious about death than young adults (Belsky, 1984). When asked how they would spend the last six months of their life, for example, young adults state they would devote the time to doing things they haven't yet done and to traveling. Older people report they would spend the time with family and friends and in contemplation. The elderly seem to fear the process of dying and the pain that is often associated with it rather than death itself (Belsky, 1984; Kimmel, 1980). However, changes in the perception of prescribing pain medication to the dying is allowing for more pain control at the end of life. Although doctors used to shy away from generously prescribing pain medication in general, they now accept that there is little fear in prescribing it to those facing death because developing an addiction to pain medication is not really a concern (Lague, 2000).

## *Biological Death*

**Biological death**

Historically defined as when the heart stopped beating and respiration ceased, leading to the cessation of brain function.

There is no longer one universally accepted definition of biological death. **Biological death** historically has been defined to take place when a person can no longer breathe independently and the heart stops beating. Until recently, the cessation of respiration and heartbeat resulted in death of the brain and all observable or measurable physical signs of life (Black, 1953; Blank, 2001; Monaghan, 2002; Rubenstein, Cohen & Jackson, 2006). However, advances in medical care have given us the technology for resuscitating heartbeat and respiration, even if the brain is irreparably damaged.

The ability to assist an individual with respiration or electrically restart the heart coincided with the development of immunosuppressant drugs that allows for organ transplantation. Hence, the need for fresh organs for transplant sparked discussion in the mid-1900s about redefining biological death to include brain death (Monaghan, 2002).

Brain death can occur due to injury or disease (Blank, 2001; Monaghan, 2002; Rubenstein, Cohen & Jackson, 2006). Two early problems with which medical personnel grappled, with was how to define brain death and how to actually test for it with any precision. A group commonly referred to as the Harvard Medical School committee created the early criteria to define and diagnose brain death in 1968. These criteria stated that brain death results in the following:

- Unresponsiveness and unreceptivity (lack of consciousness)

- Lack of spontaneous movements or breathing

- Lack of reflexes

Although not part of the official criteria, it was recommended that doctors check for lack of electrical activity in the cerebral cortex (using an EEG) prior to a final judgment of brain death. Additionally, twenty-four hours should be given to see if any improvement is shown prior to removal of any life-support machines (Blank, 2001; Monaghan, 2002; Rubenstein, Cohen & Jackson, 2006).

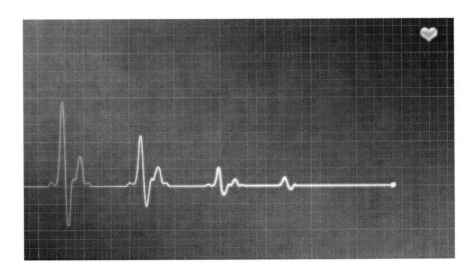

*Biological death happens when a person is no longer able to breathe on their own, and their heart stops beating. (iStock)*

These criteria were electively used by some physicians; however, many physicians still struggled with deciding when to declare someone brain dead and allow organ removal for donation.

The Uniform Determination of Death Act (1980) was the first comprehensive statement developed by governmental agencies, the American Medical Association, and the American Bar Association defining when death can be declared. Below is the definition:

> An individual who has sustained either (1) irreversible cessation of circulatory and respiratory functions, or (2) irreversible cessation of all functions of the entire brain, including the brainstem, is dead. A determination of death must be made in accordance with accepted medical standards (NCCUSL, 1980).

This definition seems to make sense. If your heart is not beating, you are not breathing, and your entire brain is not functioning, you are considered dead. However, proponents of "brain death" balk at this definition because it requires **"whole-brain" death** (Monaghan, 2002). Instead, they seek a **"partial-brain" death** or "cerebral brain" death definition. They seek a definition that would allow for a breathing person who lacks consciousness (presumably permanently) to be considered dead; therefore, allow for organ donation before the blood ceases to pump through the veins. Such partial-brain death can happen when the cerebral cortex loses functionality, but the brain stem continues to function in support of vital functions such as respiration (Blank, 2001; Monaghan, 2002; Rubenstein, Cohen & Jackson, 2006). Such individuals can be referred to being in a persistent vegetative state (PVS) or in a minimal conscious state (MCS).

An international survey that included seventy countries with guidelines about diagnosing brain death found that all of them require irreversible coma and a lack of reflexes associated with brain stem activity (Monaghan, 2002). However, there was considerable variation as to whether cessation of breathing was necessary, how long a patient should be watched for improvement, and how many doctors must concur that the individual is brain dead. Whereas some countries require a confirmatory EEG showing lack of electrical activity in the brain, the United States does not. Hence, a person may be considered dead in one country, yet be considered alive in another.

This redefinition of death that the medical community is currently struggling with will probably persist for the foreseeable future. As with any controversial topic, thorny questions will need to be addressed if movement continues in the direction of allowing for a "partial-brain" death criteria for death (Blank, 2001; Monaghan, 2002; Rubenstein, Cohen & Jackson, 2006). For example, if a person is partially-brain dead, should they be given pain killers as the organs are removed for donation? "Some patients with dead brain stems still have electrical activity in other parts of their brains, and there is no way to test whether the pain perceiving area of the brain still functions" (Monaghan, 2002, p. 38). Should people in a persistent vegetative state be considered brain dead, because there is little to no hope of them regaining consciousness though the body may function for years in some cases? If yes, should they be given anti-anxiety medications when on the table having their organs removed? Research indicates that people in a persistent vegetative state con-

**Spotlight**

How did the Uniform Determination of Death Act define death?

**"Whole-brain" death**

When the entire brain, including the brain stem, ceases to function.

**"Partial-brain" death**

A concept that a person should be considered dead if his or her higher cognitive functions no longer function, but parts of the brain still function and maintain physical life.

tinue to show physiological emotional responses in reaction to events in their environment (such as a relative's presence) (Dolce et al., 2008). Can you imagine their distress if they realize their death is imminent as their organs are removed? What about individuals in the last stage of Alzheimer's, the profoundly retarded, or anencephalic infants? Should they be considered dead or even have their death hastened by withholding life-sustaining measures such as food? Will parents of the anencephalic infants (those born without most of the brain) be pressured to allow the organs to be harvested immediately and cheated of what little time they have to cradle their child before natural death? Should there be a conscience clause so that individual religious beliefs can be honored even if it runs counter to the medical culture? Finally, how much say should third-party payers have in the determination of death? If a person uses the conscience clause to maintain care for their "dead" loved one, will insurance be required to pay? Such issues make you wish for the days when cessation of heartbeat and breathing were the only criteria for determining death.

## Psychological Death

**Psychological death**

The thoughts and emotional reactions experienced by the dying individuals and his or her family and friends.

**Psychological death** refers to the thoughts and emotional reactions experienced by the dying individuals and his or her family and friends. Most people who know they are dying react in particular ways that allow death to function as a developmental event in their life span. We will discuss psychological death in more depth later in this chapter.

## Social Death

**Social death**

The institutional and cultural events and processes that relate to a deceased individual, such as the bereavement of family and friends and the funeral.

**Social death** refers to the institutional and cultural events and processes that relate to a deceased individual, such as the bereavement of family and friends and the funeral. The execution of the deceased person's will is one of the few widely accepted societal events to formally recognize an individual's death. There are few institutionalized practices that accompany someone's death. The funeral or memorial service, although no longer universally practiced in our society, is diverse in form and purposes. We will discuss different religious traditions in dealing with death in the next chapter.

> *Pause and process:*
> 1. Distinguish between biological death, psychological death, and social death.
> 2. What is the difference between whole-brain death and partial-brain death.

# DYING TRAJECTORIES

Each person experiences death in his or her own way. Death may come suddenly and unexpectedly, as the result of a fatal accident, or it may be a long process, as with terminal diseases such as cancer and AIDS.

**Trajectory**

A path or pattern that is followed in some particular process.

**Dying trajectories**

Representations of the duration and shape of the dying process.

**Duration**

The time the process takes.

**Lingering pattern**

The person is expected to die, but clings to life for an indeterminate time.

**Short-reprieve pattern**

The person's death is postponed unexpectedly, but only for a short period of time.

**Abrupt-surprise pattern**

The person is expected to recover but dies instead.

**Suspended-sentence pattern**

The person is discharged from medical care and is expected to live for several years.

**Entry-reentry pattern**

The person experiences steady decline, but is able to remain at home between periods of hospitalization.

**Acute phase**

A crisis accompanied by high personal stress associated with increasing awareness of the inevitability of death.

A **trajectory** is a path or pattern that is followed in some particular process. **Dying trajectories** differ depending on the circumstances that cause and influence this condition. Researchers outline the process of dying in several ways. For example, Glasser and Strauss (1968) see dying as a passage from being alive to being dead. They refer to dying trajectories as representations of the duration and shape of the dying process. **Duration** refers to the time the process takes, and shape to its rate of progression. Some patterns of dying are of short duration, whereas others are extended. The shape of some dying patterns is a steady decline, whereas that of others alternates between times of decline and times of stability. Glasser and Strauss outlined five dying trajectories:

1. The **lingering pattern** in which the person is expected to die, but clings to life for an indeterminate time.

2. The **short-reprieve pattern** in which the person's death is postponed unexpectedly, but for only a short period of time.

3. The **abrupt-surprise pattern** in which the person is expected to recover but dies instead.

4. The **suspended-sentence pattern** in which the person is discharged from medical care and is expected to live for several years.

5. The **entry-reentry pattern** in which the person experiences steady decline, but is able to remain at home between periods of hospitalization.

Among the terminally ill, dying may be experienced as a series of phases (see Figure 10-1). Three periods have been proposed (Pattison, 1977; Kaufman & Kaufman, 2006):

1. The **acute phase** is a crisis accompanied by high personal stress associated with increasing awareness of the inevitability of death.

2. In the **chronic living-dying phase**, the person adjusts to the idea of approaching death, and experiences a variety of feelings such as grief, fear of the unknown, and isolation.

3. The **terminal period** is characterized by withdrawal from others and general disengagement from the world.

| **FIGURE 10-1** | **PHASES OF DYING** |

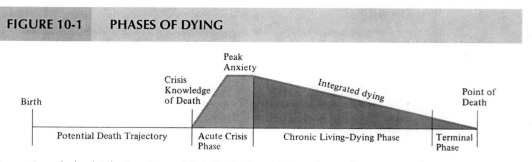

Source: From the book, *The Experience of Dying* by E. Mansel Pattison © 1977 by Prentice-Hall, Inc.

**Chronic living-dying phase**

The person adjusts to the idea of approaching death, and experiences a variety of feelings such as grief, fear of the unknown, and isolation.

**Terminal period**

Characterized by withdrawal from others and general disengagement from the world.

**Terminal decline**

The official term used to describe the accelerated cognitive degeneration as elderly individuals approach death.

Several researchers report that there are a number of indicators associated with the closeness of death (Bäckman & MacDonald, 2006; Lieberman, 1965; Lieberman & Coplan, 1970; MacDonald, Hultsch & Dixon, 2008; Reigel & Reigel, 1972). These indicators include a decline in the quality of cognitive functioning; a decline in the degree of introspection; a less aggressive self-image; a decline in intelligence test scores; and a decline in energy. These factors were often observed among people who died within one to three years of a terminal diagnosis.

**Terminal decline** is the official term used to describe the accelerated cognitive degeneration as elderly individuals approach death (MacDonald, Hultsch & Dixon, 2008). Longitudinal research has found that lower speed of cognitive processing and higher inconsistency of speed are measures predictive of impending death. What is unclear is the nature of the relationships between biological, neurological, and cognitive processes that allow for cognitive measures to predict death (Bäckman & MacDonald, 2006; MacDonald, Hultsch & Dixon, 2008). Bäckman and MacDonald are two developmentalists currently working to develop and test models to help explain the curious relationship between terminal decline and imminent death.

*Pause and Process:*

1. What is meant by a dying trajectory?

2. Define terminal decline in your own words.

# LEADING CAUSES OF DEATH

> *"When a person's death outshines his life it's a dad blame pity."*
> —*Dancing in Cadillac Light* **by Kimberly Willis Holt**

The above quote comes from an awarding winning novel for children, which focuses on a young girl's struggle with death and grief. Statistically, most of us will die of the common and expected illnesses that come with aging. However, one out of ten of us will die unexpectedly and suddenly (Lague, 2000). These unexpected, sudden deaths are those that tend to overshadow the person's life. The person is remembered for how they died, not for how they lived.

Further, the deaths of the young are particularly difficult to comprehend. "When the young precede elders in death it is an unnatural event. When children die, it is as if life's promise and potential has been abruptly terminated. We mourn their loss differently from those who have attained maturity and lived a full life" (Jalongo, 2005, p. 46). There is said to be no greater, all-consuming grief than that of a parent losing a child to death (Utne, 2005).

The leading causes of death change throughout the life span. Additionally, the leading causes of death vary according to historical time period, geographical location, ethnicity, and even gender. In this section, we will consider some of the leading causes of death in the United States in 2006 (the most recent data available at press time by the Center for Disease Control).

## *Death During Prenatal Development*

It is extremely difficult to have sound statistics on death during the prenatal period for two reasons. First, it is estimated that approximately 50 percent of zygotes miscarry prior to implantation; hence, many women who have miscarriages never even know they are pregnant (Vorvick, 2009). These early miscarriages can occur either due to natural causes (such as fertilization occurring in the uterus instead of in the fallopian tube) or due to unnatural causes such as the hormones in the birth control pill or "day after" pill. Second, approximately one million pregnancies are electively terminated through abortions each year in the United States; subsequently, it is impossible to know what percentage of those pregnancies would have resulted in natural fetal death (Figa-Talmanca & Repetto, 1988; Guttmacher Institute, 2005).

Of those pregnancies where women know they are pregnant and choose to continue the pregnancy, fetal death is divided into two periods. Unborn babies between conception and nineteen weeks of development are considered miscarried (sometimes called spontaneous abortion). Somewhere between 15–20 percent of all pregnancies miscarry during this period, with most occurring before seven weeks (Vorvick, 2009).

Those twenty weeks or beyond in prenatal development are considered stillborn (sometimes called fetal demise) (Lindsey, 2008). The death rate for stillbirths is approximately 6.9 deaths for every 1000 births, diagnosed by the absence of a heartbeat (Lindsey, 2008). The death rate for elective abortions is approximately 233 deaths for every 1,000 births (Gamble et al., 2008).

The cause of natural death during the prenatal period is unknown in up to 60 percent of all cases (Lindsey, 2008). When the cause can be identified, it can be placed in one of three categories: maternal causes, fetal causes, or placental pathology. The most common cause is chromosomal abnormalities in the baby (Vorvick, 2009). Other fetal causes include infection and congenital abnormalities (such as a heart defect) (Lindsey, 2008; Vorvick, 2009). Maternal causes include advanced maternal age, Rh disease, preeclampsia, hypertension, and diabetes (Lindsey, 2008). Placental causes include cord accidents, hemorrhages, and placental insufficiency. Regardless of the cause, the loss can be overwhelming to the expectant parents, which we will discuss in the section on grief.

## *Death During Infancy*

**Congenital anomalies**

Birth defects or chromosomal abnormalities that are incompatible with life.

If a child survives until birth, there are several factors that may lead to his or her death before the first birthday. The primary leading cause of death for infants is **congenital anomalies**. These are birth defects or chromosomal abnormalities that are incompatible with life and are responsible for 20.4 percent of infant deaths. A short gestation—or preterm birth—is the second leading cause of death, responsible for 17.0 percent of infant deaths. Sudden infant death syndrome (SIDS) is the third leading cause of death, responsible for 8.1 percent of infant deaths. Finally, maternal pregnancy complications (5.9 percent) and unintentional injury (4.0 percent) round out the top five leading causes of death in infancy. An unintentional injury is the official term for accidents. Suffocation is the most common cause of unintentional injury deaths, accounting for 73.5 percent of all unintentional deaths.

## *Death During Early Childhood*

Between the ages of one and five, the primary leading cause of death is unintentional injury, accounting for 35.4 percent of all early childhood deaths. Below are the major types of injuries leading to death for this age group:

- Motor vehicle accidents (31.2 percent of all unintentional injury deaths)
- Drowning (27.0 percent of all unintentional injury deaths)
- Fire or burn injuries (12.4 percent of all unintentional injury deaths)
- Suffocation (8.0 percent of all unintentional injury deaths)
- Pedestrian accidents (6.4 percent of all unintentional injury deaths)

Beyond those listed above, falls, being struck, natural/environmental events, poisoning, and firearms are some other categories that also contribute to unintentional injury deaths in early childhood.

The second leading cause of death is congenital anomalies, accounting for 10.8 percent of all early childhood deaths. Finally, **malignant neoplasms** (8.9 percent), homicide (7.7 percent), and heart disease (3.4 percent) round out the top five leading causes of death. Malignant neoplasm is the technical term for cancer.

**Malignant neoplasms**

Technical term for cancer.

*The leading cause of death during early childhood is unintentional injuries such as motor vehicle accidents. (iStock)*

## *Death During Middle and Late Childhood*

Unintentional injury is also the primary leading cause of death between the ages of six and twelve. However, the subcategories and percentages shift slightly for this age group. Below are the major types of injuries leading to death in middle and late childhood:

- Motor vehicle traffic accidents (53.7 percent)

- Drowning (10.5 percent)

- Fire or burn injuries (9.3 percent)

- Other land transportation accidents (such as buses) (5.7 percent)

- Suffocation (4–6 percent)

Beyond the leading causes of unintentional injury deaths listed above, the same sorts of events and occurrences listed in the early childhood section also contribute to these deaths in middle and late childhood (e.g., firearms, falls, and poisoning).

The second leading cause of death in middle and late childhood is malignant neoplasms (16.9 percent). Congenital anomalies (5.8 percent), homicide (5.2 percent), and heart disease (3.5 percent) round out the top five leading causes of death for this age range.

## *Death During Adolescence*

Unintentional injury is the primary leading cause of death in adolescence (44.5 percent). However, as was true in middle and late childhood, the subcategories and percentages shift once again. Below are the subcategories responsible for the most unintentional injury deaths in adolescence:

- Motor vehicle traffic accidents (70.7 percent)

- Poisoning (7.1 percent)

- Drowning (6.5 percent)

- Other land transportation accidents (2.6 percent)

- Suffocation (2.2 percent)

The second leading cause of death in adolescence is homicide (13.7 percent). Sadly, suicide is the third leading cause of death in adolescence (11.0 percent). Finally, malignant neoplasms (6.9 percent) and heart disease (3.6 percent) round out the top five leading causes of death for this stage of the life span.

## *Death During Early Adulthood*

Because the leading causes of death shift between emerging adulthood (eighteen to twenty-five years of age), and the rest of early adulthood (twenty-six to thirty-nine years of age), each substage will be considered separately.

The top five leading causes of death in emerging adulthood are the same as those in adolescence, although the percentages are different. Unintentional injuries account for 45.8 percent of all deaths in emerging adults, with motor vehicle traffic accidents and poisoning accounting for the vast majority of them. Homicide is the second leading cause of death in emerging adulthood, responsible for 16.3 percent of all deaths. Finally, suicide (12.3 percent), malignant neoplasms (4.6 percent), and heart disease (3.4 percent) round out the top five leading causes of death for emerging adults.

For the latter part of early adulthood, unintentional injuries are once again the primary leading cause of death; however, this category accounts for less deaths overall at only 29.9 percent. As in emerging adulthood, motor vehicle traffic accidents and poisoning account for the vast majority of these deaths. Interestingly, the second leading cause of death changes for this age group to malignant neoplasms (11.1 percent). Suicide is still the third leading cause of death (10.7 percent), although heart disease (10.0 percent) becomes a close fourth leading cause of death. Homicide (8.2 percent) is the fifth leading cause of death for those between the ages of twenty-six and thirty-nine.

## *Death During Middle Adulthood*

For the first time since infancy, unintentional injuries are not the leading cause of death. For those between the ages of forty and sixty-five, malignant neoplasms are the primary leading cause of death at 31.5 percent. Heart disease is the second leading cause of death at 21.7 percent. Unintentional injuries drop to the third leading cause of death at just 7.6 percent. Curiously, poisoning edges out motor vehicle traffic accidents as the predominant cause of unintentional injury death. Falls also increase to be the third most likely type of unintentional injury death. Diabetes and cerebrovascular disease tie as the fourth and fifth leading cause of death in middle adulthood, each at 3.6 percent of all deaths. **Cerebrovascular disease** is a category for death related to the blood vessels in the brain, such as a stroke.

**Cerebrovascular disease**

A category for death related to the blood vessels in the brain such as a stroke.

## *Death During Late Adulthood*

As in early adulthood, the leading causes of death change between the beginning part of late adulthood and the latter part of late adulthood. For this reason, we will consider those between the ages of sixty-five and seventy-five separate from those aged seventy-five and beyond. We will see chronic respiratory disease appear in the top five for the first time, which refers to illnesses such as emphysema, asthma, or chronic obstructive pulmonary disease.

Between the ages of sixty-five and seventy-five, the primary leading cause of death is malignant neoplasms at 34.7 percent. Heart disease comes in second at 23.9 percent. Chronic respiratory disease (7.3 percent), cerebrovascular disease (4.8 percent), and diabetes mellitus (3.9 percent) round out the top five leading causes of death for this age range. You may have noticed that for the first time since birth, unintentional injury is not one of the top five leading causes of death. Indeed, it slips to the sixth position for this age range, accounting for just 2.1 percent of all deaths. However, within this small percentage, motor vehicle traffic accidents and falls nearly tie as the leading cause for such accidental deaths.

For those seventy-five and older, heart disease becomes the primary leading cause of death at 30.5 percent. Malignant neoplasms are the second leading cause of death at 18.3 percent. Cerebrovascular disease (7.2 percent), chronic respiratory disease (5.7 percent), and Alzheimer's disease (5.0 percent) complete the list for the top five leading causes of death. Unintentional injury falls to ninth on the list at 2.1 percent of all deaths, with influenza/pneumonia, diabetes mellitus, and nephritis coming in at sixth, seventh, and eighth respectively. However, of those who die of unintentional injury during this age span, 50.9 percent die due to a fall, whereas 13.5 percent die from a motor vehicle traffic accident.

## A Historical Perspective on Causes of Death

We have just learned about the leading causes of death across the stages of the life span. However, it is sometimes interesting to see the leading causes of death from a historical perspective. There have been significant changes in the leading causes of death in the United States since the turn of the twentieth century. Prior to 1900, communicable diseases such as tuberculosis, influenza, and diphtheria were responsible for the majority of deaths (see Table 10-1). By the late 1960s, these diseases accounted for less than 1 percent of all deaths in the United States, quite a shift in statistics. As discussed above, the leading causes of death in mid to late adulthood have shifted from communicable diseases to those classified as chronic degenerative diseases. These include the malignant neoplasms, cardiovascular diseases, chronic respiratory diseases, and cerebrovascular diseases discussed previously.

| TABLE 10-1 | THE LEADING CAUSES OF DEATH IN THE UNITED STATES; 1900 | |
|---|---|---|
| **RANK** | **CAUSES OF DEATH** | **PERCENTAGE OF ALL DEATHS** |
| 1 | Influenza and pneumonia | 11.8 |
| 2 | Tuberculosis (all forms) | 11.3 |
| 3 | Gastroenteritis | 8.3 |
| 4 | Diseases of the heart | 8.0 |
| 5 | Vascular lesions affecting the central nervous system | 6.2 |
| 6 | Chronic nephritis | 4.7 |
| 7 | All accidents | 4.2 |
| 8 | Malignant neoplasms (cancer) | 3.7 |
| 9 | Diseases of early infancy | 3.6 |
| 10 | Diphtheria | 2.3 |

Source: National Center for Health Statistics (19830). *Monthly Vital Statistics Report, 37*, No. 13. Washington, DC: U.S. Government Printing Office.

Changes have also occurred in the place where most individuals die. Prior to 1900, death commonly occurred in the home. Medical care was administered there rather than in a clinic or hospital. As medical technology became more complex, medical care for the dying shifted from the home to an institution such as a hospital. This change has affected how families participate in the dying process of a family member, which will be discussed later in this chapter.

*Pause and Process:*

1. How do the causes of unintentional injury death change across the life span?

2. How do you think cognitive processes and emotional control during adolescence contribute to unintentional injury, homicide, and suicide being the top three causes of death during this age span?

# ADVANCED DIRECTIVES

**Advanced directive**

A written document explicating what medical measures you would like employed if you lose the capacity to make such decisions. You can also elucidate who you would like to make these decisions for you if you become incapacitated.

**Basic nursing care**

Basic care provided to all hospital patients (such as food and cleaning of wounds).

## *Advanced Directives*

An **advanced directive** is a "document that allows you to designate under what conditions you would want life-sustaining treatment to be continued or terminated" (Lague, 2000, p. 139). If you are ninety years old and your heart stops beating, do you want CPR to be administered? If you are thirty-five years old and suffer a heart attack, do you want CPR to be administered? Do you want a respirator if you are unable to breathe on your own? In an advanced directive you can define what treatments you would want administered and what treatments you would want withheld given any specific circumstance or situation (Lague, 2000; McGirt, 2005). Feeding tubes become a complicated ethical and moral issue, because they are not technically a medical treatment (Orr & Meilaender, 2004). Instead, feeding tubes (which provide basic nutritional nourishment) are **basic nursing care** along the same lines as getting a bath or cleaning a wound.

*Pause and Process:*

1. What is an advanced directive?

2. What is the difference between a medical treatment and basic nursing care?

# END OF LIFE CARE

*"What is a good death? ... lack of fear, openness to spirit, and love of community ... those same qualities that lie at the heart of a good life."*

**—Utne, 2005**

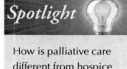

How is palliative care different from hospice care?

There has been a steady increase in the last few decades in the number of people who die in an institution rather than at home. Most deaths occur in a hospital or a nursing home (U.S. Bureau of the Census, 1991b). The manner in which death is managed in these institutions is sometimes criticized as impersonal and callous toward both the dying individual and that person's family. Palliative and hospice care has helped address these criticisms.

## Palliative Care

**Palliative care**

Treatment for those suffering from illness that focuses on pain management, symptom control, and emotional support in the face of stress.

**Palliative care** is treatment for those suffering from illness that focuses on pain management, symptom control, and emotional support in the face of stress (Center to Advance Palliative Care, 2009). Palliative care can be provided at any point during an illness, whereas hospice care (discussed below) can be provided only to those with less than six months to live. Palliative care also provides emotional support for the family of the ill person.

## Hospice Care

**Hospice care**

Care that is provided in a person's home or hospice home to those with less than six months to live.

**Hospice care** has emerged in recent years as a humane way to assist dying individuals and their families. The original meaning of hospice was a rest station for weary travelers, or place of healing for those injured in the Crusades during the Middle Ages. Today, hospice care is a way of providing end-of-life care to those with less than six months to live. This care can be provided in the person's home or in a hospice home; however, keep in mind that it has provided many the opportunity to die at home in accordance with their wishes. Palliative care is always a part of hospice care (Center to Advance Palliative Care, 2009).

Within the hospice environment, the dying person is made as peaceful and comfortable as possible (Lague, 2000). Medication to control pain is given only when the person wishes to control the sensations. The dying person's autonomy is carefully respected, and the dignity of the person is uppermost in the minds of the staff providing care.

One of the principal goals of hospice agencies is to help dying people have a "happy death"—one that is typically conceptualized to be as free of pain as possible and in which the dying make major decisions regarding their care and well-being. Further, a happy death usually involves an atmosphere that embraces the value of the dying person, promotes closure and family interactions, and honors religious beliefs (Kehl, 2006).

Hospice agencies also provide support to families after the death. Families given such assistance in working through the bereavement process have been found to manage their grief more effectively and achieve a better adjustment than families whose loved ones died in a hospital (Crawford, 1980).

## Physician-Assisted Suicide

**Physician-assisted suicide**

When a doctor provides a patient with the means to commit suicide at the patient's request. The doctor provides the lethal dose, but the patient is responsible for actually taking the medication.

**Physician-assisted suicide** is a topic of growing discussion in the United States today, despite the fact that the majority of medical and nursing associations are against legalizing it. It can be defined as when a doctor provides a patient with the means to commit suicide at the patient's request (Harrigan, 2000).

Oregon was the first state to legalize physician-assisted suicide with the 1997 Death with Dignity Act. People with less than six months to live may request a lethal dose of medication, which two physicians must approve (Yeoman, 2003). You would think that uncontrollable pain would be the leading cause for such requests; remarkably, that has never been cited as the reason for the request (Nightingale Alliance, 2003). Instead, every applicant has cited psychological and social reasons for seeking the lethal dose, with 94 percent citing the loss of independence as the major factor (Nightingale Alliance, 2003; Yeoman, 2003).

Physician-assisted suicide falls under the broader spectrum of euthanasia. **Euthanasia** is the willful ending of a life that is not a consequence of a disease, illness, or injury (Harrigan, 2000). Voluntary euthanasia is when a patient requests to die and the doctor administers the lethal dose. As mentioned above, physician-assisted suicide is when a patient requests to die, the doctor provides the lethal dose, but the patient is responsible for actually taking the medication. **Non-voluntary euthanasia** is when a doctor administers a deadly dose of medication without the patient requesting it. All three are considered active forms of euthanasia.

There is a long history of euthanasia in the modern world. Euthanizing the socially and physically undesirables was so common in the 1930s in Germany that it was openly discoursed in their medical journals (Harrigan, 2000). Many mentally disabled and physically disabled individuals were victims of nonvoluntary euthanasia, as were individuals of certain ethnic or religious groups.

The Netherlands is one European country with a long history of legal euthanasia (Nightingale Alliance, 2003; Watt, 1994). Studies show that between 50–64 percent of all individuals euthanized in the Netherlands were conducted without the explicit request of patients. Indeed, it is reported that more than ten thousand citizens in the Netherlands

### Euthanasia

The willful ending of a life that is not a consequence of a disease, illness, or injury.

### Non-voluntary euthanasia

A doctor administers a deadly dose of medication without the patient requesting it.

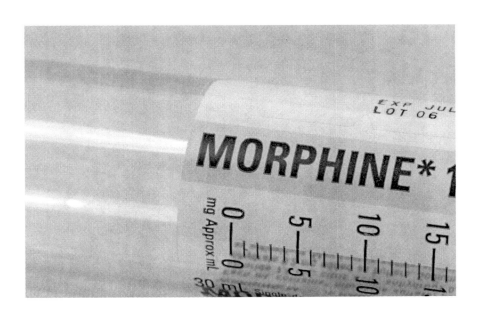

*Palliative care focuses on pain management and symptom control. (iStock)*

carry a "Do Not Euthanize Me" card in their wallet in the event they have the misfortune of needing emergency care. There are growing reports of newborns and infants with disabilities being euthanized without parental request (*Associated Press,* 2005; Nightingale Alliance, 2003). Further, the chronically depressed are considered worthy candidates for physician-assisted suicide. In recent years, 9 percent of all deaths in the Netherlands were due to some form of euthanasia (that is almost one out of every ten deaths). With great consequence for the study of development we watch the brewing intense debate about euthanasia and physician-assisted suicide in the United States.

*Pause and Process:*

1. What are the various forms of active euthanasia?

2. What is the most common reason the people of Oregon request a physician-assisted suicide?

# COGNITIVE ASPECTS OF DYING AND DEATH

**LEARNING OBJECTIVES:**

1. *Explain how the understanding of death changes with cognitive development.*
2. *Discuss communication strategies for interactions with dying individuals.*
3. *Discuss how an individual copes when facing his or her own death.*

Benjamin Franklin once remarked that the only things certain in life are death and taxes. It is perhaps the certainty of death that motivates us to avoid thinking of it, preparing adequately for it, and understanding its place in the life span. Most people have great difficulty comprehending that one day they will cease to be alive on this planet. The desire for life makes death seem the antithesis of our purposes for living and continuing to deal with the challenges of life. Yet death and dying are as important as birth in the growth and development of an individual.

**Dying** and death may be the last taboo topics of discussion in our society. Our ideas about the process of dying, what death is like, what happens after death, the treatment of the body after death, and the reactions of people to someone's death have only recently come to be discussed openly, if still with some trepidation. Covering dying, death, and bereavement in a life span textbook are important for a few reasons. Dying, like being born, is recognized today as a stage in the life span. It is an event that must be faced by everyone someday. It has its own particular developmental tasks, not only for individuals, but for families as well. Dying and death present both with changes that call for a series of adjustments and means for coping with these changes. Our greatest fears often are of things and events that we do not understand. By learning about death and the process of dying, we may humanize this experience and, in turn, further humanize the experience of living (Kimmel, 1980).

**Dying**

The complex process leading to death, characterized by an individual's particular dying trajectory.

# UNDERSTANDING DYING AND DEATH

## *General Awareness and Acceptance of Death*

Those who are dying perhaps realize what is happening and accept the inevitability of death. People differ, however, in how they cope with this inevitability. Psychologically, acceptance is a willing embrace of reality. It is awareness of "the way it is," the final step in dealing with the dying process. Liebermann and Coplan (1970) suggest that individuals first confront the issue of personal death in middle age. Elderly people appear to have resolved this issue or are in the process of realizing that death is not so far off. In one sense, this realization is a significant step toward the development of the sense of integrity described by Erikson (1950). The relation between advancing age and fear of impending death is demonstrated graphically in a study by Bengston, Cueller, and Ragan (1977). In middle age, people start to deal with their growing awareness of death, then gradually become less afraid of death through the years of adulthood. Children may experience dying as a developmental task in different ways, depending upon their age and the cause of their dying.

Individuals can be expected to experience certain needs as part of the dying process, although this process is unique to each individual (Cook & Oltjenbruns, 1989). These needs may be physical, emotional, social, psychological, or spiritual.

**DEVELOPMENTAL DIFFERENCES IN ATTITUDES ABOUT DEATH**    Our initial attitudes about dying and death are formed in early childhood. These attitudes become modified and refined as our capacity for cognitive functioning improves through the subsequent stages of childhood, adolescence, and adulthood. Socialization processes also affect the manner in which our attitudes are modified throughout the life span. These changes are

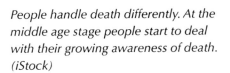

*People handle death differently. At the middle age stage people start to deal with their growing awareness of death. (iStock)*

outlined in this section. You may notice that some of the dates for the studies cited in this section seem quite old. The reason for this is two-fold. First, these studies were well conducted and the findings are still valid. Second, the focus of research on death, dying, and grieving has turned away from studying developmental differences in attitudes about death, and tend to focus more on areas such as terror management, physician-assisted suicide, and the grieving process.

*Early Childhood*    Understanding of death in childhood is dependent upon cognitive development and changes drastically across the years (Children's Grief Network, 2003). Cook and Oltjenbruns (1989) identify four components of young children's understanding of dying and death:

- NONFUNCTIONALITY    This term refers to the cessation of physical functions such as breathing and heart rate. One of the earliest studies of children's concepts of death was performed by Nagy (1948). She found that young children believed that individuals who were dead were capable of some but not all physical activities. This is shown in their belief that dead people are in a sleep state and can be awakened by an adult. Young children's belief in nonfunctionality is not complete, which is attributed to their level of cognitive development. They have animistic concepts, attributing life to inanimate objects. This belief in animism is a normal aspect of preoperational cognitive development in early childhood discussed earlier in this book.

- FINALITY    This term relates to the permanence of death and the understanding that the state cannot be reversed. Psychologist Gerald Koocher (1973, 1974) questioned children ranging in age from six to fifteen years about causes and events related to death and dying. As children grow older, they shift from giving magical and egocentric reasons for death to more abstract, reality-based reasons. Only the younger (preoperational children) believed that "dead things" could be revived. They even told of ways this could occur. None of the older (concrete or formal operational) children believed this. Again, this finding supports Piaget's ideas about animistic thought among young children.

- UNIVERSALITY    This term refers to the fact that everyone will eventually die; no one is exempt from death. Young children have a particularly difficult time understanding this concept. One study reports that about 62 percent of children between two and seven surveyed thought that some people will not die (White, Elsom & Prawat, 1978).

- CAUSALITY    Causality refers to those factors that are responsible for death, such as disease, accident, or injury. Young children's ideas about the causes of death reflect their egocentric understanding of the world. For example, when the young children in Koocher's (1973, 1974) study were asked, "What makes things die?" many responded with statements such as "You can die if you swallow a dirty bug."

*Middle Childhood*    Cook and Oltjenbruns (1989) used the components of the concept of death just discussed to describe how school-age children have modified their cognitive scheme of death. These changes reflect a more advanced level of cognitive development that Piaget labeled concrete operational.

- NONFUNCTIONALITY    School-age children have formed the notion that when people die, they do not have physical functions such as breathing or a heart rate (Nagy, 1948).

- FINALITY    Koochers (1973, 1974) work demonstrates that school-age children understand the finality of death and comprehend that once something is dead, it cannot be brought back to life.

- UNIVERSALITY    When the school-age children in White, Elsom & Prawat's (1978) study were asked, "Do you think that everyone will die someday?" 62 percent of them answered correctly. This compares with 38 percent of the preschool children.

- CAUSALITY    School-age children are able to provide specific examples of what can cause death. This also reflects their level of cognitive functioning. Responses typically are concrete, such as fires, guns, or illnesses (Koocher, 1973, 1974).

*Adolescence*    Cognition among adolescents is labeled formal operational thought by Piaget. Briefly, thought from adolescence into the years of adulthood is characterized by improving intellectual abilities. These include employing logic and reasoning to reach decisions, flexibility in using abstractions and hypotheses, lessened egocentrism, and increasing use of symbolism. Adolescent thinking has its flaws, however, which may influence thought as well as behavior and may account for some of their risk-taking behaviors. Some flaws in adolescents' thinking stand out: the ideation that they are exempt from danger and rules (the personal fable) and the belief that everyone is paying strict attention to their behavior (the imaginary audience). Because of their advanced abilities in logic and reasoning, adolescents can grasp the notions of eternity, the meaning of life, and mastery of the components of death discussed earlier in this section. Their ability to pose "if, then" situations allows them to ponder such hypothetical questions as, "What are five things you would do if you were told you had six months to live?"

Compared to younger children, high school students are interested in many philosophically oriented questions about dying and death (Cook & Oltjenbruns, 1982). For example, older adolescents apparently understand that dying is a process rather than an event and wonder about how to treat someone who is terminally ill. Adolescents also address ethical issues in their thinking about death as part of their development of formal operational thought patterns. For example, teenage cancer patients are insistent on being honestly dealt with by their caregivers (Orr, Hoffmans & Bennetts, 1984).

The notion that death can occur in adolescence is problematic for most teenagers. Normally, they perceive death as something that can happen to them only in the distant future. Their difficulty in grasping the possibility of their own death can be traced to

*Adolescents tend to believe that they are exempt from danger and rules. This may be a reason for risk-taking behavior. (iStock)*

adolescent flaws in cognitive development such as the personal fable. It is this very inability to conceptualize their own death that allows teenagers with terminal illnesses to cope and use hope as a survival technique (Susman, Pizzo & Poplack, 1981).

*Early Adulthood*    By the time an individual reaches early adulthood, he or she has acquired the basic beliefs, attitudes, and components of our culture's concept of dying and death. Although attitudes toward life generally take a more prominent position in the young adult's thinking, awareness of ideas of death does occur during this time of life. For example, the traditional marriage ceremony includes the vow for commitment "until death do us part," which brings into consciousness the possibility of the loss of a loved one.

The birth of children and parenting them through childhood also brings young adults an awareness of the fragility of life. The loss of a child is a tragedy for a family and involves a very difficult grieving and adjustment process. Some infants and children die of illness, birth defects, or accidental injury. Others die before they are born. Similar grief reactions may be experienced when someone has an intentional abortion.

Losses of other kinds can be experienced as symbolic deaths. Young adults learn to deal with the loss of relationships, the termination of jobs, leaving home, and the loss of social roles such as parenting when children are grown. Mastery of these challenges equips them with new skills, maturity, and confidence for facing the challenges of middle and late adulthood. Perhaps these losses also help to prepare them for the physical deaths of family and friends in the future. However, during this period, it is still difficult for most young adults to think about the possibility of their own death (Kastenbaum, 1975, 1977).

*Middle Adulthood*    The midlife transition in the early part of middle adulthood precipitates a change in a person's perception of time. Time is now seen in terms of length left to live rather than in terms of length passed since birth (Neugarten, 1968). This and other changes in perception cause middle-aged people to confront the possibility of their death in the near future. In a deep part of the self, personal death is more of a reality than it was before. Major life changes are often motivated by this awareness.

People begin to experience the aging process more rapidly and in more obvious ways during middle adulthood. Loss is experienced in a variety of ways during this period: the death of friends of similar ages, the death of a spouse, loss of major parenting responsibilities, and retirement from the work force toward the end of this stage. Some people react to the midlife transition with its change in perspectives by discarding goals and behaviors they no longer see as enhancing the self. They may get divorced, change career paths, and discard unhealthy behavior patterns such as addictions in favor of more health-promoting behaviors.

Middle age may be experienced as the time for making a last-ditch effort to achieve personal happiness. Many individuals realize that personal happiness is not to be looked for in external sources or material belongings, but must come from within and has spiritual connections.

**Spotlight**

Define death anxiety in your own words.

**Death anxiety**

A fundamental fear of death shared by most people.

*Late Adulthood*   The elderly might be expected to be especially fearful of death and to experience high **death anxiety** because of their close proximity to death. Research does not support this assumption. The most common orientation to death among the elderly is not fear but acceptance of its inevitability (Bengston et. al, 1977; Kalish, 1981; Munichs, 1966). Erikson (1950) notes that a fear of death in an elderly person is indicative of the lack of ego integration. An important developmental task at this stage of life—and one that promotes a sense of integrity—is to become less fearful of death. Older people may be less afraid of death than younger people because of its increasing prevalence among their acquaintances. The elderly attend more funerals, read the obituaries more frequently, and visit grave sites more regularly than younger people.

As people progress through late adulthood and experience the effects of the aging process, their impending death is brought more and more to mind. This may account for their preoccupation with preparing a will and disposing of their personal property. They need to be allowed to discuss their views on death and how they wish their own death to be handled.

*Pause and Process:*

1. How do attitudes toward death change between early childhood and middle childhood?

2. Why do older adults think about death more than younger adults?

# COMMUNICATION DURING THE DYING PROCESS

## *Needs and Concerns of the Dying*

Individuals facing impending death experience a variety of needs and concerns. These needs can include physical, emotional, social, psychological, and spiritual needs. It is important to be mindful of the fact that just as grieving is an individualized process, so is the dying process. Said another way, each individual facing death has their own unique set of needs and concerns; we address only the more common and general ones here. The needs discussed in this section do not prescribe an appropriate dying process any more than the needs experienced at any other stage prescribe an appropriate developmental path. Rather, they assist individuals to develop a healthy approach to the end of their life. The following information is based upon the research and findings of Cook & Oltjenbruns (1989).

**PHYSICAL NEEDS AND CONCERNS**    Two main areas of concern within the physical domain include pain management and body image. Many individuals fear the pain that may infest their body in the final days of life on this planet. As mentioned earlier in this chapter, doctors are more willing than ever to assist in the alleviation of pain through medication and palliative care. With proper medical interventions, pain should be able to be managed for most individuals in their final days. Additionally, just as social and emotional support help mitigate the pain of child birth, so too does such support assist in the pain of dying.

Body image is a bit more difficult to manage in comparison to pain. Body image can be conceptualized as how one sees his or her body and how that body compares to their ideal body image and the bodies of others. The body is often ravaged when succumbing to a terminal illness. Weight drops and bodily function declines. Psychological, physical, and social support can assist dying individuals to cope with these physical changes.

**EMOTIONAL NEEDS AND CONCERNS** Emotional needs may focus upon the unknown—what is on the other side of death? There may also be fears of pain or loneliness due to isolation or rejection. Further, a person may be worried about unfulfilled responsibilities.

**SOCIAL NEEDS AND CONCERNS** Issues in this domain center upon awareness of impending death. The more aware a person is of their upcoming death, the better he or she can interact with caretakers and express his or her needs. Once an individual becomes aware of their imminent death and accepts it, he or

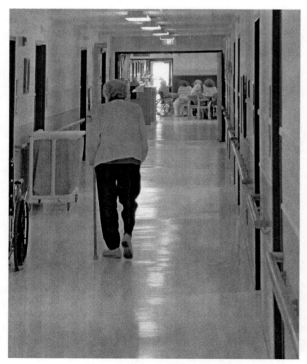

*Nursing homes may make social interactions more difficult. (iStock)*

she may become socially withdrawn. Conversely, social isolation may occur due to societal avoidance of death or physical settings (such as a nursing home) that make social interactions more difficult.

**PSYCHOLOGICAL NEEDS AND CONCERNS**    Dying individuals like to be informed, maintain some sense of control (such as where they will die and how the funeral will be handled), and conduct a life review in which they can find meaning from their journey through life.

**SPIRITUAL NEEDS AND CONCERNS**    Spiritual and religious beliefs assist many in facing death. Those from various religious convictions often believe that suffering brings them closer to God and is not in vain. Further, religious beliefs can provide a context that gives significance to life.

**HOW TO INTERACT WITH SOMEONE WHO IS DYING**    If you live long enough, you will eventually experience watching a loved one die. We often feel awkward in this situation, uncertain as to how we should act or what we should say (Lague, 2000). We should keep in mind that people don't want to die alone, and are often desperate for the support and company of family and friends during this last transition in life.

Research has found the following behaviors helpful when interacting with someone who is dying (Lague, 2000):

- Sit close and provide the comfort of holding hands or hugs.

- Allow the conversation pace to be set by the dying person. Silence is okay too.

- Listen to the person non-judgmentally and empathetically. This is not the time to correct any mistakes in his or her memory or knowledge. It is also not the time to tell them that you have heard a particular story one hundred times already, which leads us to the next point.

- Allow the person to reminiscence about their life. Laugh, cry, and ruminate together.

- Support the person to make as many decisions about what should happen after his or her death as possible, if they want.

- Say your goodbyes and express your feelings of love and attachment if possible.

**HOW TO SUPPORT A PERSON WHO HAS LOST A LOVED ONE**    In the next section, we will discuss grief and mourning in detail. In general, it is best to allow the grieving individual to set the course of discourse. Listen. Never say that you understand what they are going through; everyone experiences grief differently. Offer actual, practical help, such as cooking a meal, making phone calls, or watching the kids. Often, the little things mean the most.

*Pause and Process:*

1. What are some of the needs and concerns of the dying?

2. How should you interact with a dying person?

# COPING WITH DYING AND DEATH

Death anxiety, or fear of death, is a fundamental feeling shared by almost all individuals, according to existential philosophers and psychologists. These scholars believe that people search for meaning to their lives. The choice of life over death, or vice versa, is always possible for individuals throughout the life span. According to this view, choosing death is the ultimate freedom, but death remains threatening because it destroys the person's known existence and renders life meaningless (May, 1958).

The fear of death is deeply ingrained in Western culture (Haoward & Scott, 1965). Death is commonly regarded as a defeat and as a separation from loved ones. For others, it is seen as a journey home to be with their God. In general, death represents the unknown to many individuals.

## *Kübler-Ross' Stages of Dying*

**Thanatology**

The study of dying, death, and grief.

The psychiatrist Elizabeth Kübler-Ross has made one of the most significant contributions to the field of **thanatology** (the study of dying, death, and grief). She interviewed people who knew they had a terminal illness, such as cancer, and these individuals provided her with insights about the death process among those who are aware of their impending death. Kübler-Ross (1969) identified five stages experienced by people going through the process of dying: *denial, anger, bargaining, depression,* and *acceptance.* All these stages are not experienced by everyone who is dying, nor are they always experienced in the sequence Kübler-Ross outlined. People may shift from one stage to another during this involved and complex process.

Denial, the first stage in this model, is characterized by the unwillingness to accept the diagnosis of impending death. A common reaction is, "No, not me. It can't be true." Some people believe that a mistake has been made in the diagnostic tests or that someone else's records were confused with their own. Some react by seeking opinions from other physicians—which, even if the diagnosis is accurate, is a good step to make.

In the second stage, initial attempts to cope with the idea of impending death are replaced by feelings of anger. People rage, "Why me?" These harsh feelings are directed at anyone who is accessible; including family, friends, and medical personnel. Such reactions are understandable, according to Kübler-Ross, because the person feels cheated of the basic right to life and is resentful of what seems to be a cruel twist of fate.

Kübler-Ross calls the next stage bargaining. The person decides that anger is an ineffective means for securing additional time to live. What may work instead, the person now reasons, are requests addressed to God and to medical personnel for help in postponing death. The person tries to strike a deal by agreeing to be good, to dedicate remaining time to service to others in exchange for a lifting of the death sentence. Kübler-Ross sees this stage as a positive step toward coping with the stress of dying.

When people begin to show signs of a great sense of loss, Kübler-Ross notes, they are experiencing another step in the dying process she labels depression. She describes two types of depressive reactions: **reactive depression**, or feelings of loss and disfigurement of the body from surgery or from the ravages of disease; and **preparatory depression**, or beginning to prepare for death by grieving for the separation from loved ones. Kübler-Ross notes that

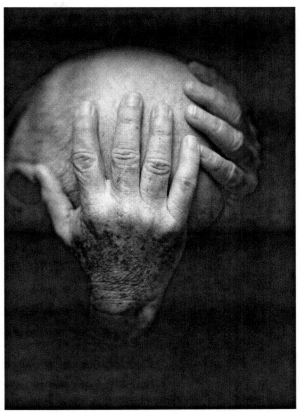

*Denial is the first stage of dealing with dying and death. (iStock)*

**Reactive depression**

Feelings of loss and disfigurement of the body from surgery or from the ravages of disease.

**Preparatory depression**

Beginning to prepare for death by grieving for the separation from loved ones.

preparatory depression is often silent and calls for quiet demonstrations of reassurance from others. Reactive depression is often verbalized and requires visible signs of "cheering up" from others.

The final stage is acceptance. At this time the person is almost without expression of negative feelings. Neither depression, anger, or grief is evident. The person has become reconciled to the inevitability of death. There is general fatigue and weakness. The stage is characterized by efforts to contemplate death with a "certain degree of quiet expectation." Kübler-Ross believes that at this stage the dying person has come to terms with his or her approaching death, but family members have not. There is a discrepancy between where the dying individual is and where loved ones are in the process.

A number of criticisms have been directed at this model of dying. Several investigators have questioned the validity of these stages for all dying persons, as well as the sequence that Kübler-Ross outlines (Hinton, 1963; Lieberman, 1965; Metzger, 1980; Schulz & Aderman, 1974). Kübler-Ross based her model on data from subjective interviews with people who were terminally ill. Other investigators used more objective methods to collect data. All who have studied the terminally ill individuals observe that they experience depression prior to death, but only Kübler-Ross describes a series of stages in a sequence that culminates with death. For example, Kastenbaum (1975) suggests exploration of ethnic differences in people who are dying; personality types and styles that may influence coping with dying; the effects of age and developmental level of the dying; and so on. The model described by Kübler-Ross does not adequately address such issues; however, it did provide an excellent start on this area of research.

*Pause and Process:*

1. What is death anxiety?

2. Explain the stages of dying.

# SOCIOEMOTIONAL ASPECTS OF DYING AND DEATH

### *LEARNING OBJECTIVES:*

*1. Describe the stages of grief and complicated grief*

*2. Explain American death rituals, the role of religion, and cultural-historical perspectives on death*

Death can occur at any point in the life span. When death is not accidental or unexpected, people experience changes and events that help to prepare them for the end of their life. These may be the death of associates or friends, a chronic illness, and other occurrences. For example, one of the authors watched one of her children stare death in the face at the tender age of ten. Luckily, the child lived; however, the lesson of the fragility of life has never been forgotten.

Neugarten (1968b) points out that people shift their perception of time in the middle years of life from "time since birth" to "time left to live." Perhaps this realization prepares individuals for the approach of death long before it usually occurs.

# EMOTIONAL ASPECTS OF DEATH

A person's attitude often predicts or guides behavior. Attitudes are acquired as a person grows and progresses through the various stages of the life span. An individual is socialized to have certain feelings, values, and beliefs by parents, peer groups, and the culture at large. These are communicated through a variety of methods, such as books, television, movies, and events in the family and community. Hence, the emotional aspects of death are intertwined with social influences.

Many people's impressions about death come from first-hand experiences. These influence both current and future understanding and feelings about death. In a report by Kübler-Ross and Worden (1977) of the results of a questionnaire completed by 5,274 individuals who attended workshops and lectures on dying and death, the average age at first contact with a death experience was 11.4 years. For almost half the respondents, the death of a grandparent was the first death experience. Next, was the death of a parent, friend, or other family member. Sadness and grief were the most frequently mentioned reactions. Confusion, denial, and shock were also frequent reactions.

## *The Experience of Grief and Loss*

When a person we love or feel close to dies, our reaction is painful and very emotional. We experience this death as one of the most stressful events in life. **Grief** and **bereavement** are terms that are used interchangeably to refer to the normal response to the loss of someone or something that is important to us. **Mourning** describes the socially prescribed ways people display grief (Pine, 1976).

All of us experience a number of losses as part of our growth and development throughout the life span and we often react to them by grieving. For example, people may experience grief when they move from one location to another, lose their job or valuable possessions, or get divorced. Some of these losses are more painful than others. Reactions to them vary, not only in degree and nature, but also in duration (Kimmel, 1980).

Theories of grief and loss often describe people's reactions in terms of the degree of their attachment to the object lost (Bowlby, 1980; Freud, 1917). Because of our psychological makeup, we human beings form strong attachments to others as well as to things. Need fulfillment has a strong emotional base and motivates much human behavior. Separation from the object (person or thing) that fulfills such emotional needs causes a variety of distressing reactions and generates anxiety.

Although dealing with the death of any loved one is difficult, it is said that the death of a child is particularly difficult. Although people expect young parents to experience grief after the death of an infant from conditions such as sudden infant death syndrome (SIDS), parents also suffer loss of a child through miscarriage, stillbirth, or even abortion. Below, we will discuss the loss of the very young and the grief such loss triggers. Then, we will move on to the grief process experienced in reaction to all losses, whether the deceased is a fetus, child, or adult.

## *Miscarriage*

**Miscarriage**, also known as spontaneous abortion, is the loss of an unborn child before it is viable (officially defined as before twenty weeks of prenatal development) (Lindsey, 2008). As discussed in the first section, a miscarriage can be caused by a variety of factors, such as fetal factors or maternal factors. It is particularly frustrating and devastating because it, by and large, cannot be predicted or prevented

Both parents experience grief after a miscarriage (Belkin, 1985; Borg & Lasker, 1981; Leitar, 1986). The intensity of grief is not determined by the amount of time that has passed since conception. Rather, it depends on the meaning the couple attributed to the pregnancy, their motivation to become parents, and the values and status of parenthood in the couple's culture. Tragically, many young couples undergoing this experience do not receive adequate support and understanding from either the medical community or their

---

**Grief**

The natural or expected response to personal loss; often used interchangeably with bereavement.

**Bereavement**

A term used interchangeably with grief to describe a natural or expected response to personal loss.

**Mourning**

The socially prescribed ways of expressing grief.

**Miscarriage**

The natural loss of an embryo, usually before the tenth week of pregnancy.

*Bereavement refers to the normal response of the loss of someone. (iStock)*

social networks (Leff, 1987). The medical community is guilty of great insensitivity when it places a woman whose miscarriage requires hospitalization on the maternity floor—sometimes even in the same room with women who have just delivered a healthy baby. Although this practice is changing, its once routine use is a statement about society's ignorance of the effects of a miscarriage on couples.

Guilt is a common reaction in women who have miscarried (Seibel & Graves, 1980). They erroneously personalize what has happened, blaming themselves for not exercising enough, working too long and hard, or eating the "wrong" kinds of food. Because many women connect the ability to reproduce with their femininity and personal competence, a miscarriage may make them feel like failures. A miscarriage also motivates many couples to rush into initiating another pregnancy without allowing sufficient time for physical and psychological healing. Community support groups or church ministries may help couples to work through their grief successfully before they attempt another pregnancy.

**Stillbirth**

Death of a fetus before birth due to any one of several reasons.

**Neonatal death**

Death of a baby during the neonatal period (birth to 2 weeks of age).

**Perinatal deaths**

A term that includes deaths from 20 weeks gestation to four weeks after birth.

## *Stillbirth and Neonatal Death*

Sometimes a fetus dies inside the mother's uterus and is not expelled from the mother's uterus until the normal time for delivery. This is known as **stillbirth** (twenty plus weeks of prenatal development) (Lindsey, 2008). When a newborn dies immediately after birth, it is called **neonatal death**. Both classes of death are known as **perinatal deaths**, because they occur in relation to birth. The frustrating aspect of these deaths is that they frequently happen for unexplainable reasons.

Society tends to discount the effect that a stillbirth or death of a newborn has on parents because it is commonly believed that people do not develop a significant attachment to their offspring before birth. Those who have experienced such a loss disagree. They find them very hard to accept because they have developed an attachment to the child during prenatal development, even though it may be less intense than the attachment parents feel toward an older child.

A perinatal death constitutes a crisis for the young couple, especially in their marriage relationship. Many women blame themselves. Men, too, sometimes feel guilty or responsible for the death in some way. If the couple has a history of losses of this nature, the situation is exacerbated. Counseling may be necessary to work through the grief and save the marriage (Leff, 1987; Wing et al., 2001).

## *Sudden Infant Death Syndrome (SIDS)*

Sometimes an infant dies suddenly for no apparent reason. It is impossible to describe the shock of discovering a child dead in its crib when hours or minutes before it was in apparent good health.

SIDS is the third leading cause of death among infants in their first year of life. It used to be the leading cause; however, public education about laying an infant to sleep on their back without pillows and blankets has helped lower the incidence some. That said, even after years of intensive study, researchers and medical providers continue to debate the causes of SIDS (ACOG, 2005; Bass, Kravath & Glass, 1986; Mackintosh, 1982).

*(iStock)*

Although it is known that the immediate cause of SIDS is the cessation of the infant's breathing; the million dollar question is why the infant ceases to breathe. As mentioned above, sleeping on the stomach, having soft bedding, or sleeping with pillows and blankets contributed to the high incidence of SIDS. However, infants continue to die of SIDS without these contributing factors. One possible cause of SIDS (and there is probably more than just one cause) is a condition known as **idiopathic protracted apnea** (Naeye, 1980). Idiopathic protracted apnea is an interruption in breathing during sleep. It is thought to be caused by a disturbance in the functioning of neurotransmitters within those areas of the brain that regulate breathing and other functions (Sahni, Fifer & Myers, 2007). For some reason, a chemical imbalance may occur, causing breathing to stop and not to be resumed. Other proposed explanations include a genetic propensity for SIDS, viral infections, enzyme abnormalities, or reactions to medications.

**Idiopathic protracted apnea**

An interruption in breathing during sleep.

There are some risk factors that increase the likelihood of SIDS. Exposure to second hand smoke is a risk factor for SIDS (ACOG, 2005). Infants should never be around an individual smoking or near clothing or furniture that smells of cigarette smoke. Low birthweight infants are at an increased risk of SIDS, as are infants that suffer from sleep apnea. Infants who have siblings that have died from SIDS are also at risk for SIDS themselves.

As previously discussed, there are a few steps that can be taken to try to prevent SIDS (ACOG, 2005). Avoidance of soft bedding, blankets, and pillows is an important step in preventing SIDS, as is placing the infant to sleep on the back. Allowing the infant to fall asleep using a pacifier seems to lower the risk of SIDS. Not smoking during pregnancy and avoiding second hand smoke after birth help prevent SIDS. Additionally, sleeping under a ceiling fan may help prevent SIDS. The unexpected death of an infant causes grief reactions that are very hard to resolve (Cook & Oltjenbruns, 1989). Parental reactions range from shock to denial, guilt, anger, and self-reproach. It is not unusual for the young parents to assume full responsibility for this type of death, though they rarely have anything for which to blame themselves. Many parents are subjected to homicide investigations by the police and social service agency officials. Because child abuse is so common in our society, this is a necessary precaution. However, it adds a great deal more stress to an already devastating situation.

One of the more comprehensive studies about the effects of sudden infant death upon family members finds the following (DeFrain & Ernst, 1978): (1) Sudden infant death was the most severe crisis ever experienced by parents in the study. (2) It required about six months for the family to recover to earlier levels of functioning. (3) It took about sixteen months for the adults to regain the level of personal happiness they enjoyed prior to the death. (4) Most adults experienced feelings of personal guilt as well as physiological and psychological disorders while they were grieving. (5) Within two and a half years, 60 percent of the families had moved from the residence where the infant's death occurred.

Many couples find the support they need by participating in groups designed to assist them, some of which are sponsored by the National SIDS Foundation (Williamson, 1986). As the public becomes more educated about the unpredictability of SIDS, attitudes are changing. People are less likely to blame parents for causing SIDS (Chng, 1982).

## Stages of Grief and Mourning

Many do not realize that there is a difference between grief and the grieving process. Grief is the term used to express the raw emotion associated with loss, whereas the grieving process is the means of coping with grief (Leming & Dickinson, 2006). Emotions associated with grief include a sense of hopelessness, meaninglessness, helplessness, and complete and utter pain and suffering. The grieving process can encompass several stages and one learns to muddle through and manage a life without their loved one.

One must keep in mind that there are many faces to the grieving process. Grieving has emotional, cognitive, cultural, sociological, spiritual, and physical components (Attig, 1991; Leming & Dickinson, 2006). Whereas grief is a passive emotion in which the inflicted has had no choice in partaking, the grieving process provides a means through which grief can be actively addressed.

At the heart of any grieving process is the coping of the loss of a relationship (Leming & Dickinson, 2006). There is now only a "me" instead of a "we," and this shatters one's sense of self. There is no one "right" way to grieve; it is a highly individualized process.

Models of grieving describe not only the stages that individuals go through in reaction to some type of loss, but also the manifestations of grief during those stages (Brasted & Callahan, 1984; Jacobs et al., 1987; James & Cherry, 1988; Spangler & Demi, 1988). One of the primary conclusions of such models is that grieving is a complex, multidimensional process that takes varying periods of time and is experienced with varying degrees of intensity. Its manifestations are physical, emotional, and behavioral. Below, we will examine two different models for the stages of grief. You will notice that there is considerable overlap between the two models; yet, some noticeable differences as well.

## *The Grief Wheel*

**Grief wheel**

A model of the grieving process described by Spangler and Demi.

Spangler and Demi (1988) present one of the more easily understood models of the grief process (see Figure 10-2). Called the **grief wheel**, it parallels to a certain degree the stages of dying described by Kübler-Ross (1969). The difference is that this model describes grief reactions to any kind of loss and is therefore applicable to people who are affected by the death of a close friend or relative.

According to the grief wheel model, the life path theoretically proceeds in a fairly uneventful manner until, at some point, a loss of some type is experienced. Then there is a period of personal decline and disorganization, until finally, the grieving person is reconciled to the loss and achieves a redefinition of life. The steps in the grieving process of this model are outlined briefly here:

**FIGURE 10-2    THE "GRIEF WHEEL" REPRESENTATION OF THE BEREAVEMENT PROCESS**

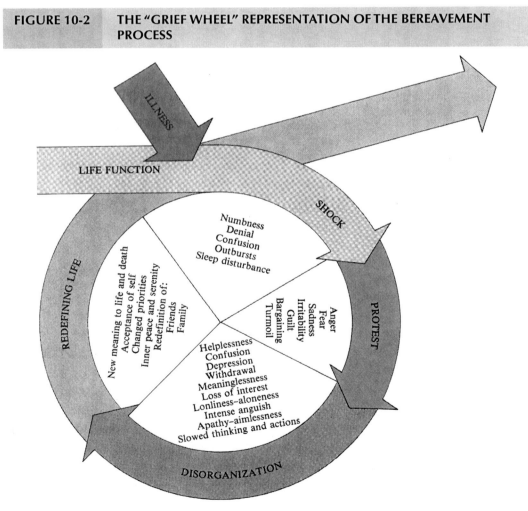

Source: Spangler, J., & Demi, E. (1988) *Bereavement support groups: Leadership annual* (3rd ed.) Denver, CO: Grief Education Institute.

1. *Shock*   The first reaction to loss is shock or confusion and denial. These intrapsychic (emotional and psychological) reactions are health-promoting at this time because they protect people against the initial severity of the loss. The outward manifestations range from the common reaction of crying to symptoms ordinarily associated with depression, such as loss of appetite and sleep disturbances.

2. *Protest*   This next step is characterized by further symptoms of depression, such as guilt and fear. Anger is a prominent outward expression of grief. As people allow themselves to experience the pain of their loss, their adjustment and recovery are enhanced.

3. *Disorganization*   This is the low point of dealing with grief, the "bottoming out" period during which most people must either accept the reality of their loss or continue to function in a disorganized manner. Apathy and withdrawal are hallmarks of the attempt to draw on inner resources to deal with the grief. Depression may be fully symptomized at this time. Toward the end of this step, people desire to recover the object of their loss. This may explain why people who are grieving have a strong preoccupation with what or whom they have lost. For those who have lost a loved one through death, this preoccupation may be manifested by frequent visits to the grave site, keeping the person's room and belongings exactly as they were when the person died, or being reluctant to discard anything that belonged to the person.

4. *Redefining Life*   Almost all theories of grief address the notion that emotional attachment to the love object must be severed for recovery from the loss to be completed. Freud (1917) terms this final aspect **grief work**. It is at this stage that people accept the reality of their loss and begin the business of rebuilding their lives. In order for them to do so, however, they must take the time to be introspective, to fully experience the pain of the loss. Then feelings are freed and they come to terms with a life that does not include the lost person (Worden, 1982). People at the early part of this step may appear to be emotionally sterile and closed off to relationships. Then they begin to feel again and to come to terms with reality, which enhances recovery. They reassess and redefine personal priorities and goals. Upon completion of this step, the life path or function recovers to the point where it was at the time of the loss. In fact, for those who fully experience grief and use it as an opportunity for personal growth, the model suggests that functioning resumes at a level greater than that known prior to the loss. In other words, adversity has been turned to self-enhancement.

**Grief work**

The stage in which people accept the reality of their loss and begin the business of rebuilding their lives.

Although this model is useful for understanding the grief process, several cautions should be issued for clarification (Bugen, 1979). First, the stages are not sequential—people may move forward and then regress to an earlier stage, and intrapsychic reactions from more than one stage can be experienced simultaneously. Second, components of the stages tend to blend or overlap; there are often no definite beginnings or endings in time. It is possible for people to spend an indefinite period at each stage as they work through their grief. Third, this model fails to allow for individual differences in the process of grieving. Finally, some people never progress through all the stages of this model and adjust completely to their loss. For them, full recovery may require professional help.

**SEVEN BEHAVIORS AND FEELINGS IN THE GRIEVING PROCESS** Kavanaugh (1972) identified seven behaviors and emotions associated with the grieving process, which may be experienced by individuals coping with grief (Leming & Dickinson, 2006). These seven behaviors and emotions are similar in nature to Kübler-Ross's stages of the dying process. We will discuss Kavanaugh's seven components to the grieving process below.

1. *Shock and Denial* Although unexpected deaths are often devastating, even expected deaths can lead to a period of shock and denial. There is a feeling of surrealism and disbelief. The shock provides a sort of safe place to function in until denial sets in for a person. Although often conceived of as a negative process, denial can be adaptive for short periods of time when dealing with death. Denial provides an escape from the feelings of loneliness and devastation that a death can cause. Death causes multiple disruptions and problems that must be dealt with—for example, the loss of a husband may mean the loss of a primary breadwinner, best friend, lover, and father of their children. With denial, each of these individual losses can be addressed slowly and separately as cognitive coping ability allows (Leming & Dickinson, 2006).

2. *Disorganization* In many ways, the period of disorganization after a death can be perceived as a period of existential crisis. The death has caused the person to feel a sense of meaninglessness, purposelessness, and loss of identity. There is a pervading feeling of disconnect with reality and death is somewhat viewed as preferable to life (Leming & Dickinson, 2006).

3. *Volatile Reactions* Emotions run high during this stage of grief. With the loss of identity suffered during disorganization, a sense of being attacked or facing utter destruction can set in. Such "under siege" feelings may be experienced and expressed as anger, horror, resentment, or dread. Some individuals may even go through a period of

*The shock of a death is the precursor to denial. (iStock)*

experiencing feelings of hatred toward their deceased loved one. Other objects of such negative emotions include doctors, God, friends, family members, clergy members, or funeral personnel. Occasionally, negative emotions may become internalized and manifest themselves as physical symptoms, such as headaches or stomach issues (Leming & Dickinson, 2006).

4. *Guilt*   When the emotions associated with grief are internalized, more than just physical symptoms may emerge. In fact, the feeling of guilt is one common manifestation from the internalization of resentment, anger, or trepidation (Leming & Dickinson, 2006). Depression, anxiety, or self-loathing may result.

Guilt is far from rare when coping with the death of a loved one. Cognitive dissonance in regards to why a loved one had to die while you still live may develop. One way to cope with such cognitive dissonance is to blame the victim. Blaming the victim allows an individual to mitigate the experience of guilt by transferring the negative emotions to either the person who has died or to someone who may (at least in the grieving individual's mind) have prevented the death (Leming & Dickinson, 2006).

5. *Loss and Loneliness*   As denial wanes, the reality of loss edges into the grieving person's consciousness. As the grieving individual resumes daily life, the loss of the loved one is experienced at a whole new level. Holidays, traditions, and regular social outings become a regular reminder of the person's death. The grieving individual may recognize the void in his or her life and encounter loneliness. This loneliness may manifest itself as emotions of self-pity, depression, or woe. Even loved ones that were abusive, cruel, or emotionally unavailable are missed, because anyone is better than no one.

The experience of loss and loneliness in the grief process is ultimately unavoidable. Some individuals may seek refuge again in denial. Others may unwisely seek refuge in shallow or superficial "replacement" marriages, friendships, or relationships. However, genuine relationships alone will help provide any long-term release from loss and loneliness (Leming & Dickinson, 2006).

6. *Relief*   Sometimes in the midst of the grieving process, a sense of relief is experienced. It is not uncommon for someone who has watched a loved one slowly die to think to him or herself, "at least they are at peace now," and experience relief. Occasionally, these feelings of relief can trigger guilt. However, it is important to realize that this relief is not due to negative feelings toward the deceased, but due to an end of suffering and a search for peace and growth in the future (Leming & Dickinson, 2006).

7. *Reestablishment*   Reestablishment is concerned with regaining a sense of purpose and meaning in life, a new sense of normalcy. This process takes time and a person may not even be aware that they are on the path of reestablishment until it is com-

plete and he or she has time to reflect upon the time between the death and the present (Leming & Dickinson, 2006).

It is important to realize that these seven behaviors and feelings neither occur in a linear nor mutually exclusive fashion. A person experiencing relief may suddenly be plunged back into the experience of guilt and loss, then retreat back into denial until he or she is ready to once again deal with the death. The process of grief is highly individualized and no two people grieve in exactly the same manner (Leming & Dickinson, 2006). Bereavement is a messy emotional, cognitive, behavioral, social, and spiritual process; however, as the cliché goes, whatever doesn't kill us makes us stronger in the end.

## Tasks of Mourning

Sometimes, the mourning process is conceptualized as having four necessary tasks that must be addressed before closure can occur (Leming & Dickinson, 2006). These tasks emphasize the necessarily active nature of the mourning process and assert that these tasks must be completed in order for reestablishment to develop. These four tasks, based upon research by the National Institute of Health, include the following:

List and describe the four tasks of mourning.

1. Accept that the loss is real

2. Suffer through the emotional turmoil and misery of grief

3. Adapt to daily life without the deceased

4. Redirect the emotional energy once focused upon the deceased loved one and that relationship to a new and viable relationship

**ACCEPTANCE THAT THE LOSS IS REAL**    When a death is expected, we can engage in anticipated or preparatory grieving. However, when a death occurs unexpectedly, the reality of the situation and loss can take some time to accept (Leming & Dickinson, 2006). Viewing the body, talking about the person and his or her death, viewing photographs of the deceased, looking upon the deceased's personal belongings, and passing on these belongings to friends and loved ones are all activities that can assist in this task of mourning.

**EXPERIENCE THE PAIN OF GRIEF**    The pain of grief is both physical and emotional (Leming & Dickinson, 2006). Tears, deep, soul-wrenching sobbing, headaches, stomach pains, and the like may all be experienced during this task of mourning.

**ASSUME NEW SOCIAL ROLES**    Someone must assume the social roles previously occupied by the deceased (Leming & Dickinson, 2006). Some social roles include hosting the yearly Thanksgiving meal for the family, organizing family reunions, being the fix-it handyman, or being the fun grandparent who takes the grandkids fishing and camping every summer. Redesignating these social roles is necessary for this task of mourning.

*Viewing photographs of the deceased may help one accept the loss of a loved one. (iStock)*

**REINVEST IN NEW RELATIONSHIPS**    The energy that was previously invested in the relationship with the now deceased person must be redirected during this task of mourning (Leming & Dickinson, 2006). This does not mean that one stops loving the person who has died, but that as humans we crave social interactions and emotional connections. To make relationships work, they require energy, and the energy once devoted to the previous relationship can now be invested in a different relationship.

## Factors Affecting the Grief Process

Researchers have identified at least four factors that influence how the grief process is experienced and affect its duration and intensity (Cook & Oltjenbruns, 1989). These are briefly outlined here.

**SEX**    Researchers find that men and women differ in their reactions to death, especially to the death of a spouse (Galatzer-Levy & Cohler, 1993). After the death of a spouse, women experience more health problems than men (Parkes & Brown, 1972; Sanders, 1979), as well as more death anxiety, feelings of anger, social isolation, depersonalization, and symptoms of depression. Women also feel a greater sense of abandonment after a spouse's death than men do (Glick et al., 1974). Despite all of these problems experienced by women, overall, men have more difficulty adjusting to the death of a spouse than women (Galatzer-Levy & Cohler, 1993). Whereas women feel abandoned, men feel that they have lost a part of themselves. Men take longer to ultimately adjust to life without their soul mate.

Reactions to children's deaths are also dissimilar for men and women. Mothers tend to have a more extreme reaction to the death of a newborn child than fathers do (Peppers & Knapp, 1980; Wing et al., 2001). They also experience more difficulty during the first year following the child's death as they attempt to cope with the holidays, the child's birthday, and the anniversary of the child's death (Cook, 1983; Wing et al., 2001).

There are several speculations as to why men and women differ in their reaction to a child's death, and to grief in general (Wing et al., 2001). Attachment differences between a mother/child and father/child relationship may lead to differences in grief when a loss of the child is experienced. Sex differences in how one orients his or herself to stress and coping in general may lead to sex differences in grieving. Finally, gender roles and social norms and expectations may lead to sex differences in the emotional expression of grief.

**AGE**    Although painful for both children and adults, expressing bereavement differs with age and level of development (Kaufman & Kaufman, 2006). Because children conceptualize death differently than adults, their reactions are also different (Goldman, 1998; Kaufman & Kaufman, 2006). Young children experience grief even when they do not have an accurate understanding of death. They show physical and psychological manifestations of grief, as discussed in the models of grieving; however, the forms are more appropriate to a child's level of development. For example, bedwetting, regressive overdependent-type behaviors, aggressiveness, temper tantrums, and exaggerated death fantasies are not uncommon (Elizur & Kaffman, 1983). Generally, reactions to grief are intense in young children.

School-age children have a somewhat more refined concept of death than preschoolers, and thus a different pattern of grief. Their reactions to the death of a parent range from feelings of guilt to a desire to protect the surviving parent (Berlinsky & Biller, 1982; Ikeman et al., 1987; Kaffman & Elizur, 1979). One out of five bereaving children shows significant problems two years after a parent's death (Kaufman & Kaufman, 2006). Reactions to the death of a sibling include fears related to illnesses, a desire to learn more about death, and inappropriate acting-out behaviors (Kock-Hatten, 1986; Spinette, Swarner & Sheposh, 1981). Dealing with a death during childhood or the teenage years can increase the risk for academic problems, depression, social withdrawal, anxiety, and a variety of behavioral problems (Kaufman & Kaufman, 2006).

Adolescents might be expected to follow the more adult grief reaction pattern described by Lamers (1978). However, researchers find that behavioral problems occur if adolescents are not encouraged to deal with their grief in an open manner (Aubrey, 1977; Shoor & Speed, 1976). This suggests that adolescents may be helped in their recovery process when they are treated more like adults than children (e.g., by recognizing their ability to participate in funerals or memorial services).

Adult mourning is characterized by the realization that significant social interaction is lost by the death and may vary according to the mourner's personality (e.g., the degree of maturity versus immaturity) (Gut, 1974). When Catherine Sanders (1980a) studied the bereavement of forty-five adults who had lost a spouse, she found differences between the younger (less than sixty-three years) and older (more than sixty-five years) people. Younger surviving spouses showed greater grief for as long as eighteen months after the death of a spouse, but older spouses demonstrated more aggravated reactions. Among people this age, it is probably harder to regain optimism and feelings of belonging.

Sanders (1980b) also reports different intensities of grief according to the age and relationship of the deceased. The parents of a child who has died show greater grief reactions than people who have lost a spouse or an older parent. This researcher reports that frequent church attendees were less likely to respond with great outward pessimism, but showed more repressed bereavement responses. Most interesting was the finding of no differences in bereavement intensities between those adults whose loved one died after a chronic illness and those whose loved one died suddenly and unexpectedly. Additionally, middle-aged people show greater declines in health status than young adults or the elderly (Perkins & Harris, 1990). They may be more vulnerable to the hazards placed on their health by bereavement than the young or the old because of the multiple types of stresses in their lives.

**PERSONALITY**   In general, those who have a dependent personality are more vulnerable to a difficult grief reaction than others (Gut, 1974; Parkes & Brown, 1972). These individuals generally rely on significant others for approval, have a low tolerance for frustration, and have high levels of anxiety. They tend to center their emotional lives and well-being around their relationship with a significant other. When this person dies or is otherwise lost from their life, they are likely to experience severe depression, a lengthy bereavement, and a less optimistic prognosis for recovery.

**CULTURE**   Cultural guidelines for appropriate grieving behavior tell people how to express their grief. For example, our culture as a whole generally tends to prescribe that mourning the dead should be done in private.

Some funeral homes or mortuaries even provide what is termed a "grieving room" for family members. This room may be fitted with a large window covered by a mesh curtain so the family can view the funeral but the audience cannot view the family. The intent is to protect the family's privacy during the highly emotional event of their loved one's funeral. Exceptions to this practice of private mourning can be found, however. Some African-American subcultures, for example, permit unrestrained emotional reactions at funerals (Charmaz, 1980).

*Those that are more vulnerable to a loss tend to center their lives and well-being around their relationship with a significant other. (iStock)*

## Family Rituals

Rituals are used by a culture to formalize certain events and to give them meaning. We have a variety of rituals that recognize birth and other life events. Birthdays, for instance, are recognized in a ritualized manner by celebrations, special cakes, making a wish before blowing out the cake candles, and singing "Happy Birthday." These rituals are known to virtually everyone in the United States (a very small percentage of religious groups reject the birthday ritual).

A number of rituals are associated with death, although the United States seems to be currently experiencing a crisis in regards to death rituals. These rituals have traditionally assisted families and friends to formally recognize the close of their relationship as it had been known with the person who has died. Rituals are important because they promote acceptance of death rather than denial. They also are important because they help people to express feelings in nonverbal ways, which facilitates the bereavement process (Conley, 1987).

A fading, yet perhaps best-known, ritual associated with death is the funeral or memorial service. This ritual serves certain functions for families and friends. It recognizes the person's life; sanctions public mourning of the person's death; facilitates the bereavement process; allows the functioning of social support networks such as kinship groups to the immediate family; and establishes new social statuses for both the person who has died (the deceased) and those who survive (the bereaved) (Charmaz, 1980; Fulton, 1987).

Traditionally, other rituals accompany the funeral or memorial service. These may include internment of the ashes in a respectful manner; having a military tribute; throwing a fistful of dirt on the person's casket as it is lowered into the ground; participating in a wake prior to the funeral; selecting certain pieces of clothing for the deceased person's burial; placing mementos in the person's casket before the burial; viewing the person's body as it lies in state; and releasing helium-inflated balloons at the conclusion of the funeral to symbolize the release of the person's spirit through death.

Customarily, other rituals may follow the funeral or memorial service: the reading of the person's will; sorting through and disposing of the dead person's personal effects; voluntary removal of a wedding ring by the widow or widower; visiting the grave and supervising the installation of the headstone; and responding to gestures of sympathy made by family and friends. All of these traditional rituals are thought to help people in their grief work.

## Grief Therapy

At some time in our lives, most of us will feel called upon to provide support for someone who is grieving some loss. Fortunately, most people are able to successfully accomplish their grief work. However, it is useful to know some general guidelines when called upon to help someone in this process. Cook and Oltjenbruns (1989) suggest that anyone who wants to provide support to a grieving person should:

1. Give the person permission to grieve by listening and providing appropriate supportive statements.

2. Support the grief work in ways that are meaningful to the person.

3. Encourage expressions of grief by appropriately recognizing them.

4. Support the person's acceptance of the loss by acting as a mirror of reality.

5. Listen as the person shares his or her grief work.

6. Share any information known about the normal grief responses and process.

7. Assist in ways that are meaningful to the person, such as helping with housework and taking care of children.

All of these gestures show care, concern, and sympathy for the surviving person's well-being and assist that person through the grief process. Sometimes, however, people need professional assistance because their grieving is blocked or inhibited or because they are "stuck" at one step in the grief process. **Grief therapy** consists of specific psychotherapeutic methods for helping people move toward recovery (James & Cherry, 1988). Besides individual therapy work with a professional, self-help books and support groups can greatly aid people to deal with a difficult grieving process. In the next section, we will explore a type of grief, **complicated grief**, which may require such intervention.

## Helping Children Cope with Loss

A child's stage of development (cognitively and socioemotionally) greatly influences his or her ability to recognize the finality of death and the grief response (Bagshaw, 1998; Graham, 2004). A child's adaptive capacities are challenged when facing a loss. Protective fac-

**Grief therapy**

Professional counseling specifically aimed at helping individuals who experience difficulty in completing their grief process.

**Complicated grief**

Grief that involves an adjustment disorder or interferes with a person's ability to function in everyday life.

*Children face many challenges when they suffer a loss. It is important to be supportive during this time. (iStock)*

tors such as a sense of purpose and problem-solving abilities are taxed. A child's resiliency is tested in ways never before imagined. Social support is of paramount importance.

When children are coping with a death, be it a pet, a classmate, or a relative, it is important to answer their questions honestly. It is best to follow a grieving child's lead and to respect his or her process of coping (Jalongo, 2005).

Programs, such as Seasons for Growth, have been developed to help children cope with loss due to death or divorce (Graham, 2004). Individual bereavement counseling is also an option. The goal is to assist the child to adapt to the loss by recognizing emotions, appropriately sharing and expressing emotions, reducing a sense of isolation, and teaching healthy problem-solving, decision-making, and coping strategies.

Below are some strategies for helping a child to express and work through grief (Children's Grief Network, 2006; Cunningham, 2009; Graham, 2004; Kaufman & Kaufman, 2006):

- Art therapy

- Mime

- Role-playing

- Stories

- Discussion

- Playdough

- Music

- Journaling

- Doll or puppet play

- Poetry

- Creating a family tree

- Memory boxes or collages

- Creating a loss timeline

- Children's stories about death and grieving

- Bibliotherapy

The goal is to express emotions and to develop a new sense of normalcy (Graham, 2004). To have healthy grief, a child must be provided the opportunity to express their loss in a meaningful way (Kaufman & Kaufman, 2006). Research has shown that grief programs and social support groups promote positive outcomes for children and adolescents dealing with loss. Some outcomes include a more positive attitude, a greater sense of happiness, better communication and coping skills, and a lower sense of isolation.

Complicated grief and bereavement counseling: Sometimes the grieving process becomes blocked or unresolved. When grief is not being actively dealt with and is interfering with one's ability to function in daily life, complicated grief could be the cause. It is as though there is a wall between a person's grief and mind, and counseling can help break the wall down (Children's Grief Network, 2006).

Complicated grief may develop for several reasons (Children's Grief Network, 2006; Kaufman & Kaufman, 2006). Contributing factors include: a sudden or traumatic death (such as homicide or suicide); a social stigma attached to the death (such as AIDS or abortion); when a person has experienced multiple losses within a short window of time; if the relationship with the deceased was conflict-ridden; or when there is a lack of social support to assist with grieving. Therapy can help individuals of all ages work through their complicated grief and learn to be happy again.

*Pause and Process:*

1. What is the difference between grief and the grieving process?

2. What are the tasks of grieving?

# SOCIAL ASPECTS OF DEATH

## *American Death Rituals*

Although there is no set standard that all Americans prescribe to in terms of a death ritual, there tends to be a common process most Americans experience. Funerals and memorial services serve multiple purposes following the death of a loved one (Dickinson & Leming, 2008). First, they provide a means of disposing of the body. Second, family and friends are provided a forum in which to remember and reminisce about the person's life. Third, seeing the body or casket assists in accepting the reality of the death. Fourth, the funeral or memorial service is a rite of passage, after which, mourners are expected to return to their daily life and tasks.

Most Americans (79 percent) choose to have a traditional ground burial (Dickinson & Leming, 2008). Cremation, although growing in popularity, is chosen by 21 percent of Americans. Regardless, our cultural norms require that the deceased be treated with dignity and regard; burials and internment of ashes fulfill this norm (Leming & Dickinson, 2006; Lynch, 2007).

Children benefit emotionally by being allowed to participate in the death rituals, such as eulogies, writing the obituary, or attending the funeral (Kaufman & Kaufman, 2006; Leming & Dickinson, 2006). Once again, children's questions should be answered honestly, but at their level (i.e., you don't need to go into the intricate details of how the person died). Children often provide emotional support to the grieving adults (Jalongo, 2005; Leming & Dicksonson, 2006).

**Green burials**

The use of biodegradable caskets and integrating forests and conservation efforts with graveyards.

Death rituals are in a time of transition in America (Basler, 2004; Whalen, 1990). There is a movement toward "green" burials. **Green burials** and graveyards work to support the environment while still respecting the deceased. Examples include using biodegradable caskets and integrating forests and conservation efforts with graveyards.

There is also a move toward "quicky" funerals (Whalen, 1990). A current fad includes drive-up windows at funeral homes through which mourners can quickly view the body and sign the condolence book (the culture of convenience at its finest). Other places offer time-share cemetery plots, where the body is placed and mourned for a specified amount of time, after which that body is disposed of and the plot is made available for the next fresh body (scary, but true).

## *Religious Traditions*

In the previous section, we discussed the bare bones of the death rituals in America. However, many religious traditions offer richer and more intricate death rituals (Whalen, 1990). We will highlight just a few here.

The Hindu people traditionally have a ceremony called the Shraddha (Whalen, 1990). The body is washed, clothed in a shroud covered with flowers, and carried to a pyre. A male relative lights the fire and engages in reciting sacred verses as he walks around the body. The body must be cremated so that the spirit moves on to its next life. After three days pass, the ashes are collected and temporarily buried. About a week and a half later, the ashes are retrieved and placed in a sacred river. The son of the deceased recites prayers and invokes the spirits and support of ancestors (which is one reason why male babies are desired more than female babies).

Whereas the Hindu and Buddhists embrace cremation, Jews, Muslims, and Baha'i forbid it (Whalen, 1990). People of the Jewish, Muslim and Baha'i faith bury the body shortly after death. In some Muslim communities, the cultural norm is for women to wail at the funeral loudly in a show of their grief.

*Religious traditions regarding death are varied. For example, the Hindu ceremony called the Shraddha calls for the body to be washed, clothed in a shroud and covered in flowers. It is then carried to a pyre to be cremated. (iStock)*

The Catholic Church has funeral rites laid out in the Order of Christian Funerals. The focus is upon the person's soul entering purgatory or heaven (Johnson, 1994). In the Catholic faith, purgatory can be conceptualized as "a temporary state of purification for those destined for heaven but not yet totally free from the effects of sin and selfishness" (Whalen, 1990, p. 153). Additionally, the Church recognizes that this is a time of terrible grief for family and friends and works to help them in their suffering. Below we will discuss the three steps of the Catholic funeral rite, in which the family and friends are encouraged to help. These steps help provide a process of support and healing for the bereaved (Johnson, 1994).

The first step in a Catholic funeral is a **vigil** (Johnson, 1994). The vigil can take place in a funeral parlor, a home, or a church. The body may or may not be there, it is open to personal preferences. The vigil is short in duration and focuses mainly on prayer, although readings and music are also included.

The second step in a Catholic funeral is the funeral liturgy, which takes place at a Catholic church (Johnson, 1994). This liturgy (which includes readings and a homily) may take place within a mass or on its own. The body may or may not be present, depending on personal preferences. There is not, however, any eulogy. The focus is on God's love and mercy and the promise of eternal life. "You're supposed to console and strengthen the community in their loss, not to dwell on somebody's past accomplishments in the face of the great equalization of death" (Johnson, 1994, p. 89).

The third and final step in the Catholic funeral is the **rite of committal**. Here, the person's body or ashes is sprinkled with holy water, possibly incensed, and placed in its final resting place.

In Judaism the body is buried as rapidly as possible in a simple shroud and coffin. The mourners then gather at the home of the deceased and the immediate relatives begin a seven day period of mourning.

Although we have touched upon the religious death rituals for the Hindu, Muslim, Buddhist, Baha'i, Jewish, and Catholic faiths, these are just the tip of the iceberg. Protestants, Mormons, and Freemasons all have their own religious death traditions that offer comfort during a time of distress and loss (Whalen, 1990).

## *Historical and Cultural Perspectives on Death*

We cannot begin to do justice to the rich history and diversity of death perspectives and traditions in this small space. From the mummification of Egyptians to the Viking kings set afloat on burning ships, cultures across history have found ways to show respect to the dead and send them on their journey to the afterlife (Whalen, 1990).

Although culture shapes death rituals, death can shape culture. The black death of the Middle Ages brought about a child's rhyme that is still popular today: Ring around the rosies, a pocketful of posies, ashes, ashes, we all fall down. "The meaning of the rhyme was that life could be unimaginably beautiful—and the reality unbearably horrible" (Cantor, 2001, p. 40). The bubonic plague killed around one-third of Western Europe's population

**Vigil**

The first step in a Catholic funeral that may take place in a funeral parlor, a home, or a church. The vigil is short in duration and focuses mainly on prayer, although readings and music are also included.

**Rite of committal**

The third and final step in a Catholic funeral where the person's body or ashes is sprinkled with holy water, possibly incensed, and placed in its final resting place.

and contributed to shifts in politics and religion that are still evident in the culture today. Hence, death shapes life as much as life shapes death.

*Pause and Process:*

1. What does the traditional American death ritual entail?

2. What are some religious traditions in regard to death?

---

# SUMMARY

1. The definition of death has changed from earlier times to reflect advances in medical technology used to sustain life. Dying is understood today to be the final stage of the life span, a process in which certain steps are taken to prepare for impending death. Death can occur at any point of the life span for reasons related to age and developmental stage of the individual. The leading causes of death changed during the twentieth century (from infections to chronic degenerative diseases), as has the place where death usually occurs (from the home to an institution).

2. There are different dying trajectories and phases of death. Each trajectory and phase has its own characteristics and issues that must be addressed. Terminal decline is the curious occurrence that cognitive declines can predict impending death.

3. Advance directives allow you to dictate what medical interventions and treatment you would want if incapacitated. The Terri Schindler-Schiavo case highlighted the importance of writing down your wishes in the event that some tragic accident or illness happens.

4. End of life care is better than ever. Pain can be managed more than in the past, and palliative and hospice care help address the dying person's physical, emotional, psychological, social, and spiritual needs. Physician-assisted suicide is gaining

momentum in the United States; however, it may prove a slippery slope as we watch our European nations report its use on newborns without parental consent and the mentally ill who cannot possibly give informed consent.

5. Attitudes about dying and death are formed early in the life span but are modified as individuals experience refinements in their cognitive abilities and develop maturity. Attitudes about dying and death among older individuals differ from those of children and adolescents. Many life events in adulthood assist people to prepare for their own eventual death. By learning to cope with change and loss throughout the years of adulthood, individuals may come to have less death anxiety in late adulthood.

6. Most individuals experience dying as a process. This process varies from person to person. The stages that many people go through before death happens are highly individualistic. That said, Kübler-Ross offered a theory for five stages of facing death that is useful in understanding certain stages that an individual may experience.

7. Grief and bereavement are interchangeable terms that refer to the normal response to personal loss. Mourning refers to the ways people express grief.

8. One hazard of pregnancy is the chance of loss through miscarriage, stillbirth, or SIDS. Because

these are unanticipated events, they are highly problematic to parents and other family members. Parents' grief reactions include anger, guilt, confusion, preoccupation with thoughts of the child, sadness, loss of appetite, sleeping disorders, and irritability. Participation in community support groups or church ministry groups may assist parents to work through their grief.

9. Grieving is a process that involves several stages characterized by internal and external behaviors. There is no set duration or intensity for bereavement, but grief recovery is a realistic goal. Factors that influence the grief process include the person's sex, age, personality, and cultural background. Social rituals help people in their grieving process. Some of these are associated with the funeral or memorial services, whereas others take place afterward. When people are unable to resolve their grief on their own, specialized therapy aimed at alleviating blocks to progress toward recovery can be very helpful.

10. The traditional, generic death ritual in America is a funeral or memorial service. This ritual assists individuals to accept the death and find closure. Different religions have different rites. Death has shaped history and death rites vary across time and culture.

## SELF-QUIZ

1. What was the historical definition of biological death? How has this definition changed in recent decades?
2. Explain the Harvard Medical School criteria for declaring someone dead.
3. How did the Uniform Determination of Death Act define death?
4. What is the difference between whole-brain death and partial-brain death?
5. Describe what is meant by psychological death and social death.
6. What are the leading causes of death across the childhood and adolescent years?
7. What are the leading causes of death across the adult years?
8. Explain how the Terri Schindler-Shiavo case taught the American public about the importance of having an advanced directive.
9. What characterizes a "good death"?
10. How is palliative care different from hospice care?
11. Describe developmental changes in attitudes toward death.
12. What are some of the physical needs and concerns of the dying?
13. Explain the emotional needs and concerns of the dying.
14. Describe the social needs and concerns of the dying.
15. What are some of the psychological needs of the dying?
16. Discuss the spiritual needs and concerns of the dying.
17. What are some suggestions on how to interact with a dying person?
18. How can you support a person in mourning?
19. Define death anxiety in your own words.
20. Describe the stages of dying.
21. Explain what is meant by bereavement.
22. What is the difference between grief and mourning?
23. Clarify the distinction between a miscarriage and a stillbirth.
24. Define what is meant by neonatal death.
25. List the factors associated with contributing to SIDS.
26. Describe the stages of the grief wheel.
27. Explain the seven behaviors and feelings involved in the grieving process.

28. List and describe the four tasks of mourning.
29. Describe and characterize the developmental differences in bereavement across the life span.

30. How do the traditional American death rituals compare with some of the religious death rituals described in this chapter?

## — TERMS AND CONCEPTS —

# Glossary

**Abrupt-surprise pattern**   The person is expected to recover but dies instead.

**Accommodation**   Altering existing schemas to help in understanding new information.

**Acne**   A chronic inflammation of the oil glands and hair follicles located in the facial area.

**Acquisition period**   A shift in cognition seen in childhood and adolescence.

**Active genotype-environment correlation**   An environment that the child seeks due to genetic preferences.

**Acute**   A form of organic brain syndrome that is reversible in many cases.

**Acute phase**   A crisis accompanied by high personal stress associated with increasing awareness of the inevitability of death.

**Adaptive expertise**   An approach to problems that is characterized by flexibility and promotes life-long learning.

**Adaptive features**   Those features that are conducive to survival in a given environment, whatever those features may be.

**Adaptive reflexes**   This group of reflexes aids the neonate to locate and obtain food, thus helping to ensure its survival.

**Adolescence**   The fifth stage of the life span, occurring between thirteen and eighteen years of age.

**Adult stem cells**   Stem cells obtained from patients or donors found in numerous tissues and organ systems, even fat.

**Adulthood**   The period of the life span following adolescence.

**Advanced directive**   A written document explicating what medical measures you would like employed if you lose the capacity to make such decisions. You can also elucidate who you would like to make these decisions for you if you become incapacitated.

**Affect intensity**   One's intensity of emotion.

**Affective complexity**   The appearance of older adults having more complex emotional experiences compared with younger adults.

**Afterbirth**   The final stage of labor which involves the expulsion of the placenta and the membranes as well as any remaining amniotic fluid from a woman's uterus.

**Age of viability**   The point in prenatal development where the baby stands a chance of surviving outside of the womb.

**Ageism**   Unreasonable or irrational beliefs about aging and older individuals.

**Aggression**   Any hostile act that causes fear in others and leads to forceful contact; may be verbal or physical and directed at people as well as objects.

**Aging**   A complex process involving a decline in physiological competence that inevitably increases the incidence and intensifies the effects of accidents, disease, and other forms of environmental stress.

**Agreeableness**   The degree to which a person is trusting, giving, and kind.

**Alzheimer's disease**   A degenerative chronic brain disorder occurring commonly in late adulthood. It is characterized initially by forgetfulness, later by serious cognitive dysfunction; and eventually by complete loss of mental functioning and death.

**Ambivalent attachment style**    An infant who seeks proximity to his/her mother with extreme distress and hyperactivity of closeness.

**Amniocentesis**    The withdrawal of a sample of amniotic fluid (which includes the baby's sloughed off skin cells) from the mother's uterus.

**Amniotic fluid stem cells**    Stem cells found in amniotic fluid.

**Aneurysm**    A rupture of an artery wall within the brain.

**Animism**    The belief of young children that all things, including objects, are alive.

**Anorexia nervosa**    An eating disorder involving complex emotional and body image disturbances that lead to an obsession with limiting dietary intake in order to control body weight. The condition is life-threatening if left untreated.

**Anoxia**    Oxygen starvation of tissues.

**Anterior attention system**    Includes the brain areas such as the prefrontal cortex.

**Apgar score**    An evaluation method for assessing the health status of a newborn.

**Apparent hypocrisy**    The considerable incongruence between what they say they believe and how they behave.

**Armored-defended**    A personality type where the individual strives to maintain control over their lives.

**Arteriosclerosis**    A condition usually occurring in advanced cases of atherosclerosis in which there is a gradual loss of elasticity in arterial vessels. The end result is high blood pressure or hypertension.

**Arthritis**    Inflammation of the joint area between bone junctions.

**Articulation disorders**    Disorders in which a person struggles to produce appropriate speech.

**Association**    The ability to form a connection between a stimuli and a response.

**Assimilation**    Incorporating information from the environment into previously known ideas.

**Associative play**    Engaging in a common activity and interacting with others.

**Atherosclerosis**    A cardiovascular disease in which plaques of fatty material form along arterial walls in the body and especially in the heart. This leads to blockage of blood flow and the possibility of clots, increasing the likelihood of heart attack and stroke.

**Attachment**    A strong affectional tie or emotional or emotional bond between two individuals.

**Attachment theory**    Intense emotional tie between two individuals, such as an infant and a parent.

**Attention deficit/hyperactivity disorder**    A disorder that causes children to be highly distractible and energetic. It is caused by a chemical imbalance in the brain leading to difficulties in regulating attention, impulsivity, and hyperactivity.

**Attitude of initiative**    A feeling of confidence.

**Authoritarian parenting style**    Parents that display discipline, but show little affection.

**Authoritative parenting style**    Parents that display both affection and discipline.

**Autoimmune responsiveness theory**    As people grow older their immune system begins to attack the body's own tissues.

**Autonomy**    Refers to establishing personal boundaries and self-differentiation from things and others.

**Autosomes**    A single chromosome; any one of the forty-six chromosomes found in the nucleus of a human cell.

**Average**    A child with a small group of friends, who is neither greatly disliked nor considered popular.

**Avoidant attachment style**    An infant who does not seek out his/her mother and exhibits a detached pattern o closeness.

**Avoidant-insecure attachment style**    An infant does not seem to care if the mother leaves or returns.

**Axon**    Takes information from the neuron away to be sent to other neurons.

**Babinski reflex** Named for its discoverer, this reflex occurs when the sole of the baby's foot is stroked along the outer edge. In response, the neonate's toes spread wide in a fanning action, relax somewhat, curl forward tightly closed, and return to their original position.

**Baby blues** Feelings of sadness and exhaustion that over 70 percent of women experience the first week or two after birth.

**Baby boomer generation** Individuals born between 1946 and 1964.

**Baby colic** A condition in which a healthy baby cries or screams frequently for extended periods of time for no apparent reason.

**Balance** The ability to maintain equilibrium and stability.

**Basic nursing care** Basic care provided to all hospital patients (such as food and cleaning of wounds).

**Basic processes** "Frequently used, rapidly executed, memory activities such as association, generalization, recognition, and recall. They are among the building blocks of cognition, in the sense that all more complex cognitive activities are built by combining them in different ways."

**Basic trust** The sense that others are predictable and can be relied on.

**Bereavement** A term used interchangeably with grief to describe a natural or expected response to personal loss.

**Big five factors personality theory** A theory that posits that there are five super-traits that are the foundation of personality.

**Bilateral coordination** The coordinated, integrated use of both sides of the body in performing motor acts.

**Bioecological theory** A theory by Bronfenbrenner that emphasizes the nested environments that influence human development.

**Biological age** How old an individual's body is based on health.

**Biological death** Historically defined as when the heart stopped beating and respiration ceased, leading to the cessation of brain function.

**Birth order** The order in which children are born in a family.

**Blended family** A family unit consisting of an adult male and female couple, one of whom has remarried, and the children of one or both from a previous marriage; a new term for stepfamily.

**Bodily-kinesthetic intelligence** The mental ability to control one's body in a purposeful way.

**Body transcendence versus body preoccupation** The necessity of finding happiness and satisfaction in relating to others and in creative or mental endeavors for healthy development to occur.

**Braxton-Hicks contractions** Practice contractions by the uterus.

**Breech** When a child is upside down for delivery, with the bottom being delivered first.

**Bulimia** An eating disorder involving emotional and body image disturbances that lead to intake of large amounts of food that are then purged by vomiting or use of laxatives to control body weight.

**Bullying** An aggressive behavior (words, actions, or social exclusion) which intentionally hurts or harms another person; the behavior occurs repetitiously and creates a power imbalance such that it is difficult for the victim to defend him or herself.

**Caring** Having empathy and concern for others.

**Cataracts** A change in the lens of the eye causing it to become opaque to entering light, which reduces vision considerably

**Cell body** Contains the parts of the cell to keep it alive and functioning (such as the nucleus).

**Cellular clock theory** When biological errors in the DNA genetic code accumulate, the cells are unable to function at all and die.

**Centering** A cognitive trait in early childhood that limits information processing to only one aspect or characteristic rather than several simultaneously.

**Cephalic presentation** Head first delivery.

**Cephalocaudal growth pattern**   Changes occur in the head region of the body, both internally and externally in advance of those occurring toward the abdominal region.

**Cerebrovascular disease**   A category for death related to the blood vessels in the brain such as a stroke.

**Character**   Having a moral compass and integrity.

**Childproofing**   Arranging and adapting housing and physical space (e.g., by capping electrical outlets) to meet safety concerns for infants.

**Chorionic villus sampling**   A procedure by which chorionic villi (hairlike structures that are the predecessors of the placenta) are removed and analyzed to determine if genetic disease is present.

**Chromosomal disorder**   A disorder due to a chromosomal abnormality or defect.

**Chromosomes**   A collection of genes contained within a cell nucleus; the total number per cell is constant for each species, with humans having forty-six in each cell, except for the gametes, which have twenty-three.

**Chronic**   A form of organic brain syndrome that is not reversible.

**Chronic living-dying phase**   The person adjusts to the idea of approaching death, and experiences a variety of feelings such as grief, fear of the unknown, and isolation.

**Chronological age**   The number of years that have passed since an individual's birth (or conception in some cultures).

**Circular reactions**   Actions that occur by chance and then are repeated and modified through practice.

**Class inclusion**   A cognitive ability of middle childhood that allows a child to consider the whole as well as its parts in classification operations.

**Classical conditioning**   The pairing of a neutral stimulus with an unconditioned stimulus in order to achieve a desired response.

**Classification**   The cognitive ability to group objects according to traits of similarity or likeness.

**Classification and categorization skills**   The ability to use salient features to place objects or constructs into distinct groups.

**Client-centered therapy**   Also known as person-centered therapy, it is a non-directive approach to therapy based upon humanistic theory. This approach believes that the client has the necessary inner resources to cope with his or her problems.

**Climacteric**   Decline in sexual functioning among middle-aged men.

**Clique**   A smaller group of friends that are similar in appearance, demographics, and activities.

**Codified**   Math that is written.

**Codominance**   Occurs when both alleles are fully expressed.

**Cognition**   Those processes, such as perception, thinking, reasoning, and problem solving, by which one comes to know and understand the world.

**Cognitive conceit**   A characteristic of thought in middle childhood in which individuals perceive situations and people in black-and-white, all-or-nothing.

**Cognitive domain**   Changes in intellectual or mental functioning.

**Cognitive flexibility**   The ability to shift from one thinking style to another.

**Cohabitation**   Living with a romantic partner prior to marriage.

**Cohabitation effect**   The increased risk for divorce associated with cohabitation.

**Cohort**   A group of individuals having a statistical factor (as age or class membership) in common in a demographic study.

**Collagen**   A fibrous protein that is a basic component of connective tissue.

**Colostrum**   The first liquid secreted by the mammary glands, full of antibodies and nutrition.

**Communicative disorders**  Any disorder that impairs one's ability to communicate.

**Companionate relationship**  A grandparent-grandchildren relationship described as an easy-going, friendly relationship that involves emotionally-satisfying leisure-time.

**Competence**  An individual's skills, abilities, and proficiency within a specific domain, such as school, relationships, or sports.

**Complicated grief**  Grief that involves an adjustment disorder or interferes with a person's ability to function in everyday life.

**Conception**  The fertilization of an ovum by a sperm cell.

**Concrete operations**  The stage of cognitive development experienced in middle childhood in which thought becomes more logical and based on immediate physical realities and mental imagery abilities become more refined.

**Conditionalized knowledge**  The skill experts have in retrieving the specific information that they need for any given problem.

**Confidence**  Having certainty in one's ability.

**Congenital anomalies**  Birth defects or chromosomal abnormalities that are incompatible with life.

**Connections**  An individual's relationships with others and feelings as though one belongs.

**Conscientiousness**  The degree to which a person values and/or needs organization, precision, and self-discipline.

**Conservation**  The understanding that the essential characteristics of something are preserved even though it is rearranged in different ways.

**Contagion**  The second stage for understanding of illness as "caused by people or objects that are proximate to, but not touching, the child."

**Continuous variation**  When a trait or variation is distributed on a continuum or spectrum.

**Control group**  The group that receives the placebo.

**Control phase**  The period where necessary changes and or adaptations are made in the approach to the learning task.

**Controversial**  Children who are liked by many peers, and disliked by many peers.

**Conventional level**  Moral reasoning that consists of conformity to the rules of important groups.

**Cooperative play**  The integration of several children into group play where different roles are assumed.

**Cooperatively**  The willingness to play with one another.

**Coordination**  The ability to use various muscle groups together to accomplish specific actions.

**Co-regulation**  The shift to greater sharing and balance of social power between parents and children during the Family and School-age Children stage of the family life career.

**Correlational research**  The study of relationship existence between two or more variables.

**Co-sleeping**  Parents and children sleep in the same bed.

**Crawling**  Locomotion with the abdomen on a surface.

**Creeping**  Locomotion by moving the hands and knees with the abdomen off the surface.

**Cross-sectional**  A research design that compares measurements or observations of some particular trait or behavior between groups of people of different ages at the same time.

**Crowds**  A large mixed-sex group of older children or adolescents who have similar values and attitudes and are known by a common label.

**Cruising**  Walking using the assistance of objects or people.

**Crystallized intelligence**  Skills acquired through education and socialization such as verbal skills, mathematical skills, inductive reasoning, and interpersonal skills; the ability to recall and use information.

**Curvilinear relationship**  In this type of correlation, two variables increase or decrease together up to a point, then switch to a negative correlation where one variable increases while the other decreases.

**Death anxiety**    A fundamental fear of death shared by most people.

**Death**    The cessation of all observable or measurable physical signs of life (physical death); related aspects are social and psychological death.

**Decentering**    The cognitive ability that allows a school-age child to attend to more than one aspect simultaneously in performing classification operations.

**Deciduous teeth**    The primary or first set of sixteen teeth that erupt when an infant is between five and seven and one half months of age.

**Deductive reasoning**    Beginning with the big picture and developing conclusions.

**Delay gratification**    The ability to put off something pleasurable and rewarding and work hard in the here and now.

**Dementia**    A type of organic brain syndrome that is a neuropsychiatric disorder related to brain cell impairment.

**Dendrites**    Receives information from other neurons.

**Dentition**    The shedding of one set of teeth and the eruption of another.

**Deoxyribonucleic acid (DNA)**    A complex molecule composed of four basic nucleotides that is the carrier of genetic inheritance.

**Dependent variable**    A variable that is measured in an experimental study; the outcome of an experimental study.

**Depression**    A disease that involves a person's thoughts, emotions, and feelings.

**Descriptive research**    Research that seeks to describe a phenomenon.

**Developmental tasks**    The unique characteristics and tasks that help define each stage of life span.

**Diabetes**    The failure of the pancreas gland cells to secrete an adequate amount of an enzyme (insulin) that is essential for metabolizing sugars.

**Dialectical reasoning**    The deliberate coordination of inferences for the purpose of making cognitive progress.

**Dialectical thinking**    A style of thinking in adulthood in which individuals appear to accept and may even relish contradictions and conflicts in values.

**Difficult temperament**    The resisting of physical handling, crying inconsolably, and showing irregular sleeping and eating patterns.

**Discontinuous variation**    When a trait or variation can be placed into distinct categories.

**Disenchantment stage**    In the aftermath of the honeymoon phase, emotional depression settles in as people come to realize that they have actually fully withdrawn from a constant and fulfilling social role in their lives.

**Disorganized/disoriented attachment style**    An infant that lacks a cohesive strategy in coping with the strange situation.

**Diverticulitis**    An inflammation of a portion of an intestine that causes pain, nausea, and a change in bowel habits.

**Dominant**    A gene from one parent that controls or suppresses the influence of the complementary (recessive) gene from the other parent in the offspring.

**Dopamine**    A neurotransmitter that is responsible for smooth and coordinated movement of the muscles in the body.

**Double-blind study**    An experiment where neither the researcher nor the participants are aware of who is receiving the actual treatment or who is receiving the placebo.

**Doula**    A professional labor coach.

**Duration**    The time the process takes.

**Dying**    The complex process leading to death, characterized by an individual's particular dying trajectory.

**Dying trajectories**    Representations of the duration and shape of the dying process.

**Easy temperament**   A baby who is adaptable, cheerful and happy, and responsive to others and situations.

**Ectopic**   A pregnancy that develops in a location outside the uterus.

**Ego**   The rational part of our psyche which tries to balance the needs of the id and superego.

**Ego differentiation versus work-role preoccupation**   The adjustments that must be made to retirement from work roles.

**Ego transcendence versus ego preoccupation**   Recognizing and accepting one's impending death by living life as fully as possible and attempting to make life more secure, more satisfying, and more meaningful for those who will survive after one's death.

**Egocentrism**   A cognitive trait that limits a child's understanding of the world to their own perceptions.

**Elderly**   The term describing individuals in late adulthood who are sixty-five years of age or older.

**Elderspeak**   A style of speech used when speaking with older adults. It is similar to infant-directed speech in which speech is simplified, spoken slowly, and higher in pitch and intonation.

**Embryo**   The name of the developing individual during the embryonic period.

**Embryonic period**   The two weeks after conception until around eight weeks after conception.

**Embryonic stem cells**   Stem cells obtained from human embryos that result in the death of the embryo.

**Emotional intelligence**   The ability to recognize the emotions of others and regulate one's own emotions while effectively utilizing emotions in adaptive and skillful ways.

**Emotions**   Subjective feelings such as love or joy that help to define our existence as human beings.

**Empathy**   The ability to comprehend accurately the thoughts, feelings, and actions of others.

**Emphysema**   A condition involving destruction of lung tissue that results in lowered lung elasticity.

**Empty nest**   The period of the post-parental stage of the family life cycle when a couple phase out their active parenting responsibilities.

**Encoding**   Developing an internal, mental representation of the situation.

**Entry-reentry pattern**   The person experiences steady decline, but is able to remain at home between periods of hospitalization.

**Epigenetic information**   A characteristic of developmental changes meaning that changes that are currently observed were determined by those that occurred earlier in time, and changes that follow will be influenced by the ones currently being observed.

**Episodic memory**   Specific life event memories.

**Equipotentiality**   The ability for a cell to develop into any type of cell in the body.

**Ethnic harassment**   A workplace environment where verbal assaults are targeted toward individuals because of their ethnicity.

**Ethnographic research**   A specific type of naturalistic research largely used in anthropology, education, and cultural studies.

**Ethology**   The field of inquiry that studies the biological bases of behavior patterns in animals and humans.

**Euthanasia**   The willful ending of a life that is not a consequence of a disease, illness, or injury.

**Evocative genotype-environment correlation**   An environment in which the child elicits certain environments or behaviors due to his or her genetics.

**Evolutionary theory**   Those theories of developmental change that are founded on Darwin's theory of evolution; these theories stress the role of biological factors in the individual's adaptation to the environment.

**Existential intelligence**   The mental ability to contemplate the purpose and meaning of life and issues surrounding death and what comes after death.

**Experimental group**   The group that receives the experimental treatment.

**Experimental research**     Seeks to establish cause and effect relationships.

**Experimenter bias**     The influence of the experimenter's expectations or behavior in an experiment.

**Expertise**     Having extensive experience, knowledge, and understanding within a specific area of interest.

**Explicit memories**     Conscious memories that can be visualized as well as provide a verbal account.

**Explicit memory**     The information that you purposely try to recall, such as when you tell a friend about a movie you just watched.

**Explicit-theoretical approaches**     Seek to empirically study wisdom in an objective and scientific way.

**Exploratory play**     Object oriented play.

**Extrinsic motivation**     A person's drive to learn because of what he or she will receive in doing so.

**Extroversion**     The degree to which a person is outgoing.

**Fair-weather cooperation**     The second stage of friendship perception that typically occurs between the ages of eight to ten where ideas of reciprocity and adapting to friends' likes and dislikes govern the early friendship.

**Family systems theory**     The approach that theorizes that families operate as a system in the ways they make decisions and take actions that govern behavior, help the group meet its goals, and enable the group to maintain stability over time.

**Fast-mapping**     A language skill used by young children; the meaning of a new word is acquired by comparing it with one that is familiar.

**Fear**     A reaction that involves physical and/or psychological agitation and dreadful anticipation of real or imagined danger to one's safety.

**Fertilization**     The penetration of the ovum by a sperm cell.

**Fetal alcohol syndrome**     A disorder that may include physical abnormalities and cognitive deficits due to a mother drinking alcohol during pregnancy.

**Fetal medicine**     Any medical intervention or care directed at the developing, in utero individual.

**Fetal period**     The phase of prenatal development that spans from eight weeks after conception to birth (at around forty weeks).

**Fetal surgery**     Surgery that is conducted while the child is still developing prenatally.

**Fetus**     The name of the developing individual beginning in the ninth week after conception until birth.

**Figurative language**     The use of similies, proverbs, idioms, and metaphors.

**Fine motor skills**     Those motor acts that require the use of small muscle groups and hand-eye coordination.

**Fitness**     How well an individual is suited for his or her environment and the ability to survive and reproduce.

**5-to-7 shift**     A transition period in cognitive development between the preoperational and concrete operations stages; thinking is based more on intuition than logic.

**Fixation**     Occurs when attempts to satisfy needs at a certain stage of personality development are continually frustrated.

**Flexibility**     The freedom to bend or move the body in various directions.

**Fluency disorders**     Disorders in which a person struggles to communicate smoothly.

**Fluid intelligence**     The ability to perceive relationships, reason logically and abstractly, and form concepts and interpretations.

**Formal operations**     The fourth stage of cognitive development proposed by Piaget that commences in adolescence; thought is characterized as less rigid, more flexible, and less dependent on perceptions and past experiences.

**Free-radicals**     Unstable oxygen molecules that are released when cells metabolize energy.

**Game of thinking**     Divorcing oneself from reality and playfully considering various hypothetical possibilities in certain situations.

**Gender harassment** A workplace environment that is hostile, degrading, or insulting toward one particular gender.

**Gender identity** One's knowledge of being either male or female.

**Generation X** Individuals born between 1965 and 1979.

**Generation Y** Individuals born after the year 1980.

**Generativity versus stagnation** The seventh psychosocial attitude described by Erikson; It is developed optimally between twenty-four and fifty-four years of age. Generativity is an interest in caring for others and sharing one's knowledge, skills, and information. Stagnation (self-absorption) is directing all one's interest inward to oneself.

**Genes** The basic agents of heredity from one generation of humans to the next.

**Genetic imprinting** The repression or expression of a gene or chromosome in an offspring that is dependent upon which parent it is inherited from.

**Genotype** The total genetic makeup of an individual.

**Germinal period** The phase of prenatal developing lasting from conception until implantation in the uterus (around ten to fourteen days).

**Gerontophobia** The unreasonable and irrational fear of the elderly; related to ageism.

**Gingivitis** Inflammation of gum tissue that contributes highly to tooth loss.

**Glaucoma** A group of diseases resulting in increased pressure within the eyeball and leading to blindness if left untreated.

**Goodness-of-fit** How adaptable a child's environment is to his or her temperament.

**Gout** A metabolic disorder that results from uric acid crystals forming at joint areas, especially in the feet.

**Green burials** The use of biodegradable caskets and integrating forests and conservation efforts with graveyards.

**Grief** The natural or expected response to personal loss; often used interchangeably with bereavement.

**Grief therapy** Professional counseling specifically aimed at helping individuals who experience difficulty in completing their grief process.

**Grief wheel** A model of the grieving process described by Spangler and Demi.

**Grief work** The stage in which people accept the reality of their loss and begin the business of rebuilding their lives.

**Gross motor skills** Those motor acts that require the use of large muscle groups.

**Group politics** Those social skills that facilitate a child's participation in peer groups.

**Growth** Behaviors meant to increase functioning and adaptation.

**Guilt** Feeling shame and remorse.

**Habituation/dishabituation** An experimental technique that allows researchers to measure recognition in babies.

**Hand skills** The ability to explore and manipulate a wide variety of objects with the hands.

**Healthy behavior** Any behavior that reduces the susceptibility to disease and enhances physical and psychological function and well-being.

**Hiatal hernia** A condition in which a portion of the stomach slides up next to the esophagus.

**Highly competent experts** Experts who exhibit great adaptability, flexibility, and creativity in utilizing their expertise across a variety of situations.

**Hitching** Crawling or creeping backward using the buttocks rather than the hands and knees.

**Holophrases** An early speech form used by infants in which single words convey a wide number of meanings.

**Honeymoon phase** Immediately following the formal event of retirement, most people feel happy and peaceful initially as they experience the independence of retirement.

**Horizontal decalage**  Unevenness in applying an understanding of conservation problems across different contexts.

**Hormonal stress theory**  As the hormone system ages, it is less effective at managing stress.

**Hospice care**  Care that is provided in a person's home or hospice home to those with less than six months to live.

**Hostile attributional bias**  The thinking that bullies are always suspect of the intentions of others and see hostility where there is none.

**Human development**  The changes that occur in individuals between conception and death.

**Hypertension**  Abnormally high blood pressure caused by constriction of arteries; it increases the likelihood of kidney damage, heart failure, and brain damage via strokes.

**Hypothesis**  Generically, hypothesis means educated guess. A hypothesis should come from a theory, be a statement, and be testable.

**Hypothetical reasoning**  The ability to think and reason about ideas in the abstract.

**Id**  The drives that seek gratification of elemental needs for food, water, sex, and warmth.

**Identity**  The fifth attitude proposed by Erikson. Identity is the notion, acquired in adolescence, that the self is composed of different aspects having distinct boundaries that constitute a whole, integrated personality.

**Identity foreclosure**  The inability to commit to any role or idea of direction for their lives.

**Idiopathic protracted apnea**  An interruption in breathing during sleep.

**Imaginary audience**  The adolescent egocentric belief that other people are obsessed and consumed with his or her appearance and behavior.

**Imitation**  The basic process of a newborn being capable of immediately imitating your behavior.

**Implantation**  Occurs when the zygote burrows into the uterus.

**Implicit memories**  Unconscious memories that influence our behavior.

**Implicit memory**  Unconscious memory that guides your behavior, thoughts, and feelings.

**Implicit-theoretical approaches**  Approach to the study of wisdom that investigates people's common understanding of wisdom

**Impulsion**  The rate at which body movement begins from a stationary position.

**Incomplete dominance**  Occurs when one allele is not completely dominant over the second allele.

**Incompletely launched young adults**  Young adults who return home to live with their parents.

**Incontinence**  The inability to retain urine in the bladder until voluntarily released.

**Independent variable**  A variable that is controlled and/or manipulated.

**Individual difference**  Any quality, trait, or characteristic that distinguishes one person from others.

**Individuation**  The process by which an adolescent recognizes and develops his or her personal identity as an individual who is distinct from other family members. It is characterized by developing one's own values and belief systems and having the courage to make decisions and live by these.

**Inductive reasoning**  Reasoning from specific facts to general conclusions.

**Infant-directed speech**  Speech that is more accentuated and of a higher pitch.

**Infantile amnesia**  The inability to remember much about the first two or so years of life after birth.

**Infertility**  The inability to conceive a child after consistently having intercourse without contraception for at least a year.

**Information-processing**  How information is represented, processed, and applied in reference to memory constraints at any given age.

**Informed consent** Providing research participants with enough information about a study that they can knowledgeably agree or disagree to participate.

**Inherited disorder** A disorder or disease that develops due to a gene mutation, chromosomal problem, or other genetic factor.

**Inhibitory deficit theory** A theory that examines what aspects of cognitive processing declines with age, and what aspects of cognitive processing remain stable.

**Institutional Review Board (IRB)** A committee that evaluates whether a research study is ethical and allowed to be conducted.

**Integrated** A personality type in late adulthood that may be thought to resemble the sense of integrity described by Erikson.

**Interpersonal intelligence** The mental ability to understand one's own emotional self.

**Intimacy versus isolation** The sixth psychosocial attitude described by Erikson; it is developed optimally between eighteen and twenty-four years of age. Intimacy is the ability to have a close and loving relationship with another. Isolation is the refusal to allow oneself to become vulnerable enough to establish intimate relationships.

**Intimate and mutually shared relationships** The third stage of friendship perception that typically occurs at the end of middle childhood, between the ages of 10 to twelve where children value the continuity and longevity of friendship.

**In-time leavers** Individuals that move out of their parents homes permanently before the age of twenty-five.

**Intrinsic motivation** A person's internally generated drive to learn because it is inherently enjoyable.

**Inventive strategies** Making use of one's own knowledge and current strategies in answering a novel problem.

**Involved relationship** A grandparent-grandchildren relationship that focuses on an active role of raising grandchildren and conducting the role as an active caretaker much like a parent.

**Irreversibility** The inability of young children to comprehend that some processes and operations can be reversed in sequence.

**Job simplification** Work that is repetitive, simplified, and fragmented.

**Kyphosis** A "humpback" posture.

**Labor** The process by which the cervix is opened prior to birth and the fetus is moved from the uterus through the birth canal; accomplished by means of contractions of the uterus, which increase in strength, duration, and frequency as delivery nears.

**Laboratory studies** Allow for better variable control and manipulation than naturalistic studies.

**Language** "A system of abstract symbols and rule-governed structures, the specific conventions of which are learned."

**Language Acquisition Device (LAD)** An innate brain structure proposed by Chomsky that regulates the means by which an individual learns language.

**Lanugo** A fine down-like hair covering the baby's body.

**Late adulthood** The eighth stage of the life span and final stage of adulthood; traditionally, the stage begins at age sixty-five or retirement from the work force and continues until near-death.

**Late leavers** Individuals that are still living at home after the age of twenty-five.

**Life history** All the changes experienced by a living organism, from its conception to its death.

**Lightening** Occurs when the fetus' head drops down into the pelvis.

**Lingering pattern** The person is expected to die, but clings to life for an indeterminate time.

**Linguistic intelligence** Involves the mental abilities in the semantics, syntax, and overall expression of language.

**Logical-mathematical intelligence** Involves mental abilities in pattern recognition, relationships, reasoning, and mathematical operations.

**Longitudinal design**    A study that makes repeated measurements or observations of the same individuals over an extended period of time.

**Long-term memory**    The final memory location in the brain where information is stored indefinitely; recall of events in the distant past.

**Macular degeneration**    A decreased blood supply to the retina, causing loss of visual sharpness when looking directly ahead but not in the peripheral vision areas.

**Maintenance**    Behaviors striving to keep functioning at current levels despite declines in processes or ability.

**Malignant neoplasms**    Technical term for cancer.

**Maturationism**    The belief that changes in development are due only to heredity; changes result from the execution of genetic programming.

**Maturity**    Completion of all growth and developmental changes; associated with attaining adulthood in the past.

**Meconium**    A newborn's first bowel movement.

**Meiosis**    The process by which the gametes (sperm and ova) are produced in the male testicles and the female ovaries.

**Menarche**    The first menstrual period experienced by a girl, marking the beginning of puberty.

**Menopause**    The climacteric in females; cessation of all reproductive functions that begins at about age forty-five to forty-eight and is completed by about age fifty-five.

**Mental health**    A state of psychological well-being in which an individual is able to behave according to cultural standards.

**Merely skill experts**    Expertise that functions largely on routine.

**Meta-analysis**    The data from numerous studies on a particular topic are synthesized and analyzed.

**Metacognition**    The ability to be aware of and understand the changes occurring in one's own cognitive processes.

**Metalinguistic-awareness**    The capacity to use language to analyze, study, and understand language.

**Metamemory**    An awareness of the extent of one's memory.

**Microgenetic studies**    A study that only lasts a matter of days or weeks.

**Middle adulthood**    The seventh stage of the life span, occurring between forty-five and sixty-five years of age.

**Middle age**    A term synonymous with middle adulthood. Middle age can bring about new perceptions, redefinitions of roles, and different means for achieving personal happiness.

**Miscarriage**    The unwanted ending of a pregnancy, usually within the first three months of pregnancy.

**Mitochondrial theory**    The inability of the mitochondria to properly function as the cell's powerhouse and failure to provide enough energy for the cell to function. Damage to the mitochondria is caused by free-radicals released into the cell.

**Mitosis**    The splitting of each chromosome in the body cell to form a new pair.

**Modeling**    The process by which behavior is acquired and modified through observing and replicating the behavior of others.

**Momentary playmates**    Temporary playmates, typically because they happen to be in the same physical location.

**Monitoring phase**    Maintaining awareness of what is being learned and thinking.

**Moro reflex**    This reflex is associated with a sudden change in movement or support of the newborn. If a neonate is raised or lowered suddenly or if support of its head is released, the baby responds by raising its arms upward very quickly and curling its fingers. Moving of the legs accompanies these reflex motions.

**Morphemes**    Meaningful units of speech.

**Mourning**    The socially prescribed ways of expressing grief.

**Multifactorial disorder**    A disorder that results from the interaction of genetics with the environment.

**Multiple intelligences** A theory in which there are various domains or abilities in which a person can be intelligent.

**Multiple regression** A statistical method that allows researchers to predict one variable based on the values of other variables.

**Musical intelligence** The mental ability to understand the components of music, such as tone, melody, pitch, and rhythm.

**Mutation** A change in the chemical structure of the gene or genes and can occur during cell division or as a result of environmental influences.

**Myelin (myelin sheath)** A fatty material deposited around axons.

**Myelinated** A layer of fat that can surround the axon.

**Naturalist intelligence** The mental ability to recognize plant and animal life in the environment and the relationships and interconnections between these species.

**Naturalistic observation method** A method of conducting research on human development that usually occurs in the "real" world where behavior happens spontaneously.

**Needs hierarchy** A person's need to satisfy certain basic needs before they attempt to realize self-actualization.

**Negative correlation** As one variable increases, the other decreases.

**Neglected** Children who are neglected by peers and describe themselves as having no friends.

**Neonatal death** Death of a baby during the neonatal period (birth to two weeks of age).

**Neuron** The information processing cell of the nervous system.

**Neuroticism** The degree to which a person is insecure, emotional, and anxious.

**Neurotransmitters** Chemical messengers that carry information to other neurons.

**Non-voluntary euthanasia** A doctor administers a deadly dose of medication without the patient requesting it.

**Novice** A person with limited experience, knowledge, or understanding within a specific area of interest.

**Obesity** A body weight that exceeds by 20 percent of what is considered to be appropriate for one's age.

**Observational learning** Learning that occurs through observing others.

**Observer bias** Different accounts given by people who observe the same event.

**Off-target verbosity** The tendency for some older adults to drift to irrelevant topics during conversation.

**Off-time** When a person experiences puberty earlier or later than most of his or her same-age peers.

**One-way assistance** The first stage in friendship perception that occurs early in middle childhood where friends must match a child's personal standard.

**Onlooker play** Observing others at play.

**Openness** The degree to which a person is comfortable with variety, autonomy, and change.

**Operant conditioning** The use of reinforcers and punishers to control behavior.

**Operational definition** How a variable is defined in a measurable way.

**Oppositional defiant disorder** A mental disorder characterized by a pattern of disobedience, hostility, and deviant behavior.

**Organogenesis** The formation of organs during the embryonic period.

**Osteoporosis** Inflammation of bone tissue causing softness and porous structure; the condition can lead to bone breakage and tooth loss.

**Ostracism** A social control mechanism used by peer groups to enforce group rules and conformity to behavior standards; it is seen, for example, when children are ignored and rejected on the school playground.

**Overextension** When a child applies the meaning of a word too broadly.

**Overlaps** When a word is underextended on some occasions and overextended on other occasions.

**Palliative care** Treatment for those suffering from illness that focuses on pain management, symptom control, and emotional support in the face of stress.

**Palmar (hand) and plantar (foot) grasping reflex** These reflex movements are produced by touching or stroking the palm of the newborn's hands or the soles of its feet. Both fingers and toes curl in the grasping manner in response. The strength of these reflexes is remarkable.

**Parallel play** Playing alongside others who are doing the same or a different activity.

**Parallel processing** Refers to the ability to cognitively process and complete two or more tasks at a time.

**Parkinson's disease** A chronic degenerative brain disorder commonly occurring in late adulthood. It is characterized initially by tremors, muscle weakness, and a peculiar gait; then speech becomes slurred; death eventually results from severe brain cell damage.

**"Partial-brain" death** A concept that a person should be considered dead if his or her higher cognitive functions no longer function, but parts of the brain still function and maintain physical life.

**Passive genotype-environment correlation** An environment in which the child passively receives an environment.

**Passive smoking** Inhaling air in an area where someone has been smoking.

**Passive-dependent** A personality type with two basic variations that may be observed: (a) those whom are succorance-seeking in having strong dependency needs on others; and (b) those who a4re apathetic or having little or no interest in others or in their surroundings.

**Peak experiences** The feeling of great joy, ecstasy, and cosmic identification with the whole universe.

**Pediatric psychology** The area of psychology that studies the interactions and relationships among health, illness, physical development, cognitive development, and socioemotional development across the life-span.

**Peer group** A (usually) same-sex group of children of similar ages and developmental abilities that significantly influences social changes in middle childhood.

**Perceptual skill** The ability to perceive through sight and sound; especially those skills related to motor skill development, such as depth perception and pattern perception, that emerge in infancy.

**Perfection principle** An internalized judge or parent figure guiding the person's behavior according to social and moral ideals.

**Perinatal deaths** A term that includes deaths from twenty weeks gestation to four weeks after birth.

**Perinatology** Concerned with the detection and treatment of illness in developing individuals before birth.

**Periodontal disease** Disease of the gums caused by improper hygiene; it can lead to significant tooth loss.

**Permissive style** Parents that are affectionate, but display little discipline.

**Personal or Invincibility fable** The belief that one is immune from all harm or injury.

**Personality** The inner behavior that represents the true inner self as well as to outward actions manifesting that inner self.

**Phenomenism** The first stage for understanding illness "as an external concrete phenomenon that is spatially and temporally remote from the condition of illness."

**Phenotype** The traits and characteristics such as hair color, skin color, and behavior that can be observed.

**Philosophical approaches** Values the history of wisdom discourse in philosophy.

**Phonemes** The simplest and most elementary sounds in speech, or the building blocks of speech.

**Phonics** An approach to teaching reading and spelling based upon phonetics, or the sound of letters.

**Physical (biological) domain** Changes in the body or physical appearance.

**Physician-assisted suicide**   When a doctor provides a patient with the means to commit suicide at the patient's request. The doctor provides the lethal dose, but the patient is responsible for actually taking the medication.

**Physiologic**   The fifth stage for understanding illness; described as the malfunctioning of an internal physiologic organ or process and is explained as a step-by-step sequence of events.

**Placebo**   An inert or innocuous substance used especially in controlled experiments testing the efficacy of another substance (as a drug).

**Planning phase**   A person sets goals and considers what they already know and what they need to still learn.

**Play therapy**   The use of play to assist a child with psychological, behavioral, or emotional problems.

**Pleasure principle**   Attraction to those things which are enjoyable and repelled by those things that produce discomfort.

**Pneumonia**   An inflammation of the lungs.

**Polygenic process**   The interaction of alleles from more than one gene.

**Popular**   Children who are liked by many peers.

**Positive correlation**   As one variable increases, the other variable increases.

**Positive regard**   Characterized as being warm, genuine, and giving total attention and acceptance to the client.

**Postconventional level**   Moral reasoning based upon internalized and personalized values.

**Posterior attention system**   Includes the brain areas such as the posterior parietal cortex and the thalamus.

**Post-formal operational thought**   A possible fifth stage of cognitive development, in early adulthood.

**Postpartum depression**   The feelings of sadness and exhaustion persist or even worsen past the two week mark.

**Postpartum psychosis**   When a woman is afraid to be left alone with the baby and has thoughts of hurting herself or the baby.

**Pragmatics**   The ability to adjust speech in socially and culturally appropriate ways.

**Precausal thinking**   A type of logic unique to young children based on intuition rather than fact.

**Precision**   The dexterity and accuracy of movements.

**Preconventional level**   Moral reasoning based upon physical consequences and the power of those in authority.

**Prediction**   A statement of what somebody thinks will happen in the future.

**Premature baby**   A baby who weighs five and one half pounds or less at birth and has a gestational age of less than thirty-seven weeks.

**Preoccupied-insecure attachment**   An infant is terribly upset when the mother leaves and is inconsolable when she returns.

**Preoperational**   The kind of thinking young children do when they begin to use mental imagery but are not yet able to use logic; intuition is often used in reaching decisions.

**Preparatory depression**   Beginning to prepare for death by grieving for the separation from loved ones.

**Prepubertal growth spurt**   A rapid increase in height and weight preceding puberty (at about age ten to twelve).

**Pre-retirement**   The period preceding retirement during which a person may make plans and arrangements for his or her retirement.

**Presbycusis**   The loss of hearing of high-frequency tones.

**Presbyopia**   Difficulty in accurately perceiving objects that are close.

**Primary emotions**   Emotions which are present at birth or shortly thereafter. They are believed to be hard-wired into the brain and serve an adaptive purpose.

**Primary short-term memory**   The conscious process of keeping information in short-term memory.

**Private speech**   A speech form prevalent in early childhood in which children talk to themselves or continue to talk even when no one is listening to what they are saying.

**Problem solving**    The development of strategies to overcome an obstacle in order to achieve a goal.

**Procedural memory**    Knowledge about how to perform certain tasks, like riding a bike or driving a car, or even walking.

**Prosocial**    A growing sense of others (e.g. comforting other children who seem sad or worried).

**Prosocial behaviors**    Those behaviors that promote helpfulness and show concern for others, such as altruism or empathy.

**Proximodistal growth pattern**    Changes happen first in the center, innermost area of the body and then move outward to the ends of extremities.

**Pruning**    The elimination of unnecessary excess neuron connections between millions of neuron cells over time.

**Pseudostupidity**    The tendency of young adolescents to interpret situations in more complex ways than called for.

**Psychological age**    Based upon an individual's adaptive capacities in relation to their chronological age.

**Psychological death**    The thoughts and emotional reactions experienced by the dying individuals and his or her family and friends.

**Psychopathology**    The branch of medicine dealing with the causes and processes of mental disorders.

**Psychophysiologic**    The sixth stage for understanding illness; illness is understood physiologically, but the child also can consider the influence of psychological factors.

**Psychosocial crisis**    A central problem that the person is expected to master in order to make healthy progress to the next stage.

**Psychotropic medication**    Any medication capable of altering cognition, or behavior.

**Puberty**    The developmental event occurring in early adolescence in which the sexual organs become functional. It is associated with other significant physical changes in the body.

**Punishers**    Are meant to decrease the behaviors they follow.

**Quickening**    The first detection by mother of movements made by a fetus.

**Randomly assigned**    Assignment of research participants to groups in an experimental study by chance.

**Reactive depression**    Feelings of loss and disfigurement of the body from surgery or from the ravages of disease.

**Reality principle**    According to Freud, the tendency to behave in ways that are consistent with reality.

**Recall**    The basic process of a newborn being capable of recalling observed behavior experiences.

**Recessive**    A gene from one parent whose influence is repressed by the complementary (dominant) gene from the other parent in the offspring.

**Recognition**    Awareness or recollection of having seen something before.

**Reflection phase**    The time to judge one's own work, make attributions in regards to the quality of the work, and evaluate the outcomes within the given context.

**Reflexes**    A response controlled by the autonomic nervous system, over which an individual has no willful control.

**Regulation of loss**    Behaviors that allow for reorganization or functioning at lower levels because maintenance is no longer possible.

**Rehearsal**    Practicing something over and over again.

**Reinforcers**    Are meant to increase the behavior they follow.

**Rejected**    Children who are rejected by peers are disliked, and are at risk of many serious problems that include clinical depression.

**Rejecting-neglecting parenting style**    Parents that display little affection or discipline.

**Religiosity**    Incorporates spirituality, but includes the additional dimension of living the faith.

**Remote relationship**    A grandparent-grandchildren relationship characterized by infrequent contact governed by behavior that is ritualistic and highly symbolic.

**Reorientation stage**   People attempt a more realistic appraisal of their options for the future.

**Returners**   Young adults who had ventured out to independent living, but subsequently returned to live with their parents at some point between the ages of twenty-one and twenty-five years of age.

**Reversibility**   The cognitive ability of school-age children to understand that certain operations can occur in their reverse order (e.g., subtraction is the reverse of addition).

**Rheumatism**   A variety of conditions resulting in stiffness and soreness in tissues associated with bone joints.

**Rhythm**   Regular body movements.

**Risky behavior**   Any behavior that detrimentally effects health or increases the likelihood of disease, although they typically increase an individual's sense of well-being at the moment.

**Rite of committal**   The third and final step in a Catholic funeral where the person's body or ashes is sprinkled with holy water, possibly incensed, and place in its final resting place.

**Role confusion**   The disjointed, fragmented notion of self resulting from an inability to integrate the various aspects of personality into a unified whole.

**Rooting reflex**   This is a searching reflex motion that helps the neonate to locate a breast or bottle nipple. It occurs when the baby's cheeks are stroked or the corner of its mouth is touched. The response is "rooting," in which the baby turns its head in the direction of the stimulation, and as it does so, opens its mouth. The baby's tongue begins to move forward and backward in its mouth.

**Rough-and-tumble play**   Physically active play.

**Sample**   A subset of a population.

**Sandwich generation**   The term sometimes used to describe middle-aged individuals, referring to their divided loyalties and responsibilities toward the younger and the older generation within their family systems.

**Scaffolding**   An instructional strategy in which a learning task is structured whereby a lot of support is offered early on, but as the student begins to learn, less and less support is given.

**Schema**   Any consistent, reliable pattern or plan of interaction with the environment.

**School bilingualism**   The offering of courses in a secondary language in the elementary schools.

**Science**   The marriage of rationalism and empiricism that provides a mechanism allowing for understanding the world within a system of checks and balances.

**Scientific method**   A series of steps that scientists from any field use as a process to test theories and gain knowledge within their field.

**Scientific-inductive reasoning**   Starting with an observation or thought that generates a hypothesis about something.

**Scoliosis**   S-curved spinal column.

**Scripts**   An organized series of acts committed to memory (e.g., getting dressed, brushing the teeth).

**Secondary emotions**   Emotions that develop during the second year or so after birth, as cognitive development advances. They can be a blend of two or more primary emotions, culturally-specific, or self-conscious/self-evaluative in nature.

**Secular trend**   The trend, inferred from observation of several generations, toward achieving sexual maturity at earlier ages than in the past.

**Secure attachment style**   An infant who misses his/her mother when she leaves the room and greets her upon returning.

**Selection, optimization, and compensation (SOC) theory**   A theory that examines how selection, optimization, and compensation assist individuals in coping with the declines associated with aging. It is often considered a theory of successful aging.

**Selective attention**   A cognitive ability to tune out distracting stimulation while performing a task.

**Self-actualization**   A person's drive to achieve their personal full potential.

**Self-awareness**   A child's use of self-referencing pronouns, using their own name, and occasionally labeling themselves by sex and age.

**Self-concept**   One's basic ideas about one's inner self.

**Self-regulated learning**   When a person keeps track of what they have learned, what they still need to learn, and have a strategy for how to learn it.

**Semantic memory**   General knowledge.

**Semantics**   The ability to express meaning through language.

**Senescence**   The process of aging.

**Senility**   Marked deterioration in mental organization characterized by confusion, memory loss, information-processing difficulties, and disorientation.

**Sense of industry**   A positive, healthy attitude toward work and the need to master certain basic skills.

**Sense of inferiority**   A pervasive attitude of worthlessness.

**Sense of integrity versus a sense of despair**   The final psychosocial attitude proposed by Erikson; it is developed in late adulthood. Integrity is characterized by completion of the task of integrating the various aspects of the self-concept and identity and evaluation of one's life as having been a meaningful and fulfilling experience. Despair is characterized by a feeling of loss, disappointment, and deep dissatisfaction with the way one's life was lived.

**Sensory register**   The first memory storage location where sensory information is stored in the brain before becoming short- or long-term memory.

**Sequential design**   A compromise that minimizes the disadvantages of both cross-sectional and longitudinal designs.

**Seriation**   A cognitive ability that allows objects to be scaled according to various dimensions (e.g., large to small).

**Sex chromosomes**   The twenty-third pair of chromosomes which determines a person's gender.

**Sexual harassment**   Unwanted sexual attention.

**Sexualization**   A person's value comes only from his or her sexual appeal or behavior, to the exclusion of other characteristics; a person is held to a standard that equates physical attractiveness (narrowly defined) with being sexy; a person is sexually objectified—that is, made into a thing for others' sexual use, rather than seen as a person with the capacity for independent action and decision making; and/or sexuality is inappropriately imposed upon a person.

**Shame**   The feeling that one's inner self is exposed as being flawed in some manner.

**Shame and doubt**   Refers to the belief that one is unable to be autonomous and that one's inner self is basically flawed and defective.

**Short-reprieve pattern**   The person's death is postponed unexpectedly, but only for a short period of time.

**Short-term memory**   An initial memory storage location in the brain where information remains for about one minute before being erased or placed into long-term memory; recall of information, events, and so on that are relatively recent.

**Significant others**   Those people who are singularly important at each particular stage of a person's psychosocial development.

**Silent generation**   Individuals born between 1922 and 1945.

**Slow-to-warm-up temperament**   The display of quiet activity levels, somewhat fussy, and wary around others and situations.

**Social age**   Based upon social norms and expectations in relation to what an individual "should" be doing at a specific chronological age.

**Social cognition**   The skills involved in understanding the dynamics of human social interaction patterns. Self-understanding is also related to these skills.

**Social death**   The institutional and cultural events and processes that relate to a deceased individual, such as the bereavement of family and friends and the funeral.

**Social hierarchy**   An organizational ranking of peers based on how much a child is liked or disliked by others.

**Social norms**   Expectations in a given society about how an individual should behave, feel, and think.

**Social policy**   Typically, a government policy regarding a social issue.

**Social referencing**   When infants look at their parents' faces and behavior for information about something.

**Social smile**   Smiling in response to social stimulation from others.

**Socialization**   The process by which individuals are taught to conform to social rules, to acquire personal values, and to develop attitudes typical of their culture.

**Sociobiology**   The study of the biological bases of social behavior.

**Sociocultural theory**   A theory that cognitive development is dependent upon social interactions.

**Socioemotional domain**   Changes in emotion, personality, and relationships.

**Socioemotional selectivity theory**   A theory that as age increases, so does the desire to be more selective in one's social relationships, optimizing positive interactions.

**Solitary play**   Children are alone or are playing independently of others.

**Somatic stem cells**   Another term for adult stem cells.

**Source memory**   The ability to remember where you heard, saw, or learned something.

**Spatial intelligence**   Involves mental abilities in perception of objects and the ability to mentally transform and manipulate these objects.

**Spatial reference memory**   The aspect of memory that stores information about one's environment and spatial orientation.

**Speech**   Orally expressed language.

**Speed**   The rate of movement once the body is in action.

**Spina bifida**   A birth defect in which the tissue surrounding the spinal cord does not properly close during prenatal development

**Spirituality**   A sense of connectedness with God (or some other higher spiritual being).

**Stability stage**   The routine of established behaviors.

**Startle reflex**   This reflex is most often elicited by loud noises and unexpected, sudden touching of the newborn's trunk area.

**Still in the nest**   Individuals who are still living at home between the ages of twenty-one to twenty-five years, but are actively working towards moving out, and are out by the end of this age-range.

**Stillbirth**   Death of a fetus before birth due to any one of several reasons.

**Stochastic processes**   The probability of random accidental injury to cellular DNA.

**Stranger wariness**   Or stranger anxiety, which is observable around six months of age.

**Strength**   The ability to exert force.

**Stress**   The physiological and psychological reactions of an organism to demands placed upon it.

**Stressors**   Events that can cause stress reactions.

**Strokes**   A cerebrovascular accident occurring when a blood vessel in the brain ruptures or is obstructed by a blood clot.

**Structural equation modeling**   A model that is developed to explain patterns of relationships among variables.

**Sucking reflex**   The sucking reflex is closely associated with both the rooting and swallowing reflexes. It is produced when the soft palate in the baby's mouth is stimulated.

**Sudden infant death syndrome (SIDS)**   A condition of unknown cause resulting in the sudden and unexpected death of an infant.

**Superego**   Functions to control and override the id's attempts to express basic drives in ways that are socially unacceptable.

**Suspended-sentence pattern**   The person is discharged from medical care and is expected to live for several years.

**Swimming reflex**    This unusual reflex occurs when the neonate is submerged on its abdomen in water. The baby holds its breath and makes swimming motions with both arms and legs.

**Symbolic play**    Using objects in a pretend fashion (e.g. like tea parties).

**Sympathy**    The ability to feel the same way that others do; learning to sympathize is the first step toward developing empathy.

**Synaptic gap (synapses)**    The tiny gaps between neurons.

**Syntax**    The rules for making grammatical sentences.

**Task analysis**    The careful examination of a problem and consideration of what steps will be necessary in order to solve it.

**Temperament**    A baby's general approach to the world and behavioral orientation.

**Teratogen**    Anything that can cause abnormal development.

**Teratology**    A branch of science that studies the causes, mechanisms, and patterns of abnormal development.

**Terminal decline**    The official term used to describe the accelerated cognitive degeneration as elderly individuals approach death.

**Terminal period**    Characterized by withdrawal from others and general disengagement from the world.

**Termination**    The last stage which is marked by a role shift from retiree either to being employed again, or to being disabled in advanced age.

**Thanatology**    The study of dying, death, and grief.

**Theoretical eclecticism**    The approach of investigating the varied models and concepts and choosing the best to apply to a particular issue.

**Theory**    A collection of ideas used to explain observations.

**Theory of mind**    The ability to understand your own mental state, as well as the mental state of others.

**Time-series analysis**    A study of the same variable across time.

**Tonic neck reflex**    This reflex usually occurs when the neonate is placed on its back. The arms, legs, and head move to a characteristic "fencing" position in which the arm and leg on one side are extended, while those on the other side are flexed. The baby's head turns to one side, usually in the direction of its extended limbs.

**Toxemia**    An acute hypertensive disease of pregnancy characterized by high blood pressure, retention of body fluids, and the presence of protein in the urine.

**Trait**    A distinguishing feature or characteristic.

**Trajectory**    A path or pattern that is followed in some particular process.

**Transductive reasoning**    Seeing a relationship between two objects or events, when in fact no relationship exists.

**Transverse**    When a child is sideways during labor (requires either that the child is physically moved to the head-down position, or delivered C-section).

**"Type A" personality**    Highly competitive, restless, and achievement oriented.

**"Type B" personality**    A personality that is low in hostility and aggression, and moderately ambitious.

**"Type C" personality**    Associated with an increased risk for cancer, this personality type tends to be introverted and eager to please.

**Umbilical cord blood and placental stem cells**    Stem cells found in the umbilical cord blood and placenta after birth.

**Underextension**    When a child limits the meaning of the word too narrowly.

**Unintegrated**    A personality type where individuals may be described as experiencing dementia.

**Unoccupied play**    Play that seems random and without purpose.

**Values**    A person's belief about what is right and what is wrong.

**Variables**    Anything that can vary.

**Vernix caseosa**    A thick, cold cream-like substance covering the baby's skin. It serves to protect the skin and lubricate the fetus for passage through the birth canal.

**Vernix**    The lubricating, creamlike substance that has formed during the fetal period.

**Vestigial reflexes**    Several reflexes present at birth that seem to be relics of adaptive experiences sometime in our vast evolutionary past.

**Vigil**    The first step in a Catholic funeral that may take place in a funeral parlor, a home, or a church. The vigil is short in duration and focuses mainly on prayer, although readings and music are also included.

**Visual acuity**    Sharpness or clarity of vision

**Visualization**    The ability to organize and process visual materials.

**Visuomotor flexibility**    The ability to shift from familiar to unfamiliar tasks involving hand-eye coordination.

**Voice disorders**    Persistent difficulties with the quality of voice.

**Walking reflex**    Step-like motions of the legs occur reflexively when the neonate is held in an upright position and allowed to touch a flat surface with its feet. The legs respond by flexing alternately as if the child is walking.

**"Whole-brain" death**    When the entire brain, including the brain stem, ceases to function.

**Widowhood**    A label applied to both men and women who survive the death of a spouse.

**Working memory**    The workbench of memory where simultaneous cognitive processes can be attended to and handled.

**Zone of proximal development**    The range between what a child can accomplish alone and what can be accomplished with assistance.

**Zygote**    The name of the developing individual during the germinal period.

# References

Abraham, S. (1979). Weight and height of adults 18–74 years of age, United States 1971–1974. *Vital and Health Statistics, Series 11, No. 211.* DHEW Publication No.(PHS) 79–1659.

Abraham, S. (1979). Mean weight in pounds of adults 18–74 years by age and sex: United States, 1971–1974. *Vital and Health Statistics, Series 11, No. 211.* DHEW Publication No. (PHS) 799–1659.

Acredolo, L. P., & Goodwyn, S. (1988). Symbolic gesturing in normal infants. *Child Development, 59,* 450–466.

Acredolo, L. P., & Hake, J. K. (1982). Infant perception. In B. B. Wolman (Ed.), *Handbook of developmental psychology.* Englewood Cliffs, NJ: Prentice Hall.

Ad Hoc Committee of the Harvard Medical School. (1968). A definition of irreversible coma: Report of the Ad Hoc Committee of the Harvard Medical School to Examine the Definition of Brain Death. *Journal of the American Medical Association, 205,* 337–340.

Adams, C. G., & Turner, B. F. (1985). Reported change in sexuality from young adulthood to old age. *Journal of Sex Research, 21,* 126–141.

Adeyanju, M. (1990). Adolescent health status, behaviors, and cardiovascular disease. *Adolescence, 25,* 155–169.

Ainsworth, M. (1973). The development of infant-mother attachment. In B. Caldwell & H. Riciuti (Eds.), *Review of child development research.* Vol. 3. Chicago: University of Chicago Press.

Ainsworth, M. (1977). Attachment theory and its utility in cross-cultural research. In P. Leiderman, S. Tulkin, & A. Rosenfield (Eds.), *Culture and infancy: Variations in the human experience.* New York: Academic Press.

Ainsworth, M. D. S., Blehar, M. C., Waters, E., & Wall, S. (1978). *Patterns in attachment: A psychological study of the strange situation.* Hillsdale, NJ: Erlbaum.

Ainsworth, M. D. S., & Wittig, B. A. (1969). Attachment and exploratory behavior of one-year-olds in a Strange Situation. In B. M. Foss (Ed.), *Determinants of Infant Behavior, 4,* (pp. 111-136). London: Methuen.

Alam, S. E. (1978). The aging parent and the adult child. *Journal of Home Economics, 71,* 26–28.

Albert, M. S., & Killiany, R. J. (2001). Age-related cognitive change and brain-behavior relationships. In J. E. Birren & K. W. Schaie (Eds.), *Handbook of the psychology of aging.* San Diego, CA: Academic Press.

Aldous, J. (1978). *Family careers: Developmental change in families.* New York: Wiley.

Aldous, J. (1987). Family life of the elderly and the near-elderly. *Journal of Marriage and the Family, 49,* 227–234.

Aldwin, C. M. (1994). *Stress, coping, and development: An integrative perspective.* NY: The Guilford Press.

Alessandri, S., & Wozniak, R. (1989). Perception of the family environment and interfamilial agreement in belief concerning the adolescent. *Journal of Early Adolescence, 9,* 67–81.

Alexander, J. F., & Malouf, R. E. (1983). Problems in personality and social development. In P. Mussen (Ed.), *Handbook of child psychology.* Vol. 4. New York: Wiley.

Allegeier, E. R., & Murnen, S. K (1985). Perceptions of parents as sexual beings: Pocs & Godow revisited. *Siecus Reports, 13,* 11–12.

Allport, G. W. (1961). *Pattern and growth in personality.* New York: Holt, Rinehart, Winston.

American Association of Retired Persons. (1986). *A profile of older Americans.* Washington, DC: American Association of Retired Persons.

American Cancer Society. (1988). *Cancer facts and figures.* New York: American Cancer Society.

American College of Obstetricians and Gynecologists (2005). *Your pregnancy and birth* (4th ed.). Washington, DC: The American College of Obstetricians and Gynecologists and Meredith Books.

American Heart Association. (1984). *Eating for a healthy heart: Dietary treatment for hyperlipidemia.* Dallas, TX: American Heart Association.

American Psychiatric Association. (1980). *Diagnostic and statistical manual of mental disorders* (3rd ed.). Washington, DC: American Psychiatric Association.

Ames, L. B. (1986). Ready or not. *American Educator, 10,* 30–34.

Anastasi, A. (1958). Heredity, environment, and the question "how." *Psychological Review, 65,* 197–208.

Anderson, D. (1987). Family and peer relations of gay adolescents. *Adolescent Psychiatry, 14,* 162–178.

Anderson, T. (1984). Widowhood as a life transition: Its impact on kinship ties. *Journal of Marriage and the Family, 46,* 105–114.

Andrew, E., Clancy, K., & Katz, M. (1980). Infant feeding practices of families belonging to a prepaid group practice health care plan. *Pediatrics, 65,* 978–987.

Anglin, J. M. (1977). *Word, object, and conceptual development.* New York: Norton.

Anrig, G., Jr. (1988). How to retire early and comfortably. *Money, 17(12),* 58–60.

Ansbacher, R. (1983). Median age for menopause. *Medical Aspects of Human Sexuality, 17,* 143.

Antonucci, T. C. (2001). Social relations: An examination of social networks, social support, and sense of control. In J. E. Birren & K. W. Schaie (Eds.), *Handbook of the psychology of aging.* San Diego, CA: Academic Press.

Aries, P. (1962). *Centuries of childhood* (Translated by R. Baldick). New York: Knopf.

Ary, D. V., & Biglan, A. (1988). Longitudinal changes in adolescent cigarette smoking behavior: Onset and cessation. *Journal of Behavioral Medicine, 11,* 361–382.

Asher, S., & Gottman, J. (Eds.). (1981). *The development of children's friendships.* New York: Cambridge University Press.

Ashner, L., & Meyerson, M. (1990). *When parents love too much: What happens when parents won't let go.* New York: William Morrow.

Aslin, R. N. (1987). Motor aspects of visual development in infancy. In P. Salapatek & L. Cohen (Eds.), *Handbook of infant perception.* Vol. 1. New York: Academic Press.

Astin, A. (1977). *Four critical years.* San Francisco: Josey-Bass.

Atchley, R. C. (1971). Retirement and work orientation. *The Gerontologist, 2,* 29–32.

Atchley, R. C. (1976). *The sociology of retirement.* Cambridge, MA: Schenkman.

Athey, I. (1983). Language development factors relating to reading development. *Journal of Educational Research, 76,* 197–203.

Attie, I., & Brooks-Gunn, J. (1989). Development of eating problems in adolescent girls. *Developmental Psychology, 25,* 70–79.

Aubrey, R. R. (1977). Adolescents and death. In E. R. Prichard et al., (Eds.), *Social work with the dying patient and family* (pp. 131–145). New York: Columbia University Press.

Auerbach-Fink, S. (1978). Mothers' expectations of child care. *Young Children, 32,* 12–21.

Aukett, R. (1988). Gender differences in friendship patterns. *Sex Roles, 19,* 57–63.

Ault, R. (1983). *Children's cognitive development* (2nd ed.) New York: Oxford University Press.

Avery, M. E. (1989). *Pediatric medicine.* Baltimore: Williams and Wilkins.

Babchuck, N., Peters, G., Hoyt, D., & Kaiser, M. (1979). The voluntary associations of the aged. *Journal of Gerontology, 34,* 579–587.

Babladelis, G. (1987). Young persons' attitudes toward aging. *Perceptual and Motor Skills, 65,* 553–554.

Backett, L. (1986). *Mothers and fathers.* New York: St. Martin's Press.

Backman, L., Small, B. J., & Wahlin, A. (2001). Age and memory: Cognitive and biological perspectives. In J. E. Birren & K. W. Schaie (Eds.), *Handbook of the psychology of aging.* San Diego, CA: Academic Press.

Bailey, D. A. (1977). The growing child and the need for physical activity. In R. Smart & M. Smart (Eds.), *Readings in child development and relationships* (2nd ed.). New York: Macmillan.

Bailey, G. W. (1989). Current perspectives on substance abuse in youth. *Journal of the American Academy of Child and Adolescent Psychiatry, 28,* 151–162.

Baillargeon, R. (1987). Object permanence in 3 1/2 and 4 1/2 month old infants. *Developmental Psychology, 23,* 655–664.

Baltes, P. B., Lindenberger, U., & Staudinger, U. M. (1998). Life-span theory in developmental psychology. In W. Damon & R. M. Lerner (Eds.), *Handbook of child psychology (Vol. 1): Theoretical models of human development* (5th ed.). NY: John Wiley & Sons, Inc.

Baltes, P., & Schaie, K. (1974). Aging and the IQ: The myth of the twilight years. *Psychology Today, 7,* 35–40.

Baltes, P. B., & Smith, J. (1990). Toward a psychology of wisdom and its ontogenesis. In R. J. Sternberg (Ed.), *Wisdom: Its nature, origins, and development.* NY: Cambridge University Press.

Bandura, A. (1973). *Aggression: A social learning analysis.* Englewood Cliffs, NJ: Prentice Hall.

Bandura, A. (1977). *Social learning theory.* Englewood Cliffs, NJ: Prentice Hall.

Bandura, A. (1986). *Social foundations of thought and action.* Englewood Cliffs, NJ: Prentice Hall.

Bandura, A. (1989). Human agency in social cognitive theory. *American Psychologist, 44,* 1175–1184.

Bandura, A., & Walters, R. H. (1963). *Social learning and personality development.* New York: Holt, Rinehart, and Winston.

Banks, M. S., & Salapatek, P. (1983). Infant visual perception. In M. M. Haith & J. Campos (Eds.), *Handbook of child psychology.* Vol. 2. New York: Wiley.

Baptiste, D. A., Jr. (1987). The gay and lesbian stepparent family. In F. Bozett (Ed.), *Gay and lesbian parents.* New York: Praeger.

Barber, C. E. (1980). Gender differences in experiencing the transition to the empty nest. *Family Perspective, 14,* 87–95.

Barglow, P., Vaughn, B., & Molitor, N. (1987). Effects of maternal absence due to employment on the quality of infant-mother attachment in a low-risk sample. *Child Development, 58,* 945–954.

Barling, J. (1990). *Employment, stress, and family functioning.* Chichester, England: John Wiley.

Barnes, K. E. (1971). Preschool play norms: A replication. *Developmental Psychology, 5,* 99–103.

Barnes, G., & Welte, J. (1988). Predictors of driving while intoxicated among teenagers. *Journal of Drug Issues, 18,* 367–384.

Barranti, C. C. R. (1985). The grandparent/grandchild relationship: Family resource in an era of voluntary bonds. *Family Relations, 34,* 343–352.

Barrera, M., & Maurer, D. (1981). Discrimination of strangers by the three month old. *Child Development, 52,* 558–563.

Barret, R. L., & Robinson, B. L. (1990). *Gay fathers.* Lexington, MA: DC Heath.

Bart, P. (1971). Depression in middle age women. In V. Gornick & B. Moran (Eds.), *Women in sexist society.* New York: Basic Books.

Bart, P. (1975). The loneliness of the long distance mother. In J. Freeman (Ed.), *Women: A feminist perspective.* Palo Alto, CA: Mayfield.

Bass, M., Kravath, R., & Glass, L. (1986). Death-scene investigation in sudden infant death. *New England Journal of Medicine, 315,* 100–105.

Baughman, E. (1971). *Black Americans.* New York: Academic Press.

Baumeister, R., & Senders, P. (1989). Identity development and the role structure of children's games. *Journal of Genetic Psychology, 150,* 19–37.

Baumrind, D. (1966). Effects of authoritative parental control on child behavior. *Child Development, 37,* 887–907.

Baumrind, D. (1967). Child care practices anteceding three patterns of preschool behavior. *Genetic Psychology Monographs, 75,* 43–88.

Baumrind, D. (1971). *Current patterns of parental authority.* Developmental Psychology Monographs, 4(1).

Baurer, D. H. (1976). An exploratory study of developmental changes in children's fears. *Journal of Child Psychology and Psychiatry, 17,* 69–74.

Bayley, N. (1969). *Bayley scales of infant development.* New York: Psychological Corporation.

Bayley, N. (1970). Development of mental abilities. In P. Mussen (Ed.), *Carmichael's manual of child psychology.* (3rd ed.). Vol. 1. New York: Wiley.

Bayley, N., & Oden, M. (1955). The maintenance of intellectual ability in gifted adults. *Journal of Gerontology, 10,* 91–107.

Beattie, M. (1987). *Codependent no more.* New York: Harper/Hazelden.

Beattie, M. (1989). *Beyond codependency and getting better all the time.* San Francisco, CA: Harper & Row.

Beck, S. (1982). Adjustment to and satisfaction with retirement. *Journal of Gerontology, 37,* 616–624.

Beck, M. (1990). *The geezer boom.* Newsweek, Special edition Winter/Spring, 63–68.

Beck, R., & Beck, S. (1989). The incidence of extended households among middle-aged black and white women. *Journal of Family Issues, 10,* 147–168.

Becker, W. (1964). Consequences of different kinds of parental discipline. In M. Hoffman & L. Hoffman (Eds.), *Review of child development research,* Vol. 1. New York: Russell Sage.

Becvar, R. J., & Becvar, D. S. (1982). *Systems theory and family therapy: A primer.* New York: University Press of America.

Belgrave, L. L. (1990). The relevance of chronic illness in the everyday lives of elderly women. *Journal of Aging and Health, 2,* 475–481.

Belkin, L. (1985). *Counseling and support following miscarriage.* New York Times (June 6), 20.

Bell, R. Q. (1968). A reinterpretation of the direction of effects in studies of socialization. *Psychological Review, 75,* 81–95.

Bell, R. Q. (1971). Stimulus control of parent or caretaker behavior by offspring. *Developmental Psychology, 4,* 63–72.

Bell, R. R. (1981). Friendships of women and men. *Psychology of Women Quarterly, 5,* 402–417.

Bell, A. P., & Weinberg, M. S. (1978). *Homosexualities: A study of diversity among men and women.* New York: Simon and Schuster.

Belsky, J. (1978). The effects of day care: A critical review. *Child Development, 49,* 929–949.

Belsky, J. (1981). Early human experience: A family perspective. *Developmental Psychology, 17,* 3–23.

Belsky, J. (1984). *The psychology of aging: Theory and research and practice.* Monterey, CA: Brooks/Cole.

Belsky, J. (1988). The "effects" of infant day care reconsidered. *Early Childhood Research Quarterly, 3,* 235–273.

Belsky, J. (1990). Child care and children's socioemotional development. *Journal of Marriage and the Family, 52,* 885–903.

Belsky, J. (1990). Parental and nonparental child care and children's socioemotional development: A decade in review. *Journal of Marriage and the Family, 52,* 885–903.

Belsky, J., & Rovine, M. J. (1988). Nonmaternal care in the first year of life and the security of infant-parent attachment. *Child Development, 59,* 157–168.

Belsky, J., Lang, M. E., & Rovine, M. (1985). Stability and change in marriage across the transition to parenthood: A second study. *Journal of Marriage and the Family, 47,* 855–865.

Belsky, J., Robins, E., & Gamble, W. (1984). The determinants of parental competence: Toward a contextual theory. In M. Lewis (Ed.), *Beyond the dyad.* New York: Plenum.

Belsky, J., Spanier, G. B., & Rovine, M. (1983). Stability and change in marriage across the transition to parenthood. *Journal of Marriage and the Family, 45,* 567–577.

Belsky, J., Steinberg, L. D., & Walker, A. (1982). The ecology of day care. In M. Lamb (Ed.), *Nontraditional families: Parenting and child development.* Hillsdale, NJ: Erlbaum.

Belsky, J. K. (1988). *Here tomorrow: Making the most of life after fifty.* New York: Ballantine Books.

Bengston, V. (1985). Diversity and symbolism in grandparental roles. In V. Bengston & J. Robertson (Eds.), *Grandparenthood.* Beverly Hills, CA: Sage.

Bem, S. (1989). Genital knowledge and gender constancy in preschool children. *Child Development, 60,* 649–662.

Bengston, V. (1975). Generation and family effects in value socialization. *American Sociological Review, 40,* 358–371.

Bengston, V. L., Cuellar, J. B., & Ragan, P. K. (1977). Stratum contrasts and similarities in attitudes toward death. *Journal of Gerontology, 32,* 76–88.

Bengston, V., Dowd, J., Smith, D., & Inkeles, A. (1975). Modernization, modernity, and perceptions of aging: A cross-cultural study. *Journal of Gerontology, 30,* 688–695.

Bengston, V. L., Rosenthal, C. J., & Burton, L. M. (1990).Families and aging: Diversity and heterogeneity. In R. H. Binstock & L. George (Eds.), *Handbook of aging and the social sciences* (3rd ed.). San Diego, CA: Academic Press.

Benoliel, J. Q. (1975). Childhood diabetes: The commonplace in living becomes uncommon. In A. L. Strauss & B. G. Glaser (Eds.), *Chronic illness and the quality of life.* St. Louis, MO: Mosby.

Beresin, E. V., Gordon, C., & Herzog, D. B. (1989). The process of recovering from anorexia nervosa. *Journal of the American Academy of Psychoanalysis, 17,* 103–130.

Bergstrom, L. R. (1990). Retiring with security. *Security Management, 34,* 97–100.

Berk, L. E. (1986). Private speech: Learning out loud. *Psychology Today,* (May), 34–42.

Berlinsky, E., & Biller, H. B. (1982). *Parental death and psychological development.* Lexington, MA: Lexington Books.

Berman, A. L. (1986). Helping suicidal adolescents: Needs and responses. In C. A. Cort & J. M. McNell (Eds.), *Adolescence and death* (pp. 151–166). New York: Springer.

Bernard, J. (1981). The good provider role: Its rise and fall. *American Psychologist, 36,* 1–12.

Berndt, T., Hawkins, J., & Hoyle, S. (1986). Changes in friendship during a school year: Effects on children's and adolescents' impressions of friendship and sharing with friends. *Child Development, 57,* 1284–1297.

Bernstein, B. E. (1978). Generational conflict and the family. *Adolescence, 13,* 751–754.

Bertenthal, B, & Campos, J. (1987). New directions in the study of early experience. *Child Development, 58,* 560–567.

Bianchi, S. M., & Spain, D. (1986). *American women in transition.* New York: Russell Sage Foundation.

Bieber, I., Dain, H., Dince, P., Drellich, M., Grand, H.,Gundlach, R., Kremer, M., Rifkin, A., Wilbur, C., & Bieber, T. (1962). *Homosexuality: A psychoanalytical study.* New York: Basic Books.

Bigner, J. J. (1972a). Parent education in popular literature: 1950–1970. *Family Coordinator, 21,* 313–319.

Bigner, J. J. (1972b). Sibling influence on sex-role preference of young children. *Journal of Genetic Psychology, 121,* 271–282.

Bigner, J. J. (1974a). A Wernerian developmental analysis of children's descriptions of siblings. *Child Development, 45,* 317–323.

Bigner, J. J. (1974b). Second-born's discrimination of sibling role concepts. *Developmental Psychology, 10 ,* 564–573.

Bigner, J. J. (1980). *Preliminary report: Development of social competencies in children.* Ft. Collins, CO: Colorado State University Experiment Station.

Bigner, J. J. (1989). *Parent-child relations: An introduction to parenting* (3rd ed.). New York: Macmillan.

Bigner, J. J., & Bozett, F. W. (1989). Parenting by gay fathers. *Marriage and Family Review, 14,* 155–176.

Bigner, J. J., & Jacobsen, R. B. (1980). Children's perceptions of "goodness" and "badness" in sibling roles. *Home Economics Research Journal, 8,* 274–280.

Bigner, J. J., & Jacobsen, R. B. (1989a). The value of children to gay and heterosexual fathers. *Journal of Homosexuality, 18,* 163–172.

Bigner, J. J., & Jacobsen, R. B. (1989b). Parenting behaviors of homosexual and heterosexual fathers. *Journal of Homosexuality, 18,* 173–186.

Bigner, J. J., Jacobsen, R. B., & Heward, L. (1987). *Developmental changes in the value of children for adults.* Unpublished manuscript.

Bigner, J. J., Jacobsen, R. B., & Miller, J. A. (1982). The value of children for farm families. *Psychological Reports, 50,* 793–794.

Bigner, J. J., Jacobsen, R. B., & Phelan, G. K. (1981). Cultural correlates of parent-nonparent stereotypes: A multivariate analysis. *Home Economics Research Journal, 9,* 184–192.

Binstock, R. H. (1987). Health care: Organization, use, and financing. In G. Maddox (Ed.), *Encyclopedia of aging.* New York: Springer.

Birch, L. L. (1987). Children's food preferences: Developmental patterns and environmental influences. *Annals of Child Development, 4,* 171–208.

Birch, L. L., McPhee, L., & Sullivan, S. (1989). Children's food intake following drinks sweetened with sucrose or aspartame: Time course effects. *Physiology and Behavior, 45,* 387–395.

Birnholz, J., & Benacerraf, B. (1983). The development of human fetal hearing. *Science, 222,* 516–518.

Birren, J. E., Kinney, D. K., Schaie, K. W., and Woodruff, D. S. (1981). *Developmental psychology.* Boston: Houghton Mifflin.

Birren, J. E., & Schaie, K. W. (Eds.) (2001). *Handbook of the psychology of aging.* San Diego, CA: Academic Press.

Birren, J. E., Woods, A., & Williams, M. (1980). Behavioral slowing with age: Causes, organization, and consequences. In L. Poon (Ed.), *Aging in the 1980s.* Washington, DC: American Psychological Association.

Black, C., & DeBlassie, R. R. (1985). Adolescent pregnancy: Contributing factors, consequences, treatment, and plausible solutions. *Adolescence, 47,* 671–678.

Black, H. (1953). *Black's law dictionary* (4th ed.). St. Paul, MN: West.

Blakeslee, S. (1986). Rapid changes seen in young brain. *New York Times, June 24,* C1, C10.

Blank, R. H. (2001). Technology and death policy. In G. E. Dickinson & M. R. Leming, (Eds.), *Dying, death, and bereavement* (10th ed.). NY: McGraw-Hill.

Blau, Z. S. (1973). *Old age in a changing society.* New York: Franklin Watts.

Blieszner, R., & Alley, J. (1990). Family caregiving for the elderly: An overview of resources. *Family Relations, 39,* 97–102.

Block, C., Norr, K., Meyering, S., Norr, J., & Charles, A. (1981). Husband gatekeeping in childbirth. *Family Relations, 30,* 197–204.

Blood, R. O., & Wolfe, D. M. (1960). *Husbands and wives: The dynamics of married living.* New York: Free Press.

Bloom, B. S. (1964). *Stability and change in human characteristics.* New York: Wiley.

Bloom, L. (1970). *Language development: Form and function in emerging grammar.* Cambridge, MA: MIT Press.

Bloom, L., & Lahey, M. (1978). *Language development and language disorders.* New York: Wiley.

Bloom, M. V. (1987). Leaving home: A family transition. In J. & S. Bloom-Feshbach (Eds.), *The psychology of separation and loss: Perspectives on development, life transitions, and clinical practice.* San Francisco: Josey-Bass.

Blumberg, R. L., & Winch, R. F. (1977). Societal complexity and familial complexity: Evidence for the curvilinear hypothesis. *American Journal of Sociology, 77,* 898–920.

Blumenfield, M., Levy, N. B., & Kaufman, D. (1978). The wish to be informed of a fatal illness. *Omega, 9,* 323–326.

Bohannan, P. (1970). The six stations of divorce. In P. Bohannan (Ed.), *Divorce and after.* New York: Doubleday.

Boivin, M., & Begin, G. (1989). Peer status and self-perception among early elementary school children: The case of the rejected children. *Child Development, 60,* 591–596.

Bok, S. (1976). Personal directions for the care at the end of life. *The New England Journal of Medicine, 295,* 367–368.

Boldt, M. (1982). Normative evaluations of suicide and death: A cross generational study. *Omega, 13,* 145–157.

Borg, S., & Lasker J. (1981). *When pregnancy fails: Families coping with miscarriage, stillbirth, and infant death.* Boston: Beacon Press.

Borhek, M. V. (1988). Helping gay and lesbian adolescents and their families: A mother's perspective. *Journal of Adolescent Health Care, 9,* 123–128.

Borke, H. (1975). Piaget's mountains revisited: Change in the egocentric landscape. *Developmental Psychology, 12,* 185–191.

Bornstein, M., & Sigman, M. (1986). Continuity in mental development from infancy. *Child Development, 57,* 251–274.

Boss, P. (1980). Normative family stress: Boundary changes across the life span. *Family Relations, 29,* 445–452.

Botwinick, J. (1977). Intellectual abilities. In J. E. Birren & K. Schaie (Eds.), *Handbook of the psychology of aging.* New York: Van Nostrand.

Boukydis, C., & Burgess, R. (1982). Adult physiological response to infant cries: Effects of temperament of infant, parental status, and gender. *Child Development, 53,* 1291–1298.

Bower, T. (1975). Infant perception of the third dimension and object concept development. In L. Cohen & P. Salapatek (Eds.), *Infant perception: From sensation to cognition.* Vol. 2. New York: Academic Press.

Bower, T. (1976). Repetitive processes in child development. *Scientific American, 235,* 38–47.

Bower, T. (1977). *A primer of infant development.* San Francisco: Freeman.

Bowlby, J. (1952). *Maternal care and mental health.* Monograph Series No. 2. Geneva: World Health Organization.

Bowlby, J. (1969). *Attachment and loss: Attachment* (Vol. 1). NY: Basic Books.

Bowlby, J. (1980). *Attachment and loss: Loss, sadness, and depression.* (Vol. 3). New York: Basic Books.

Bowlby, J. (1982). Attachment and loss: Retrospect and prospect. *American Journal of Orthopsychiatry, 52,* 664–678.

Bowman, M. L. (1990). Coping efforts and marital satisfaction: Measuring marital coping and its correlates. *Journal of Marriage and the Family, 52,* 463–474.

Boyden, T., Carroll, J., & Maier, R. (1984). Similarity and attraction in homosexual males: The effects of age and masculinity-femininity. *Sex Roles, 10,* 939–948.

Boysson-Bardies, B., Sagart, L., & Durand, C. (1984). Discernible differences in the babbling of infants according to target language. *Journal of Child Language, 11,* 1–15.

Bozett, F. W., & Sussman, M. B. (1989). Homosexuality and family relations: Views and research issues. *Marriage and Family Review, 14,* 1–8.

Brackbill, Y. (1977). Long-term effects of obstetrical anesthesia on infant autonomic function. *Developmental Psychology, 10,* 529–535.

Brackbill, Y., Adams, G., Drowell, D. H., & Gray, M. L. (1966). Arousal levels in neonates and preschool children under continuous auditory stimulation. *Journal of Experimental Child Psychology, 4,* 178–188.

Bradbard, M. R., & Endsley, R. C. (1986). Sources of variance in young working mothers' satisfaction with child care. In S. Kilmer (Ed.), *Advances in early education and day care.* Vol. 4. Greenwich, CT: JAI.

Bradshaw, J. (1988). *Bradshaw on: The family.* Deerfield Beach, FL: Health Communications.

Bransford, J. D., Brown, A. L., & Cocking, R. R. (Eds.) (2000). *How people learn: Brain, mind, experience, and school* (Expanded ed.). Washington, DC: National Academy Press.

Brasted, W. S., & Callahan, E. J. (1984). Review article: A behavioral analysis of the grief process. *Behavioral Therapy, 15,* 529–543.

Bratcher, W. (1982). The influence of the family on career selection: A family systems perspective. *Personnel and Guidance Journal, October,* 87–91.

Brazelton, T. B. (1969). *Infants and mothers: Differences in development.* New York: Delacorte.

Brazelton, T. B. (1978). Introduction. In A. J. Sameroff (Ed.), Organization and stability of newborn behavior: A commentary on the Brazelton Neonatal Behavior Assessment Scale. *Monographs of the Society for Research in Child Development, 43* (177), 1–13.

Brazelton, T. B. (1987). Behavioral competence in the newborn infant. In G. B. Avery (Ed.), *Neonatalogy: Pathophysiology and management of the newborn.* (Pp. 379–399). Philadelphia: Lippincott.

Brehm, S. S. (1992). *Intimate relationships* (2nd ed). NY: McGraw-Hill, Inc.

Bretschneider, J. G., & McCoy, N. L. (1988). Sexual interest and behavior in healthy 80 to 102-year-olds. *Archives of Sexual Behavior, 17,* 109–129.

Bridges, K. (1930). A genetic theory of emotions. *Journal of Genetic Psychology, 37,* 514–527.

Bridges, K. (1932). Emotional development in early infancy. *Child Development, 3,* 324–341.

Broccolo, A. (1989). How to select the right nursing home. *Family Safety and Health, 48,* 7–13.

Brock, D. W. (2006). How much is more life worth? In G. E. Dickinson & M. R. Leming, (Eds.), *Dying, death, and bereavement* (10th ed.). NY: McGraw-Hill.

Broderick, C. (1979). *Marriage and the family.* Englewood Cliffs, NJ: Prentice Hall.

Brody, E. (1981). Women in the middle and family help to older people. *The Gerontologist, 21,* 471–480.

Brody, E. B., & Brody, N. (1976). *Intelligence.* New York: Academic Press.

Brody, J. (1990). *Preventing children from joining yet another unfit generation.* New York Times, May 24, B14.

Broman, S. (1986). Obstetric mediation: A review of the literature on outcomes in infancy and childhood. In M. Lewis (Ed.), *Learning disabilities and prenatal risk.* Urbana, IL: University of Illinois Press.

Bronfenbrenner, U. (1977a). Nobody home: The erosion of the American family. *Psychology Today, 10* (May), 41–47.

Bronfenbrenner, U. (1977b). Toward an experimental ecology of human development. *American Psychologist, 32,* 513–531.

Bronfenbrenner, U., & Morris, P. A. (1998). The ecology of developmental processes. In W. Damon & R. M. Lerner (Eds.), *Handbook of child psychology (Vol. 1): Theoretical models of human development* (5th ed.). NY: John Wiley & Sons, Inc.

Brook, J., Whiteman, M., Gordon, A., & Cohen, P. (1986). Some models and mechanisms for explaining the impact of maternal and adolescent characteristics on adolescent stage of drug use. *Developmental Psychology, 22,* 460–467.

Brooke, V. (1989). Nursing home life: How elders adjust. *Geriatric Nursing, 10,* 66–74.

Brooks, R., & Obrzut, J. (1981). Brain lateralization: Implications for infant stimulation and development. *Young Children, 26,* 9–16.

Brooks-Gunn, J., & Furstenberg, F. (1990). Coming of age in the era of AIDS: Puberty, sexuality, and contraception. *Milbank Quarterly, 68,* 59–84.

Brooks-Gunn, J., & Petersen, A. (1983). *Girls at puberty.* New York: Plenum.

Brooks-Gunn, J., & Ruble, D. (1982). The development of menstrual-related beliefs and behavior during adolescence. *Child Development, 53,* 1567–1577.

Brooks-Gunn, J., Boyer, C., & Hein, K. (1988). Preventing HIV infection and AIDS in children and adolescents. *American Psychologist, 43,* 958–964.

Brophy, J. (1986). Teacher influences on student achievement. *American Psychologist, 41,* 1069–1077.

Brown, A. (1982). Learning and development: The problems of compatibility, access, and induction. *Human Development, 25,* 89–115.

Brown, A., Bransford, J., Ferrarar, R., & Campione, J. (1983). Learning, remembering, and understanding. In P. Mussen (Ed.), *Handbook of child psychology* (4th ed.). Vol. 3. New York: Wiley.

Brown, J. M., O'Keefe, J., Sanders, S., & Baker, B. (1986). Developmental changes in children's cognition to stressful and painful situations. *Journal of Pediatric Psychology, 11,* 343–357.

Brown, R. A. (1973). *First language.* Cambridge: Harvard University Press.

Brown, S. (1989). Life events of adolescents in relation to personal and parental substance abuse. *American Journal of Psychiatry, 146,* 484–489.

Brown, S. L., & Booth, A. (1996). Cohabitation versus marriage: A comparison of relationship quality. *Journal of Marriage and Family, 58,* 668–678.

Brubaker, T. H. (1990). Families in later life. *Journal of Marriage and the Family, 52,* 959–982.

Bruch, H. (1978). *The golden cage: The enigma of anorexia nervosa.* Cambridge, MA: Harvard University Press.

Bruner, J. (1971). *The relevance of education.* New York: Norton.

Bruner, J. (1983). *Child's talk.* New York: Norton.

Bruner, J., Olver, R., & Greenfield, P. (1966). *Studies in cognitive growth.* New York: Wiley.

Bryant, B. K., & Crockenberg, S. (1980). Correlates and dimensions of prosocial behavior: A study of female siblings with their mothers. *Child Development, 51,* 529-544.

Buell, S. J., & Coleman, P. D. (1979). Dendritic growth in the aged human brain and failure of growth in senile dementia. *Science, 206,* 854–856.

Bugen, L. A. (1979). *Death and dying: Theory/research/practice.* Dubuque, IA: William C. Brown.

Bugental, D. B. (1986). Unmasking the "polite smile:" Situational and personal determinants of managed affect in adult-child interaction. *Personality and Social Psychology Bulletin, 12,* 7–16.

Bullock, M. (1985). Animism in childhood thinking: A new look at an old question. *Developmental Psychology, 21,* 217–226.

Bullock, M., & Lutkenhaus, P. (1988). The development of volitional behavior in the toddler years. *Child Development, 59,* 664–675.

Bumpass, L. L. (1984). Children and martial disruption: A replication and update. *Demography, 21,* 71–81.

Bumpass, L. L., & Lu, H. H. (2000). Trends in cohabitation and implications for children s family contexts in the United States. *Population Studies, 54,* 29–41.

Burden, D. S. (1986). Single parents and the work setting: The impact of multiple job and home life responsibilities. *Family Relations, 35,* 37–44.

Burger, S., Miller, B., & Mauney, B. (1986). *A guide to management and supervision of nursing homes.* Springfield, IL: Charles C. Thomas.

Burns, D. D. (1980). *Feeling good: The new mood therapy.* New York: William Morrow and Co., Inc.

Burns, D. D. (1989). *The feeling good handbook: Using the new mood therapy in everyday life.* New York: William Morrow.

Burnside, I. M., Ebersole, P., & Monea H. E. (Eds.). (1979). *Psychological caring through the life cycle.* New York: McGraw-Hill.

Burt, R. D., Vaughan, T. L., & Daling, J. R. (1988). Evaluating the risks of Cesarean section: Low Apgar score in repeat C-section and vaginal deliveries. *American Journal of Public Health, 78,* 1312–1314.

Buss, D. M. (1989). Sex differences in human mate preferences: Evolutionary hypotheses tested in 37 cultures. *Behavior and Brain Sciences, 12,* 1-49.

Busse, E. W. (1987). Primary and secondary aging. In G. Maddox (Ed.), *The encyclopedia of aging.* New York: Springer.

Butler, L. (1989). Sexual problems in the elderly, II: Men's vs. women's. *Geriatrics, 44,* 75–82.

Butler, R. N. (1963). The life review: An interpretation of reminiscence in the aged. *Psychiatry, 26,* 65–76.

Button, R. (1990). Self-esteem in girls aged 11–12: Baseline findings from a planned prospective study of vulnerability to eating disorders. *Journal of Adolescence, 13,* 407–413.

Cahan, S., & Cohen, M. (1989). Age versus schooling effects on intelligence development. *Child Development, 60,* 1239–1249.

Cain, W. S., Reid, F., & Stevens, J. C. (1990). Missing ingredients: Aging and the discrimination of flavor. *Journal of Nutrition for the Elderly, 9,* 3–9.

Cairns, R. B. (1998). The making of developmental psychology. In W. Damon & R. M. Lerner (Eds.), *Handbook of child psychology (Vol. 1): Theoretical models of human development* (5th ed.). NY: John Wiley & Sons, Inc.

Caldwell, M., & Peplau, L. (1984). The balance of power in lesbian relationships. *Sex Roles, 10,* 587–599.

Caldwell, B. M., Wright, C., Honig, A., & Tannenbaum, J. (1970). Infant day care and attachment. *American Journal of Orthopsychiatry, 40,* 397–412.

Calhoun, L. G., & Selby, J. W. (1980). Voluntary childlessness, involuntary childlessness, and having children: A study of social perceptions. *Family Relations, 29,* 181–183.

Callari, E. S. (1986). *A gentle death: Personal caregiving to the terminally ill.* Greensboro, N.C.: Tudor.

Cameron, E. (1988). Old, needy, and black. *Nursing Times, August 10,* 38.

Campbell, D., Bunker, V. W., & Thomas, A. J. (1989). Selenium and vitamin E status of healthy and institutionalized elderly subjects: Analysis of plasma, erthyrocytes and platelets. *British Journal of Nutrition, 61,* 221–225.

Candib, L. M. (1989). Point and counterpoint: Family life cycle theory: A feminist critique. *Family Systems Medicine, 7,* 473–487.

Cantor, N. F. (2001). Studying the Black Death. In G. E. Dickinson & M. R. Leming, (Eds.), *Dying, death, and bereavement* (10th ed.). NY: McGraw-Hill.

Cantor, P. (1977). Suicide and attempted suicide among students: Problem, prediction, and prevention. In P. Cantor (Ed.), *Understanding a child's world.* New York: McGraw-Hill.

Cantor, D., Fischel, J., & Kaye, H. (1983). Neonatal conditionability: A new paradigm for exploring the use of interoreceptive clues. *Infant Behavior and Development, 6,* 403–413.

Caputo, D. V., & Mandell, W. (1970). Consequences of low birth weight. *Developmental Psychology, 3,* 363–383.

Carey, S. (1978). The child as word learner. In M. Halle, J. Bresnan, & G. Miller (Eds.), *Linguistic theory and psychological reality.* Cambridge, MA: MIT Press.

Carey, R. G., & Posavac, E. J. (1978). Attitudes of physicians on disclosing information to and maintaining life for terminal patients. *Omega, 9,* 67–77.

Carroll, J., & Rest, J. (1982). Moral development. In B. Wolman (Ed.), *Handbook of human development.* Englewood Cliffs, NJ: Prentice Hall.

Carruth, B. R., & Goldberg, D. L. (1990). Nutritional issues of adolescents: Athletics and the body image mania. *Journal of Early Adolescence, 10,* 122–140.

Carter, D., & Welch, D. (1981). Parenting styles and children's behavior. *Family Relations, 30,* 191–195.

Carver, C. S., & Gaines, J. G. (1987). Optimism, pessimism, and postpartum depression. *Cognitive Therapy and Research, 11,* 449–462.

Cassady, G., & Strange, M. (1987). The small-for-gestational age (SGA) infant. In G. B. Avery (Ed.), *Neonatology: Pathophysiology and management of the newborn.* (pp. 299–331). Philadelphia: Lippincott.

Cassel, C. K. (Ed.). (1990). *Geriatric medicine.* New York: Springer-Verlag.

Cassidy, J. (1986). The ability to negotiate the environment: An aspect of infant competence as related to quality of attachment. *Child Development, 57,* 121–134.

Cataldo, C., & Whitney, E. (1986). *Nutrition and diet therapy: Principles and practices.* St. Paul, MN: West Publishing Co. Center for Disease Control. (1991).

Cernoch, J., & Porter, R. (1985). Recognition of maternal axillary odors by infants. *Child Development, 56,* 1593–1598.

Chance, P., & Fischman, J. (1987). The magic of childhood. *Psychology Today, 21* (May), 48–60.

Chand, I., Crider, D., & Willets, F. (1975). Parent-youth disagreement as perceived by youth: A longitudinal study. *Youth and Society, 6,* 365–375.

Charmaz, K. (1980). *The social reality of death: Death in contemporary America.* Reading, MA: Addison-Wesley.

Chasnoff, I. J. (1988). *Drugs, alcohol, pregnancy, and parenting.* Hingham, MA: Kluwer.

Chatters, L. M. (1988). Subjective well-being evaluations among older blacks. *Psychology and Aging, 3,* 184–190.

Chavance, M., Herbeth, B., & Fournier, C. (1989). Vitamin status, immunity, and infections in an elderly population. *European Journal of Clinical Nutrition, 43,* 827–833.

Cherlin, A., & Furstenberg, F. (1986). *The new American grandparent: A place in the family.* New York: Basic Books.

Cherry, L., & Lewis, M. (1976). The preschool teacher-child dyad: Sex differences in verbal interaction. *Child Development, 46,* 532–535.

Chilman, C. (1968). Families in development at mid-stage of the family life cycle. *Family Coordinator, 17,* 297–312.

Chilman, C. (1980). Parental satisfactions, concerns, and goals for their children. *Family Relations, 29,* 339–345.

Chilman, C. (1983). *Adolescent sexuality in a changing American society* (2nd ed.). New York: Wiley.

Chiriboga, D., & Cutler, L. (1980). Stress and adaptation: Life span perspectives. In L. W. Poon (Ed.), *Aging in the 1980s.* Washington, DC: American Psychological Association.

Chiriboga, D. (1981). The developmental psychology of middle age. In J. Howells (Ed.), *Modern perspectives in the psychiatry of middle age.* New York: Bruner/Mazel.

Chiriboga, D., & Cutler, L. (1980). Stress and adaptation: Life span perspectives. In L. W. Poon (Ed.), *Aging in the 1980s.* Washington, DC: American Psychological Association.

Chisholm, J. S. (1983). *Navajo infancy: An ethological study of child development.* New York: Aldine.

Chitwood, D. G., & Bigner, J. J. (1980). Young children's perceptions about old people. *Home Economics Research Journal, 8,* 369–374.

Chng, C. (1982). Sudden infant death syndrome: An inexplicable tragedy for the family. *Family Perspective, 16,* 123–128.

Choi, J. W. (1978). Exercise and participation in sports among persons 20 years of age and over. *Advance Data from Vital and Health Statistics, No. 19,* March 15.

Chomsky, N. (1957). *Syntactic structures.* The Hague: Mouton.

Chomsky, N. (1959). A review of B. F. Skinner's Verbal behavior. *Language, 35,* 26–58.

Chomsky, N. (1965). *Aspects of a theory of syntax.* Cambridge, MA: MIT Press.

Chomsky, N. (1968). *Language and mind.* New York: Harcourt, Brace, Jovanovich.

Chomsky, N. (1975). *Reflections on language.* New York: Pantheon Books.

Chown, S. (Ed.). (1972). *Human aging.* Baltimore: Penguin.

Chugani, H., & Phelps, M. (1986). Maturational changes in cerebral function in infants determined by FDG positron emission tomography. *Science, 231,* 840–843.

Chumlea, W. C. (1982). Physical growth in adolescence. In B. Wolman (Ed.), *Handbook of developmental psychology.* Englewood Cliffs, NJ: Prentice Hall.

Cicirelli, V. (1983). Adult children and their elderly parents. In T. Brubaker (Ed.), *Family relationships in later life.* Beverly Hills, CA: Sage.

Claperede, E. (1912). Jean Jacques Rousseau et la conception functionelle de l'enfance. *Revue de Metaphysique et de Morale, 20,* 391–416.

Clapp, G. (1988). Television: Today's most important socializer? In G. Clapp (Ed.), *Child study research.* Lexington, MA: Lexington Books.

Clark, E. V. (1982). The young word maker: A case study of innovation in the child's lexicon. In E. Warner & L. Gleitman (Eds.), *Language acquisition: The state of the art.* Cambridge, England: Cambridge University Press.

Clark, D. (1988). *As we are.* Boston, MA: Alyson Publications.

Clarke, J. I., & Dawson, C. (1989). *Growing up again: Parenting ourselves, parenting our children.* Minneapolis, MN: Hazelden.

Clarke-Stewart, K. A. (1984). Day care: A new context for research and development. In M. Perlmutter (Ed.), Parent-child interactions and parent-child relations in child psychology. *The Minnesota symposium on child psychology.* Vol. 17. Hillsdale, NJ: Erlbaum.

Clarke-Stewart, K. A. (1988). Parents effects on children's development: A decade of progress? *Journal of Applied Developmental Psychology, 9,* 41–84.

Clarke-Stewart, K. (1989). Infant day care: Maligned or malignant? *American Psychologist, 44,* 266–273.

Clasen, D., & Brown, B. (1985). The multidimensionality of peer pressure in adolescence. *Journal of Youth and Adolescence, 14,* 451–468.

Clavan, S. (1978). The impact of social class and social trends on the role of grandparent. *Family Coordinator, 27,* 351–357.

Clemens, A. W., & Axelson, L. J. (1985). The not-so-empty nest: Return of the fledgling adult. *Family Relations, 34,* 259–264.

Clinton, H. R. (1990). *In France, day care is every child's right.* New York Times, April 7, 25.

Cohan, C. L., & Kleinbaum, S. (2002). Toward a greater understanding of the cohabitation effect: Premarital cohabitation and marital communication. *Journal of Marriage and Family, 64,* 180–192.

Cohen, E. (2005). What living wills won't do. In G. E. Dickinson & M.R. Leming, (Eds.), *Dying, death, and bereavement* (10th ed.). NY: McGraw-Hill.

Cohen, G. (1987). Alzheimer's disease. In G. Maddox (Ed.),The encyclopedia of aging. New York: Springer. Comfort, A. (1976). *A good age.* New York: Crown.

Cohen, D., & Zigler, E. (1977). Federal day care standards: Rationale and recommendations. *American Journal of Orthopsychiatry, 47,* 456–465.

Cohen, J., Coburn, K., & Pearlman, J. (1980). *Hitting our stride: Good news about women in their middle years.* New York: Delacorte.

Coie, J. D., & Kuperschmidt, J. B. (1983). A behavioral analysis of emerging social status in boys' groups. *Child Development, 54,* 1400–1416.

Coleman, J. (1961). *The adolescent society.* Glencoe, IL: Free Press.

Coleman, M., & Ganong, L. H. (1985). Remarriage myths: Implications for the helping professions. *Journal of Counseling and Development, 64,* 116–120.

Coleman, M., & Ganong, L. H. (1990). Remarriage and stepfamilies. *Journal of Marriage and the Family, 52,* 925–940.

Colligan, R. C., & Offord, K. P. (1990). MacAndrew versus MacAndrew: The relative efficacy of the MAC and the SAP scales for the MMPI in screening male adolescents for substance abuse. *Journal of Personality Assessment, 55,* 708–716.

Colombo, J. (1982). The critical period concept: Research, methodology, and theoretical issues. *Psychological Bulletin, 91,* 260–275.

Comer, J., & Schraft, C. (1980). Working with black parents. In R. Abidin (Ed.), *Parent education and intervention handbook.* Springfield, IL: Charles C. Thomas.

Comfort, A. (1970). Biological theories of aging. *Human Development, 13,* 127–139.

Condon, W. S., & Sander, L. W. (1974). Synchrony demonstrated between movements of the neonate and adult speech. *Child Development, 45,* 456–462.

Condon, J. T., & Watson, T. L. (1987). The maternity blues: Exploration of a psychological hypothesis. *Acta Psychiatrica Scandinavia, 76,* 164–171.

Condry, J., Bence, P., & Scheibe, C. (1988). Nonprogram content of children's television. *Journal of Broadcasting and Electronic Media, 32,* 255–269.

Conley, B. H. (1987). Funeral directors as first responders. In E. J. Dunne, J. L. McIntosh, & K. Dunne-Maxim (Eds.), *Suicide and its aftermath: Understanding and counseling pediatric illness* (pp. 171–181). New York: Norton.

Cook, J. A. (1983). A death in the family: Parental bereavement in the first year of life. *Suicide and Life Threatening Behavior, 13,* 42–61.

Cook, S. (1985). Experimenting on social issues: The case of school desegregation. *American Psychologist, 40,* 452–460.

Cook, A. S., & Oltjenbruns, K. A. (1982). A cognitive developmental approach to death education for adolescents. *Family Perspective, 16,* 9–14.

Cook, A. S., & Oltjenbruns, K. A. (1989). *Dying and grieving: Life span and family perspectives.* New York: Holt, Rinehart, Winston.

Cook, T. H., & Miller, N. (1985). The challenge of Alzheimer's disease. *American Psychologist, 40,* 1245–1250.

Coopersmith, S. (1967). *The antecedents of self-esteem.* San Francisco: Freeman.

Corbin, C. (1980). The physical fitness of children. In C. Corbin (Ed.), *A textbook of motor development.* Dubuque, IA: W. C. Brown.

Cordell, A., Parke, R., & Sawin, D. (1980). Fathers' views of fatherhood with special reference to infancy. *Family Relations, 29,* 331–338.

Coverman, S., & Sheley, J. (1986). Change in men's housework and childcare time, 1965–1975. *Journal of Marriage and the Family, 48,* 413–422.

Cowan, C., Cowan, P., Heming, G., Garrett, E., Coysh, W., Curtis-Boles, H., Boles, A. (1985). Transitions to parenthood: His, hers, and theirs. *Journal of Family Issues, 6,* 451–482.

Cowgill, D. (1986). *Aging around the world*. Belmont, CA: Wadsworth.

Cox, F. D. (1990). *Human intimacy: Marriage, the family, and its meaning* (5th ed.). St. Paul, MN: West.

Cox, H. (1977). Eastern cults and western culture: Why young Americans are buying oriental religions. *Psychology Today, July*, 43–47.

Cox, H. (Ed.) (2006). *Annual editions: Aging* (18th ed.). Dubuque, IA: McGraw-Hill/Dushkin.

Cox, M. J., Owen, M. T., Lewis, J., Riedel, C., Scalf-McIver, L., & Suster, A. (1985). Intergenerational influences on the parent-infant relationship in the transition to parenthood. *Journal of Family Issues, 6*, 543–564.

Cozby, P. C. (2001). *Methods in behavioral research* (8th ed.). NY: McGraw Hill.

Craik, F., Byrd, M., & Swanson, J. (1987). Patterns of memory loss in three elderly samples. *Psychology and Aging, 21*, 79–86.

Crain, W. C. (2005). *Theories of development: Concepts and applications* (5th ed.). Englewood Cliffs, NJ: Prentice Hall.

Cratty, B. J. (1986). *Perceptual and motor skill development in infants and children* (3rd ed.). Englewood Cliffs, NJ: Prentice Hall.

Crawford, J. K. (1980). The role of hospice services in family members' adjustment to death. Unpublished master's thesis, University of Nebraska.

Crilly, R. G., Willems, D. A., & Trenholm, K. J. (1989). Effect of exercise on postural sway in the elderly. *Gerontology, 35*, 137–145.

Crockett, W., & Hummert, M. (1987). Perceptions of aging and the aged. In K. Schaie & K. Eisdorfer (Eds.), *Annual review of gerontology and geriatrics*. Vol. 7. New York: Springer.

Crone, T. M. (1990). The aging of America: Impacts on the marketplace and workplace. *Business Review, May 1*, 3.

Crook, C. (1978). Taste perception in the newborn infant. *Infant Behavior and Development, 1*, 52–69.

Crook, C., & Lipsett, L. (1976). Neonatal nutritive sucking: Effects of taste stimulation on sucking rhythm and heart rate. *Child Development, 47*, 518–522.

Crosby, J. (1985). *Reply to myth: Perspectives on intimacy*. New York: Wiley.

Cross, D., & Paris, S. (1988). Developmental and instructional analyses of children's metacognition and reading comprehension. *Journal of Educational Psychology, 80*, 131–142.

Crouter, A., MacDermid, S., McHale, S., & Perry-Jenkins, M. (1990). Parental monitoring and perceptions of children's school performance and conduct dual--and single-earner families. *Developmental Psychology, 26*, 649–657.

Crouter, A., Perry-Jenkins, M., Huston, T., & McHale, S. (1987). Processes underlying father involvement in dual-earner and single-earner families. *Developmental Psychology, 23*, 431–441.

Csikszentimihalyi, M., & Larson, R. (1984). *Being adolescent: Conflict and growth in the teenage years*. New York: Basic Books.

Cuber, J. F., & Haroff, P. B. (1965). *Sex and the significant Americans*. Baltimore: Penguin Books.

Cumming, E. (1963). Further thoughts on the theory of disengagement. *International Social Science Journal, 15*, 377–393.

Cumming, E., & Henry, W. E. (1961). *Growing old*. New York: Basic Books.

Cunningham, F. G., MacDonald, P. C., & Gant, N. F. (1989). *Williams' obstetrics* (18th ed.). Norwalk, CN: Appleton & Lange.

Cutler, S. (1977). Aging and voluntary association participation. *Journal of Gerontology, 32*, 470–479.

Cutler, W., Garcia, C., & McCoy, N. (1987). Perimenopausal sexuality. *Archives of Sexual Behavior, 16*, 225–234.

Daly, M. P., & Sobal, J. (1990). Vitamin/mineral supplement use by geriatric outpatients in the United Kingdom. *Journal of Nutrition for the Elderly, 10*, 55–60.

Damon, W. (1983). Self-understanding and moral development from childhood to adolescence. In W. Kurtines & J. Gewirtz (Eds.), *Morality, moral behavior, and moral development*. New York: Wiley.

Damon, W., & Hart, D. (1982). The development of self-understanding from infancy through adolescence. *Child Development, 53*, 841–864.

Damon, W., & Lerner, R. M. (1998). *Handbook of child psychology (Vol. 1): Theoretical models of human development* (5th ed.). NY: John Wiley & Sons, Inc.

Dannemiller, J., & Stephens, B. (1988). A critical test of infant pattern preference models. *Child Development, 59*, 210–216.

Davidoff, J. B. (1975). *Differences in visual perception: The individual eye*. New York: Academic Press.

Davidson, J. K., & Darling, C. A. (1988). The stereotype of single women revisited: Sexual practices and sexual satisfaction among professional women. *Health Care for Women International, 9*, 317–322.

Davies, L., & Carr, K. (1991). Warning signs for malnutrition in the elderly. *Journal of the American Dietetic Association, 91*, 1413–1420.

Dawson, D. A., & Cain, V. S. (1990). Child care arrangements: United States, 1988. *Advance Data From Vital and Health Statistics, No. 187*. Hyattsville, MD: National Center for Health Statistics.

Dawson, D., & Hendershot, G. (1987). Aging in the Eighties: Functional limitations of individuals age 65 and over. *Advance Data from Vital and Health Statistics, No. 133, June 10*. DHHS Publication No. (PHS) 87–1250. Hyattsville, MD: U. S. Public Health Service. ]

Deaux, K. (1985). Sex and gender. *Annual Review of Psychology, 36*, 49–81.

DeCasper, A. J., & Carstens, A. A. (1981). Contingencies of stimulation: Effects on learning and emotion in neonates. *Infant Behavior and Development, 4*, 19–35.

DeFrain, J. (1979). Androgynous parents tell who they are and what they need. *Family Coordinator, 28*, 237–243.

DeFrain, J., & Ernst, L. (1978). The psychological effects of sudden infant death syndrome on surviving family members. *Family Practitioner, 6*, 985–988.

DeLozier, J. E., & Gagnon, R. O. (1991). National ambulatory medical care survey: 1989 summary. *Advance Data From Vital and Health Statistics, No. 203*. Hyattsville, MD: National Center for Health Statistics.

deMonteflores, C., & Schultz, S. (1978). Coming out: Similarities and differences for lesbians and gay men. *Journal of Social Issues, 34*, 59–72.

Demos, J., & Demos, V. (1969). Adolescence in historical perspective. *Journal of Marriage and the Family, 31*, 632–638.

Dennis, W., & Dennis, M. (1940). The effect of cradling practices upon the onset of walking in Hopi children. *Journal of Genetic Psychology, 56*, 77–86.

Derdeyn, A. (1985). Grandparent visitation rights: Rendering family dissension more pronounced. *American Journal of Orthopsychiatry, 55*, 277–287.

DeVito, J. (1970). *The psychology of speech and language*. New York: Random House.

deVos, S. (1990). Extended family living among older people in six Latin American countries. *Journal of Gerontology, 45*, 87–94.

DeVries, M. W., & Sameroff, A. J. (1984). Culture and temperament: Influence on infant temperament in three East African societies. *American Journal of Orthopsychiatry, 54*, 83–96.

Dickinson, G. E. & Leming, M. R., (Ed.) (2008). *Dying, death, and bereavement* (10th ed.). NY: McGraw-Hill.

Dick-Reed, G. (1944). *The principles and practice of natural childbirth*. New York: Harper.

Dickson, S., & Parke, R. D. (1988). Social referencing in infancy: A glance at fathers and marriage. *Child Development, 59*, 506–511.

DiClemente, R. J. (1990). The emergence of adolescents as a risk group for human immunodeficiency virus infection. *Journal of Adolescent Research, 5*, 7–17.

DiMatteo, M., Morton, S., Lepper, H., Damush, T., Carney, M., Pearson, M., & Kahn, K. L. (1996). Cesarean childbirth and psychosocial outcomes: A meta-analysis. *Health Psychology, 15*, 303-314.

Dixon, R., & Baltes, P. (1986). Toward life span research on the functions and pragmatics of intelligence. In R. Sternberg & R. Wagner (Eds.), *Practical intelligence: Nature and origins of competence in the everyday world*. New York: Cambridge University Press.

Dixon Jr., W. E. (2003). *Twenty studies that revolutionized child psychology*. Upper Saddle River, NJ: Prentice Hall.

Dodge, K., & Frame, C. (1982). Social cognitive biases and deficits in aggressive boys. *Child Development, 53*, 620–635.

Doering, M. R., & Rhodes, S. R. (1989). Changing careers: A qualitative study. *Career Development Quarterly, 37,* 316–322.

Dohrenwend, B. S., & Dohrenwend, B. P. (1974). *Stressful life events: Their nature and effects.* New York: Wiley.

Donaldson, S., & Westerman, M. (1986). Development of children's understanding of ambivalence and causal theories of emotions. *Developmental Psychology, 22,* 655–662.

Douglas, K., & Arenberg, D. (1978). Age changes, cohort differences, and cultural changes on the Guilford-Zimmerman Temperament Survey. *Journal of Gerontology, 33,* 737–747.

Dowd, J. (1975). Aging as exchange: A preface to theory. *Journal of Gerontology, 30,* 584–594.

Dowd, J. (1980). Exchange rates and old people. *Journal of Gerontology, 35,* 596–602.

Dowd, J. (1984). Beneficence and the aged. *Journal of Gerontology, 39,* 102–108.

Dowd, J., & Tronick, E. Z. (1986). Temporal coordination of arm movements in early infancy: Do infants move in synchrony with adult speech? *Child Development, 57,* 772–776.

Dreeben, R., & Gamoran, A. (1986). Race, instruction, and learning. *American Sociological Review, 51,* 660–669.

Dreyer, P. H. (1982). Sexuality during adolescence. In B. Wolman (Ed.), *Handbook of developmental psychology.* Englewood Cliffs, NJ: Prentice Hall.

Drury, T. F., & Howie, L. J. (1979). Prevalence of selected chronic digestive conditions. *Vital and Health Statistics, Series 10, No. 123,* DHEW Publication No.(PHS) 79–1558.

DuBard, C., & Newton, W. (1999). Elective Cesarean delivery to prevent vertical transmission of HIV. *Journal of Family Practice, 48,* 493–494.

Dubrow, E., & Tasak, J. (1989). The relation between stressful life events and adjustment in elementary school children: The role of social support and social problem-solving skills. *Child Development, 60,* 1412–1424.

Dudley, D. L. (1991). Coping with retirement: Stress and lifechange. *Cupa Journal, 42,* 1–4.

Dukes, R. L., & Lorch, B. D. (1989). The effects of school, family, self-concept, and deviant behavior on adolescent suicide ideation. *Journal of Adolescence, 12,* 239–251.

Duncan, T. E., Duncan, S., & Hops, H. (1996). The role of parents and older siblings in predicting adolescent substance use: Modeling development via structural equation latent growth curve methodology. *Journal of Family Psychology, 10,* 158–172.

Dunn, J., Brown, J. R., Slomkowski, C., Telsa, C., & Youngblade, L. M. (1991). Young children's understanding of other people's feelings and beliefs: Individual differences and their antecedents. *Child Development, 62,* 1352-1366.

Dunphy, D. (1963). The social structure of urban adolescent peer groups. *Sociometry, 26,* 230–246.

Duvall, E. (1977). *Marriage and family development.* 5th ed. Philadelphia: Lippincott.

Duvall, E. M., & Miller, B. (1985). *Marriage and family development* (6th ed.). New York: Harper & Row.

Dyer, E. (1963). Parenthood as crisis: A restudy. *Journal of Marriage and the Family, 25,* 196–201.

Eakins, P. S. (1986). *The American way of birth.* Philadelphia: Temple University Press.

East, P., Hess, L., & Lerner, R. (1987). Peer social support and adjustment in early adolescent peer groups. *Journal of Early Adolescence, 7,* 135–163.

East, P. L., & Khoo, S. (2005). Longitudinal pathways linking family factors and sibling relationship qualities to adolescent substance use and sexual risk behaviors. *Journal of Family Psychology, 19,* 571-580.

Eaton, W. O., & Ennis, L. R. (1986). Sex differences in human motor activity level. *Psychological Bulletin, 100,* 19–28.

Eder, R. A. (1989). The emergent personalist: The structure and content of 3 1/2, 5 1/2, and 7 1/2-year-olds' concepts of themselves and other persons. *Child Development, 60,* 1218–1229.

Eggerman, S., & Dustin, D. (1985). Death orientation and communication with the terminally ill. *Omega, 16,* 255–265.

Ehrlich, C. (2009). Hebrew/Israelite literature. In C. Ehrlich (Ed.) *From an antique land: An introduction to ancient Near Eastern literature* (pp. 313-392). Rowman and Littlefield. Lanham, MD.

Eisele, J., Hertsgaard, D., & Light, H. (1986). Factors related to eating disorders in young adolescent girls. *Adolescence, 21,* 283–290.

Eisenberg, N. (1989). The development of prosocial values. In N. Eisenberg, J. Reykowski, & E. Staub (Eds.), *Social and moral values: Individual and social perspectives.* Hillsdale, NJ: Erlbaum.

Eisenberg, N., Wolchik, S. A., Hernandez, R., & Pasternack, J. (1985). Parental socialization of young children's play: A short-term longitudinal study. *Child Development, 56,* 1506–1514.

Elder, G. (1962). Structural variations in the childrearing relationship. *Sociometry, 25,* 233–245.

Elder, G. H. (1998). The life course and human development. In W. Damon & R. M. Lerner (Eds.), *Handbook of child psychology (Vol. 1): Theoretical models of human development* (5th ed.). NY: John Wiley & Sons, Inc.

Elia, E. A. (1991). Exercise and the elderly. *Clinics in Sports Medicine, 10,* 141–147.

Elizur, E., & Kaffman, M. (1983). Factors influencing the severity of childhood bereavement reactions. *American Journal of Orthopsychiatry, 53,* 669–676.

Elkind, D. (1967). Egocentrism in adolescence. *Child Development, 38,* 1024–1038.

Elkind, D. (1974). *Children and adolescents: Interpretative essays on Jean Piaget.* New York: Oxford University Press.

Elkind, D. (1976). *Child development and education.* New York: Oxford University Press.

Elkind, D. (1978). Understanding the young adolescent. *Adolescence, 13,* 127–134.

Elkind, D. (1981). *The hurried child.* Reading, MA: Addison-Wesley.

Elkind, D. (1987). *Miseducation.* New York: Knopf.

Ellis, L., Ames, M. Peckham, W., & Burke, D. (1988). Sexual orientation of human offspring may be altered by severe maternal stress during pregnancy. *Journal of Sex Research, 25,* 152–157.

Eng, L., & O'Laughlin, M. (1989). The next generation. *San Francisco Examiner, June 24,* 58.

Enns, J. T., & Girgus, J. S. (1985). Developmental changes in selective and integrative visual attention. *Journal of Experimental Child Psychology, 40,* 319–337.

Entwisle, D. R., & Alexander, K. L. (1987). Long-term effects of Cesarean delivery on parents' beliefs and children's schooling. *Developmental Psychology, 23,* 676–682.

Entwisle, D., & Doering, S. G. (1980). *The first birth.* Baltimore, MD: Johns Hopkins University Press.

Erikson, E. (1950). *Childhood and society.* New York: Norton.

Erikson, E. (1964). *Insight and responsibility.* New York: Norton.

Erikson, E. (1982). *The life cycle completed.* New York: Norton.

Erikson, E., Erikson, J., & Kivnick, H. (1986). *Vital involvement in old age.* New York: Norton.

Eron, L. (1987). The development of aggressive behavior from the perspective of a developing behaviorism. *American Psychologist, 42,* 435–442.

Espenshade, T. (1984). *Investing in children: New estimates of parental expenditures.* Washington, DC: Urban Institute Press.

Espino, D. V., Neufeld, R. R., Mulvihill, M., & Libow, L. S. (1988). Hispanic and non-Hispanic elderly on admission to the nursing home: A pilot study. *The Gerontologist, 28,* 821–827.

Evans, M. A., Esbenson, M., & Jaffe, C. (1981). Expect the unexpected when you care for a dying patient. *Nursing, 11,* 55–56.

Eveleth, P. B., & Tanner, J. M. (1976). *Worldwide variation in human growth.* Cambridge, England: Cambridge University Press.

Everitt, A. V. (1976). Conclusion: Aging and its hypothalamic-pituitary control. In A. V. Everitt & J. A. Burgess (Eds.), *Hypothalamus, pituitary, and aging.* Springfield, OH: Charles C. Thomas.

Fabricius, W., & Cavalier, L. (1989). The role of causal theories about memory in young children's memory strategy choice. *Child Development, 60,* 298–308.

Fabricius, W., & Wellman, H. (1983). Children's understanding of retrieval cue utilization. *Developmental Psychology, 19,* 15–21.

Fagan, J. F., & McGrath, S. K. (1981). Infant recognition memory and later intelligence. *Intelligence, 5,* 121–130.

Fagot, B. (1978). The influence of sex of child on parental reactions to toddler children. *Child Development, 49,* 459–465.

Fagot, B. (1985). Beyond the reinforcement principle: Another step toward understanding sex-role development. *Developmental Psychology, 21,* 1097–1104.

Fagot, B., Hagan, R., Leinbach, M., & Kronsberg, S. (1985). Differential reactions to assertive and communicative acts of toddler boys and girls. *Child Development, 56,* 1499–1505.

Fairchild, T. N. (1986). Suicide prevention. In T. N. Fairchild (Ed.), *Crisis intervention strategies for school-based helpers* (pp. 321–369). Springfield, IL: Charles C. Thomas.

Faltermayer, E. (1991). Ready to retire: Decisions galore. *Fortune, 124(10),* 137–140.

Fantz, R. I. (1958). Pattern vision in young infants. *Psychological Record, 8,* 43–47.

Fantz, R. I. (1961). The origin of form perception. *Scientific American, 36,* 66–72.

Fantz, R. I., Fagan, J. F., & Miranda, S. B. (1975). Early visual selectivity. In L. B. Cohen & P. Salapatek (Eds.), *Infant perception: From sensation to cognition.* Vol. 1. New York: Academic Press.

Farley, R., & Allen, W. R. (1987). *The color line and the quality of life in America.* New York: Russell Sage Foundation.

Farrell, M., & Rosenberg, S. (1981). *Men at midlife.* Boston: Auburn.

Fasteau, M. F. (1975). *The male machine.* New York: McGraw-Hill.

Faust, M. S. (1960). Developmental maturity as a determinant of prestige of adolescent girls. *Child Development, 31,* 173–186.

Fay, R. E., Turner, C. F., Klasen, A., & Gagnon, J. (1989).Prevalence and patterns of same-gender sexual contact among men. *Science, 243,* 338–348.

Feather, N. T. (1980). Values in adolescence. In J. Adelson(Ed.), *Handbook of adolescent psychology.* New York: Wiley.

Feldman, H. (1981). A comparison of intentional parents and intentionally childless couples. *Journal of Marriage and the Family, 43,* 593–600.

Feldman, S., & Gehring, T. (1988). Changing perceptions of family cohesion and power across adolescence. *Child Development, 59,* 1034–1045.

Feldman, S., & Nash, S. (1979). Sex differences in responsiveness to babies among mature adults. *Developmental Psychology, 15,* 430–436.

Feldman, S., & Quatman, T. (1988). Factors influencing age expectations for adolescent autonomy: A study of early adolescents and their parents. *Journal of Early Adolescence, 8,* 325–343.

Ferguson, K., Yesalis, C., Pomrehn, P., & Kirkpatrick, M. (1989). Attitudes, knowledge, and beliefs as predictors of exercise intent and behavior in schoolchildren. *Journal of School Health, 59,* 112–115.

Fernandez, E. (1989). *Coming out is hard to do.* San Francisco Examiner, June 20, 47.

Fine, M. A., Moreland, J. R., & Schwebel, A. (1983). Long-term effects of divorce on parent-child relationships. *Developmental Psychology, 5,* 703–714.

Finn, S. (1986). Stability of personality self-ratings over 30 years: Evidence for an age/cohort interaction. *Journal of Personality and Social Psychology, 50,* 813–818.

Fischer, K. W. (1987). Relations between brain and cognitive development. *Child Development, 58,* 623–632.

Fischer, C. A., Crockett, S. J., & Heller, K. E. (1991). Nutrition knowledge, attitudes, and practices of older and younger elderly in rural areas. *Journal of the American Dietetic Association, 91,* 1398–1404.

Fitting, M., Rabins, P., Lucas, M. J., Eastham, J. (1986). Caregivers for demented patients: A comparison of husbands and wives. *Gerontologist, 26,* 248–252.

Flavell, J. H. (1985). *Cognitive development* (2nd ed). Englewood Cliffs, NJ: Prentice Hall.

Flavell, J. H. (1986). The development of children's knowledge about the appearance-reality distinction. *American Psychologist, 41,* 418–426.

Flavell, J., & Ross, L. (1981). *Social cognitive development: Frontiers and possible futures.* Cambridge, England: Cambridge University Press.

Flavell, J. (1985). *Cognitive development* (2nd ed.). Englewood Cliffs, NJ: Prentice Hall.

Flavell, J., Beach, D., & Chinsky, J. (1966). Spontaneous verbal rehearsal in memory tasks as a function of age. *Child Development, 37,* 283–299.

Flavell, J., Flavell, E., Green, F., & Wilcox, S. (1981). The development of three spatial perspective-taking rules. *Child Development, 52,* 356–368.

Fleming, A. S., Ruble, D. N., Flett, G. L., & Shaul, D. L. (1988). Postpartum adjustment of first-time mothers: Relations between mood, maternal attitudes, and mother-infant interactions. *Developmental Psychology, 24,* 71–81.

Folkman, S., & Lazarus, R. (1980). An analysis of coping in a middle-aged community sample. *Journal of Health and Social Behavior, 21,* 219–239.

Forrest, J. D., & Singh, S. (1990). The sexual and reproductive behavior of American women, 1982–1988. *Family Planning Perspectives, 22,* 206–214.

Forward, S. (1989). *Toxic parents: Overcoming their hurtful legacy and reclaiming your life.* New York: Bantam Books.

Fozard, J. L., & Gordon-Salant, S. (2001). Changes in vision and hearing with aging. In J. E. Birren & K. W. Schaie (Eds.), *Handbook of the psychology of aging.* San Diego, CA: Academic Press.

Fozard, J., Wolf, E., Bell, B., McFarland, A., & Podosky, S.(1977). Visual perception and communication. In J. Birren & K. Schaie (Eds.), *Handbook of the psychology of aging.* New York: Van Nostrand Reinhold.

Fraiberg, S. (1977). *Insights from the blind: Comparative studies of blind and sighted infants.* New York: Basic Books.

Fraley, R., & Shaver, P. (2000). Adult romantic attachment: Theoretical developments, emerging controversies, and unanswered questions. *Review of General Psychology, 4,* 132-154.

Frankenburg, W. K., & Dodds, J. (1967). The Denver developmental screening test. *Journal of Pediatrics, 71,* 181–191.

Frankenburg, W. K., Frandal, A., Sciarillo, W., & Burgess, D. (1981). The newly abbreviated and revised Denver Developmental Screening Test. *The Journal of Pediatrics, 99,* 995–999.

Frauenglass, M., & Diaz, R. (1985). Self-regulatory functions of children's private speech: A critical analysis of recent challenges to Vygotsky's theory. *Developmental Psychology, 21,* 357–364.

Freeman, D. (1983). *Margaret Mead and Samoa.* Cambridge, MA: Harvard University Press.

French, D. (1988). Heterogeneity of peer-rejected boys: Aggressive and nonaggressive subtypes. *Child Development, 59,* 976–985.

Freud. S. (1917). Mourning and melancholia. In J. Strachey (Ed.), *The standard edition of the complete psychological works of Sigmund Freud.* London: Hogarth Press.

Freudenberger, H., & Richelson, G. (1980). *Burnout: The high cost of high achievement.* New York: Anchor/Doubleday.

Fried, P. A., Watkinson, B., Dillon, R. F., & Dulberg, C. S. (1987). Neonatal neurological status in a low-risk population after prenatal exposure to cigarettes, marijuana, and alcohol. *Journal of Developmental and Behavioral Pediatrics, 8,* 318–326.

Friedman, W. (1986). The development of children's knowledge of temporal structure. *Child Development, 57,* 1386–1400.

Friedrich, O. (1983). What do babies know? *Time, August 15,* 52–59.

Friel, J., & Friel, L. (1988). *Adult children: The secrets of dysfunctional families.* Deerfield Beach, FL: Health Communications.

Frisch, R. E. (1983). Fatness, puberty, and fertility: The effects of nutrition and physical training on menarche and ovulation. In J. Brooks-Gunn & A. Petersen (Eds.),*Girls at puberty: Biological and psychosocial aspects.* New York: Plenum.

Frodi, A., & Lamb, M. (1978). Sex differences in responsiveness to infants: A developmental study of psychophysiological and behavioral responses. *Child Development, 49,* 1182–1188.

Froggatt, K. (2006). A survey of end-of-life care in care homes. In G. E. Dickinson & M. R. Leming, (Eds.), *Dying, death, and bereavement* (10th ed.). NY: McGraw-Hill.

Fromm, E. (1970). *The art of loving.* New York: Bantam.

Fulton, R. (1987). Death, grief, and the funeral. In M.A. Morgan (Ed.), *Bereavement: Helping the survivors* (pp. 123–126). London, Ontario: King's College.

Furstenberg, F. F. (1983). The life course of children of divorce: Marital disruption and parental contact. *American Sociological Review, 52,* 656–668.

Gaddis, A., & Brooks-Gunn, J. (1985). The male experience of pubertal change. *Journal of Youth and Adolescence, 14,* 61–69.

Galatzer-Levy, R. M. & Cohler, B. J. (1993). *The essential other: A developmental psychology of the self.* New York: Basic Books.

Galper, M. (1978). *Coparenting: Sharing your child fully.* Philadelphia: Running Press.

Galvin, K. M., & Brommel, B. J. (1986). *Family communication: Cohesion and change.* Glenview, IL: Scott, Foresman.

Gamoran, A. (1989). Rank, performance, and mobility in elementary school grouping. *Sociological Quarterly, 30,* 109–123.

Gannon. J. P. (1989). *Soul survivors: A new beginning for adults abused as children.* New York: Prentice Hall Press.

Garbarino, J. (1980). Changing hospital childbirth practices: A developmental perspective on prevention of child maltreatment. *American Journal of Orthopsychiatry, 50,* 588–597.

Garbarino, J., Guttman, E., & Seeley, J. W. (1986). *The psychologically battered child: Strategies for identification, assessment, and intervention.* San Francisco: Jossey-Bass.

Gardner, J. M., & Karmel, B. (1984). Arousal effects on visual preference in neonates. *Developmental Psychology, 20,* 374–377.

Gardner, D. B. (1979). *Preventing childhood accidents.* Ft. Collins, CO: Commercial Printing.

Gardner, H. E. (1998). Extraordinary cognitive achievements (ECA): A symbol systems approach. In W. Damon & R. M. Lerner (Eds.), *Handbook of child psychology (Vol. 1): Theoretical models of human development* (5th ed.). NY: John Wiley & Sons, Inc.

Garn, S., Sandusky, S., Nagy, J., & Trowbridge, F. Negro-caucasoid differences in permanent tooth emergence at a constant income level. *Archives of Oral Biology, 18,* 609–615.

Garrod, A., Beal, C., & Shin, P. (1989). The development of moral orientation in elementary school children. Paper presented at the biennial meeting of the Society for Research in Child Development, Kansas City.

Garvey, C. (1977). *Play.* Cambridge, MA: Harvard University Press.

Geary, D. (1989). A model for representing gender differences in the pattern of cognitive abilities. *American Psychologist, 44,* 1155–1156.

Geber, M. (1958). The psychomotor development of African children in the first year, and the influence of maternal behavior. *Journal of Social Psychology, 47,* 185–195.

Gee, A. S. (1978). Understanding cohabitation: Implications for home economists. *Journal of Home Economics, 13,* 38–42.

Gelman, R., & Baillargeon, R. (1983). A review of some Piagetian concepts. In P. Mussen (Ed.), *Handbook of child psychology* (4th ed.). Vol. 3. New York: Wiley.

General Mills Corp. (1981). *Raising children in contemporary America.* Minneapolis, MN: General Mills.

George, L. K., & Weiler, S. J. (1981). Sexuality in middle and late life. *Archives of General Psychiatry, 38,* 919–923.

Gerard, H. (1983). School desegregation. *American Psychologist, 38,* 869–877.

Gesell, A., & Ames, L. B. (1947). The development of handedness. *Journal of Genetic Psychology, 70,* 155–175.

Gesell, A. & Ilg, F. (1946). *The child from five to ten.* New York: Harper & Row.

Gesell, A., & Thompson, H. (1929). Learning and growth in identical infant twins: An experimental study by the method of co-twin control. *Genetic Psychology Monographs, 6,* 1–124.

Ghodsian-Carpey, J., & Baker, L. (1987). Genetic and environmental influences on aggression in 4 to 7-year-old twins. *Aggressive Behavior, 13,* 173–186.

Gibson, E. (1969). *Principles of perceptual learning and development.* New York: Appleton-Century-Crofts.

Gibson, R. C. (1986). Older black Americans. *Generations, 10,* 35–39.

Gibson, E., & Walk, R. D. (1960). *The visual cliff. Scientific American, 202,* 64–71.

Gilbert, E., & DeBlassie, R. (1984). Anorexia nervosa: Adolescent starvation by choice. *Adolescence, 19,* 839–846.

Gilchrist, L. D., Schinke, S. P., & Maxwell, J. S. (1987). Life skills counseling for preventing problems in adolescence. *Journal of Social Service Research, 10,* 73–84.

Gilford, R. (1984). Contrasts in marital satisfaction throughout old age: An exchange theory analysis. *Journal of Gerontology, 39,* 325–333.

Gilligan, C. (1982). *In a different voice: Psychological theory and women's development.* Cambridge, MA: Harvard University Press.

Ginsburg, H., & Opper, S. (1979). *Piaget's theory of intellectual development* (2nd ed.). Englewood Cliffs, NJ: Prentice Hall.

Glaser, K. (1978). The treatment of depressed and suicidal adolescents. *American Journal of Psychotherapy, 32,* 252–269.

Glass, J. (1983). Prebirth attitudes and adjustment to parenthood: When "preparing for the worst" helps. *Family Relations, 32,* 377–386.

Glasser, B. G., & Strauss, A. L. (1965). *Awareness of dying.* Chicago: Aldine.

Glasser, B. G., & Strauss, A. L. (1968). *Time for dying.* Chicago: Aldine.

Glenn, N. D. (1975). Psychological well-being in the postparental stage: Some evidence from national surveys. *Journal of Marriage and the Family, 37,* 105–110.

Glenn, N. D., & McLanahan, S. (1981). The effects of offspring on the psychological well-being of older adults. *Journal of Marriage and the Family, 41,* 409–421.

Glenn, N. D., & Weaver, C. N. A note on family situation and global happiness. *Social Forces, 57,* 960–967.

Glenwick, D. S., & Mowrey, J. D. (1986). When parent becomes peer: Loss of intergenerational boundaries in single parent families. *Family Relations, 35,* 57–62.

Glick, P., & Lin, S. (1986). More young adults are living with their parents: Who are they? *Journal of Marriage and the Family, 48,* 107–112.

Glick, I., Weiss, R., & Parkes, C. (1974). *The first year of bereavement.* New York: Wiley.

Goetting, A. (1982). The six stations of remarriage: Developmental tasks of remarriage after divorce. *Family Relations, 31,* 213–222.

Goetting, A. (1986). The developmental tasks of siblingship over the life cycle. *Journal of Marriage and the Family, 48,* 703–714.

Goldberg, H. (1976). *The hazards of being male: Surviving the myth of masculine privilege.* New York: Nash.

Goldfarb, W. (1945). Effects of psychological deprivation in infancy and subsequent adjustment. *American Journal of Psychiatry, 102,* 18–33.

Goleman, C. (1986). Major personality study finds that traits are mostly inherited. *New York Times, (July 29),* 17–18.

Goleman, D., & Gurin, J. (Eds.) (1993). *Mind body medicine: How to use your mind for better health.* NY: Consumer Reports Books.

Gonzalez-Mena, J. (1986). Toddlers: What to expect. *Young Children, 42,* 85–90.

Goodenough, F. (1939). A critique of experiments on raising the IQ. *Educational Methods, 19,* 73–79.

Goodnow, J. (1977). *Children drawing.* Cambridge, MA: Harvard University Press.

Goodwin, J. S. (1989). Social, psychological, and physical factors affecting the nutritional status of elderly subjects: Separating cause and effect. *American Journal of Clinical Nutrition, 50,* 1201–1210.

Gordon, S. (1981). Preteens are not latent, adolescence is not a disease. In L. Brown (Ed.), *Sex education*. New York: Plenum.

Gottfried, A., Gottfried, A., & Bathurst, K. (1988). Maternal employment, family environment, and children's development: Infancy through the school years. In A. Gottfried & A. Gottfried (Eds.), *Maternal employment and children's development: Longitudinal research*. New York: Plenum.

Gould, R. (1978). *Transformations: Growth and change in adult life*. New York: Simon and Schuster.

Gould, L. A. (1990). Cardiovascular health and sexual function. *Medical Aspects of Human Sexuality, 24*, 27–29.

Graham, C. (1991). Exercise and the aging. *Diabetes Forecast, 44*, 34–40.

Graham, J. W., Marks, G., & Hansen, W. B. (1991). Social influence processes affecting adolescent substance use. *Journal of Applied Psychology, 76*, 291–298.

Graziano, A., DeGiovanni, I. S., & Garcia, K. A. (1979). Behavioral treatment of children's fears: A review. *Psychological Bulletin, 86*, 804–830.

Greenberg, M., & Morris, N. (1974). Engrossment: The newborn's impact on the father. *American Journal of Orthopsychiatry, 44*, 520–531.

Greenberger, E., & Steinberg, L. D. (1986). When teenagers work. New York: Basic Books. Grinder, R. (1973). *Adolescence*. New York: Wiley.

Greenleaf, P. (1978). *Children through the ages*. New York: McGraw-Hill.

Greyson, B., & Stevenson, I. The phenomenology of near death experiences. *American Journal of Psychiatry, 137*, 1193–1196.

Grinder, R. (1973). *Adolescence*. New York: Wiley.

Grotevant, H. D., & Cooper, C. R. (1985). Patterns of interaction in family relationships and the development of identity exploration in adolescence. *Child Development, 56*, 415–428.

Grotevant, H. D., & Cooper, C. R. (1986). Individuation in family relationships. *Human Development, 29*, 82–100.

Gullotta, T. P., Adams, G. R., & Alexander, S. J. (1986). *Today's marriages and families*. Monterey, CA: Brooks/Cole.

Gut, E. (19974). Some aspects of adult mourning. *Omega, 5*, 323–342.

Gutteling, B., Weerth, C., Zandbelt, N., Mulder, E., Visser, G., & Buitelaar, J. (2006). Does Maternal Prenatal Stress Adversely Affect the Child's Learning and Memory at Age Six?. *Journal of Abnormal Child Psychology, 34*, 787-796.

Guttman, D. (1969). *The country of old men: Cross-cultural studies in the psychology of later life*. Ann Arbor, MI: Institute of Gerontology, University of Michigan-Wayne State.

Guttman, D. (1977). The cross-cultural perspective. In J. E. Birren & K. Schaie (Eds.), *Handbook of the psychology of aging*. New York: Van Nostrand.

Hagestad, G. (1985). *Continuity and connections*. In V. Bengston & J. Robertson (Eds.), Grandparenthood. Beverly Hills, CA: Sage.

Hagestad, G. (1986). *The family: Women and grandparents as kin keepers*. In A. Pifer & L. Bronte (Eds.), Our aging society. New York: Norton.

Haith, M. M. (1980). *Rules that babies look by: The organization of newborn visual activity*. Hillsdale, NJ: Erlbaum.

Hall, G. S. (1882). *The moral and religious training of children*. Princeton Review, 26–48.

Hall, G. S. (1904). *Adolescence*. Vols. 1 and 2. New York: D. Appleton & Co.

Halpern, D. (1989). The disappearance of cognitive gender differences: What you see depends on where you look. *American Psychologist, 44*, 1156–1158.

Halpern, H. W. (1990). *Cutting loose: An adult's guide to coming to terms with your parents*. New York: Simon & Schuster.

Halpert, E. (1991). Aspects of a dilemma of middle age: Whether or not to place aged, failing parents in a nursing home. *The Psychoanalytic Quarterly, 60*, 426–435.

Halverson, H. M. (1931). An experimental study of prehension in infants by means of systematic cinema records. *Genetic Psychology Monographs, 10*, 107–286.

Hamill, P. V. (1977). NCHS Growth curves for children. *Vital Health Statistics, Series 11*, No. 165. (DHEW Publication No. 78–1650). Washington, DC: U. S. Government Printing Office.

Hamilton, E., & Whitney, E. (1982). *Nutrition: Concepts and controversies* (2nd ed.). St. Paul, MN: West Publishing.

Handler, E. (1973). Expectations of day care parents. *Social Service Review, 47*, 266–277.

Hannson, R., Nelson, R., Carver, M., NeeSmith, D., Dowling, E., Fletcher, W., & Suhr, P. (1990). Adult children with frail elderly parents: When to intervene? *Family Relations, 39*, 153–158.

Hansen, D. A., & Hill, R. (1964). Families under stress. In H. Christensen (Ed.), Handbook of marriage and the family. Chicago: Rand-McNally.

Hanson, S. (1986a). Healthy single parent families. *Family Relations, 35*, 125–132.

Hanson, S. (1986b). Single custodial fathers. In S. Hanson & F. W. Bozett (Eds.), *Dimensions of fatherhood*. Beverly Hills, CA: Sage.

Hanson, S. L., Myers, D. R., & Ginsburg, A. (1987). The role of responsibility and knowledge in reducing teenage out-of-wedlock childbearing. *Journal of Marriage and the Family, 49*, 241–256.

Hapgood, C. C., Elkind, G. S., & Wright, J. J. (1988). Maternity blues: Phenomena and relationship to later postpartum depression. *Australian and New Zealand Journal of Psychiatry, 22*, 299–306.

Harkins, E. (1978). Effects of empty nest transition on self-report of psychological and physical well-being. *Journal of Marriage and the Family, 40*, 549–556.

Harkins, E. (1978). Effects of empty nest transition on self-report of psychological and physical well-being. *Journal of Marriage and the Family, 40*, 549–556.

Harlow, H. (1958). The nature of love. *American Psychologist, 13*, 673–685.

Harlow, H., Harlow, M., & Hansen, E. (1963). The maternal affectional system of rhesus monkeys. In H. Rheingold (Ed.), *Maternal behavior in animals*. New York: Wiley.

Harper, L., & Huie, K. (1985). The effects of prior group experience, age, and familiarity on the quality of organization of preschoolers social relations. *Child Development, 56*, 704–717.

Harper, L. V., & Sanders, K. M. (1978). Preschool children's use of space: Sex differences in outdoor play. In M. Smart & R. Smart (Eds.), *Preschool children: Development and relationships*. New York: Macmillan.

Harris, A., & Harris, T. (1985). *Staying OK*. New York: Harper & Row.

Harris, K. R. (1990). Developing self-regulated learners: The role of private speech and self-instructions. *Educational Psychologist, 25*, 38–45.

Harris, M. (1985). The three career life. *Money, May*, 108–110.

Harry, J. (1982). Decision-making and age differences among gay male couples. *Journal of Homosexuality, 8*, 9–21.

Hart, L., & Goldin-Meadow, S. (1984). The child as a nonegocentric art critic. *Child Development, 55*, 2122–2129.

Hart, N. A., & Keidel, G. C. (1979). The suicidal adolescent. *American Journal of Nursing, 79*, 80–84.

Harter, S. (1982). Children's understanding of multiple emotions: A cognitive developmental approach. In W. Overton (Ed.), *The relationship between social and cognitive development*. Hillsdale, NJ: Erlbaum.

Harter, S. (1983). Developmental perspectives on the self-system. In P. Mussen (Ed.), *Handbook of child psychology*, Vol. 4. New York: Wiley.

Hartup, W. (1983). Peer relations. In P. Mussen (Ed.), *Handbook of child psychology*, Vol. 4. New York: Wiley.

Hartup, W. (1989). Social relationships and their developmental significance. *American Psychologist, 44*, 120–126.

Hatton, C. L., Valente, S. M., & Rink, A. (1977). *Suicide: Assessment and intervention*. New York: Appleton-Century-Crofts.

Hatwell, Y. (1987). Motor and cognitive functions of the hand in infancy and childhood. *International Journal of Behavioral Development, 10*, 509–526.

Hausman, P. (1983). *Foods that fight cancer: A diet and vitamin program that protects the entire family*. New York: Rawson Associates.

Hausman, P., & Hurley, J. B. (1989). *The healing foods: The ultimate authority on the curative power of nutrition*. Emmaus, PA: Rodale Press.

Havighurst, R. (1964). Stages of vocational development. In H. Borrow (Ed.), *Man in a world at work*. Boston: Houghton Mifflin.

Havighurst, R. J. (1972). *Developmental tasks and education* (3rd ed.). New York: David McKay.

Havighurst, R. F., & Albrecht, R. (1953). *Older people.* New York: Longmans, Green.

Havighurst, R. F., Neugarten, B. L., & Tobin, S. S. (1968). Disengagement and patterns of aging. In B. L. Neugarten (Ed.), *Middle age and aging.* Chicago: University of Chicago Press.

Hay, D., Murray, P., Cecire, S., & Nash, A. (1985). Social learning of social behavior in early life. *Child Development, 56,* 43–57.

Hayflick, L. (1974). Cyrogerontology. In M. Rockstein (Ed.), *Theoretical aspects of aging.* New York: Academic Press.

Hayflick, L. (1977). The cellular base for biological aging. In C. E. Finch & L. Hayflick (Eds.), *Handbook of the biology of aging.* New York: Van Nostrand.

Hayflick, L. (1980). The cell biology of aging. *Scientific American, 242,* 58–65.

Hazan, C., & Shaver, P. (1994). Attachment as an organizational framework for research on close relationships. *Psychological Inquiry, 5,* 1-22.

Hazard, W. R. (Ed.). (1990). *Principles of geriatric medicine and gerontology* (2nd ed.). New York: McGraw-Hill.

Heaney, R. P. (1989). Nutritional factors in bone health in elderly subjects: Methodological and contextual problems. *American Journal of Clinical Nutrition, 50,* 1182–1187.

Heddescheimer, J. C. (1976). Multiple motivations for mid-career changes. *Personnel and Guidance Journal, 55,* 109–111.

Hegner, B. R. (1991). *Geriatrics: A study of maturity* (5th ed.). Albany, NY: Delmar.

Heibeck, T. H., & Markman, E. M. (1987). Word learning in children: An examination of fast mapping. *Child Development, 58,* 1021–1034.

Hein, K. (1989). AIDS in adolescent: Exploring the challenge. *Journal of Adolescent Health Care, 10,* 10S–35S.

Heller, M. (1986). Commuter marriages: A growing necessity for many couples in academe. *The Chronicle of Higher Education, 31.*

Helson, R., & Moane, G. (1987). Personality change in women from college to midlife. *Journal of Personality and Social Psychology, 53,* 176–186.

Hendrix, H. (1988). *Getting the love you want: A guide for couples.* New York: Henry Holt.

Herek, G. (1985). On doing, being, and no being: Prejudice and the social construction of sexuality. *Journal of Homosexuality, 12,* 135–151.

Hergenhahn, B. R. (2000). *An introduction to the history of psychology* (3rd ed.). NY: Wadsworth Publishing.

Herman, E. (1976). Senile hypophyseal syndromes. In A. V. Everitt & J. A. Burgess (Eds.), *Hypothalamus, pituitary, and aging.* Springfield, OH: Charles C. Thomas.

Hess, E. H. (1962). Ethology: An approach toward the complete analysis of behavior. *In New Directions in Psychology.* Vol. 1. New York: Holt, Reinhart, & Winston.

Hess, E. (1972). Imprinting in a natural laboratory. *Scientific American, 226,* 24–31.

Hess, R. D., & Camara, K. A. (1979). Post-divorce family relationships as mediating factors in the consequences of divorce for children. *Journal of Social Issues, 35,* 79–96.

Hetherington, E. M. (1972). Effects of father absence on personality: Development in adolescent daughters. *Developmental Psychology, 7,* 313–321.

Hetherington, E. M. (1979). Divorce: A child's perspective. *American Psychologist, 34,* 851–859.

Hetherington, E. M., Cox, M., & Cox, R. (1976). Divorced fathers. *Family Coordinator, 25,* 417–427.

Hetherington, E. M., Cox, M., & Cox, R. (1979). Family interaction and the social, emotional, and cognitive development of children following divorce. In C. Vaughn & T. B. Brazelton (Eds.), *The family: Setting priorities.* New York: Science and Medicine Publications.

Hetherington, E. M., Stanley-Hagan, M., & Anderson, E. R. (1989). Marital transitions. *American Psychologist, 44,* 303–312.

Higgins, A., & Turnure, J. (1984). Distractibility and concentration of attention in children's development. *Child Development, 55,* 1799–1810.

Hill, E., & Dorfman, L. (1982). Reaction of housewives to the retirement of their husbands. *Family Relations, 31,* 195–200.

Himes, C. L. (2001). Elderly Americans. In H. Cox (Ed.), *Annual editions: Aging* (18th ed.). Dubuque, IA: McGraw-Hill/Dushkin.

Hine, V. H. (1979). Dying at home: Can families cope? *Omega, 10,* 175–187.

Hinton, J. M. (1963). The physical and mental distress of dying. *Quarterly Journal of Medicine, 32,* 1–21.

Hirschman, C., & Hendershot, G. (1979). Trends in breast-feeding among American mothers. *Vital and Health Statistics, Series 23* (3), DHEW Publication No. (PHS) 79–1979.

Hobbins, J., & Mahoney, M. (1974). In utero diagnosis of hemoglobinopathies: Technic for obtaining fetal blood. *New England Journal of Medicine, 290,* 1065–1067.

Hobbs, D. (1965). Parenthood as crisis: A third study. *Journal of Marriage and the Family, 27,* 367–372.

Hobbs, D., & Wimbish, J. (1977). Transition to parenthood by black couples. *Journal of Marriage and the Family, 39,* 677–689.

Hodges, W. F., Tierney, C. W., & Buchsbaum, H. K. (1984). The cumulative effect of stress on preschool children of divorced and intact families. *Journal of Marriage and the Family, 46,* 611–617.

Hoff-Ginsberg, E. (1986). Function and structure in maternal speech: The relation to the child's development of syntax. *Developmental Psychology, 22,* 155–163.

Hoffman, L. (1977). Changes in family roles, socialization, and sex differences. *American Psychologist, 32,* 644–657.

Hoffman, L. (1979). Maternal employment. *American Psychologist, 34,* 859–865.

Hoffman, L. (1986). Work, family, and the child. In M. Pallak & R. Perloff (Eds.), *Psychology and work: Productivity, change, and employment.* Washington, DC: American Psychological Association.

Hoffman, L. (1989). Effects of maternal employment in the two-parent family. *American Psychologist, 44,* 283–293.

Hoffman, L. W., & Manis, J. D. (1979). The value of children in the United States: A new approach to the study of fertility. *Journal of Marriage and the Family, 41,* 583– 596.

Hogan, D. (1980). The transition to adulthood as a career contingency. *American Sociological Review, 45,* 261.

Holden, C. (1983). OTZ cites financial disaster of Alzheimer's. Science, 233, 839–841.

Holland, J. (1973). *Making vocational choices: A theory of careers.* Englewood Cliffs, NJ: Prentice Hall.

Holmes, L. D. (1987). *Quest for the real Samoa: The Mead-Freeman controversy and beyond.* South Hadley, MA: Bergin & Garvey.

Holmes, T. H., & Rahe, R. H. (1967). The social readjustment scale. *Journal of Psychosomatic Research, 11,* 213–218.

Holt, J. (1964). *How children fail.* New York: Pitman.

Hooker, E. (1969). *Final report of the task force on homosexuality.* Bethesda, MD: National Institute of Mental Health.

Hopkins, J., Campbell, S. B., & Marcus, M. (19870. Role of infant-related stressors in postpartum depression. *Journal of Abnormal Psychology, 96,* 237–241.

Hopkins, J., Marcus, M., & Campbell, S. B. (1984). Postpartum depression: A critical review. *Psychological Bulletin, 95,* 498–515.

Hopson, J. A. (1984). A love affair with the brain: PT conversation with Marian Diamond. *Psychology Today, 18,* 62.

Horan, M. A., & Brouwer, A. (Eds.). (1990). *Gerontology: Approaches to biomedical and clinical research.* London: Edward Arnold.

Horn, J. L., & Donaldson, G. Y. (1980). Cognitive development in adulthood. In D. G. Brim & J. Kagan (Eds.), *Constancy and change in human development.* Cambridge, MA: Harvard University Press.)

Horowitz, A., & Shindelman. (1983). Reciprocity and affection: Past influences on present caregiving. *Journal of Gerontological Social Work, 5,* 5–20.

Horwath, C. C. (1989). Chewing difficulty and dietary intake in the elderly. *Journal of Nutrition for the Elderly, 9,* 17–25.

Households and families. (1985). *Family Economics Review, 1,* 19–20.

Houseknecht, S. (1979). Childlessness and marital adjustment. *Journal of Marriage and the Family, 41,* 249–265.

Houseknecht, S. (1987). Voluntary childlessness. In M. B. Sussman & S. K. Steinmetz (Eds.), *Handbook of marriage and the family.* New York: Plenum.

Houser, B. B., & Berkman, S. L. (1984). Aging parent/mature child relationships. *Journal of Marriage and the Family, 46,* 295–299.

Hoving, K., Spencer, T., Robb, K., & Schulte, D. (1978). Developmental changes in visual information processing. In P. Ornstein (Ed.), *Memory development in children.* Hillsdale, NJ: Erlbaum.

Howard, A., & Scott, R. (1965). Cultural values and attitudes toward dying. *Journal of Existentialism, 6,* 161–174.

Howe, N., & Ross, H. S. (1990). Socialization, perspective-taking, and the sibling relationship. *Developmental Psychology, 26,* 160-165.

Howes, C. (1990). Can the age of entry and the quality of infant child care predict adjustment in kindergarten? *Developmental Psychology, 26,* 292–303.

Howes, C., & Stewart, P. (1987). Child's play with adults, toys, and peers: An examination of family and child care influences. *Developmental Psychology, 23,* 423–430.

Howes, C., Rodning, C., Galluzzo, D., & Myers, L. (1988). Attachment and child care: Relationships with mother and caregiver. Early *Childhood Research Quarterly, 3,* 403–316.

Hoy, E. A., Sykes, D. J., Bill, J. M., & Halliday, H. L. (1991). The effects of being born of very-low-birth-weight. *Irish Journal of Psychology, 12,* 182–197.

Hrdy, S. B. (1999). *Mother nature: Maternal instincts and how they shape the human species.* NY: Ballantine Books.

Hubel, D. H., & Weisel, T. N. (1970). The period of susceptibility to the physiological effects of unilateral eye closure in kittens. *Journal of Physiology, 206,* 419–436.

Hudson, J., Pope, H., & Jonas, J. (1983). Treatment of bulimia with antidepressants: Theoretical considerations with clinical findings. In A. Stunkard & E. Stellar (Eds.), *Eating and its disorders.* New York: Ravan Books.

Hulit, L. M. & Howard, M. R. (1997). *Born to talk: An introduction to speech and language development* (2nd ed.). Needham Heights, MA: Allyn & Bacon.

Humphreys, A. P., & Smith, P. K. (1987). Rough and tumble friendship and dominance in school children: Evidence for continuity and change with age in middle childhood. *Child Development, 58,* 201–212.

Hunt, M. (1974). *Sexual behavior in the 1970s.* Chicago: Playboy Press.

Hunt, R. J. (1988). Incidence of tooth loss among elderly Iowans. *American Journal of Public Health, 78,* 1330–1336.

Hunter, F. T., & Younis, J. (1982). Changes in functions of three relations during adolescence. *Developmental Psychology, 18,* 806–811.

Hurlock, E. (1980). *Developmental psychology* (5th ed.). New York: McGraw-Hill.

Husain, S., & Vandiver, T. (1984). *Suicide in children and adolescents.* New York: SP Medical and Scientific Books.

Huttunen, M. O., & Niskanen, P. (1973). Prenatal loss of father and psychiatric disorders. *Archives of General Psychiatry, 35,* 429–431.

Ikeman, B., Block, R., Avery, J., Niedra, R., Sulman, J., Tretowsky, S., & Yorke, E. (1987). Grief work with children: Access, clinical issues, community advocacy. In M. A. Morgan (Ed.), *Bereavement: Helping the survivors* (pp. 105–119). London, Ontario: King's College.

Ilg, F. L., & Ames, L. B. (1955). *Child behavior.* New York: Harper & Brothers.

Illingworth, R. (1975). *The development of the infant and young child* (6th ed.). London: Churchill Livingstone.

Inhelder, B., & Piaget, J. (1958). *The growth of logical thinking from childhood to adolescence.* New York: Basic Books.

Institute for Social Research. (1985). *Time, goods, and well-being.* Ann Arbor, MI: University of Michigan Press.

Izard, C., Huebner, R., Resser, D., McGinness, G., & Doughterty, L. (1980). The young infant's ability to produce discrete emotional expressions. *Developmental Psychology, 16,* 132–140.

Izard, C., Hembree, E., Doughterty, L., & Spizziri, C. (1983). Changes in two to nineteen month old infants' facial expressions following acute pain. *Developmental Psychology, 19,* 418–426.

Izard, C., Hembree, E., & Huebner, R. (1987). Infants' emotion expressions to acute pain: Developmental change and stability of individual differences. *Developmental Psychology, 23,* 105–113.

Jacklin, C. (1989). Female and male: Issues of gender. *American Psychologist, 44,* 127–133.

Jacobs, L. (1980). Variations in penile tumescence during sex activity. *Medical Aspects of Human Sexuality, 14,* 11.

Jacobs, S. C., et al. (1987). Attachment theory and multiple dimensions of grief. *Omega, 18,* 41–52.

Jacobsen, R. B. (1971). An exploration of parental encouragement as an intervening variable in occupational-educational learning of children. *Journal of Marriage and the Family, 33,* 174–182.

Jacobsen, R. B., Bigner, J. J., & Hood, S. (1991). Black versus white single parents and the value of children. *Journal of Black Studies,* 21, 302–312.

Jacobson, S. W. (1979). Matching behavior in the young infant. *Child Development, 50,* 425–430.

Jahoda, M. (1982). *Employment and unemployment: A social-psychological perspective.* Cambridge: Cambridge University Press.

Jalongo, M. R. (2005). Editorial: On behalf of children. In G. E. Dickinson & M. R. Leming, (Eds.), *Dying, death, and bereavement* (10th ed.). NY: McGraw-Hill.

James, J. W., & Cherry, F. (1988). *The grief recovery handbook.* New York: Harper & Row.

James, M., & Jongeward, D. (1971). *Born to win.* New York: Addison-Wesley.

Jensen, A. (1969). How much can we boost IQ and scholastic achievement? *Harvard Educational Review, 39,* 1–123.

Jersild, A. (1960). *Child psychology* (5th ed.). Englewood Cliffs, NJ: Prentice Hall.

John-Roger, & McWilliams, P. (1990). *You can't afford the luxury of a negative thought.* Los Angeles, CA: Prelude Press.

Johnson, M. A. (1989). Variables associated with friendship in an adult population. *Journal of Social Psychology, 129,* 379–384.

Johnson, M. T., & Roberts, J. (19778). Prevalence of dermatological disease among persons 1–74 years of age: United States. *Advance Data from Health and Vital Statistics, No. 4,* January 26.

Johnson, V., & Pandina, R. J. (1991). Effects of the family environment on adolescent substance use, delinquency, and coping styles. *American Journal of Drug and Alcohol Abuse, 17,* 71–88.

Jones, B. (1986). Quality and equality through cognitive instruction. *Educational Leadership, April,* 4–11.

Jones, G., & Smith, P. (1984). The eyes have it: Young children's discrimination of age in masked and unmasked facial photographs. *Journal of Experimental Child Psychology, 38,* 328–337.

Jones, H. (1957). The later careers of boys who were early- or late-maturing. *Child Development, 28,* 113–128.

Jones, H., & Bayley, N. (1950). Physical maturing among boys as related to behavior. *Journal of Educational Psychology, 41,* 129–148.

Jones, H., & Mussen, P. (1958). Self-conceptions, motivations, and interpersonal attitudes of early and late-maturing girls. *Child Development, 29,* 491–501.

Jones, W. (1979). Grief and involuntary career change: Its implications for counseling. *Vocational Guidance Quarterly, 27,* 196–201.

Jones, D. C., Bloys, N., & Wood, M. (1990). Sex roles and friendship patterns. *Sex Roles, 23,* 133–139.

Jorgensen, S. R., & Sonstegard, J. S. (1984). Predicting adolescent sexual and contraceptive behavior: An application and test of the Fishbein model. *Journal of Marriage and the Family, 46,* 43–55.

Judson, F. N. (1989). What do we really know about AIDS control? *American Journal of Public Health, 79,* 878–882.

Jussim, L. (1989). Teacher expectations: Self-fulfilling prophecies, perceptual biases, and accuracy. *Journal of Personality and Social Psychology, 57,* 469–480.

Justice, E. (1985). Categorization as a preferred memory strategy. *Developmental Psychology, 21,* 1105–1110.

Jylha, M., & Jokela, J. (1990). Individual experiences as cultural: A cross-cultural study on loneliness among the elderly. *Aging and Society, 10,* 295–306.

Kach, J. A., & McGhee, 1982). Adjustment to early parenthood: The role of accuracy of preparenthood experiences. *Journal of Family Issues, 3,* 375–388.

Kachigan, S. K. (1986). *Statistical analysis: An interdisciplinary introduction to univariate and multivariate methods.* NY: Radius Press.

Kaffman, M., & Elizur, E. (1979). Children's bereavement reactions following death of the father. *International Journal of Family Therapy, 1,* 203–229.

Kagan, J. (1970). The determinants of attention in the infant. *American Scientist, 58,* 298–306.

Kagan, J. (1972). Do infants think? *Scientific American, 226,* 74–82.

Kagan, J. (1984). *The nature of the child.* New York: Basic Books.

Kagan, J., Reznick, J. S., Clarke, C., Snidman, N., & Garcia-Coll, C. (1984). Behavioral inhibitions to the unfamiliar. *Child Development, 55,* 2212–2225.

Kalish, R. (1963). An approach to the study of death attitudes. *American Behavioral Scientist, 6,* 68–80.

Kalish, R. (1981). *Death, grief, and caring relationships.* Monterey, CA: Brooks/Cole.

Kalish, R. (1987). Death. In G. L. Maddox et al., (Eds.), *The encyclopedia of aging.* New York: Springer.

Kalish, R., & Reynolds, D. (1976). *Death and ethnicity: A psychocultural study.* Los Angeles, CA: University of California Press.

Kalish, R., & Reynolds, D. (1981). *Death and ethnicity: A psychological study.* Farmington, N. Y.: Baywood.

Kalnins, I., & Bruner, J. (1973). Infant sucking to change the clarity of a visual display. In L. Stone, H. Smith, & L. B. Murphy (Eds.), *The competent infant: Research and commentary.* New York: Basic Books.

Kamin, L. J. (1974). *The science and politics of IQ.* Potomac, MD: Erlbaum.

Kamp Dush, C. M., Cohan, C. L., & Amato, P. R. (2003). The relationship between cohabitation and marital quality and stability: Change across cohorts? *Journal of Marriage and Family, 65,* 539–549.

Kandel, D. B., Davies, M., Karus, D., & Yamaguchi, K. (1986). The consequences in young adulthood of adolescent drug involvement. *Achives of General Psychiatry, 43,* 746–754.

Kandel, D. B., Raveis, V. H., & Davies, M. (1991). Suicidal ideation in adolescence: Depression, substance use, and other risk factors. *Journal of Youth & Adolescence, 20,* 289–309.

Kaplan, B. J. (1986). A psychobiological review of depression during pregnancy. *Psychology of Women Quarterly, 10,* 35–48.

Kaplan, H., & Dove, H. (1987). Infant development among the Ache of East Paraguay. *Developmental Psychology, 23,* 190–198.

Kaplan, P. (1990). *Educational psychology for tomorrow's teacher.* St. Paul, MN: West Publishing Co.

Kaplan, F., & Kaplan, T. (1973). *The power of play.* Garden City, NJ: Anchor Press.

Kaplan, S., Nessbaum, M., Skomoronsky, P., Shenker, I., & Ramsey, P. (1980). Health habits and depression in adolescence. *Journal of Youth and Adolescence, 9,* 299–304.

Kart, C., Metress, E. S., & Metress, J. F. (1978). *Aging and health: Biologic and social perspectives.* Menlo Park, CA: Addison-Wesley.

Kastenbaum, R. J. (1975). Is death a life crisis? On the confrontation with death in theory and practice. In N. Datan & L. Ginsberg (Eds.), *Life-span developmental psychology: Normative life crises.* New York: Academic Press.

Kastenbaum, R. J. (1977). Death and development through the life span. In H. Feifel (Ed.), *New meanings of death.* New York: McGraw-Hill.

Kastenbaum, R. J. (1986). *Death, society, and human experience* (3rd ed.). Columbus, OH: Charles E. Merrill.

Kastenbaum, R. J., & Aisenberg, R. (1972). *The psychology of death.* New York: Springer.

Katch, B. (1981). Fathers and infants: Reported caregiving and interaction. *Journal of Family Issues, 2,* 275–296.

Katchadourian, H. A. (1977). *The biology of adolescence.* San Francisco: Freeman.

Katchadourian, H. A. (1985). *Fundamentals of human sexuality* (4th ed.). New York: Holt, Rinehart, Winston.

Kaufman, K. R. & Kaufman, N. D. (2006). And then the dog died. In G. E. Dickinson & M.R. Leming, (Eds.), *Dying, death, and bereavement* (10th ed.). NY: McGraw-Hill.

Kehl, K. A. (2006). Moving toward peace. In G. E. Dickinson & M. R. Leming, (Eds.), *Dying, death, and bereavement* (10th ed.). NY: McGraw-Hill.

Keller, W. D., Hildebrandt, K. A., & Richards, M. E. (1985). Effects of extended father-infant contact during the newborn period. *Infant Behavior and Development, 8,* 337–350.

Keller, S. E., Bartlett, J. A., Schleifer, S. J., & Johnson, R. L. (1991). HIV-relevant sexual behavior among a healthy inner-city heterosexual adolescent population in an endemic area of HIV. *Journal of Adolescent Health, 12,* 44–48.

Kellett, J. M. (1991). Sexuality of the elderly. *Sexual and Marital Therapy, 6,* 147–160.

Kelley, K., & Byrne, D. (1992). *Exploring human sexuality.* Englewood Cliffs, NJ: Prentice Hall.

Kellogg, R. (1970). *Analyzing children's art.* Palo Alto, CA: Mayfield.

Kellogg, R., & O'Dell, S. (1967). *The psychology of children's art.* San Francisco: CRM.

Kelly, A. (1988). Gender differences in teacher-pupil interactions: A meta-analytic review. *Research in Education, 39,* 1–23.

Kelly, J. E., & Harvey, C. R. (1979). Basic dental examination findings of persons 1–74 years. *Vital and Health Statistics, Series 11,* No. 214. DHEW Publication No. (PHS) 79–1662.

Kemper, S., & Mitzner, T. L. (2001). Language production and comprehension. In J. E. Birren & K. W. Schaie (Eds.), *Handbook of the psychology of aging.* San Diego, CA: Academic Press.

Kennedy, J. (1989). Determinants of peer social status: Contributions of physical appearance, reputation, and behavior. Paper presented at the annual meeting of the Society for Research in Child Development, Kansas City.

Kennedy, E., Spence, S., & Hensley, R. (1989). An examination of the relationship between childhood depression and social competence among primary school children. *Journal of Child Psychology and Psychiatry, 30,* 561–573.

Kennedy, M. M. (1980). *Office politics: Seizing power, wielding clout.* Chicago: Follett.

Kennedy, M. M. (1982). *Salary strategies: Everything you need to know to get the salary you want.* New York: Rawson, Wade.

Kennedy, M. M. (1985). *Office warfare: Strategies for getting ahead in the aggressive 80s.* New York: Macmillan.

Kennell, J., Slyter, H., & Klaus, M. (1970). The mourning response of parents to the death of a newborn infant. *New England Journal of Medicine, 283,* 344–349.

Kenniston, K. (1971). *Youth and dissent: The rise of a new opposition.* New York: Harcourt, Brace, Jovanovich.

Kerckhoff, R. L. (1976). Marriage and middle age. *Family Coordinator, 20,* 5–11.

Kessen, W., Haith, M. M., & Salapatek, P. (1970). Infancy. In P. Mussen (Ed.), *Carmichael's manual of child psychology* (3rd ed.). Vol. 1. New York: Wiley, 1970.

Ketcham, C. J., & Stelmach, G. E. (2001). Age-related declines in motor control. In J. E. Birren & K. W. Schaie (Eds.), *Handbook of the psychology of aging.* San Diego, CA: Academic Press.

Kett, J. (1977). *Rites of passage: Adolescence in America.* New York: Basic Books.

Kimball, M. (1989). A new perspective on women's math achievement. *Psychological Bulletin, 105,* 198–214.

Kimmel, DC (1980). *Adulthood and aging.* (2nd ed.). New York: Wiley.

Kinard, E. M., & Reinherz, H. (1986). Effects of marital disruption on children's school aptitude and achievement. *Journal of Marriage and the Family, 48,* 285–294.

Kinney, D., Hyman, W., Greetham, C., & Tramer, S. (1999). Increased relative risk for schizophrenia and prenatal exposure to a severe tornado. *Schizophrenia Research, 13,* 45–46.

Kinsey, A. C., Pomeroy, W. B., & Martin, C. E. (1948). *Sexual behavior in the human male*. Philadelphia: Saunders.

Kinsey, A. C., Pomeroy, W. B., Martin, C. E., & Gebhard, P. H. (1953). *Sexual behavior in the human female*. Philadelphia: Saunders.

Kirkpatrick, D. (1989). Will you be able to retire? *Fortune, 120*(3), 56–59.

Kitson, G. C., Babri, K. B., & Roach, M. J. (1985). Who divorces and why. *Journal of Family Issues, 6,* 255–294.

Kitson, G. C., & Morgan, L. A. (1990). Consequences of divorce. *Journal of Marriage and the Family, 52,* 913–924.

Kitzinger, S. (1983). *The complete book of pregnancy and childbirth.* New York: Knopf.

Klaus, M., & Kennell, J. H. (1976). *Maternal-infant bonding.* St. Louis, MO: Mosby.

Kline, G. H., Stanley, S. M., Markman, H. J., Olmos-Gallo, P. A., St. Peters, M., Whitton, S. W., et al. (2004). Timing is everything: Pre-engagement cohabitation and increased risk for poor marital outcomes. *Journal of Family Psychology, 18,* 311–318.

Kline, R. B., Canter, W. A., & Robin, A. (1987). Parameters of teenage alcohol use: A path analytic conceptual model. *Journal of Consulting and Clinical Psychology, 55,* 521–528.

Klinnert, M. D., Emde, R., Butterfield, P., & Campos, J. (1986). Social referencing: The infant's use of emotional signals from a friendly adult with mother present. *Developmental Psychology, 22,* 427–432.

Knaub, P. K., Hanna, S. L., & Stinnett, N. (1984). Strengths of remarried families. *Journal of Divorce, 7,* 41–55.

Knox, A. (1977). *Adult development and learning.* San Francisco: Josey-Bass.

Knox, T. A., Kassarkian, Z., & Dawson-Hughes, B. (1991). Calcium absorption in elderly subjects on high and low-fiber diets: Effect of gastric acidity. *American Journal of Clinical Nutrition, 53,* 1480–1487.

Kobasa, S., Maddi, S., & Kahn, S. (1982). Hardiness and health: A prospective study. *Journal of Personality and Social Psychology, 42,* 168–177.

Koblinsky, S. A., & Todd, C. M. (1989). Teaching self-care skills to latchkey children: A review of research.

Koch, H. (1956). Sissiness and tomboyishness in relation to sibling characteristics. *Journal of Genetic Psychology, 88,* 231–244.

Koch-Hattem, A. (1986). Siblings' experience of pediatric cancer: Interviews with children. *Health and Social Work, 11,* 107–117.

Kohlberg, L. (1966). Development of moral character and moral ideology. In M. Hoffman & L. Hoffman (Eds.), *Review of child development research.* Vol. 1. New York: Russell Sage.

Kohlberg, L. (1969). Stage and sequence: The cognitive-developmental approach to socialization. In D. Goslin (Ed.), *Handbook of socialization theory and research.* Chicago: Rand McNally.

Kohlberg, L. (1984). *Essays on moral development,* Vol. 2. San Francisco: Harper & Row.

Kohlberg, L., & Gilligan, C. (1971). The adolescent as a philosopher: The discovery of the self in a postconventional world. *Daedalus, Fall,* 1051–1086.

Kohlberg, L., Yaeger, J., & Hjertholm, E. (1968). Private speech: Four studies and a review of theories. *Child Development, 39,* 817–826.

Kolata, G. (1986). Obese children: A growing problem. *Science, 232,* 20–21.

Kolata, G. (1987). Associations or rules in acquiring language? *Science, 237,* 133–134.

Kolb, B. (1989). Brain development, plasticity, and behavior. *American Psychologist, 44,* 1203–1212.

Koocher, G. P. (1973). Childhood, death, and cognitive development. *Developmental Psychology, 9,* 369–375.

Koocher, G. P. (1974). Talking with children about death. *American Journal of Orthopsychiatry, 44,* 405–411.

Kopp, C. (1982). Antecedents of self-regulation. *Developmental Psychology, 18,* 199–214.

Korner, A. (1971). Individual differences at birth: Implications for early experience and later development. *American Journal of Orthopsychiatry, 41,* 608–619.

Kourany, R. F. (1987). Suicide among homosexual adolescents. *Journal of Homosexuality, 13,* 111–117.

Krogman, W. M. (1980). *Child growth.* Ann Arbor, MI: University of Michigan Press.

Kovar, M. G. (1986a). Aging in the eighties. *Advance Data From Vital and Health Statistics, No. 115.* DHHS Publication No. (PHS) 86–1250. Hyattsville, MD: Public Health Service.

Kovar, M. G. (1986b). Aging in the eighties: Age 65 years and over and living alone: Contacts with family, friends, and neighbors. *Advance Data From Vital and Health Statistics, No. 116, May 9.* DHHS Publication No. (PHS) 86–1250. Hyattsville, MD: U. S. Public Health Service.

Kovar, M. G. (1988). Aging in the eighties: People living alone—two years later. *Advance Data From Vital and Health Statistics, No. 149, April 4.* DHHS Publication No. (PHS) 88–1250. Hyattsville, MD: U. S. Public Health Service.

Kovar, M. G., & LaCroix, A. Z. (1987). Aging in the eighties: Ability to perform work-related activities. *Advance Data From Vital and Health Statistics, No. 136.* DHHS Publication No. (PHS) 87–1250. Hyattsville, MD: Public Health Service.

Kowles, R. V. (1985). *Genetics, society, and decisions.* Columbus, OH: Charles Merrill.

Kozma, A., & Stones, M. J. (1983). Prediction of happiness. *Journal of Gerontology, 38,* 626–628.

Kreutler, P. A. (1980). *Nutrition in perspective.* Englewood Cliffs, NJ: Prentice Hall.

Kriesberg, L. (1970). *Mothers in poverty: A study of fatherless families.* Chicago: Aldine.

Krogman, W. M. (1980). *Child growth.* Ann Arbor, MI: University of Michigan Press.

Kubler-Ross, E. (1969). *On death and dying.* New York: Macmillan.

Kubler-Ross, E., & Worden, J. W. (1977). Attitudes and experiences of death workshop attendees. *Omega, 8,* 91–106.

Kuhn, M. (1978). Insights on aging. Journal of Home Economics, 71, 18–20.

Kupersmidt, J. (1989). Socially rejected children: Bullies, victims, or both? Paper presented at the annual meeting of the Society for Research in Child Development, Kansas City.

Kurdek, L. A. (1981). An integrative perspective on children's divorce adjustment. *American Psychologist, 36,* 856–866.

Kurdek, L. (1989). Relationship quality in gay and lesbian cohabitating couples: A 1-year follow-up study. *Journal of Social and Personal Relationships, 6,* 39–59.

Labaree, D. (1987). Politics, markets, and the compromised curriculum. *Harvard Educational Review, 57,* 483–494.

Labouvie-Vief, G., & Schell, D. (1982). Learning and memory in later life. In B. Wolman (Ed.), *Handbook of developmental psychology.* Englewood Cliffs, NJ: Prentice Hall.

Labouvie-Vief, G. (1985). Intelligence and cognition. In J. E. Birren & K. Schaie (Eds.), *Handbook of the psychology of aging* (2nd ed.). New York: Van Nostrand.

Labouvie-Vief, G. (1986). Modes of knowledge and the organization of development. In M. Commons, L. Kohlberg, F. Richards, & J. Sinnot (Eds.), *Beyond formal operations 3: Models and methods in the study of adult and adolescent thought.* New York: Praeger.

Lagercrantz, H., & Slotkin, T. A. (1986). *Scientific American, 254*(4), 100–107.

Lamanna, M. A., & Reidmann, A. (1988). *Marriages and families: Making choices and facing change* (3rd ed.).Belmont, CA: Wadsworth Publishing Co.

Lamaze, F. (1958). *Painless childbirth: Psychoprophylactic method.* New York: Harper & Row.

Lamb, M., & Goldberg, W. (1982). The father-child relationship. In L. Hoffman et al., (Eds.), *Parenting.* Hillsdale, NJ: Erlbaum Associates.

Lamb, M. E., Hwang, C. P., Broberg, A., & Bookstein, F. (1988). The effects of out of home care on the development of social competence in Sweden: A longitudinal study. *Early Childhood Research Quarterly, 3,* 379–402.

Lang, A., & Brody, E. (1983). Characteristics of middle-aged daughters and help to their elderly parents. *Journal of Marriage and the Family, 45,* 193–202.

LaRossa, R. (1986). *Becoming a parent*. Beverly Hills, CA: Sage Publications.

LaRossa, R., & LaRossa, M. (1981). *Transition to parenthood*. Beverly Hills, CA: Russell Sage Foundation.

Larsen, E. (1985). *Stage II recovery*. San Francisco: Harper & Row.

Larsen, E. (1987). *Stage II relationships: Love beyond addiction*. San Francisco, CA: Harper & Row.

Laury, G. V. (1981). Difficulty in reaching orgasm by aging men. *Medical Aspects of Human Sexuality, 15*, 29, 32.

Laury, G. V. (1982). Ejaculatory changes in aging men. *Medical Aspects of Human Sexuality, 16*, 136, 145.

Leboyer, F. (1976). *Birth without violence*. New York: Knopf.

Leff, P. (1987). Here I am, Ma: The emotional impact of pregnancy loss on parents and health-care professionals. *Family Systems Medicine, 5*, 105–114.

Leifer, M. (1980). *Psychological effects of motherhood: A study of first pregnancy*. New York: Praeger.

Leitar, E. (1986). Miscarriage. In T. Rando (Ed.), *Parental loss of a child*. Champaign, IL: Research Press.

LeMasters, E. E. (1957). Parenthood as crisis. *Marriage and Family Living, 19*, 352–355.

LeMasters, E. E. (1974). *Parents in modern America* (Rev. ed.). Homewood, IL: Dorsey.

LeMasters, E. E. (1983). Parents in contemporary America: *A sympathetic view* (4th ed.). Homewood, IL: Dorsey.

Lennenberg, E. H. (1969). On explaining language. *Science, 164*, 635–643.

Lerner, J. V., & Galambos, N. L. (1985). Maternal role satisfaction, mother-child interaction, and child temperament: A process model. *Developmental Psychology, 21*, 1157–1164.

Lerner, M. (1980). When, why, and where people die. In E. S. Shneidman (Ed.), *Death: Current perspectives* (pp. 87–106). Palo Alto, CA: Mayfield.

Lerner, R. M. (1998). Theories of human development: Contemporary perspectives. In W. Damon & R. M. Lerner (Eds.), Handbook of child psychology (Vol. 1): *Theoretical models of human development* (5th ed.). NY: John Wiley & Sons, Inc.

Lerner, R. M., Karson, M., Meisels, M., & Knapp, J. R. (1975). Actual and perceived attitudes of late adolescents and their parents: The phenomenon of the generation gap. *Journal of Genetic Psychology, 126*, 195–207.

Lester, B., Hoffman, J., & Brazelton, T. B. (1985). The rhythmic structure of mother-infant interaction in term and preterm infants. *Child Development, 56*, 15–27.

Leung, E., & Rheingold, H. (1981). Development of pointing as a social gesture. *Developmental Psychology, 17*, 215–220.

LeVay, S. (1991). A difference in hypothalamic structure between heterosexual and homosexual men. *Science, 253*, 1034.

Leventhal, H., Rabin, C., Leventhal, E. A., & Burns, E. (2001). Health risk behaviors and aging. In J. E. Birren & K. W. Schaie (Eds.), *Handbook of the psychology of aging*. San Diego, CA: Academic Press.

Levin, I. (1982). The nature and development of time concepts in children: The effects of interfering cues. In W. Friedman (Ed.), *The developmental psychology of time*. New York: Academic Press.

Levin, I., Wilkening, F., & Dembo, Y. (1984). Development of time quantification: Integration and nonintegration of beginnings and endings in comparative durations. *Child Development, 55*, 2160–2172.

Levine, R. (1980). Adulthood among the Gusii of Kenya. In N. J. Smelser & E. H. Erikson (Eds.), *Themes of work and love in adulthood*. Cambridge, MA: Harvard University Press.

Levinson, D., et. al. (1978). *The seasons of a man's life*. New York: Ballentine.

Levinson, D. (1980). Toward a conception of the adult life course. In N. J. Smelser & E. Erikson (Eds.), *Themes of work and love in adulthood*. Cambridge, MA: Harvard University Press.

Levinson, D. (1986). A conception of adult development. *American Psychologist, 41*, 3–13.

Levy, J. C., & Deykin, E. Y. (1989). Suicidality, depression, and substance abuse in adolescence. *American Journal of Psychiatry, 146*, 1462–1467.

Levy, M. H. (1988). Pain control research in the terminally ill. *Omega, 18*, 265–275.

Lewis, C., Battistich, V., & Schaps, E. (1990). School-based primary prevention: What is an effective program? *New Directions for Child Development, Winter*, 35–59.

Lewis, C. B. (Ed.). (1990). *Aging: The health care challenge* (2nd ed.). Philadelphia: F. A. Davis.

Lewis, M. (1987). Social development in infancy and early childhood. In J. Osofsky (Ed.), *Handbook of infant development*. New York: Wiley.

Lewis, R., Feneau, P., & Roberts, C. (1979). Fathers and the postparental transition. *Family Coordinator, 28*, 514–520.

Lieberman, M. A. (1965). Psychological correlates of impending death: Some preliminary observations. *Journal of Gerontology, 20*, 181–190.

Lieberman, M. A., & Coplan, A. S. (1970). Distance from death as a variable in the study of aging. *Developmental Psychology, 2*, 71–84.

Lindsey, R. (1987). Colleges accused of bias to stem Asians' gain. *New York Times, January 25*, 10.

Locke, J. (1689). *Essay Concerning Human Understanding*. New York: Macmillan.

Loehlin, J., Lindzey, G., & Spuhler, J. (1975). *Race differences in intelligence*. San Francisco: Freeman.

Logan, B. N. (1991). Adolescent substance abuse prevention: An overview of the literature. *Family and Community Health, 13*, 25–36.

Logan, D. (1980). The menstrual experience in 23 foreign countries. *Adolescence, 15*, 247–256.

Lomax, R. G. (2001). *Statistical concepts: A second course for education and the behavioral sciences* (2nd ed.). Mahwah, NJ: Lawrence Erlbaum Associates, Publishers.

Lopata, H. Z. (1973). *Widowhood in an American city*. Cambridge, MA: Schenkman.

Lorenz, K. (1965). *Evolution and modification of behavior*. Chicago: University of Chicago Press.

Lowenthal, M. F., Thunher, M., & Chirigoa, D. (1977). *Four stages of life*. San Francisco: Josey-Bass.

Lowik, M. R. H., Hofman, Z., & Kok, F. J. (1991). Nutrition and blood pressure among elderly men and women. *Journal of the American College of Nutrition, 10*, 149–153.

Lowrey, C. R., & Settle, S. A. (1985). Effects of divorce on children: Differential impact of custody and visitation patterns. *Family Relations, 34*, 455–463.

Lumpkin, C., Jr., McClung, J., Pereira-Smith, O., & Smith, J. (1986). Existence of high abundance antiproliferative mRNAs in senescent human diploidfibroblasts. *Science, 232*, 393–395.

Lynch, T. (2007). Into the oblivion. In G. E. Dickinson & M. R. Leming, (Eds.), *Dying, death, and bereavement* (10th ed.). NY: McGraw-Hill.

Maccoby, E. (1980). *Social development: Psychological growth and the parent-child relationship*. New York: Harcourt Brace Jovanovich.

Maccoby, E. (1984). Middle childhood in the context of the family. In W. Collins (Ed.), *Development during middle childhood: The years from six to twelve*. Washington, DC: National Academy of Sciences.

Maccoby, E. (1990). Gender and relationships: A developmental account. *American Psychologist, 45*, 513–520.

Maccoby, E., & Jacklin, C. (1974). *The psychology of sex differences*. Stanford, CA: Stanford University Press.

Maccoby, E., & Hagen, J. (1965). Effect of distraction upon central versus incidental recall: Developmental trends. *Journal of Experimental Child Psychology, 2*, 280–289.

Maccoby, E., & Jacklin, C. N. (1987). Gender segregation in childhood. In *Advances in child development and behavior*. Vol. 20. New York: Academic Press.

Mace, D. (Ed.) (1983). *Prevention in family services: Approaches to family wellness*. Beverly Hills, CA: Sage.

MacEwen, K. E., & Barling, J. (1991). Effects of maternal employment experiences on children's behavior via mood, cognitive difficulties, and parenting behavior. *Journal of Marriage and the Family, 53*, 635–644.

Mackintosh, E. (1982). Mysteries. *Science, 82*, 108.

Mackintosh, N. J. (1983). *Conditioning and associative learning*. Oxford: Clarendon Press.

Macklin, E. (1987). Alternative family forms. In M. B. Sussman & S. K. Steinmetz (Eds.), *Handbook of marriage and the family*. New York: Plenum.

Macrae, J., & Herbert-Jackson, E. (1976). Are behavioral effects of infant day care program specific? *Developmental Psychology, 12,* 269–270.

Madden, D. J. (2001). Speed and time of behavioral processes. In J. E. Birren & K. W. Schaie (Eds.), *Handbook of the psychology of aging*. San Diego, CA: Academic Press.

Maddox, G. L. (1968). Persistence of life style among the elderly: A longitudinal study of patterns of social activity in relation to life satisfaction. In B. L. Neugarten (Ed.), *Middle age and aging*. Chicago: University of Chicago Press.

Magai, C. (2001). Emotions over the life span. In J. E. Birren & K. W. Schaie (Eds.), *Handbook of the psychology of aging*. San Diego, CA: Academic Press.

Maier, H. W. (1965). *Three theories of child development*. New York: Harper & Row.

Major, B., Appelbaum, M., Beckman, L., Dutton, M., Russo, N., & West, C. (2009). Abortion and mental health: Evaluating the evidence. *American Psychologist, 64,* 863–890.

Makinodan, T. (1977). Immunity and aging. In C. E. Finch & L. Hayflick (Eds.), *Handbook of the biology of aging*. New York: Van Nostrand.

Malaspina, D., Corcoran, C., Kleinhaus, K., Perrin, M., Fennig, S., Nahon, D., et al. (2008). Acute maternal stress in pregnancy and schizophrenia in offspring: A cohort prospective study. *BMC Psychiatry,* 81–9. doi:10.1186/1471-244X-8-21.

Malinak, D. P., Hoyt, M. F., & Patterson, V. (1979). Adults' reactions to the death of a parent: A preliminary study. *American Journal of Psychiatry, 136,* 1152–1156.

Mancini, J., & Bleiszner, R. (1991). Aging parents and adult children: Research themes in intergenerational relations. In A. Booth (Ed.), *Contemporary families: Looking forward, looking back*. Minneapolis, MN: National Council on Family Relations.

Mandell, F., McAnulty, E., & Reese, R. M. (1980). Observations of parental response to sudden unanticipated infant death. *Pediatrics, 65,* 221–224.

Manning, B. H. (1990). Task-relevant private speech as a function of age and sociability. *Psychology in the Schools, 27,* 365–372.

Manning, C., & Lieux, E. (1991). Volunteer labor contribution in nutrition programs for the elderly. *Journal of Nutrition for the Elderly, 10,* 5–10.

Marcia, J. E. (1980). Identity in adolescence. In J. Adelson (Ed.), *Handbook of adolescent psychology* (pp. 159–187).New York: Wiley.

Marciano, T. (1979). Male influences on fertility: Needs for research. *Family Coordinator, 28,* 561–568.

Markusen, E., Owen, G., Fulton, R., & Bendiksen, R. (1978). SIDS: The survivor as victim. *Omega, 84,* 277–283.

Margolin, G., Huster, G., & Glueck, C. J. (1991). Blood pressure lowering in elderly subjects: A double-blind cross-over study of omega-3 and omega-6 fatty acids. *American Journal of Clinical Nutrition, 53,* 562–566.

Maris, R. (1985). The adolescent suicide problem. *Suicide and Life Threatening Behavior, 15,* 91–109.

Markides, K. S., & Krause, N. (1986). Older Mexican Americans. *Generations, 10,* 31–34.

Markman, E. M., & Wachtel, G. F. (1988). Children's use of exclusivity to constrain the meanings of words. *Cognitive Psychology, 20,* 121–157.

Marlatt, G., Baer, J., Donovan, D., & Kivlahan, D. (1988). Addictive behaviors: Etiology and treatment. *Annual Review of Psychology, 39,* 223–252.

Marshall, S., & Smith, J. (1987). Sex differences in learning mathematics: A longitudinal study with item and error analysis. *Journal of Educational Psychology, 79,* 372–381.

Marshall, V., (1986). A sociological perspective on aging and dying. In V. Marshall (Ed.), *Later life: The social psychology of aging*. Beverly Hills, CA: Sage.

Martin, L. G. (1988). The aging of Asia. *Journal of Gerontology, 43,* 99–113.

Martin, A. D., & Hetrick, E. S. (1988). The stigmatization of the gay and lesbian adolescent. *Journal of Homosexuality, 15,* 163–183.

Martin, J. (1987). The impact of AIDS on gay male sexual behavior patterns in New York City. *American Journal of Public Health, 75,* 493–496.

Martinez, G., & Nalezwinski, J. (1981). 1980 update: The recent trend in breast-feeding. *Pediatrics, 67,* 260–263.

Martocchio, B. C. (1986). Agendas for quality of life. *The Hospice Journal, 2,* 11–21.

Maslow, A. (1968). *Toward a psychology of being*. Princeton, NJ: Van Nostrand.

Maslow, A. (1970). *Motivation and personality* (2nd ed.). New York: Harper & Row.

Masters, W. H., & Johnson, V. E. (1966). *Human sexual response*. Boston: Little, Brown.

Masters, W. H., & Johnson, V. E. (1970). *Human sexual inadequacy*. Boston: Little, Brown.

Masters, W. H., & Johnson, V. E. (1979). *Homosexuality in perspective*. Boston: Little, Brown.

Masters, W. H., Johnson, V. E., & Kolodny, R. C. (1985). *Human sexuality* (2nd ed.). Boston: Little, Brown.

Maultsby, H. (1979). Rational rules for making rules. *Interaction, 7,* 3–4.

Maurer, D., & Maurer, C. (1988). *The world of the newborn*. New York: Basic Books.

Mauritzen, J. (1988). Pastoral care for the dying and bereaved. *Death Studies, 12,* 111–122.

May, R. (1958). Contributions to existential psychotherapy. In R. May, E. Angel, & H. F. Ellenberger (Eds.), *Existence: A new dimension in psychiatry and psychology*. New York: Basic Books.

McCandless, B. (1970). *Adolescents: Behavior and development*. New York: Holt, Rinehart, & Winston.

McCann, I., & Holmes, D. (1984). Influence of aerobic exercise on depression. *Journal of Personality and Social Psychology, 46,* 1142–1147.

McCarthy, M. (1991). Family caregivers of the frail elderly: Impact of caregiving on their health and implications for interventions. *Family and Community Health, 14,* 48–55.

McCartney, K. (1984). Effect of quality of day care environment on children's language development. *Developmental Psychology, 20,* 244–260.

McClearn, G. (1964). Genetics and behavior development. In M. Hoffman and L. Hoffman (Eds.), *Review of child development research*. Vol. 1. New York: Russell Sage.

McClearn, G. (1970). Genetic influences on behavior and development. In P. Mussen (Ed.), *Carmichael's manual of child psychology* (pp. 39–76). Vol. 1. New York: Wiley.

McClearn, G. E., & Vogler, G. P. (2001). The genetics of behavioral aging. In J. E. Birren & K. W. Schaie (Eds.), *Handbook of the psychology of aging*. San Diego, CA: Academic Press.

McClelland, D., Constantian, C., Regalado, D., & Stone, C. (1978). Making it to maturity. *Psychology Today, 18(June),* 42.

McClelland, K. A. (1982). Adolescent subculture in the schools. In T. Field et al., (Eds.), *Review of human development*. New York: Wiley.

McCoy, N., Cutler, W., & Davidson, J. (1985). Relationships among sexual behavior, hot flashes, and hormone levels in perimenopausal women. *Archives of Sexual Behavior, 14,* 385–394.

McCubbin, H. I. (1979). Integrating coping behavior in family stress theory. *Journal of Marriage and the Family, 41,* 237–244.

McCubbin, H. I., & Patterson, J. M. (1983). Family stress and adaptation to crisis: A double ABCX model of family behavior. In D. H. Olson & B. C. Miller (Eds.), *Family Studies Review Yearbook*. Vol. 1. Beverly Hills, CA: Sage Publications.

McGrory, A. (1978). *A well model approach to the care of the dying client*. New York: McGraw-Hill.

McKim, M. (1987). Transition to what? New parents' problems in the first year. *Family Relations, 36,* 22–25.

McNally, J. W., & Mosher, W. D. (1991). AIDS-related knowledge and behavior among women 15–44 years of age: United States, 1988. *Advance Data from Vital and Health Statistics, No. 200.* Hyattsville, MD: National Center for Health Statistics.

McNeil, K. J., LeBlanc, E. M., & Joyner, M. (1991). The effect of exercise on depressive symptoms in the moderately depressed elderly. *Psychology and Aging, 6,* 487–491.

McNemar, Q. (1940). A critical examination of the University of Iowa studies of environmental influence upon the IQ. *Psychological Bulletin, 37,* 63–92.

McWhirter, D., & Mattison, A. (1984). *The male couple: How relationships develop.* Englewood Cliffs, NJ: Prentice Hall.

McWilliams, J-R., & McWilliams, P. (1990). *Life 101: Everything we wish we had learned about life in school—but didn't.* Los Angeles, CA: Prelude Press

Mead, M. (1928). *Coming of age in Samoa.* New York: William Morrow & Co., Inc.

Mead, M. (1935). *Sex and temperament in three primitive societies.* New York: William Morrow & Co., Inc.

Mead, M., & MacGregor, F. (1951). *Growth and culture: A photographic study of Balinese children.* New York: Putnam.

Mellendick, G. (1983). Nutritional issues in adolescence. In A. Hoffman (Ed.), *Adolescent medicine.* Reading, MA: Addison-Wesley.

Meltzhoff, A. N., & Moore, M. K. (1977). Imitation of facial and manual gestures by human neonates. *Science, 198,* 75–78.

Meltzhoff, A. N., & Moore, M. K. (1979). Interpreting "imitative" responses in early infancy. *Science, 205,* 217–219.

Meltzhoff, A. N., & Moore, M. K. (1983). Methodological issues in studies of imitation: Comments on McKenzie & Over and Koepke et al. *Infant Behavior and Development, 6,* 103–108.

Menaghan, E. G., & Parcel, T. L. (1990). Parental employment and family life: Research in the 1980s. *Journal of Marriage and the Family, 52,* 1079–1098.

Mendelson, B., & White, D. (1985). Development of self-body in overweight youngsters. *Developmental Psychology, 21,* 90–97.

Mercier, L. R., & Berger, R. M. (1989). Social service needs of lesbian and gay adolescents: Telling it their way. *Journal of Social Work and Human Sexuality, 8,* 75–95.

Meredith, N. V. (1969). Body size of contemporary groups of eight-year-old children studied in different parts of the world. *Monographs of the Society for Research in Child Development, 34,* Whole No. 1.

Mergenhagen, P. (1991). Doing the career shuffle. *American Demographics, 13,* 42–47.

Messer, D. J., McCarthy, M. E., McQuiston, S., MacTurk, R. H., Yarrow, L. J., & Vietze, P. M., (1986). Relation between mastery behavior in infancy and competence in early childhood. *Developmental Psychology, 22,* 366–372.

Mattessich, P., & Hill, R. (1987). Life cycle and family development. In M. Sussman & S. Steinmetz (Eds.), *Handbook of marriage and the family.* New York: Plenum.

Metzger, A. M. (1980). A Q-methodological study of the Kubler-Ross stage theory. *Omega, 10,* 291–301.

Meuleman, J. (1989). Osteoporosis and the elderly. *Medical Clinics of North America, 73,* 1455–1460.

Meyer, K. (1987). The work commitment of adolescents: Progressive attachment to the work force. *Career Development Quarterly, 36,* 140–147.

Milevsky, A. (2003, April). *Sibling Support in Preadolescence and Adolescence.* Paper presented at the meeting of the Society for Research in Child Development, Tampa, Florida.

Milevsky, A., & Levitt, M. J. (2005). Sibling support in early adolescence: Buffering and compensation across relationships. *European Journal of Developmental Psychology, 2,* 299-320.

Miller, A. (1990). *For your own good: Hidden cruelty in childrearing and the roots of violence.* New York: The Noonday Press.

Miller, B. C., & Moore, K. A. (1990). Adolescent sexual behavior, pregnancy, and parenting: Research through the 1980s. *Journal of Marriage and the Family, 52,* 1025–1044.

Miller, C. A. (1987). A review of maternity care programs in western Europe. *Family Planning Perspectives, 19,* 207–211.

Miller, J., Williamson, E., Glue, J., Gordon, Y., Grudzinskas, J., & Sykes, A. (1980). Fetal loss after implantation: A prospective study. *The Lancet, 83,* 554–556.

Miller, L., & Reynolds, J. (2009). Autism and vaccination—The current evidence. *Journal for Specialists in Pediatric Nursing,* 14, 166–172.

Miller, M. (1978). Geriatric suicide: The Arizona study. *Gerontologist, 18,* 488–496.

Miller, S. A. (1988). Parents' beliefs about children's cognitive development. *Child Development, 59,* 259–286.

Miller, S. (1986). Certainty and necessity in the understanding of Piagetian concepts. *Developmental Psychology, 22,* 3–18.

Miller, P., & Aloise, P. (1989). Young children's understanding of the psychological causes of behavior: A review. *Child Development, 60,* 257–285.

Miller, P., Danaher, D., & Forbes, D. (1986). Sex-related strategies for coping with interpersonal conflict in children aged five to seven. *Developmental Psychology, 22,* 543–548.

Miller, V., Onotera, R. T., & Deinard, A. S. (1984). Denver developmental screening test: Cultural variations in southeast Asian children. *Journal of Pediatrics, 104,* 481–482.

Miller-Jones, D. (1989). Culture and testing. *American Psychologist, 44,* 360–366.

Millstein, S. (1989). Adolescent health: Challenges for behavioral scientists. *American Psychologist, 44,* 837–843.

Millstein, S. (1990). Risk factors for AIDS among adolescents. *New Directions for Child Development, Winter,* 3–15.

Mindel, C. H., & Vaughn, C. E. (1978). A multidimensional approach to religiosity and disengagement. *Journal of Gerontology, 33,* 103–108.

Minix, N. A. (1987). Drug and alcohol prevention education: A developmental social skills approach. *The ClearingHouse, 61,* 162–165.

Minuchin, P. P., & Shapiro, E. K. (1983). The school as a context for social development. In E. Hetherington (Ed.), *Handbook of child psychology,* Vol. 4. New York: Wiley.

Mischel, W. (1974). Processes in delay of gratification. In L. Berkowitz (Ed.), *Advances in experimental psychology.* Vol. 7. New York: Academic Press.

Mischel, W., Shoda, Y., & Rodriguez, M. (1989). Delay of gratification in children. *Science, 244,* 933–938.

Mohs, R., Breitner, J., Silverman, J., & Davis, K. (1987). Alzheimer's disease. *Archives of General Psychiatry, 44,* 405–408.

Molloy, D. W., Richardson, L. D., & Grilly, R. G. (1988). The effects of a three-month exercise program on neuropsychological function in elderly institutionalized women: A randomized controlled trial. *Age and Aging, 17,* 303–309.

Monaghan, P. (2002). The unsettled question of brain death. In G. E. Dickinson & M. R. Leming, (Eds.), *Dying, death, and bereavement* (10th ed.). NY: McGraw-Hill.

Montemayer, R. (1983). Parents and adolescents in conflict: All families some of the time and some families most of the time. *Journal of Early Adolescence, 3,* 83–103.

Montemayer, R. (1986). Family variation in parent-adolescent storm and stress. *Journal of Adolescent Research, 1,* 15–31.

Moody, H. R. (1984). Can suicide on grounds of old age be ethically justified? In M. Tallmer, et al., (Eds.), *The life-threatened elderly* (pp. 64–92). New York: Columbia University Press.

Moody, R. A. (1975). *Life after life.* New York: Bantam.

Moore, K. L. (1988). *The developing human: Clinically oriented embryology* (4th ed.). Philadelphia: Saunders.

Moore, S., & Rosenthal, D. A. (1991). Adolescent invulnerability and perceptions of AIDS risk. *Journal of Adolescent Research, 6,* 164–180.

Mor-Barak, M. E., & Miller, L. S. (1991). Social networks, life events, and health of the poor, frail elderly: A longitudinal study of the buffering versus the direct effects. *Family and Community Health, 14,* 1–14.

Morbidity and Mortality Weekly Report (MMWR). (1985, June 21). Suicide —U.S., 1970–1980.

Morgan, V., & Dunn, S. (1988). Cameleons in the classroom: Visible and invisible children in nursery and infant classrooms. *Educational Review, 40,* 3–12.

Morisey, P. G. (1990). Black children in foster care. In S. M. Logan, E. M. Freeman, & R. G. McRoy (Eds.), *Social work practice with black families.* New York: Longman.

Morley, J. E. (1990). Anorexia in older patients: Its meaning and management. *Geriatrics, 45,* 59–65.

Morrison, D. (1985). Adolescent contraceptive behavior: A review. *Psychological Bulletin, 98,* 538–568.

Morrison, R. S., & Meier, D. E. (2004). Palliative care. In G. E. Dickinson & M. R. Leming, (Eds.), *Dying, death, and bereavement* (10th ed.). NY: McGraw-Hill.

Mosher, W. D. (1990). Use of family planning services in the United States: 1982 and 1988. *Advance Data from Vital and Health Statistics, No. 184.* Hyattsville, MD: National Center for Health Statistics.

Mosher, W. D., & Pratt, W. F. (1990). Contraceptive use in the United States, 1973–88. *Advance Data from Vital and Health Statistics, No. 182.* Hyattsville, MD: National Center for Health Statistics.

Moskowitz, B. (1978). The acquisition of language. *Scientific American, 239,* 92–108.

Mounts, N., Lamborn, S., & Steinberg, L. (1989). Relations between family processes and school achievement in different ethnic contexts. Paper presented at the biennial meeting of the Society for Research in Child Development, Kansas City.

Mulligan, T. (1990). Chronic disease and impotence in the elderly. *Medical Aspects of Human Sexuality, 24,* 33–34. National Center for Health Statistics.

Mulligan, T., & Moss, C. (1991). Sexuality and aging in male veterans: A cross-sectional study of interest, ability, and activity. *Archives of Sexual Behavior, 20,* 17–25.

Munnichs, J. (1966). *Old age and finitude.* Basel, Switzerland: Karger.

Murdock, G. P. (1949). *Social structure.* New York: Macmillan.

Murphy, J. M., & Gilligan, C. (1980). Moral development in late adolescence and adulthood: A critique and reconstruction of Kohlberg's theory. *Human Development, 23,* 77–104.

Murray, S. F., Dolby, R. M., Nation, R. L., & Thomas, D. B. (1981). Effects of epidural anesthesia on newborns and their mothers. *Child Development, 52,* 71–82.

Murstein, B., Chalpin, M., Heard, K., & Vyse, S. (1989). Sexual behavior, drugs, and relationship patterns on a college campus over thirteen years. *Adolescence, 24,* 125–139.

Mussen, P., & Jones, M. (1957). Some conceptions, motivations and interpersonal attitudes of late and early-maturing boys. *Child Development, 28,* 242–256.

Muuss, R. E. (1985). Adolescent eating disorder: Anorexia nervosa. *Adolescence, 20,* 525–536.

Muuss, R. E. (1986). Adolescent eating disorder: Bulimia. *Adolescence, 21,* 257–267.

Myers, B. (1982). Early intervention using Brazelton training with middle-class mothers and fathers of newborns. *Child Development, 53,* 462–472.

Nader, P. R., Wexler, D. B., Patterson, T. L., & McKusick, L. (1989). Comparison of beliefs about AIDS among urban, suburban, incarcerated, and gay adolescents. *Journal of Adolescent Health Care, 10,* 413–418.

Naeye, R. (1980). Sudden infant death. *Scientific American, 242,* 56–62.

Nagy, M. (1948). The child's theories concerning death. *Journal of Genetic Psychology, 73,* 3–27.

National Academy of Sciences. (1982). *Marijuana and health.* Washington, DC: National Academy Press.

National Association of State Boards of Education (1990). *Code blue: Uniting for healthier youth.* Alexandria, VA: National Association of State Boards of Education.

National Center for Health Statistics (1980). Basic data on hearing levels of adults. *Vital and Health Statistics, Series 11, No. 215.*

National Center for Health Statistics (1986). Maternal weight gain and the outcome of pregnancy, United States, 1980. *Vital Statistics (DHHS Publication No. 86–1922).* Washington, DC: U. S. Government Printing Office.

National Center for Health Statistics. (1990). Advance report of final mortality statistics, 1988. *Monthly Vital Statistics Report, 39(7).* Hyattsville, MD: U. S. Public Health Service.

National Center for Health Statistics. (1990). *Annual summary of births, marriages, divorces, and deaths: United States, 1989. Monthly Vital Statistics Report, Vol. 38 (13).* Hyattsville, MD: Public Health Service.

National Center for Health Statistics. (1991). Births, marriages, divorces, and deaths for 1990. *Monthly Vital Statistics Report, 39(12).* Hyattsville, MD: U. S. Public Health Service.

National Committee for Citizens in Education (NCCE). (1986). Don't be afraid to start a suicide prevention program in your school. *Network for Public Schools, Winter Holiday,* 1–4.

National Institute on Drug Abuse (NIDA). (1987). Cocaine use remains steady, other drug use declines among high school seniors. *NIDA Notes, 2(2),* 1.

National Research Council (2000). *How people learn: Brain, mind, experience, and school* (Expanded ed.). Washington, DC: National Academy Press.

National Research Council and Institute of Medicine (2000). *From neurons to neighborhoods: The science of early childhood development.* Committee on Integrating the Science of Early Childhood Development. Jack P. Shonkoff and Deborah A. Phillips, eds. Board on Children, Youth, and Families, Commission on Behavioral and Social Sciences and Education. Washington, DC: National Academy Press.

Nelson, K. (1978). How children represent knowledge of their world in and out of language: A preliminary report. In R. Siegler (Ed.), *Children's thinking: What develops.* Hillsdale, NJ: Erlbaum.

Nelson, K., Rescorla, L., Gruendel, J., & Benedict, H. (1978). Early lexicons: What do they mean? *Child Development, 49,* 960–968.

Nelson, K., & Gruendel, J. (1981). Generalized event representations: Basic building blocks of cognitive development. In M. E. Lamb & A. Brown (Eds.), *Advances in developmental psychology,* Vol. 1. Hillsdale, NJ: Erlbaum.

Nelson, N. M., Enkin, M. W., Saigal, S., Bennett, K. J., Milner, R., & Sackett, D. L. (1980). A randomized clinical trial of the Leboyer approach to childbirth. *New England Journal of Medicine, 302,* 655–660.

Nelson-LeGall, S., & Gumerman, R. (1984). Children's perceptions of helpers and helper motivation. *Journal of Applied Developmental Psychology, 5,* 1–12.

Neugarten, B. (1968). The awareness of middle age. In B. L. Neugarten (Ed.), *Middle age and aging.* Chicago: University of Chicago Press.

Neugarten, B. (1968). Adult personality: Toward a psychology of the life cycle. In B. L. Neugarten (Ed.), *Middle age and aging.* Chicago: University of Chicago Press.

Neugarten, B. (1970). The old and the young in modern societies. *American Behavioral Scientist, 14,* 18–24.

Neugarten, B. (1973). Personality change in later life: A developmental perspective. In C. Eisdorfer & M. P. Lawton (Eds.), *The psychology of adult development and aging.* Washington, DC: American Psychological Association.

Neugarten, B. (1978). *The wise of the young-old.* In R. Gross, B. Gross, & S. Seidman (Eds.), *The new old: Struggling for decent aging.* Garden City, NY: Doubleday-Anchor.

Neugarten, B. L., Havighurst, R. J., & Tobin, S. S. (1968). Personality and patterns of aging. In B. L. Neugarten (Ed.), *Middle age and aging.* Chicago: University of Chicago Press.

Neugarten, B. L., & Moore, J. W. (1968). The changing age-status system. In B. L. Neugarten (Ed.), *Middle age and aging.* Chicago: University of Chicago Press.

Neugarten, B., & Neugarten, D. (1987). The changing meanings of age. *Psychology Today, 21,* 29–33.

Newberger, C. M., Milnicoe, L. H., & Newberger, E. H. (1986). *The American family in crisis: Implications for children.* New York: Year Book Medical Publishers.

Newcomb, M. D., & Bentler, P. M. (1988a). The impact of family context, deviant attitudes, and emotional distress on adolescent drug use: Longitudinal latent-variable analyses of mothers and their children. *Journal of Research in Personality, 22,* 154–176.

Newcomb, M. D., & Bentler, P. M. (1988b). Impact of adolescent drug use and social support on problems of young adults: A longitudinal study. *Journal of Abnormal Psychology, 97,* 64–75.

Newcomb, M. D., & Bentler, P. M. (1989). Substance use and abuse among children and teenagers. *American Psychologist, 44,* 242–248.

Newcomb, M. D., Fahy, B., & Skager, R. (1990). Reasons to avoid drug use among teenagers: Associations with actual drug use and implications for prevention among different demographic groups. *Journal of Alcohol and Drug Education, 36,* 53–81.

Newcomb, M. D., McCarthy, W. J., & Bentler, P. M. (1989). Cigarette smoking, academic lifestyle, and social impact efficacy: An eight-year study from early adolescence to young adulthood. *Journal of Applied Social Psychology, 19,* 251–281.

Newman, P. R., & Newman, B. M. (1991). *Development through life: A psychosocial approach* (5th ed.). Pacific Grove, CA: Brooks/Cole.

NICHD Early Child Care Research Network. (2001). Nonmaternal care and family factors in early development: An overview of the NICHD Study of Early Child Care. *Journal of Applied Developmental Psychology, 22,* 457–492.

Nobles, W. W. (1984). Alienation, human transformation and adolescent drug use: Toward a reconceptualization of the problem. *Journal of Drug Issues, 14,* 243–252.

Noelker, L., & Wallace, R. (1985). The organization of family care for impaired elderly. *Journal of Family Issues, 6,* 23–44.

Norton, A. J., & Glick, P. C. (1986). One parent families: A social and economic profile. *Family Relations, 35,* 356–361.

Norton, A. J. (1983). Family life cycle: 1980. *Journal of Marriage and the Family, 45,* 267–275.

Noyes, R. (1980). Attitude change following near death experiences. *Psychiatry, 43,* 234–242.

Noyes, R., & Clancy, J. (1977). The dying role: Its relevance to improved medical care. *Psychiatry, 40,* 41–47.

Noyes, R., & Kletti, R. (1977). Panoramic memory: A response to the threat of death. *Omega, 8,* 181–194.

Nunnally, J. C. (1973). Research strategies and measurement methods for investigating human development. In J. R. Nesselroade and H. W. Reese (Eds.), *Life span developmental psychology* (pp. 87–110). New York: Academic Press.

Nye, F. I. (1957). Child adjustment in broken and in unhappy, unbroken homes. *Marriage and Family Relations, 19,* 356–361.

O'Connor, S., Vietze, P. Sherrod, K., Sandler, H., & Alteneier, W. (1980). Reduced incidence of parenting inadequacy following rooming-in. *Pediatrics, 66,* 176–182.

O'Mahony, J. (1989). Development of thinking about things and people: Social and nonsocial cognition during adolescence. *Journal of Genetic Psychology, 150,* 217–224.

O'Neill, N., & O'Neill, G. (1972a). *Open marriage: A new lifestyle for couples.* New York: Evans & Co.

O'Neill, B., & O'Neill, G. (1972b). Open marriage: A synergic model. *Family Coordinator, 21,* 403–409.

O'Rand, A. M., & Krecker, M. L. (1990). Concepts of the life cycle: Their history, meanings, and use in the social sciences. *Annual Review of Sociology, 16,* 241–262.

Oates, D. S., & Heinicke, C. M. (1985). Prebirth prediction of the quality of the mother-infant interaction: The first year of life. *Journal of Family Issues, 6,* 523–542.

Oetting, G. R., & Beauvais, F. (1991). Orthogonal cultural identification theory: The cultural identification of minority adolescents. *International Journal of Addictions, 25,* 655–685.

Ogborn, W. F. (1933). *Recent social trends in the United States.* New York: McGraw-Hill.

Okun, B. (1984). *Working with adults: Individual, family, and career development.* Monterey, CA: Brooks/Cole.

Olson, D. H., & McCubbin, H. I. (1983). *Families: What makes them work?* Beverly Hills, CA: Sage Publications.

Olson, D. H., McCubbin, H., Barnes, H. L., Larsen, A. S., Muxen, M. J., & Wilson, M. A., (1983). *Families: What makes them work.* Beverly Hills, CA: Sage.

Olson, D. H., Sprenkle, D., & Russell, C. (1979). Circumplex model of marital and family systems I: Cohension and adaptability dimensions, family types, and clinical applications. *Family Process, 18,* 3–28.

Olson, D. H. (1986). What makes families work? In S. Van Zandt et al., (Eds.), *Family strengths 7: Vital connections.* Lincoln, NE: Center for Family Strengths, University of Nebraska.

Orgel, L. (1970). The maintenance of the accuracy of protein synthesis and its relevance to aging: A correction. *Proceedings of the National Academy of Science, 67,* 1476.

Orr, D. P., Hoffmans, M. A., & Bennetts, G. (1984). Adolescents with cancer report their psychological needs. *Journal of Psychosocial Oncology, 2,* 47–59.

Osgood, N. J. (1989). Aging in America: Preventing suicide in the elderly. *Medical Aspects of Human Sexuality, 23,* 27–29.

Overpeck, M. D., & Moss, A. J. (1991). Children's exposure to environmental cigarette smoke before and after birth: Health of our nation's children, United States, 1988. *Advance Data From Vital and Health Statistics. No. 202.* Hyattsville, MD: National Center for Health Statistics.

Overton, W. F. (1998). Developmental psychology: Philosophy, Concepts, and Methodology. In W. Damon & R. M. Lerner (Eds.), Handbook of child psychology (Vol. 1): *Theoretical models of human development* (5th ed.). NY: John Wiley & Sons, Inc.

Padawer, J. A., Fagan, C., Janoff-Bulman, R., Strickland, B. R., & Chorowski, M. (1988). Women's psychological adjustment following emergency Cesarean versus vaginal delivery. *Psychology of Women Quarterly, 12,* 25–34.

Palmore, E. (1975). *The honorable elders.* Durham, NC: Duke University Press.

Palmore, E., & Maeda, D. (1985). *The honorable elders revisited: A revised cross-cultural analysis of aging in Japan.* Durham, NC: Duke University Press.

Parcel, G., Simons-Morton, B., O'Hara. N., Baranowski, T., Kolbe, L., & Bee, D. (1987). School promotion of healthful diet and exercise behavior: An integration of organizational change and social learning theory interventions. *Journal of School Health, 57,* 150–156.

Parke, R. (1979). Perspectives on father-infant interaction. In J. D. Osofsky (Ed.), *Handbook of infant development.* New York: Wiley.

Parke, R., & Sawin, D. (1976). The father's role in infancy: A reevaluation. *Family Coordinator, 25,* 365–371.

Parke, R., & Tinsley, B. (1987). Family interaction in infancy: In J. Osofsky (Ed.), *Handbook of infant development.* New York: Wiley.

Parke, R. D., & Slaby, R. G. (1983). The development of aggression. In P. H. Mussen (Ed.), *Handbook of child psychology.* Vol. 4. New York: Wiley.

Parker, W. A. (1980). Designing an environment for childbirth. In B. L. Blum (Ed.), *Psychological aspects of pregnancy, birthing, and bonding.* New York: Human Sciences Press.

Parkes, C. M. (1975). Determinants of outcome following bereavement. *Omega, 6,* 303–323.

Parkes, C. M., & Brown, R. J. (1972). Health after bereavement: A controlled study of young Boston widows and widowers. *Psychosomatic Medicine, 34,* 449–461.

Parmalee, A. H., & Stern, E. D. (1972). Development of states in infants. In C. Clemente, D. Purpura, & F. Mayer (Eds.), *Sleep in the maturing nervous system.* New York: Academic Press.

Parmelee, A. H., Jr., & Sigman, M. (1983). Perinatal brain development and behavior. In P. Mussen (Ed.), *Handbook of child psychology. Vol. 2. Infancy and developmental psychobiology.* New York: Wiley.

Parsons, J., Adler, T., & Kaczala, C. (1982). Socialization of achievement attitudes and beliefs: Parental influences. *Child Development, 53,* 310–321.

Parten, M. B. (1932). Social participation among preschool children. *Journal of Abnormal and Social Psychology, 27,* 243–269.

Pasley, K., & Ihinger-Tallman, M. (1987). *Remarriage.* Beverly Hills, CA: Sage.

Patten, B. M. (1976). *Patten's human embryology: Elements of clinical development.* New York: McGraw-Hill.

Patterson, J., & McCubbin, H. (1983). Chronic illness: Family stress and coping. In C. Figley & H. McCubbin (Eds.), *Stress and the family: Coping with catastrophe.* Vol. 2. New York: Bruner/Mazel.

Pattison, E. M. (1977). The dying experience. In E. M. Pattison (Ed.), *The experience of dying*. Englewood Cliffs, NJ: Prentice Hall.

Peck, R. D. (1968). Psychological developments in the second half of life. In B. L. Neugarten (Ed.), *Middle age and aging*. Chicago: University of Chicago Press.

Pedersen, G., & Mehl, L. (1979). Some determinants of maternal attachment. *American Journal of Psychiatry, 135,* 1168–1173.

Pellegrini, A. D. (1987). Rough and tumble play: Developmental and educational significance. *Educational Psychologist, 22,* 23–32.

Pelletier, K. R. (1993). Between mind and body: Stress, emotions, and health. In D. Goleman & J. Gurin (Eds.), *Mind body medicine: How to use your mind for better health*. NY: Consumer Reports Books.

Pennington, S. B. (1987). Children of lesbian mothers. In F. W. Bozett (Ed.), *Gay and lesbian parents*. New York: Praeger.

Peppers, L., & Knapp, R. (1980). Maternal reactions to involuntary fetal-infant death. *Psychiatry, 43,* 155–159.

Peppers, L. G., & Knapp, R. S. (1980). *Motherhood and mourning: Perinatal death*. New York: Praeger.

Perdue, C. W., & Gurtman, M. B. (1990). Evidence for the automaticity of ageism. *Journal of Experimental Social Psychology, 26,* 199–206.

Peretz, A., Neve, J., & Desmedt, J. (1991). Lymphocyte response is enhanced by supplementation of elderly subjects with selenium enriched yeast. *American Journal of Clinical Nutrition, 53,* 1323–1329.

Perkins, H. W., & Harris, L. B. (1990). Family bereavement and health in adult life course perspective. *Journal of Marriage and the Family, 52,* 233–242.

Perlmutter, M. (1987). Aging and memory. In K. W. Schaie & K. Eisdorfer (Eds.), *Annual review of gerontology and geriatrics*. Vol. 7. New York: Springer.

Perry, W. G., Jr. (1970). *Forms of intellectual and ethical development in the college years: A scheme*. New York: Holt, Rinehart, Winston.

Peskin, H. (1967). Pubertal onset and ego functioning. *Journal of Abnormal Psychology, 72,* 1–15.

Peskin, H. (1973). Influence of the developmental schedule of puberty on learning and ego functioning. *Journal of Youth and Adolescence, 2,* 273–290.

Petersen, A. C. (1988). Adolescent development. *Annual Review of Psychology, 39,* 583–607.

Peterson, G. W., & Rollins, B. C. (1987). Parent-child socialization. In B. Sussman & S. Steinmetz (Eds.), *Handbook of marriage and the family*. New York: Plenum.

Pfannenstiel, J., & Seltzer, D. (1989). New parents as teachers: Evaluation of early parent education programs. *Early Childhood Research Quarterly, 4,* 1–18.

Phelps, L., & Bajorek, E. (1991). Eating disorders of the adolescent: Current issues in etiology, assessment, and treatment. *School Psychology Review, 20,* 9–22.

Phillips, J. L., McCartney, K., & Scarr, S. (1987). Child care quality and children's social development. *Developmental Psychology, 23,* 537–543.

Phillips, D. A. (Ed.) (1987). *Quality in child care: What does research tell us?* Washington, DC: National Association for the Education of Young Children.

Piaget, J. (1926). *The language and thought of the child*. New York: Harcourt, Brace Jovanovich.

Piaget, J. (1932). *The moral judgment of the child*. London: Kegan Paul, Trench, & Trubner.

Piaget, J. (1952a). *The child's conception of number*. New York: Humanities Press.

Piaget, J. (1952b). *The origins of intelligence in children*. New York: International Universities Press.

Piaget, J. (1967). *Six psychological studies*. New York: Random House.

Piaget, J. (1969). *The child's conception of time*. New York: Basic Books.

Piaget, J. (1972). Intellectual evolution from adolescence to adulthood. *Human Development, 15,* 1–12.

Piaget, J., & Inhelder, B. (1969). *The psychology of the child*. New York: Basic Books.

Piaget, J., & Inhelder, B. (1967). *The child's concept of space*. (F. Langdon & E. Lunzer, Trans.). New York: Norton.

Piernot, C. (1978). Parental expectations of day care centers. Unpublished Master's thesis, Colorado State University.

Pike, K. M. (1991). Mothers, daughters, and disordered eating. *Journal of Abnormal Psychology, 100,* 198–204.

Pine, V. R. (1976). Grief, bereavement, and mourning: The realities of loss. In V. R. Pine et al., (Eds.), *Acute grief and the funeral* (pp. 105–114). Springfield, IL: Charles C. Thomas.

Pines, M. (1983). Can a rock walk? *Psychology Today, 17(November),* 46–54.

Piper, T. (2003). *Language and learning: The home and school years* (3rd ed.). Upper Saddle River, NJ: Merrill Prentice Hall.

Pleck, J. (1985). *Working wives/working husbands*. Beverly Hills, CA: Sage.

Pollak, C. P., Perlick, D., & Linsner, J. P. (1990). Sleep problems in the community elderly as predictors of death and nursing home placement. *Journal of Community Health, 15,* 123–133.

Pollock, M. L., Carroll, J. F., & Graves, J. E. (1991). Injuries and adherence to walk/jog and resistance training programs in the elderly. *Medicine and Science in Sports and Exercise, 23,* 1194–1199.

Pomery, E., Gibbons, F., Gerrard, M., Cleveland, M., Brody, G., & Wills, T. (2005). Families and risk: prospective analyses of familial and social influences on adolescent substance use. *Journal of Family Psychology, 19,* 560-570.

Poon, L. W. (1985). Differences in human memory with aging: Nature, causes, and clinical implications. In J. E. Birren & K. Schaie (Eds.), *Handbook of the psychology of aging* (2nd ed.). New York: Van Nostrand.

Pope, H., Hudson, J., Jonas, J., & Yurgelun-Todd, D. (1983). Bulimia treated with imipramine: A placebo controlled, double-blind study. *American Journal of Psychiatry, 140,* 554–558.

Porter, L., Miller, R. H., & Marshall, R. (1986). Neonatal pain cries: Effects of circumcision on acoustic features and perceived urgency. *Child Development, 57,* 790–802.

Post, S. G. (1990). Nutrition, hydration, and the demented elderly. *Journal of Medical Humanities, 11,* 185–191.

Poznansky, E. O. (1973). Children with excessive fears. *American Journal of Orthopsychiatry, 43,* 428–438.

Prevention Research Center. (1986). *Prevention index '86: A report card on the nation's health*. Emmaus, PA: Rodele.

Price-Bonham, S., & Addison, S. (1978). Families and mentally retarded children: Emphasis on the father. *Family Coordinator, 27,* 221–230.

Protinsky, H., & Shilts, L. (1990). Adolescent substance use and family cohesion. *Family Therapy, 17,* 173–175.

Pruett, K. D. (1987). *The nurturing father*. New York: Warner.

Pulaski, M. (1980). *Understanding Piaget* (revised and expanded edition). New York: Harper & Row.

Putallaz, M., & Gottman, J. (1981). Social skills and group acceptance. In S. Asher & J. Guttman (Eds.), *The development of children's friendships*. New York: Cambridge University Press.

Quilligan, E. J. (1983). *Pregnancy, birth, and the infant*. NIH Publication No. 82-2304. Washington, DC: U. S. Government Printing Office.

Quinn, P., & Allen, K. R. (1989). Facing challenges and making compromises: How single mothers endure. *Family Relations, 38,* 390–395.

Rabin, A. (1965). Motivation for parenthood. *Journal of Projective Techniques, 29,* 405–411.

Radke-Yarrow, M., Zahn-Waxler, C., & Chapman, M. (1983). Children's prosocial dispositions and behavior. In M. E. Hetherington (Ed.), *Handbook of child psychology*. Vol. 4. New York: Wiley.

Rainone, G., Deren, S., Fleinman, P., & Wish, E. (1987). Heavy marijuana users not in treatment: The continuing search for the "pure" marijuana user. *Journal of Psychoactive Drugs, 19,* 353–359.

Reading, J., & Amateo, E. S. (1986). Role deviance or role diversification: Reassessing the psychosocial factors affecting the parenthood decision of career-oriented women. *Journal of Marriage and the Family, 48,* 255–260.

Reichard, S., Livson, F., & Peterson, P. G. (1962). *Aging and personality*. New York: Wiley.

Rende, R., Slomkowski, C., Lloyd-Richardson, E., & Niaura, R. (2005). Sibling effects on substance use in adolescence: social contagion and genetic relatedness. *Journal of Family Psychology, 19,* 611-618.

Rescorla, R. A. (1987). A Pavlovian analysis of goal-directed behavior. *American Psychologist, 42,* 119–129.

Resnick, L. (1989). Developing mathematical knowledge. *American Psychologist, 44,* 162–169.

Rest, J. (1983). Morality. In P. Mussen (Ed.), *Handbook of child psychology, Vol. 3.* New York: Wiley.

Reznick, J. S., Kagan, J., Snidman, N., Gersten, M., Baak, K., & Rosenberg, A. (1986). Inhibited and uninhibited children: A follow-up study. *Child Development, 57,* 660–680.

Rheingold, H. (1966). Development of social behavior in human infants. In H. Stevenson (Ed.), The concept of development. *Monographs of the Society for Research in Child Development, 31,* Whole. No. 107.

Rheingold, H. (1985). Development as the acquisition of familiarity. *Annual Review of Psychology, 36,* 1–17.

Rhoades, G. K., Stanley, S. M., & Markman, H. J. (2006). Pre-engagement cohabitation and gender asymmetry in marital commitment. *Journal of Family Psychology, 20,* 553–560.

Ribble, M. (1943). *The rights of infants.* New York: Columbia University Press.

Rice, M. L. (1982). Child language: What children know and how. In T. Field et al. (Eds.), *Review of human development.* New York: Wiley.

Richards, L. N. (1989). The precarious survival and hard-won satisfactions of white single-parent families. *Family Relations, 38,* 396–403.

Richards, M., Boxer, A., Petersen, A., & Albrecht, R. (1990). Relation of weight to body image in pubertal girls and boys from two communities. *Developmental Psychology, 26,* 313–321.

Richardson, D., & Short, R. (1978). Time of onset of sperm production in boys. *Journal of Biosocial Science, 5,* 15–25.

Richardson, J., Dwyer, K. (1989). Substance use among eighth-grade students who take care of themselves after school. *Pediatrics, 84,* 556–566.

Ricks, S. (1985). Father-infant interactions: A review of empirical research. *Family Relations, 34,* 505–511.

Riegel, K. (1973). Dialectic operations. The final period of cognitive development. *Human Development, 16,* 346–370.

Riegel, K. (1975). Adult life crisis: A dialectical interpretation of development. In N. Datan & H. Ginsberg (Eds.), *Life span developmental psychology: Normative life crises.* New York: Academic Press.

Riegel, K., F., & Riegel, R. M. (1972). Development, drop, and death. *Developmental Psychology, 6,* 306–319.

Rierdan, J., & Koff, E. (1980). The psychological impact of menarche: Integrative versus disruptive changes. *Journal of Youth and Adolescence, 9,* 49–58.

Ries, P. (1991). Characteristics of persons with and without health care coverage: United States, 1989. *Advance Data from Vital and Health Statistics, No. 201.* Washington, DC: U. S. Government Printing Office.

Ries, P., & Brown, S. (1991). Disability and health: Characteristics of persons by limitation of activity and assessed health status. *Advance Data From Vital and Health Statistics, No. 197. DHHS Publication No. (PHS)91–1250.* Hyattsville, MD: National Center for Health Statistics.

Ring, K. (1980). *Life at death: A scientific investigation of the near death experience.* New York: William Morrow.

Ringwalt, C. L., & Palmer, J. H. (1990). Differences between white and black youth who drink heavily. *Addictive Behaviors, 15,* 455–460.

Risman, B. J. (1986). Can men "mother?" Life as a single father. *Family Relations, 35,* 95–102.

Rizzo, T., & Corsaro, W. (1988). Toward a better understanding of Vygotsky's process of internalization: Its role in the development of the concept of friendship. *Developmental Review, 8,* 219–237.

Roberts, J. (1975). Eye examination findings among children and youths aged 12–17 years: United States. *Vital and Health Statistics, Series 11, No. 157. DHEW Publication No. (HRA) 76–1639.* Washington, DC: U. S. Government Printing Office.

Roberts, J., & Ahuja, E. M. (1975). Hearing sensitivity and related medical findings among youth 12–17 years: United States. *Vital and Health Sta-*

*tistics, Series 11, No. 154. DHEW Publication No. (HRA) 76–1637.* Washington, DC: U. S. Government Printing Office.

Roberts, J., & Rowland, M. (1978). Refraction status and motility defects of persons 4–74 years. *Vital and Health Statistics, Series 11, No. 206.* Hyattsville, MD: National Center for Health Statistics.

Roberts, J., & Ludford, J. (1976). Skin conditions of youth aged 12–17: United States. *Vital and Health Statistics, Series 11, No. 157. DHEW Publication No. (HRA) 76–1639.* Washington, DC: U. S. Government Printing Office.

Roberts, P., & Newton, P. (1987). Levinsonian studies of women's adult development. *Psychology and Aging, 2,* 154–163.

Robertson, J. F. (1978). Women in mid-life crisis: Reverberations and support networks. *Family Coordinator, 27,* 375–382.

Robinson, B., & Barret, R. L. (1986). *The developing father: Emerging roles in contemporary society.* New York: Guilford Press.

Roche, A. F. (1979). Secular trends in stature, weight, and maturation. In A. F. Roche (Ed.), Secular trends in growth, maturation, and development of children. *Monographs of the Society for Research in Child Development, 44,* 3–27.

Roche, J. (1986). Premarital sex: Attitudes and behavior by dating stage. *Adolescence, 81,* 107–121.

Rodin, J. (1986). Aging and health: Effect of the sense of control. *Science, 233,* 1217–1276.

Rodman, H., & Cole, C. (1987). Latchkey children: A review of policy and resources. *Family Relations, 36,* 101–105.

Roffwarg, H., Muzio, J., & Dement, W. (1966). Ontogenetic development of the human sleep-dream cycle. *Science, 152,* 604–619.

Rogers, C. R. (1961). *On becoming a person.* Cambridge, MA: Riverside Press.

Rogers, W. A., & Fisk, A. D. Understanding the role of attention in cognitive aging research. In J. E. Birren & K. W. Schaie (Eds.), *Handbook of the psychology of aging.* San Diego, CA: Academic Press.

Rogoff, B. (2003). *The cultural nature of human development.* NY: Oxford University Press.

Rolfes, S., & DeBruyne, L. (1990). *Life span nutrition.* St. Paul, MN: West Publishing Co.

Rollins, B., & Cannon, K. (1974). Marital satisfaction over the family life cycle: A reevaluation. *Journal of Marriage and the Family, 36,* 271–282.

Rollins, B., & Feldman, H. (1970). Marital satisfaction over the family life cycle. *Journal of Marriage and the Family, 32,* 20–28.

Romeo, F. (1984). Adolescence, sexual conflict, and anorexia nervosa. *Adolescence, 19,* 551–555.

Roscoe, B., & Peterson, K. (1989). Age-appropriate behaviors: A comparison of three generations of females. *Adolescence, 23,* 39–46.

Roosa, M. W. (1984). Maternal age, social class, and the obstetric performance of teenagers. *Journal of Youth and Adolescence, 13,* 365–374.

Rose, S. A., & Wallace, I. F. (1985). Visual recognition memory: A predictor of later cognitive functioning in preterms. *Child Development, 56,* 843–852.

Rosel, N. (1978). Toward a social theory of dying. *Omega, 9,* 49–55.

Rosenfeld, A., & Stark, E. (1987). The prime of our lives. *Psychology Today, 21,* 62–72.

Rosenman, R. (1974). The role of behavioral patterns and neurogenic factors on the pathogenesis of coronary heart disease. In R. Eliot (Ed.), *Stress and the heart.* New York: Futura.

Rosenthal, R., & Jacobson, L. (1968). *Pygmalion in the classroom.* New York: Holt, Rinehart, & Winston.

Rosenthal, P. A., & Rosenthal, S. (1984). Suicidal behavior by preschool children. *American Journal of Psychiatry, 141,* 520–525.

Rosett, J., & Sander, L. (1979). Effects of maternal drinking on neonatal morphology and state regulation. In J. Osofsky (Ed.), *Handbook of infant development.* New York: Wiley.

Rosinski, R., Pellegrini, J., & Siegel, A. (1977). Developmental changes in the processing of pictures and words. *Journal of Experimental Child Psychology, 23,* 382–391.

Roskos, K. (1990). A taxonomic view of pretend play activity among 4 and 5-year-old children. *Early Childhood Research Quarterly, 5,* 495–500.

Ross, C. E., Mirowsky, J., & Goldsteen, K. (1990). The impact of the family on health: The decade in review. *Journal of Marriage and the Family, 52,* 1059–1078.

Ross, C. P. (1985). Teaching children the facts of life and death: Suicide prevention in the schools. In M. L. Peck, N. L. Faberow, & R. E. Litman (Eds.), *Youth suicide* (pp. 147–169). New York: Springer.

Ross, H., & Lollis, S. (1987). Communication within infant social games. *Developmental Psychology, 23,* 241–248.

Rossi, A. (1968). Transition to parenthood. *Journal of Marriage and the Family, 30,* 26–39.

Rossi, A. S. (1977). A biosocial perspective on parenting. *Daedalus, 106,* 1–31.

Rossi, A. (1980). Aging and parenthood in the middle years. In P. Baltes & O. Brim (Eds.), *Life-span development and behavior.* Vol. 3. New York: Academic Press.

Rossi, S., & Wittrock, M. (1971). Developmental shifts in verbal recall between mental ages two and five. *Child Development, 42,* 333–340.

Rotenberg, K., & Sliz, D. (1988). Children's restrictive disclosure to friends. *Merrill-Palmer Quarterly, 34,* 163–184.

Rousseau, J. J. (1762) *The Social Contract.* London: Penguin Books.

Routh, D. K., Schroeder, C. S., & O'Tuama, L. A. (1974). Development of activity level in children. *Developmental Psychology, 10,* 163–168.

Rowe, D.C., & Rodgers, J. L. (1991). Adolescent smoking and drinking: Are they "epidemics?" *Journal of Studies on Alcohol, 52,* 110–117.

Rowe, G. P., & Meredith, W. H. (1982). Quality in marital relationships after twenty-five years. *Family Perspectives, 16,* 149–155.

Rowland, M. (1980). Basic data on hearing levels of adults, 25–74 years: United States, 1971–1975. *Vital and Health Statistics, Series 11, No. 215.* DHEW Publication No. (PHS) 80–1663.

Rubin, K. H., Fein, G. G., & Vandenberg, B. (1983). Play. In M. Hetherington (Ed.), *Handbook of child development* (4th ed.). New York: Wiley.

Rubin, K. H., Maioni, T. L., & Hornung, M. (1976). Free play behaviors in middle and lower class preschoolers: Parten and Piaget revisited. *Child Development, 47,* 414–419.

Ruff, C. C., & Reaves, E. L. (1989). Diagnosing urinary incontinence in adults. *The Nurse Practitioner, 14,* 8–15.

Russell, C. S. (1974). Transition to parenthood: Problems and gratifications. *Journal of Marriage and the Family, 36,* 294–301.

Rutter, M. (1979). Protective factors in children's responses to stress and disadvantage. In M. Kent & J. Rolf (Eds.), *Primary prevention of psychopathology, Vol. 3.* Hanover, NH: University Press of New England.

Rutter, M. (1980). *Changing youth in a changing society.* Cambridge, MA: Harvard University Press.

Rutter, M. (1981). Social-emotional consequences of day care for preschool children. *American Journal of Orthopsychiatry, 51,* 4–28.

Rutter, M. (1983a). School effects on pupil progress: Research findings and policy implications. *Child Development, 54,* 1–29.

Rutter, M. (1983b). Stress, coping, and development: Some issues and some questions. In N. Garmezy & M. Rutter (Eds.), *Stress, coping, and development in children.* New York: McGraw-Hill.

Rutter, M. (1984). Resilient children. *Psychology Today, 18,* 57–65.

Rutter, M. (1985). Resilience in the face of adversity: Protective factors and resistance to psychiatric disorder. *British Journal of Psychiatry, 147,* 598–611.

Ryan, R., & Lynch, J. (1989). Emotional autonomy versus detachment: Revising the vicissitudes of adolescence and young adulthood. *Child Development, 60,* 340–356.

Ryff, C. D., Kwan, C. M. L., & Singer, B. H. (2001). Personality and aging: Flourishing agendas and future challenges. In J. E. Birren & K. W. Schaie (Eds.), *Handbook of the psychology of aging.* San Diego, CA: Academic Press.

Sacher, G. A. (1977). Life table modifications and life prolongation. In C. E. Finch & L. Hayflick (Eds.), *Handbook of the biology of aging.* New York: Van Nostrand.

Sager, S. J., Steer, H., Crohn, H., Rodstein, E., & Walker, E. (1980). Remarriage revisited. *Family and Child Mental Healthy Journal, 6,* 19–33.

Sahyoun, N.R., Lentzner, H., Hoyert, D., & Robinson, K. N. (2001). Trends in causes of death among the elderly. In G. E. Dickinson & M.R. Leming, (Eds.), *Dying, death, and bereavement* (10th ed.). NY: McGraw-Hill.

Salmon, C. F., & Salmon, F. C. (1978). Housing the elderly. *Journal of Home Economics, 71,* 23–35.

Salthouse, T. (1985). Speed of behavior and its implications for cognition. In J. E. Birren & K. W. Schaie (Eds.), *Handbook of the psychology of aging* (2nd ed.). New York: Van Nostrand.

Saluter, A. F. (1989). Changes in American family life. *Current Population Reports, Series P–23, No. 163.* Washington, DC: U. S. Bureau of the Census.

Saluter, F. (1989). Singleness in America. In Studies in marriage and the family. *Current Population Reports, Series P–23, No. 162.* Washington, DC: Bureau of the Census.

Sameroff, A. J. (1968). The components of sucking in the human newborn. *Journal of Experimental Child Psychology, 6,* 607–623.

Sanchez-Ayendez, M. (1988). Puerto Rican elderly women: The cultural dimension of social support networks. *Women & Health, 14,* 239–244.

Sanders, C. M. (1979). A comparison of adult bereavement in the death of a spouse, child, and parent. *Omega, 10,* 217–232.

Sanders, C. M. (1980a). Comparison of younger and older spouses in bereavement outcomes. *Omega, 10,* 217–232.

Sanders, C. M. (1980b). A comparison of adult bereavement in the death of a spouse, child, and parent. *Omega, 10,* 303–322.

Sanik, N. M., & Mauldin, T. (1986). Single versus two parent families: A comparison of mothers' time. *Family Relations, 35,* 53–56.

Sarason, S. B. (1977). *Work, aging, and social change: Professionals and the one life-one career imperative.* New York: Free Press.

Sassen, G. (1980). Success anxiety in women: A constructivist interpretation of its source and significance. *Harvard Educational Review, 50,* 13–24.

Satir, V. (1972). *Peoplemaking.* Palo Alto, CA: Science and Behavior Books.

Saunders, C. (1978). Terminal care. In C. A. Garfield (Ed.), *Psychosocial care of the dying patient* (pp. 22–33). New York: McGraw-Hill

Savin-Williams, R. (1979). Dominance hierarchies in groups of early adolescents. *Child Development, 50,* 923–935.

Savin-Williams, R. (1980). Dominance hierarchies in groups of middle to late adolescent males. *Journal of Youth and Adolescence, 9,* 75–85.

Savin-Williams, R. (1988). Theoretical perspectives accounting for adolescent homosexuality. *Journal of Adolescent Health Care, 9,* 95–104.

Savin-Williams, R. (1989). Gay and lesbian adolescents. *Marriage and Family Review, 14,* 197–216.

Savin-Williams, R., & Demo, D. (1984). Developmental change and stability in adolescent self-concept. *Developmental Psychology, 20,* 1100–1110.

Savin-Williams, R., & Small, S. A. (1986). The timing of puberty and its relationship to adolescent and parent perceptions of family interactions. *Developmental Psychology, 22,* 342–348.

Sawin, D., & Parke, R. (1979). Fathers' affection stimulation and caregiving behaviors with newborn infants. *Family Coordinator, 28,* 509–513.

Saxon, S. V., & Etten, M. J. (1978). *Physical change and aging.* New York: Tiresias Press.

Saxton, L. (1990). *The individual, marriage, and the family* (7th ed.). Belmont, CA: Wadsworth.

Scanzoni, L., & Scanzoni, J. (1976). *Men, women, and change: A sociology of marriage and the family.* New York: McGraw-Hill.

Scanzoni, L., & Scanzoni, J. (1981). *Men, women, and change* (2nd ed.). New York: McGraw-Hill.

Schneider, S. G., Farberow, N. L., & Kruks, G. N. (1989). Suicidal behavior in adolescent and young adult gay men. *Suicide and Life-Threatening Behavior, 19,* 381–394.

Scarf, M. (1980). *Unfinished business: Pressure points in the lives of women.* Garden City, NY: Doubleday.

Scarr, S. (1984). *Mother care/Other care.* New York: Basic Books.

Scarr, S., Phillips, D., & McCartney, K. (1989). Working mothers and their families. *American Psychologist, 44,* 1402–1409.

Schachter, F. f. (1981). Toddlers with employed mothers. *Child Development, 52,* 958–964.

Schaffer, H., & Emerson, P. E. (1964). The development of social attachments in infancy. *Monographs of the Society for Research in Child Development, 29,* Whole No. 3.

Schaie, K. W. (1983). The Seattle longitudinal study: A twenty-one year exploration of psychometric intelligence in adulthood. In K. W. Schaie (Ed.), *Longitudinal studies of adult psychological development.* New York: Guilford Press.

Schaie, K. W., & Willis, S. (1986). *Adult development and aging* (2nd ed.). Boston: Little, Brown.

Schantz, C. U. (1983). Social cognition. In P. Mussen (Ed.), *Handbook of child psychology, Vol. 3.* New York: Wiley.

Schlossberg, N. (1987). Taking the mystery out of change. *Psychology Today, 21,* 74–75.

Schmidt, D. F., & Boland, S. M. (1986). Structure of perceptions of older adults: Evidence for multiple stereotypes. *Psychology and Aging, 1,* 255–260.

Schneider, E., Vining, E., Hadley, E., & Farnham, S. (1986). Recommended dietary allowances and the health of the elderly. *New England Journal of Medicine, 314,* 157–160.

Schoenborn, C. A., & Danchik, K. M. (1980). Health practices of young adults. *Advance Data from Vital and Health Statistics, No. 64.* Hyattsville, MD: National Center for Health Statistics.

Schrier, R. W. (1990). *Geriatric medicine.* Philadelphia: Saunders.

Schultz, D. & Schultz, S. E. (2010). *Psychology and work today* (10th ed.). Old Tappan, NJ: Prentice Hall.

Schulz, R., & Aderman, D. (1974). Clinical research and the stages of dying. *Omega, 5,* 137–143.

Schuster, C. S. (1986). Intrauterine development. In C. S. Schuster & S. S. Ashburn (Eds.), *The process of human development.* Boston: Little, Brown.

Schwarz, J., Strickland, R., & Krolick, G. (1974). Infant day care: Behavioral effects at preschool age. *Developmental Psychology, 10,* 502–506.

Sears, R., Maccoby, E., & Levin, H. (1957). *Patterns of child rearing.* New York: Harper & Row.

Sebald, H. (1981). Adolescents' concepts of popularity and unpopularity, comparing 1960 with 1976. *Family Coordinator, 18,* 361–371.

Seccombe, K., Ryan, R., & Austin, C. D. (1987). Care planning: Case managers' assessment of elders' welfare and caregivers' capacity. *Family Relations, 36,* 171–175.

Seibel, M., & Graves, W. (1980). The psychological implications of spontaneous abortion. *Reproductive Medicine, 24,* 161–165.

Seibel, M. M. & McCarthy, J. A. (1993). Infertility, pregnancy, and the emotions. In D. Goleman & J. Gurin (Eds.), *Mind body medicine: How to use your mind for better health.* NY: Consumer Reports Books.

Siegler, R. S. (1998). *Children's Thinking* (3rd ed.). Upper Saddle River, NJ: Prentice Hall.

Selman, R. (1981). The child as friendship philosopher. In. S. Asher & J. Gottman (Eds.), *The development of children's friendships.* New York: Cambridge University Press.

Selman, R., Beardslee, W., Schultz, L., Krupa, M., & Podorefsky, D. (1986). Assessing adolescent interpersonal negotiation strategies: Toward the integration of structural and functional models. *Developmental Psychology, 22,* 450–459.

Seltzer, G. B., Begun, A., Seltzer, M. M., & Krauss, M. W. (1991). Adults with mental retardation and their aging mothers: Impacts of siblings. *Family Relations, 40,* 310–317.

Selye, H. (1956). *The stress of life.* New York: McGraw-Hill.

Serock, K., Seefeldt, C., Jantz, R., & Galper, A. (1977). As children see old folks. *Today's Education, March-April,* 70–73.

Settles, B. H. (1987). A perspective on tomorrow's families. In M. Sussman and S. Steinmetz (Eds.), *Handbook of marriage and the family.* New York: Plenum.

Shaffer, J. B. (1978). *Humanistic psychology.* Englewood Cliffs, NJ: Prentice Hall.

Shanas, E., Townsend, P., Wedderburn, D., Fries, H., Milhoj, P., & Stejouwer, J. (1968). *Old people in three industrial societies.* New York: Atherton.

Shantz, C. (1983). Social cognition. In J. Flavell & E. Markman (Eds.), *Handbook of child psychology* (4th ed.). Vol. 3. New York: Wiley.

Shaughnessy, P. W. (1989). Quality of nursing home care: Problems and pathways. *Generations, 13,* 17–25.

Shaver, J., & Strong, W. (1976). *Facing value decisions: Rationale-building for teachers.* Belmont, CA: Wadsworth.

Sheehy, G. (1976). *Passages: Predictable crises of adulthood.* New York: Dutton.

Sheehan, N., & Nuttall. (1988). Conflict, emotion, and personal strain among family caregivers. *Family Relations, 37,* 92–98.

Sheehy, G. (1976). *Passages: Predictable crises of adult life.* New York: Dutton.

Sherman, E. (1987). *Meaning in mid-life transitions.* Albany, NY: State University of New York Press.

Shirley, M. (1931). *The first two years.* Vol 2. Minneapolis: University of Minnesota Press.

Shock, N. (1977). Biological theories of aging. In J. E. Birren & K. W. Schaie (Eds.), *Handbook of the psychology of aging.* New York: Van Nostrand.

Shock, N. W., & Norris, A. H. (1970). Neuromuscular coordination as a factor in age change in muscular exercise. In E. Jokl & E. Brunner (Eds.), *Physical activity and aging.* Vol. 4. Basel, Switzerland: S. Karger.

Shoenborn, C. A., & Danchik, K. M. (1980). Health practices among adults. *Advance Data From Vital and Health Statistics, No. 64,* November 4.

Shonkoff, J. (1984). The biological substrate and physical health in middle childhood. In W. Collins (Ed.), *Development during middle childhood.* Washington, DC: National Academy Press.

Shoor, M., & Speed, M. H. (1976). Death, delinquency, and the mourning process. In R. Fulton (Ed.), *Death and identity.* Bowie, MD: Charles Press.

Shore, C. (1986). Combinatorial play, conceptual development, and early multiword speech. *Developmental Psychology, 22,* 184–190.

Shostak, A. (1987). Singlehood. In M. B. Sussman & S. K. Steinmetz (Eds.), *Handbook of marriage and the family.* New York: Plenum.

Shulman, N. (1975). Life cycle variations in patterns of close relationships. *Journal of Marriage and the Family, 37,* 813–821.

Sidney, K. (1981). Cardiovascular benefits of physical activity in the exercising aged. In E. Smith & R. Serfass (Eds.), *Exercise and aging: The scientific basis.* Hillsdale, NJ: Enslow.

Siegal, D. (1990). Women's reproductive changes: A marker, not a turning point. *Generations, 14,* 31–32.

Siegel, D. J. (1999). *The developing mind: Toward a neurobiology of interpersonal experience.* NY: The Guilford Press.

Siegel, K., & Tuckel, P. (1984). Rational suicide and the terminally ill cancer patient. *Omega, 15,* 263–269.

Siegler, R. S. (1986). *Children's thinking.* Englewood Cliffs, NJ: Prentice Hall.

Silverstone, B., & Hyman, H. K. (1976). *You and your aging parents.* New York: Pantheon.

Simon, M. (1959). Body configuration and school readiness. *Child Development, 30,* 493–512.

Singer, J., & Singer, D. (1981). *Television, imagination, and aggression: A study of preschoolers.* Hillsdale, NJ: Erlbaum.

Singh, S., Forrest, J. D., & Torres, A. (1989). *Prenatal care in the United States.* New York: Alan Guttmacher Institute.

Skinner, B. F. (1938). *The behavior of organisms.* New York: Appleton-Century-Crofts.

Skinner, B. F. (1948). *Walden two.* New York: Macmillan.

Skinner, B. F. (1957). *Verbal behavior.* New York: Appleton-Century-Crofts.

Skinner, B. F. (1971). *Beyond freedom and dignity.* New York: Knopf.

Slackman, E., & Nelson, K. (1984). Acquisition of an unfamiliar script in story form by young children. *Child Development, 55,* 329–340.

Slavin, R. (1987). Ability grouping and student achievement in elementary schools: A best-evidence synthesis. *Review of Educational Research, 57,* 293–336.

Sluckin, W., Herbert, M., & Sluckin, M. (1983). *Maternal bonding*. Oxford, England: Blackwell.

Small, M. (1990). *Cognitive development*. San Diego, CA: Harcourt Brace Jovanovich.

Smith, C., & Lloyd, B. (1978). Maternal behavior and perceived sex of infant: Revisited. *Child Development, 49*, 1263–1265.

Smith, P. K. (1978). A longitudinal study of social participation in preschool children: Solitary and parallel play reexamined. *Developmental Psychology, 14*, 517–523.

Smith, T. (1981). Adolescent agreement with perceived maternal and paternal educational goals. *Journal of Marriage and the Family, 43*, 85–93.

Smith, T. E. (1993). Growth in academic achievement and teaching younger siblings. *Social Psychology Quarterly, 56*, 77-85.

Smock, P. J. (2000). Cohabitation in the United States: An appraisal of research themes, findings, and implications. *Annual Review of Sociology, 26*, 1–20.

Smoll, F. L., & Schutz, R. W. (1990). Quantifying gender differences in physical performance: A developmental perspective. *Developmental Psychology, 26*, 360–370.

Snarey, J. (1985). Cross-cultural universality of social-moral development: A critical review of Kohlbergian research. *Psychological Bulletin, 97*, 202–232.

Snarey, J., Reimer, J., & Kohlberg, L. (1985). Development of social-moral reasoning among kibbutz adolescents: A longitudinal cross-cultural study. *Developmental Psychology, 21*, 2–18.

Snyder, J., Bank, L., & Burraston, B. (2005). The consequences of antisocial behavior in older male siblings for younger brothers and sisters. *Journal of Family Psychology, 19*, 643-653.

Snyder, J., Dishion, T., & Patterson, G. (1986). Determinants and consequences of associating with deviant peers during preadolescence and adolescence. *Journal of Early Adolescence, 6*, 29–43.

Sobesky, W. (1983). The effects of situational factors on moral judgments. *Child Development, 54*, 575–584.

Sokolov, Y. N. (1969). The modeling properties of the nervous system. In M. Coles & I. Maltzman (Eds.), *A handbook of contemporary Soviet psychology*. New York: Basic Books.

Solomon, G. F. (1991). Psychosocial factors, exercise, and immunity: Athletes, elderly persons, and AIDS patients. *International Journal of Sports Medicine, 12*, 250–255.

Sommer, B. (1984). The troubled teen: Suicide, drug use, and running away. *Women & Health, 9*, 117–141.

Sommer, R. (1988). Two decades of marijuana attitudes: The more it changes, the more it is the same. *Journal of Psychoactive Drugs, 20*, 67–70.

Sorce, J., Emde, R., Campos, J., & Klinnert, M. (1985). Maternal emotional signaling: Its effect on the visual cliff behavior of 1-year-olds. *Developmental Psychology, 21*, 195–200.

Sorensen, R. C. (1973). *The Sorensen report: Adolescent sexuality in contemporary America*. New York: World Publishing.

Spangler, J., & Demi, E. (1988). *Bereavement support groups: Leadership manual*. (3rd ed.). Denver, CO: Grief Education Institute.

Spanier, G. (1983). Married and unmarried cohabitation in the United States: 1980. *Journal of Marriage and the Family, 45*, 277–288.

Spence, A. P., & Mason, E. B. (1987). *Human anatomy and physiology* (3rd ed.). Menlo Park, CA: Benjamin/Cummings.

Spence, D., & Lonner, T. (1971). The "empty nest:" A transition within motherhood. *Family Coordinator, 19*, 369–375.

Spence, D. A., & Wiener, J. M. (1990). Nursing home length of stay patterns: Results from the 1985 national nursing home survey. *The Gerontologist, 30*, 16–24.

Spence, J. T., & Helmreich, R. L. (1978). *Masculinity and femininity: Their psychological dimensions, correlates, and antecedents*. Austin, TX: University of Texas Press.

Spiker, C. (1966). The concept of development: Relevant and irrelevant issues. In H. W. Stevenson (Ed.), Concept of development (pp. 40–54). *Monographs of the Society for Research in Child Development, 31*, Whole No. 107.

Spinette, J., Swarner, J., & Sheposh, J. (1981). Effective parental coping following the death of a child from cancer. *Journal of Pediatric Psychology, 6*, 251–263.

Spirito, A., Hart, K., Overholser, J., & Halverson, J. (1990). Social skills and depression in adolescent suicide attempters. *Adolescence, 25*, 543–552.

Spitz, R. (1945). Hospitalism. In O. Fenichel et al. (Eds.), *The psychoanalytical study of the child*. Vol. 1. New York: International Universities Press.

Sroufe, L. A. (1985). Attachment classification from the perspective of infant-caregiver relationships and infant temperament. *Child Development, 56*, 1–14.

Sroufe, L. A., Egeland, B., & Kreutzer, T. (1990). The fate of early experience following developmental change: Longitudinal approaches to individual adaptation in childhood. *Child Development, 61*, 1363-1373.

Sroufe, L. A., & Waters, E. (1976). The ontogenesis of smiling and laughter: A perspective on the organization of development in infancy. *Psychological Review, 83*, 173–189.

Sroufe, L. A., & Wunsch, J. (1972). The development of laughter in the first year of life. *Child Development, 43*, 1326–1344.

Stanley, S. M., Amato, P. R., Johnson, C. A., & Markman, H. J. (2006). Premarital education, marital quality, and marital stability: Findings from a large, random, household survey. *Journal of Family Psychology, 20*, 117–126.

Stanley, S. M., & Markman, H. J. (1992). Assessing commitment in personal relationships. *Journal of Marriage and Family, 54*, 595–608.

Stanley, S. M., Markman, H. J., & Whitton, S. W. (2002). Communication, conflict and commitment: Insights on the foundations of relationship success from a national survey. *Family Process, 41*, 659–675.

Stanley, S. M., Rhoades, G. K., & Markman, H. J. (2006). Sliding vs. deciding: Inertia and the premarital cohabitation effect. *Family Relations, 55*, 499–509.

Stanley, S. M., Whitton, S. W., & Markman, H. J. (2004). Maybe I do: Interpersonal commitment and premarital or nonmarital cohabitation. *Journal of Family Issues, 25*, 496–519.

Staples, R., & Mirande, A. (1980). Racial and cultural variations among American families: A decennial review of the literature on minority families. *Journal of Marriage and the Family, 42*, 887–903.

Starfield, B., Katz, H., Gabriel, A., Livingston. G., Benson, P., Hankin, J., Horn, S., & Steinwachs, D. (1984). Morbidity in childhood — a longitudinal view. *The New England Journal of Medicine, 310*, 824–829.

Starling, B. P., & Martin, A. C. (1990). Adult survivors of parental alcoholism: Implications for primary care. *The Nurse Practitioner, 15*, 16–23.

Steckel, A. (1987). Psychosocial development of children of lesbian parents. In F. W. Bozett (Ed.), *Gay and lesbian parents*. New York: Praeger.

Steinberg, L. (1987). Impact of puberty on family relations: Effects of pubertal status and pubertal timing. *Developmental Psychology, 23*, 451–460.

Steinberg, L. (1988). Reciprocal relation between parent-child distance and pubertal maturation. *Developmental Psychology, 24*, 122–128.

Steiner, H. (1990). Defense styles in eating disorders. *International Journal of Eating Disorders, 9*, 141–151.

Steinmetz, S. (1988). *Duty bound: Elder abuse and family care*. Newbury Park, CA: Sage.

Steinmetz, S., & Stein, K. F. (1988). Traditional and emerging families: A typology based on structures and functions. *Family Science Review, 1*, 103–114.

Steinmetz, S., Clavan, S., & Stein, K. F. (1990). *Marriage and family realities: Historical and contemporary perspectives*. New York: Harper & Row.

Steinmetz, S. K., Clavan, S., & Stein, K. F. (1990). *Marriage and family realities: Historical and contemporary perspectives*. New York: Harper & Row.

Stenback, A. (1980). Depression and suicidal behavior in old age. In J. E. Birren & R. B. Sloan (Eds.), *Handbook of mental health and aging* (pp. 616–652). Englewood Cliffs, N. J.: Prentice-Hall.

Stern, L. (1985). *The structures and strategies of human memory*. Homewood, IL: Dorsey.

Sternberg, R. J. (1987). The uses and misuses of intelligence testing: misunderstanding meaning, users over-rely on scores. *Education Week, September 23*, 22.

Sternberg, R. J. (Ed.) (1990). *Wisdom: Its nature, origin, and development.* NY: Cambridge University Press.

Sternberg, R. J., & Lubart, T. I. (2001). Wisdom and creativity. In J. E. Birren & K. W. Schaie (Eds.), *Handbook of the psychology of aging.* San Diego, CA: Academic Press.

Sternglanz, S., Gray, J., & Murakami, M. (1977). Adult preferences for infantile facial features: An ethological approach. *Animal Behavior, 25,* 108–115.

Stevens-Long, J. (1979). *Adult life: Developmental processes.* Palo Alto, CA: Mayfield.

Stevens-Long, J. (1988). *Adult life* (3rd ed.). Palo Alto, CA: Mayfield.

Stevenson, H., Azuma, H., & Hazkuta, K. (Eds.). (1986). *Child development and education in Japan.* New York: Freeman.

Stevenson, H., Lee, S.-Y., & Stigler, J. (1986). Mathematics and achievement of Chinese, Japanese, and American children. *Science, 231,* 693–699.

Stigler, J., Lee, S.-Y., & Stevenson, H. (1987). Mathematics classrooms in Japan, Taiwan, and the United States. *Child Development, 58,* 1272–1285.

Stinnett, N., Walters, J., & Kaye, E. (1984). *Relationships in marriage and the family,* 2nd ed. New York: Macmillan.

Stinnett, N., Walters, J., & Stinnett, N. (1991). *Relationships in marriage and the family* (3rd ed.).New York: Macmillan.

Stipek, D. (1984). Sex differences in children's attributions of success and failure on mathematics and spelling tests. *Sex Roles, 11,* 969–981.

Stockdale, D., Hegland, S., & Chiaromonte, T. (1989). Helping behaviors: An observational study of preschool children. *Early Childhood Research Quarterly, 4,* 533–544.

Stockman, L., & Graves, C. S. (1990). *Adult children who won't grow up: How to finally cut the cord that binds you.* Rocklin, CA: Prima Publishing & Communications.

Streib, G. F. (1977). Changing roles in later years. In R. A. Kalish (Ed.), *The later years: Social applications of gerontology.* Monterey, CA: Brooks/Cole.

Streissguth, A. P., Burr, H. M., Sampson, P. D., Darby, B. L., & Martin, DC (1989). IQ at age 4 in relation to maternal alcohol use and smoking during pregnancy. *Developmental Psychology, 25,* 3–11.

Strobino, D. (1987). *The health and medical consequences of adolescent sexuality and pregnancy: A review of the literature in risking the future.* Vol. 2. Washington, DC: National Academy Press.

Suitor, J., & Pillemer, K. (1988). Explaining intergenerational conflict when adult children and elderly parents live together. *Journal of Marriage and the Family, 50,* 1037–1047.

Sullivan, T., & Schneider, M. (1987). Development and identity issues in adolescent homosexuality. *Child and Adolescent Social Work Journal, 4,* 13–24.

Sullivan-Bolyai, J., Hull, H. F., Wilson, C., & Corey, L. (1983). Neonatal herpes simplex virus infection in King County, Washington: Increasing incidence and epidemiologic correlates. *Journal of the American Medical Association, 250,* 3059–3062.

Super, D. E. (1957). *The psychology of careers.* New York: Harper.

Super, D. E. (1963). *Career development: Self-concept theory.* New York: College Entrance Examination Board.

Surra, C. A. (1990). Research and theory on mate selection and premarital relationships in the 1980s. *Journal of Marriage and the Family, 52,* 844–865.

Susman, E. J., Pizzo, P. A., & Poplack, D. G. (1981). Adolescent cancer: Getting through the aftermath. In P. Ahmed (Ed.), *Living and dying with childhood cancer* (pp. 99–117). New York: Elsevier.

Sutton-Smith, B. (1985). The child at play. *Psychology Today, 19* (October), 64–65.

Sutton-Smith, B., & Rosenberg, B. G. (1970). *The sibling.* New York: Holt, Rinehart, & Winston.

Suzuki-Slakter, N. (1988). Elaboration and metamemory during adolescence. *Contemporary Educational Psychology, 13,* 206–220.

Swaim, R., Oetting, E., Edwards, R., & Beauvais, F. (1989). Links from emotional distress to adolescent drug use: A path model. *Journal of Consulting and Clinical Psychology, 57,* 227–231.

Sweet, J. A., & Bumpass, L. L. (1987). *American families and households.* New York: Russell Sage Foundation.

Swyer, P. R. (1987). The organization of perinatal care with particular reference to the newborn. In G. B. Avery (Ed.), *Neonatology: Pathophysiology and management of the newborn.* Philadelphia: Lippincott.

Tan, L. E. (1985). Laterality and motor skills in four-year-olds. *Child Development, 56,* 119–124.

Tanner, J. M. (1978/1990). *Foetus into man: Physical growth from conception to maturity.* Cambridge: Harvard University Press.

Taras, H., Sallis, J., Patterson, T., Nader, P., & Nelson, J. (1989). Television's influence on children's diet and physical activity. *Developmental and Behavioral Pediatrics, 10,* 176–180.

Targ, D. (1979). Toward a reassessment of women's experience at middle age. *Family Coordinator, 28,* 377–382.

Tautermannova, M., (1973). Smiling in infants. *Child Development, 44,* 701–704.

Taveris, C. (1983). *Anger: The misunderstood emotion.* New York: Simon & Schuster.

Taylor, M. (1988). Conceptual perspective taking: Children's ability to distinguish what they know from what they see. *Child Development, 59,* 703–718.

Taylor, R. J., Chatters, L. M., Tucker, M. B., & Lewis, E. (1990). Developments in research on black families: A decade review. *Journal of Marriage and the Family, 52,* 993–1014.

Taylor, M., & Bacharach, V. (1981). The development of drawing rules: Meta-knowledge about drawing influences performances on nondrawing tasks. *Child Development, 52,* 373–375.

Taylor, E. (1989). Time is not on their side. *Time, February, 27,* 74.

Teachman, J. (2003). Premarital sex, premarital cohabitation and the risk of subsequent marital dissolution among women. *Journal of Marriage and Family, 65,* 444–455.

Tennov, D. (1979). *Love and limerance.* New York: Stein & Day.

The Carolina Consortium on Human Development (1996). Developmental science: A collaborative statement. In R. B. Cairns, G. H. Elder & E. J. Costello (Eds.), *Developmental science* (pp. 1-6). New York: Cambridge University Press.

Thelen, E. (1981). Rhythmical behavior in infancy: An ethological perspective. *Developmental Psychology, 17,* 237–257.

Thelen, E. (1986). Treadmill elicited stepping in seven month old infants. *Child Development, 57,* 1498–1506.

Thomas, A. (1986). Gender differences in satisfaction with grandparenting. *Psychology and Aging, 1,* 215–219.

Thomas, A., & Chess, S. (1984). Genesis and evolution of behavioral disorders: From infancy to early adult life. *American Journal of Psychiatry, 141,* 1–9.

Thomas, A., & Chess, S. (1987). Roundtable: What is temperament? *Child Development, 58,* 505–529.

Thomas, A., Chess, S., & Birch, H. G. (1968). *Temperament and behavior disorders in childhood.* NY: New York University Press.

Thomas, L. (1979). Causes of midlife change from high status careers. *Vocational Guidance Quarterly, 27,* 202–208.

Thomas, R. M. (1979). *Comparing theories of child development.* Belmont, CA: Wadsworth.

Thompson, M., Alexander, K., & Entwisle, D. (1988). Household composition, parental expectations, and school achievement. *Social Forces, 67,* 424–451.

Thompson, R. F., Crist, D. M., & Osborn, L. A. (1990). Treadmill exercise electocardiography in the elderly with physical impairments. *Gerontology, 36,* 112–118.

Thornburg, H. D., & Aras, Z. (1986). Physical characteristics of developing adolescents. *Journal of Adolescent Research, 1,* 47–78.

Thorndike, E. L. (1898). Animal intelligence: An experimental study of the associative processes in animals. *Psychological Review, 2* (Supplement No. 8).

Tienda, M., & Angel, R. (1982). Headship and household composition among blacks, Hispanics, and other whites. *Social Forces, 61,* 508–531.

Timiras, P. S. (1972). *Developmental physiology and aging.* New York: Macmillan.

Tobin, J., Wu, D., & Davidson, D. (1989). *Preschools in three cultures: Japan, China, and the United States.* New Haven, CT: Yale University Press.

Tobin-Richards, M., Boxer, A., & Petersen, A. (1983). The psychological significance of pubertal change: Sex differences in perceptions of self during early adolescence. In J. Brooks-Gunn & A. Petersen (Eds.), *Girls at puberty.* New York: Plenum.

Tognoli, L. (1980). Male friendship and intimacy across the life span. *Family Relations, 29,* 273–297.

Tomasello, M., Mannle, S., & Kruger, A. (1986). Linguistic environment of 1 to 2-year old twins. *Developmental Psychology, 22,* 641–653.

Toner, I., & Smith, R. (1977). Age and verbalization in delay maintenance behavior in children. *Journal of Experimental Child Psychology, 24,* 123–128.

Tower, R. (1987). *How schools can help combat student drug and alcohol abuse.* Washington, DC: NEA Professional Library.

Trevathan, W. (1983). Maternal "en face" orientation during the first hour after birth. *American Journal of Orthopsychiatry, 53,* 92–99.

Troen, S. K. (1985). Technological development and adolescence: The early twentieth century. *Journal of Early Adolescence, 5,* 429–440.

Troll, L. E. (1986). Parents and children in later life. *Generations, 10,* 23–25.

Trotter, R. (1983). Baby face. *Psychology Today, 17(8),* 14–20.

Trotter, R. (1987). You've come a long way, baby. *Psychology Today, 21(5),* 34–45.

Turner, R., & Avison, W. (1985). Assessing risk factors for problem parenting: The significance of social support. *Journal of Marriage and the Family, 47,* 881–892.

U. S. Bureau of the Census. (1983). *Current population report.* Washington, DC: U. S. Government Printing Office.

U. S. Bureau of the Census (1989). Changes in American family life. *Current Population Reports, Series P–23, No. 163.* Washington, DC: U. S. Government Printing Office.

U. S. Bureau of the Census. (1989). Studies in marriage and the family: Singleness in America, single parents and their children, married-couple families with children. *Current Population Reports, Series P–23(162).* Washington, DC: U. S. Government Printing Office.

U. S. Bureau of the Census (1990a) *Statistical abstract of the United States* (110th ed.). Washington, DC: U. S. Government Printing Office.

U. S. Bureau of the Census. (1990b). Household and family characteristics: March 1990 and 1989. *Current Population Reports, Series P–20, No. 447.* Washington, DC: U. S. Government Printing Office.

U. S. Bureau of the Census. (1991a). Cohabitation, marriage, marital dissolution, and remarriage: United States, 1988. *Advance Data, No. 194. DHHS Publication No. (PHS) 91–1250.* Washington, DC: U. S. Government Printing Office.

U. S. Bureau of the Census (1991b). *Statistical abstract of the United States* (111h ed.). Washington, DC: U. S. Government Printing Office.

U. S. Bureau of Labor. (1986). *Consumer expenditure survey, 1982–1983. Bulletin No. 2246.* Washington, DC: U. S. Government Printing Office.

U. S. Department of Agriculture. Updated estimates of the cost of raising a child, 1987. *Family Economic Review, 4,* 36–37.

U. S. Department of Health and Human Services (1987). *Smoking and health: A national status report* (HHS/PHS/CDC Publication No. 87–8396). Washington, DC: U. S. Government Printing Office.

U. S. Senate, Special Committee on Aging. (1986). *Aging America: Trends and projections.* Washington, DC: U. S. Government Printing Office.

Utne, N. (2005). To live with no regrets. In G. E. Dickinson & M.R. Leming, (Eds.), *Dying, death, and bereavement* (10th ed.). NY: McGraw-Hill.

Vaillant, G. E. (1977). *Adaptation to life.* Boston: Little, Brown.

Van Camp, S. P., & Boyer, J. L. (1989). Cardiovascular aspects of aging. *Physician and Sports Medicine, 17,* 120–125.

Vandell, D. L., Henderson, V. K., & Wilson, K. S. (1988). A longitudinal study of children with day-care experiences of varying quality. *Child Development, 59,* 1286–1293.

Vandenberg, B. (1978). Play and development from an ethological perspective. *American Psychologist, 33,* 724–739.

Veevers, J. E. (1973). The social meanings of parenthood. *Psychiatry, 36,* 291–310.

Vega, W. A. (1990). Hispanic families in the 1980s: A decade of research. *Journal of Marriage and the Family, 52,* 1015–1024.

Vega, W. A., Patterson, T., Sallis, J., Nader, P., Atkins, C., & Abramson, I. (1986). Cohesion and adaptability in Mexican-American and Anglo families. *Journal of Marriage and the Family, 48,* 857–867.

Verbrugge, L. M. (1977). The structure of adult friendship choices. *Social Forces, 56,* 576–597.

Verbrugge, L. M. (1979). Multiplexity in adult friendships. *Social Forces, 57,* 1286–1309.

Vetere, V. (1982). The role of friendship in the development and maintenance of lesbian love relationships. *Journal of Homosexuality, 8,* 51–65.

Vincent, C. (1972). An open letter to the "caught" generation. *Family Coordinator, 21,* 143–146.

Vinters, H. V. (2001). Aging and the human nervous system. In J. E. Birren & K. W. Schaie (Eds.), *Handbook of the psychology of aging.* San Diego, CA: Academic Press.

Vogt, W. P. (1993). *Dictionary of statistics and methodology: A nontechnical guide for the social sciences.* Newbury Park, CA: SAGE Publications.

von Bertalanffy, L. (1974a). General systems theory and psychiatry. In S. Arieti (Ed.), *American handbook of psychiatry, Vol. 1* (2nd ed.). New York: Basic Books.

von Bertalanffy, L. (1974b). *General systems theory.* New York: Braziller.

von Hofsten, C. (1983). Catching skills in infancy. *Journal of Experimental Psychology, 9,* 75–85.

von Hofsten, C., & Fazel-Zandy, S. (1984). Development of visually guided hand orientation in reaching. *Journal of Experimental Child Psychology, 38,* 208–219.

Voydanoff, P. (1990). Economic distress and family relations. *Journal of Marriage and the Family, 52,* 1099–1115.

Vurpillot, E. (1968). The development of scanning strategies and their relation to visual differentiation. *Journal of Experimental Child Psychology, 6,* 632–650.

Vygotsky, L. S. (1962). *Thought and language.* Cambridge, MA: MIT Press.

Vygotsky, L. S. (1978). *Mind in society: The development of higher psychological processes.* Cambridge, MA: Harvard University Press.

Waas, G. (1988). Social attributional biases of peer-rejected and aggressive children. *Child Development, 59,* 969–975.

Wadsworth, B. (1971). *Piaget's theory of cognitive development.* New York: David MacKay.

Wadsworth, B. J. (2004). *Piaget's theory of cognitive and affective development* (5th ed.). NY: Pearson Education, Inc.

Walbroehl, G. S. (1988). Effects of medical problems on sexuality in the elderly. *Medical Aspects of Human Sexuality, 22,* 56–57.

Walford, R (1983). *Maximum life span.* New York: Norton.

Walker, A. J. (1985). Reconceptualizing family stress. *Journal of Marriage and the Family, 47,* 827–838.

Walker, A. J., Pratt, C. C., Martell, L. K., & Martin, S. K. (1991). Perceptions of aid and actual aid in intergenerational caregiving. *Family Relations, 40,* 318–323.

Walker, B. A., & Mehr, M. (1983). Adolescent suicide—a family crisis: A model for effective intervention by family therapists. *Adolescence, 18,* 285–292.

Waller, G., Calam, R., & Slade, P. (1988). Family interaction and eating disorders: Do family members agree? *British Review of Bulimia and Anorexia Nervosa, 3,* 33–40.

Wallerstein, J. S. (1983). Children of divorce: The psychological tasks of the child. *American Journal of Orthopsychiatry, 53,* 230–243.

Wallerstein, J. S. (1987). Children of divorce: Report of a ten-year follow-up of early latency-age children. *American Journal of Orthopsychiatry, 57,* 199–211.

Wallerstein, J., & Blakeslee, S. (1989). *Second chances.* New York: Ticknor & Fields.

Wallerstein, J., Corbin, S., & Lewis, J. (1988). Children of divorce: A 10-year study. In E. Hetherington & J. Arasteh (Eds.), *Impact of divorce, single parenting, and stepparenting.* Hillsdale, NJ: Erlbaum.

Wallerstein, J. S., & Kelly, J. B. (1975). The effects of parental divorce: Experiences of the preschool child. *Journal of the American Academy of Child Psychiatry, 14,* 600–616.

Wallerstein, J. S., & Kelly, J. B. (1976). The effects of parental divorce: Experiences of the child in later latency. *Journal of the American Academy of Child Psychiatry, 15,* 257–269.

Wallerstein, J. S., & Kelly, J. B. (1980). Effects of divorce on the visiting father-child relationship. *American Journal of Psychiatry, 137,* 1534–1539.

Wareham, K., Lyon, M., Glenister, P., & Williams, E. (1987). Age-related reactivation of an X-linked gene. *Nature, 327,* 725–727.

Waterman, A. S. (1982). Identity development from adolescence to adulthood: An extension of theory and a review of research. *Developmental Psychology, 18,* 341–358.

Waters, E., Merrick, S., Treboux, D., Crowell, J., & Albersheim, L. (2000) Attachment security in infancy and early adulthood: A twenty year longitudinal study. *Child Development, 71,* 684-689.

Watson, J. B. (1924). *Behaviorism.* New York: Norton.

Watson, R. (1983). Premarital cohabitation vs. traditional courtship: Their effects on subsequent marital adjustment. *Family Relations, 32,* 139–147.

Wattenberg, B. (1984). *The good news is bad news.* New York: Simon & Schuster.

Wattleton, F. (1987). American teens: Sexually active, sexually illiterate. *Journal of School Health, 57,* 379–380.

Watts, W. D., & Wright, L. S. (1990). The relationship of alcohol, tobacco, marijuana, and other illegal drug use to delinquency among Mexican-American, Black, and White adolescent males. *Adolescence, 25,* 171–181.

Weatherly, D. (1964). Self-perceived rate of physical maturation and personality in late adolescence. *Child Development, 35,* 1197–1210.

Weg, R. (1983). Changing physiology of aging. In D. Woodruff & J. E. Birren (Eds.), *Aging: Scientific perspectives and social issues.* Monterey, CA: Brooks/Cole.

Wegscheider-Cruse, S. (1985). *Choicemaking.* Pompano Beach, FL: Health Communications.

Weinberg, A. D., Engingro, P. F., & Miller, R. L. (1989). Death in the nursing home: Senescence, infection, and other causes. *Journal of Gerontological Nursing, 15,* 12–17.

Weiner, A. S. (1977). Cognitive and social-emotional development in adolescence. *Journal of Pediatric Psychology, 2,* 87–92.

Weisfeld, G. E. (1982). The nature-nurture issue and the integrating concept of function. In B. B. Wolman (Ed.), *Handbook of developmental psychology.* Englewood Cliffs, NJ: Prentice Hall.

Weisman, A. D. (1972). *On dying and denying.* New York: Behavioral Publications.

Weistein, S. (1991). Retirement planning should be done now. *The Practical Accountant, 24,* 28–35.

Wellen, C. (1985). Effects of older siblings on the language young children hear and produce. *Journal of Speech and Hearing Disorders, 50,* 84–99.

Weller, R. H., & Bouvier, L. F. (1983). *Population: Demography and policy.* New York: St. Martin's Press.

Wellman, B. (1932). The effects of preschool attendance upon intellectual development. *Journal of Experimental Education, 1,* 48–69.

Wellman, H. M. (1985). The origins of metacognition. In D. Forrest-Pressley, G. McKinnon, & T. Waller (Eds.), *Cognition, metacognition, and performance.* New York: Academic Press.

Wellman, H. M., Ritter, K., & Flavell, J. H. (1975). Deliberate memory behavior in the delayed reactions of very young children. *Developmental Psychology, 11,* 781–787.

Wenger, J. E. (1989). Finding a nursing home. *Diabetes Forecast, July 1,* 78.

Werner, E. E. (1984). Resilient children. *Young Children, 24,* 686–692.

Werner, E. E., & Smith, R. (1982). *Vulnerable but not invincible: A study of resilient children.* New York: McGraw-Hill.

Werner, P., Middlestadt-Carter, S., & Crawford, T. (1975). Having a third child: Predicting behavioral intentions. *Journal of Marriage and the Family, 37,* 348–358.

Wertlieb, D., Weigel, C., & Felstein, M. (1989). Stressful experiences, temperament, and social support: Impact on children's behavior symptoms. *Journal of Applied Developmental Psychology, 10,* 487–505.

Wertlieb, D., Weigel, C., Springer, T., & Feldstein, M. (1987). Temperament as a moderator of children's stressful experiences. *American Journal of Orthopsychiatry, 57,* 234–245.

West, J. R. (1986). *Alcohol and brain development.* London: Oxford University Press.

Whisnant, L., Brett, E., & Zegans, L. (1975). Implicit messages concerning menstruation in commercial educational materials prepared for young adolescent girls. *Journal of Psychiatry, 132,* 815–820.

White, S. H. (1975). Commentary. In L. B. Miller & J. L. Dyer, (Eds.), Four preschool programs: Their dimensions and effects. *Monographs of the Society for Research in Child Development, 40,* 168–170.

White, T. G. (1982). Naming practices, typicality, and underextension in child language. *Journal of Experimental Child Psychology, 33,* 324–346.

White, L. K., & Booth, A. (1985). The quality and stability of remarriages: The role of stepchildren. *American Sociological Review, 50,* 689–698.

White, C. B. (1982). A scale for the assessment of attitudes and knowledge regarding sexuality in the aged. *Archives of Sexual Behavior, 11,* 491–502.

White, E., Elsom, B., & Prawat, B. (1978). Children's conceptions of death. *Child Development, 49,* 307–311.

Whitehead, W. E., Drinkwater, D., & Cheskin, L. J. (1989). Constipation in the elderly living at home: Definition, prevalence, and relationship to lifestyle and health status. *Journal of the American Geriatrics Society, 37,* 423–430.

Whitfield, C. L. (1987). *Healing the child within: Discovery and recovery for adult children of dysfunctional families.* Deerfield Beach, FL: Health Communications.

Whitney, E., & Hamilton, E. (1987). *Understanding nutrition* (4th ed.). St. Paul, MN: West Publishing Co.

Wilcox, B. L., Millstein, S. G., & Gardner, W. (1990). Protecting adolescents from AIDS. *New Directions for Child Development, Winter,* 71–75.

Wilkie, C., & Ames, E. (1986). The relationship of infant crying to parental stress in the transition to parenthood. *Journal of Marriage and the Family, 48,* 545–550.

Williams, H. (1983). *Perceptual and motor development.* Englewood Cliffs, NJ: Prentice Hall.

Williams, E. R., & Caliendo, M. A. (1984). *Nutrition: Principles, issues, and applications.* New York: McGraw-Hill.

Williams, J. W., & Stith, M. (1980). *Middle childhood: Behavior and development* (2nd ed.). New York: Macmillan.

Williams, S. R. (1989). *Nutrition and diet therapy* (6th ed.). St. Louis, MO: Times Mirror/Mosby College Publishing.

Williamson, P. (1986). National Sudden Infant Death Syndrome Foundation. In T. Rando (Ed.), *Parental loss of a child.* Champaign, IL: Research Press.

Wilson, E. O. (1975). *Sociobiology: The new synthesis.* Cambridge, MA: Harvard University Press.

Wilson, E. O. (1978). *On human nature.* Cambridge, MA: Harvard University Press.

Wilson, R. S. (1985). Risk and resilience in early mental development. *Developmental Psychology, 21,* 795–805.

Windle, M. (1991). The difficult temperament in adolescence: Associations with substance use, family support, and problem behaviors. *Journal of Clinical Psychology, 47,* 310–315.

Windle, M. (2000). Parental, sibling, and peer influences on adolescent substance use and alcohol problems. *Applied Developmental Science, 4,* 98–110.

Wingfield, A., & Byrnes, D. (1981). *The psychology of human memory.* New York: Academic Press.

Winick, M., & Brasel, J. (1977). Early malnutrition and subsequent brain development. *Annals of the New York Academy of Science, 300,* 280–282.

Winterton, M. (1991). Strategies for promoting physical fitness. *Nursing Clinics of North America, 26,* 855–890.

Wise, T. (1978). Variations in male orgasm. *Medical Aspects of Human Sexuality, 12,* 72.

Wolff, P. H. (1966). The causes, controls, and organization of behavior in the neonate. *Psychological Issues, 5,* 496–503.

Wolff, P. (1969). The natural history of crying and other vocalizations in early infancy. In B. Foss (Ed.), *Determinants of infant behavior.* Vol. 4. London: Methuen.

Woods, L. N., & Emery, R. E. (2002). The cohabitation effects on divorce: Causation or selection? *Journal of Divorce and Remarriage, 37,* 101–119.

Worden, J. W. (1982). *Grief counseling and grief therapy.* New York: Springer

Yager, J. (1988). The treatment of eating disorders. *Journal of Clinical Psychiatry, 49,* 18–25.

Yamamoto, K., Soliman, A., Parsons, J., & Davies, O.L. (1987). Voices in unison: Stressful events in the lives of children in six countries. *Journal of Child Psychology and Psychiatry, 28,* 855–864.

Yang, R. K., Zweig, A. R., Douthitt, T. C., & Federman, E. J. (1976). Successive relationships between maternal attitudes during pregnancy, analgesic medication during labor and delivery, and newborn behavior. *Developmental Psychology, 12,* 6–14.

Yarrow, M., Scott, P., & Waxler, C. (1973). Learning concern for others. *Developmental Psychology, 8,* 240–260.

Yeaworth, R. C., York, J., Hussey, M. A., Ingle, M. E., & Goodwin, T. (1980). The development of an adolescent life change event scale. *Adolescence, 15,* 91–97.

Yonas, A., Granrud, C. E., & Pettersen, L. (1985). Infants' sensitivity to relative size information at distance. *Developmental Psychology, 21,* 161–167.

Young, C. (1991). Alcohol, drugs, driving, and you: A comprehensive program to prevent adolescent drinking, drug use, and driving. *Journal of Alcohol and Drug Education, 36,* 20–25.

Zahn-Waxler, C., Radke-Yarrow, M., & Brady-Smith, J. (1977). Perspective-taking and prosocial behavior. *Developmental Psychology, 13,* 87–88.

Zelazo, P. (1983). The development of walking: New findings and old assumptions. *Journal of Motor Behavior, 15,* 99–137.

Zelnik, M., & Kim, Y. (1982). Sex education and its association with teenage sexual activity, pregnancy, and contraceptive use. *Family Planning Perspectives, 14,* 117–126.

Zheng, J. J., & Rosenberg, I. H. (1989). What is the nutritional status of the elderly? *Geriatrics, 44,* 57–44.

Zill, N., & Rogers, C. C. (1988). Recent trends in the well-being of children in the United States and their implications for public policy. In A. J. Cherlin (Ed.), *The changing American family and public policy.* Washington, DC: Urban Institute Press.

Zimet, G. D., Hillier, S. A., Anglin, T. M., & Ellick, E. (1991). Knowing someone with AIDS: The impact on adolescents. *Journal of Pediatric Psychology, 16,* 287–294.

Zinker, J.C., & Fink, S. l. (1966). The possibility of psychological growth in a dying person. *Journal of General Psychology, 74,* 185–199.

Zuckerman, B., Frank, D., Hingson, R., AMaro, H., Levenson, S. M., Kayne, J., Parker, S., Vinci, R., Aboagye, K., Fried, L., Cabral, H., Timperi, R., & Bauchner, H. (1989). Effects of maternal marijuana and cocaine use on fetal growth. *The New England Journal of Medicine, 320,* 762–768.

Zuger, B. (1989). Homosexuality in families of boys with effeminate behavior: An epidemiological study. *Archives of Sexual Behavior, 18,* 155–166.

Zuger, B. (1989). Homosexuality in families of boys with effeminate behavior: An epidemiological study. *Archives of Sexual Behavior, 18,* 155–166.

# Index

LaVergne, TN USA
02 September 2010

195555LV00001BA/2/P